A

HISTORY

OF

THE LAW, THE COURTS,

AND

THE LAWYERS

Of Maine,

FROM ITS FIRST COLONIZATION TO THE EARLY PART OF THE PRESENT CENTURY.

By WILLIAM WILLIS.

THE LAWBOOK EXCHANGE, LTD.
Clark, New Jersey
2006

ISBN-13: 978-1-58477-628-4
ISBN-10: 1-58477-628-5

Printed in the United States of America on acid-free paper

THE LAWBOOK EXCHANGE, LTD.
33 Terminal Avenue
Clark, New Jersey 07066-1321

Please see our website for a selection of our other publications and fine facsimile reprints of classic works of legal history:
www.lawbookexchange.com

Library of Congress Cataloging-in-Publication Data

Willis, William, 1794-1870.
A history of the law, the courts, and the lawyers of Maine : from its first colonization to the early part of the present century / William Willis.
p. cm.
Originally published: Portland : Bailey & Noyes, 1863.
Includes bibliographical references and index.
ISBN 1-58477-628-5 (alk. paper)
1. Law--Maine--History. 2. Courts--Maine--History. 3. Lawyers--Maine--Biography. I. Title.
KFM78.W55 2005
349.74109--dc22

2005029069

A HISTORY OF THE LAW, THE COURTS, AND THE LAWYERS Of Maine,

FROM ITS FIRST COLONIZATION TO THE EARLY PART OF THE PRESENT CENTURY.

By WILLIAM WILLIS.

PORTLAND:
BAILEY & NOYES.
M DCCC LXIII.

PRINTED BY BROWN THURSTON,

COR. OF EXCHANGE AND MIDDLE STS.

Dedication.

TO THE

LEGAL PROFESSION IN MAINE,

THIS WORK,

DEVOTED TO THE HISTORY OF THE

Law and the Lawyers of our State,

IS RESPECTFULLY

DEDICATED

BY THEIR BROTHER,

WILLIAM WILLIS.

PREFACE.

THE present work originated in the preparation of a lecture for the Maine Historical Society, in which I proposed to present brief sketches of the early lawyers, with anecdotes of the bar, in Maine. The materials became so copious that they stretched far beyond the limits of a discourse, and have assumed the shape in which they now appear.

I had for a long time desired that some aged member of our bar would collect and preserve, for the instruction and amusement of his brethren and successors in the profession, reminiscences of the early lawyers and practice, as well as of the usages which prevailed at the bar, in former days. I had hoped that Judge Mellen, who was very free and felicitous with his pen, and was more familiar with these subjects, with perhaps one exception, than any of our old lawyers, would have favored the profession with his recollections and observations, during the half century in which he was an active and leading member of the profession. Or that Judge Whitman, who had a similar experience, and a keen relish for the curious anecdotes, the peculiar customs and racy jokes, which lingered around the courts, and in the memory of the old practitioners, long after the eccentric characters, who had not only wit in themselves, but were the cause of wit in others, had passed to a higher bar, would have rendered this service. But these honored brethren were unwilling to undertake the task of transmitting these valuable memorials.

Solicitor General Davis, more competent perhaps, than any one, kindly replied to my letters. In one of his answers, dated in February, 1828, he writes, "If I were to give you a full answer to all your inquiries, it would amount to a volume of the size of Butler's Reminiscences. I am so much engaged at present, that I cannot write a book of reminiscences, but I will answer some of your inquiries." The next extract will show how much we have lost in the failure of Mr. Davis to record his observations. "From my earliest acquaintance with the country, in every part of which I have discharged my professional duties, I can recollect and furnish more sketches of the nature you request, than any other man now alive, because I am the oldest of the whole of them; but I cannot do it at present." In another letter he says, "If I should ever think of putting my reminiscences on paper, they would embrace a work of more extensive character, in what relates to the professional gentlemen in Maine, than could easily be obtained." Mr. Davis was at that time seventy years old, and still filling the office of Solicitor General. Before he left it, his health and memory failed, and the profession and the public lost anecdotes and reminiscences of the bar which can never be recovered.

At this late day, I have undertaken to preserve some of the memorials of the past. I have been obliged to range over a wide field, and to ask the contribution of facts, and even memoirs, from gentlemen who have had large experience at the bar and in general society. Among these, I must not fail to acknowledge my obligations to my good friends, the venerable Jacob McGaw of Bangor, John H. Sheppard of Boston, Robert H. Gardiner of Gardiner, William Allen of Norridgewock, and William B. Sewall and Judge Bourne of Kennebunk. These, with Mr. Dummer of Hallowell, Mr. Abbot of Castine, Dr. Bradley of Fryeburg, and Governor Crosby and Judge Williamson of Belfast, and others, have rendered me cheerful and valuable services, for which the profession, as well as myself, are their debtors.

I have traced the history of the law and of the courts from the founding of the first colony on the shores of Maine to the present time, and have accompanied the progress of the courts by a chapter on reports and reporters, from the origin of this important department of the law down to our day. I have also, as I believe, presented a sketch of every lawyer who practiced in our courts to the year 1800, with memoirs of prominent members of the profession from that time to the period of our separation from Massachusetts.

I should have been glad to extend my notices to all the principal lawyers who entered the practice previous to 1820, when we became an independent State. Many of those gentlemen have, in years subsequent to that event, taken the highest positions at the bar, on the bench, and in public life, and have honored the profession by distinguished talents and upright lives. But my work had already so much exceeded my original design and reasonable dimensions, that I felt obliged to deny myself the pleasure of speaking of those eminent men as their standing and merits deserve. Their names will endure, and some future gleaner will transmit them to the coming time.

I could wish that my labors might be justly entitled to the commendation which Lord Bacon, in the dedication of his Essays to the Duke of Buckingham, bestows upon that nobleman,—"You have planted things that are like to last." If mine do not last, I hope that they may, at least, interest the passing generation.

NOTE.

While this volume was going through the press, some changes took place on the bench of the Supreme Court. The constitutional terms of Chief Justice Tenney and Justice Goodenow, having expired in October, 1862, their places were supplied by the appointment of Justice John Appleton of Bangor, as chief justice, and Edward Fox of Portland and Jonathan G. Dickerson of Belfast, as associates.

Judge Tenney had held a seat upon the bench of the Supreme Court twenty-one years, having been appointed a justice in 1841, and chief in 1855. He was born in Rowley, Massachusetts, graduated at Bowdoin College in 1816, and after a successful and brilliant practice of twenty years in Norridgewock, he was raised to the bench. In 1850, he received from Bowdoin College the degree of LL. D., and has been a lecturer at the college, on Medical Jurisprudence, thirteen years.

Judge Goodenow was born in Henniker, New Hampshire, in 1793, and came to Maine with his father in 1802. He was awhile at Dartmouth College, but left before taking his degree. He pursued his professional studies with Mr. Holmes at Alfred, and commenced practice there in 1818.

He became the partner of Mr. Holmes, and married his daughter. In 1838, he was appointed attorney general of the State, and held the office four years. In 1841, he was appointed judge of the District Court for the western district, which office he held during the constitutional term of seven years. In 1855, he was raised to the bench of the Supreme Court. Bowdoin College conferred upon him, in 1820, the degree of A. M., and in 1860, that of LL. D. In 1838, he was chosen one of the trustees of that institution, and continues in the office. Judge Goodenow has taken a distinguished part in the politics as well as the law of the State, is, and ever has been, a firm supporter of all its good institutions: he retires to private life with unsullied reputation.

Since the above note was prepared, another change has taken place on the bench of the Supreme Court, by the resignation, in February, 1863, of Judge Fox, who had been appointed from the Cumberland Bar to the place made vacant by the elevation of Judge Appleton to the chief justiceship. Mr. Fox is a native of Portland, a graduate of Harvard College in the class of 1834, and of the Cambridge Law School in 1837. He occupied a prominent position at the Cumberland Bar, to which he again returns: he had been solicitor of the city of Portland several years previous to his appointment as judge.

PORTRAITS.

CONTENTS.

LAW AND LAWYERS.

LAW AND LAWYERS.

CHAPTER I.

THE EARLIEST JURISPRUDENCE IN MAINE.

THE adventurers who first settled on the coast of Maine, from the Piscataqua River to Pemaquid, were detached companies, without government or any bond of union. They were pursuing their private gains, and were generally employed in lumbering, fishing, and traffic with the Indians. The largest of these companies, those at Agamenticus, Winter Harbor, and Richmond's Island, adopted certain regulations for their government, called combinations. We have some fragments of records referring to such documents, and to the existence of a court among the colonists at the mouth of Saco River, prior to the arrival, in the summer of 1636, of Wm. Gorges, the nephew and deputy of the chief proprietor, of which the following is a specimen: "Feb. 7, 1636. It is ordered that Mr. Thomas Lewis shall appear the next court day at the now dwelling house of Thomas Williams (Winter Harbor), there to answer his contempt, and to shew cause why he will not deliver up the *combination* belonging to us, and to answer such actions as are commenced against him."

In consequence of freedom from restraint, and the roving life of the adventurers, there were, among the settlers, great dissipation and dissoluteness of manners, which is amply testified to by the early records; and was made one of the causes assigned by Sir Ferdinando Gorges for the appointment of a Governor General of all North Virginia, or New England, as the territory was then called. In a paper from the King, under date of Nov. 3, 1634, endorsed by Gorges, it is declared, "Since the undertaking of the plantations, complaints of various abuses have been received, to remedy which, advice has been taken with the Council of State, and directions given for a Governor to be sent over, to take charge of public affairs," &c.[1] Although this, I think, has primary reference to the Plymouth and Massachusetts companies, whose agitations in politics and religion were particularly offensive to the royal and episcopal government, yet it may well embrace all those separate companies which were then occupying the coast of Maine, whether with or without title. In another paper, under date of Nov., 1634, endorsed by Gorges, entitled "Considerations necessary to be resolved upon in settling the Governor for N. E.," it is stated that a number of discontented persons are got into the best parts of the country, and are having their supporters there; it is asked whether it would not be policy to lay a restraint upon this until license could be obtained that those who go over should be bound to conform to the rites and ceremonies of the church.[1] This restraint was imposed by the king.

Early in 1635, Gorges was expecting to receive the appointment of Governor General of New England, and made arrangements for an early departure; he was not appointed until 1637; a movement was also made to revoke the charter of the Massachusetts Company. But political agitations

[1] Early Doc. relating to Maine. Sainsbury's Col. Papers.

commencing at this time, both in Scotland and England, withdrew attention from colonial affairs, and the governor, instead of coming to America, followed the king to Scotland. The charter was consequently not disturbed. In a letter to the Secretary of State, Sir Francis Windebank, March, 1635, Gorges writes, "I beseech you to do me the favor to let their lordships know that for as much as I perceive it is his majestie's gracious pleasure to assign me Gov. in N. E." he desired them to give order for repealing the "Patents of those already planted in the Bay of Massachusetts, that there be no just cause left of contention by reason thereof, when I arrive in those parts."

Ferdinando Gorges, grandson and heir of Sir Ferdinando, in a petition to the king, 1675, says, "The king, by reason of complaints against the settlers in Mass., &c., resolved to take to himself the gov't of N. E., and to have one general gov. there. That thereupon, he nominated Sir Ferdinando Gorges to be Governor. All which appears by the king's declarations and commissions, (July, 1637). That shortly after, the troubles which arose in Scotland and in England prevented pet'rs grandf. from going to his gov'nt, but he attended the king into Scotland." (Early Doc. 22.)

The declaration referred to is called the "King's Manifesto," and is dated July 23, 1637. (Sainsbury's Col. Papers, 1,256.) "The king declares his resolution to provide for the future good of those adventuring in any such undertakings by appointing Sir Fer. Gorges Governor, and commands that none be permitted to go into those parts without Gorges' knowledge or license, and directions where to settle." (Ib.)

Massachusetts, with a perseverance and ingenuity never exceeded, baffled all the efforts of her numerous and powerful enemies at home to annul her act of incorporation. She pursued steadily and successfully her settled purpose of maintaining her independence through a period of 140 years, until the final triumph of the Revolution.

On the surrender of their grand charter by the Plymouth Company in June, 1635, the country was divided among the several members. Gorges received the portion lying between the Piscataqua and the Kennebec Rivers, which he named New Somersetshire, from the county in England where his estates were situated. He immediately sent over his nephew, Capt. Wm. Gorges, to take formal possession of his Province, and to establish his authority there. The deputy held his first court at Saco, March 21, 1636. This is the first legal tribunal, constituted by authority, which existed in Maine. The members of the court are styled commissioners; they were seven in number, and resided in different parts of the Province: Purchase came from Brunswick, Cammock and Josselyn from Scarboro', Bonithon and Lewis from Saco, and Godfrey from York: these are historical names, and all but Lewis and Cammock lived many years, to partake of the agitations and trials which awaited the foundation of this now flourishing commonwealth.

Previous to the arrival of Wm. Gorges, some kind of government must have existed in the different settlements which had been established at Kittery, York, the mouth of Saco River, at Spurwink, and Casco. It is probable that they were held together by voluntary associations, as at Exeter and other places where the proprietors had provided no legal government. A few scattered fragments on the records of York County, indicate such to be the fact. By these it appears that courts were held, in which civil causes were tried and verdicts rendered by a jury. One of these fragments of the date, Feb. 7, 1636, is an order that Thomas Lewis, who was one of the original patentees of Saco, should appear on next court day, to shew cause why he will not deliver up the combination belonging to us.

The court established by Wm. Gorges assumed general jurisdiction over the whole Province, not only of the rights of parties but of government, and endeavored to introduce something of order out of the very discordant materials which had been gathered upon the different points of the territory. Actions of trespass, slander, incontinency, for drunkenness, and "rash speeches," occurred frequently, and were generally determined by the intervention of a jury of six or more persons. The forms of proceeding were of the simplest character, and the absence of lawyers is found in the entire freedom from all technicalities in the pleadings and verdicts: they are marked by plainness of speech and special application. A single specimen may be cited in illustration: "Sept. 7, 1636. Whereas Mr. George Cleeve hath not paid the sum of £5. 16. 8. unto Wm. Riall according to the order above specified, these are therefore to authorize you in his majestie's name, to make seizure and attach any manner of goods and chattels then belonging to the said Cleeve, for the full satisfaction of the debt and penalty above specified, and this shall be your warrant." This was directed to the constable of Saco, and signed by four members of the court: viz., Vines, Bonithon, Cammock, and Lewis.

The criminal proceedings were equally simple: "March 25, 1636. There was this day presented by Mr. Theophilus Davis, officer for this place, (Saco), John Wotton for being drunk and giving ill tearms to the officer, John the carpenter for being drunk, James Coale for being drunk, Wm. Scadlock for being drunk. John Wotton is by order of court to make a pair of stocks by the last of April or to pay 40s. 8d. in money. Also he is fined 5s. 8d. for being drunk." Each of the others was fined 5s. 8d. for drunkenness.

But none of the charters to the original proprietors contained any powers of government; they were merely territorial grants. And Sir Ferdinando Gorges perceiving how ineffectual these were, had never ceased to importune the king to confirm his charter, with the necessary powers to enforce his jurisdiction. This he succeeded in accomplishing, and a patent was issued to him under the Great Seal, dated April 3, 1639, which conferred upon him unlimited power. By this charter the name of his territory was changed to the Province of Maine, which is its first appearance in our history. Power was conferred, "with the assent of the greater part of the free-holders of said Province," to make, ordain, and publish laws, ordinances, and constitutions: to erect courts of justice, ecclesiastical, civil, and temporal: the church of England to be the religion of the Province: to appoint magistrates, judges, and officers, with appeal to the Lord Proprietor: to raise troops, prosecute war, build forts, towns, and cities: to establish markets: to erect manors: to fit out a navy with admiral rights, jurisdictions, &c. More ample powers were never bestowed upon a subject. Gorges immediately set himself to work to organize a government under his charter. His commission to his new councillors, and his ordinances, bear date Sept. 2, 1639. By these Sir Thomas Josselyn was nominated deputy governor, and Vines, Champernoon, Henry Josselyn, Bonithon, Hooke, and Godfrey, his councillors. Sir Thomas declined the appointment of deputy, and the office was conferred by Gorges on his cousin, Thomas Gorges, who arrived at his Province in the spring of 1640. This was an able board. Thomas Gorges was educated at the Inns of Court, and was a lawyer, the first and only one, so far as we have any knowledge, who resided in the Province for the first hundred years after its settlement, except one, Thomas Morton, who was driven from Massachusetts and came to

York in 1644. Vines had long experience of the country: he was the steward and confidential agent of the proprietor, and had a grant embracing the present town of Biddeford, in which he resided. Champernoon was a nephew of Sir F. Gorges, and was of an ancient family in the county of Devon. Henry Josselyn had been in the country from six to nine years, was of a good family, the son of Sir Thomas Josselyn of Kent, and was placed in responsible positions as early as 1634 in New Hampshire and Maine, and continued to sustain his character in various fortunes, as a prominent actor in our provincial affairs, until his death in 1682. Bonithon was here in 1632 as one of the two grantees of the territory on the east side of Saco River, now embraced in the town of Saco. He was a man of energy and enterprise, and strenuously opposed the extension of the Massachusetts jurisdiction over this province in 1652, and the following years, for which he was proscribed. Wm. Hooke was son of Alderman Hooke of Bristol, England, and an early settler of York, as was also the remaining councillor, Godfrey, who was connected with our political affairs forty years. He was the first to occupy the large tract of land at the mouth of York River, where was the principal plantation of Gorges, on which he expended much money, early erecting a manor house and a mill there, and stocking the place with cattle. Gorges in his "Narrative," written in 1640, p. 50, says, "I have not sped so ill, I thank my God for it, but I have a house and home there, and some necessary means of profit, by my saw mills and corn mills, besides some annual receipts, sufficient to lay the foundation of greater matters, now the government is established."

These were the men to whom the Lord Proprietor confided the affairs of his large domain; they composed not only an executive council for the province, but a court for the trial of all criminal offenses, and, as he quaintly said, to determine all differences arising between party and party, for *meum* and *tuum*. His commission to them was, to hold courts, to administer oaths, to determine all causes, civil and criminal, public and private, according to justice and equity. This power also embraced admiralty and probate jurisdiction. And so much did he enter into details in the affairs of his government that he even prescribed the forms of proceeding, which, to prevent embarrassment among a people removed from all technicalities and legal appliances, were of the most simple kind, as the following summons prescribed in his ordinances will show: "To our well beloved, A. B., Greeting. These are to will and command you to come and appear before us, the council established in the Province of Maine, upon the —— day of ——, to answer to the complaint of ——. Given under our hands and seals."

The same simplicity in form was carried into other proceedings of the court, of which the following declaration and verdict in the year 1647 are examples. "To the worshipful Henry Josselyn, Esq., with the rest of the commissioners and assistants now assembled at Wells. Captain Francis Champenoone Plf. against Wm. Paine of Ipswich, declareth against the said Wm. Paine for certain monies due for a cable or hawser delivered unto his servant Wm. Quirke to the value of twenty pounds or there about." The verdict is equally plain: "We find for the Plf. fourteen pounds sterling and cost of court."

The following forms of a declaration and plea show a degree of point and plainness worthy of imitation. "Ambrose Berry Plf. v. John Smith Dft. in an action of account. The Plf. declareth that the Deft. oweth him on account between them the 11th day of May last, the sum of £4. 11. 8. which the Deft. refuseth to pay, notwithstanding he hath been often thereto required, and thereupon he brings his action and craveth for his damages, &c."

"The answer of John Smith Deft. The Deft. hereunto answereth and saith that he doth not owe the Plf. the aforesaid sum of £4. 11. 8. in manner and form as the Plf. declareth, and thereupon puts himself upon the trial of twelve men." This record indicates the hand of a lawyer, and that was probably Thomas Gorges.

The people of the several plantations had been summoned by warrant from "Richard Vines, Steward General to Sir Ferdinando Gorges," "to appear at a General Court to be holden at Saco on the 25th June next, for the settling of government within said province." The inhabitants of Agamenticus responded by sending four deputies "to appear for us at said courte, and do hereby give unto said parties full power and authority for us to treate and conclude of any thing which in their discretion shall be for the good and benefit of this plantation."

The first session of the court under the charter was held June 25th, 1640. The following officers were then sworn: Richard Vines, Esq., Richard Bonithon, Esq., Henry Josselyn, Esq., and Edward Godfrey, Gentleman, Counsellors; Roger Garde, Register, Robert Sankey, Provost Marshal, besides an under marshal and constables.

There were eighteen entries of civil actions, and nine complaints. At the September session, the Deputy Governor, Thomas Gorges, presiding, there were pending twenty-eight civil actions, of which nine were jury trials, and thirteen indictments. This first general court divided the Province into two parts, the western extending from the Piscataqua to Kennebunk, the eastern to the Sagadahoc: and in each an inferior court was established, to be held three times a year; and provided that there be one general court for the whole Province, to be held at Saco every year on the 25th day of June.

Among the proceedings of this first court was an action

of trespass between two of the most considerable men of the Province, — Richard Foxwell, the son-in-law of Capt. Richard Bonithon, one of the proprietors of the eastern side of Saco River, now Saco, and Capt. Thomas Cammock, nephew of the Earl of Warwick, and proprietor of the tract on the eastern side of Blackpoint River, now Scarboro'. We may therefore suppose that the best legal skill of the province was employed in the case. We quote the record: "The Plaint. here declares that he hath for these foure years or thereaboute lived at Blackpoynt in the right of Capt. Richard Bonithon, his father-in-law, who settled him there, and gave him as much freedom and privilege as by virtue of his patent he could, ether for planting, fishing, fowling or the like, which was the main cause of his settling there. Now the Plf. further declareth that the deft., Capt. Thomas Cammock, hath often times and still doth, both to himself and others, forbid, and by violence oppose the said privilege of fishing for Basse and lobsters in the said river of Blackpoynt and the shoales thereof, to the great damage and hindrance of himself and many others, it being the greatest part of his reliefe for himself and family for the yeare, and hath also assaulted and taken away the goods of the Plf., and further threateneth him: to the damage of 20 shillings sterling at the least, for which the Plf. humbly desireth this court for a * * according to law."

"The answer of Capt. Thomas Cammock the deft.

"Hereunto the defendant answereth and saith, that by virtue of his patent, the Royaltie of fishing and fowling belongeth to him, and not to be violently trespassed by force, and hath sustained great damage by their fishing and comming on his ground and otherwise. Though he never denied any that came with leave or in a fayre way, with acknowledgement, but thinketh it intrusion to be diffringed of his grant which all pattentees enjoy: for redress referreth himself to the court."

"The Plf. and deft. hereupon joyne issue, and put themselves upon the trial of a jury of twelve men: viz., Mr. Thomas Page, Mr. Arthur McWorth, Mr. George Frost, Mr. Richard Tucker, Mr. Thomas Williams, Mr. Wm. Cole, John Heard, Edward Robinson, George Puddington, Francis Robinson, Edward Small, and John West, good men and true."

"The jury give in here their verdict, and find with the Plf. and give him for damage twenty shillings with a restauration of the goods again which were taken from him by the deft. Judgment is given by the court upon this verdict, and execution awarded."

The records of the administration of estates and wills are intermingled in the same books with other proceedings, the court having jurisdiction in Probate as well as in other matters. In the first book is the inventory of the estate of "Richard Williams servant to Mr. Matthew Craddock Merchant," dated June 15, 1635: he died in March, 1635. The following is the record in this case, and is interesting as being the *first* administration granted in this territory:

"At this court (1640) commeth Payton Cooke, gent., in the behalf of himself and others the creditors of Richard Williams, late of this plantation, who died here intestate, aboute foure years since. And craveth of this court power and authority to take into his custody, all the goods and chattels of the said Richard Williams. Whereupon the court hath granted to the said Payton Cooke letters of Administration, and thereby given him power to take the said goods and chattels into his custody and the same to administer to himself and the said creditors proportionally, so far as the same shall extend, according to the law of England in that case provided, and the true intent and meaning of this court. The said Payton Cooke to certify at the next courte holden here of his proceedings herein."

As we have given the first probate record of our State, we will close this portion of our judicial history by a transcript of the *first bill in equity* in Maine, and probably the first in New England. It was entered June, 1640:

"The complainant humbly sheweth, that whereas about the 14th day of November, 1637, there was an account passed, between the complainant and George Cleeves and Richard Tucker, upon which account * * among other goods the said George Cleeves and Richard Tucker, for satisfaction, did sell and deliver to the complainant one thousand of clapboards, receiving then from him a general acquittance, which the said complainant did then likewise give; the said George Cleeves and Richard Tucker then promising the complainant, that if he could not enjoy the said clapboards, that they would, notwithstanding the said acquittance, give him satisfaction for them, according to the rate he took them; notwithstanding the said George Cleeves and Richard Tucker did formerly know that the said clapboards were in controversy, neither can the Plf. enjoy them; and they utterly refuse to give the complainant any satisfaction for the same. Whereupon he humbly entreateth this court to take the same into consideration and to grant him the like privilege, which the honorable court of Chancery affordeth all his majestie's subjects in cases of this nature.

Your humble petitioner, JOHN HINKFORD."

"The court hath ordered the defts. to answer to this bill, at the next court to be holden here."

The records have not preserved any answer.

Cleeves and Tucker were the first settlers of the Neck, now Portland, in 1632.

Besides the general and inferior courts, commissioners, corresponding to justices of the peace or municipal judges of the present day, were appointed in each town for the trial of small causes; their jurisdiction in civil matters being limited to forty shillings. From their judgments an appeal lay to the higher court.

After near forty years of incessant effort in the cause of colonization, and at the cost of a large portion of his estate, the noble founder of Maine had the satisfaction, at last, of seeing established in his extensive and beautiful domain, an administration of government which was giving protection to the scattered colonists, and binding them together under the security of laws, which, by the charter, they would have the privilege of enacting.

But at this juncture, new and alarming difficulties arose, which soon disturbed the order which had been established, and blasted the hopes of the unfortunate proprietor. In the spring of 1642, the civil war broke out in England. A long course of arbitrary measures on the part of the king, and irritating encroachments and bold assertions in Parliament, of the rights of the people, brought the contending parties to the end of negotiations, and to an open and severe conflict. The king fled to York and was joined by his loyal friends, while Parliament, supported by the city of London, the representative and center of the popular sentiment, made active preparations to maintain the principles of freedom they had so nobly advanced.

Gorges gave his person and his fortune to the royal cause, and devoted the remainder of his life to active duty for his master's service, in which he died in 1647: we have no information in regard to his age, but from the part he took in the insurrection of the Earl of Essex in 1601, forty-six years prior to his death, he must have been at least seventy-five years old.

The troubles in the mother country could not fail to be felt in her colonies. Massachusetts, with her strong Puritan tendency, secretly rejoiced in every movement undertaken in the cause of civil and religious liberty; while Maine was equally loyal to the king and the church. It was not long, however, before the agitations in England began to disturb the harmony of the people here. George Cleeves, the first settler of Portland, and all his life an agitator, went home and induced Sir Alexander Rigby, an active republican and Parliamentarian, to interest himself in the affairs of this Province. He persuaded him to get a foot-hold here by the purchase of the Plough Patent, as it was called, a grant made by the council of Plymouth in 1630 to John Dy and others, extending from Cape Porpoise to Cape Elizabeth. The title was wholly invalid, and had never been enforced. But it afforded a sufficient color under which to hoist the Puritan flag, which, sustained by the Puritan power in England, and the sympathies of the Puritan Commonwealth adjoining, succeeded in exercising a brief authority, and distracting the counsels of the people in the eastern part of Gorges' Province. Cleeves was sent over by Rigby as his deputy in 1643, and succeeded in holding courts at Casco and Scarboro' for seven or eight years, in conflict with the courts of Gorges, which still kept up their claim over the whole territory, and the exercise of their jurisdiction in the western part of the Province, under Vines, the faithful servant and deputy of Gorges. In 1645, Vines, weary of conflict and agitation, left the Province and settled in Barbadoes, and was succeeded by the veteran emigrant, Edward Godfrey, the first settler of York, who valiantly and persistently maintained the rights of Gorges and his heirs, until overpowered by a superior force.

This new power was no other than Massachusetts, who, taking advantage of the triumph of her principles in England, and dreading and hating the Episcopal power in Maine, under a forced construction of the language of her charter, assumed title and jurisdiction over all the territory lying southerly of a line drawn from Lake Winnepiseogee to Casco Bay. She was not long in asserting her pretended title: in 1652 she demanded of Godfrey, the governor, a submission of the people to her jurisdiction and laws. After a strenuous, but ineffectual opposition by the governor, the inhabitants, receiving no aid nor encouragement from the proprietor in England, yielded to the necessity of the case. Those in the western part of the Province submitted to her jurisdiction in November, 1652, those in the central part, Cape Porpoise and Saco, in July, 1653; and in July, 1658, after a most desperate resistance by the sturdy Episcopalians and loyalists, the Rev. Robert Jordan, Henry Josselyn, Arthur McWorth, and others, a majority of the inhabitants, weary with the conflict, acknowledged themselves "to be subject to the government of Massachusetts Bay."

This usurpation of the Bay colony corresponded with that of the Parliament at home; and though successful, it had no foundation in right. I will not say that it was not eventually best for the people here; it resulted in giving them a good and permanent government and stable and just laws. The Restoration in England in 1660 brought with it new complicities in this Province; it revived the hopes and exertions of the grandson and heir of Sir Ferdinando Gorges. Encouraged by the king, and confirmed by repeated decisions of the council and the courts, he made strenuous efforts to recover his power. He appointed his deputy governor and commissioners, and re-established his courts, which were in constant conflict with those of Massachusetts. The commissioners of Gorges, in 1662, Henry Josselyn and Nicholas Shapleigh, protested against the acts and authority of Massachusetts; Jordan and Neale, and many of the most substantial men of the Province, joined with them, while they were opposed by Cleeves, Munjoy, and others, who adhered to Massachusetts, and a state of violence and anarchy pervaded the whole territory.

The king's commissioners came over in 1664 with an order from the king to Massachusetts, to deliver to the agent of Gorges quiet possession of his Province. The general court, through their agent, replied, claiming the territory by their patent, which they say was ten or eleven years prior to that of Gorges, and transmitted the report of their surveyors, who run the line from Winnepiseogee to Casco Bay, as evidence of their title. This controversy was kept up by Massachusetts for twelve or fifteen years, notwithstanding decrees of court, orders in council, and peremptory demands of the king, uniformly against her, until that persistent colony, finding her own charter in danger by a longer contest, finally employed an agent to negotiate with Gorges for the purchase of his whole title, and succeeded in procuring a conveyance of all his interests in the Province in 1677, for £1250 sterling. She thus established a just claim to the jurisdiction and territory, which was acknowledged by the inhabitants, and her supremacy recognized.

During this long period of thirty years, while this triangular controversy was raging, law had but feeble sway; its voice could not be heard above the strife of passion and the din of war. Courts indeed were kept up, commissioners and judges held their terms, sometimes guarded by soldiers, and sometimes driven by them from their seats; but it was one thing to decide and decree, and quite another to execute, where authority and jurisdiction were denied and resisted. It may, however, be affirmed that during this interregnum of a stable and recognized government, the forms of proceedings remained of the simplest kind, and no person presiding in the courts under any of the governments that claimed title in the Province, was educated to the law, or familiar with its principles. The law did not exist among the people as a science, nor was its practice regulated by men trained to the profession.

CHAPTER II.

THE ADMINISTRATION OF THE PROVINCIAL LAWS UNDER MASSACHUSETTS.

At the time of the purchase of Maine by Massachusetts, 1677, the whole Province was lying desolate under the scourge of the Indian war. Massachusetts had defended various parts in it, had kept the savages at bay, and brought them to sue for peace. The cost to her was eight thousand pounds sterling. And when the people came back at the close of the war in 1678, they returned as the lawful and acknowledged subjects of Massachusetts. Jordan, her most intelligent and active opponent, did not return; he died, in 1679, at Great Island in Portsmouth harbor, N. H., to which he had fled from the Indians, in the 68th year of his age; and Episcopalianism, to whose service he had given the best years of his life, may be said to have died with him in Maine. Cleeves and Munjoy were also dead. Godfrey had returned to England, and Josselyn, the constant and energetic opponent of Massachusetts, found service, and an important position, in the Duke of York's province at Pemaquid. Thus the way was fairly opened for the peaceful rule of the Bay Colony, and she was not long in improving it. Courts were immediately established, over which

Thomas Danforth presided; and in 1680, Danforth was appointed President of the Province. He at once proceeded to York, and held an assembly composed of the representatives of the people, for the reorganization of the government.

Under the Colonial charter of Massachusetts to the year 1692, when the Province charter went into effect, there had been in Massachusetts no Supreme or Superior Court, technically so called. The jurisdiction, which by the Provincial charter was granted to that Court, had been exercised by the magistrates or assistants, the upper branch of the General Court. They assumed supreme judicial power, and jurisdiction in all matters of divorce, the probate of wills, and the settlement of the estates of deceased persons. And as their object was the establishment of a religious commonwealth, they regarded the laws of Moses "better precedents than the common law, or the decisions of Westminster."

As the population and the complicities of business multiplied, it was found necessary to establish local courts; and a tribunal was organized in each county, consisting of magistrates residing in the county, appointed by the General Court, together with "such persons of worth as the freemen of the county should nominate," not to exceed five in all. The courts thus constituted had power to appoint clerks, summon juries, issue precepts, and render judgment, having jurisdiction in all cases except those of a capital nature. They also had probate jurisdiction, and the regulation of highways and other county matters. This tribunal, called the County Court, combined the jurisdiction of the Common Pleas and the General Sessions of the Peace. An appeal lay to the Court of Assistants, always held in Boston.

This system continued in Massachusetts during the existence of the colony, but was not extended over Maine, as it was decided that the purchased territory must be governed according to the charter granted to Gorges.

Under the new organization, provision was made for appeals in all cases from the Superior Courts, and that no sentence should be given in capital trials without the concurrence of the major part of the Assembly; that either party was at liberty to object, before pleading, to any of the justices or deputies. And it was ordered that the laws, orders, and precedents that had been before practiced and were of use in the Province, should remain in full force until the General Assembly or Council should take order therein.

This jurisdiction continued eleven years from the purchase, until it was interrupted by the second Indian war, which devastated the whole eastern country. During the existence of the colonial government, no educated lawyer practiced in the courts of Maine, or sat upon the bench, with the exception of Thomas Gorges, the first deputy of the proprietor, who was educated at the Inns of Court in London, and presided in the General Court of the Province in 1640, and for three years after.

There was also for the brief period of two years from 1643, another educated lawyer in the Province, Thomas Morton, who had been master of the revels in Merry Mount, now Quincy, Massachusetts, in 1625, and wrote many satirical pieces upon the colony. He was driven out of Massachusetts in 1628, and went back to England; but returning in 1643, he was imprisoned and fined. On being set at liberty, he thought it expedient to abandon the Bay Colony for one where he could have a larger liberty. He came to Agamenticus, now York, where he died two years after, neglected and poor. The Memorialist of Plymouth calls him "a pettifogger at Furnival's Inn." It is not probable that he had any practice in our courts. In the council minutes, May 5, 1635, relating to the surrender of the charter of New England, and the division of the territory, *Thomas Morton* is appointed solicitor to prosecute a suit for repealing the patent of the Massachusetts Company.[1] It is not improbable that he is the lawyer before referred to, and probably had a better reputation at home than in this country, where his conduct was criticised by hostile judges. His satirical "rhymes and verses," on the peculiarities of New England, gave great offense, and for which the government of Massachusetts had him "set him in the Bilbows" in 1628.

---

1 Sainsbury's Colonial Papers, i. p. 206.

CHAPTER III.

PEMAQUID PROVINCE — ITS JURISDICTION AND JURISPRUDENCE.

THE remarks we have made in the preceding pages apply particularly to the Province of Gorges, embracing the territory between the Piscataqua and Kennebec Rivers. The central portion of our State, lying between the Kennebec and Penobscot Rivers, was under different jurisdictions. All east of the Penobscot, with the exception of the Castine Peninsula, remained a wilderness, in its native condition, during the entire 17th century.

Pemaquid and the adjacent territory were occupied by permanent settlers as early as 1625; several years before, it had been the frequent resort of fishermen from Europe, who had found this coast, and the island of Monhegan, lying twelve miles from Pemaquid Point, the most convenient station to pursue their profitable occupation.

We presume no government or administration of law existed among these adventurers, until after the charter granted by the Council of New England to Aldworth and Elbridge of Bristol, England, in 1632; although as early as 1630, the very year that Boston was founded, it had a population of about five hundred persons; except it may have been by voluntary association, as is found to have been the case in most of the other settlements on the coast. It was one of the considerations of the grant to Aldworth and Elbridge, that they had undertaken to build a town on their grant, and "settle divers inhabitants there for the general good of that country."[1]

By that charter, powers of government were granted to the proprietors; and they were authorized to "establish such laws and ordinances as are for the better government of the said persons so transported, and the same by such officer or officers, as they shall by most voices elect and choose, to put in execution."

By this provision, a representative government was established, the inhabitants being authorized to elect their executive officers by a majority of votes. Abraham Shurt, the agent of the proprietors, was long the chief magistrate of the colony, and, with a board of assistants, administered the government. What courts were established, or what laws enacted, no record remains to inform us. But that there was need of laws, and an efficient administration of them, we cannot doubt, from the magnitude of the trade and business of the colonists, and the intercourse they had with the mother country and the other colonies. It was at one time the seat of the most considerable transactions of any settlement upon the New England coast. Shurt was sent over by his employers in 1626, to take charge of their interest at Monhegan, and afterwards as the manager of their affairs under the new patent. He appears to have been active, intelligent, and faithful; and Mr. Thornton, in his interesting account of ancient Pemaquid, in the fifth volume of the Maine Historical Collections, attributes to him the authorship of the brief and comprehensive formula by which the acknowledgment of the deeds in Maine and Massachusetts

---

[1] Sainsbury's Colonial Papers, i. 141.

has ever been certified. The deed from the Indian sachems, of the Pemaquid territory, to John Brown, dated July 15, 1625, bears the certificate of acknowledgment in the well known terms, "personally appeared and acknowledged this instrument to be their act and deed, at Pemaquid, July 24, 1626. Before me, Abraham Shurt." We know of no such form prior to that. Shurt was living in 1662, at the age of 80, "or thereabout," as he expresses it in a deposition given in December of that year.[1]

This grant passed out of the hands of the heir of the original proprietors in 1650, and the controverted titles, in various sources, from the Indians, English patentees, and under possessory rights, became the subject in after years of a furious and most bitter controversy, which was only settled by the interference of the government of Massachusetts, and then by compromise, in 1812.

During a period of twenty years from this time, there seems to have been a very inefficient administration of law in that Province. The commissioners of Charles II., in 1664, visited this portion of the State, and give a very unfavorable view of its condition at that time. They say, "Upon Shipscot River and upon Pemaquid 8 or 10 miles asunder, are three small plantations belonging to his royal highnesse, the biggest of which hath not above 30 houses in it and those very mean ones. The people for the most part are fishermen, and never had any government among them." The commissioners endeavored to establish order and civil government there, and for that purpose appointed most respectable persons, living in other parts of the State, as magistrates, among whom were Henry Josselyn of Scarboro',

---

[1] Mr. Williamson, in his History of Maine, says, "Abraham Shurt, Esq., died at Pemaquid about 1680." i. 603. We know not upon what authority; it is probably an error.

Robert Jordan and George Munjoy of Falmouth. It is evident that the commissioners underrated both the population and condition of that colony.

At this time it had passed into the hands of James, Duke of York, brother of the king, by a double title, first in 1663, by purchase from Lord Stirling, who had a grant of it from the Council for New England, and second, by a grant from the king, March, 1665. But this, from various reasons, did not become available until 1673; and when the Governor of New York, which was also granted to the Duke, assumed the administration of government there, it became an appendage of the Colony of New York, and was represented in its General Assembly. Courts were established by the Council sitting in New York, as follows: "June 24, 1680. In Council, Ordered, that some persons be appointed to go from here to Pemaquid for holding courts." "June 26. Sagadahock magistrates or officers to continue, the courts to try only for 40s. instead of £5 formerly granted them." "Mr. Potter, Lawrence Dennis, and Richard Redding to be commissioners and assistants in the courts of session to try to £20." The noted Sir Edmund Andros was governor at this time, of the Duke of York's possessions on this continent; and, as such, issued a commission to Henry Josselyn, who had formerly been one of Gorges' commissioners, residing in Scarboro', and others, to be a court of session, and "to act according to law and former practise." This court held its sessions in June and November. Justices of the Peace were also appointed from time to time, with authority to hear and determine causes civil and criminal.

Thomas Gyles lived, at the time of the first Indian war, at Merry Meeting Bay; he afterwards settled at Pemaquid, and was made chief justice of the court there, as his son, John, affirms. He was killed by the Indians in 1689.

John Jordan, the eldest son of the Rev. Robert Jordan

of Cape Elizabeth, was appointed by Governor Andros, a special justice for Cornwall, in 1680.

None of these persons were educated to the law, but we may suppose from their rank, position, and opportunities, that they were well qualified to discharge the duties required of them. Josselyn, in particular, had for more than forty years served as assistant, commissioner, and judge, under the various governments which had existed in the western part of the State; and from his high birth as a son of Sir Thomas Josselyn, we may suppose that he had been well instructed in the learning of his day, before he came to the country. He always maintained a high character, and died at an advanced age in the confidence and respect of all who knew him.

The governors, for the time being, Andros and Dongan, occasionally visited the Province, which was called the County of Cornwall: the principal place was Pemaquid, which was constituted a port of entry, and made a shire town: it had paved streets, was defended by one of the best forts on the coast, and was surrounded by a respectable and busy population. The county embraced all the settlements between the Kennebec and Penobscot Rivers, over which the Governor of New York exercised almost despotic jurisdiction. Quite a large commerce was carried on with Europe, and the other English colonies on the coast, of which masts, lumber, furs, and fish constituted the principal exports, and for which wines, liquors, coin, and various kinds of merchandise were received in exchange. A collector was appointed for Pemaquid City, and his instructions from the Council in New York are minute, and as formal as those emanating from our own Secretary of the Treasury. The people were jealous to maintain the character and importance of that place; and in a petition to the Governor and Council of New York, they ask that "Pemaquid may still remain the metropolitan of these parts because it ever have been so, before Boston was settled."

The Province of Pemaquid included the thriving settlements on the eastern side of the Kennebec River, with Arrowsic and Parker's Islands. At the commissioners' court, held at Sheepscot in September, 1665, their principal inhabitants, among whom were Hammond and Parker, took the oath of allegiance to the proprietor. And Lawrence Denny, or Dennis, a resident there, was afterwards commissioned one of the justices of the court in the Province.

Before this time, however, the inhabitants on the Kennebec had been under the government of the Plymouth Colony, by virtue of the charter granted to William Bradford, in 1620; and by him, in 1640, assigned to the colony. It was used by that colony for forty years, merely as a source of revenue from the salmon and shad fisheries, and traffic in lumber and furs. They had a magistrate and agents there to preserve order and regulate their trade; but never regarded it as the place of a permanent settlement. In 1661 the colony sold the patent to some wealthy men in Massachusetts, Antipas Boies, Edward Tyng, Thomas Brattle, and John Winslow; but the inhabitants were few and scattered, and no regular government was established in it, until the Duke of York took possession of the country.

In September, 1686, the Duke of York, who had now become James II., transferred the jurisdiction of his eastern territory to Massachusetts, which immediately assumed the government over it. His order is thus headed, "Royal order for the surrender of Pemaquid to Massachusetts," and goes on to say, "Whereas we have thought fit to direct that our port and country of Pemaquid, in regard of its distance from New York, be for the future annexed to and be continued under the government of our territory and dominion of New England," he orders, &c.

There was, undoubtedly, disaffection and insubordination among the people, and it was difficult for a government so far removed, to keep them in subjection. They had, from the roving habits of the people, their freedom from a regular system of law, and their distance from any controlling authority, acquired ideas of liberty and a free, democratic spirit, which made them hard subjects for such a desultory jurisdiction as was exercised over them. The better part had long desired a firm and stable government, and had applied to Massachusetts to take them under her protection. Massachusetts had now attained the object of her pursuit and ambition. She felt that her own security, in a measure, depended upon her power and right to control the unquiet spirits which occupied the territories adjacent to her, and with whom she had long had intimate commercial and political relations. Her efforts were at last crowned with success, and she lost no time in giving stability to the institutions in her new acquisitions.

The second Indian war, which broke out soon after, 1689, interrupted her plans, and instead of establishing a peaceful government, she was called upon to defend the territory, and to rescue the inhabitants from imminent peril. And before it was over, the new charter of 1691 was granted, which united with the old Bay Colony, that of Plymouth, the whole territory of Maine, and also Nova Scotia.

CHAPTER IV.

MAINE UNDER THE CHARTER OF 1691. COURTS AND JUDGES.

THE course, now, of Massachusetts was more plain and easy; instead of incessant controversy, and the embarrassment of adapting her policy to various systems of jurisprudence, and to the irregular habits of lawless adventurers, her excellent charter gave union and force to her government. Her wise statesmen, and she had many, immediately set themselves to work, to strengthen the rights and liberties of the people, and to confirm the foundations already laid for republican institutions. Her laws were hereafter to be uniform, and to have the same application and execution in Plymouth and in Maine, as in Suffolk and Middlesex.

The first act she passed, under the new charter, June, 1692, was to continue the existing laws in force, until the 10th of the ensuing November. The second act was a declaration of principles, so just and simple, and such a foreshadowing of the great doctrines enunciated emphatically, eighty-four years afterwards, as the basis of the Revolution, that I think they ought to be recalled to our notice. They say:

"Be it declared and enacted by the governor, council and representatives of their majesties province of the Massachusetts Bay, That all and every the rights and liberties of the people shall be firmly and strictly holden and observed: That is to say, That no freeman shall be taken and imprisoned, or be disseized of his freehold, or liberties, or his free customs, or be outlawed or exiled, or in any manner destroyed, nor shall be passed upon, adjudged or condemned, but by the lawful judgment of his peers, or the law of this province.

"Justice nor right shall be neither sold, denied or deferred to any man within this province.

"No man shall be twice sentenced for one and the same crime, offence or trespass.

"No tax, assessment, custom, or imposition whatsoever shall be laid, assessed, imposed or levied on any of their majesties subjects in this province, or their estates, on any color or pretense whatsoever, but by the act and consent of the governor, council and representatives of the people, assembled in general court.

"No man of what state or condition soever, shall be put out of his lands or tenements, nor be taken nor imprisoned, nor disinherited nor banished, * * without being brought to answer by due process of law.

"All trials shall be by the verdict of twelve men, peers or equals, and of the neighborhood, and in the county or shire where the fact shall arise.

"In all capital cases there shall be a grand inquest.

"In all cases whatsoever, bail by sufficient sureties shall be allowed and taken, unless for treason or felony."

A "Habeas Corpus" act was passed at the same session.

These noble sentiments embody an extraordinary advance in civil liberty, — the cardinal principles of the Declaration of Independence, and of the bill of rights adopted in our constitutions; and show the flavor of the spirit and the watchful temper of the men who were molding the institu tions of New England, and preparing the way for the independence of foreign sovereignty, afterwards so gloriously achieved.

They followed this declaration with acts for quieting men's possessions of land, and settling the titles to estates, a most needed enactment in those disturbed times; another made lands and tenements liable for the payment of debts; the next established courts of justice, and these were substantially the same as they now exist. They were the justices of the peace for the trial of small causes; the Quarter Sessions held by the justices of the peace for the county, corresponding to our courts of county commissioners; the Inferior Court of Common Pleas; the Superior Court; and, strange to say, a Court of Chancery. The last, however, was disallowed by the home government, and never went into effect. The governor and council were by the charter made a Court of Probate; a Court of Admiralty was also established by the crown.

The Superior Court, thus established for the first time in the Province, consisted of a chief and four associate justices, who were Wm. Stoughton, chief justice, Thomas Danforth, who had been the President of Maine before the charter, Wait Winthrop, John Richards, and Samuel Sewall. None of these had been educated as lawyers, and there was not at that time an educated lawyer on the bench or at the bar! Stoughton had been a popular and successful preacher; after graduating at Harvard, he went to England and became a fellow of Oxford University; he was a man of learning and ability. Danforth was a politician and a statesman; had been Deputy Governor and President of Maine, and had discharged, for many years, important offices with integrity and wisdom. Winthrop was the grandson of the first Governor Winthrop: he was educated a physician, but was also a popular military leader and statesman. Richards was a wealthy merchant, and had been long in public life. Sewall, son of the first Henry Sewall, was born in England, and educated for the ministry, but was drawn away from his profession by the superior attractions of politics: in 1718 he was appointed chief justice of this court. He was a man of learning, and the most accurate lawyer upon the bench; he did much to introduce a correct and uniform practice in the courts; he recommended, in 1690, the form of case on book accounts instead of debt; the admission of books of account as evidence originated in Massachusetts before 1650. He was the ancestor of Chief Justice Samuel Sewall, who died in 1814; and his name in collateral branches has given lustre and dignity to the bench and bar in Massachusetts and Maine.

No educated lawyer held a seat upon the bench, during the existence of the Province charter, with the exception of Benjamin Lynde of Salem, Dudley of Roxbury, Trowbridge of Cambridge, and William Cushing, who, at the time of his appointment in 1772, resided in Maine. Judge Lynde, elevated to the bench in 1712, was the first educated lawyer placed upon it. Since the Revolution, the usage has been invariable to place no one on the bench but regularly trained lawyers.

This court held two sessions a year in the principal counties, but the trials of causes arising in Maine, which formed but one county till 1760, were held in Boston or Charlestown. It was not until 1699 that a term was granted to this State, which was held at Kittery until 1743, when it was removed to York. This continued to 1760, when the counties of Cumberland and Lincoln were established: a term of the Superior Court was first held in Cumberland in 1761; in Lincoln not until 1786; both held in June, but only for jury trials.

The judges who held the first term at Falmouth for

Cumberland, were Lieutenant-Governor Hutchinson, chief justice; Benjamin Lynde, John Cushing, and Peter Oliver, associates. This court, established in 1699, consisted of a chief and four other justices, and so constituted, continued during the existence of royal authority in the colony. The constitution of 1780 changed the title of this court to that of the "Supreme Judicial Court," but with the same powers and jurisdiction as its predecessor had, and with the same number of judges. The judges first appointed by the new government were William Cushing, Nathaniel Peaslee Sargent, James Sullivan, David Sewall, and Jedediah Foster. The court thus constituted continued until 1800, and was held in the several counties by a full bench for all purposes, three members forming a quorum. So that "all jury trials were in effect trials at bar, were conducted in the presence of the full court, and not less than three were competent to preside at such trials." This system was found to be embarrassing, as questions of law were discussed and decided in the hurry of the trial, without much examination, and, as often happened, with a divided court. It was the practice also for different members to charge the jury, and they often gave contradictory opinions upon points of law arising in the case. But as the circuits extended and business increased, it was found that the court could not dispatch the constantly increasing business, it being impossible for the full court to travel into each county and dispose of all the actions. The consequence was, a large accumulation of causes on the dockets, and great delay in disposing of them. But the people had become attached to this system, and were reluctant to have their cases tried other than by a full court; and the legislature, instead of adopting the only practicable remedy, which was the *nisi prius* system, by which jury trials are conducted by one judge, enlarged the number of judges to *seven*, in 1800, and made two quorums, so that the court could be held in two places at the same time. They also divided the Commonwealth into two circuits, an eastern and western, and authorized the court to be held in each county, except Suffolk, by three judges, but requiring the attendance of the whole seven in Suffolk.

But this change not relieving the difficulty, an act was passed in 1804, by which the number of judges was reduced to five, four of whom to constitute a quorum; to hold one term a year in each county, except Nantucket, Duke's, and Washington. It provided that, in case of disability, three might hold this term, and that another term should be held in those counties by two or more of the judges; but that any one might hold the court and discharge its duties, except in certain cases, among which were all criminal proceedings.

Under the guidance of the able and intelligent men who occupied seats upon this high tribunal, this department of government was gradually acquiring the form and finish which placed it upon a foundation of efficiency and security, and made it an honored and highly ornamental pillar of the State. In 1805, the *nisi prius* system was completely introduced, with five judges, of whom three might hold the *law* term, and one or more the *trial* terms, as it now exists in the old Commonwealth.

The judges of this court, until 1792, appeared on the bench in robes and wigs; in summer the robes were of black silk, in winter, of scarlet cloth. The judges of the United States Supreme Court, in the sessions at Washington, still retain the robe; the wig disappeared with the venerable William Cushing.

The records of this court for all the counties were kept in Boston, until 1797, when they were transferred to the custody of the clerks of the Common Pleas of the several counties, except those of Lincoln, Hancock, and Washington in Maine, and Duke's and Nantucket in Massachusetts. It was made the duty of the justices of the Supreme Court to appoint a clerk for the counties of Lincoln, Hancock, and Washington, to reside in and keep the records in such place in the county of Lincoln as the court should direct. The court appointed Jonathan Bowman, Jr., the clerk for these counties, his residence to be at Pownalborough. The duties of clerk had been divided between a stationary clerk and a circuit clerk: the former made up and kept the records, issued executions, certified copies, &c.: the latter attended the judges on their circuit, and discharged the duties incident to that office. John Tucker, of Boston, was the circuit clerk throughout the Commonwealth for many years; and Charles Cushing, brother of Judge William, sheriff of Lincoln before and during the Revolution, was the local clerk of Suffolk and Nantucket, which office he held from the close of the Revolution to his death in 1810.

By these various advances, the system of jurisprudence in Massachusetts and Maine had acquired its maturity, and was administered in its highest court by men of learning and of the purest integrity. The accomplished Chief Justice Dana retired from the bench, after a judicial service of twenty-one years, and was succeeded by the more learned Chief Justice Parsons. He was followed in 1813, by the amiable, just, and upright Sewall, who, after a year's labor in his high office, was suddenly cast down by death; and the accomplished, wise, and judicious Parker, who had begun his professional life at Castine, and continued it in Portland, was elevated to the station, which he honored and adorned for a period of sixteen years. He was succeeded by Shaw, his peer in all the high qualities which give lustre to the bench: whose recent retirement and death were deeply lamented.

In Maine, the *nisi prius* system was retained, and administered by a chief and two associate justices, until 1847, when an additional justice was appointed. In 1852 a radical change was made in the judicial system of the State: the Common Pleas was abolished, and all the litigation of the State, even appeals from justices of the peace, was cast upon the Supreme Court, then increased to seven judges. The effect of this system has been to clog the machinery of this tribunal with petty causes of little value or consequence, but which occupy as much time as those involving high principles and large values; and by occupying the time of the court, has deprived it of that leisure for research and deliberation which is needed to give it a high intellectual character, and confidence in its legal decisions; and by lowering the standard of legal attainment, has had a tendency to impair the authority of its judgments, and the reliance which is due to the tribunal of final resort.

COURT OF COMMON PLEAS.

A Common Pleas, called the Inferior Court, consisting of four judges, was organized for each county. The judges, in the language of the statute, were to be "substantial persons;" practically they were not "learned in the law," but they were generally prominent, well-to-do men, who had occupied political or municipal stations, and had acquired the reputation of honesty and capacity for public employment. Prior to the beginning of the present century, so far as my examination has extended, there had not been in Maine one educated lawyer on this bench. The first that I have found was John Frothingham, who was a regular practitioner of the Cumberland Bar, and appointed in 1804. The first judges of this court all resided west of Biddeford;

two terms a year were held in York, and two in Wells, until 1736, when, on the urgent application of the people in the central portion of the Province, a term was annually held, in June, at Falmouth, now Portland. Mr. Pepperell, afterwards Sir William, was then its chief justice. In 1760 the counties of Cumberland and Lincoln were incorporated, on which occasion two terms of the Common Pleas were established in each county. Lincoln then embraced the old Sagadahoc, or Duke of York's Province, and also all of the State lying east of the Penobscot River.

This court continued with the same jurisdiction, and the same number of judges, to the end of the royal government in Massachusetts, and was revived under the Constitution, with all its powers, in 1782. In 1804 the number of justices was reduced to three in each county; and in 1811, in the administration of Gov. Gerry, the old system, which had continued unimpaired for one hundred and twelve years, was abrogated, in form, at least, but not in jurisdiction or substance, and the circuit system adopted: by which the Commonwealth, including Maine, was divided into six circuits, of which three were in Maine; viz., the first, second, and third eastern circuits, in each of which a chief justice and two associate justices were appointed. Thus constituted, they remained until the separation of Maine from Massachusetts; when, after the machinery of the new government was well under way, the legislature, in 1822, established a court consisting of a chief justice and two associate justices, whose jurisdiction extended over the whole State; either one to hold the terms, and to receive a fixed salary, instead of the fees of court, which had, for the hundred and twenty years previous, been divided between the judges and their clerk for their compensation. The justices first appointed for this court, were, — chief justice, Ezekiel Whitman of Portland; Samuel E. Smith of Wiscasset, and David Perham of Bangor, associates.

The judges appointed by Governor Gerry, under the act of 1811, for Maine, were, for York, Cumberland, and Oxford, Benjamin Greene, chief; Judah Dana of Fryeburg, and William Widgery of Portland, associates: for Lincoln, Kennebec, and Somerset, Nathan Weston, Jr., chief; Benjamin Ames and Judah McLellan, associates: for Hancock and Washington, William Crosby, chief; Martin Kinsley and James Campbell, associates. These were all lawyers but Widgery, Kinsley, and Campbell.

This intermediate system continued, according to the constant usage of the country, for more than one hundred and fifty years, until the radical change took place by the act of 1852, when the court was abolished, and its duties transferred entire to the Supreme Court.

The trials in these courts were by the intervention of a jury. This institution came in with the first settlers, both in Massachusetts and Maine. In the first court held in Maine under the charter to Gorges in 1639, there were nine *jury* trials, and some cases of presentment by a grand jury. The jury for trials consisted generally of twelve men, although there are instances where it was composed of a less number. The indictments were brief and distinct: "Mr. Arthur Browne presented by the Grand Enquest for swearing two oathes, is therefore fined by the bench two shillings." "Mr. George Burdett, minister of Agamenticus, is Indicted by the whole bench for a man of ill name and fame: infamous for incontinency, a publisher and broacher of divers dangerous speeches, the better to seduce that weak sex of women to his incontinent practices, contrary to the peace of our sovereign lord the King as by depositions and evidences appear," &c. Four indictments were found against Burdett at this court, on which he was fined forty-five pounds sterling.

The General Court, which had jurisdiction over all public

and private concerns of the Province, granted the first *act of incorporation* which was established in Maine. It is as follows: "Whereas there were certain propositions preferred to the general court by —— and others for their better encouragement to goe on with the work of making iron, Itt is granted and ordered that they shall have the sole managing of the work for twenty-one years, allowing iron for £20 per tunn, and furnishing the country with bar iron within three years, and permitting any man to come into the company within one month, he underwriting 50 shillings. 2d, tis granted that they shall have liberty on all waste ground to have stone, earth, wood, way, water courses, and on all appropriated land to have stone, wood and earth giving reasonable satisfaction as two indifferent men shall judge and ways and water courses free."

3rd. To have certain land and plantation privileges.

4th. To be free from taxes for seven years.

5th. The regular laborers in the works to be free from "watching and training."

6th. All the adventurers, agents, and assigns to have the privilege of planters.

It was not until after the new charter went into effect, that the forms of writs and procedure in court acquired any system, and it was much later that the forms of declaration were settled. In 1701, the General Court established forms of writs, and authorized the courts to frame rules of practice. But so fixed had become the habits of the judges and the practitioners, that it was several years later that strict legal forms and technical rules were adopted. In 1721, Dummer, in his defense of the New England charters, says: "No special pleadings are admitted, but the general issue is always given, and special matters brought in evidence." Declarations, different from the English practice, were then as now made parts of the writs, as Dummer says, for quicker dispatch; and if the action is on account, the bill is annexed.

No rules of practice were adopted by the courts until after the Revolution; although the bar of Suffolk, particularly, had found it necessary, for their protection, to adopt some regulations in regard to irregular practitioners, as will be noticed in another place. In 1701, the attorney's oath was prescribed, and was the same now used.

COURT OF GENERAL SESSIONS OF THE PEACE.

This court did not exist in Massachusetts or Maine under that name, previous to the adoption of the charter of 1691. In Massachusetts, the "County Court," as it was called, held by magistrates living in the respective counties, or such magistrates as the General Court should appoint, "with such persons of worth as may be appointed, at the nomination of the freemen of the county," "to be joined in commission with the magistrates, so there be five in all, three whereof may keep a court, provided there be one magistrate," embraced the jurisdiction of the Common Pleas and Sessions.

The jurisdiction of this court extended to all cases, civil and criminal, except divorce, and crimes whose punishment extended to life, limb, or banishment; with power to summon juries, appoint clerks and other officers. They also had jurisdiction as a Court of Sessions, to lay out highways, issue licenses to innholders, &c.; also probate powers in the settlement of estates. They combined the principal jurisdiction and duties of the Superior, Inferior, and Probate Courts, as subsequently established, — the Court of Assistants retaining original and appellate powers in certain cases. In Maine, during the government of the proprietor, the General Court exercised the principal jurisdiction in all matters; but from the commencement of the civil war in England, a state of great confusion and anarchy existed here, in which various contestants were contending for supremacy, one triumphing one day and some other the next, in which the administration of justice was a mockery, and the rights and interests of the people wholly disregarded. The king himself became a party, and by his commissioners, in 1664, endeavored to restore the rights and jurisdiction of the heir of Gorges. The commissioners divided the territory into two districts, one embracing the western portion to the Kennebec, the other the Duke's province; and they established courts in them, but they had no power to enforce their decrees. Where Massachusetts could be heard, she planted her county courts, and exercised a divided sway. This conflict was kept up until the Indian war scattered courts and people, and put an end to the exercise of all jurisdiction, until 1679, when the old Bay Colony restored, under her right as a purchaser, a stable government, which continued over the few inhabitants who returned to the desolate country, for the period of twelve years, when the new charter went into effect.

In the distribution of judicial authority under the charter, a court was established by the name of "A Court of General Sessions of the Peace," to be held in each county "by the justices of the peace of the same county, or so many of them as are, or shall be limited in the commission of the peace," who were "empowered to hear and determine all matters relating to the conservation of the peace and punishment of offenders, and whatsoever is by them cognizable according to law." They had their clerks and officers, and power to summon juries, and establish rules of practice. On this court was conferred the power of laying out highways, superintending houses of correction, granting licenses to innholders and retailers, and the charge of the financial and prudential affairs of their several counties, in addition to such jurisdiction in criminal matters as related to the conservation of the peace. These powers continued without essential alteration, during the existence of the provincial government, and were revived by the act of the legislature of Massachusetts in 1782, in nearly the terms of the original act. This court was established on the same principle as the English "Court of General Quarter Sessions of the Peace," and its powers were similar. But in the rapid progress which took place in the public and private affairs of the Commonwealth, the courts were gradually adapted to the altered circumstances and wants of the people. In 1804, all the jurisdiction of this court was transferred to the Common Pleas, except as to erecting and repairing jails and other county buildings, allowing and settling county accounts, assessing county taxes, granting licenses, laying out highways and town ways, and determining the damages. This was an important and radical change which has continued to the present time under the various forms of the court. In 1807, the organization of the court was altered by substituting a fixed number of judges, instead of the crowd of justices of the peace, which had before occupied its bench,—one chief justice for each county, and associates differing in number according to the extent of the counties: in York, Cumberland, Oxford, and Lincoln, there were four each; in Kennebec and Hancock, six; Washington, two; who had the same powers as were conferred by the act of 1804, and received three dollars a day while in actual attendance, and two dollars for every ten miles' travel. In 1808, the name of the court was altered to that of "Court of Sessions;" retaining the same powers. In 1809, an act was passed to transfer the duties of this court to the Common Pleas; but this failed to give satisfaction, and the old "Court of Sessions" was re-established in 1811. It was, however, again abolished in 1814, and all its "powers, authorities, and duties," except in Suffolk, Nantucket, and Duke's Counties, were transferred to the Circuit Court of Common Pleas ; and the governor was authorized to appoint "two discreet persons, being freeholders within each county," to be "Session Justices of the Circuit Court of Common Pleas in their respective counties." They were to be associated with the justices of the Circuit Court for the purpose of hearing and determining all matters of which the previous Court of Sessions had cognizance. In 1819, the Court of Sessions was again restored, consisting of a chief justice and two associate justices for each county. There were then nine counties in Maine, in which twenty-seven judges were appointed, only five of whom were lawyers; viz., Joseph Thomas of Kennebunk, Peleg Chandler of New Gloucester, Ebenezer Clapp of Bath, Calvin Selden of Norridgewock, and Samuel M. Pond of Bucksport: Thomas, Clapp, and Selden were chief justices.

The changes, after the separation of Maine, were no less frequent in the organization of this court than they had been in Massachusetts. Under the first revision of the laws in 1821, it was provided that the court should consist of "one chief justice, and not exceeding four nor less than two associate justices," in the several counties, — who were to receive three dollars each day they attended court, and one dollar for every ten miles' travel. In 1825, the old organization was restored, of a chief and two associate justices. In March, 1831, a radical change took place: the governor, with advice of council, was authorized to appoint, "three suitable persons as county commissioners in each of the several counties of the State," to "hold their offices for the term of four years." The commissioners were invested with the powers and duties of the Court of Sessions, and received the same compensation. This tribunal, thus constituted, we are happy to say, has retained its organization and powers until the present time; except that, in 1842, the office was made elective, and some changes have been made in the compensation of the commissioners.

PROBATE COURT.

Under the colony charter of Massachusetts, of 1628, the first assistants, who were appointed by the king, eighteen in number, to assist the governor in the exercise of his executive powers, were, with the governor and deputy governor, invested with authority to take care for the disposing and ordering of the general business and affairs of the plantation, and the government of the people there. The assistants were subsequently chosen by the freemen of the colony; and they exercised jurisdiction in matters of probate, until the establishment of county courts in 1639, when it was transferred to those courts, with the right of appeal to the Court of Assistants. By an act of the General Court, in 1639, it was provided, "that there be records kept of all wills, administrations, and inventories: as also of the days of every marriage, birth and death of every person within this jurisdiction." The same act made the first provision in New England, if not in America, for a registry of deeds. "Item, to record all men's houses and lands, being certified under the hands of the men of every town, deputed for the ordering of these affairs." In 1641, this provision was made more definite.

In 1652, any two magistrates, with the clerk of the county court, were authorized to admit a will to probate on the oath of two witnesses, and to grant administration; and the clerk was required to report the same to the next county court, and make record of it. By act of 1641, it was ordered that the county court of the county, where the intestate had his last residence, should have power to assign to the widow such part of the estate of her husband as they should deem just and equal; and in the division among the children, the oldest son should have a double portion. If no son, the daughters shared equally. By another act, the same year, the widow's right of dower was established.

In short, the provisions of probate jurisdiction were gradually brought, under the colonial government, into the system, substantially, in which it now exists. The sound, practical common sense of the wise founders of Massachusetts went directly to the accomplishment of the objects desired; and they framed their enactments and their institutions so as best to carry those objects into effect.

In Maine, the General Court assumed jurisdiction on all subjects of the administration of estates, and continued to exercise it until the Province was absorbed into that of Massachusetts. We fortunately have a record remaining in the archives of York County, which proves the manner in which this jurisdiction was exercised from the first inception of the government in Maine. In June, 1635, the inventory of the "estate of Richard Williams servant to Mr. Matthew Craddock" was taken by Mr. George Frost, John Wadleigh, and Robert Edwards, which is confirmed by the deposition of John Wadleigh in 1660. In the conflict of jurisdiction which harassed the Province from the commencement of the revolution in England, 1642, to the acquisition of the legal title by Massachusetts, Col. Alexander Rigby, a staunch republican, was recognized as the lawful proprietor of the Province of Ligonia, extending from Cape Porpoise to Cape Elizabeth. George Cleeves was appointed his deputy, under the style of Deputy President, and held his court, under the name of "The General Assembly of the Province of Ligonia," which took cognizance of all matters of government, as well as private rights. In this court, in 1648, was an elaborate trial, on the petition of Rev. Robert Jordan, administrator of the estate of his father-in-law, John Winter, against the executors of Mr. Robert Trelawny, the proprietor of the plantation of Cape Elizabeth, on which, after a full hearing, a specific decree was passed. In May, of the same year, in the same court, was brought forward a record from a general court held under Gorges' authority, in 1640, granting administration to Payton Cooke on the estate of Richard Williams, above mentioned, for confirmation, which was decreed as follows: "Wee the judges for the Province of Ligonia do, by our authority ratify and confirme unto the said Payton Cooke the above said administration, according to the full terms thereof. Witness our hands, under our provincial seal at the day and year above written. George Cleeves, Henry Jocelyn, Robert Jordan." "Recorded by Edward Rishworth, 11th March, 1667—8."

After the colonial charter of Massachusetts was annulled, the president, Joseph Dudley, and after him, Andros, from 1686 to 1689, assumed supreme probate jurisdiction, introduced the forms of the Spiritual Court in England, and attended personally to all cases of administration, where the estate exceeded fifty pounds sterling. He introduced order and system into this branch of the law, but greatly increased the fees, and required all estates to be settled in Boston.

By the charter of 1691, probate jurisdiction was conferred on the governor and council; but they, by virtue of their power of substitution, appointed Judges of Probate in each county.

Governor Pownal, in 1760, in a statement to the council, represented that the Courts of Probate had no seal, kept no records, had no rules, and did not observe the common formalities of a judicial court. After this time, Registers were appointed and seals adopted. Very little regularity existed in their proceedings previous to the Revolution, and no material change was made in the organization of the courts.

Before 1692, the Recorder of the Province of Maine, who was generally the clerk of the County Court, recorded wills and administrations with the records of that court.

The constitution of Massachusetts, adopted in 1780, made provision that "the Judges of Probate of Wills, and for granting letters of administration, shall hold their courts at such place or places, on fixed days, as the convenience of the people shall require." And until such times and places were appointed by the legislature, the courts were to be held as the respective judges should direct. The constitution also provided that, "All causes of marriage, divorce and alimony, and all appeals from Judges of Probate, shall be heard and determined by the Governor and Council, until the legislature shall, by law, make other provision," — thus retaining the practice which had prevailed under the charter. But in March, 1784, the legislature passed the first Probate Act, which established a Court of Probate in the several counties, to be "held by some able and learned person in each county, to be appointed judge, to whom was assigned the jurisdiction of which Probate Courts have, or hereafter, by the laws of the Commonwealth, shall have cognizance." An appeal was allowed to the Supreme Court. The judge and register by the constitution were to be appointed by the Governor and Council.

Thus was established this important court, through which all the estates in the community pass, in substantially the same form and with the same powers as they exist at this day. The act in Maine, of March 20, 1821, embraced, in seventy sections, running through thirty-five octavo pages, the provisions and improvements in detail, which the experience of more than a third of a century had engrafted on the original stock of primitive principles, rendered expedient, if not necessary, by the advancing population and wealth of so prosperous and enterprising a community as that of Massachusetts and Maine. The principles remained the same in jurisdiction and powers, but expanded to meet the larger exigencies.

Judges of Probate had the same tenure of office by the constitution as the judges of the common law courts, but were paid, as were also the Registers, by fees assessed upon the business of their courts. In 1826, the legislature of Maine, by a most beneficent provision, abolished all fees in those courts, and appointed fixed salaries for the judges and registers, varying in the different counties with the amount of their business.

In 1839, the judges of this court shared the fate of those in the other courts, by an abridgment of their life tenure to that of seven years; and this was followed by a still more democratic rule, by which both judges and registers, by an amendment of the constitution in 1855, were made elective by the people every four years.

The Judges of Probate appointed in Maine under the charter were:

Joshua Scottow,	1687—1693
Francis Hook,	1693—1695
Samuel Wheelwright,	1695—1700
Joseph Hammond,	1700—1710
Ichabod Plaisted,	1710—1715
John Wheelwright,	1715—1745
Jeremiah Moulton,	1745—1765
John Hill,	1765—1772
Jonathan Sayward,	1772—1775

In Cumberland:

Samuel Waldo,	1760—1770

Enoch Freeman, ...	1770—1782
In Lincoln:	
William Cushing, ...	1760—1772
Jonathan Bowman, ...	1773—1804

REGISTERS.

Thomas Scottow, ...	1687—1693
John Wincol, ...	1693—1695
Joseph Hammond, ...	1695—1700
Charles Frost, ...	1700—1733
Rob't Elliot Gerrish, . . .	1733—1744
Simon Frost, ...	1744—1776
David Sewall, ...	1766—1781
In Cumberland:	
J. Stockbridge, ...	1760—1761
Stephen Longfellow, ...	1761—1775
Samuel Freeman, ...	1775—1804
In Lincoln:	
William Bryant, ...	1760—
Roland Cushing, ...	1773—1778

CONDITION AND PROGRESS OF THE BAR—ADMISSION OF MEMBERS.

During the exercise of royal authority in Massachusetts and Maine, under the charter of 1691, the administration of justice went on pretty uniformly, and without essential changes. In none of the common law courts were any lawyers on the bench, except in the Superior Court; and in that, at intervals, but four, viz., Lynde, Dudley, Trowbridge, and William Cushing. Benjamin Lynde studied in the Temple at London, and was judge and chief justice, from

1712, thirty-three years. Paul Dudley was one of the most cultivated men and learned lawyers of the ante-Revolution period; educated to the bar at the Temple, he was appointed judge in 1718, and chief justice in 1745, as successor to Lynde, and held that office till his death in 1751. Trowbridge was not appointed until 1767, and Cushing in 1772. The rules of practice were few and simple; and, although the courts were authorized to establish "rules for the more orderly practise and proceedings," they do not seem to have thought it necessary to go largely into that subject. We have no evidence that the bars of the Province established any formal regulations, or formed any associations of their members.

The first act relating to attornies was one of restraint, passed in 1663, to render them ineligible as deputies to the General Court. The next was passed in 1701, prescribing the form of an oath to be taken on admission to the bar, and their fees. From 1720, onward, there were able, cultivated, and richly endowed lawyers, who gradually raised the level of the bar to a high standard, and improved the forms of proceedings and the practice in the courts. Dudley, the Auchmutys, Reed, Lynde, Shirley, Otis, Jonathan Sewall, Gridley, Pratt, Dana, Farnham, Trowbridge, &c., were among those who adorned the bar of that period, and would have done credit to any bar of recent times. But they were more addicted to routine, and restrained by the narrow limits of the institutions under which their destinies were cast. They could not expand their wings freely for a flight among the stars: a colonial and dependent government was not the sphere for high aspirations or renowned achievement.

When free institutions were established in the state, and all stations were open to all men, the effects of an independent and self-relying condition began to be manifest, in the general advance of society, and progress in all our institutions, which reached to the staid, sedate, and conservative precincts of the courts of law. All the judges of the highest court from that time, were educated and able lawyers, who gradually introduced improvements in the forms of proceedings and the practice of the courts. Clear and concise rules of practice were introduced in 1806, which were published in the second volume of the reports; these, among other things, had reference to maintaining the character and purity of persons who desired to enter into practice.

Examiners were appointed in each county, consisting of the best lawyers, who were carefully to examine candidates for admission, both as attornies to the Common Pleas, and as counsellors to the Supreme Court. These regulations were an expansion of an act passed in 1785, providing for the admission of attornies, similar to the Province act. The bars of the several counties also adopted stringent rules to purge themselves, and to keep their associations free from unworthy members, and to elevate the character and position of the profession. The acts and regulations concerning attornies were adopted in Maine on the separation, and were enforced, keeping up the standard of the profession and its professors. The requisitions for admission were,— good moral character, three years' study with a counsellor at law, if having received a degree from college; or, without that, the candidate was to have faithfully devoted seven years, at least, to the acquisition of scientific and legal attainments, of which three years should have been spent in professional studies with some counsellor at law. These requirements were persisted in until 1843, when the legislature of Maine, under some strange influence, swept all these salutary regulations away, and, by a single sentence, removed those just restraints which enabled the bar to preserve a respectable standard of professional merit, and to guard itself, as well as society, from the bad effects of ignorant and unqualified practitioners. The clause is as follows: "Any citizen of this State of good moral character, on application to the Supreme Court, shall be admitted to practice as an attorney in the judicial courts of this State." Thus it will be perceived, that no discretion was left to the court to judge of merit or qualification. Any person who produced a certificate of fair character, might enter the practice, whether he had any knowledge of law, or skill in practice, or not. The effect of this law was, undoubtedly, to lower the standard of merit in the legal profession, and to break up the bar associations, which had for many years been a source of legal improvement and pleasant social intercourse. These evils became apparent in a few years, and made so deep an impression on the public mind, that the legislature, in 1859, passed an act, requiring all candidates for admission to the bar to be examined by a committee, annually appointed in each county by the Supreme Court, of "three or more persons learned in the law, whose duty it shall be to examine thoroughly touching his qualifications as a lawyer, any applicant to be admitted to practice;" and "no person shall be admitted thus to practice, until he submits to such examination, and produces to the court a certificate of such examination," pays the dues, and takes the oath, which is the one originally adopted, and before mentioned.

But this return to more stringent requirements for admission to practice, did not restore the social and profitable reunions of the bar, in which the judges and the lawyers were wont to lay aside the ermine and the robe, and give free play to their genial and cultivated minds. The wit and humor which flashed on these occasions, relieved the prosaic dullness of official station, and the tediousness of a routine life.

COUNTY OFFICERS IN 1800.

YORK COUNTY.

Judges of the Common Pleas:

Nathaniel Wells of Wells,
Edward Cutts of Kittery,
Jonas Clark of Wells,
Simon Frye of Fryeburg.

Daniel Sewall, Clerk.
Edward Cutts, Judge of Probate.
Daniel Sewall, Register of Probate.
William Frost of York, Register of Deeds.
Ichabod Goodwin of Berwick, Sheriff.

CUMBERLAND COUNTY.

Judges of the Common Pleas:

John Lewis of North Yarmouth,
William Gorham of Gorham,
Stephen Longfellow of Gorham,
Robert Southgate of Scarboro'.

Samuel Freeman of Portland, Clerk.
William Gorham, Judge of Probate.
Samuel Freeman, Register of Probate.
Isaac Ilsley, Register of Deeds.
John Waite of Portland, Sheriff.

LINCOLN COUNTY.

Judges of the Common Pleas:

Thomas Rice of Wiscasset.
Nathaniel Thwing of Woolwich.

Jonathan Bowman of Dresden.
Orchard Cook of Pownalboro'.

Jonathan Bowman, Jr., of Pownalboro', Clerk.[1]
Jonathan Bowman, Judge of Probate.
Jonathan Bowman, Jr., Register of Probate.
Thomas Rice, Register of Deeds.
Edmund Bridge of Dresden, Sheriff.

KENNEBEC COUNTY.

Judges of the Common Pleas:

Joseph North of Augusta,
Daniel Cony of Augusta,
Nathaniel Dummer of Hallowell,
Chandler Robbins of Hallowell.

John Davis, Clerk.
James Bridge, Judge of Probate.
Thomas Bowman, Register of Probate.
Henry Sewall, Register of Deeds.
Arthur Lithgow of Winslow, Sheriff.

HANCOCK COUNTY.

Judges of the Common Pleas:

Paul Dudley Sargent of Sullivan,
Oliver Parker of Castine,
William Vinal of Vinalhaven.

Warren Hall, Clerk.
Paul Dudley Sargent, Judge of Probate.
Jonathan Eddy of Eddington, Register of Probate.

---

1 Also Clerk of the Supreme Court for the counties of Lincoln, Hancock, and Washington.

Joseph Perkins, Register of Deeds.
Thomas Phillips of Castine, Sheriff.

WASHINGTON COUNTY.

Judges of the Common Pleas:

Stephen Jones of Machias,
Alexander Campbell of Steuben,
John Crane of Columbia.

Ralph Hart Bowles, Clerk.
Stephen Jones, Judge of Probate.
Stephen Jones, Jr., Register of Probate.
George Stillman, Register of Deeds.
John Cooper of Machias, Sheriff.

CHAPTER V.

REPORTS AND REPORTERS.

Among the improvements which were introduced within the first quarter century of the new government, was the appointment of a reporter of the decisions of the Supreme Court. This judicious measure, which has proved so valuable to the profession and to the people, was cautiously adopted in 1804, the act limiting the office to three years. In 1806, it was continued to 1811, when it was again continued to 1815; after which it was made a permanent institution, or during the pleasure of the legislature, the experiment having been found entirely beneficial and successful. Although reporting had been practiced many years in England, it was done, for the most part, by individuals on their own responsibility. East was the reporter in the King's Bench, when the law was passed in Massachusetts establishing the office of reporter. He was of the firm of Durnford & East, who commenced their reports in 1786, and modestly styled them, "Notes of Cases adjudged in the Court of King's Bench." Lord Ellenborough was then chief justice. The reports of Durnford & East were the first which were published regularly, "within a short time after each term," and were, therefore, called the Term

Reports; and the success which attended them so increased the number of such publications, as that the profession was overwhelmed with them. The various reports during the reign of George III. amount to upwards of sixty; and the whole number of volumes published in England down to 1825, was five hundred.

The first reports published in England were the Year-Books, which contain reports of cases in a tolerably regular series, from the beginning of the reign of Edward II., 1307, to sometime into the reign of Henry VIII., about the year 1520. The study of the Year-Books was part of the discipline of law students, until after the middle of the last century. Lord Mansfield said, "that when he was young, few persons would confess that they had not read a considerable part, at least, of the Year-Books; but at the time at which he was speaking, few would pretend to more than an occasional recourse to them, in very particular cases." After the suspension of the publication of these books, no reports were published for a considerable period. "It was then thought by the sages of the law," says Lord Coke, "that the Reports of the Law were sufficient." The next collection, after the Year-Books, was that of Plowden, compiled from his private notes, and published in the age of Elizabeth. They only contained points of law determined upon demurrers or special arguments; and "have always been deservedly esteemed of the highest authority." In the year 1585, appeared the Reports of Sir James Dyer, from a collection of notes published after his death, which were held in high estimation, from the eminent character of the author. In the latter part of the reign of Elizabeth, 1600, Lord Coke commenced the publication of his reports, which, from their high value, were called "The Reports." He says, in his preface to the first part, "I have, since the 22d year of her majesty's reign, which is now twenty years complete, observed the true reasons, as near as I could, of such matters in law, wherein I was counsel, and acquainted with the state of the case, as have been adjudged upon mature deliberation." The first eleven parts of these reports appeared in the lifetime of their author, from 1600 to 1615, the twelfth and thirteenth at subsequent periods. Of their great value, we cannot better speak than in the language of Lord Bacon, in his Proposal for amending the laws of England: "Of this I say no more, but that, to give every man his due, had it not been for Sir Edward Coke's reports, — which though they may have errors and some peremptory and extra-judicial resolutions more than warranted, yet they contain infinite good decisions and ruling over of cases, — the law by this time had been a ship almost without ballast; for that the cases of modern experience are pled from those that are adjudged and ruled in former time." Next after Coke, came Sir Henry Hobart, his successor also on the bench of the Common Pleas. He left, on his death, a collection of valuable MSS. notes of cases determined in that court. These were afterwards edited and published by Sir Heneage Finch, twenty-two years after Coke's, and were considered by the profession, "accurate and lucid expositions of the law which they contain." During the twelve years of the Commonwealth, there were twenty-one volumes of reports published by judges, sergeants at law, and other lawyers, — among them, Popham, Coke, Noy, and Bulstrode. This was a period when much freedom was given to the press; so much so, that "its fertility was accounted a fault," even at that time, and led, on the Restoration, to the passage of a statute, passed 1661, prohibiting all law books to be printed, without a license from the Chancellor or one of the chief justices. Notwithstanding this restriction, there were sixteen volumes published in the twenty-three years of

Charles II., from 1660 to 1683, which included Yelverton, Croke, Eliz., Moore, 1st and 2d Anderson, 1st Rolle, and 1st Modern. In the four years of James II., there were seven volumes published, including Saunders, and three of Keble. From that time to 1711, thirteen volumes were published, "most of which," as the writer of the preface to v. Modern says, "to express myself in my Lord Coke's words, set open the windows of the law to let in the gladsome light." Among these were two, three, four, and five Modern, Lutwich, and Shower.

In the intermediate period, between 1711 and 1765, when the first volume of Burrow's reports was published, appeared the seven remaining volumes of Modern Reports, Raymond, and Sir John Strange; the last two, after the death of their authors, and all from notes of cases decided long previous. The desire for *recent* decisions was strongly expressed by the profession, and induced Sir James Burrow to undertake the gratification of this wish. He says, "Late cases are most sought after. I was subject to continued interruption, and even persecution, by incessant application for searches into my notes, for transcript of them. * * This inconvenience grew from bad to worse, till it became quite insupportable;" and he published, in 1765, his first volume containing cases from 1756 to 1758, inclusive, commencing with the first appearance of Lord Mansfield on the bench. His preface to the first volume is dated November, 1765, in which he makes this remarkable statement: "Since the 11th day of November, 1756, to this day, there never has appeared in court the least difference of opinion; every rule, order, certificate and judgment have been *unanimous.* There never was more business. The reasonings and opinions of the judges never gave more satisfaction. *All* the seats were never so filled together." The judges were,— Lord Mansfield, Sir Thomas Denison, Sir Michael Foster, and Sir John Eardly Wilmot. In regard to this remarkable statement, and fact, as it no doubt was, there was a different explanation given. Robert Morris, in a letter to Sir Richard Ashton, a judge in the King's Bench, says: "It is not uncommon abilities, integrity, and temper, as Mr. Burrow would persuade us, but sheer fear of Lord Mansfield, the Scottish chief, which produces this miracle in the moral and intellectual world." The five volumes of Burrow came down to 1772. Cowper extends from 1774 to 1778, and is followed by Douglass from 1779 to 1781. Durnford & East commenced in 1786 their regular series, which was continued by East to 1812. In 1792, Durnford published a volume from the MSS. of Lord Chief Justice Willes, of cases decided during his time, from 1737 to 1758, in one volume. But the volumes of reports now thicken so fast in England, that we do not propose to follow them any farther; and content ourselves with a brief survey of the early American reports.

The first volume of reports of the decisions of any court in the United States, was one published by Ephraim Kirby, in 1789, of cases adjudged in the Supreme Court of Connecticut, from 1785 to 1788, in one volume. Kirby was afterwards appointed the first judge of the United States District Court at New Orleans, and died at Fort Stoddard in 1804. The next reports which appeared were those of Dallas, of cases in the courts of the United States and Pennsylvania, before and since the Revolution, four volumes, octavo: the first volume was published in 1790: with the exception of Kirby, these are the oldest reports in the United States. Alexander J. Dallas was born in Jamaica, 1759, came to Philadelphia in 1783, and within ten days took the oath of allegiance to the United States. He became an eminent lawyer, author, and politician, was several years Secretary of State for Pennsylvania, and afterwards Secretary of the Treasury of the United States, in the administration of Mr. Madison, and for a time, in 1815, discharged the additional duties of Secretary of War. He died in January, 1817. He was father of George M. Dallas, late Minister to England. In 1797, appeared Judge Martin's North Carolina Reports, and the next year, those of Judge Heywood, of the same State, embracing cases from 1789. The same year were published Judge Jesse Root's Connecticut Reports, of cases in the Supreme Court, from 1789 to 1798, in two volumes — the second published in 1802; and the first volume of Bushrod Washington's Reports, of cases in the Court of Appeals in Virginia. In 1799, appeared the first volume of Heywood's Tennessee Reports. In 1800, Alexander Addison, of Pittsburg, published a volume containing cases decided in the county courts and the High Court of Errors and Appeals in Pennsylvania. These, we believe, were all the reports published in this country during the last century, except some of scattered and prominent cases, as Hogan's State Trials, of Hopkinson and Nicholson, in 1794, which we do not embrace in our catalogue.

With the present century commenced a more rapid career of publications in this as well as other departments of law. In 1801, appeared the first volume of Call's Reports, of cases in the Court of Appeals in Virginia, from 1797 to 1802, in three volumes; and Wallace's Circuit Court Reports in the Third Circuit United States Court. In 1802, was published Taylor's North Carolina Reports; and, in 1803, the Reports of James Hughes, of cases in the Supreme Court of Kentucky, from 1785 to 1801, in one volume, quarto. In 1804, appeared Caines's Cases in Error, one volume, and the first volume of Judge Cranch's valuable series in nine volumes, of cases adjudged in the Supreme Court of the United States, from 1801 to 1815; and Bay's South Carolina Reports, of cases from 1783 to 1804, in two volumes. In 1805, George Caines commenced the publication of the New York Term Reports, by appointment of the State, which have been continued through numerous volumes, by himself, Johnson, Cowen, Wendell, and others, to the present time. The same year witnessed the commencement of that remarkable and unbroken series of Reports of the Supreme Court of Massachusetts, contained in seventy-seven volumes, to 1862. The first volume was published by Ephraim Williams, a distinguished lawyer of Berkshire County, who was appointed reporter in 1803, and in October of the following year, published his volume. He resigned the office, as too laborious, after the publication of the first volume; and was succeeded by Dudley Atkins Tyng, who published sixteen volumes, to 1822, including the last year of Chief Justice Dana, the whole judicial life of Chief Justice Parsons, the year of Chief Justice Sewall, and eight years of Chief Justice Parker. His successors have been Octavius Pickering, who published twenty-four volumes; Judge Metcalf, twelve volumes; Cushing, twelve volumes; Gray, ten volumes; and Allen, the present reporter, two volumes. In 1805, was also published Cameron & Norwood's North Carolina Reports, in one volume, octavo; and Kentucky Reports, one volume; and Bay's South Carolina Reports, since the Revolution; second edition in New York, 1809—1811, in two volumes. In 1806, Judge Thomas Day commenced the publication of his valuable reports of cases decided in the Supreme Court of Connecticut. On the publication of the sixteenth volume, the Law Reporter of February, 1847, observes: "Mr. Day is unquestionably the oldest living reporter. As early as 1806, the first volume of 'Day's Reports' were issued, and from that time to the present, for forty years and upwards, he has continued in the service of the public, recording and preserving the opinions of an able court. His twenty-one volumes of Reports comprise a body of decisions on questions of Common Law, of equity, and of ecclesiastical and maritime law, from which may be drawn a more complete system of jurisprudence in all its departments, probably, than from the reports of the decisions of any other single court in this country, the Supreme Court of the United States alone excepted."

In 1807, appeared Pennington's New Jersey Reports; in 1809, Harris's Maryland; which were the first published in those States. Harris was associated with McHenry, in the publication of this work in four volumes, embracing cases from 1658 to 1799, in the Provincial, General, and Appeals Courts of Maryland. Judge Martin commenced the same year, the publication of his Louisiana Reports, which extended to twenty volumes, from 1809 to 1830; and Royal Tyler his Vermont Reports, from 1800 to 1803, in two volumes; which were the first published in those States, and by persons who were, for a time, chief justices of their highest courts. In 1810, appeared Bee's Admiralty Reports, of cases in the District of South Carolina.

We have now given a brief *resume* of the earliest reports published in most of the States to 1810: it would require too much space and time to follow their successors through subsequent years. I will, therefore, only mention the first reporters who engaged in this duty in the other States, in the order of their publication. In Tennessee were, Cooke, one volume, 1811 to 1814; Heywood continued to 1818, four volumes, 1816 to 1818; Overton, 1791 to 1817, two volumes. Blackford's Indiana Reports, 1817. Bruse's Illinois, 1819. Hammond's Ohio, series from 1813. Adams's

New Hampshire, from 1816 to 1819, published in 1819, and continued under the name of New Hampshire Reports. Alabama, Minor's Reports, 1820, one volume. Georgia, Charlton, one volume, from 1805 to 1810, published in 1824.

To these should be added, the valuable reports of cases decided in the First Circuit of the United States Court, during the period of thirty-three years that Judge Story presided, with eminent ability, in that tribunal. These were commenced by John Gallison, in 1815, who published two volumes, embracing decisions from 1812. They were continued, after the lamented death of Mr. Gallison, by William P. Mason, in five volumes; Charles Sumner, in three volumes; and William W. Story, son of the judge, in three volumes, — making a series of fifteen volumes. Woodbury & Minot reported the decisions of Justice Woodbury, in three volumes, after the death of Judge Story, in 1845. Two volumes have also been published of the decisions of Judge Ware, in the Admiralty Court of Maine, from 1822 to 1849, under the revision of that able judge; which are standard authority on the numerous questions therein determined. The second volume was edited by Edward H. Davies.

We are now brought to a consideration of the Maine Reports, embracing the decisions in the Supreme Court of Maine, from 1820 to 1860, in forty-six volumes. The office of reporter was established in 1820: the governor was required, as soon as practicable after the passage of the law, to appoint "a suitable person, learned in the law, to be a Reporter of the decisions of the Supreme Judicial Court," who was to receive a salary of six hundred dollars a year, and the profits arising from the publication of the reports. It was a fortunate circumstance, for the honor of the new

State and the character of the judiciary, that so accurate a lawyer, and so ingenious a scholar, as Simon Greenleaf, was appointed to that office. The first volume of his reports was published in 1822, and was followed by eight additional volumes, extending to 1832, inclusive. The ninth volume contains a digest of the nine volumes, with a table of cases alphabetically arranged. During the whole period of these reports, the learned Chief Justice Mellen presided in the court, assisted during the whole period by Justice Weston, who succeeded Judge Mellen in the chief justiceship; and Judge Preble, who being appointed Minister to Holland, in 1828, was succeeded by Judge Parris. Mr. Greenleaf, having been appointed professor in the Law School at Cambridge, in 1833, left Portland in that year for his new duties, and was succeeded by John Fairfield, afterwards Member of Congress, Governor of the State, and Senator in Congress, who published three volumes; and was succeeded by John Shepley, who published seventeen volumes, from 1835 to 1849. His successors have been John Appleton, now judge of the Supreme Court, Asa Redington, late judge of the Common Pleas, Solomon Heath, John M. Adams, Timothy Ludden, and the present reporter, Wales Hubbard. The merit of these reports is various, depending both on the qualifications and legal ability of the court, and the manner in which the points of the case, the arguments, and the rulings are presented. It cannot but be considered an unfortunate circumstance, that the fluctuations of politics should be allowed to enter into the consideration of an appointment, which, next to that of the judge on the bench, is of eminent importance to the pure and intelligent administration of justice.

The multiplication of the volumes of reports has become excessively burdensome. Mr. Hoffman, in his Course of

Legal Study, second edition, published in 1836, furnishes a table of reports of the several States and the United States, by which it appears, up to that time, 1836, the whole number of volumes was four hundred and seventy-three, — this number included about twenty volumes of reports of separate trials, such as Burr's two volumes, the impeachment of Judge Chase, &c., leaving four hundred and fifty-two volumes of reports in the usual course of proceedings. Since that time, a period of twenty-six years, we may safely estimate that the number of volumes has been more than doubled; so that now they will probably come up to one thousand volumes of reports published in this country alone, of the decisions of our own courts, besides the numerous reprints of foreign reports. To lawyers who are desirous of keeping informed of the progress of the law, and the course of practice, this accumulation is really oppressive. The evil, we think, is much increased by the diffusive and vicious manner of reporting, the verbose opinions which are given in many cases, and the publication of cases which present no new or important principles of law. This ought to be reformed altogether.

We may conclude this branch of our subject by adopting the language of the writer of the preface to the fifth volume of Modern Reports, published in 1711, who says: "Thus I have given an historical account of our reports, which a country lawyer, who was afterwards advanced to a seat of justice, told the bar were too voluminous; for when he was a student, he could carry a complete library of books in a wheelbarrow; but that they were so wonderfully increased, in a few years, they could not then be drawn in a wagon."

The proceedings of court, after the statute of Edward III., were carried on in English, reported in French, and recorded in Latin. It continued customary to report in French until the time of the Commonwealth. In 1649, was passed "An

Act for turning the Books of the Law and all processes and proceedings in Courts of Justice into English." The Latin continued to be the language of the records until the reign of George II.

JUDGES OF THE SUPREME COURT—ATTORNEY GENERALS.

The succession of chief justices in the Supreme Court of Maine has been as follows:

Prentiss Mellen, LL. D., ...	1820—1834
Nathan Weston, LL. D., ...	1834—1841
Ezekiel Whitman, LL. D., . . .	1841—1848
Ether Shepley, LL. D., ...	1848—1855
John S. Tenney, LL. D., ...	1855—

In 1839, the constitution of Maine was altered so as to make the term of the judicial office *seven* years, instead of "during good behavior, but not beyond 70 years." Under the original provision, Chief Justice Mellen retired from the office at the age of seventy, while in the full ripeness of his powers. The other chiefs fell under the seven years' rule, although Judge Whitman resigned before the completion of his term, at the age of seventy-two and one-half years.

The associate judges in this court have been as follows:

Nathan Weston, ...	1820—1834
William P. Preble, ...	1820—1828
Albion K. Parris, ...	1828—1836
Nicholas Emery, ...	1834—1841
Ether Shepley, ...	1836—1848
John S. Tenney, ...	1841—1855
Samuel Wells, ...	1848—1854
Joseph Howard, ...	1848—1855
Richard D. Rice, ...	1852—

Joshua W. Hathaway, ...	1852—1859
John Appleton, ...	1852—
Jonas Cutting, ...	1854—
Seth May, ...	1854—1862
Daniel Goodenow, ...	1855—
Woodbury Davis, ...	1855—1856
Woodbury Davis, ...	1857—
Charles W. Walton, ...	1862—

ATTORNEY GENERALS.

Erastus Foote, ...	1820—1832
Jonathan P. Rogers, ...	1832—1833
Nathan Clifford, ...	1833—1838
Daniel Goodenow, ...	1838—1842
Otis L. Bridges, ...	1842—1845
Wyman B. S. Moor, ...	1845—1847
Samuel H. Blake, ...	1847—1848
Henry Tallman, ...	1849—1852
George Evans, ...	1852—1855
John S. Abbott, ...	1855—1857
Nathan D. Appleton, ...	1857—1860
Josiah H. Drummond, ...	1860—

By an amendment of the constitution, in 1855, the office of Attorney General is made elective annually by the legislature. His salary is fixed at one thousand dollars a year: in 1820 it was eight hundred dollars. The salaries of the judges, as established in 1820, were,— for the chief justice, eighteen hundred dollars; the associates, fifteen hundred dollars each. In 1834, the salaries were all put at sixteen hundred dollars each. In 1836, they were raised to eighteen hundred dollars, at which they have since remained.

CHAPTER VI.

THE PRACTITIONERS IN THE COURTS — CHECKLEY — WATSON — BULLIVANT — RICHARDSON — READ — AUCHMUTY. FEES — SALARIES — EARLIEST PRACTITIONERS IN MAINE.

It has been observed that the attornies who practiced in the courts, were men not educated to the bar, but taken from other professions. This continued to be the case for some years into the last century, even in Massachusetts, and very much later in Maine. Anthony Checkley had been a merchant, and was afterwards chosen attorney general. Watson had been a merchant in London ; "but not thriving there, he left the Exchange for Westminster Hall ; and in Boston, as Dunton observes, had become as dexterous in splitting of causes, as if he had been bred to it." Bullivant had been an apothecary and physician, and left these pursuits for the law, in which he became skillful and prominent. Richardson, another attorney under the colony, was a tailor. Douglass, in his "Summary," written about 1747, says, "Generally, in our colonies, particularly in New England, people are much addicted to quirks of the law. A very ordinary countryman in New England is almost qualified for a country attorney in England."

Some opinion may be formed of the estimation in which attornies were held in the first century of the colony, by their exclusion from the General Court, as well as by the common sarcasms, which have not ceased to this day. Randolph, the noted secretary of Andros, in a letter to Povey, in England, January, 1688, says, "I have wrote you of the want we have of two or three honest attornies, if any such thing in nature. We have but two, one is West's creature, come with him from New York, and drives all before him. He also takes extravagant fees, and for want of more, the country cannot avoid coming to him, so that we had better be quite without them than not to have more."[1]

John Read, who was admitted to the Suffolk Bar, about 1720, was the most eminent lawyer of his day, and did more than any other man to give harmony and consistency to the practice, and to establish correct forms of procedure in court. Many of his forms are contained in modern books of precedents, and are constantly used. He simplified the prolix and obscure forms of conveyance used in the English system, and gave us a noble gift, the concise and comprehensive form of deeds now used by us. His arguments to court and jury were formed upon the same model; they were concise, pertinent, and logical; and, although he was full of wit and irony, he permitted no more of these qualities to enter into his addresses than was suited to give point or illustration to his logic. The goodness of his nature was equal to his ability. In an eccentric mood, on one occasion, he sallied forth on foot, in the plainest garb, to make a journey, in which he gave free vent to his frolicsome nature. He was passing through a village in which a

---

[1] Washburn's Judicial History.

court was sitting: he entered the court room, in which a cause was about to come on. The plaintiff was poor; his claim, though just, was somewhat involved. The defendant was rich, with many friends and able counsel. Read collected the facts, and thinking the plaintiff had a good cause, he offered him his services. The offer was accepted, notwithstanding the uncourtly dress of the person. When the case came on, the court and the bar were surprised by the appearance of the strange counsel. His outward appearance was soon, however, forgotten, as he went on stating what induced him to engage in the cause, — to advocate the rights of a poor but honest man. As he continued, unfolding the case, ridding it of its obscurities, and showing in a clear light, its merits, the audience and the court were astonished and charmed. He so clearly expounded the law, and applied to it the facts, that no one had any doubt of the justice of his case. As soon as it was won, he pursued his journey in quest of new adventures. [1]

He was the first lawyer who was ever chosen to the General Court, which was in 1738. By a colony law, 1663, an attorney of the courts was not eligible as a deputy.

Robert Auchmuty, educated in Dublin and the Temple, and admitted to practice in Boston, in 1720, was another of the prominent lawyers of his time; and did much to elevate the character of the profession, and to give system and order to its proceedings. He was appointed Judge of Admiralty in 1733, and died in 1750. After this period, the eminent lawyers followed, who continued to and after the Revolution, and, by their learning and brilliant deeds, illustrated that period of our history, — Otis, the younger Auchmuty,

---

1 The foregoing anecdote I borrow from S. L. Knapp's interesting "Sketches," published in Boston, 1821.

Quincy, Trowbridge, Gridley, Hawley, Paine, Sargent, Sewall, Adams ; and, in Maine, Cushing, Bradbury, David Sewall, and the Sullivans, John and James.

Attornies were recognized by the act of 1701 ; and before they could charge fees for services, or act in court, they were required to take an oath to do no falsehood, &c., in the form which has been retained to this day. The same act prescribed the fee for an attorney in the *Superior* Court at twelve shillings ; in the *Inferior*, ten shillings, "and no more, any usage to the contrary notwithstanding." This could not be complained of, as the judges, at this time, did not receive over fifty pounds a year for their services. And as late as the middle of the last century, their salaries did not exceed three hundred and fifty dollars. They complained, and, we may well suppose, justly, that the compensation hardly paid their traveling expenses. They usually made their circuits in great state. As they approached the shire town, they were met by the sheriff, with an escort and a flourish of trumpets : their arrival was announced by the firing of a cannon ; and the daily summons of the court, before bells were introduced, was by beating the drum.

In Maine, the profession of law made slow progress, as well in its forms as in the persons who ministered at its altars. The Province had not been permitted, for more than a century after its colonization, to enjoy a period of repose sufficiently long to allow any institutions of civil government to become settled and consolidated. It was not until after all fear of Indian depredations had been removed, that encouragement was given for permanent occupation and extensive improvement. And it was not, therefore, until that very period, that educated lawyers began to seek our territory for the practice of their profession.

William Cushing,—distinguished and venerable name!—was the first of these; he came to the Province in 1760,[1] and settled on the Kennebec River, in that part of Pownalboro' which is now Dresden, where the Plymouth proprietors afterwards erected, in 1761, a court-house, spacious for that day, three stories high, and which may still be seen by those who pass by rail or river, near the head of Swan Island. Mr. Cushing was son of Judge John Cushing, and grandson of another judge of the same name,— both of the Superior Court. He was born in Scituate, Massachusetts, 1733, graduated at Harvard College, 1751, kept school in Roxbury a year, and, after finishing his studies with the eminent lawyer, Jeremiah Gridley, he established himself in Maine. He was made the first Judge of Probate of Lincoln County in 1760, as his brother Charles, a graduate of 1755, was made the first sheriff. Daniel Davis, the distinguished solicitor, said in a letter to me, that "Mr. Cushing commenced practice in the ancient town of Pownalboro', which then comprehended the towns of Dresden and Wiscasset. He was translated to the bench, during his practice as a lawyer in Pownalboro'. He resided in the family of his brother Charles, who was sheriff of the County of Lincoln, and afterwards Clerk of the Supreme Court for 'a time whereof the memory of man runneth not to the contrary.'"

At the time Mr. Cushing commenced practice in Dresden, there was no house on the Kennebec River, from two miles above that place, to the settlements in Canada, except the block-houses at Augusta and Winslow, then called Forts Weston and Halifax. The whole country, as a witness once said in court, was an "eminent wilderness." Of all the judges and officers of the courts in the three counties, and

1 Governor Washburn, in his valuable "Judicial History of Massachusetts," says he went there in 1755. I think he is in error in that date. He went there, as I have reason to believe, in 1760, as Judge of Probate.

of the county officers, he was the solitary lawyer,— he stood alone as an educated lawyer in this spacious territory. How extensive his practice, or what was his standing as a lawyer, can only be inferred from the marks of favor which he received from the governments, before and after the Revolution; and from the distinguished ability with which for thirty-eight years he discharged his duties as a judge. In 1772, he was appointed successor of his father on the bench of the Superior Court; and, in 1777, was appointed chief justice of the Supreme Court of Massachusetts by the Revolutionary government, — the first to hold that office. In 1789, Washington appointed him to the bench of the Supreme Court of the United States, which office he held at the time of his death, in 1810. He was a man of tall and dignified presence, and as he moved along the streets, with his cocked hat, bush wig, and small clothes, he made an imposing appearance, which attracted general attention.

Noah Emery, a native of Kittery, was the earliest resident lawyer in Maine; who, although not educated for the bar, seems to have possessed much legal acumen and accuracy. He was a cooper by trade, and came to the bar about 1725. He was descended from Anthony Emery, who was a carpenter, and came to this country from Romsey, England, with his brother John, and settled in Kittery, where, and through this State and New Hampshire, his descendants are numerous, and many of them distinguished.

Noah Emery was the son of Daniel Emery and Eliza, daughter of William Gowen, and was born in that part of ancient Kittery which is now Elliot, December 11, 1699. He married for his first wife, Elizabeth Chick of Kittery, January 22, 1722; and for his second wife, Mrs. Sarah Cooper of Berwick, October 30, 1740. His will, dated January 1, 1761, was approved January 6, 1762: in this he names but five children; viz., his eldest son, Daniel, Noah, Richard, Japheth, and John. To Noah and Richard he devised lands in New Hampshire, from which I infer that he was the ancestor of the Exeter family, in which the grandfather and father of Judge Nicholas Emery, late of Portland, were named Noah; and, I think, were the son and grandson of the subject of this notice. Mr. Emery was a ready draftsman, of quick perceptions and considerable ability, which gave him an extensive practice. He was on several occasions, from 1741 to 1759, appointed King's Attorney. He died in 1762.

CALEB EMERY, a kinsman of Noah, either a brother or a cousin, succeeded him in his practice. He was admitted to the bar of the Common Pleas, in York County, in 1750, as a copy of the record before me shows, and "took the oath appointed by law," the judges present being Sir William Pepperell, Jeremiah Moulton, and Simon Frost. Mr. Emery was generally employed in agricultural pursuits. He commenced practice in Kittery, but moved to York. In 1761, he was appointed, by the Common Pleas, King's Attorney. The duty of this officer was similar to that of County or District Attorney, at the present day; they were appointed from term to term by the court to attend to the criminal and county business. He retired from practice during the Revolutionary War, and never resumed it.

JOHN EMERY, another of this family, was in practice in 1752, but not educated, and he seldom appears upon the records: it is probable that his business and legal merits were not prominent. I have been unable to obtain any definite knowledge concerning him.

CHAPTER VII.

IRREGULAR PRACTITIONERS — BAR RULES AGAINST THEM — DAVID SEWALL — DISTRICT COURT — LAWYERS FROM OTHER COLONIES.

In Cumberland County there was no regular lawyer until after the county was organized; but there were several persons in Falmouth, now Portland, of education and clerical habits, who, no doubt, attended the court, — the Common Pleas being the only one sitting there, — to assist parties in their suits: these were, — Jabez Fox, Enoch Freeman, and the elder Stephen Longfellow, who were all graduates of Harvard. At a later period, Samuel Freeman, the son of Enoch, was largely employed in this kind of business. After regular lawyers were established there, a severe bar rule was adopted to cut off such practice.

I find on the York dockets numerous entries made by irregular practitioners. In July term, 1767, out of twenty-five entries, Thomas Bragdon, John Frost, Colonel Donnell, and Colonel Sparhawk made ten, while John Sullivan made five; James, two; David Sewall, eight. In April term, 1774, Wyer, of Falmouth, made twenty entries; Caleb Emery, seven; Sewall, thirty-two; James Sullivan, twenty-four; John, nine; irregular practitioners but six.

Enoch Freeman, in Cumberland, filled twenty-eight writs for April term, 1758; fourteen for October term, and eleven for the next January term. His fee for writ and summons was eight shillings. John Adams, in his diary, speaks repeatedly of the evil arising from the practice of uneducated and ignorant men, as deputy sheriffs, &c., drawing writs and other proceedings: he mentions three in his neighborhood. It became so great an abuse, that it was prohibited by law. Under 1763, he says the bar agreed upon four rules: 1st, That nobody should answer to a suit, but the plaintiff himself, or some sworn attorney, and that a general power should not be admitted. 2d, That no attorney fee should be allowed where the declaration was not drawn by the plaintiff, or a sworn attorney. 3d, That no attendance should be taxed unless the party attend personally, or by a sworn attorney. 4th, That no attorney be allowed to practice in the Superior or Inferior Courts, unless duly sworn. When these rules were presented to the court for adoption, James Otis sharply opposed them, on the ground that "all schemes to suppress pettifoggers, must rest on the honor of the bar." The members of the bar were filled with indignation against Otis for his opposition, and abused him without measure. Thacher moved, that, in the invitations to the judges, the expression should be, — the bar, — exclusive of Mr. Otis, — invites, &c.

Mr. Adams says, soon after he was admitted to the bar, 1758, "He found the practice of law was grasped into the hands of deputy sheriffs, pettifoggers, and even constables, who filled all the writs upon bonds, promissory notes, and accounts, and received the fees established for lawyers, and stirred up many unnecessary suits."

David Sewall, a native of York, born in 1735, was the second educated lawyer, resident in Maine; he descended from Henry Sewall, the first emigrant of the name, through his son John, a brother of Chief Justice Stephen Sewall. He graduated at Harvard, in 1755, a classmate of John Adams, the second President of the United States, and of Sheriff Charles Cushing. He studied law with Judge William Parker of Portsmouth, whose daughter Mary he afterwards married. He established himself in the practice at York, in 1759, and pursued it, in connection with the office of Register of Probate, to which he was appointed in 1766, with much success, until his appointment as associate justice of the Supreme Court of Massachusetts, in 1777. After an honorable service of twelve years in this court, he was appointed by President Washington, in 1789, a judge of the United States Court for the District of Maine; this Court then had the jurisdiction of the Circuit Court of the United States.

We insert the commission of judge, with the commencement of the records of the court, in the elegant writing of Henry Sewall, the first clerk:

"Records of the District Court of the U. S., begun and held at Portland, within and for the District of Maine on the first Tuesday of December, A. D. 1789, being the fifth day of the same month.

"The court being opened, the commissions following were read —

[SEAL.] "George Washington President of the U. S. of A.

"To all who shall see these presents, Greeting:

"Know ye, that reposing special trust and confidence in the wisdom, uprightness and learning of David Sewall of Maine District, Esq., I have nominated, and by and with the advice and consent of the Senate, do appoint him, Judge of the District Court in and for the said District: and do authorize and empower him to execute and fulfil the duties of that office according to the Constitution and Laws of the U. S. And to have and to hold said office, with all the powers, privileges and emoluments to the same of right appertaining unto him the said David Sewall during his good behavior."

The commission is dated September 26, 1789, and signed, "George Washington."

December 1, 1789, Judge Sewall took the oath prescribed by the law, before Samuel Freeman, Richard Codman, John Frothingham, and Daniel Davis, Justices of the Peace.

On the same day, the oaths prescribed by law were respectively administered by Judge Sewall to William Lithgow, Jr., as District Attorney, and to Henry Dearborn, as Marshal, whose commissions also bear date, September 26, 1789.

The next year after his appointment, it fell to his lot to have the first trial for piracy which had occurred under the new government. The prisoner, Thomas Bird, was convicted and executed in Portland, in June, 1790, — General Henry Dearborn was Marshal, and officiated at the execution.

Judge Sewall held this office until 1818, discharging its duties with great fidelity and urbanity, when the infirmities of age admonished him to retire from all active labor. He was President of the Board of Overseers of Bowdoin College fourteen years, and near seventeen years Register of Probate in York County. He died in 1825, at the age of ninety, having filled the office of judge forty-one years. He left no family. Judge Sewall was a man of great benevolence, unassuming in his deportment, social and amiable in his manners, and of great purity of character. He remarked to a friend near the close of his days, that if he were to lead his life over again, he did not know that he should wish to alter it. Fontenellê, the celebrated French philosopher and author, expressed a similar sentiment: "Had I again to begin my career, I would do as I have done." He might more justly have said, "I would do better." He was, however, a man of genial temperament, of benevolent character, and led a happy life. He died in 1757, one hundred years old.

The District Court of Maine furnishes a remarkable instance of the conservative character of the United States judiciary department. In this court there have been but three judges from its organization in 1789, when Judge Sewall was appointed, to the present day, seventy-three years. Judge Sewall presided in it twenty-nine years, Judge Parris three years, and was succeeded by Judge Ware, in 1822, who now, after forty years' service, ably discharges its duties. The District Court of Massachusetts presents a similar example, that having had but three judges; viz., John Lowell, John Davis, and the present incumbent, Judge Sprague, who has held, since 1841, the office, which was filled by Judge Davis, with great ability and fidelity, forty years.

In cases of importance, as well as on ordinary occasions, regularly educated lawyers from New Hampshire and Massachusetts attended the courts in Maine. Among these we find Matthew Livermore, William Parker, and Samuel Livermore, of Portsmouth; Daniel Farnham and John Lowell, of Newburyport; John Chipman, of Marblehead; John Sullivan, of Durham, New Hampshire; James Otis, Jeremiah Gridley, Jonathan Sewall, and John Adams, of Boston.

In the great case of the Plymouth and Pejepscot proprietors, involving valuable titles on the Androscoggin and Kennebec Rivers, tried in the Common Pleas at Falmouth, in 1754, Otis and Gridley, the two most distinguished lawyers in Massachusetts, were present as counsel for the parties. At the July term, 1768, of the Superior Court, in Falmouth, Mr. Chipman, who was in attendance, was seized with an apoplectic fit in the court room, and died within three hours.

The late President John Adams attended the courts in Maine for twelve successive years prior to the Revolution. The worthy Judge Bailey of Wiscasset, a short time before his death, which took place in 1853, observed to me, "In a call I made upon the elder President Adams, at Quincy, not long before he died, he stated that in his early law practice, he once attended the Superior Court at Pownalboro', now Dresden, in the County of Lincoln, where the old court house is yet standing on the bank of the Kennebec River; and that from Brunswick to the ferry over that river, he was guided by marked trees, and by the same kind of guide up the river to the court house." It was at one of the last terms of his attendance on the court in Falmouth, that the separation took place between him and his intimate friend, Jonathan Sewall, who had yielded to the blandishments and patronage of the Government, and adhered to the royal party. They walked together upon Munjoy's Hill, in Portland, in July, 1774, before breakfast, and earnestly discussed the great questions which were agitating the country. They could not convince each other, and Mr. Adams terminated the conversation by saying, "I see we must part; and with a bleeding heart I say it, I fear forever; but you may depend upon it, that this adieu is the sharpest thorn on which I ever set my foot." After this, they did not meet again until Mr. Adams called upon him in London, in 1788 as ambassador of the free American States. Sewall died in Halifax, in 1796, aged about sixty-two.

Jeremiah Gridley was a very able lawyer: he died in 1767, and was succeeded in his office of Attorney General by Jonathan Sewall. The celebrated John Gardiner, of whom we shall have something to say, by and by, in a speech in the legislature of Massachusetts, on special pleading, said, "This erroneous opinion of the profession here was taken from a mere *dictum* of the late Mr. Gridley, who, though a mighty pompous man, was a man of considerable learning and abilities — in learning and genius, however, almost infinitely inferior to that great giant of learning and genius, the law member from Newburyport," (Theophilus Parsons). The Diary of John Adams confirms this judgment, taken on the spot by him, just entering the bar, — "Gridley's grandeur consists in his great learning, his great parts, and his majestic manner; but it is diminished by stiffness and affectation."

Matthew Livermore, of Portsmouth, was son of Samuel Livermore, of Watertown, Massachusetts, where he was born in 1703. He graduated at Harvard College, 1722, and went to Portsmouth, in 1724, to take charge of a school, and, at the same time, pursue his legal studies. He was admitted to the bar in 1731, at which time there was no regularly educated lawyer in that town. He was an accomplished lawyer, and had an extensive business in Maine as well as New Hampshire. He was appointed by Governor Belcher, Attorney General of the Province, and King's Advocate in the Admiralty Court; and was afterwards judge of the Superior Court of New Hampshire. He died February 14, 1776.

Samuel Livermore, also a distinguished practitioner in Maine, lived in Portsmouth. He descended from John Livermore, of Watertown, and was the son of Samuel Livermore, of Waltham, Massachusetts, where he was born May 15, 1732. He graduated at Princeton College, in 1752, pursued his law studies with Judge Trowbridge, and commenced practice in Portsmouth. He was appointed Attorney General of New Hampshire, in 1769, and was re-appointed by the Revolutionary government. He was several times delegate to the Continental Congress, and was made chief justice of New Hampshire, in 1782; was a member of the convention for adopting the Federal Constitution, and afterwards successively representative and senator in Congress. He died full of honors in 1803. His sons, Edward St. Loe and Arthur, were long judges of the Superior Court of New Hampshire. Arthur was chief justice fifteen years. Elijah Livermore, brother of Samuel, was chief proprietor of the town of Livermore, in Maine, and the first settler,—taking with him emigrants from Waltham and neighboring towns, and inducing others to migrate. Bond, in his History of Watertown, says, "He was a man of great worth."

William Parker, also from Portsmouth, had a large practice in Maine. He was by trade a tanner, and had received only such an education as was furnished by the common schools of his native town. When he became twenty-one, he commenced the study of the law, and was admitted to the bar in 1732. He early distinguished himself in his profession by great natural abilities and liberal culture, and rose rapidly in his business and reputation. He was successively appointed Register of Probate, King's Attorney for Maine, Judge of Admiralty, and, in 1771, Judge of the Superior Court of New Hampshire. But being a loyalist, he relinquished that office at the opening of the Revolution. He was the father of Bishop Parker of Boston, Judge William of Exeter, of Mrs. Judge Sewall of York, and of

Lydia, the grandmother of Senator John P. Hale of New Hampshire.

Daniel Farnham graduated at Harvard College, in 1739; he had an extensive practice in the courts, both of York and Cumberland, up to the period of the Revolution. He was an able lawyer, and was occasionally appointed King's Attorney in York County. He died in 1776, aged fifty-six. His daughter, Sybil, married Dr. Micajah Sawyer, a celebrated physician in Newburyport, and was the mother of Dr. William Sawyer, Harvard College, 1788, who died in Boston, 1859, aged eighty-eight. He also left a son, William. Levi Lincoln, the elder, of Worcester, studied law with Mr. Farnham.

In a trial in Cumberland County, 1763, between the Rev. Mr. Smith of Falmouth and the Brackett family, where the title to a large island in Portland Harbor was involved, we find the counsel employed, were, — for the plaintiff: Mr. Chipman of Marblehead, David Sewall of York, and David Wyer of Falmouth; for the defense, Samuel Livermore of Portsmouth, and Daniel Farnham. Mr. Livermore's fee for arguing the cause for Mr. Smith was six pounds, thirteen shillings, and four pence, lawful, — twenty-two dollars and twenty-three cents, — as appears by the receipt in my possession.

Mr. Chipman was a son of the Rev. John Chipman of Beverly, who was grandson of John of Barnstable and Hope Howland. He graduated at Harvard College, 1738; was father of Ward Chipman, a refugee, and agent of the British government in settling the eastern boundary line; and grandfather of the late Ward Chipman, chief justice of New Brunswick. His daughter married the late William Gray of Boston.

CHAPTER VIII.

TRAVELING THE CIRCUIT — RESIDENT LAWYERS PRIOR TO THE REVOLUTION — BRADBURY — WYER — PARSONS — THE SULLIVANS — LANGDON — CUSHING — STOCKBRIDGE.

I HAVE thus given the names of all the persons who practiced in the courts of Maine, to the year 1760, when the counties of Cumberland and Lincoln were incorporated. It appears that, of the regularly educated lawyers, but two were residents in the Province, the others were from the two neighboring colonies. It was the custom, which continued many years after the Revolution, for the judges to travel their circuits on horseback; and the lawyers attended the circuits in the same manner. This mode of conveyance was rendered necessary, where they could not conveniently reach their destination by water, on account of the impassable nature of the roads by carriages, through the forests which then covered the country. Some of the prominent lawyers of the State, such as Mellen, Wilde, Davis, Orr, Lee, Holmes, McGaw, Wilson, Crosby, &c., were in the habit of attending the courts holden out of their own counties, down to the time of the separation of the State.

After the organization of the counties of Cumberland and Lincoln, and the establishment of additional courts, young and enterprising lawyers dared to venture into this almost unexplored territory.

THEOPHILUS BRADBURY was the first of these adventurers: he was a descendant of Thomas Bradbury, who settled in Salisbury, Massachusetts, about 1638; and was born in Newbury, in 1739. His parents were Theophilus Bradbury and Ann Woodman. He graduated at Harvard in 1757, in the class with Revs. Tristam Gilman and Edward Brooks, ministers of North Yarmouth; and was admitted to practice in May, 1761, at the first term held for Cumberland County: previous to which time he had kept the grammar school in Portland. He was the first educated lawyer who established himself in the territory lying between the towns of York and Pownalboro'. He was soon followed by

DAVID WYER, a native of Charlestown, Massachusetts, and a graduate of Harvard, in the class of 1758; who studied his profession with James Otis of Boston, and was admitted to the bar here, October term, 1762. He also had taught a school in the town before his admission. John Adams, in his Diary, page 269, says that Wyer was his chum. This must have been in Wyer's freshman year, as Adams graduated in 1755.

As these were the only lawyers in the county, until 1774, they engrossed the business, and were always employed on opposite sides. Their characters were as much at variance as was the current of their practice: Bradbury was grave and dignified; Wyer, gay and full of satire, and the shafts of his wit did not always fall harmless from the shield of his adversary. They were both good lawyers, and their forensic struggles afforded gratification, and often amusement, to the attendants upon the courts. Bradbury was a better special pleader, and his character and manners gave him much influence with the jury. Wyer, by his brilliant sallies, often carried the audience, if he did not win his cause. Bradbury was an earnest Congregationalist, while Wyer gave a no less warm support to the growth of Episcopacy, which was then just planting its roots in this virgin soil. Wyer died at the early age of thirty-six, in 1776, leaving a family which is transmitted in the female line. Bradbury was driven away by the destruction of Falmouth, in 1775, and established himself in his native town, where, in 1796, he was elected a member of Congress, and the next year appointed on the bench of the Supreme Court. He died in 1803.

Mr. Davis, to whose letter I have before referred, remarks, "I have heard about David Wyer from the late Gov. Sullivan, and some of his cotemporaries, who were refugees from Falmouth, and who returned after the peace of 1783. They said he was a high-minded, sterling fellow, of strong talents, an able and eloquent advocate, and extremely independent in his opinions and character. He and the late Judge Bradbury were always antagonists in their professional career, and as there was a great difference in the two gentlemen, I have heard many anecdotes of them that would not be proper for the public eye. Bradbury was always grave and judicious, and had great influence with the court and jury. Wyer was full of wit and vivacity. This contrast frequently gave birth to scenes in the forum, very much to the amusement of their mutual friends."

Mr. Wyer married Miss Russell, a niece of Thomas Russell of Charlestown, October, 1764, by whom he left a son and daughter; the daughter married Samuel Waite, a son of Stephen Waite of Portland, and had a family.

Mr. Bradbury married a daughter of Ephraim Jones of Falmouth, by whom he had several sons and daughters.

His son Charles was long a respectable merchant in Boston; and George, a graduate of Harvard, 1789, was a lawyer at Newburyport and Portland, and was a representative in Congress from the Cumberland District two terms, 1813—1817. He died in 1823.

While these young and ardent advocates were pursuing their eminent career, another aspirant came among them, destined to eclipse both, and to take his stand pre-eminently at the head of the bar and the bench in New England,—

THEOPHILUS PARSONS, who, after leaving college in 1769, came to Falmouth as a teacher of the grammar school, and commenced the study of his profession with Theophilus Bradbury. He began his school in June, 1770, and kept it till September, 1773. He was admitted to the bar in July, 1774, and had already begun to distinguish himself, when the Revolution and the destruction of Falmouth removed from our State one of the brightest lights of jurisprudence which the annals of our country have furnished.

These were all the lawyers who were settled in Cumberland prior to the commencement of the Revolution. In Lincoln County, three promising young men established themselves.

JAMES SULLIVAN, the first of these, born in Berwick, in 1744, studied law with his brother John, in Durham, New Hampshire, and opened an office in Georgetown, on the Kennebec, in 1767. He remained there but two years, when he removed to Biddeford, and during the war, 1778, to Massachusetts. From the commencement of the Revolution to the close of his life, in 1808, he was constantly in official stations, as member of the legislature, commissary of the troops, judge of the Superior Court, Attorney General, commissioner of the United States, and died in his second term as governor of Massachusetts, December 10, 1808. Amid all these duties he found time to engage largely in literary labors, as the historian of Maine, a contributor to the collections of the Massachusetts Historical Society, of which he was a prime mover and first president, and, as a politician, to the public press. No man of his time was more full of active and successful duty, than this accomplished lawyer and able advocate.

At a meeting of gentlemen from several towns, held in Falmouth, November 4, 1775, at Colonel Tyng's house, Colonel Mitchell, Moderator, "Mr. James Sullivan was chosen commander-in-chief over the militia and the other companies now in pay in the province." "Voted that 4 persons be appointed to assist Mr. Sullivan. Voted that Col. Mitchell be second in command — Col. Fogg third." Mr. Sullivan was then but thirty-one years old.

The following characteristic language is from a letter in my possession, from him to S. Freeman, then in the Provincial Congress, January 21, 1776: "I am surprised the militia bill is where you mention in your last. I fear our country will owe its destruction to the squeamishness of our Gen. Court. Bold and manly strides are necessary in war: what is done amiss in war, may be set right in time of peace."

No lawyer was thought better able than he to compete with the ablest jurist of Massachusetts; and he and Parsons were very often engaged on opposite sides of a controversy, when the conflict was severe, and in a high degree interesting. Their strong antagonism in politics also gave a zest to their encounters; which, however, from men of such superior intellect, were generally courteous and respectful. On one occasion, Sullivan became much excited in a cause, in which he was opposed by Parsons, and exclaimed, — "I thank God, I never took a bribe from any man." Parsons coolly replied, — "I thank God, I never met a man who dared offer me one."

It has been told me, that Mr. Sullivan, when engaged in the examination of aged witnesses in court, would often lead his inquiries into an historical line, in order to extract information which enabled him to accumulate materials for his History of the State.

Biographies of these distinguished men have recently been published in an extended form; that of Parsons by his son, the Professor of Law at Harvard; and of Sullivan, by his grandson, Mr. Amory of Boston.

JOHN SULLIVAN, elder brother of James, after trying his hand at sea, at the age of seventeen or eighteen, entered the office of Mr. Livermore of Portsmouth, where he very successfully and honorably pursued his legal studies, acquiring thus early a reputation for ability, wit, and acuteness, which he carried through life, in the many high stations which he occupied, as a lawyer, a general, member of Congress, Attorney General, and President of New Hampshire. These qualities pertained to the three sons, John, Ebenezer, and James, which they inherited from both father and mother, who were natives of Ireland, and migrated to Maine in 1723. The father, William Sullivan, was a highly educated man, well skilled in classical literature, and a teacher of the classics. He died at Berwick, in 1796, at the age of one hundred and five years. The son, John, commenced practice in Newmarket, New Hampshire, whence he soon moved to Durham, where he died, in 1795, aged fifty-four. He often visited his parents, on which occasions he came from Durham, in his spacious family chariot, with two horses, and servants, and dressed in the best style of the times.

Two other lawyers of much promise commenced practice in Lincoln before the Revolution; but whose bright words of promise were broken to their hopes.

TIMOTHY LANGDON and ROLAND CUSHING were both graduates of Harvard, one in 1765, the other in 1768. Langdon read law with Mr. Gridley in Boston, and was connected with some of the first families in Massachusetts and New Hampshire. He was brother of Governor John Langdon, and was born in Portsmouth. President John Adams, in his Diary, under date, "Falmouth, July term, 1771," says, "dined with David Wyer in company with his father, Farnham, Sewall, Cushing, Lowell, &c. Spent the evening with the bar at Shattuck's (the tavern) in high spirits. Agreed unanimously to recommend Tim. Langdon to be sworn. All in good spirits, very cheerful and chatty; many good stories. This day argued the cause of Freeman and Child, a suit for £10 penalty, for taking greater fees in the custom house than allowed by the Province law. Freeman got a verdict, and I was congratulated."

Langdon commenced practice in that part of Pownalboro' which is now Wiscasset; he was appointed Crown Lawyer before the Revolution; represented Pownalboro' in the Provincial Congress, in 1776; and was appointed Admiralty Judge for Maine by the Provisional government of Massachusetts, in 1778. Maine was constituted by the Provincial Congress a separate Admiralty District, from which circumstance it was ever after called, "The District of Maine," until its organization as a State.

Langdon was able, eloquent, and brilliant; but in a few years, he became very dissipated, and was spoken of by those who knew him, as the shattered remains of a once sound lawyer. Losing character and business in Wiscasset, he wandered off to Norridgewock, in 1793; but he met with no better success there, from his irregularities. He then tried Farmington, where he remained five or six years, leading a vagrant and destitute life,—occasionally filling a writ or picking up a law job; and finally died, in 1808, in a bar room at Hinkley's Plains, in Hallowell, of *delirium tremens*.

Roland Cushing was a younger brother of Judge William and Sheriff Charles Cushing. He was born in Scituate, Massachusetts, in 1750, and, on leaving college, in 1768, he pursued the study of law in the office of his brother William. He possessed rare talents, a fine education, person, and manners. He settled first at Dresden, then at Gardiner, from which he moved to Waldoboro', a half-shire town of Lincoln County from 1787 to 1809, having been appointed Register of Probate. Here he found himself in the midst of a German population, where he could have but little business, and no congenial society. His talents and cultivation were wasted for want of the necessary stimulus and opportunity; and he fell into habits of intemperance, which hurried him to an early grave, in 1788, at the age of thirty-eight. He was never married.

Mr. Deane, in his History of Scituate, says of him, "He was a man of talents, and celebrated for his beauty and gracefulness." It is said that he would argue most eloquently when he could hardly stand without being supported. This was told to me by the Hon. Thomas Rice, a native of Wiscasset, who added, "Tradition a few years ago was filled with praises of his beauty, eloquence, and popularity. In force and brilliancy he exceeded his more fortunate, because more wise and virtuous, brothers, William and Charles." He was not spared by the stern retributions which inevitably and inexorably come upon all who live in violation of the fundamental laws of our being. These two brilliant men,—Langdon and Cushing, are sad examples of the utter waste of moral and intellectual power. Our profession, as I have had it deeply impressed upon my observation in these inquiries, furnishes too many similar examples of premature ruin by drunkenness.

JOSEPH STOCKBRIDGE. I believe I have introduced into these desultory sketches, notices of all the lawyers who practiced in Maine prior to the Revolution, except Joseph Stockbridge, who died in Falmouth, within a year after he commenced practice in Cumberland County. He was son of David Stockbridge of Hanover, Massachusetts; graduated at Harvard College, 1755, and was appointed the first Register of Probate for Cumberland County. He ingratiated himself in public favor during the short time he lived in the county, and died much lamented, April 5, 1761, in the twenty-fourth year of his age. The following notice of Mr. Stockbridge's death, appeared in the Falmouth paper, April 13, 1761: "On the 5th ins. Mr. Joseph Stockbridge died here, to the great grief of the people in general; for though he had lived here but a few months, his civil, religious, and prudent behavior gained him the esteem of all that knew him, and great satisfaction was expected from his knowledge and capacity in the offices he sustained in the county."

CHAPTER IX.

SOCIAL USAGES OF THE BAR — FROTHINGHAM — TYLER — THACHER — LITHGOW — BARRISTERS.

THE social usages of that, and a more recent period, were unfavorable to the habits of lawyers. Their number was small, their meetings rare, and their spirits genial; and when they met on occasions of the assembling of the courts, it was natural that they should unbend, and relax the conventional habits which their position in general society required them to maintain. It was their custom while on the circuits to have evening gatherings, at which the favorite beverages of the day, flip and punch, were freely circulated; and the gay sessions were often protracted through the long hours of the night. On these occasions, they frequently held mock courts, in which one of their number was appointed judge, and trials took place for breaches of good fellowship, or some imaginary offenses. On one of these occasions, in York County, Mr. Lowell, afterwards United States Judge, arrived during the session of the court at Biddeford, and tying his horse at the door of the tavern, went in to seek lodgings; but the landlord being unable to accommodate him, he was obliged to obtain other quarters; and inadvertently left his horse all night at the door where he was first fastened. This was considered in the mock court a high offense, for which he was called to answer; the landlord was also placed on trial for his neglect of the horse. David Farnham was appointed judge. After a long hearing and argument, the landlord was fined a bowl of good punch for his neglect, and Lowell was fined twice as much for suffering the poor animal to remain all night at the door. The sentence was carried into immediate execution. Mr. Lowell, born in Newbury, in 1743, became a distinguished judge of the United States Court, and father of the no less distinguished sons, John, Francis C., and Charles Lowell. He died in 1802.

On another occasion, Noah Emery was accused of calling the high sheriff, Leighton, a *fool*. For this weighty offense he was brought before the court, and the allegation being proved, the court, taking into consideration the circumstances of the offense, ordered Emery to pay one *pipe of tobacco;* and the sheriff to pay one *mug of flip* for deserving the appellation. The equity of this admirable institution will be at once perceived in the exact justice that was measured out to both parties, the penalties always enuring to the benefit of the company, of which both accuser and accused were partakers.

Meetings of members of the bar were first held in Boston, in 1759, at the suggestion of John Adams, who had been recently admitted to practice, to take some measures against irregular practitioners. He says, in his Diary, "Many of these meetings were the most delightful entertainments I ever enjoyed. The spirit that reigned was that of solid sense, generosity, honor, and integrity; and the consequences were most happy; for the courts and the bar, instead of scenes of wrangling, chicanery, quibbling, and ill manners, were soon converted to order, decency, truth, and candor. Mr. Pratt was so delighted with these meetings, and their effects, that when we all waited upon him to Dedham on his way to New York to take his seat as chief justice of that State, he said to us, "Brethren, above all things, forsake not the assembling of yourselves together."

At the time of the Revolution there was no lawyer in our territory north or east of Gardiner; and it is stated in the Diary of John Adams, that of the eight persons actively engaged at the bar in Boston, in 1763, Mr. Adams was the only one who was found there at the close of the Revolution: Thacher died in 1765, Gridley in 1767, Otis incapacitated in 1771, and died 1783; Auchmuty, Kent, Sewall, and two others adhered to Great Britain.

The Revolution swept as a desolating scourge over our land, and all material interests were, for the time, prostrated. It was no longer a field for lawyers to till. William Cushing in Lincoln, Sullivan and Sewall in York, were appointed judges of the Superior Court; in Cumberland, Wyer died in 1776, and Bradbury and Parsons fled from the smoldering ruins of ill-fated Falmouth; Roland Cushing and Langdon, in Lincoln, only remained to sustain the falling pillars of the law. Sullivan left Maine, in 1778, as a judge of the Superior Court, having since 1775 acted in a military capacity.

John Frothingham. The field did not long lie fallow: it must indeed be barren which would discourage a lawyer from entering it. The first who had the courage to adventure upon this apparently forlorn hope, was John Frothingham, who came to Falmouth in 1773, or '74, as Bradbury, Wyer, and Parsons did before him, as a school-master. He descended from William Frothingham, one of the first settlers of Charlestown, Massachusetts, through his sixth son Samuel, the grandfather of the subject of this notice. His father was Deacon John Frothingham. He was born in Charlestown, in 1750, and graduated at Harvard College, in 1771. While pursuing his avocation as a teacher, he read law with Mr. Bradbury, and was a fellow-student with Parsons. He was admitted to practice at the Cumberland Bar, in March, 1779; but did not abandon his vocation as teacher, which he must have found more profitable than the bar.

Mr. Frothingham spent the remainder of his life in Portland. In 1780, he was appointed County Attorney; was collector of the excise for Maine; one of the trustees of Bowdoin College twenty-four years, and its secretary; a representative to the General Court, 1786; thirty-four years clerk of the First Parish; twelve years Register of Probate; and eight years judge of the Court of Common Pleas, until its reorganization in 1811. He was a faithful, upright, intelligent, and honest man; and closed his long career of usefulness, in 1826. He left several children by his wife, Martha May, sister of the late Colonel Joseph May, and of the venerable Samuel May of Boston; three of whom survive, — John, a respected merchant in Montreal; Lucretia, the widow of Franklin Tinkham; and Abigail, the wife of the distinguished Dr. Ray, of the Butler Asylum in Providence, Rhode Island.

The business of the profession in that county may be inferred from the number of entries upon the docket during the dark days of the Revolution: in 1778, they were eighteen; 1779, twenty-six; 1780, twenty; and the whole number for the seven years of the war, to 1783, was but one hundred and ninety-eight. The population of the county was, in 1780, then including a part of Oxford, but about fourteen thousand; and of the State, about forty-three thousand.

ROYAL TYLER came to Falmouth the same year that Mr. Frothingham was admitted to the practice, 1779. He was born in Boston, his father having been of the King's Council; was a graduate of Harvard, in the class of 1776. He was a fine scholar and an accomplished man. He continued but about two years in our State, when he moved to Vermont, and became a distinguished lawyer, and the chief justice of the Superior Court of that State. In 1809 and 1810 he published two volumes of reports of the decisions of her highest tribunal. An incident occurred during his practice in Cumberland, which was not a little annoying to him. He commenced an action against an officer of a privateer then lying in the harbor, and went on board with the sheriff to have the writ served. But the privateersman, not liking the process, took up his anchor and sailed out of the precinct, carrying the attorney and his officer with him, whom he landed safely at Boothbay, and kept on his cruise; acting upon the classical dictum,—*inter arma, leges silent.*

Mr. Tyler died in August, 1826, at the age of sixty-six. He had been judge twelve years, of which six were as chief justice. He published, besides the two volumes of reports, several poems and comedies. He was a man of elegant manners, fine literary taste, and a learned judge.

WILLIAM LITHGOW, JR., son of Judge William Lithgow of Georgetown, commenced practice during the Revolution. He was not educated at college, but read law with Mr. Sullivan at Biddeford. On the breaking out of the war, he entered the military service; was an officer in the army which captured Burgoyne, and served with credit during the war, in which he had his arm shattered, and retired with the rank of major. He returned to his profession, after these stirring scenes were over, and established himself at Augusta, having his office in the only plastered room of the block-house of Fort Weston, which had been used as a defense against the Indians. He is said to have been an able advocate, and a lawyer of much ability and extensive practice. He was appointed, in 1789, the first United States Attorney for Maine, and was twice elected a senator to the legislature of Massachusetts, and a major-general in the militia. He was a man of fine personal appearance, of military bearing, and accomplished manners. He died in February, 1796, at the age of forty-six, never having been married. The father of General Lithgow came from Scotland in early life, with his father, and settled in Georgetown on the Kennebec. Before the Revolution, he had command by turns of the three forts at Richmond, Augusta, and Winslow; and was employed by the government in its intercourse with the Indians. After the Revolution, he was many years a magistrate and judge of the Court of Common Pleas. He was a man of good sense, fine manners, a genial temper, and great hospitality. He died December 20, 1798, aged eighty-six years. He married a daughter of Colonel James Noble, by whom he had four sons and six daughters: three of the daughters married Samuel Howard of Augusta, Rev. John Murray of Boothbay, and Major James Davidson of Bath; the other three died single; one of them, Jane, a handsome and accomplished woman, was engaged to Roland Cushing, but died suddenly before marriage. His sons were James, Arthur, Robert, and William. Arthur was several years sheriff of Kennebec; he married a daughter of Sheriff Bridge. James married the only daughter of John Gardiner, the barrister, of Dresden, and had two sons, and a daughter who married Colonel E. Williams.

George Thacher. We have the name of but one more who, during the existence of the war, adventured into the

State as a practitioner: that was George Thacher of Biddeford. He too had been a school-master, after taking his degree at Harvard, in 1776; and this seems to have been the common path from the college to the bar; for generally the young men of that day who had persevered in obtaining an education, had exhausted their means, and came out into the world embarrassed by debt, and had to struggle long to free themselves from those iron fetters. While keeping school, they could be acquiring means of subsistence, and the payment of their debts, and at the same time be preparing for the professions to which they were looking for future support and advancement in life.

Mr. Thacher was descended from Anthony, the common ancestor, who came to this country in 1633; was of the fourth degree from him, and was born in Yarmouth, Cape Cod, April 12, 1754. His father was Peter Thacher, and his mother a daughter of George Lewis of Barnstable. He studied his profession with Shearjashub Bourne of Barnstable, and commenced practice in York, in 1780 or '81; in 1782 he moved to Biddeford, where the principal part of his life was spent, succeeding James Sullivan in the practice at that place. In 1788, Mr. Thacher was elected a member of the old Congress. On the adoption of the constitution of the United States, Maine constituted one district, and he was elected the first representative from Maine in the new congress. He held the office by successive elections, until 1801, when, on being appointed a judge of the Supreme Court of Massachusetts, he resigned his seat. He was the only representative from Maine until 1793, when it became entitled to three representatives, and Peleg Wadsworth of Portland, and Henry Dearborn of Gardiner, were chosen as his colleagues. While in Congress, Judge Thacher took an active part in the important debates of the time, and his speeches contain useful information and sound argument, seasoned by genuine "Attic salt."

He continued upon the bench until January, 1824, and died in April of the same year. Judge Thacher was a sound and acute lawyer, and a good general scholar. He carried to the bench a mind well stored with legal principles, and a memory always ready to furnish, from its ample stores, authority of unreported cases, and illustration from general literature. His integrity and impartiality were never questioned; but his manner was not agreeable upon the bench, for he was constantly interrupting the lawyers and arguing points with them, and was sometimes fretful and impatient. Yet he was a man, in private life, of a genial temper and agreeable social habits; had fine conversational powers, and was full of anecdotes, which he had a happy manner of relating. He had infinite humor, and his wit often created merriment at the bar, as well as in his social intercourse. I recollect being in court when Judge Thacher interrupted a lawyer who was earnestly pressing a point,—"You need not argue that point, sir, for to my mind it has no more weight than the lightest feather upon a bumble-bee's wing." The anecdote of the challenge sent to him while in Congress is familiar. A member had offered a proposition that the coin to be issued from the mint should bear the figure of an eagle. Mr. Thacher, by way of banter, offered an amendment, that the effigy should be a goose, for the old bird, said he, could be represented upon the large pieces, while the goslings would be suitable for the small ones. This he sustained in a humorous speech, which kept the house in a merry mood; he alluded to the fact that Rome had once been saved from the barbarians by the cackling of geese. The mover of the bill, assuming that this was an attempt to insult him, sent a challenge. Mr. Thacher told the bearer, that he had no right to hazard his life on such a chance, but would write to his wife, and if she consented, he would accept the challenge; but, as a compromise, he proposed that his figure might be marked on a barn door, and if the challenger, standing at the proper distance, hit it, he would acknowledge himself shot. The gentleman's friends, finding that they could do nothing with Mr. T., abandoned the matter.

An anecdote to which Mr. Thacher, when at the bar, was a party, is told by an old lawyer. He was managing a cause against the Attorney General, in which the counsel were considerably excited: the Attorney General said to Mr. Thacher, "You are no gentleman." Thacher rose and said, "Well, now, I admit, Mr. Attorney, that I am no gentleman, — I am no gentleman." The venerable Judge Strong, who was holding the court, interrupted, and with his peculiar arch manner, said, "Well, gentlemen, I think you need not go to the jury about that."

Judge Thacher had a peculiar way of charging the jury. He would dissect and analyze the case, and so mix up the facts that the jury were perplexed to know the views of the court upon them. Mr. Orr once characterized this peculiarity by this graphic description, — he said, "Thacher would take his fish, and make it into a chowder, and then turn the chowder back again into a fish."

July 20, 1784, Judge Thacher married Mary Savage, a daughter of Samuel Phillips Savage of Weston, Massachusetts, by whom he had five sons and five daughters, all of whom, but one daughter, survived their father. Of the sons, George and Samuel Phillips Savage were educated for the bar, and after many years' practice, are both dead. One of his daughters married Joseph Adams, a late respected member of the Cumberland Bar. In his domestic relations, Judge Thacher was a most kind and indulgent husband and father, and his dwelling was the abode of peaceful enjoyment, and a large though frugal hospitality; of which the humble as well as the noblest in the land have been partakers. The President of the United States, and his classmate, Governor Gore, have been his guests, as they passed through our State. His invitation to Governor Gore was by the familiar address by which his classmates knew him in college, — "Kitty Gore."

CHAPTER X.

FIRST LAWYERS AFTER THE REVOLUTION — DAVIS — GARDINER —BARRISTERS—WETMORE — RAPID PROGRESS OF MAINE IN BUSINESS AND POPULATION — EBENEZER SULLIVAN.

WE have passed in review the members of the profession, who before and during the Revolution, upheld the feeble arms of the law in Maine. They have faded from the knowledge and the memory of those who are filling their places, and deriving benefit from their labors. They assisted to bring order and system into our jurisprudence; to adapt it to the altered circumstances of our country, and the free institutions which had been established upon the ruins of colonial dependency. Others have labored, and we have entered into their labors.

We now propose to speak of the lawyers who, during the closing twenty years of the last century, exercised a commanding influence upon the social institutions and the political and legal systems of our State.

DANIEL DAVIS. 1782—1804.

The first lawyer who came into Maine on the close of the Revolution, was Daniel Davis, who was son of Daniel Davis, a respectable farmer, and born in Barnstable, Cape Cod, May 8, 1762. The early part of his life was spent on his father's farm. But having an earnest desire for an education, his father made efforts and sacrifices to accomplish this object. After a very crude preparation, he offered himself for admission at Harvard College, and was rejected. This, though it disconcerted him, did not extinguish his desire for a profession; and, abandoning a college course, he was placed with an attorney at Barnstable for his legal training. In three years from that time he was admitted to the Barnstable Bar, before he was twenty-one years old. Mr. Davis studied his profession in the office of Shearjashub Bourne of Barnstable, who took great pride in this student, after he rose to distinction, and was wont to say, when recurring to his success in after life, "*I took special pains with Daniel.*" Judges Thacher and Mellen of Maine, and Hall of Vermont, were also students in Mr. Bourne's office.

The perplexing inquiry now came what he should do with himself. He was not long in making his decision; full of confidence and hope, he mounted his horse, with all his worldly gear upon his back, and turning his head toward the rising sun, he found himself on a pleasant autumn day of 1782, in the village of Falmouth, now Portland. He was light of purse, as he was light of heart, having only a pistareen in his pocket. But he had a ready wit, a handsome person, and engaging manners. An introductory letter to Dr. Deane, the minister of the only parish in the village, put him on a good footing, and he speedily commenced a most successful career. The only other lawyer in the town or county was Mr. Frothingham, and there were but four others in the whole State; viz., Mr. Thacher in York; Roland Cushing, Timothy Langdon, and William Lithgow in Lincoln. In a letter written in 1828, he thus speaks of Maine, "When I went into that country, in every part of which I have discharged my professional duties, the face of it, the habits and manners of the people, and those circumstances which are peculiar to a new country, where all the institutions of society were disregarded and neglected, would form a picture, that would astonish the present generation." Again, he says, "As a specimen of the change since my time, I recollect that when I went to Falmouth, there was no settled minister of the Gospel between that town and the British territories, except in North Yarmouth, New Gloucester, Wiscasset, and I believe one in Townsend. I was going to say, the sheep were without shepherds, — but then there were no sheep, but plenty of wolves all over the country." * * "I am the only survivor of the Maine bar who lived in that State at the time I went into it," — this was in 1828. The sarcasm contained in the above remark must be set down to the wit of Mr. Davis, and not taken for sober truth.

Mr. Davis was an able advocate, and of easy and pleasant address. As a consequence, his business and reputation rapidly increased. He was no student, and not a profound lawyer; but he had the faculty of showing all he had, and of seizing upon the points of a cause with facility and tact: he gathered up materials in the progress of the trial to construct an argument, which he had the happy talent to present to the jury in a most attractive form. By his readiness on all occasions, and his address, he became very popular through the county. In 1792, he was one of the candidates for Congress, at the first election, for Cumberland District; and received in Portland one hundred and twenty-four votes, to thirty-seven given for General Wadsworth; the General, however, run better in the country, and obtained the position, which he held, by successive elections, until 1806. Mr. Davis was representative to the General Court six years, and six years a member of the senate of Massachusetts from Cumberland. In the legislature, he was a distinguished debater, and ranked with the eloquent Harrison Gray Otis. In 1796, he was appointed United States Attorney for Maine, as successor to William Lithgow, and held the office until removed by Mr. Jefferson, in 1801. Silas Lee succeeded him. In 1800, while holding the above office, he was appointed Solicitor General of the Commonwealth, by Governor Strong; an office created especially for him, as, in 1767, it had been for Jonathan Sewall. This position he held until 1832, when, from age and infirmity, being no longer able to perform the responsible duties of a criminal lawyer, the law establishing the office was repealed. It is but just to say, that he discharged all its duties with great ability and fidelity, for which he seemed to have a peculiar aptitude. In 1800, he was chosen President of the Board of Overseers of Bowdoin College, which he held five years. In 1804, finding that his services as Solicitor General required his presence more frequently in Massachusetts than in Maine, he moved to Boston, where he resided while he continued in office. On its being taken from him, he retired from practice, and removed to Cambridge, where he died October 27, 1835. He published two works on criminal law, which are esteemed by the profession; one called, "Davis's Justice;" the other, "Precedents of Indictments." Of the former work, a writer in the Law Reporter, volume x., page 232, says, "The work of the late Mr. Solicitor Davis took at once the high rank which it long sustained among the safe and useful law books for the many. Its author was one of the best prosecuting officers that ever practiced in Massachusetts, and neatness and accuracy characterized all his literary and professional efforts."

In 1786, he made a long and perilous journey to Quebec to consummate a matrimonial engagement previously formed with Miss Louisa Freeman of his native town, a sister of Dr. James Freeman, D. D., of King's Chapel, Boston. A narrative of this long journey through the unbroken wilderness and forest, which then spread between the Atlantic and the lower St. Lawrence, would embellish the pages of a tale with romantic interest. By this charming and accomplished lady he had a family of talented and amiable children. His eldest daughter married William Minot of Boston; and his only surviving son is the distinguished Charles H. Davis, of the United States Navy, and of the Coast Survey, who has made himself illustrious by his skill and valor in feats of arms during the rebellion, as well as by his scientific attainments and works.

I am able to add from one of the early cotemporaries of Mr. Davis, not at all given to laudation, the following characteristics of him: "He was eloquent and graceful, and a charming companion; he was not a student, nor a book lawyer, but was quick in his perceptions, and argued his cases well."

Mr. Davis was in the habit of quoting Scripture in his addresses to the jury, and did not always remember accurately. In the trial of Jacob Cochran, in Cumberland, for lewdness, a predecessor of the Mormons in his doctrines, against whom there was considerable prejudice in the community, he quoted the passage, "Put off thy shoes," &c., in order to disarm this prejudice, citing the passage as spoken *of* the Hebrew prophet, instead of *to* him. On another occasion, he was counsel in the Supreme Court, in York County, in an action by the mother of a boy against a school-master, for an excessive flogging of her son in school. Bradbury, one of the judges, suggested that there should be more proof of the offense of the boy. To which Mellen, for the defendant, replied, that if a school-master was obliged to hunt up evidence among his pupils to justify his manner of governing his school, he would be placed in a more difficult position than any officer of government. Davis answered, — "Brother Mellen was probably educated 'in the school of one Tyrannus.'" "Well," says Judge Paine, "he was a good master, wan't he?"

Harrison Gray Otis, at a meeting of the Cape Cod Association, in Boston, 1839, in his usual pleasant manner, thus alluded to Mr. Davis, — "I also formed the acquaintance of the then future Solicitor General of the State; he was somewhat my senior, and assumed some little pretensions over his school-mates in consequence of having been chief volunteer fifer to the Barnstable minute men: in the rudiments of which art as well as of agriculture, he was instructed by a Patagonian sybil, named Phillis, his father's servant, who taught him alternately to play the fife and plough potatoes."

Mr. Minot has furnished me a further illustration of this anecdote. He says, Mr. Davis and George Thacher, the late judge, when boys were neighbors in Barnstable. The day after the battle of Bunker Hill, the militia company of that town set off for Boston. The boys accompanied the soldiers, — Davis acting as fifer. A few miles out of Barnstable, an order came directing the company to return home. In their retreat, Thacher and Davis, tired of their march, mounted an old horse they met in the road, without saddle or bridle. After riding some miles, they dismounted, and abandoned their steed in the highway. Many years after, Davis, as Solicitor General, was prosecuting a horse thief, before Thacher as judge, in the county of Kennebec. In the course of the trial, the judge leaned over the bench, and said, in an undertone, to the solicitor, "Davy, this reminds me of the horse you and I stole together in Barnstable."

JOHN GARDINER. 1786—1793.

The next lawyer who came into Maine was John Gardiner, who established himself in Pownalboro', in 1786. He was son of Dr. Sylvester Gardiner, and was born in Boston, about the year 1731. He received his education in England; and at the Inner Temple he had the benefit of the legal instruction of the distinguished Sir Charles Pratt, afterwards the Lord Chancellor, Camden. Admitted to the bar of the King's Bench, and the courts at Westminster Hall, he practiced before Lord Mansfield, and acquired a brilliant reputation. He was appointed Attorney General of the Island of St. Christopher, and practiced there, and at another island, until the conclusion of the Revolutionary War. In 1784, he returned to this country, where he and his family were recognized as citizens of Massachusetts, by a special law of the Commonwealth. This act was passed February 13, 1784, and is so honorable to his character that I quote from it:

"An Act declaring and confirming the citizenship of John Gardiner, Esq., Barrister at Law, Margaret Gardiner his wife, and of Ann, John Sylvester John, and Wm. Gardiner, their children.

"Whereas the said John Gardiner was born in Boston, the metropolis of this Commonwealth, and while a minor, was, by his father, sent to Great Britain for his education, where for a succession of years he remained a distinguished friend to, and through a vicissitude of fortune, hath continued an avowed and inflexible assertor of the rights and liberties of his native country, and a bold opposer of the enemies thereof; and having lately returned to reside in the said metropolis, and soon expecting his said wife and children, he and they ought to be declared free citizens of the said Commonwealth."

He continued two years in Boston, when he moved into Maine, and occasionally appeared as counsel in the Supreme Court, where he invariably attracted attention from his copious learning, his polished manners, and his attractive elocution. He used to appear on such occasions in his barrister's gown. He was the most learned and cultivated lawyer in Maine; and no one at the bar of Massachusetts excelled him as a general scholar, or in the variety of his information. In 1789, he was elected a representative from Pownalboro' to the legislature of Massachusetts, and was successively re-elected until his death in 1793. Here he took a very conspicuous part in proposing improvements in the legal system of the State, and advocated his measures with great earnestness and ability.

In January, 1790, he introduced a resolution, that the House would resolve itself into a committee of the whole, to take into consideration "the present state of the law and its professors in the Commonwealth." He prefaced his resolution by spirited remarks against lawyers and abuses of the law. He objected to associations of members of the bar, and the formation of bar rules; the mode of taxing cost, and other practices, which he termed illegal and unwarrantable usurpations. He thought the law ought to be simplified; and that many customs which had crept in from the English system, should be eradicated. Most of the bills which he introduced were rejected by large majorities; the one to abolish special pleading was debated with great earnestness.

From these circumstances he was called the "Law Reformer," and was evidently in advance of his age. The measure proposed by him, and urged ably and eloquently, to abolish *special pleading*, and to simplify the practice in the courts, was opposed, with zeal equal to his own, by Parsons and other lawyers, who feared to touch the old and time-honored forms, lest the whole fabric should fall into confusion. Forty years after, this measure was adopted, to general acceptance in Massachusetts and Maine. He aided effectually in abolishing the law by which the oldest son inherited a double portion of his parent's estate; and another to abolish the clumsy process of common recovery, so that a tenant in tail could by deed dock the entailment. He was a prominent actor and debater on all subjects of interest which came before the legislature, and displayed copious resources of knowledge and illustration. In the midst of this activity he suddenly perished, at the age of sixty-three, on a voyage from the Kennebec to Boston to take his seat in the General Court.

Mr. Gardiner, before he left England, practiced for a time at Haverford West, in Wales, where he married a Welsh lady, Margaret Harris, by whom he left three children. His daughter Ann married James Noble Lithgow, son of Judge William Lithgow of Georgetown: they had two sons and one daughter. The daughter, Louisa, married Colonel Edward Williams of Augusta, and died in 1824, aged twenty-six. The sons, Alfred G. and Llewellen Lithgow, are now living, but without issue. His son, the Rev. John Sylvester John Gardiner, long rector of Trinity Church in Boston, who was also educated in England, was distinguished for classical learning and high culture. A daughter of his married John P. Cushing, Esq., of Watertown, lately deceased; his son William, a lawyer in Boston, married a daughter of Thomas H. Perkins, and inherits the genius of his family.

Since writing the above, I have been favored with an interesting sketch of this extraordinary man, from his nephew, the Hon. Mr. Gardiner of Gardiner, which I could not forgive myself, and my readers would not forgive me, if I did not present in his own words:

"John Gardiner, the eldest son of Dr. Sylvester Gardiner,

was born in Boston in 1731. He was sent at an early age by his father to Scotland, for his education, and from thence he went to London and pursued his legal studies at the Inner Temple. Upon being admitted to the bar, he commenced practice on the Welsh Circuit, and married Miss Harris, sister of the wife of Sir. Watkin Williams Wynne, distinguished in English political life. He then removed to London, where he attracted the notice of Lord Mansfield, and with his patronage and his own talents he had a fair prospect of rising to distinction. He, however, became intimate with Churchill, Wilkes, and characters of that description, and was junior counsel in the defense of Wilkes when he was arrested on a general Secretary of State's warrant. The cause excited great and very general interest at the time. A handsome piece of plate was presented to him on the occasion, by Wilkes's political friends, with a long inscription congratulating him upon the success of his effort in proving the illegality of a '*Secretary of State's warrant.*' The plate is still in possession of the counsellor's grandson, William H. Gardiner of Boston. In gaining his case, Gardiner lost the favor of Lord Mansfield, who procured him the appointment of Attorney General of St. Kitts as an honorable banishment. He here took such an active part in politics as a Whig as to make it expedient for him to quit the island, and after remaining a short time in Jamaica, he removed to Martinique, where he took office under the French. After the peace of 1783, he returned to his native place, and in a letter to his father, dated Boston, July 14, 1783, he says that 'Gov. Hancock, Samuel Harris, and Dr. Cooper have all received me with the greatest cordiality; and General Washington, in consequence of letters from the French Ministry, overwhelmed me with civility during the four days I staid with him.' In Boston he resumed the practice of his profession, and induced his brethren to resume the legal costume, which had been laid aside. To prevent walking through the street in their gowns, they agreed to robe at the house of Judge Tudor, which was next to the court house. The custom was not of long continuance. It was said to have been given up from a countryman hearing Hitchborn, in his gown, utter a volley of oaths to a man with whom he was bargaining for a load of wood, and expressing his astonishment to all his friends how the Boston parsons would swear.

"John Gardiner's opinions were opposed to those of his father in religion as well as in politics. In the former he was an Arian, and took an active part in the alteration of the liturgy of King's Chapel, of which his father had been for many years warden and an active member. I remember his giving my mother a prayer book of the altered liturgy, in which he had written his name to the preface to show its authorship. He would attend services at Trinity Church, where his son, adhering to the ancient faith, was assistant minister, for he said he must hear Jack preach, and would make the responses from his altered book while the people were repeating from the Book of Common Prayer.

"In 1786, his wife being deceased, he removed to Pownalboro' with his three children, to property bequeathed to him by my grandfather. With great learning, a highly cultivated taste, and accustomed to move in the most polished circles, it is difficult to conceive the motive that should have induced him to fix his residence among an uneducated people in a comparative wilderness. Many anecdotes are related of his eccentricity while residing there, and of the petty frauds which the low cunning of some of the people were enabled to practice upon him. He was chosen to the General Court as representative from Pownalboro', and was so active in his exertions to have the English law so altered as to be adapted to the circumstances of our country, as to obtain the name of law reformer, and succeeded in obtaining the abolition of the law of primogeniture and virtually the law of entail, but was not equally successful in abolishing special pleading, where he was before his age. He took an active part in obtaining a repeal of the law prohibiting theatrical performances. He was persuaded not to deliver the speech he had prepared for the occasion, as being too learned for his audience. He had it printed, and it makes an octavo volume of one hundred and fifty pages, full of Latin and Greek quotations. He was a very fine classical scholar, and with a remarkable memory would repeat, as he went along, whole books from his favorite Greek authors.

"In 1793 he took passage for Boston in a vessel with a heavy deck load. The wind blew violently from the northwest, and she was overset immediately on leaving the river, and all on board perished."

BARRISTERS—INNS OF COURT.

Mr. Gardiner was admitted to the degree of barrister in June, 1761, by the "Honorable Benchers of the Inner Temple," London. The term *Barrister* is derived from the Latin, Barra, Bar, and signified those persons who were admitted to plead the cause of their clients at the bar of the courts. It is equivalent to what was formerly understood here as counsellor at law, and distinguished from an attorney, who, in legal contemplation, prepares the details of causes. This distinction has gradually passed away, and among us, a counsellor performs the duties of barrister, attorney, and scrivener. In England, no person could be admitted a barrister, unless he had resided three years in one of the Inns of Court, if a graduate of Cambridge or Oxford, and five years if not such graduate. The same rule prevailed in Massachusetts before the Revolution, and some years after. A sergeant at law, a title never adopted in this country, was the highest rank, next to the judges, and corresponds to doctor in the civil law. The "Inns of Court," viz., the "Inner Temple," the "Middle Temple," "Lincoln's Inn," and "Gray's Inn," were anciently regarded as a sort of university, to which the sons of the nobility and gentry resorted, after leaving Oxford or Cambridge, to acquire a general knowledge of law and politics. These young men being liberally furnished with money, rendered these establishments places of riot and dissipation, which was not cured until this class of persons withdrew, and left them for those whose objects were study and improvement.

The only lawyers in Maine who were raised to the degree of barrister, were John Gardiner, William Cushing, David Sewall, Theophilus Bradbury, David Wyer, and William Wetmore.

Mr. Adams, in his valuable and piquant Diary, gives us some interesting notices on this subject, and the forms of that day. He says, "1761, Nov. 14, Brother Quincy and I sworn into the Superior Court. It is now about three years since I was sworn into the Inferior Court. About this time the project was conceived, I suppose by Mr. Hutchinson, the chief justice, of clothing the judges and lawyers with robes. Mr. Quincy and I were directed to prepare our gowns and bands and the tie wigs, and were admitted barristers, having practiced three years at the Inferior Courts, according to one of our new rules." Again, in July, 1766, he says, "A meeting of the bar at the coffee house for the admission of three young gentlemen. Lawyers swarm and multiply, but the country grows, &c. Four years must pass before the three young gentlemen admitted this night will assume the gown." * * "The bar has at last introduced a regular progress to the gown, and seven years must be the state of probation."

Joseph Willard, in his valuable address to the Bar in Worcester County, in 1829, informs us that Judge John Sprague of Lancaster, Worcester County, "at the Feb. term of the Supreme Court in Suffolk, 1784, was called up by the *first writ* that issued for barrister in this Commonwealth; the previous mode being without writ."

I think no barristers were created in Massachusetts after 1794, and at the close of the century but twelve remained. The barristers, according to English custom, which continued sometime after the Revolution, appeared in court in robes, as did also the judges, who also retained the wig. But these official appendages gradually disappeared before the progress of republican ideas. Judge William Cushing, who died in 1810, was the last to dispense with the wig. The robe, or gown, is still retained by the judges of the Supreme Court of the United States in their annual session at Washington; and it must be confessed that it lends dignity to the official station, which inspires respect, especially when worn with the gravity which becomes a judge of so august a tribunal.

The following description of a court scene in 1761, given by the first President Adams, on occasion of the application for "Writs of Assistance," presents a vivid picture of the court and bar of that day: "In this chamber near the fire, were seated the five judges, with Lieut. Gov. Hutchinson at their head, as chief justice, all in their new fresh robes of scarlet English cloth, in their broad bands and immense judicial wigs. In this chamber were seated at a long table all the Barristers of Boston and its neighboring county of Middlesex, in their gowns, bands, and tie wigs. They were not seated on ivory chairs, but their dress was more solemn and more pompous than that of the Roman Senate, when the Gauls broke in upon them."

The court consisted of Chief Justice Hutchinson, Benjamin Lynde, John Cushing, father of our William Cushing, Peter Oliver, and Chambers Russell.

In 1800, the number of barristers in England was seven hundred and seventy-three; but they increased very rapidly in the fifty succeeding years, numbering in 1851, three thousand two hundred and seventy-four.

WILLIAM WETMORE.

William Wetmore, of whom we have spoken as one of the barristers of Maine, resided several years on the banks of the Penobscot River, and practiced his profession there during the latter portion of the last century and the beginning of the present. He was born in Connecticut, in 1749, graduated at Harvard College in 1770, and practiced law in Salem, Massachusetts; but having a large property in Maine, in right of his wife, who was a Waldo, he established himself upon it and managed it several years; a portion of it was Orphan's Island, in the Penobscot River. He was several years Judge of Probate of Hancock County, until 1804, when he returned to Boston, and was Judge of the Court of Common Pleas in that city; an office which he filled acceptably many years. He died in 1830, aged eighty-one. Judge Story married his daughter.

RAPID PROGRESS IN BUSINESS AND POPULATION.

After the peace of 1783, the advance of Maine was very rapid in business and population. The old Commonwealth was a large owner in her territory, and many extensive tracts were held by private persons for speculation and settlement. Great exertions were made by public and private owners to bring their lands into the market, and increase the number of settlers. In the seven years after the peace, the population nearly doubled, rising to about one hundred thousand souls; and commercial business all along the line of her coast was in active operation, giving employment to lumber men and mechanics, and building up thriving towns upon her whole sea border. In 1789, the counties of Hancock and Washington were incorporated; and, though the former contained but five thousand seven hundred inhabitants, and the latter but two thousand five hundred, yet from the activity and energy of the people, and their prospective growth, enterprising young men were induced to embark their hopes and prospects in this new and uncultivated field of labor.

Lawyers were not backward in following these sure indications of business. In 1787, Manasseh Smith went to Wiscasset; in 1789, Salmon Chase and Samuel Cooper Johonnot established themselves in Portland; Isaac Parker, afterwards chief justice of Massachusetts, in Castine, and was the first lawyer settled in the State east of Wiscasset; Dudley Hubbard in Berwick, where Ebenezer Sullivan, an elder brother of Governor Sullivan, was practicing, a brilliant and talented man, but prematurely ruined by intemperance. In 1789, George Stacy settled in Biddeford, and Silas Lee in Wiscasset; in 1790, Phineas Bruce in Machias, the first lawyer who went to Washington County; William Symmes in Portland; James Bridge in Augusta; and Sylvanus Wildes in Kennebunk.

EBENEZER SULLIVAN.

Ebenezer Sullivan was a man of varied talents and pursuits. He first engaged in trade; then served in the army; he commanded a company against the Indians in the West; and finally became a member of the bar. "He was a man," says one who knew him well (General Hodsdon), "of a very fine frame and figure, straight, and about six feet high; and his walk, looks, speech, and every motion of him, were indications of being an active, energetic, and dignified military commander. According to my best knowledge, he was, if not the first lawyer that practiced in Berwick, the only one there for several years, until Dudley Hubbard opened an office in the same place. His inordinate use of ardent spirit, together with the zealous perseverance of Dudley Hubbard, his professional competitor, diminished his practice, and he left the State; went to New York City, where he died shortly after.

CHAPTER XI.

LAWYERS FROM 1790 TO 1800 — PARKER — CHASE — JOHONNOT — HUBBARD — STACY.

DURING the ten years from 1790 to 1800, lawyers came into the State with an accelerated movement; they more than kept pace with the population. The number of inhabitants, which in 1790 was ninety-six thousand five hundred and forty, came in 1800 to be one hundred and fifty-one thousand seven hundred and nineteen. The number of lawyers in 1790 was sixteen, or one to six thousand thirty-three of the population; in 1800 there were fifty-four lawyers, or one to two thousand eight hundred and nine of the population. Among those who came into the State in that period of ten years, were Prentiss Mellen; the late Judge Wilde; Joseph Thomas of Kennebunk; Nathaniel Perley of Hallowell; Samuel Thatcher at New Gloucester, still living, and the oldest lawyer in the State; Judge Bailey of Wiscasset; Allen Gilman, of Bangor; William Wetmore at Castine; Edward P. Hayman of Berwick, many years Clerk of the Supreme Court in this circuit; Judge Stebbins of Alna; Chief Justice Whitman, now living in Massachusetts; Cyrus King, John Holmes, Nicholas

Emery, George W. Wallingford, in York County; Peter O. Alden at Brunswick; and Benjamin Hasey at Topsham.

It is worthy of remark, that of the fifty-four lawyers in practice in 1800, forty-nine were immigrants from other States. Benjamin Hasey of Topsham, James Bridge of Augusta, Nathan Bridge of Gardiner, and Thomas Rice of Winslow, were natives. Of these fifty-four, it may again be observed, that three became chief justices of the Supreme Court, — Parker, Mellen, Whitman; four, associate justices of the same court, — Thacher, Parker, Wilde, Emery; three, chief justices of the Common Pleas,— Whitman, Silas Lee, Wetmore; six, judges of the Common Pleas, — Frothingham, Dana, Widgery, Stebbins, Wetmore, Whitman; one, judge of the Admiralty Court during the Revolution,— Timothy Langdon; four, Judges of Probate, — James Bridge, Silas Lee, Jeremiah Bailey, Judah Dana; one, Solicitor General, — Davis; two, United States Attornies, — Davis and Silas Lee; one, United States Marshal of the District, — Parker; three, senators in Congress, — Mellen, Holmes, Dana; and eleven, members of the lower house of Congress, — George Thacher, Judge Parker, Lee, Bruce, Rice, Samuel Thatcher, Widgery, Whitman, King, Holmes, Bailey. Two had been members of the convention of Massachusetts on the Constitution of the United States, — Symmes and Widgery; and several were members of the convention which prepared the Constitution of Maine. Many were distinguished, not only at the bar, but in public life; and adorned various spheres of usefulness by high social, mental, and manly qualities.

Only two are now living, of all who were in practice in the State in 1800: the survivors are Chief Justice Whitman, who was born March 11, 1776, and Samuel Thatcher, born in July of the same year, — they are consequently both eighty-six years old. The former removed to East

Bridgewater, his native place, in 1852; the other lives in Brewer.

For convenient reference, I insert a list of all the resident lawyers who practiced in Maine prior to 1800, with the years of commencing and ending practice in Maine, where I have been able to ascertain the facts—

Thomas Gorges,	1640—1643
Thomas Morton,	1643—1645
Noah Emery,	1725—1762
Caleb Emery,	1750—1775
John Emery,	1752—
William Cushing,	1755—1772
David Sewall,	1759—1777
Theophilus Bradbury,	1761—1775
David Wyer,	1762—1776
Timothy Langdon,	1768—1808
James Sullivan,	1768—1778
Roland Cushing,	1768—1789
Theophilus Parsons,	1774—1775
Ezra Taylor,	1779—
John Frothingham,	1779—1804
Royal Tyler,	1779—1781
William Lithgow, Jr.,	1780—1796
George Thacher,	1781—1801
Daniel Davis,	1782—1804
Samuel Dagget,	1783—1798
Manasseh Smith,	1788—1823
George Stacy,	1789—1792
Dudley Hubbard,	1789—1816
Samuel C. Johonnot,	1789—1791
Salmon Chase,	1789—1806
Isaac Parker,	1789—1806

Silas Lee, ...	1789—1814
Sylvanus Wildes, ...	1790—1792
James Bridge, ...	1790—1834
William Symmes, ...	1790—1807
Phineas Bruce, ...	1790—1805
Ebenezer Sullivan, ...	—
William Widgery, ...	—1801
Prentiss Mellen, ...	1792—1840
Joseph Thomas, ...	1792—1830
George Warren, ...	1792—1796
Samuel S. Wilde, ...	1793—1815
Amos Stoddard, ...	1793—1798
Job Nelson, ...	1793—1850
Benjamin Hasey, ...	1794—1851
John Bagley, ...	1794—1795
Thomas Rice, ...	1794—1854
Reuben Kidder, ...	1795—1816
Nathaniel Perley, ...	1795—1824
William Hodge, ...	1795—1798
Moses Gill, ...	1795—1798
Ebenezer Bradish, ...	1796—1799
Thomas S. Sparhawk, ...	1796—1807
Allen Gilman, ...	1796—1846
Edward P. Hayman, ...	1796—1831
Oliver Leonard, ...	1796—1828
Benjamin Whitwell, ...	1796—1812
John Hathaway, ...	1796—1799
Cyrus King, ...	1797—1817
Josiah Stebbins, ...	1797—1829
Peter O. Alden, ...	1797—1843
James D. Hopkins, ...	1797—1840
Jeremiah Bailey, ...	1797—1853
Samuel P. Glidden, ...	1797—1818
Charles Angier, ...	1798—1803

Samuel Thatcher, ...	1798 —
George E. Vaughan, ...	1798 —
Nicholas Emery, ...	1798 — 1862
Judah Dana, ...	1798 — 1845
Thomas Bowman, ...	1798 — 1800
John Merrill, ...	1798 — 1816
Nathan Bridge, ...	1798 — 1825
Isaac Story, ...	1798 — 1801
George W. Wallingford, ...	1798 — 1824
John Holmes, ...	1799 — 1843
Ezekiel Whitman, ...	1799 — 1822
Andrew Greenwood, ...	1799 — 1816
Leonard Morse, ...	1799 — 1823
John Park Little, ...	1799 — 1809
Bohan P. Field, ...	1800 — 1843
Temple Hovey, ...	1800 — 1803
Daniel P. Upton, ...	1800 — 1805
John Winslow, ...	1800 — 1803
Henry V. Chamberlain, ...	1800 — 1808

ISAAC PARKER. 1789—1806.

Having presented the names of all the lawyers who came to Maine prior to the close of the last century, and described most of them, it will be an agreeable duty to continue my sketches through the remaining portion of this varied group, on which we shall find the lights and shadows of life have fallen with no less intenseness than on other fields of human struggle and ambition.

None of the persons we have named were more conspicuous, in all the qualities of a lawyer and a gentleman, than Chief Justice Parker. His first American ancestor was John Parker, who came from Biddeford, in Great Britain, to Saco in Maine. In 1650, he purchased the island in Kennebec River, which afterwards, and now, bears his name, — Parker's Island. He died there, in 1661. His son John became a large purchaser of lands on the Kennebec River, and is said, in ancient records, to "have been the first of the English nation to subdue the said tract." He was driven from his possessions on the Kennebec by the Indians in 1689, and was killed at the fort in Casco, now Portland, with his son James, in an assault by the French and Indians, in 1690, at the age of fifty-six. The surviving members of his family established themselves in Charlestown, Massachusetts. The chief justice was in the sixth degree of descent from the first John, and was born in Boston, June 17, 1768. He graduated at Harvard College in 1786, at the age of eighteen, with high honor. Among his classmates were Timothy Bigelow, Alden Bradford, Dudley Hubbard, and John Lowell. He maintained at school and college a high rank in scholarship. He pursued his law studies in Boston, in the office of Judge Tudor; and, on being admitted to the bar, in 1789, moved to that part of the town of Penobscot which is now Castine. Hancock County, of which that was the shire-town, was incorporated the same year; and he was the first, and for some years, the only lawyer in it. His talents and industry soon gave him a high rank, and his genial temper and manners made him a universal favorite. In 1791, 1793, 1794, and 1795, he represented his town in the legislature; and from this period to the close of his life, in July, 1830, there was scarcely a year in which he was not in some important public office. From 1796 to 1798 he was one of the three representatives in Congress from Maine, succeeding General Dearborn: his colleagues were George Thacher and Peleg Wadsworth. He declined a re-election, and the place was filled by Silas Lee. In 1799, he was appointed United

States Marshal for Maine District; and then moved to Portland, as the courts were there held, and it was the most convenient place to discharge the duties of his office. In December, 1803, Mr. Jefferson removed him, and gave the office to Dr. Thornton of Saco, who held it to the time of his death, in 1824. These offices did not withdraw him from his profession, which he pursued successfully in the common law courts, being engaged in the most important causes which were pending in the tribunals of the State. He took high rank as a counsellor and an advocate; and enjoyed a lucrative practice, until his appointment as an associate judge of the Supreme Court of Massachusetts, in January, 1806. He took his seat at the following March term in Suffolk. In December, of the same year, he presided alone at the important trial of Thomas O. Selfridge for the killing of Charles Austin; in which he had to withstand the forensic skill and ingenuity of the ablest lawyers in Massachusetts, on an issue invenomed by a harsh party spirit. Attorney General Sullivan and Solicitor General Davis were for the government; Samuel Dexter, Christopher Gore, Harrison G. Otis, and Charles Jackson, for the prisoner. He came out of this severe ordeal with unqualified approbation for dignity and impartiality.

The appointment of so young a man, being then but thirty-seven years old, to so important an office, by a governor eminently qualified to estimate character and qualifications, as was Governor Strong, and by the side of such aged and prominent men as the accomplished Chief Justice Dana, and Justices Sedgwick, Sewall, and Thacher, is a sufficient indication of the legal ability and standing of Judge Parker at the bar of the Commonwealth. But we learn from his cotemporaries, that his qualifications for the office were fully equal to its demands, and are amply attested by his judicial career of twenty-four years. The testimony of a cotemporary to me, a short time ago, will throw an agreeable light upon the private character of this estimable man; of his public career we need say nothing,—that is already brilliantly recorded. Judge Whitman said, "Parker was one of the pleasantest men I ever knew,—kind, courteous, and amiable. He was not sanguine or over confident in his cases; and was often embarrassed in arguing them. "He told me," said Judge W., "that he frequently suffered from this diffidence and embarrassment. At times he was very eloquent, and always, from his candid, honest manner, had great weight with the jury." He further observed that Judge Parker once said to him, that his performances depended very much upon the state of his feelings.

Chief Justice Sewall having died suddenly at Wiscasset, in 1814, he was immediately appointed his successor; and as Chief Justice Shaw remarks, "to the universal satisfaction of the community." This sentiment was in no wise abated through the sixteen years during which he presided in the court, to his own sudden and lamented death in 1830, at the age of sixty-two. His most enduring monument is to be found in the twenty-six volumes of the Massachusetts Reports, beginning at the second; they record his clear and learned opinions, in all branches of the law, which under the profound labors of Chief Justice Parsons and himself, were molded and formed to that mature system of jurisprudence which is the pride and security of the ancient Commonwealth. No man was ever more free from affectation or pretension than Judge Parker; modest, unassuming, unaffectedly great, he despised all the accessories and expedients to which weak and mean men resort to acquire notoriety.

Judge Parker was a graceful and polished writer, as well as speaker. In 1800, he delivered an eulogy on the death of Washington, at Portland, which was published: his beautiful tribute to the memory and character of his predecessor, Chief Justice Parsons, was also published. He was eleven years one of the trustees of Bowdoin College, and twenty years one of the overseers of Harvard, from which college he received the degree of LL. D., in 1814. In 1816, he was appointed Royall Professor of Law in Harvard University,— the first on that foundation,—and held the office until 1827.

His popularity as a man, and his reputation as a lawyer and advocate, attracted young students to his office for their law education, after he moved to Portland. Among these, were Samuel D. Freeman and John Wadsworth, talented townsmen; William B. Sewall, now of Kennebunk; James Savage, the venerable antiquary, of Boston; and Abraham Eustis, afterwards Brigadier General in the United States army; these were all graduates of Harvard, and are dead, except Sewall and Savage.

Judge Parker married Rebecca, a daughter of Joseph Hall of Medford, Massachusetts, who was a descendant from John Hall of Concord, 1658, afterwards of Medford, which became the seat of the family. His grandson, John Hall, was the father of Joseph and grandfather of Mrs. Parker. Her mother was Abigail Brooks, a member of the honored family of that name in that ancient town. By her he had several children; sons,—Edward, Charles A., and John; daughters,—Ann, married to Henry Wainwright of Boston; Margaret, who died before her father, unmarried; and Emily, married to Mr. Davis of Boston. Charles graduated at Harvard in 1819, was a lawyer in Boston, and many years Clerk of the Supreme Judicial Court in Suffolk County.

SALMON CHASE.

Salmon Chase, another distinguished lawyer, came into the State, and to the practice in 1789, the same year with Judge Parker. Mr. Chase was born in Cornish, New Hampshire, in 1761, a descendant from Aquila Chase, who was born in 1618, and came from Cornwall, England, to Newbury, Massachusetts. Mr. Chase had six brothers, all of whom were highly respected. Among them were Dudley Chase, Chief Justice of the Supreme Court of Vermont, and a distinguished Senator in Congress; and the Right Rev. Philander Chase, Bishop of Ohio and Illinois. Mr. Chase graduated at Dartmouth College in 1785, after which he went to Portsmouth, New Hampshire, to take charge of a school, and became a student at law with Judge Sherburne. On completing his studies, he established himself in Portland, where he continued in the quiet and uninterrupted pursuit of his profession until his death, in 1806, at the age of forty-five. Mr. Chase was a sound, well-read lawyer, and had such a reputation through the country as to be called the "Law Book." In the great deficiency of reports and books of reference, his opinions were much relied on in cases of doubt and difficulty. Mr. Hopkins, who was at the bar with him ten years, in a notice of him, says, "He was not only an able lawyer, but he was well versed in all the branches of solid learning; in legal science, in mathematical and metaphysical learning, he had few superiors." He further says, "Mr. Chase was held by all his cotemporaries in very high respect as a lawyer." His practice was very extensive, more so than any lawyer of the time in the State, and confidence in him was unlimited; in the midst of this success, he was suddenly removed, and a brilliant light of the bar extinguished. One of his cotemporaries thus spoke of him, "Salmon Chase was a sound lawyer, but not an eloquent advocate. He was wont to say, that let him prepare himself as thoroughly as he might, and be possessed of all the law and facts of his case, when he arose to address the jury, his mind seemed to be in chaos, he could not collect and arrange his thoughts, nor satisfy himself in the presentation of his cause." I learn from the same respected authority, that "He was a kind and amiable man, easy and accessible in his manners, and of fine personal appearance. From his sincerity and frank manner, he always had great influence with the jury. On one occasion he was engaged in a cause in the Common Pleas, before Chief Justice Lewis, an old man, with Mellen and Hopkins, who, being both excited, were continually sparring with each other, to the great annoyance of the bar; in the midst of which the judge was quietly enjoying his nap. Chase, out of patience, jumped up, and said, "Pray, your Honor, stop this jabber, jabber, jabber."

Mr. Chase was the uncle of the respected Secretary of the Treasury of the United States, who was named for his uncle, and to prevent all mistake in the case, the name of "Portland" was added, and "Salmon *Portland* Chase" perpetuates the name and residence of the honored subject of our notice.

The two eminent lawyers of whom I have been speaking, Parker and Chase, together with their cotemporary, William Symmes, of whom a brief notice will follow, stand now vividly before me, as I saw them in my youthful days, in the court room and streets of Portland. All were of dignified mein and carriage, Chase much the tallest, but all portly, erect, and handsome. They were well-preserved specimens of the old school gentlemen and lawyers, all born before the commencement of the Revolution.

Mr. Chase's death was very sudden; he was at his office on Monday, and the next Sunday he died of bilious fever.

He left a son and a daughter, remarkably fine children. George, the son, graduated at Harvard College in 1818, with high promise, and gave every indication of honor and usefulness. He commenced the study of law in Portland, but the next year, November 11, 1819, in the midst of brilliant expectations, his numerous friends and companions were summoned to pay the last tribute of affection and esteem at the grave of their friend. His sister, Elizabeth, married Dr. Howard of Boston, a grandson of Rev. Simeon Howard, the beloved pastor of the West Church, Boston.

Mr. Chase was twice married, first to Miss Mary Stinson of Portsmouth, by whom he had one son, George, before mentioned, born September 29, 1800. She died in 1801. In 1804 he married Sarah Tyng Waldo, widow of Samuel Waldo, a merchant in Portland, by whom he had the daughter before spoken of, who, with the mother, survived him.

SAMUEL C. JOHONNOT.

My next sketch will be of one whose name is not even known to persons of the last two generations, — a man who rose upon our horizon with a brilliancy which gave token of eminent success, but who was consumed in his own brightness. I refer to Samuel Cooper Johonnot. He was born in Boston, graduated at Harvard College in 1783, and was admitted to the bar of Cumberland in October, 1789, the same year which introduced Mr. Chase, Dudley Hubbard, and others to the practice in Maine. He had previously studied and been admitted in Boston. In portraying his character I adopt the language of Solicitor General Davis, in a letter to me in the year 1828. "Johonnot was the grandson of the celebrated Samuel Cooper, D. D., of Boston, for whom he was named and by whom he was adopted. His grandfather discovered his extraordinary genius when he was quite a child. At an early age he sent him to France and Geneva for his education; he remained many years in those countries, and when he returned he had nothing of the appearance, manners, or habits of an American. He was a complete Frenchman in everything. But his education was as thorough as any young man at that time could acquire in Europe. He was an elegant scholar. Spoke the modern languages, was full of wit, vivacity, and Latin, and one of the pleasantest companions I ever met with. But with all this, his European education ruined him for an American. He had no feelings, notions, or manners in common with us Yankees. For these reasons he could never succeed in his profession, though he had great natural endowments for it; he accordingly quit it, and went to the West Indies. The last I heard of him he was an auctioneer. He studied with the late Governor Sullivan, by whom he was introduced to the bar, and who was extremely fond of him."

To this graphic notice from Mr. Davis, I will add the testimony of Mr. Hopkins, who knew him well. "His satirical powers rendered him dangerous to those who fell under his censure, and ultimately proved injurious to himself; for, entering into a newspaper quarrel upon the subject of a political election in 1791, his satire bore very severely upon several of the most considerable persons in Portland; their resentment rendered his longer stay so perilous, that he found it necessary to make a hasty removal. He resided in Portland only about two years; he afterwards went to Demarara, where he was appointed American Consul in 1793, and accumulated a handsome estate."[1] He died in 1806.

---

[1] Hopkins's Address to the Cumberland Bar, 1833.

MANASSEH SMITH.

Manasseh Smith was a son of Abijah Smith of Leominster, Massachusetts, where he was born in 1749, and graduated at Harvard College in 1773. For awhile he was chaplain in the army; he afterwards pursued the study of law, and commenced practice in Leominster, and was for a time Clerk of the Court. He moved to Hollis in New Hampshire, and married there Hannah, a daughter of Daniel Emerson of that place, where several of his children were born. In 1788 he established himself in Wiscasset, Maine, where he ever after resided. He was wont to say that his whole library, at the commencement of his practice, consisted of the Statutes of Massachusetts and Blackstone's Commentaries. Law books were rare and expensive in that day, very few had been published in this country; the first American edition of Blackstone was issued at Philadelphia in 1772, and was a great enterprise; the books then to be found in the principal cities, Boston, New York, and Philadelphia, were Bacon's Abridgment, Burrows, Plowden, Hobart, 2d Raymond, and Pere Williams's Reports, and the Law Dictionaries of Cunningham and Jacobs. It was not until some years after the Revolution, that any law books, except a few of forms, were published in this country: among the first were several prepared by Samuel Freeman of Portland; viz., the Clerk's Assistant, Town Officer, Probate Manual, and Justice's Assistant: these, as an old practitioner informed me, were in general use by the profession, and with the Statutes, Blackstone's Commentaries, and Espinasse's Nisi Prius, were about all the books which a lawyer's library contained at the close of the last century. Mr. Freeman was competent to the task he had undertaken, for, before the Revolution, he had been one of the irregular practitioners at the bar, and afterwards had filled all the offices, the forms of which his books contained. He was forty-six years Clerk of the Court to 1820, with the exception of one year, and for forty-six years was Register and Judge of Probate, passing from one to the other in 1804; he was Postmaster twenty-nine years, and twenty-five years a Selectman of the town. For a portion of the time he held nearly all these offices at once, — that is, Clerk, Judge or Register of Probate, Postmaster, and Selectman. Such an experience qualified him to prepare acceptable books of forms, and their merit was proved by their extensive use.

John Adams, admitted to practice in 1758, speaking of the law books of that time, in his Diary, says, "At this time the study of the law was a dreary ramble. The name of Blackstone had not been heard, whose Commentaries, together with Sullivan's Lectures, and Reeves's History of the Law, have smoothed the path of the student, while the long career of Lord Mansfield, his many investigations and decisions, the number of modern reporters in his time, and a great number of writers on particular branches of the science, have greatly facilitated the acquaintance of it. I was desirous of seeking the law as well as I could in its fountains, and I obtained as much knowledge as I could of Bracton, Britton, Fleta, and Glanville, but I suffered very much for want of books."

Mr. Willard, in his address to the Worcester Bar in 1829, says, "In the seventeenth century it may well be doubted whether there were any books of the common law in the country, excepting two copies of the following works, which the Governor and assistants ordered to be imported in 1647; viz., Coke's Entries and Reports, his Commentaries and Reading on Magna Charta, the New Terms of the Law, and Dalton's Justice."

Mr. Rice, who established himself in Winslow in 1795, informed me that he opened an office in Wiscasset in 1794, at which time Silas Lee and Manasseh Smith were in practice there. He says, "There they lived and there they died. Smith had formerly been a minister and afterwards Clerk of the Court in Massachusetts or New Hampshire. He accumulated a handsome property, and left a large family. I believe he never had any library except the Statutes of the State and Blackstone. He wrote so bad a hand that it was almost impossible to read it. It is said that Judge Paine, trying to read a special plea of his, was brought to a stand, and scolded him heartily. Smith said he had been, as a minister, in the habit of writing fast, which led him to be careless."

Mr. Smith was not distinguished as a lawyer or advocate, but devoted himself to office business with assiduity, intelligence, and success. He gave more honor and service to the profession by his four sons, all of whom were educated at Harvard, and became successful and honorable practitioners; viz., Manasseh, who graduated in 1800, and established himself in Warren, where he died a worthy and prominent citizen in 1822; Joseph Emerson, 1804, a respected practitioner in Boston, and died there in 1837; his classmate, Judge Ware of the United States District Court of Maine, pursued, for a time, his law studies with him. Samuel Emerson, a graduate in 1808, admitted to practice at the Suffolk bar in 1812, became a prominent lawyer at Wiscasset, was made Chief Justice of the Court of Common Pleas in 1821, and in 1822 an associate of the new court, with Chief Justice Whitman at its head; and in 1831 was elected Governor of the State, which office he held, by subsequent elections, three years.[1] The fourth of this series of honored descendants is Edwin, a graduate of 1811, who,

---

[1] A more extended notice of Governor Smith will be found in subsequent pages.

after discharging the duties of his profession many years in Warren, enjoying the confidence and respect of the community in which he has long resided, retired with honor from the bar.

Besides these sons, Mr. Smith left four daughters; viz., Hannah, who married Colonel Samuel Seavey of Wisconsin; Mary, married Ivory Hovey of Berwick; Lydia and Lucy, who died in Wiscasset. He died at Wiscasset, May 23, 1823, at the age of seventy-four.

DUDLEY HUBBARD.

Dudley Hubbard, the first regularly educated lawyer who settled in South Berwick, was born in Ipswich, Massachusetts, March 3, 1763. He was probably descended from Colonel Nathaniel Hubbard; I infer this because the Colonel married a daughter of Rev. Samuel Dudley of Exeter;—the two names uniting in Dudley Hubbard, seem to point to such an origin, and being a native of Ipswich, long the residence of the Hubbard family, confirms the conjecture. He graduated at Harvard College in 1786, in the class with Timothy Bigelow, Alden Bradford, and Chief Justice Parker. On leaving college, he immediately commenced the study of his profession with Daniel Davis in Portland, was admitted to the bar in Cumberland County at the October term, 1789, and established himself in that part of Berwick which, in 1814, was incorporated as South Berwick. This was a beautiful and prosperous village, containing an unusual number of well-educated and cultivated persons. Ebenezer Sullivan, a brother of John and James, was then in practice there; he was brilliant and eloquent like his brothers, but irregular and desultory in his habits; he had served in the army of the Revolution, and was captain of one of the two companies raised in South Berwick at the beginning of the war. He afterwards commanded a company on the western frontiers. He was not a rival to stand much in the way of an intelligent and persevering attorney; Mr. Hubbard, therefore, soon left him far behind in the race for business, and had the whole field to himself. His clients multiplied, many of them from Boston, with which Berwick was much connected in trade, and his engagements rapidly increased. He was for many years leader at the York bar, and he occasionally practiced in Cumberland. He was an eloquent advocate; which, united with a very handsome person, pleasing address, and dignified manners, introduced him to an extensive and lucrative practice. He also was for sometime attorney for the county. His large business and standing at the bar drew numerous students to his office, among whom were some who became prominent in subsequent years; viz., Edward P. Hayman, Benjamin Greene, George W. Wallingford, William A. Hayes, William Lambert, and Ether Shepley, late Chief Justice of Maine, all of whom but Judge Shepley are dead.

The following anecdote will give an impression of the imposing appearance of Mr. Hubbard in term time. The late Judge Dana of Fryeburg, on his first attendance at the court in York, near the close of the last century, took a letter of introduction to Mr. Hubbard; but he found him so formal and distant in his demeanor that he did not deliver it. Dana met there his classmate, the late Judge Emery, who had just established himself at Parsonsfield, and was also attending his first term. As they were jogging on together toward home, on horseback, Dana told Emery about his letter to Hubbard; Emery replied that he also had a similar letter, which he had declined presenting for the same reason. This may have been the reserve of modest young men, at a period when the intercourse between the elder and junior members of the bar was much less free than at the present day.

Mr. Hubbard's fine conversational powers and his agreeable address gave him the *entree* into the best society, not only of his own place of residence, but of Portsmouth, Boston, and of Montreal, where he went occasionally to visit his wife's friends. His social qualities and his fondness for society drew him too much from his professional duties in the latter part of his life, in consequence of which his pecuniary resources were much diminished, while his expensive habits did not follow the same ratio of reduction. He also built a handsome house, the one which Judge Hayes afterwards owned and occupied. These expenditures outrun his income, and he became embarrassed and despondent; having a proud, ambitious spirit, his affairs pressed heavily upon him, and he died suddenly, April 26, 1816, at the age of fifty-three. His wife was Olivia Dame, whom he married at *Trois Rivieres*, in Canada. She was educated in a convent at Montreal, and was a woman of great personal beauty and accomplished manners. She survived her husband but a few years. Mr. Hubbard left one daughter, who married Benjamin Nason of South Berwick, and their daughter is the wife of Edward E. Bourne, Jr., a lawyer in Kennebunk, and son of Judge Bourne. Thus the blood of Mr. Hubbard is transmitted, though not his name.

GEORGE STACY.

Another York lawyer, cotemporary of Mr. Hubbard, was George Stacy. He, too, was a native of Ipswich, born in 1764, and graduated at Harvard College in 1784. After being admitted to the bar he established himself at Biddeford in 1789 or the year before. But soon getting into some disagreeable entanglement with the other sex, and becoming dissipated, he was obliged to make a sudden departure from that place. He afterwards became Consul for the Isle of France, and died at St. Mary, Georgia, in 1808. He was a tall and well-proportioned man, but acquired no distinction as a lawyer or advocate ; and his name, many years ago, passed out of the recollection of the people of Saco.

In making a survey of the lives and characters of the lawyers who have moved through the plane of our history for the past one hundred years, we are deeply impressed with the retributions which have been meted out according to their lives and acts. To the industrious, virtuous, and honorable practitioners, — honor, success, applause, and friends have been awarded; while those who have pursued the phantoms of pleasure and indulged in the social vices of the period, have fallen into untimely and unhonored graves, or lived to be objects of reprobation and contempt. The examples of each class are numerous, and could easily be recalled; but it were an invidious task to exhibit the dark shadows which have settled heavily on many of our brethren. The moral to be drawn from the contrast would be useful to young practitioners, but at an expense of wounded feeling which it were not worth while to incur.

CHAPTER XII.

WILLIAM SYMMES — PHINEAS BRUCE — SILAS LEE — JAMES BRIDGE — PRENTISS MELLEN — SAMUEL S. WILDE — GEORGE WARREN — AMOS STODDARD — WILLIAM HODGE — THOMAS RICE — JOSEPH THOMAS — JOB NELSON.

WILLIAM SYMMES. 1790—1807.

AMONG the distinguished lawyers who came into practice in the State in 1790, were William Symmes, at Portland; James Bridge, at Augusta; and Phineas Bruce, at Machias. Mr. Symmes came with a reputation acquired as a member of the Convention of Massachusetts which adopted the Constitution of the United States. He was descended from the Rev. Zachariah Symmes, who was rector of the Parish of Dunstable in Bedfordshire, England, from 1625 to 1633. In the latter year he came to this country, and was immediately settled in Charlestown, Massachusetts, where he died in 1671. His son Zachariah, and his grandson Thomas, were ministers in Bradford. The subject of this notice was the son of the Rev. Zachariah Symmes of Andover, and of the sixth generation from the first immigrant. He was born in 1762, graduated at Harvard College in 1780, and after pursuing his regular course of study, was admitted to practice at the Essex Bar. Previous to this, he spent some time in Virginia as a private tutor, during which he kept up a correspondence with his classmates and friends: his letters are said to have been interesting and instructive: a friend who had seen them pronounced them beautiful. In 1788 he was a member of the Convention of Massachusetts which adopted the Constitution of the United States, and in the first instance took part in opposition to it under the instructions of his constituents; he afterwards, on hearing the arguments of Parsons and others, changed his views, and voted in favor of its adoption, for which he received the commendation of his town. He came to Portland in 1790, and entered at once upon a successful practice, and took high rank at the bar; he was a good classical scholar, a sound lawyer, and an able advocate. His manner was formal and stately, but graceful. One of his students,—William Freeman,—now living at an advanced age in Cherryfield, has given me his impressions of Mr. Symmes, which, coming from so reliable a source, are justly apppreciated; he says, "The personal appearance of Mr. Symmes was stately and dignified. He was, in all respects, a gentleman in his manners, and emphatically one of the old school. He was affable and polite, and commanded affection as well as respect. He may truly be said to have been one of the most imposing and influential men at that time in Portland. As a lawyer and advocate he was unsurpassed. In his efforts as a speaker there was perhaps more of the *fortiter in re*, than the *suaviter in modo*. He always touched the right string. He had great discriminating powers; no one brought out the root and truth of the case so effectually as he did, whether at the bar or any public meeting. Great confidence was felt in his opinions on all occasions, and especially on legal questions. He was unquestionably the best and most reliable lawyer in the State of his time." He then speaks of the cloud which was cast upon his latter days by the use of intoxicating drinks; and adds, "Often, when mellow with brandy, his favorite drink, he was brilliant, and threw more light on a subject under discussion than any other speaker." It was probably under the influence of his favorite beverage that a scene between him and Judge Thacher took place. Mr. Symmes had made a motion to the court, which he was zealously arguing, notwithstanding frequent interruptions by the judge. Thacher at last became impatient, and said, "Mr. Symmes, you need not persist in arguing the point, for I am not a court of errors, and cannot give a final judgment." "I know," replied Symmes, "that you can't give a final judgment, but as to your not being a *court of errors*, I will not say."

Mr. Symmes often attended the courts in York, as did other prominent members of the Cumberland Bar, and was frequently engaged in important cases. In the course of a trial in an action of trespass concerning a lot of boards, Symmes, in his formal, dignified manner, spoke of the "sanctity" of this pile of lumber. Ebenezer Sullivan and other members of the bar were amused with the use of the word in that connection, and Sullivan wrote an impromptu, nearly as follows:

"Moses of old, who led the Jewish race,
Forbid but one, and that the holy place;
Even God himself forbade that wood or stone
Should have the homage due to him alone,
But Symmes, with wisdom greater than divine,
Finds sanctity in boards and slabs of pine."

It was very common for the wits of the bar, at that time, to amuse themselves in writing squibs and bon mots during the tedious processes of trials.

Mr. Hopkins, a cotemporary, in his address to the Cumberland Bar in 1833, thus speaks of Mr. Symmes: "Mr. Symmes was a well-read lawyer, and an able and eloquent advocate. He ranked among the first of his cotemporaries. He was also a fine classical scholar, of cultivated literary taste, and uncommonly learned as a historian. His productions in the newspapers of the time were honorable testimony to his literary character, particularly a series of numbers, entitled 'Communications,' about the year 1795, in defense of the common law. These numbers were published in the principal newspapers throughout the Union. Mr. Symmes, with Judge Thacher and two or three others, rendered the newspapers of that period very interesting by their valuable contributions." It may not be improper for me to say that Mr. Hopkins himself, as also Johonnot, Mr. Mellen, and Solicitor Davis, were among the contributors who made the Portland papers of that day exceedingly interesting.

Mr. Symmes was never married; he died January 7, 1807, aged forty-five. He had a brother, a physician in New Gloucester, who died in the early part of this century, about the year 1804.

PHINEAS BRUCE. 1790—1809.

We come now to speak of Phineas Bruce: and who, you ask, is Phineas Bruce? No wonder that his name is not remembered by a living member of the bar in Maine; yet, sixty years ago, he had a name and a fame. He was the first lawyer that entered into practice in the county of Washington. He descended from George Bruce, who settled in Woburn, Massachusetts, about 1650, and was son of George Bruce, born in 1732, and Hannah Lovett, born in 1738. His father died in Leicester, May 3, 1785, and his mother at Billerica, December 18, 1821, having had ten children, six sons and four daughters. Phineas was the second child, and was born at Mendon, Massachusetts, June

7, 1762. He graduated at Yale College in 1786, and commenced his legal studies with William Caldwell of Rutland, ending them with Benjamin Hitchborn of Boston. After being admitted to the bar, he came to Machias, in 1790. He was a good lawyer, and highly esteemed for his integrity, and his ability to investigate and analyze any subject to which he applied his powers; but from excessive modesty and diffidence he never became a successful advocate. He represented the town of Machias in the legislature eight years, from 1793, and was the only representative to the General Court during that time from the county. In 1803, he was elected to the Eighth Congress, which commenced its term in 1804. His colleagues from Maine were Richard Cutts from York, Peleg Wadsworth from Cumberland, and Samuel Thatcher from Lincoln. But a violent attack of hypochondriasis, to which he had been subject, occurring at this time, prevented his taking his seat; and before the close of his term he became of unsound mind, and continued insane until his death, which took place in Uxbridge, October 4, 1809.

In March, 1795, he married Jane Savage, sister of the Hon. James Savage of Boston, by whom he had five sons and one daughter. His widow died in Cambridge, Massachusetts, in 1854, at the age of eighty-six.

SILAS LEE.

Silas Lee was son, and the eighth child, of Dr. Joseph Lee of Concord, Massachusetts, and was born there July 23, 1760. Mr. Lee pursued his preliminary studies under some difficulties: his native town was one of the earliest battle fields of the Revolution, and letters and arms alternately occupied his thoughts; and it was not until he was twenty years old, and near the close of the great struggle, that he was able to enter Harvard College, from which he graduated in 1784, having for his classmates the late Professor Abbott of Bowdoin College, and Chief Justice Mellen. He pursued his legal studies with Judge Thacher at Biddeford, whose niece, Temperance Hedge of Dennis, Cape Cod, he afterwards married. He established himself in Wiscasset in 1789, and having the whole field to himself, and being a skillful lawyer, he soon acquired a large and profitable practice. He zealously pursued his professional business, while at the same time he engaged in political life. In 1794, 1798, and 1799, he represented his town in the General Court, the first time as successor to Mr. Gardiner, who was wrecked and drowned in 1793. In 1799 he was elected to Congress from the Eastern District to succeed Mr. Parker, who had been appointed Marshal of the district. He held this place one term, when, in 1801, he was selected by Mr. Jefferson to take the place of Daniel Davis as United States Attorney for Maine. This office he held in conjunction with that of Judge of Probate, to which he was appointed in 1804 as successor to Judge Bowman, until his death, which took place March 3, 1814, at the age of fifty-four. He also held the office of chief justice of the Common Pleas in 1810, and until the new court went into operation in 1811. He died of a nervous fever caused by a continued and excessive strain upon his constitution in the severe duties of his offices. From 1807 to the close of the war with England in 1815, during the non-intercourse and non-importation laws, the embargo and all the restrictive measures of government, the United States courts were crowded with business; large amounts of property were held under seizure for violation of law, and the novelty and importance of the suits rendered the duties of the District Attorney exceedingly arduous. Opposition to the restrictive measures arrayed against him the whole commercial interest, which employed the ablest advocates to embarrass and foil the government officers. These kept the attorney in a state of constant excitement and exertion, and were too great a burden for Mr. Lee to bear; he perished in the midst of them, a martyr to official duty.

Mr. Lee was a well-read lawyer, was quick and full of energy, and, as one of his cotemporaries informed me, few persons more fully enjoyed the confidence of the public or were more sincerely mourned. He was a good special pleader, but a poor advocate; in his address to the jury he was long, prosy, and tedious; but, notwithstanding this defect, he had a very large business, which may be accounted for by his good sense and ability as a lawyer, his genial disposition and gentlemanly manners. He left no children.

Mr. Rice, a cotemporary of Mr. Lee, in a letter to me a short time before his death, made the following remarks: "Mr. Lee was a good lawyer, but was too tedious in his long speeches, greatly attached to special pleading, and would, in drawing a plea under the statute of limitations, occupy a sheet or two of closely written paper. He had a large business, made a good deal of money, but died poor."

JAMES BRIDGE. 1790—1834.

About the same time that Mr. Lee settled in Wiscasset, James Bridge commenced practice in Augusta, then a part of Lincoln County. He was the son of Edmund Bridge, who was born in Lexington, Massachusetts, in 1739.

The Bridges are of ancient lineage; they go back to classical times; we learn that a contest for some time existed in Italy between the houses of *Ponti* and *Canali* as to the antiquity of their families; the former contended that the *Bridges* were above the *Canals*, the latter, that Canals existed before Bridges. Our classical friends need not be told

HON. JAMES BRIDGE

AT THE AGE OF 35

James Bridge

that the Italian names Ponti and Canali are interpreted in English by Bridge and Canal.

The plain English family of Bridge, their first coming to America, and the descent of James Bridge from the American ancestor, are fully spoken of in a notice of Sheriff Bridge, which is contained in another part of our book. His mother was Phebe Bowman, by whom he was connected with Judge Bowman of Lincoln County. His father was Sheriff of Lincoln from 1781 to 1815, a period of thirty-four years. James, his eldest son, was born in Dresden, September 21, 1765. He graduated at Harvard College in 1787, a classmate of John Quincy Adams, Judge Cranch, Dr. Hezekiah Packard, father of Professor Packard of Bowdoin College, and the late Judge Putnam of Massachusetts. He was the chum of Mr. Adams and a fellow-student at law with him in the office of Theophilus Parsons at Newburyport. On being admitted to practice in 1790, he first opened an office at Bucksport on the Penobscot, but soon after removed to Augusta, where he ever after lived.

He entered on the profession with the reputation of being a good scholar, and he soon acquired that of being a good lawyer. The time was remarkably favorable for a practitioner. General Lithgow was the only lawyer who occupied that field, and he was soon disabled by disease. Land titles were then in great confusion; large proprietors,—absentees,—had neglected their estates; many persons were coming into the district, and not knowing where to apply to make purchases, had entered upon favorable locations, and pitched their habitations without title. Vexing questions were constantly arising in regard to boundaries as well as to rights of title and possession. Into the midst of this practice Mr. Bridge entered with intelligence, zeal, and activity, acquired the confidence of landed proprietors and of the community, and became the leader at the bar. It was particularly as the agent and attorney of the Proprietors of the Kennebec Purchase, that his business was extended, and a large property accumulated. He associated with him in practice a young lawyer who had been his student, then just coming on the stage, Reuel Williams, as a partner, who laid, in this connection, the foundation of a fortune and political distinction.

Mr. Bridge found his partner so able to take charge of the business that he gradually retired from it; and although the partnership continued in name for thirty years, yet Mr. Bridge did very little in it after 1810; he had a disrelish for courts, his circumstances were easy, and he was sharing considerable profits from the office for the benefit of having introduced a young friend on a most successful career, and for his own occasional attendance.

Mr. Bridge was so much engrossed by professional duties for the first twenty years of his practice, that he did not engage in political life; in 1799 he represented his town in the legislature, probably with a view to effect the establishment of Kennebec County, which was separated from Lincoln in that year. He was appointed the first Judge of Probate of the county, which he resigned in 1804, and was succeeded by Judge Daniel Cony. He was a member of the Executive Council of Massachusetts in 1818, and a delegate to the convention which prepared the Constitution of Maine in 1819, and one of the committee to draft that instrument.

Judge Bailey of Wiscasset observed to me that when he came to Maine in 1794, "Mr. Bridge was at the head of the bar in Augusta, and his practice was very extensive, especially in landed matters." He also said of Mr. Bridge's father, that "he was an excellent officer and much respected. He had a long range to attend to; all the country now comprised in the counties of Lincoln, Kennebec, Somerset, and part of

Waldo was then in one county." And this was before the counties of Sagadahoc, Androscoggin, and Knox were taken off.

He was appointed in 1820 one of the joint commissioners of Massachusetts and Maine, "to adjust the personal concerns of the two States," and to make division of the public lands. The commissioners, consisting of Levi Lincoln, George Bliss, and Silas Holman of Massachusetts, and James Bridge, Benjamin J. Porter, and Lathrop Lewis of Maine, made their report concerning the personal rights in May, 1822, which they declared to be a full and final adjustment of all personal property and of liabilities and claims between the two States. December 28, 1822, they made a report "on the division of the public lands under the act of separation," a long and able document, and they made a final report of their doings in May, 1823. Judge Bridge was also appointed in 1820 with Albert Newhall and William Swan, a commissioner to investigate the doings of certain banks which had become bankrupt.

The office business of this gentleman was so extensive and lucrative that it occupied his time too much to enable him to make a distinguished figure as an advocate, yet he was an easy, graceful speaker, and capable of taking a high position in that character if he had given attention to it. Not long after his connection with Mr. Williams, he gradually withdrew from the courts and practice, and found sufficient employment as President of one of the Augusta Banks and in the management of his private affairs. He was eminently a practical man, and by a steady application to the duties of private life he secured to himself a competency, of which his children after his death, in 1834, became partakers. A persistent solicitor for a society once was urging with great earnestness his subscription to some object, and took occasion to say that a liberal donation would bear honorable testimony to his generosity. Mr. Bridge heard him through, then coolly replied that he could not agree with him, for from his experience in life, which had been considerable, he had found that people were respected more for what they had than for what they gave away.

This was not quite so good as Douglass Jerrold's reply. A not very deserving character had been frequently aided by subscription, and an appeal was again made. "Well," said Jerrold, "how much does he want this time?" "Why, just a four and two naughts I think will make him straight." "Well," said he, "put me down for one of the naughts." Another reply of Jerrold's is equally good. Tom Dibbin said to him the first time he saw him, "Young man, have you sufficient confidence in me to lend me a guinea?" "O yes," said Jerrold, "I have the confidence, but not the guinea."

Judge Bridge married Hannah, a daughter of Judge Joseph North of Augusta, who died before him, leaving the reputation of great benevolence of character and most pleasing manners. Their children were as follows:

1. Edmund Theodore, born in 1799, graduated at Bowdoin College in 1818. He studied law and opened an office in Augusta, was sometime United States Mail Agent for New England, moved to New York, opened an office, and there died in 1854, aged fifty-five. He left two daughters, and had a son in the practice of law in New York, who is dead.

2. Margaret, born about 1801, married a son of General North, aid of the Baron Steuben. She is now a widow residing in the city of New York.

3. James, born about 1803, merchant of Augusta. He married a daughter of Hon. Reuel Williams, and is living in Augusta.

4. Horatio, born 1805, graduated at Bowdoin College in

1825, studied law and opened an office in Augusta, and is now "Chief of Bureau of Clothing and Provision," at Washington.

5 and 6. William and Mary, twins, born in 1808. Mary is dead, and William is now attached to the Navy Yard in Charlestown, Massachusetts.

7. Hannah, born in 1810, married Daniel Williams, a lawyer in Augusta, Maine.

The Hon. Jacob McGaw of Bangor has kindly furnished me the following sketch of one of his cotemporaries.

OLIVER LEONARD. 1796—1828.

Although the ancestry of any citizen of the United States exerts very little influence upon his reputation or usefulness in the period of life in which he is, or ought to be, most beneficial to society; yet all of us are so constituted, that we feel satisfaction in being able to reckon honorable names among our kindred, whether they be dead or remain in full life.

Oliver Leonard was not accustomed to recur frequently to his lineage, yet his relatives reckon their descent from the noble family of Leonard, Lord Dacre, who flourished in the twelfth century, at Pontypool, in England.

In 1652, James Leonard, with his brother, Henry Leonard, sons of Thomas Leonard, left Pontypool, and came to Taunton, Massachusetts, where James settled, and there established the first manufactory of iron that ever existed in America. Henry settled in the neighboring town of Raynham, where he remained a few years, and then removed to New Jersey. From these two gentlemen, the genealogy of all the families of Leonard in the United

States may be traced. Men of considerable eminence in the learned professions, and other dignified conditions in life, have existed in nearly every generation of this name, since the arrival of the two brothers before spoken of.

Oliver Leonard, the subject of this sketch, was a son of Jonathan Leonard, who descended from the aforenamed James Leonard, and was born at Norton, Massachusetts, in February, 1764. He entered Brown University, Providence, Rhode Island, 1783, and graduated in 1787. While Mr. Leonard was an undergraduate in college, the insurrection in Massachusetts, commonly known as "Shays's Rebellion," occurred. The patriotism of the scholar was too ardent to permit even the honors and benefits of college to detain him from joining the governmental troops under General Lincoln, and performing the duties of adjutant as long as his services could be useful to the Commonwealth. His fine personal appearance and good horsemanship induced poorly informed spectators to suppose that he was colonel of a regiment, and to apply to him the title which that rank confers on its lawful possessor. In his after life he was always addressed by the style or title of *Colonel Leonard.*

Shays's Rebellion having been quelled, Mr. Leonard returned to the university, rejoined his class, and graduated with it in good standing. Embarrassment in all kinds of business at that time presented to young men great difficulties in making choice of the most judicious pursuits for usefulness and prosperity in after life. An offer by Major Thomas Fobes to enter into partnership in trade with him, at Norton, was accepted by Mr. Leonard, but continued only about one year, when it was dissolved, and a pupilage as student at law, under the direction of Stephen Dexter, Esq., at Newport, Rhode Island, was commenced; and with the exception of a short time in Judge Padelford's office, at Taunton, pursued until his admission to the bar in 1791.

While living at Newport, he became acquainted with Mrs. Sarah Fletcher, and was married to her about the time he commenced the practice of his profession. Mrs. Fletcher was the widow of an English surgeon in the American Revolution. She had, in her own right, an annuity of one hundred guineas. With this fund to connect with professional earnings, he established himself, and opened a law office at Taunton, the shire town of Bristol County in the Commonwealth of Massachusetts. At this place he continued to reside until 1796, sharing, so far as he might with some other older and more firmly established lawyers than himself, in the business of the county.

About this time, some resolute and industrious young men who lived in the region of Mr. Leonard's nativity, but who had just begun to acquire property, determined to remove to Orrington, Maine, which was then principally in the state of nature. Mr. Leonard being favorably impressed in prospect of the future importance of the territory bordering on Penobscot River, concluded to remove from Taunton, and settle in Orrington, with the hope and expectation of participating liberally in the reward of well directed efforts for development of its capabilities of prospective wealth and honor. Pursuant to this determination, he purchased a tract of land on which the making of a farm had been commenced, in that part of Orrington which now constitutes the town of Brewer, and there conducted, through twenty years, his professional labors. There was no disappointment of hopes concerning the rapid increase of population in Orrington and circumjacent territory; but the residents were generally poor men. This characteristic produced numerous successful applications for pecuniary credit. Large profits were freely promised to creditors, which very commonly failed of fulfillment. Suits at law for collection of debts became numerous in proportion to the population. Mr. Leonard was the only lawyer, during five years, who lived within the limit that now constitutes the county of Penobscot, and enjoyed a large amount of practice in the department mentioned. In 1802, two other lawyers commenced the business of their profession in the adjoining town of Bangor, and partook largely of business that before had been performed by Mr. Leonard exclusively. The fortune of Mrs. Leonard, united to her husband's professional income, induced him to engage too largely in the purchase and manufacture of lumber, together with some other operations that were entirely foreign to the course of his previous education and pursuits; which proved unfortunate in their results.

The people of Orrington having become sufficiently numerous to be entitled to a representative in the legislature of Massachusetts, elected Mr. Leonard to that honorable office in 1798, and he was re-elected the five following years. Flattered by the confidence and respect thus manifested by his townsmen, he discharged the duties of the office promptly and with fidelity. Having undertaken to perform functions of such great and differing natures, he could not be expected to excel in his profession. Yet he remained at Orrington in the prosecution of a small portion of business until after the close of the war between the United States and England, which was commenced in 1812.

Having disposed of the estate that had belonged to him in Orrington (now Brewer), he removed to Bangor in 1817 with the intention of employing his time in more constant application to professional pursuits than he had done in several of the preceding years. But he had become so much weaned from study and the routine of business, that few

J E B[illegible]s Lith. Boston.

P. Mellen

Aged 60 years.

clients were inclined to patronize him; and this, too, at a time when increased income was very desirable.

A grievous illustration of the maxim, "Solitary woes are rare," now occurred, which served to crush the aspirations of Mr. Leonard for the comforts that a pecuniary competency affords to persons who have been accustomed to such enjoyments from their infancy up to the border of old age.

It so happened that now, when the principal dependence of Mr. and Mrs. Leonard for their ease and even sustenance in after life, was the regular and prompt payment of her annuity, the base of the fund on which that annuity, together with other annuities, rested, became the subject of a suit in Chancery. Payment of the annuities was thereby suspended for nearly or quite twenty years.

All superfluities in household affairs ceased to be attainable by Mr. and Mrs. Leonard, and the comforts of life became fewer from month to month until absolute poverty overtook them, instead of the abundance which they had previously enjoyed. His splendid figure bent, his cheerful and handsome face became gradually gloomy, and his conversation lost most of its charms under his adversity. Infinite wisdom protracted his depressed life until January, 1828, when his earthly existence ended, and his spiritual, eternal state commenced.

At the time of Mr. Leonard's death the suit in Chancery had not been closed, but Mrs. Leonard lived to enjoy, through one or two years, the fruits of a decree entirely favorable to her claims and rights.

PRENTISS MELLEN. 1792—1840.

Prentiss Mellen, the next lawyer who settled in Maine, was the eighth of the nine children of the Rev. John Mellen of Sterling, Massachusetts, and was born in that town October 11, 1764. His mother was Rebecca Prentiss, daughter of the Rev. John Prentiss of Lancaster, from which family his Christian name was derived. His grandfather was Thomas Mellen, a farmer of Hopkinton in Massachusetts. His father was born there March 14, 1722, graduated at Harvard College in 1741, and having served long and faithfully in the ministerial office at Sterling and Hanover, in the Old Colony, he died at Reading, Massachusetts, in 1807, aged eighty-five.

His elder brother Henry and himself were fitted for college by their father, and entered Harvard together in 1780, from which they took their degree in 1784, in the same class with John Abbott, long a professor in Bowdoin College; Silas Lee, a distinguished lawyer in Wiscasset; and others who have taken honorable positions in society. Henry, brilliant, witty, an attribute of the Prentiss stock, somewhat wayward, but beloved by all who knew him, established himself in the profession of law at Dover, New Hampshire, where he died in 1809. Prentiss spent a year after his graduation, in Barnstable, as a private tutor in the family of Joseph Otis; he pursued his legal studies in the same place with the eccentric lawyer, Shearjashub Bourne, and was admitted to the bar in Taunton in October, 1788. On that occasion, in conformity with an ancient custom, he treated the court and bar with half a pail of punch. His own version of this treat was as follows: "According to the fashion of that day, on the great occasion, I treated the judge and all the lawyers with about half a pail of *punch*, which *treating aforesaid* was commonly called "the colt's tail."

Mr. Mellen commenced practice in his native town, but removed in eight months to Bridgewater, where he continued until November, 1791. Not meeting with the success he desired, he again changed his domicil, and spent the winter and spring with his brother Henry in Dover. From that place, in July, 1792, he removed to Biddeford in this State, by the advice of his firm and constant friend, the late Judge Thacher, who was then a Representative in Congress from Maine. Here he commenced that sphere of successful and honorable practice which placed him at the head of the bar in Maine, and at the head of its highest judicial tribunal.

His beginning in Biddeford was of the most humble kind, and may give an idea of what professional men had to endure in that day. He thus described it to me: "I opened my office in one of old Squire Hooper's front chambers, in which were then arranged *three beds* and half a table and one chair. My clients had the privilege of sitting on some of the beds. In this room I slept, as did also sundry travelers frequently, the house being a tavern."

What his library was, may be inferred from this humble office apparatus. The population of Biddeford did not then exceed eleven hundred, and that of the whole county, which embraced a large part of Oxford, was about twenty-eight thousand; all served by three attornies; viz., Dudley Hubbard of Berwick, and Messrs. Thacher and Mellen at Biddeford. There was then one term of the Common Pleas Court held at Biddeford; and one term of the Supreme Court at York, for the year, in that county, and one term of the Supreme Court in each of the counties of Cumberland and Lincoln for jury trials;—which was all the favor the highest judicial tribunal was then permitted to extend to this District. The *law* term for Maine was held in Boston, and the records kept there. The whole population of the State was then about one hundred thousand. Governor Sullivan had formerly lived and practiced in Biddeford, but had removed to Boston, and was, at the time we are speaking of, Attorney General of Massachusetts.

From 1804, until his appointment as chief justice in 1820, Mr. Mellen practiced in every county in the State, and was engaged in every prominent cause. In 1806, his practice in Cumberland being extensive, he removed to Portland, where his professional engagements had become numerous, and where a very large commercial business was transacted. His competitors were men of high legal attainments, of great natural abilities, and able and eloquent as advocates. Daniel Davis had just before removed to Boston; there remained,—the accomplished Parker, afterwards chief Justice of Massachusetts; the patient and laborious Chase, and the scholarly Symmes, both of whom, by their untimely death, opened a wider field for the new comers; the grave and cautious Whitman, afterwards chief justice of Maine; the sensible and acute Longfellow, and the ardent Hopkins; all of them residents of Portland, and ornaments of the Cumberland Bar. He also found able rivals in other parts of the State, in the adroit and eloquent Wilde, late of the Supreme Court of Massachusetts; the sagacious Silas Lee; and Orr, shrewd, skillful, and prompt. "His most constant opponent," said Professor Greenleaf, "was Judge Wilde; their forensic warfare, adopted by tacit consent, was to place the cause on its merits, produce all the facts, and fight the battle in open field." He adds, "A generous warfare like this could not but create a generous friendship. They have often been heard to speak of each other and of those scenes in animating terms."

To take the lead among such men, in their chosen profession, required and proved Mr. Mellen to have possessed more than ordinary powers. It was often said, previous to the separation of Maine from Massachusetts, that the Bar of Cumberland was the best in the commonwealth. And certainly that must have been a bar of extraordinary quality, which could at one time boast of lawyers superior to

Parker, Symmes, Mellen, Chase, Whitman, Longfellow, Emery; and the juniors, Orr, Fessenden, Greenleaf, Davies, who came in as the others passed to the bench or to a higher tribunal.

At the bar, Mr. Mellen's manner was fervid and impassioned; his countenance lighted up with brilliancy and intelligence; his perceptions were rapid, and his mind leaped to conclusions to which other minds more slowly traveled, and, as a consequence, he was sometimes obliged to yield his suddenly formed opinions to more mature reflection. On one occasion Chief Justice Parsons remarked to him when he was ardently pressing a point, "You are aware, Mr. Mellen, that there are authorities on the other side." "Yes, yes, your Honor, but they are all in my favor."

He identified himself with the cause of his client, and never for a moment neglected it, or failed to improve every opportunity in his opponent's weakness or errors, to secure a victory. His voice was musical, his person tall and imposing, and his manner fascinating.

His life was not entirely absorbed by his profession. In 1808 and 1809, and again in 1817, he was chosen a member of the Executive Council in Massachusetts; and in 1816, an elector at large for President. In 1817, while he held the office of councillor, he was chosen a senator in Congress from Massachusetts, with Harrison Gray Otis for his colleague. This situation he held until Maine was organized as a separate State, when, in July, 1820, he was appointed chief justice of its Supreme Court. The same year he received the honorary degree of Doctor of Laws from both Harvard and Bowdoin Colleges.

He continued to discharge the laborious duties of chief justice with singular fidelity and ability until October, 1834, when, having attained the age of seventy, he became constitutionally disqualified for the office. On the bench his thorough knowledge of practice, his familiarity with decided cases, and his quick perception of the points and merits of a case, were peculiarly valuable at a time when the new State was forming its system of jurisprudence, and establishing rules for its future government. The industry and ability with which he discharged his arduous and important duties, while at the head of our highest court, appears forcibly written in the first eleven volumes of the Maine Reports; in the first nine of which he found an able exponent in his friend, the accomplished Greenleaf. Of the sixty-nine cases in the first volume of Greenleaf, in which formal reports are given, the opinions in fifty were drawn by the chief justice. A larger proportion still, appears in the second volume, where of the eighty-four formal opinions, he drew seventy-four. And this industry and application is apparent through the whole series, in the last of which, second of Fairfield, of the one hundred and six opinions, he prepared fifty-five. Nor were those decisions of a light or hasty kind; many of them involved points of the highest importance, requiring profound study, nice discrimination, and keen analysis. It may not be improper to say that in these opinions the learned chief justice did not fall behind his high reputation as a lawyer or his elevated position as a judge. And it is gratifying to be able to say that our reports were cited at that period, in other States, with great respect.

Never were stricter integrity, nor a more earnest desire to render exact justice in every case, carried to the bench; and no judge ever performed his duties more conscientiously. If any criticism may be permitted on a judicial course so pure and able, it might be said that there were times when the judge's patience gave way before the tedious prolixity of some advocates, who were unwilling to give the court credit for a knowledge of the elementary principles of law; or where witnesses were pertinaciously bent on telling all their experience before coming to the point in hand. In such cases he would sometimes be obnoxious to the censure of the worthy Fuller, according to the canon of his "good judge;" of whom he says, he is "patient and attentive in the hearing the pleading on both sides; and hearkens to the witnesses, though tedious. He may give a waking testimony who 'hath but a dreamy utterance; and many people must be impertinent before they can be pertinent; and cannot give evidence about a hen, but first they must begin with it in the egg. All which our judge is contented to hearken to." But we cannot say this always of our good chief justice; he could not sit still till this egg was hatched. In another aspect he, however, amply met this worthy's requirement: "He nips those lawyers, who, under a pretense of kindness to lend a witness some words, give him *new* matter, yea, clean contrary to what he intended."

On his retirement from the bench, the Cumberland Bar addressed a letter to Judge Mellen, through a committee of its most respected members, expressive of the high sense it entertained of his services and merits, as an upright judge, and of his qualities as a man, to which tribute of affection and respect he responded with deep sensibility.

In 1838 Judge Mellen was appointed by the executive of Maine at the head of a commission to revise and codify the public statutes of the State, which had accumulated to nearly one thousand chapters, of various, and in some instances, of inconsistent provisions. He earnestly engaged in this task with his colleagues, the Hon. Samuel E. Smith and Ebenezer Everett, Esq., and submitted their report on the first of January, 1840, embracing the whole body of the public statute law in one hundred and seventy-eight chapters under twelve titles. This was adopted by the legislature, and constituted the first volume of the Revised Statutes.

This was the last public service of our estimable citizen, who had now passed the seventy-fifth year of his age.

But our portrait would not be complete without the lights which come from his private and domestic life. And this was as free from obscurity as was the ermine of his judicial office. He married Miss Sally Hudson of Hartford, Connecticut, in May, 1795, whose acquaintance he made while practicing law in Bridgewater, and whose musical talents first attracted his attention. She was a daughter of Barzillai Hudson of Hartford. He described his engagement in the following characteristic language to me: "I left Bridgewater in 1791, having there first seen and fallen in love with my present wife, *and told her a piece of my mind.*"

She was an amiable and accomplished woman, with whom he lived in domestic happiness over forty-three years, administering, without stint, the rites of a generous hospitality. She died in 1838, aged seventy-one years. By her he had six children, all born in Biddeford; of whom two daughters only survive. The oldest son, Grenville, a graduate of Harvard, in the class of 1818, is well known as a literary man, flowering out from the legal profession: he died in 1841, at the age of forty-two. His son Frederick was educated at Bowdoin, from which he graduated in 1825; he prepared himself for the practice of law, but was seduced from it by the soft impeachment of art; he devoted himself to painting, but died in 1834, at the age of thirty, before accomplishing his high aspirations.

Judge Mellen calmly and serenely yielded up his life on the last day of the year 1840, in the midst of his own winter, having passed through seventy-six years of a busy, well-spent life; firm in the conviction of an approval by the great Judge of quick and dead. He was the last survivor of his father's family of nine children, — four sons and five daughters. His youngest sister was the mother of Governor Kent, now one of the judges of the Supreme Court of Maine.

The Cumberland Bar erected a solid and durable marble monument to his memory, with suitable inscriptions, in the cemetery in Portland, over his remains.

I believe that the remark he made in his last sickness to be perfectly true, "I have always endeavored to do do what I believed to be right." He was a religious man, a devoted attendant upon public worship, conscientious in the performance of duty, and faithful in all the relations of life. His natural temperament was cheerful and gay; full of wit and anecdote, fond of society, which he enjoyed to the last, and in which his cheerful and benevolent countenance was always acceptable.

He was a man of warm imagination and fine literary taste. He early inclined to cultivate a familiarity with the muses, and like his cotemporary, Judge Story, made poetry the sport of his idle hours from his earliest to his latest age.

The following *jeu d' esprit* was sent by Judge Mellen, in 1801, to Clerk Sewall, which is followed by Mr. Sewall's answer. They appeared in the Portsmouth Advertiser, October 17, 1801.

"'Squire Sewall, Sir,—Be pleased to lend me,
Or give,—or, at least, to send me,
Twelve blanks of Court of Common Pleas,
Touched off on paper smooth as grease,
With the great name of your great Honor
Stuck down, to sanction, at one corner.
I want them soon to keep law going,
For law sets other blessings flowing;
Because, as *love of ready rhino*
Is the root of evil, *you* and *I* know,

Law scatters wide this evil stuff,
Till the poor souls havn't half enough
To keep their bodies from the jail.
So by next post, sir, do not fail
To frank them, without further telling;
And you'll oblige your friend, P. Mellen."

The Clerk's answer:

"'Squire Mellen, Sir,—See here I send you
Twelve blank court writs, which I will lend you
Till the next court; and I expect
To fill them you will not neglect;
And if you want, I'll send you more,
By single, dozen, or by score.
You'll get them served; which done, you'll venture
On the clerk's docket all to enter
That are not settled by those fools
Who will not be confined to rules.
For *law* sets many blessings flowing,
Sends many a sheriff fast a-going;
Takes from vile folks 'the root of evil,'
Which causes them to be quite civil;
Keeps them in jail till all is spent,
And then be sure they will repent;
Thus justice runs through all the State,
'Mongst high and low, and small and great.
The commonwealth 'sends greeting' to all,
For the clerk's name is Daniel Sewall."

The cultivation of poetry is not inconsistent with the severe pursuits of the legal science. Even my Lord Coke, who, in the mind of the professional student, is the personification of dryness, often quoted from the poets, and observes, "It standeth well with the gravity of our lawyers to cite verses." Everybody, too, remembers Pope's praise of Mansfield, "How sweet an Ovid was in Murray lost." And our own days have witnessed in the eminent English lawyer, Sir Thomas Noon Talfourd, the most elaborate and polished of legal poets. The following poetical *jeu d' esprit* on the law of pauper settlement, from an old poet, may be quoted in this connection as a true legal maxim in verse:

A woman having a settlement
Married a man with none:
The question was, he being dead,
If that *she* had was gone.
Quoth Sir John Pratt, the "settlement,
Suspended doth remain,
Living the husband, but him dead,
It doth revive again.
Chorus of puisne Judges.
Living the husband, but him dead,
It doth revive again."

The calmness and patience with which our lamented friend bore his last sickness, gave ample testimony of the sincerity of his faith and the firmness of his religious principles. At this trying period he frequently uttered expressions of his entire submission to the divine will: desirous to be relieved from the burden of the flesh, yet perfectly resigned to wait. At one time he said, "I seem to be suspended between heaven and earth: the body clings to its native element, while the spirit struggles to be free." At another time he said, "I can't let go, the thread of life is too strong." It broke at length, and the spirit ascended to its congenial home.

And now, in the language of Fuller's "Holy State," "we leave our good judge to receive a just reward of his integrity from the Judge of judges, at the great assize of the world."

SAMUEL S. WILDE. 1792—1815.

Among the bright lights which have illuminated the law in Maine, none have shone with greater luster than the late Judge Wilde. He was born in Taunton, Massachusetts, February 5, 1771, the son of Daniel Wilde and Anna Sumner, the only daughter of Samuel Sumner of Taunton. Daniel, his father, was the only son of William Wilde and Anna, a daughter of the Hon. Samuel White of Taunton, who was Speaker of the House of Representatives of Massachusetts at the time of the Stamp Act. He took his first degree at Dartmouth College, in 1789; having among his classmates, Governors Crittenden of Vermont and Dinsmore of New Hampshire. He immediately entered upon the study of law with David L. Barnes of Taunton, who was afterwards Judge of the United States District Court of Rhode Island; and was admitted to the bar of Bristol County in 1792. He came to Maine soon after, and commenced practice in Waldoboro'; two years after, he moved to Warren, and was the first lawyer who commenced practice in that town. On the incorporation of Kennebec County, in 1799, he moved to Hallowell, which continued to be his place of residence until he removed to Massachusetts, on the separation of Maine in 1820, to continue the exercise of his office as Judge of the Supreme Court of the Commonwealth, to which he had been appointed by Governor Strong, in 1815.

The Hon. Frederick Allen, who was cotemporary with Judge Wilde at the Kennebec Bar, thus speaks of him as he entered on the practice in that county: "Having no superior at the bar, and, indeed, no equal, he immediately entered upon a successful course of practice, which continued to expand from year to year, as long as he resided there. The great success of Mr. Wilde consisted in his power as an advocate, which was unrivaled by any cotemporary. His clear and ready perception of all the intricate points of a cause was remarkable. He rarely failed to make himself so far master of his case as to impart his convictions to the jury. His addresses to the jury were generally brief, energetic, and rapid. His enunciation was clear and distinct. He spoke for the *cause* — not for any general effect. The main qualities of his forensic addresses were force, energy, and ingenuity. We believe he was the most popular advocate who has ever grown up in Maine. His practice extended to all the counties east of Cumberland."

We may add that he occasionally came into Cumberland; where, as in other counties, his great rivals were Mellen and Orr; who, according to the custom of that time with the principal lawyers, "traveled the circuit," or followed the Supreme Court into the several counties.

On the death of Judge Dewey, in 1815, Mellen and Wilde had rival claims for the vacant seat; which was awarded to Wilde, although the junior. Mr. Mellen was, however, not long after chosen to the senate of the United States, from which he was transferred to the bench of Maine as her first chief justice. The sharp conflicts at the bar between these eminent lawyers furnished many interesting scenes to the lookers on. Mellen was ardent, earnest, rapid, and impulsive, — seeming to carry his cause by storm. Wilde, cool, collected, ingenious, and impressive, — calmly undermining or overthrowing the arguments of his adversary. They both, for the first fifteen years of this century, had eminent success as advocates at the bar, and were leading counsel in the numerous and important land cases which were continually thronging the courts.

On the occasion of Judge Wilde's retiring from the bench, in 1851, at the age of eighty years, Benjamin Rand, a distinguished lawyer in Boston, thus spoke of the legal attainments of this jurist: "By the course of his early studies, and by extensive practice at the bar with eminent lawyers, his cotemporaries, of great attainments in the recondite learning of the day, he acquired, before his elevation to the bench, a deep and thoroughly accurate knowledge of the great principles and rules of the common law in all its various ramifications.

"Among other branches of the jurisprudence of the common law, that pertaining to real property then constituted, and still continues to constitute, a very essential part of our legal science. This seems to have been one of his early and favorite studies."

Chief Justice Shaw, on the same occasion, said, "Commencing the study of the law at a period when the law of real property was of the highest practical utility and importance, his powerful mind was early devoted to that system of rules founded deeply in the principles of the common law. Practicing in a part of the Commonwealth where great interests were drawn in question, depending on the law of real property; where the highest honors and rewards of the profession awaited the practicer who was best versed in the knowledge and practice of this branch of the law, his mind became so familiar with its minute and apparently subtle distinctions, that he could apply them promptly, like simplest principles, to complicated cases."

Again Judge Shaw remarks, "A practice of twenty-four years at the bar, and his judicial labors, during the long period of thirty-five years, have made his name and his reputation conspicuous amongst living jurists."

He held the office of Judge of the Supreme Court longer than any other judge in Massachusetts, with the exception of the first Samuel Sewall, who was appointed in 1692, and continued on the bench, as an associate and chief justice, until 1728, a period of thirty-six years. Benjamin Lynde held the two offices thirty-four years, from 1712 to 1745; and Paul Dudley thirty-four years, from 1718 to 1751. Judge Shaw held the office of chief justice thirty years, from 1830 to 1860.

Mr. Wilde was so much occupied by professional engagements that he rarely took part in political life, although he was a very earnest and strenuous adherent of the Federal party. In 1797, on the 4th of July, he delivered an oration at Thomaston, before the "Friendly Society, and in commemoration of the anniversary of American Independence," which was published, and is characterized by terseness of language and patriotism of sentiment.

In 1798 and 1799, he represented the town of Warren in the legislature; and in 1800 and 1808, he was appointed by the legislature one of the electors of President and Vice-President. In 1814, he was a member of the Executive Council; and, the same year, was appointed a delegate to the Hartford Convention, in company with some of the most illustrious men of the Commonwealth; viz., George Cabot, Harrison Gray Otis, William Prescott, Nathan Dane, and Stephen Longfellow. The next year he took his seat upon the bench, which for thirty-five years he adorned by sound legal learning, undeviating impartiality, and great dignity of deportment. "Of his absolute and entire impartiality," says Judge Shaw, "a close and daily observation of twenty years enables me to speak with entire confidence."

In 1792, the same year in which he was admitted to the bar, Judge Wilde entered into a matrimonial partnership by his marriage with Eunice, a daughter of General David Cobb, then of Taunton, but afterwards of Maine; by whom he had nine children, most of whom are dead: their mother died June 6, 1826. His eldest daughter, Eunice, married Williams Emmons of Augusta, son of the Rev. Dr. Emmons of Franklin, Massachusetts, and died in 1821. Another married the Rev. Mr. Tappan, son of Dr. Tappan of Augusta. Eleanor married John W. Mellen, son of the Rev. John Mellen of Cambridge, who are both dead. Caroline married Caleb Cushing of Newburyport, and died in 1832.

His eldest surviving son is Clerk of the Courts in Suffolk County.

In private life, Judge Wilde was social; and in early life, convivial; always genial and affable. Warmth and kindness of heart, and courtesy of manner, ever characterized him. We may sum up his merits in the language of a resolution offered to the Suffolk Bar by George S. Hillard, on occasion of Judge Wilde's death, which occurred June 25, 1855:

"The private and personal worth of this eminent magistrate was in strict harmony with his official merits, and, indeed, formed a part of them. His bearing upon the bench indicated the man. Simple in his tastes, of industrious habits, of a cheerful spirit, of warm domestic affections, and strong religious faith, he never lost his interest in life, and nothing of him but his body grew old. He was frank, direct, calmly courageous, and of unalloyed simplicity; caring as little to conceal what he was, as to affect what he was not."

His services and merits as a public man and a private citizen were universally acknowledged, and the three universities of Harvard, Dartmouth, and Bowdoin, in conferring upon him the honorary degree of Doctor of Laws, did but record the just expression of public opinion. He was also chosen a member of that select association of Massachusetts, the "American Academy of Arts and Sciences."

GEORGE WARREN.

Among the lesser lights of the Kennebec Bar which shone briefly and not brightly, and were extinguished before the opening of the present century, were George Warren, Amos Stoddard, and William Hodge. Warren was the son of General Warren; his mother was the celebrated Mercy

Warren, daughter of James Otis of Barnstable; she was author of several poetical effusions, and a history of the Revolution, in three volumes. Her son George did not receive a liberal education, but after pursuing the usual course of study prescribed to those who had not received a degree at college, he was admitted to the bar of Suffolk in 1792. The same year he went to Winslow on the Kennebec River, where his family and their friends had landed property. Winslow, then including Waterville, had a population of only about eight hundred, and their habitations were few and far between. He was the first lawyer there or in that part of the county. But law was not much to his fancy, and he only indulged in it for diversion. He was a representative to the General Court the first year of his being in Winslow; his land agency occupied much of his time, the remainder was wildly spent.

He built a cottage on the bank of the river in which he kept bachelor's hall for awhile; but the country and society were altogether too solitary for him, and he moved to Augusta, where his habits of dissipation increased to a fatal extent, and he soon died very poor.

Mr. Rice, who succeeded Warren and knew him well, thus speaks of him: "He built a cottage house on the bank of the Kennebec River, according to a plan furnished him by Dr. Bulfinch[1] of Boston; finished the outside, did a little something to the inside, lived and kept bachelor's hall in it, and kept a ferry across the river. Warren was a very popular man, very social, and soon partook of the habits of many in the country. I saw him at Augusta a few days before his death, and found him in great distress. Mr. Warren was a man of fine natural talents, and though not publicly educated, had stored his mind with much useful and pop-

1 The son of Dr. Bulfinch planned the State Houses in Boston and Augusta.

ular knowledge. His mother was one of the best informed and best educated women in Massachusetts, and wrote a history of the Revolution."

AMOS STODDARD. 1792—1798.

Amos Stoddard was the son of Anthony Stoddard of Woodbury, Connecticut, a son of the Rev. Solomon Stoddard of Northampton, a name of great note in the ecclesiastical history of his time. The subject of our notice was born in Woodbury, in 1759. At the age of twenty he entered the Revolutionary army, and served through the war. He was afterwards assistant clerk of the Supreme Court in Boston, from which place he came to Hallowell in 1792 or 1793, and opened an office as an attorney of the Common Pleas. In 1797 he represented the town of Hallowell in the legislature. He was a man of fine personal appearance, and had more taste for military life than for the quiet pursuit of his profession in a remote country village, as Hallowell then was. On the first tap of the drum as a signal to arms in 1798, against the French, his military ardor revived, and he entered the army with a captain's commission. In 1799 he had command of the fort in Portland, which had been erected on the summit of Munjoy's Hill, and called Fort Sumner. In July of that year he delivered the 4th of July oration in Portland. In October, 1802, he was again in charge of Fort Sumner; but the same month he was ordered to the Ohio, and does not appear again in our latitude. In the battle of Fort Meigs, May, 1813, he was wounded by a shell, which terminated his life, at the age of fifty-four. He had attained the rank of Major in the regular army, and was reputed to have been a man of talents. At one time he was civil commander of upper Louisiana; and a military station, Fort Stoddard, was named for him. In 1812 he published sketches of that country. He had previously published, in London, a work called "The Political Crisis."

WILLIAM HODGE. 1794—1798.

Mr. Hodge was not so fortunate as Major Stoddard, for in some pique against his friends for not furnishing him with pecuniary aid, he enlisted in Adams's army as a common soldier. He was born in Wiscasset, and graduated at Harvard College in 1791; after completing his legal studies, he opened an office in Winslow in 1794, on the point made by the Sebasticook and Kennebec Rivers, where had been erected Fort Halifax, as a frontier post to protect the country from Indian incursions. But this proved a discouraging station for a graduate of Harvard, who had been used to see people and to meet good society, and he abandoned the place the next year. He enlisted in the army in 1798, from which, although he was released by the intercession of his friends, it does not appear that he returned to the bar in Maine, and I have no knowledge as to his subsequent life.

THOMAS RICE.

In this connection I will introduce a character, — one of the cotemporaries of the last three, whose steady, quiet, and honorable life was in entire contrast to theirs. Thomas Rice, who for fifty-nine years was a member of the Kennebec Bar, and whose long life of eighty-six years was spent in Maine, was born in Wiscasset, March 30, 1763. He took his first degree at Harvard in 1791, a classmate of his townsman, Hodge, before mentioned. His ancestor who first came to this country was one of the Scotch-Irish colony that arrived in Boston from Belfast,—the grandfather of his father,—and settled in Sutton in Worcester County, where his father was brought up. In that town the Rev. John McKinstry, an immigrant of the same colony, educated at the College of Edinburgh, was the first settled minister. His father, Dr. Thomas Rice, was educated at Harvard, from which he took his degree in 1756, and having pursued his medical studies with Dr. Oliver Prescott of Groton, he established himself in his profession at Wiscasset. In addition to his labors as a physician, he was for many years a judge and chief justice of the Court of Common Pleas for Lincoln County, and Register of Deeds. He discharged the duties of these various offices with uprightness and fidelity, and died honored and respected in 1812.

His son Thomas, after leaving college, went to Groton to keep school, and at the same time to study medicine with Dr. Prescott, the teacher of his father. But after a little experience he quitted the study of medicine, and entered the office of Timothy Bigelow as a law student. After completing his three years' course, he went to Wiscasset, where the court was then sitting, and applied for admission to the bar, but was estopped by the rule which required that a portion of the preparatory study should be pursued in the county. His own simple narrative in this perplexity will show us some of the forms of that day. He says, "I knew not then what to do but to return to Groton to consult my friend Mr. Bigelow. I stopped in Boston,—the court of Common Pleas was sitting there. I saw Judge Sullivan, the president of the bar in that county, and told him my story. He said he would call a bar meeting and submit my case, which he did, and they voted immediately for my admission to practice in that county. I have the certificate of the clerk of the court, Ezekiel Price, now before me (1851), which shows that fifty-seven years since (1794), I was admitted to the practice of the law. I returned to Wiscasset, there I found Lee and Smith (Manasseh), and there I staid until the first day of the next April, 1795, when I set my face toward Winslow, including that part of it called Waterville. A classmate of mine named Hodge had just left that place, and I was desirous to occupy his stand. My brother and myself each mounted a horse, one carrying my library in his saddle bags and the other my wardrobe. After a wearisome ride through the mud, we arrived at Fort Halifax. I found, to my surprise, that the stand I had been looking to had been occupied four days by the late Reuben Kidder. I was now brought to a dead stand; which way to go I knew not; my brother had returned with our horses, and I was left moneyless and friendless. There was an acquaintance of my father's, who had been living in Winslow a year or two, who owned the only house in the place, except Fort Halifax and one or two fishermen's huts. I went to see him, told him my situation, and asked his advice. He said the prospect was dark, but as I had come, if I had a mind to try my luck, he would board me five or six months, and give me the use of a little room (about eight feet square) that he had in a small building which was occupied with a few articles that he had for the use of the fishermen. I concluded to stay and put up a small sign on my door, giving notice that a lawyer was ready to do business there. At the end of six months I paid for my board and had something left; and in the course of two years my business had increased so that I thought I was worth twelve or fifteen hundred dollars."

In another letter to me, he says, "Near by the cottage erected by Mr. Warren, and on his land, stood a small unfinished building which had been used a short time before by a man having a few goods to trade with the fishermen. This building was on the bank of Kennebec River, about a mile below where my office stood on Fort Halifax Point, between the Kennebec and Sebasticook Rivers. Here myself and wife lived about two years. During the winters of these two years, I had to break my own road up to the county road, the snow being frequently from two to three feet deep. I left my wife in the morning, and wended my way as well as I could, and returned at night tired and weary. I could find no other resting place, and necessity compelled me to take that. Soon after I went there to live, Mr. Warren left and went to Augusta. The second summer I lived there I bought of an Indian, a birch canoe. He taught me how to use it, and in it I went to and from my office daily, which saved me a good deal of trouble and some expense in not being obliged to cross the Sebasticook River."

This may justly be called the pursuit of law under difficulties. We think the young practitioners of the present day would be hardly willing to make their way into practice through such toils, embarrassments, and hardships as beset the way of our pioneer on the Kennebec. Mr. Rice was a true man, he went steadily and courageously on, patiently laboring in his profession, encouraged by gradual success, securing, by integrity, ability, and urbanity of manners, the good will of the people, independence in his pecuniary circumstances, honorable standing at the bar and in public life. In 1807 he was appointed by the Supreme Court one of the examiners of counsellors and attornies for Kennebec. In 1814 he represented his town in the legislature of Massachusetts, and was representative in Congress from the Kennebec District, two terms, from 1817 to 1821. Having faithfully lived, and discharged the duties of the various offices he was called to fill, with honorable fidelity, he laid down the burden of his long life peacefully, at the grave's mouth, with the respect of all who knew him, August 24, 1854, in the eighty-fourth year of his age.

The first President Adams, in obtaining his admission to

the bar, passed through an ordeal not unlike that of Mr. Rice. I copy from Mr. Adams's Diary as giving us a glimpse of the forms at that day: "1758, October 25. Went in the morning to Mr. Gridley's and asked the favor of his advice, what steps to take for an introduction to the practice of law in this county. He answered, 'Get sworn.' But in order to that, Sir, as I have no patron in this county,— G.—I will recommend you to the court; mark the day the court adjourns to in order to make up judgments; come to town that day, and in the meantime, I will speak to the bar; for the bar must be consulted, because the court always inquires if it be with the consent of the bar. Then Mr. Gridley inquired what method of study I had pursued, &c."

"Thursday, 26. Went in the morning to wait on Mr. Pratt. He inquired if I had been sworn at Worcester. No. 'Have you a letter from Mr. Putnam to the court?' No. 'It would have been most proper to have done one of these things first. When a young gentleman goes from me into another county, I always write in his favor to the court in that county; or, if you had been sworn there, you would have been intitled to have been sworn here. But now, nobody in this county knows anything about you, so nobody can say anything in your favor but by hearsay. I believe you have made a proper proficiency in science, and that you will do very well, but that is only hearsay.' Pratt is infinitely harder of access than Gridley; he is ill natured, and Gridley is good natured."

"Monday, November 6. Went to town; went to Mr. Gridley's office, but he had not returned to town. Went again; not returned. Attended court till after twelve, and began to grow uneasy, expecting that Quincy would be sworn and I have no patron, when Mr. Gridley made his appearance, and on sight of me he whispered to Mr. Pratt, Dana, Kent, Thacher, &c., about me. Mr. Pratt said nobody knew me. Yes, says Gridley, I have tried him, he is a very sensible fellow. At last he rose up and bowed to his right hand and said, Mr. Quincy,—when Quincy rose; then he bowed to me, Mr. Adams, when I walked out. 'May it please your Honors, I have two young gentlemen, Mr. Quincy and Mr. Adams, to present for the oath of attorney. Of Mr. Quincy, it is sufficient to say, he has lived three years with Mr. Pratt; of Mr. Adams, as he is unknown to your Honors, it is necessary to say, that he has lived between two and three years with Mr. Putnam of Worcester, has a good character from him and all others that know him, and that he was with me the other day several hours, and I take it he is qualified to study the law by his scholarship, and that he has made a very considerable, a very great proficiency in the principles of the law, and therefore that the client's interest may be safely intrusted in his hands. I, therefore, recommend him, with the consent of the bar, to your Honors for the oath.' Mr. Pratt said two or three words, and the clerk was ordered to swear. After the oath, Mr. Gridley took me by the hand, wished me much joy, and recommended me to the bar. I shook hands with the bar and received their congratulations, and invited them over to Stone's to drink some punch, where the most of us resorted and had a very cheerful chat."

JOSEPH THOMAS. 1792—1830.

Joseph Thomas was born in Pembroke, Massachusetts, November 20, 1762, graduated at Harvard College in 1786, in the class with Judge Parker, Alden Bradford, and other prominent men. He came to Portland and took charge of the grammar school after taking his degree, and afterwards studied law with his uncle, Daniel Davis. He was admitted to the bar in Cumberland at the May term, 1792, and immediately established himself in practice at Kennebunk. There was then no lawyer in that town, unless it may have been Sylvanus Wildes, who came there in 1790, but remained so short a time as to have left no traces or traditions concerning himself. A Sylvanus Wildes, a graduate of Harvard in the class of 1777, is noted on the catalogue as having died in 1829: whether the lawyer at Kennebunk was the same, we have no means of knowing. We do not find his name among the lawyers of Massachusetts or Maine in 1793. The only other lawyers in the County of York were George Thacher and Prentiss Mellen in Biddeford, and Dudley Hubbard in Berwick. Kennebunk was a part of Wells until 1820; the population of the united town in 1790 was but three thousand and seventy, of which Kennebunk contained the smallest proportion, probably not more than twelve hundred in 1792; but it was a place of considerable activity and commercial business, and became the residence of several distinguished lawyers.

Mr. Thomas was a man of sound intellect, and well versed in legal principles; which gave value and confidence to his professional advice. He rarely argued his own cases, and had no distinction as an advocate, but he had a ready wit, and was a genial, social companion. An instance of a practical joke is told of him. Judge Widgery, who was an associate justice of the Circuit Court of Common Pleas appointed in 1812 by Governor Gerry, although no lawyer, charged the jury, while holding court in York County, that a man had a right to make his mark on the ground and tell another if he stepped over it, he would knock him down. Thomas started out of court before the judge, and went to the house where the judge and several members of the bar boarded; when the judge was approaching the gate, Thomas drew a line on the ground with his cane, and when Widgery came to it, he told him if he dared step over the line, he would knock him down. The judge hesitated at this application of his own law, and after considerable parley, Thomas yielded, and let him pass.

Mr. Thomas was popular in his town, and had the confidence of the people; he was many years one of the selectmen of the town; a representative to the legislature three years,—1814, 1815, 1816; chief justice of the Court of Sessions; and a member of the convention which framed the Constitution of Maine.

In the notice of him by Mr. Hopkins, in his address to the Cumberland Bar, in 1833, he thus speaks of him: "He possessed a strong mind and highly respectable acquirements in many branches of learning. He was so entirely unassuming and unpretending that his mental acquisitions were generally under-estimated by strangers, who had but little knowledge of the man; this estimation always rose in proportion as their intimacy increased."

He died January 20, 1830, aged sixty-seven, leaving no issue. His wife was a niece of Daniel Davis.

The Hon. Jacob McGaw of Bangor has favored me with the following sketch of Mr. Nelson's life.

JOB NELSON. 1793—1850.

Job Nelson was born in Middleborough, Massachusetts, in 1766, and died in Orland, July 2, 1850.

The site of the town of Castine, where Mr. Nelson's professional life was spent, is one of as much natural beauty as exists anywhere in New England. With its beauty is connected a harbor of great capacity and entire security for ships of any supposable size. Its adaptation for ship building, the carrying trade, and fisheries, is equaled by few places.

This town was the first in the State that received permanent settlers on the eastern shore of Penobscot Bay. It had been occupied in the seventeenth century by Baron *Castine*, a French gentleman, through thirty or forty years, as a temporary place of traffic with Indians by exchanging some cloths and trinkets of small value for beaver and other furs. By means of this business he became very rich, and left the fort which had been erected by him at large expense, and which had protected him against hostile attacks of Indians when drunk, as well as against plunderers of his goods and moneys at other times. The advantages which this commanding position offered were not overlooked by England at the period of the American Revolution. She constructed, and her army occupied, an important fortification on the highest point of the peninsula. The noble harbor, too, was used as a commanding position by her navy.

In 1789, Castine was made the shire town of the new and extensive County of Hancock, and was constituted one of the ports of entry in the United States. About this time, Chief Justice Isaac Parker of Massachusetts, who was then commencing his eminent career in the practice of law, selected this town as the most suitable place for his future professional labors, and here prosecuted them about ten years. In this year, also, 1790, Mr. Nelson, having pursued a full term of collegiate study at Brown University in Providence, Rhode Island, and acquitted himself respectably as a scholar, received the honor of that literary institution in the Degree of Bachelor of Arts. Excited prospects of rapid and great prosperity that must follow the recent adoption of the Federal Constitution, filled the mind of almost every young man of the United States, and induced him to hasten in selecting the course of his future personal employment. Mr. Nelson adopted the profession of law as best adapted to his tastes, and therefore commenced its study under the guidance of Hon. Seth Paddelford, at Taunton, Massachusetts. Having finished the usual preparatory course for admission to practice in the judicial courts of Massachusetts, he took the oaths prescribed by law, and was legally qualified to perform the duties of his station. The important question of locality, where he might hope to be most useful, and meet with the best success through the vigor of his manhood, must now be determined. It so happened that some of the prominent events that had given notoriety to Castine in past time, and held out promises of prosperity for the future, beçame known to Mr. Nelson, and fixed him in the choice of that place for his residence. Thereupon, in the autumn of 1793, he proceeded to carry his choice into effect, which he speedily accomplished. By this time the reputation of Mr. Parker as an excellent advocate and sound lawyer had become so well established, that he was often absent from Castine; sometimes attending court on professional engagements, and sometimes representing his town in the General Court at Boston. The new lawyer was, therefore, well received and liberally employed. Mr. Nelson soon acquired a good reputation for promptness and fidelity in all business intrusted to him. Different agencies, also, of large tracts of land, occupied portions of his time, while they added to his everyday home business, and increased his income.

In 1795, Mr. Parker was elected to fill the office of representative in the Congress of the United States, and from that time he ceased to perform the common duties of an attorney at Castine. All of Mr. Nelson's time and powers of mind were thenceforward occupied in the discharge of various duties. His fellow-citizens desired his services as their representative in the General Court of Massachusetts, which desire he felt bound to gratify, and served them accordingly. In the autumn of 1801, the late William Abbot, Esq., having finished a regular course of preparatory study for practice of law, came to Castine, opened an office, and shared in the professional business of the place. Mr. Nelson being now well established in successful employments, purchased the handsome and thoroughly-built dwelling-house recently erected by Judge Parker. This purchase was preparatory to his marriage with Miss Margaret Farwell, a lady of uncommon personal beauty, with corresponding gracefulness of manner and ease in conversation. This marriage constituted the basis of the pride and enjoyment of his subsequent life. The office of Judge of Probate of Wills, &c., in and for the County of Hancock, became vacant about this time. Mr. Nelson's qualifications, combined with the wishes of those gentlemen who were best acquainted with him, pointed him out as the most suitable person to fill it. He accordingly received the appointment to that office by the Governor of the Commonwealth of Massachusetts, as successor to Judge William Wetmore, in 1804, and discharged its duties in a very acceptable manner through many succeeding years, until the District of Maine was separated from Massachusetts, and assumed the position of an independent State.

The functions of his office of Judge of Probate under the government of Massachusetts, therefore, ceased; but the first Governor of Maine,—Hon. William King,—disregarding the difference of political opinions between himself and Judge Nelson, replaced him in the honorable office of Judge of Probate under the new Government. The duties of his office were performed by him with all the ability he had before exercised, until the summer of 1836. At this period he attained the venerable age of seventy years, at which age the power of all judicial officers, excepting Justices of the Peace, ceased by reason of a provision which then existed in the Constitution of the State.

The duties incident to the office of Judge of Probate required only a small part of his time, and being in perfect harmony with his pursuits and employments as a lawyer, had no influence prejudicial to his professional income or improvement. But the amount of home business at Castine, of every kind, decreased in proportion to the more rapid growth in business and population of some other towns that border on the waters of Penobscot and Union Rivers. There was, therefore, a concurrence of circumstances at the time when the duties of Judge of Probate devolved upon another person, and the home business of Castine was diminished, that harmonized with the venerable years and quiet inclinations of Judge Nelson. He, therefore, withdrew from the bustle of courts, and removed with his family to Boston, where he enjoyed the society of some select friends for about two years, when he returned to Castine. At this time, feeling that a state of entire quietude was better adapted to meet the infirmities of old age, than his present place of residence, and an unfortunate occurrence happening about the same time, the destruction by fire of his fine mansion, endeared to him by many fond associations, conspired to determine him to quit entirely the scene of his early labors and cares. And with the serenity and cheerfulness becoming a good man, he retired to his farm in Orland, a town pleasantly situated on Penobscot Bay, and overlooking its waters beautifully dotted with island gems. Here the remainder of his life was calmly spent in the midst of a loving and delightful family, until he was summoned to a higher and better existence. He died July 2, 1850, aged eighty-four: his remains were taken to Castine, and buried in the sepulcher of his family.

Judge Nelson left five children, three sons, William, Horatio, and Henry, and two daughters all in respectable standing in society and unmarried. A son and daughter died before him, — the son left a family. Another son died recently.

CHAPTER XIII.

BENJAMIN HASEY — REUBEN KIDDER — NATHANIEL PERLEY — THOMAS S. SPARHAWK — ALLEN GILMAN — JOHN HATHAWAY — ISAAC STORY — EDWARD P. HAYMAN — SAMUEL P. GLIDDEN — JEREMIAH BAILEY.

BENJAMIN HASEY. 1794—1851.

Benjamin Hasey was a native of Lebanon, Maine. His father, Isaac Hasey, the first minister of that town, was born in Cambridge, Massachusetts, and graduated at Harvard in the class of 1762. He was settled in Lebanon in 1765, where his son Benjamin was born, July 5th, 1771, and was named from an uncle, who took his degree from Cambridge in that year. His mother was a daughter of William Owen of Boston. Mr. Hasey, like his father and uncle, was a graduate of Harvard, being of the class of 1790, of which one member still survives, the venerable Josiah Quincy, the oldest living graduate, who, at the age of ninety, is in possession of the ripe faculties which have given a luster to his name and age. Mr. Hasey received his preliminary education at Dummer Academy, under the tuition of the celebrated Master Moody, and entered college in 1786.

Soon after leaving college, he entered the office of the late

Judge Thacher in Biddeford as a student, and was admitted to practice in April, 1794. In June of the same year, he established himself at Topsham, where he continued to reside until his death, March 24, 1851, a period of fifty-seven years, a single, as well as a singular man. The only lawyers in Lincoln, exclusive of Kennebec County, when he commenced practice there, were Langdon, Lee, and Manasseh Smith, all in Wiscasset.

Mr. Hasey represented his town in the legislature of Massachusetts several years before the separation; but he had no taste for politics, and he withdrew from all public employment. He was fifteen years one of the trustees of Bowdoin College. Reserved and retired in his habits, he became more so as he left the common highway so much frequented by lawyers and politicians. It was not unnatural that a man of his sensitive nature should have shrunk from scenes which are often contaminated by low intrigues and self-seeking arts. Of the most rigid integrity, regular and quiet in all his modes of thought and action, nothing disturbed him more than the cant of demagogues. As may be supposed, he was strongly conservative,—change was distasteful to him. This may be a reason why he never married. For more than thirty-eight years he boarded in the same family, and for many years he occupied the same office, to which he daily resorted until within a few days of his death, in the same manner as when he was in practice. But with all his peculiarities, he was ever to be relied upon; his word was sacred, his act just, his deportment blameless. As a counsellor, his opinions were sound and much valued, and for many years he had an extensive practice in the counties of Lincoln and Cumberland. We remember the prim, snug-built, and neatly dressed gentleman, with his *green satchel* in hand, according to the usage of that day, taking his seat at the bar, and waiting calmly for the order of his business: he rarely appeared as an advocate, his natural diffidence and reserve disqualifying him for any display. Many years before his death he left the active duties of the profession; the innovations which were taking place in the manners and course of practice at the bar, were ill-suited to his delicate and conservative feelings. The want of ancient decorum and respect, the absence of forensic courtesy, fretted upon his nerves. The abolishing of special pleading annoyed him, and the revision and codification of the statutes thoroughly confused his habitual notions of practice, displaced his accustomed authorities, and cast him afloat in his old age on what seemed a new profession. He lived in the past and believed in it, and strove as much as mortal could to keep himself from the degeneracy of modern ideas. Mr. Hasey, at the time of his death, was the oldest surviving lawyer in the State; when he commenced practice the whole number was but seventeen, all of whom he survived except Judge Wilde, who had removed from the State.

The Hon. Frederic Allen, his cotemporary in Lincoln County, has furnished the following well-considered estimate of Mr. Hasey's character and standing: "He was well versed in the principles of the common law. His reading was extensive, both legal and miscellaneous. His memory was tenacious, his habits studious. In his person, though very small in stature, he was of the most perfect formation, and always most neatly attired. He had much good sense, was a strict adherent to the old federal party, from whose leading opinions, so long as the party had a distinctive existence, he never wavered, and had little charity for those who did. He was not much employed as an advocate: he generally argued not over one case a year, and that was done very well. His address to the jury was brief, free from all repetition, or copious illustration. He left the world in the same apparent quietude in which he had lived, leaving a name much honored, and a character highly respected."[1]

REUBEN KIDDER. 1795—1816.

Three graduates from Dartmouth College, in the class of 1791, established themselves in the practice of law in this State about the same time, 1795 or '96,—Reuben Kidder at Waterville, Nathaniel Perley at Hallowell, and Thomas S. Sparhawk at Bucksport. Mr. Kidder was a descendant in the fifth generation from James Kidder, who migrated to this country from East Grinsted, a considerable town in Sussex County, about thirty miles south of London. The family had long resided and maintained a respectable position in that town. James, the ancestor, was born there in 1626, and was in Cambridge, Massachusetts, in the year 1649, when he married Anna Moore of that place. He moved to Billerica, where he died, in 1676. The family remained over one hundred years in that town. The subject of this sketch was the sixth child of Reuben and Susannah (Burge) Kidder, who moved to New Ipswich, in New Hampshire, in 1750, and were among the first settlers of that place. They had twelve children, many of whom attained a great age: seven of the eight daughters, in 1844, met at the house of one of their number, whose united ages were five hundred and thirty-two years, giving an average of seventy-six years. The eldest was ninety.

Reuben Kidder was born in New Ipswich, April 3, 1768. After taking his degree in 1791, he qualified himself for the profession of the law, was admitted to practice in usual course, and established himself at Waterville in the spring of 1795, the first lawyer who adventured so far north, into what was then almost a wilderness. The town of Winslow,

---

[1] Sixth Volume Maine Historical Collections, p. 54.

of which Waterville was a part, contained in 1790 but seven hundred and seventy-nine inhabitants, and in 1800, but one thousand two hundred and fifty. Wm. Hodge, a graduate of Harvard in 1791, had preceded Kidder to Waterville a short time before, but had become discouraged, and left the place, into which Kidder stepped, in advance of Thomas Rice, who had intended to occupy it, but arrived four days too late. It would hardly seem to have been an object of much competition; but the loss of it was a sore disappointment to the young aspirant who was seeking, as is seen in our notice of him, some spot to spread his unfledged wings. Mr. Kidder sought the consolations of a companion in his solitude, and soon married Miss Lois Crosby, who became the mother of four children, of whom George and Henry died young. Camillus is settled in Baltimore, and Jerome G. is a merchant in Boston. Mrs. Kidder died in 1809. In 1816, Mr. Kidder was touched with the "western fever," which at that time prevailed in Maine, and thought to better his fortune by transferring himself to the prairies of the west. He moved to New Harmony, in Indiana, a place rendered memorable by Robert Dale Owen, as the seat of his captivating "social system." But his hopes were not realized; like many others of our people who sought to better their condition by leaving the more sterile fields, but healthy climate, of our hardy north, for the sickly though productive meadows of the west, he was doomed to sadness and disappointment. He died in 1817, the year after his removal.

Mr. Kidder was a man of good personal appearance, much general information, and fine colloquial powers. His wit and humor were conspicuous; they pervaded him, appearing in his countenance and gestures, as well as in his utterance. One who remembers him at the bar gives me the following account of him:—"He would change his countenance into such a sly, facetious expression—so unique and inimitable, that it reminded one of Drummond's famous laugh in the theater of London, which set the audience in a roar—spoken of in Cumberland's Memoirs. The most stern visage would relax the moment Mr. Kidder imagined a joke. You saw it dawning in his looks, and when it rose full upon you, you felt a glow of real pleasure. There was no ill-nature in his wit; it was brilliant, but harmless. I remember an amusing circumstance when I was a student in Wilde and Bond's office in Hallowell. The court was sitting in Augusta; the members of the bar were seated around the oblong table covered with green baize, and waiting the call of the docket; Mr. Kidder was resting his head on the table, and asleep. An action against the 'inhabitants of Waterville' was called. Mr. Kidder was the counsel, but no one answered. The call was repeated, and there being no response, the court ordered the action to be disposed of, and the crier called, in a loud, shrill voice, the inhabitants of Waterville to come into court, and show cause why their default should not be recorded, when the sleeper started up from his slumber, and rubbing his eyes, exclaimed, 'Here are the inhabitants of Waterville,' when Nat Perley, the great wit of the bar, started back, and cried out, 'For mercy's sake, Brother Kidder, don't let any of them get on me.' The court and bar joined heartily in the joke."[1]

Mr. Kidder was a man of abilities, and had considerable business at the bar, and was much respected for his gentlemanly qualities and his integrity of character; but he did not attain eminence as an advocate. He engaged in some speculations, one of which was the establishment of a smelting furnace and foundry on the Sebasticook River, near which was a bed of iron ore. It proved unfortunate, and the persons engaged in it lost the capital invested.

---

[1] Manuscript letter from John H. Sheppard, Esq.

Another cotemporary, William Allen, thus speaks of Mr. Kidder: "He was a sound and good lawyer; and in person of more than medium size, a little stooping. He was honorable in his profession, and was a man of fine tastes; he set out a grove of oaks half a mile from the village of Waterville, to which he often repaired in summer from the heat, and called it his Athenæum. He used to wear a bouquet in summer at his button hole."

I am indebted to my friend, Charles Dummer, Esq., of Hallowell, for this interesting sketch of Mr. Perley.

NATHANIEL PERLEY. 1795—1824.

Nathaniel Perley, formerly of Hallowell in the county of Kennebec, was born in the town of Boxford, county of Essex, and Commonwealth of Massachusetts, about 1770. Having passed successfully the period of preparation for a liberal education, he graduated at Dartmouth College, 1791. Entering at once upon the study of the law, he completed the term required for admission to the bar in Massachusetts, and in 1795 commenced the practice of law at Hallowell, then a thriving settlement on the Kennebec River; this place, doubtless, attracting his attention as well from the intelligence and energy of its early inhabitants as the advantages which it presented for trade and future commercial consequence. The fact, however, that others with whom he was probably acquainted, from the same county of Essex, had preceded him as residents of Hallowell, no doubt materially influenced his own determination. For some time he was the only one in the place. Intelligent, full of life, possessing high social qualities, he gathered around him many friends, and very soon he found himself actively engaged in the professional responsibilities of life. This current of business continued to enlarge with the growth of the community around him. Steadfast friends, uninterrupted health, and persevering application gave encouragement to all his hopes. He was distinguished for sound common sense; he possessed varied powers; his quickness of perception and constant good humor attracted early attention; and unfortunately, as I believe, commended him to too much notice as a wit. The progress of years in his professional life soon developed the fact that he was acquiring property. Without marked distinction for legal learning, he would be more truthfully described as a successful practitioner of law, maintaining a respectable position, whether discharging faithfully the duty which grows out of the ordinary collection of debts, or unfolding the powers of argument before a jury or the court. The course of events in his life justifies, I think, the remark, that he became too lavish of his legal opinions; his friends partook too freely of the benefit of his knowledge without compensation; he himself, at the same time, forgetful of that respect which was due both to himself and his profession. Overlooking the vital necessity of steady application, he yielded to the pleasures of mere social ease, by which the strength of his reputation as a lawyer was weakened. Insensibly to himself, he professionally lost his hold upon the better portion of the business public. Having accumulated considerable property, he was induced to embark in schemes which required much of his attention outside of his office. At first, he was successful; but entering still further upon larger operations, the results were painfully decisive upon his professional prospects. His business as a lawyer did not merely decline; it was lost: stern pecuniary difficulties met him while in the path he had now chosen. Bereft of that buoyancy of spirit which marked his temperament, without practical knowledge amidst the realities which then surrounded him, despondency settled upon his mind and prospects. Always sustained by the affections of a faithful wife and children, the cheerful light of a once happy dwelling was gradually extinguished. Mr. Perley died about the year 1824. The remote cause of his death was thought to proceed from an injury which he received, when with his workmen who were blasting stone, with the view of conducting water from a pond to a grist-mill which he was erecting in the town of Winthrop, about ten miles west of Hallowell. Unfortunately he was so near the work at the moment of explosion as to be struck upon the chest by a large stone.

Mr. Perley's position as a lawyer, during a large portion of his life, was respectable. He was in the midst of friends who were constant while he continued personally attentive to his professional business. The judges of the Supreme Court of Massachusetts, while on their tours of public duty, were frequently welcomed at his house. One, the late distinguished Chief Justice Parsons, himself a native of Essex County, held a relation to him of marked kindness and regard, — the chief justice with his wife, upon more than one occasion, sharing the cordial hospitality of Mr. Perley's household; while tradition adds, Mr. Perley's colloquial powers and wit possessed great attractions for the chief justice himself. Occasions for friendly, social intercourse readily offered, as the courts for the county of Kennebec were held at Augusta, a distance of two miles only from Hallowell.

In gathering the fragments of the past which illustrate the character of Mr. Perley as a man and a lawyer, I can add, that had he remained faithful to the noble objects of a true professional life, had he diligently strengthened his mind by study, and adhered with moral strength to his duties as a lawyer, he would have gathered the fruits of honorable labor and eminence,—all would have been finally well. Possessing great quickness of perception, his free social habits were both an attraction and temptation. Who, in the pursuits of life, can successfully dispense with industry, or habits of care and accurate attention? A marked characteristic of his mind was a sort of natural wit, or gift of repartee. Tradition supplies many of his smart and ready answers and sayings, but rarely have I found anything which could be worthily rescued from oblivion. However gratifying such utterances may be to the many, I regard this characteristic of Mr. Perley's taste and mind, a talent, not merely a questionable gift, and, as used by him, was generally highly injurious in its influence.

A celebrated ambassador of the last age, when told what a clever boy his son was, exclaimed, "I would rather you had told me how industrious he was." The same writer on law education further states, "Sir Henry Wotton, the famous Provost of Eton College, we are told by Aubrey, could not abide wits. When any young scholar was commended to him as a wit, he would say, 'Out upon him! I will have nothing to do with him; give me the plodding student!'" The well-known Judge Dodderidge declares that he found by experience, that "among a number of quick wits in youth, few are found, in the end, very fortunate for themselves, or very profitable to the commonwealth."

One characteristic of Mr. Perley's wit should be noted,—he appeared, himself, wholly unconscious of any such power of utterance. Unmoved himself, and even sedate in manner, he seemed surprised, at the moment, with the delight which the circle around him manifested. His high social qualities, united with distinguished colloquial powers and great kindness of feeling, very naturally drew around him many friends, who often beguiled him of time which should have been given to the stern duties of life.

The following incident will show Mr. Perley's prompt ability to reply. In the course of his professional duties, he was engaged in the trial of an action of replevin before Judge Weston, who was then upon the bench of the old Court of Common Pleas. Mr. Perley's client had attached a quantity of logs as belonging to Mr. N., which logs were also claimed by another Mr. N., and the letter N was the mark upon all the logs. The case was warmly contested. An important witness had been under examination between two and three hours, when the court adjourned for dinner. Immediately upon resuming the case at the opening of the court in the afternoon, Mr. Perley requested that the same witness might be called, when Judge Weston remarked that this witness had been a long time on the stand, and very closely examined, adding, "Brother Perley, what further do you expect to obtain from him?" Mr. Perley's prompt reply was, "The truth, your Honor: I have obtained everything else."

Mr. Perley was faithful and firm in advancing the public interests of the town where he resided; he represented it in the General Court in 1804 and 1816. He discharged with integrity all his political duties. Uniformly patriotic, with enlightened zeal he always upheld the best interests of our country. I find he was member of a committee of three (the other two members being the late John Davis, Esq., of Augusta, for many years clerk of the courts for the county of Kennebec, and the late Williams Emmons, Esq., then of Augusta, and at one period judge of probate for the county of Kennebec), who invited the Rev. Dr. Tappan of Augusta to deliver an address before the Washington Benevolent Society of Kennebec, at the celebration of peace with England, March 2, 1815. The only survivor of Mr. Perley's family, at this time, is a daughter, Mrs. Dumont, who married the late John P. Dumont, Esq., for many years a member of the Kennebec Bar, and a resident of Hallowell, and who served, also, both as a representative and senator, at different periods, in the legislature of Maine. Mr. Perley, at the time of his decease, left a widow and five children, all of whom, with the exception of one daughter, Mrs. Dumont, have since died, — two sons, two daughters, and his widow.

Judge Wilde, late a distinguished judge of the Supreme Court of Massachusetts, was for many years an eminent lawyer in Maine, and a resident of Hallowell, where he continued until the separation of the District of Maine, when, in 1820, he removed to Newburyport, Massachusetts. There is a tradition that soon after Judge Wilde commenced his residence at Hallowell, he proposed to Mr. Perley a professional business connection. It is possible that mutual friends may have suggested such an arrangement from considerations growing out of the facts that Judge Wilde's great ability often called him to appear before the courts in distant counties, while a prosperous collecting business required Mr. Perley to be constantly present in his office. But I do not find sufficient authority for the statement that Judge Wilde ever made such a proposal, and it is certain that such a business connection was never formed.

In presenting, for your consideration, this sketch of the character of a man of education, permit me, in conclusion, to add that Mr. Perley possessed various and vigorous powers of mind. At the outset of his professional life, many advantages met him in the way. With ability to discern the right, he could, with learning and steady application, have reached a position of high respectability among the earlier lawyers in this part of the State of Maine. When we look at what he actually accomplished, what is the admonition to the living? To the young, entering upon professional life, I would say, cherish and strengthen every moral element of character; cultivate habits of industry and careful attention; day by day discharge with fidelity every obligation of duty; never turn aside from the high and true purposes of the profession; aim to be useful rather than conspicuous; value the acquisitions of learning; hold fast your integrity, and preserve the freshness and purity of the affections. Clothed in such armor for the battle of life, a lawyer in every generation and in all his influence, will be found a blessing and a light in every community, where the bounds of his habitation are fixed. In the language of that great and good man, Chief Justice Hale, "Speed, then, the spirit of education. Let the mind be cultivated; let it be opened to see that there is the better and the right, and so expanded as to see that the right is ever the better, must ever be so, and that to find it is highest privilege, and true honor to resolve to brave any difficulty and overcome every obstacle to ascertain it; and then to do it, even at the cost of the cutting off a right hand or plucking out a right eye, is highest honor and noblest conduct, and must result in brightest attainments of excellence and happiness, giving best success in this life, and glory hereafter."

I add to this interesting notice of Mr. Perley, the testimony of a distinguished cotemporary, Mr. Allen of Gardiner. In his sketches of deceased lawyers of the Lincoln Bar, published in the Sixth Volume of the Maine Historical Collections, he says of Mr. Perley, "He was distinguished for his wit and broad humor, — for his jokes and cutting repartees at the bar. As a sample, an instance is recollected. When one of the four judges of the Court of Common Pleas, not remarkable for his profundity, coming late into court, observed, as an apology, on taking his seat, that he believed there was no member of the court less absent than himself. 'True,' replied Perley, 'and no one less present.'" Mr. Allen adds, that for many years Mr. Perley had an extensive practice at the bar, but in the latter part of his professional career, his practice declined. With many amiable and amusing qualities, he was popular with a class of clients, but those not of the first order.

The Hon. Jacob McGaw of Bangor has favored me with the following notice of Mr. Sparhawk, one of his early cotemporaries.

THOMAS STEARNS SPARHAWK. 1796—1807.

Thomas Stearns Sparhawk was a son of Rev. Ebenezer Sparhawk of Templeton, Massachusetts, the respected Congregational clergyman of that town forty-four years, from 1760; and was born there in 1769.

This parent partook largely of the noble element that characterizes New England fathers; even while struggling with poverty, they aimed to prepare their sons, by education, to rise to usefulness and honor, when they attained maturity of years. He, therefore, spared no efforts to aid this son in acquiring a collegiate education. By rigid economy he was enabled to prepare him to enter Dartmouth College, and to assist in the payment of his expenses while an under-graduate. In 1791, Thomas, having acquitted himself honorably in all respects, through the whole term of his connection with college, received the Degree of Bachelor of Arts.

From this time forward the burden of self-support devolved entirely upon himself The readiest mode of paying for present expenses and providing means for the future conditions of his life, seemed to him to be school teaching. These duties he commenced without delay, and pursued them successfully to his scholars and respectably to himself, almost two years. Then, having fixed upon the profession of law for the employment of his talents through subsequent life, as best adapted to his taste, he engaged with ardor in searching out and understanding its varied principles.

After completing a regular course of preparatory study, he was admitted at a term of the Court of Common Pleas, in the summer of 1796, to practice at the bar of the judicial courts in Massachusetts. Buckstown, now Bucksport, in the then District of Maine, had been incorporated as a town about four years. Its fine location at the head of Penobscot Bay, with an excellent harbor and sufficient depth of water for the accommodation of ships of the largest burden, had begun to attract the attention of adventurers and enterprising men of various occupations in life. Navigators, fishermen, traders, mechanics, professional men, and others were seeking, in that new country, opportunities for employment.

Mr. Sparhawk, believing in the prospective importance of the town at some future day not far distant, immediately took up his residence, and opened the first law office that was located there, and identified himself with the town, its inhabitants and interests. Having thus commenced and engaged in the activities of manhood, he received the confidence, friendship, and professional support of the existing population, both of the town and the circumjacent territory, which was sparse and scattered.

A just appreciation of the responsibilities that he had permanently assumed, induced him promptly to make arrangements for carrying out the allotments of Providence in regard to these responsibilities in the manner that, in his opinion, would best subserve his own honor and the welfare of society. He, therefore, in May, 1797, consummated the contract of marriage that he had previously entered into with Miss Mary

Kinsman of Hanover, New Hampshire, by making her his wife. She was the daughter of Colonel Kinsman, a respectable inhabitant, possessing a good estate in that town, and sister of Dr. Aaron Kinsman, an eminent physician in Portland, who died in 1808. Miss Kinsman was a young lady of handsome person, respectable attainments, well calculated to become an excellent wife and to promote the happiness of her husband. Up to this time, only two lawyers had their homes in the whole region embraced in the valley of the Penobscot Bay and River. These two gentlemen both resided in Castine, which is about twenty miles from Buckstown. The people had heretofore been little accustomed to litigation, and not much inclined to it; nor was Mr. Sparhawk disposed to encourage that pernicious habit. His inclination was to promote the permanent happiness and prosperity of everybody living within the reach of his influence, hoping and expecting to receive his full share of the blessing that would be conferred upon others through his instrumentality. The confidence, friendship, and professional support of his neighbors, as also of the inhabitants of the circumjacent settlements, were enjoyed by Mr. Sparhawk. His business, though not large, afforded himself and family a comfortable support, and enabled him to construct a respectable mansion for the present condition of his family.

Litigation not being rife within the limits of his practice, the talents of Mr. Sparhawk, as an advocate, were seldom demanded, nor did he make large pretensions in that department. Persons competent to judge, suppose that he would not have attained eminence in it even if he had attempted it. Mr. Sparhawk, through the whole period of his professional life, discharged the duties of everyday practice relating to the common concerns among neighbors in a very acceptable manner. His opinions in regard to questions of considerable intricacy were well received and respected.

His health became delicate in 1806, but he was able to perform the services that he had been accustomed to attend to from the period of his first residence in Bucksport, until 1807, when he was released from all earthly cares by a peaceful death.

Very early in the nineteenth century there was a sudden and numerous influx of population into most of the towns that bordered on the waters of Penobscot Bay and River. Lawyers of very respectable attainments and distinction settled in several of these towns, but none of them made his home at the quiet, industrious town of Bucksport, or came into conflict with Mr. Sparhawk, until the closing years of his life.

Good humor and ready wit made him a cheerful companion and pleasant neighbor to those persons who had the benefit of being acquainted with him.

Mr. Sparhawk left five children, three sons and two daughters. William, the eldest, was lost at sea. Edward Vernon was a literary gentleman, resided awhile in Montreal, and afterwards became an editor of a paper in Richmond, Virginia. Another, George, had the same tastes, and became an editor of the "Oakland Whig," in Pontiac, Michigan. His daughter Maria Louisa was a highly cultivated lady, and the author of several works; she married Charles Fox of Boston. The other daughter, Lucia K., is unmarried.

ALLEN GILMAN. 1796—1846.

Allen Gilman was the first lawyer who established himself in Bangor, where now they exist so abundantly. He went to that part of Orrington which is now Brewer in 1800, and to Bangor in 1801. That town then had less than three hundred inhabitants; he lived to see it a full-grown city, of which he became the first Mayor. Mr. Gilman was the third son of John Ward Gilman and Hannah Emery, and was born in Exeter, New Hampshire, July 16, 1773. His grandfather was Major John Gilman, who was an officer in the expedition to Louisburg in 1745, and in the French War. His maternal grandfather was the Rev. Stephen Emery of Chatham, Massachusetts, whose wife was the daughter of the Rev. Benjamin Allen, the minister of Cape Elizabeth, in the middle of the last century. Mr. Gilman's preparatory studies were pursued at Exeter Academy, and he graduated at Dartmouth College in 1791, a classmate of Chief Justice Dudley Chase of Vermont, and of Reuben Kidder and Nathaniel Perley, his cotemporary lawyers in Kennebec county. He studied law with Judge Oliver Peabody at Exeter, and commenced the practice at Gardiner, Maine, in 1796. In 1798, having just married Pamela Augusta, a daughter of Gen. Henry Dearborn, a woman of rare mental and personal attractions, he moved to Hallowell. This lovely woman died in October, 1799, leaving a daughter four months old, now the widow of the late Major Dearborn of the United States Army. This afflicting event so dispirited him that he fled from the dear familiar scenes of his wedded days to the solitude of the wilderness. He spent one year at Brewer, and in 1801 took up his residence in Bangor, where he remained the rest of his life, devoting himself assiduously to the duties of his profession. He particularly excelled in and preferred the quiet pursuits of the office, to the bustling scenes of the court room. His habits were modest and unassuming; he wrote a fine and neat hand, and was extremely accurate in conveyancing and the drafting of legal instruments. He was a sound and discriminating lawyer, of unquestioned integrity, and of easy, graceful manners. The Hon. Mr. McGaw, who is still happily living, was the cotemporary of Mr. Gilman, in Bangor, more than forty years. He says of him, that "he maintained through life an elevated standing as a lawyer; he possessed clear and rapid perceptions in cases of involved difficulties, both of law and fact, and had not only the confidence of his clients, but also of his fellow-citizens." At the time these gentlemen established themselves in Bangor, the whole of this region, extending from the sea to the Canada line, was embraced in the county of Hancock, but the inhabitants did not extend above Oldtown. The courts were held in Castine until 1814, when Bangor was made a half shire town. The lawyers consequently went down to Castine to attend court, and sometimes to Machias in the county of Washington, until the incorporation of Penobscot County, in 1816. There assembled at the sessions, especially of the Supreme Court, which was held but once a year, the choice spirits who had already pitched their tents in that far country,—Abbott of Castine, Herbert and Deane of Ellsworth, Wilson and Crosby of Belfast, and Dutton, Gilman, McGaw, and Williamson of Bangor. After the incorporation of Penobscot, Mr. Gilman seldom extended his professional visits beyond his own county. He was appointed the first Register of Probate in the new county, and held the office until the organization of the government of Maine, in 1820.

In 1834, Bangor was incorporated as a city, on which occasion his fellow-citizens selected Mr. Gilman as the first Mayor, and he was re-elected the next year. His administration was successful, and he did much to promote the welfare and beauty of the city. After this brief interruption, he continued to pursue his professional labors, to the period of his last sickness, which terminated his life April 7, 1846, in the seventy-third year of his age.

The bar of Penobscot County took honorable notice of the death of their deceased brother, who was the eldest member of that bar. They spoke of him as a man "known for the quickness of his perceptions, for his legal acumen and his general acquaintance with legal principles. Highly respectable in all the departments of practice, it is not perhaps too much to say that he was not excelled as a skillful, accurate, and accomplished conveyancer."

Mr. Gilman was small in stature, and rather frail in health; but by care and regular habits, his life was prolonged to a good old age. In October, 1806, he entered into a second marriage with a daughter of Col. John Brewer, by whom he had five sons and two daughters. His eldest son, Charles, born in 1807, was educated at Brown University, and became a prominent lawyer, and the reporter of legal decisions in Illinois, where he died in 1849. He was editor of the "Western Legal Observer," published at Quincy, Illinois, January, 1849. One of the daughters married Leonard Jones, the other died unmarried.

JOHN HATHAWAY. 1796—1799.

The same year, 1796, that Oliver Leonard established himself in that part of the town of Orrington which is now Brewer, and Thomas S. Sparhawk in Bucksport, both on the east side of the Penobscot river, as the first lawyers in those towns, John Hathaway came from the Old Colony and settled in the village of Camden, on the west side of Penobscot Bay, as the first lawyer in that region of country. The town was then part of the county of Lincoln, and contained a population of about six hundred. At the present time, it has about four thousand and six hundred.

Mr. Hathaway was the son of Abraham Hathaway, of Raynham, Massachusetts, and was born in Wrentham in 1773. He graduated at Brown University in 1793, a classmate of John Merrill, who settled in Wiscasset. After leaving college, he took a school in Hanover, Massachusetts, and commenced the study of law at the same time with Benjajamin Whitman of that place, a noted lawyer in the Old Colony, and afterwards in Boston. On completing his studies and being admitted to the bar, he was persuaded by some friends who had settled in Camden to establish himself in that town, which he concluded to do, and opened the first law office there in 1796. His early success encouraged him: there was no lawyer within hailing distance: the late Judge Wilde at Waldoboro' was the nearest, and Manasseh Smith and Silas Lee at Wiscasset, and Mr. Hasey at Topsham, were then all the lawyers in what constituted the county of Lincoln, after Kennebec was taken off. He built an office; he got married; became postmaster of the village; and by his ability and attention to business, he acquired the confidence of the absentee proprietors of that and adjacent towns under the Waldo Patent, for whom he was agent and attorney. His business extended, and he was warranted in the assurance which his prospects unfolded, of reputation, and the pecuniary rewards of a successful practice.

But in the midst of these bright promises, he was suddenly stricken with typhus fever, which terminated his life at the early age of twenty-six, October 6, 1799. Mr. Locke, in his History of Camden, speaks of his having a large practice in the courts, and says, "By doing business in the courts for the 'Twenty Associates' (proprietors of that and other towns), he became quite extensively known, and rapidly obtained the confidence and esteem of his senior brethren of the bar. As a pleader, he was forcible in argument and eloquent in style, and almost invariably engaged the attention of his auditors to the close of his plea."

In September, 1797, he married Miss Deborah Cushing, daughter of the Hon. Joseph Cushing of Hanover, Judge of Probate for Plymouth County, born in 1771. By her he had one son, who was lost at sea when twenty-three years old. She was living in 1859.

ISAAC STORY. 1797—1803.

Isaac Story was another early member of the Hancock bar, a brilliant meteor that flashed across it and expired. Mr. Story was the second son of the Rev. Isaac Story, and grandson of the Rev. Simon Bradstreet, both of Marblehead. The latter was descended from the distinguished Governor of Massachusetts of the same name. He was born in Marblehead, 1774, graduated at Harvard College in 1792, and after pursuing his regular course of study, established himself in Castine, in 1797 or '98. Here for a while he connected with his professional duties that of editor of the "Castine Journal," a weekly paper. He was more fond of literature than the law, and as the region of the Penobscot was not inspiring and encouraging in this more graceful pursuit, any more than the law, he moved back to Massachusetts, and opened an office in Rutland, Worcester County. But he did not long survive: the working of his fervid genius overtaxed his frail constitution, and he died in July, 1803, at the early age of twenty-nine. It was said of him at the time of his death, that no one of his age in Massachusetts had written more for the periodical press of his time than he. Among his publications were essays from "The Desk of Beri Hesdin," in the style of the lay preacher, which appeared in the Farmer's Museum. He published a volume in a series of letters, over the signature of "The Traveler," parts of which were printed in the Columbian Centinel. He was equally happy in poetry as in prose: a volume from his pen was published under the title of "The Parnassian Shop, by Peter Quince," in imitation of Peter Pindar, of whose wit and style he was an admirer. He received warm commendations from Joseph Dennie of the "Port Folio," and other discriminating judges of literary merit. He died at his father's house in Marblehead, and a notice of his death appeared soon after in the Salem Register, which thus speaks of him: "A gentleman well known by numerous productions in polite literature. In his manners bland, social, and affectionate; in his disposition sportive and convivial; in his morals pure, generous, and unaffected. Wit and humor were provinces in which he sought peculiar favor, though he not unfrequently mingled in his poetic effusions the gravity of sententiousness with the lighter graces." His kinsman, the late Judge Story, wrote a brief monody on his death, from which we make the following extract:—

"Spirit of him, whose chastened soul
 Could touch each chord of pure desire,
Whence, flown beyond the mind's control,
 Thy brilliant thought, thy Druid fire?
Lost in thy manhood's chariest bloom,
 O'er thee shall pity meekly mourn,
And many a sylph, who haunts the gloom,
 With twilight dews bespread thine urn."

EDWARD PAYNE HAYMAN. 1796—1831.

From this bright genius of the profession, I turn to an absolute matter-of-fact man, as dry and exact in details as the other was fresh, varied, and broad in the scope of his character. Edward Payne Hayman, better known as the circuit clerk of the Supreme Court, than in any other capacity, was born in Boston, February 22, 1771, the second son of Capt. William Hayman. After pursuing his preliminary education in his native town, he entered the office of Charles Cushing, the time-honored clerk of the courts in Boston, and who had been the sheriff of Lincoln County from its organization to his singular seizure by the tories, and made prisoner during the Revolution. This service prepared Mr. Hayman for the duties of a similar office, to which he was afterwards appointed. When he became of age, he moved to South Berwick, and entered the office of Dudley Hubbard, where he continued an attentive and close student for five years, the period then required for admission to the bar, of those who had not received a collegiate education. He was admitted to the bar in York, November term, 1796; in 1800 he was elected clerk of the Senate of Massachusetts; the same year he was appointed an assistant clerk of the Supreme Court, and the next year one of the circuit clerks—the other and chief was the venerable John Tucker, who, with Charles Cushing, the brother of Judge William, were, time out of mind, clerks of the Supreme Court. He held this office, which embraced also the county of Essex until the organization of the new government in Maine in 1820, most promptly and faithfully, discharging its responsible duties. He returned to the profession on leaving the office, but was again summoned from it in 1823, to assume the duties of Cashier of the South Berwick Bank, which had been incorporated that year, and held the post to the entire satisfaction of the stockholders and the public, to the time of his death, December 25, 1831.

Mr. Hayman was a well-read lawyer, exact in knowledge of the forms of practice, and of the utmost precision in his habits of business, as well as in his manners. A person who was well acquainted with him has furnished me with the following description of some of his peculiarities. He says, "He was exceedingly methodical and particular in everything that he said or did; he was strictly honest and correct in all his moral deportment. He never became very distinguished in his profession, but from his constant association with the court, he was a better lawyer than advocate. I do not know that he ever had an enemy. He lived about half a mile from the bank, and knew exactly how many minutes and seconds it would take him to walk from one to the other;

and he always left his house at the same moment of time, and probably for years he did not vary two minutes from his exact time of departure from his house, and his arrival at the bank." In 1809, he married Sarah, a daughter of the Rev. John Tompson, a Congregational clergyman of South Berwick, by whom he had several children who survived him; viz., Sarah, born in 1810; Edward, born in 1812; and Charles Cushing, born April 15, 1815, died July 12, 1844.

All the lawyers who practiced in the Supreme Court of the State prior to the separation from Massachusetts, cannot fail to remember his tall, prim figure, the clear tones of his voice, and the prompt and ready manner in which the circuit clerk discharged the duties of his office, and the assiduity and attention which he gave to all the business devolving upon him. He was a model in that department of life, and in fidelity to all his trusts.

SAMUEL P. GLIDDEN. 1797—1818.

Samuel P. Glidden was the first lawyer who established himself in the beautiful town of Readfield in Kennebec County. He was born in 1761, in Unity, New Hampshire, and came to Readfield in 1797, at the age of thirty-six. He does not appear to have been a graduate of any college, but received his law training in the office of Mr. West, of Charlestown, New Hampshire. He was the son of Jonathan Glidden, a native of Deerfield, who had four sons and four daughters: one of the daughters was the mother of Jonathan G. Hunton, Governor of Maine in 1830. Readfield was taken from the northerly part of Winthrop, and incorporated in 1791. In 1797, when Mr. Glidden commenced practice there, it contained a population less than nine hundred. It now has three pleasant villages, and a population of one thousand five hundred, having decreased, according to the census tables, over four hundred since 1850.

At the time Mr. Glidden opened his office, there was no lawyer between Topsham, where Mr. Hasey was established, on one side, and Hallowell and Waterville on the other. His opportunities for professional business were therefore good, and for a time he occupied a respectable position, and might have rendered himself, as my informant says, much more useful to himself and the community but for the indulgence, during the latter portion of his life, in intoxicating drinks. He died December 14, 1818, in the fifty-seventh year of his age. An aged member of the bar of Kennebec County, now living, says, "I recollect seeing Samuel P. Glidden at the bar; he was not a man of much note. He seemed to be a very quiet man, without much talent or pretension."

During the practice of Mr. Glidden at Readfield, Ex-Governor Jonathan G. Hunton, then a young man, and nephew of Mr. Glidden, studied law with him, was his successor in business there, and married his widow for his second wife, by whom he had one child, who died at the age of seven years. Mr. Hunton moved to Dixmont a few years before his death, which occurred in 1851, at the age of seventy. He had been a member of the Executive Council, and was Governor in 1830, successor to Enoch Lincoln. This lady who became his second wife was Miss Polly Mitchell. She was married to Mr. Glidden July 12, 1799, and had by him one child, who died an infant. Mr. Glidden had the reputation of being a kind and affectionate friend and neighbor, and was universally beloved by his acquaintances, and, but for his excesses, might have left an honored name.

In my investigations through the antiquities of the profession, I have been struck and saddened by the lamentable destruction of vigorous talent, noble aspirations, and brilliant prospects, by the baneful use of intoxicating liquors by professional men. The injurious usages of society, which universally prevailed on this subject, and the genial, social character of many members of the profession, seemed to have led them, beyond other classes, into the fatal snares of dissipation and ruin. And notwithstanding the earnest efforts that are now making to arrest the progress of this scourge of life and character, we fear that many young men, who might become the ornaments of the profession, and the "gladsome lights of jurisprudence," are sinking gradually into dishonored graves.

Daniel Campbell, a graduate of Dartmouth in the class of 1801, seated himself by the side of Mr. Glidden in 1808, and continued to practice there until 1817 or '18, when he moved to Winthrop. He was a member of the convention which formed the constitution of Maine. He disappeared from the bar in 1824, and entered the ministry, and was settled the first minister of the Seçond Congregational Society in Kennebunk, December 5, 1827.

JEREMIAH BAILEY. 1798—1853.

Jeremiah Bailey was the son of Ephraim Bailey and Mary Briggs, and was born at Little Compton, Rhode Island, May 1, 1773. He was educated at Brown University, from which he took his degree in 1794, and immediately came to Wiscasset and entered the office of Silas Lee. He was admitted to the bar in 1798, and commenced practice in Wiscasset, which was ever after the place of his abode. There were then in that village two other lawyers,— Mr. Lee and Manasseh Smith, and sixteen in the whole county which embraced all the country between the Kennebec and Penobscot rivers from the sea to the Canada line. The population of Wiscasset was then about one thousand seven hundred, and of the whole county about eighteen thousand.

Mr. Bailey soon acquired a high reputation for his diligence and fidelity in business, and his fine social qualities, in which he was rarely excelled. In 1808, he was appointed one of the electors of President and Vice President. His colleagues in the college, from Maine, were Andrew P. Fernald of Kittery, Samuel Freeman of Portland, and Judge Wilde of Hallowell. It is not necessary to say, from the school of politics which they represented, that they did not vote for Mr. Madison, the successful candidate, but for Charles Cotesworth Pinckney, who received but forty-seven votes, the whole Federal strength which could then be rallied. In 1810, he was elected a representative of Wiscasset to the General Court, and was returned the three following years, when in 1816 he was appointed Judge of Probate as successor to Silas Lee, who died that year. This office he held until 1834, discharging its duties with great fidelity, kindness, and urbanity. From this post of quiet, unobtrusive duty, he was transferred to a seat in Congress as the representative of Lincoln District, which he held for one term. The political character of the District becoming democratic, he was succeeded by Jonathan Cilley, who fell a martyr in 1838 to the "Code of honor," falsely so called. On leaving Congress, he returned to his profession, which he continued to pursue until his appointment by President Taylor as collector of the customs in Wiscasset, in 1849, which place he held through that Presidential term, and was removed for political considerations, by President Pierce, just previous to his death, in July, 1853, at the age of eighty. He left, as a cotemporary said of him, "an unsullied reputation, and marked for the utmost purity in the discharge of the duties of all the various offices which he was called on to fill." The same writer (F. Allen) observes, "He was much distinguished for his hospitality, and beloved for his kindness by all his numerous friends where he lived."

In 1813 he was appointed, with Benjamin Orr, a commissioner of Massachusetts, to close up the difficulties between the settlers and proprietors of lands in Lincoln, Kennebec, and Waldo Counties, whose complaints and hardships had been quieted and adjusted by arbitration, under authority of the State. The conflicting claims were satisfied by conveyances of other tracts belonging to the commonwealth, by which the vexed and alarming controversies and agitations, which had long existed, were happily compromised.

He was several years a member of the Board of Overseers of Bowdoin College, over which he presided a portion of the time; and in 1830 he was elected one of the Trustees of the College, an office which he continued to hold until his resignation, in 1838.

Judge Bailey was twice married. His first wife was Mary Seavey of Wiscasset, who died of consumption in a few years after marriage, leaving no children. In 1812, June 17th, he married Charlotte Welch, daughter of Dr. Thomas Welch of Boston. By her he had six children; viz., Charlotte, Edward, Harriet, John Q., George, and Ann. Charlotte and John Q. are not living.

I am indebted to my friend, John H. Sheppard of Boston, who was Register of Probate several years in the time of Judge Bailey, and had a constant friendly intimacy with him, for the following interesting remarks:

He was fortunate in the choice of his residence. Wiscasset is one of the finest seaports on the shores of New England. It was once the mart of busy commerce, when the harbor was filled with ships from the West Indies and Liverpool. Her streets echoed with the jovial voices of mariners, and her merchants were known far and wide, among whom the late Hon. Abiel Wood was one of the greatest ship-owners in the United States. This town suffered much from the Embargo, and the subsequent war of 1812; ceased to be the miniature of a great city; and at last became a nursery and school of many sons and daughters who have risen to wealth and honor in more prosperous places. But her natural scenery neither Embargo nor War has touched: it is beautiful as ever.

Wiscasset lies on the eastern side of a bay formed, as the late Attorney General Foote used to say, by the "deep waters of the Sheepscot"—a recess about fifteen miles from the sea. For fifty years this harbor has not been frozen over, but in two or three instances, and then only while the cold was below zero; and so eligible is the location that the Commissioner of the United States Coast Survey recommended it at Washington for a Navy Yard.

Here Judge Bailey lived to a good old age. His mansion, which he built for his own convenience, was conspicuous among the handsome houses which faced the green common, and stood on a line with the court-house and church. It was shaded by trees and shrubbery of his own planting, and near it was a garden he cultivated. Indeed, this dwelling in the midst of scenery so attractive will be long remembered for those agreeable parties and evening circles where age forgot its cares, and youth looked forward to pleasure. It was there I first saw and was introduced to DANIEL WEBSTER, Judge Story, Jeremiah Mason, and other distinguished men; for at this hospitable mansion the members of the courts held in that shire town, and strangers of distinction, were never forgotten. It seemed to be the delight of the Judge and Mrs. Bailey, who was a very interesting woman, to make others happy, and cast a sunshine of cheerfulness around them.

Judge Bailey was a sound lawyer, well-instructed in precedents and pleadings, and a very safe, peace-making counsellor; and in court a ready, sensible, but not an eloquent speaker. He never "mounted the high horse," — to quote a saying of his upon a very aspiring young advocate. His docket was never large, but always respectable, and he seemed contented with a moderate share of business. He had many rich Boston clients, and their patronage was lucrative. As a Judge of Probate he was courteous, impartial, and popular, and if in any difficult case a doubt arose, his benevolence leaned on the side of the widow and orphan; while he was so cautious and reflective in making up his decrees, that few appeals, and still fewer reverses of his opinions, ever took place in the Supreme Court of Probate. The office of Judge of Probate is not appreciated by the public. It should always be filled by some learned, upright lawyer; for though the duties are executed in a noiseless manner, and without jury or crier, yet it has been estimated that in thirty years nearly all the estates in a county come under the decree of the Probate Judiciary.

His religion was rather in an exemplary course of life than in profession. He was not a member of the church, but was habitually a church-going man, morning and afternoon of the Sabbath. Reticence on creeds and doctrines was his favorite maxim, and whatever might have been his views on those great questions that agitate society, and sometimes set their proselytes by the ears, he kept them in his own breast, and avoided all remarks on this subject. Whenever he did speak of things sacred, it was always with reverence.

The peculiar trait of his character was a kindly and honest heart. His natural abilities were good, but not great; but he was blessed with prudence and "a right judgment in all things;" self-denying and economical in his affairs; neat and methodical in his personal habits; he took delight in doing in the best manner whatever he did, even to writing the letters of his correspondence in a plain, round hand. He had by nature a very cheerful temperament, looking upon the bright side of every event, as though he could always see a piece of blue sky through the mists of our lower atmosphere. And even in his last days, when he was drawing near to the shadow of the dark mountains, he was so calm and free from all complaint and murmuring that it seemed as if his spirit saw beyond them the dawning of the life to come.

Take him for all in all, I have seldom seen a happier man. In a word, he was a perfect gentleman, "totus et rotundus." When I think of past times, and call up his image to my recollection, I feel that memory is like an ideal album of photographs. There on one of the pages in the book of reminiscence I see a spare form, not very tall, clothed in black, his habitual costume, sitting in a summer's morning by an open window in his office, shaded by an elm which he planted, a mere sapling, near the door, more than sixty years ago, and now with huge bole and broad branches bending over the street; and at this window I behold a face older in appearance than its years,—with black eyes, high forehead, bald front, and scattered gray hairs, bearing a good expression and most cordial smile; and I hear a voice somewhat musical in its very pleasant and cheerful tones, and ever ready, as the Scotch would say, with a "ceevil word for ilka bodie." This was Judge Bailey in the meridian of life.

CHAPTER XIV.

SAMUEL THATCHER — PETER O. ALDEN — CYRUS KING — JOSIAH STEBBINS — BENJAMIN WHITWELL — JOHN MERRILL — JAMES D. HOPKINS — JUDAH DANA — NICHOLAS EMERY — THOMAS BOWMAN — NATHAN BRIDGE — WILLIAM WIDGERY.

SAMUEL THATCHER. 1796—1799.

Samuel Thatcher, at the time I write (1862), is the oldest living lawyer in our State, and the oldest in his entrance on the practice. He was born in Cambridge, July 1, 1776. Mr. Thatcher was not of the celebrated Anthony and Peter Thacher families, who have scattered broadcast over the land so many eminent men in all the professions of life. He was descended from Samuel Thatcher of Watertown, Massachusetts, who was admitted a freeman, May 18, 1642, and was from the English "Old Sarum" family, of which the Thachers above named are another branch. The ancestor was deacon of the church there, often a selectman and representative to the General Court to the time of his death in 1669. His son Samuel, born 1648, died October 21, 1726, having had ten children, the youngest of whom, Ebenezer, was born in 1704. Ebenezer married in 1732, Susannah Spring, and they were the parents of seven children, the oldest of whom was Samuel, born November 5, 1732, who married Mary

Brown of Lexington, Sept. 3, 1753. These were the parents of the subject of this notice, who thus appears to be the fifth in descent from the first American ancestor. It will be perceived that this family insert *t* in their name, and are tenacious of the letter. The other branch omit it, although I noticed in a letter of Judge George Thacher, 1790, that he then retained it, but afterwards omitted it.

Mr. Thatcher graduated at Harvard College in 1793, at the age of seventeen. He is now, next to Mr. Quincy of the class of 1790, the eldest surviving graduate. Among his classmates were Judge Jackson, Francis C. Lowell, and Dr. John Pierce of Brooklyn. Mr. Thatcher, determining to qualify himself for the legal profession, entered the office of Timothy Bigelow, then living in Groton, and at the same time had charge of the Academy at that place. He remained one year, and secured a friendship with that distinguished gentleman which continued through his life. He then transferred his residence to Concord, and became a student in the office of Jonathan Fay, with whom he completed his preparatory studies, and was admitted to practice in 1798. He immediately came to Maine, and opened an office in New Gloucester, which was then a half shire town, the Common Pleas holding in it one term a year. William Widgery was then an acting justice there, and an occasional practitioner, although never admitted to the bar.

Moses Gill, a nephew of Lieut. Governor Gill, of Massachusetts, had practiced in New Gloucester, about two years before Mr. Thatcher went there. He was educated by his uncle, and had large expectations from him, was a graduate of Harvard College in the class of 1784, and the heir to a handsome estate. With encouragements sufficient to stimulate the ambition of any young man, he yielded to the blandishments of pleasure, and after a residence of two years, he returned to Massachusetts, and became irregular in his habits. He died in 1832.

But, notwithstanding the prospects of business for Mr. Thatcher at this place, were favorable, he was induced to move to Warren in October of the next year, where an opening was made by the removal of Judge Wilde to Hallowell, whose situation he purchased, and succeeded to his practice. Mr. Thatcher, in his new residence, by his pleasing address, his ability as a lawyer, and his eloquence as an advocate, soon took a commanding position at the bar, and acquired an extensive business. He obtained a reputation and popularity rarely achieved by so young a man. He had been scarcely two years in the town when he was elected its representative to the General Court, as successor to Judge Wilde, and was re-elected the next year. A vacancy occurring in the representation to Congress from Lincoln District, by the appointment of Silas Lee, in 1800, as United States Attorney for Maine, Mr. Thatcher was chosen to supply it, and was re-elected for the next Congress before he had attained the legal age. On this broader field he advocated, with great vigor and vehemence, the principles of the Federal party, which had then sunk into a hopeless minority in the national administration, from which it never afterwards recovered. Among the able men who bravely fought the battles of opposition, were Dudley Chase and Crittenden of Vermont; Timothy Pickering, Manasseh Cutler, and Josiah Quincy of Massachusetts; Tillinghast of Rhode Island; Hillhouse, Tracy, and Talmadge of Connecticut; and Drayton of New Jersey. Mr. Thatcher was with the most zealous of these in sustaining the Federal doctrines. But the influence and patronage of office, and the more popular principles of Democracy, extended the power of the dominant party through the country, and gave to it a supremacy which it held through a long series of years. Mr. Thatcher's District was not exempted from the infection, and he failed in the election of 1804. But his town, which retained its large

Federal majority down to the period of the separation from Massachusetts, immediately returned him to the Legislature, and he was re-elected the eight following years, with the exception of 1811. In February, 1814, he was appointed Sheriff of the County, and held the office until 1821, when the new government of Maine going into effect, and under different political aspects from those of Massachusetts, his place was filled by a friend of separation and of the administration. He was immediately chosen to represent his town again in the Legislature until 1824, when he left political life. He took an active part in the debates of the Legislature, and his long experience gave him influence in moulding the laws, and putting the new State into successful operation. In debate he was ardent, animated, and eloquent; the sharpness of his wit gave keenness and effect to his logic. In 1806, he delivered a eulogy on the death of General Knox. The General died in October of that year, aged fifty-six.

We cannot but think that Mr. Thatcher committed a grave error when he left his chosen profession, which he was admirably qualified to adorn, for the hackneyed and desultory paths of politics. But it is the passion of young men, and an increasing and dangerous one in this country, where more fall by the way than attain to any profitable advancement. "All rising to great place," says Lord Bacon, "is by a winding stair." How freely and constantly are now used the arts of the demagogue; and when the object is attained which is so earnestly sought, how empty and unsatisfactory is the result! — while the same earnestness in the pursuit of an honorable calling will surely lead to competency, respectability, and happiness. Lord Bacon wisely says, "Men in great place are thrice servants,—servants of the sovereign or State, servants of fame, and servants of business; so as they have no freedom, neither in their persons, nor in their actions, nor in their times. It is a strange desire to seek power and to lose liberty."

We do not think that Mr. Thatcher practiced any of the arts of a demagogue, which at that day had not risen into the rank of a power in the commonwealth. But in a community where education and high qualities were rare, his services were demanded by public exigencies; and he was too high-minded a man to stoop to the ordinary level of office-seeking. If he had not yielded to temptation of public life, we do not doubt that his own welfare and happiness would have been greatly promoted.

Mr. Thatcher was a public-spirited citizen of Warren, and labored to advance the interest and prosperity of the people: he was active in getting an academy established in that town, which was incorporated in 1808; and, with Col. Head, who died in 1861 at the age of ninety-six, he caused a principal avenue of the place to be bordered by elm trees, which now constitute a beautiful and refreshing adornment to the village.

Mr. Thatcher married, in 1799, Sarah Brown, daughter of Reuben Brown of Concord, Massachusetts, by whom he had five children; viz., Harriet Howard; Elizabeth, who died January 23, 1827; Samuel of Bangor, moved to Minnesota; George Augustus of Brewer, both married; and Benjamin Bussey, Bowdoin College, 1826, who established himself in the practice of law in Boston, and had become quite distinguished as a writer, when he was cut off in the vigor of life in 1840, at the age of thirty-one. Mr. Thatcher moved to Brewer in 1833, where he still survives.

PETER OLIVER ALDEN. 1797—1843.

Mr. Alden was a descendant of that handsome John Alden, who, at the age of twenty-two, came over to the new world in the Mayflower, 1620, and was the same who became the favored messenger of Capt. Miles Standish to Miss Priscilla Mullins, to solicit her to supply the place of his first wife, who had recently deceased. But Priscilla, who was innocent and beautiful as a Pilgrim maiden should be, preferred, as was very natural, the young agent to the aged principal. Her simple reply to the proposal of the redoubtable Captain, after listening with due respect and modesty to it, was, "Prithee, John, why do you not speak for yourself?"[1] The hint was subsequently improved, and this handsome and virtuous pair became the ancestors of a long line of descendants who have spread wide over the land, adorning all branches of industry, letters, science, and the arts.

The subject of this memoir was the son of Joseph, who was the son of John, who was the son of Joseph the second son of the first John and his wife Priscilla Mullins. The first Joseph was one of the early settlers of Bridgewater. The mother of Peter was Hannah Hall, and he was born in Middleborough, adjoining Bridgewater, in 1770. His father was a farmer in respectable circumstances, and his son, after preparing for college, entered Brown University, from which he took his degree in 1792. This college, for the ten years of the last century, furnished a number of scholars, who became prominent in the affairs of Maine: among these were Job Nelson of Castine, John Hathaway at Camden, John Merrill at Wiscasset, John P. Little at Gorham, Peleg Chandler, Ezekiel Whitman, John Holmes, Mason Shaw. He became a student in the office of Judge Padelford in Taunton, and came to Brunswick in this State near the close of 1796, or early in 1797. He was admitted to the Cumberland bar at the March term, 1797, having probably been

[1] For a dilation of this simple story, in beautiful poetic numbers, I must cite Professor Longfellow, not as an original authority, but as an accomplished commentor.

previously admitted in Bristol County, Massachusetts. He was the only lawyer in Brunswick for the remainder of that century, and for several years in the present.

In 1801, he married Mindwell, a daughter of Dr. Lyman of York, by whom he received some property. He had no children. His business for a time was very good: he was well read as a lawyer, and had fair talents and information, but he was no advocate. He was very irritable in his temper, and his manner when he undertook to argue his cases was abrupt and disagreeable. Whenever a shrewd adversary wished to gain an advantage over him, his certain way was to ruffle his temper, when he would be sure to spoil his own cause. As competitors gathered around him, in Brunswick and the neighboring towns, his business declined, and he was left almost briefless. Henry Putnam, Isaac Gates, and Ebenezer Everett, all graduates of Harvard, established themselves by his side, and divided a business that was not more than sufficient for one; while a diversion was also made by Orr in Topsham, Mitchell in Freeport, and enterprising lawyers in Bath. To make good the deficiencies arising from these causes, he engaged in commercial operations, which for a time were successful, but which were suddenly and sadly blasted by the restrictions on mercantile transactions, which took place prior to the war of 1812. The latter portion of his life was embittered by disappointment and poverty, which produced hypochondria, and left him a wreck. He died in 1843, at the age of seventy-three. His wife survived him a few years, and died among her kindred in York.

Mr. Alden was large and bulky, but not well proportioned. He was, as may be inferred from the faults of his temperament, unpopular in the community in which his life was spent; but by some reaction in 1826, perhaps from sympathy, he was elected to the House of Representatives, and re-elected the three following years, growing each time in favor until his election in 1829 was nearly unanimous.

CYRUS KING. 1797—1817.

Cyrus King was the son of Richard King of Scarborough, by his second wife, Mary, daughter of Samuel Blake of York. He was born in Scarborough, September 6, 1772. His father was an eminent citizen of that town, to which he moved, in 1746, from Watertown, Massachusetts, where he had been engaged in commercial business. He was a commissary in the army at Annapolis, Nova Scotia, in 1744; and in his new residence he became largely engaged in mercantile pursuits, in which he accumulated a fortune. A portion of his large landed estate is still enjoyed by some of his descendants. No family in the State has been so productive of distinguished persons as this. The oldest son of Richard King, by his first wife, Isabella Bragdon of York, was Rufus, eminent and prominent in the civil history of the country, from the time of his graduation at Harvard in 1717, to his death in 1829. The own brother of Cyrus, William King of Bath, was the first Governor of Maine, and held numerous other offices of high trust, under the State and general governments, which he ably discharged. The women of this family were the Doric mothers of children of much ability and usefulness. Mary married Dr. Robert Southgate, whose numerous family were conspicuous in the early part of this century; Paulina married Dr. Allen Porter; and Dorcas married Joseph Leland of Saco; and their blood flows through many channels, inspiring energy and usefulness.

Cyrus was the fourth son and youngest child of Richard, and was two years and a half old when his father died; but his mother lived to watch over and guide the expanding faculties of her son, and enjoy the honors which he acquired.

She died in 1816. Mr. King was fitted for college at Phillips Academy, Andover, and entered Columbia College, New York, in 1790, from which he graduated with the highest honors of his class. He commenced the study of law with his brother Rufus in New York, who was then a senator in Congress, and on his being appointed ambassador to England, he accompanied him as his private secretary. He remained abroad one year, when, being desirous of engaging in his chosen profession, he returned, and completed his studies in the office of the late Chief Justice Mellen at Biddeford, and was admitted to the bar in 1797.

We cannot better portray the opening career of Mr. King than by adopting the language of Mr. Folsom, in his History of Saco: "Possessing brilliant and highly cultivated powers of mind, united with habits of patient and zealous application, Mr. King soon rose to eminence in the profession. As an advocate he was unrivaled; his style of speaking was elevated and commanding; rich in the higher graces of polished oratory, and at the same time argumentative and convincing." "His addresses were more like an impetuous torrent than a smooth and gentle stream." And this was the failing of Mr. King that he could not restrain this torrent, for, as a cotemporary has said, "his ardent temperament and impetuosity of manner as an advocate sometimes carried him, in his addresses to the court and jury, beyond the limits prescribed in some of Hamlet's instructions to the players." Such was my own impression, when I have heard him argue a cause as though he would carry the court and jury by a storm of passionate utterances. But Mr. King was a sound lawyer and a safe counsellor.

At the height of party feeling growing out of the declaration of war under Madison's administration, Mr. King was elected in 1812 to the Thirteenth Congress, the representative of the York District, as successor to Richard Cutts, who had held the office from 1800; and he was re-elected for the next term.

Mr. King was an ardent and zealous member of the Federal party, and entered into all their measures in opposition to the war, with the same heartiness and vehemence which characterized his impassioned addresses at the bar. He took a very active part in the debates through the four years that he held a seat in Congress, and at times rose to a height of eloquence rarely surpassed in that body. During his first term he was a member of the Committee on Naval Affairs: at the next term, he had acquired such experience and reputation as to cause him to be placed on the important committees of Foreign Affairs and the Public Lands. His principal political associates in Congress were his brother Rufus, Christopher Gore, Jeremiah Mason, Dana of Connecticut, of the Senate, Timothy Pickering, Pitkin, Tallmadge, Baylies, and Daniel Webster, who entered Congress from New Hampshire the same year that he did. The venerable Pickering was the avowed leader of the Federal party in the House, while Calhoun of South Carolina marshaled the Administration forces. Clay was Speaker the whole period. The Federalists, though in a small minority, had great ability, and contained illustrious names: — Rufus King was a consummate orator and statesman, and none of Greek or Roman fame surpassed him; Gore, every inch a gentleman, statesman, and orator; and Webster was laying the foundation of that transcendant reputation which increased by time to his last breath at Marshfield. And the purity and integrity of Mr. Pickering, even his adversaries applauded. Let Mr. Randolph's tribute be my illustration. On the bill to reduce the compensation of members to six dollars a day, in January, 1817, Mr. Pickering made allusion to his moderate circumstances after a long life devoted to the service of his country. On a subsequent day, and on another question, Mr. Randolph said, "No man in the United States had been more misunderstood, no man more reviled — and that he said was a bold declaration for him to make—than Alexander Hamilton, unless, perhaps, it was the venerable member from Massachusetts,— Mr. Pickering —whom, whatever may be said of him, all will allow to be an honest man. The other day, when that honorable member was speaking of his own situation, on the compensation question — when his voice faltered and his eyes filled at the mention of his poverty, I thought I would have given the riches of Dives himself for his honorable feeling, when he spoke of his poverty, not that of excess or of extravagance, but an honest poverty, after a long and laborious service in the highest offices of the government. If the gentleman would take it," said Mr. Randolph, "I would give him what little I have to have inscribed on my tomb, as he may on his, 'Here lies the man who enjoyed the confidence of Washington, and the enmity of his successor.'" On this question Mr. Pickering and Mr. King took opposite sides. The subjects of principal importance after peace took place, were the Reduction of the Army, the Compensation Bill—on which Mr. Webster made a long and able report, Internal Duties, the Tariff, on a Uniform National Currency, Pensions, &c. Among the latest of Mr. King's addresses in the House, was a speech on the repeal of Internal Duties: he spoke on the 19th February 1817, at considerable length, and, it is added, with great zeal in favor of the repeal.

Mr. King returned home at the close of the session, March 3, and died suddenly in Saco, April 25th following, deeply lamented by the whole community, on which, by his eminent talents, he had conferred so much lustre.

In October, 1797, Mr. King married Hannah, the eldest daughter of Capt. Seth Storer of Saco, by whom he had one son,—William Rufus, and several daughters. His son graduated at Bowdoin College in 1823, became a lawyer, migrated west, and died there, in 1836, aged thirty-two.

JOSIAH STEBBINS. 1797—1829.

Josiah Stebbins was the son of Josiah and Martha Stebbins of Brimfield, Massachusetts, where he was born, November 19, 1766. He was a descendant of Rowland Stebbins, or Stebbings, who was born in England in 1594, came to this country from Ipswich, England, in 1634, first to Roxbury, with his wife, two sons, and two daughters, then to Springfield and Northampton, where he died in 1671. The ancestor was a man of respectable standing in England and this country, and of "gentle blood." Josiah pursued his studies preparatory for college with the Rev. Nehemiah Williams, the able and excellent minister of his native town, who was a graduate of Harvard of the class of 1769; and entering Yale College 1787, he received his first degree with the honors of the college in 1791. Among his classmates were Judge Gould, the distinguished lawyer and Judge, of Connecticut; Samuel M. Hopkins; and General Porter, Secretary of War during the administration of John Q. Adams. In 1794, Mr. Stebbins was appointed a tutor in Yale College, and at the same time pursued his legal studies in the office of the Hon. Elizur Goodrich of New Haven, one of the most eminent lawyers in that State, and afterwards Professor of Jurisprudence in the college. He was admitted to practice in 1796, and at the same time retired from his situation as tutor.

The next year, in November, he married Laura Allen of New Haven, and with this helpmeet, a stout heart, and a head full of learning, he set forth to take up the burden of life in the wilderness of Maine. He established himself in New Milford, which had been set off from Pownalboro in

1794, and afterwards, at his suggestion, named Alna. This is a rough town, and rather an unpromising location for a youthful pair accustomed to the refinements of New Haven. It contained, at the time Mr. Stebbins went there, but about six hundred inhabitants, and they, after a period of fifty years, had increased only to nine hundred and sixteen, by the census of 1850, and even this fell off during the next ten years, to eight hundred and seven. What inducements a gentleman of so much cultivation as Mr. Stebbins had to begin the practice of his profession in a place so little inviting, we do not know. It may have been for the reason that was given by Gov. Sullivan, who, when asked why he began practice in so poor a town as Arrowsic, replied, that, as he had to break into the world, he thought he would try at the weakest place. We can no better account for the fact that the Cushings and Langdon should have gone into so wild a situation as Pownalboro was, when these brilliant men made their homes there.

He was the only lawyer in the town for fifteen years, and here he pursued his professional duties with great assiduity and ability, acquiring an extensive practice and reputation. He was employed very much by the settlers, *squatters*, as they were called, who had entered upon unoccupied territory without title, and made themselves farms. These people, at the time of their entry, did not know who the proprietors were, and could find nobody who would give them a title. The whole territory was in dispute between numerous claimants, under a variety of titles, and the settlers were harassed and distracted by contradictory claims. Mr. Stebbins deeply sympathized with these tenants, secured their confidence, and managed their causes with great perseverance. So great was the embarrassment and trouble growing out of these conflicting claims, that the settlers, despairing of any remedy in the courts, resorted to arms, and resisted all attempts to survey their land by the proprietors. In one of these conflicts, in 1809, Paul Chadwick, an assistant surveyor, engaged in running some lines, was resisted in his undertakings by a party of squatters disguised as Indians, and murdered. The persons suspected of this crime, seven in number, were arrested and confined in the jail at Augusta, and so bold were the accessories of this crime that an attempt was made, or threatened, to break the jail and rescue the prisoners. The militia was called out, and the whole community was in a state of extraordinary excitement. The prisoners were indicted for murder and tried. They were defended by Mellen and Wilde with so much skill, and the popular feeling was so deeply enlisted for the guilty men, that they were acquitted by the jury. The trial commenced November 16, 1809, and occupied more than a week. The Jury returned their verdict of *not guilty*, November 25. Solicitor Gen. Davis was for the government, and the judges were Sedgwick, Sewall, Thacher, and Parker. John Merrick, Esq., of Hallowell, made and published a stenographic report of the trial, of great fullness and accuracy, which filled one hundred and eighty-six octavo pages.

To do justice to these settlers, many of whom were innocent, and to restore quiet to this large community, the Legislature, in 1808, passed an act of limitation and settlement; or, as it was commonly called, the "Betterment Act." This provided that when a tenant had been in possession of land, without title, for six years, and had made improvements upon it, the jury should be instructed to inquire into the value of the improvements, and of the land, if no improvements had been made upon it. It was then at the option of the demandant to abandon the premises to the tenant at the estimated price, or to pay to the tenant the estimated value of his improvements.

Mr. Stebbins took great interest in the adoption of this

just and salutary measure, and personally assisted in improving the system after the separation of Maine. The landed proprietors strenuously resisted the passage of the law; but the popular sentiment set so strongly in its favor, and it was so manifestly equitable to the honest and innocent settlers, that all opposition was overcome. The late Governor King, then a representative from Bath, is said to have been active in procuring the passage of the law.

In 1813, Mr. Stebbins was appointed Judge of the Court of Common Pleas for the second eastern circuit, as successor to Benjamin Ames of Bath. Nathan Weston, Jr., was chief justice, and Ebenezer Thatcher the other associate justice of this court. He held this office until the separation of the State, discharging its duties with ability and inflexible integrity.

In 1816, he was chosen a member of the Executive Council of Massachusetts, and was annually re-elected as long as Maine continued united to the old Commonwealth. In the same year he was appointed one of the electors of President and Vice President: his colleagues in Maine were Prentiss Mellen, John Low, Stephen Longfellow, William Abbott, and Timothy Boutelle. The twenty electoral votes of Massachusetts were given to Rufus King, who received thirty-four votes out of two hundred and seventeen cast: the remainder were given to Mr. Monroe.

The same year, 1816, was also conspicuous in the life of Judge Stebbins, as a member of the celebrated abortive convention at Brunswick on the separation of Maine. The majority of that convention, it is well known, adopted the famous report of the committee for counting the votes of the people for and against separation. By the law, a majority of *five* to *four* was required to carry that measure into effect. This majority was not obtained from the aggregate of votes, according to the usual construction of the language; but the committee resorted to a different method of counting the votes. The whole number cast was twenty-two thousand four hundred and sixty-six, five-ninths of which is twelve thousand four hundred and eighty-one; those in favor of separation were but eleven thousand nine hundred and twenty-seven. The committee thus finding that the law was not complied with on this construction, assumed the construction of the act to be, that the question must be decided according to the majorities of the respective *towns*. Thus, "The corporate majorities of yeas must be placed in one column, and those of nays in another, and each added. Then, as *four is to five*, so is the aggregate majority of yeas in the towns and plantations in favor, to the aggregate majority of nays in those opposed." They accordingly ciphered it out in this way,—"The whole aggregate majority of *yeas* in the towns and plantations in favor is six thousand and thirty-one. The whole aggregate majority of *nays* in the towns and plantations opposed, is four thousand four hundred and nine; then as five is to four, so is six thousand and thirty-one to four thousand eight hundred and twenty-five, the nays required. Hence it appears that upon this construction there is a majority of five to four at least of the votes returned in favor of said District's becoming an independent State."

To this report and decision, a large and highly respected portion of the convention took exception, and strenuously opposed it; but, being overborne by a majority, a *protest* against further proceeding was drawn up and signed by seventy-one members; and, on the 9th of October, Judge Stebbins presented the protest, and moved to have it entered on the journals of the convention. The following are some of the leading points of the protest: "We protest against a separation of Maine from the present government, by any means whatever, without the consent of the people.

No such consent has been given." "We protest against a reference of this subject to the General Court for the purpose expressed in the resolution; because it is, in our estimation, a request to that honorable body to enact that which cannot be reconciled with constitutional principles nor actual fact." "We protest against the report on which the resolutions are predicated, as indecorous, as not expressed in terms suitable to the respect which this convention owes itself, nor to the honor due to the Legislature." The convention, notwithstanding the protest, went on appointing a committee to prepare a constitution, others to make application to the Legislature and to Congress, and another to answer the protest.

At the next session of the Legislature, the proceedings of the convention were entirely discarded, and a resolution was adopted, "That it is not expedient for the present General Court to adopt any further measures in regard to the separation of the District of Maine."

The separation postponed at that time was accomplished in 1820: in 1821, Judge Stebbins' seat upon the bench was supplied by a friend of the separation of which he was not, and he returned to the practice of his profession, which he continued to the close of his life. In 1825, he was elected a Senator to the Legislature from Lincoln County, and re-elected the two subsequent years. In this situation, his learning and experience were valuable. He made, during this period, several important reports, two of which were in favor of appropriations for the support of deaf and dumb pupils in the Hartford Asylum, and several elaborate reports on the subject of the State's Prison. Judge Stebbins was a better counsellor and legislator than a debater, although he often engaged in debate, and was a frequent advocate at the bar. But in this line his efforts were not happy, his manner was awkward, and his style confused, overloaded, and obscure. One of his cotemporaries, Mr. Allen, who practiced in the same county with him, says, "He did not excel as an advocate. He lacked method, and the power of condensing his thoughts. His arguments were desultory, involved in parentheses, and leaving no distinct impression. He was distinguished for his affability, for his inflexible integrity, and the purity of his moral character."[1] He was extremely careless in his pecuniary transactions. He kept no accounts with his clients, and settled none; and, although economical, he permitted his claims to be barred by the statute of limitations, unless his debtors chose voluntarily to pay him. But he was a good man, a good citizen, and an able, honest lawyer. At the Lincoln bar, he stood in the front rank; in the management of his causes, he was true and faithful to his client, and permitted no part of his case to be lost by any fault of his. In private life, he was a warm and affectionate friend to those who won and deserved his confidence. A friend of learning and learned institutions, he was one of the Overseers of Bowdoin College and afterwards a Trustee, from 1816 to the time of his death. He rarely omitted attending the commencement exercises and other important occasions of the institution, and took a warm interest in its progress and success.

He died at Alna, much lamented, March 1, 1826, aged sixty-three, leaving one daughter, Laura, an only child, who inherited the literary qualities of her father, and lives unmarried in Bangor. His widow survived him a few years.

BENJAMIN WHITWELL. 1796—1812.

Benjamin Whitwell was the son of Samuel Whitwell, a hard-ware merchant in Boston, who died in 1828, aged sev-

[1] Sixth Volume Maine Historical Collections, p. 56.

enty-six, and was born there June 22, 1772. He was prepared for college in the famed Latin school of that town, which he entered in 1779, at the age of seven years, and graduated at Harvard College in 1790; of which class, one survivor, Josiah Quincy, *clarum et venerabile nomen*, yet remains, the oldest living graduate. Mr. Whitwell ranked well in college, being distinguished more in the *belles lettres* than in the profound branches of study. This was manifested by his being selected to deliver a poem at Commencement, and again when he took his second degree. On the latter occasion, he took for his subject "Seclusion." This was followed by a still higher tribute to his poetical talent, in his being selected to deliver the poem in 1806, before the Phi Beta Kappa Society. On this occasion, his subject was "Folly as it flies." He was then in the practice of law at Augusta, and this assignment shows that the stern duties of the legal practice had not hardened his imagination, nor driven the love of the muses from his heart.

On leaving college, Mr. Whitwell entered the office of Judge John Sprague, a very distinguished lawyer of Lancaster, Worcester County, whose daughter he afterward married. He was admitted to the bar, and came to Augusta in Maine, in 1796. This town was then a part of Hallowell, from which it was separated in February, 1797, and called Harrington, which name was changed to Augusta in June of the same year. It then contained a population of ten or eleven hundred, and but one lawyer, James Bridge; William Lithgow, Jr., had retired from practice, and died that year. By his connections in Boston, he had a very good business, having charge of some large tracts of land belonging to absent proprietors. But his studies and tastes were not suited to encounter the sharp conflicts of the bar in a rude state of society, and in pursuing the more gentle tendencies of his mind, he devoted to literary labors much of the time which would have made him a good lawyer, and an eloquent advocate. He wrote much for the press, and as an acquaintance happily said, "He was more fond of poetry than of pleading." It was this, perhaps, that led him to associate in business, partners more inclined to the hard tasks of the profession than he was; of these were successively, Williams Emmons, son of the celebrated preacher and controversial divine of Franklin, Massachusetts; Henry W. Fuller, and John Potter.

Mr. Whitwell remained in Augusta until 1812, when he removed to Boston, where his own family connections and those of his second wife, Lucy P., a daughter of John Scollay, a former merchant in that city, resided. There he pursued his profession, was in 1816 Assistant Secretary of State under Alden Bradford, and a representative from Boston in 1818. He was a zealous politician of the Federal school, and spoke, and wrote, and acted for the cause, as long as it kept up its organization as a party. While at Augusta, he was once or twice a candidate for representative to Congress, and in 1805 represented that town in the General Court. In his political opinions he was a co-worker with Wilde and Parker, Bailey, Orr, Abbot, Longfellow, and numerous other able and honorable men through the State; but the party was for years in a desperate minority in Maine, and adventurers in that school had little chance for advancement. His gifts as an orator and writer were often put in requisition: in 1800, on the 22d of February, he delivered a eulogy before the people of Augusta and Hallowell on the death of Washington, and on the 4th of July, 1814, he was the orator of the day before the town authorities of Boston while the war with Great Britain was at its height, in which he did not spare the administration of the General Government, and echoed the deeply felt and loudly expressed sentiment of Massachusetts against the war. The same year he was called upon to pronounce the annual address before the Massachusetts Charitable Fire Society, a celebrated institution of that day in Boston. Both of these orations were published, and were highly finished pieces of composition.

Mr. Whitwell was a distant relative of Chief Justice Parsons, and when that great jurist presided in his court at Augusta, he made Mr. Whitwell's house his home. A friend has given me an account of his interview with the Chief Justice on one of these occasions. "I called upon him," he says, "with my mother. He wore on his head a study cap, and a red bandanna about his neck. He kindly inquired about my pursuits, and when I told him I was a student at law, he gave me in conversation a most elaborate lecture on the study of the law, enumerated a list of elementary works to be read, and dwelt much on slow and repeated perusal of some of them, especially Blackstone's Commentaries, and pointed out the way to read them advantageously. On my return home I wrote down these valuable instructions, and I think they made a permanent and useful impression upon me."

In the latter part of his life, Mr. Whitwell had been feeble, and was in a decline. He was advised to spend a winter in a Southern climate, and he went to Charleston, South Carolina, near the close of 1824, without, however, material benefit, and on his return he died at sea, in April, 1825.

Several descriptions of Mr. Whitwell, and my own recollections, concur in representing him as a handsome man, and of fine personal appearance. He had a tall and graceful figure, a broad, white forehead, with a dark, heavy eyebrow, dark hair, and a full, dark eye. His style of dress was elegant, his manners, though reserved, were graceful; his whole appearance commanded respect, and indicated a high order of talents, which, in a profession more congenial to his taste, and with an active business talent, would have insured eminent success.

Mr. Whitwell, as we have intimated, was twice married. By his first wife, the daughter of Judge John Sprague of Lancaster, he had three children; viz., John, who became a professor in a college in Ohio; Samuel, settled in Lancaster; and Sarah, who married Mr. Tomkins. In May, 1808, he married Lucy P. Scollay, of Boston, whose family gave the name to the buildings at the junction of Court and Tremont streets. By her he had William S., Treasurer of the Boston and Roxbury Mill Corporation; Benjamin, deceased; Lucy, married to William Parker the distinguished engineer; and Elizabeth. His widow is still living in Boston.

JOHN MERRILL. 1798—1816.

John Merrill was the son of John Merrill, a respectable citizen of Topsham, and a Justice of the Peace for Lincoln County. He was born in Topsham in 1770. His early life was spent upon his father's farm. At a mature age he prepared for college, and entering Brown University, he took his degree in 1793, in a class of twelve members, in which he was among the best. He was regarded as a superior scholar, and particularly thorough in mathematics, for which he had both fondness and taste. Determining to become a lawyer, he entered the office of Silas Lee at Wiscasset, and having passed through the usual course with diligence, and a mind well stored with legal principles, he was admitted to the bar in 1798, and commenced practice in Hallowell. He remained in that place but about two years, when he removed to Wiscasset, and we soon after find him a partner with his former instructor, Mr. Lee, whose numerous avocations as member of Congress, United States Attorney, and Judge of Probate, called him much from his office. Mr. Merrill was a well-read lawyer, and a safe and judicious counsellor, but a natural diffidence prevented him from making any figure as an advocate. By this defect he lost the opportunities which the forum gives for the exercise and display of legal qualities, and necessarily took a lower position in the profession than his legal ability and acquirements might have justly claimed. His tastes seemed rather to have run outside of the bar. I am informed by one who knew him intimately that he had a fine genius, composed rapidly, and wrote in a polished style, and that he was very quick and expert in drawing up a legal instrument. He wrote a beautiful hand, was a great reader and deep thinker, and did not disdain to pay his court to the muses, in which gentle service he acquired no small repute. Many of his verses were circulated in manuscript among his friends, and were read with pleasure and applause. Another venerable cotemporary informs me that he was a man of good sense and general knowledge, had a fine taste, and was remarkable for his social qualities. He was a very handsome man, six feet in height, of portly figure and pleasing address. With these fine qualities, why should not this gentleman, so prepossessing in appearance and manners, and so well endowed, have left upon his times a lasting impression? He was devoid of ambition and energy, and too desultory in his efforts when he made them; he sacrificed to ease and indulgence powers and faculties, which might have given him an elevated position in the community, and conferred a permanent benefit upon his State and his profession.

It is said of Mr. Merrill that, when a young man, he was famed for his agility and strength as a wrestler. He was challenged one day by a large party in Topsham, which he did not decline, and engaged them one after another from twelve o'clock till sunset, throwing them all successively in every form of the sport. But the effort was so exhausting, that it produced an unfavorable effect upon his constitution, and led to serious consequences. Wrestling was a very fashionable exercise among young men in the last century and the beginning of the present.

It was one of the college customs at Cambridge, for the Freshmen, on the entry of the class, to be initiated into their new life by a wrestling match. The Sophomores challenged the new comers to a trial of strength in this ancient and classical exercise. The Senior class was the umpire, and the victors were treated to a supper on their invitation.

Mr. Merrill married Miss Mary Webster of Wiscasset, by whom he had a family. A son Charles is a cashier of a bank in Malden, Massachusetts; and a daughter, who married Mr. Tristram Jordan of Saco, now lives in Portland, a widow with children. Mr. Merrill died in Topsham, June, 1816, aged forty-six.

JAMES DEAN HOPKINS. 1797—1840.

James D. Hopkins was born at Axminster, a manufacturing town on the river Ax, in Devonshire, England, in 1773. He came to Portland, in this State, at the age of eleven years, with his father, Thomas Hopkins, who, with many other enterprising Englishmen, hastened to this country on the conclusion of peace, for a free air and a broader field for their energy. The father was a respectable merchant, and the owner of large landed property, which descended to his children, with an honored name. He built a large block of stores with dwellings connected, according to the English style, on Middle street in Portland, in part of which he traded and dwelt, and where he died, leaving two sons and three daughters.

James did not receive a collegiate education, but after applying himself diligently to rudimentary studies he entered the office of Daniel Davis, then the most brilliant lawyer at the bar in Maine, and earnestly devoted himself not only to acquire the knowledge of his special profession, but of gen eral literature. He became well grounded in legal principles, and particularly in that then most important branch, "special pleading," which he applied with adroitness in his subsequent practice. He was admitted to the bar in March, 1797, and immediately entered on a remunerative practice.

He was not only an adroit special pleader, but he was remarkably well read in the law of real estate, for which his skill gave him numerous engagements. In respect to special pleading, — now almost a "misnomer," and forgotten at the bar,— he may have carried his art to excess of refinement, as is apt to be the case with those who have peculiar aptitude in any subject which has taken possession of the mind. It was sometimes diverted from its legitimate purpose of opening the pathway to truth, into intricate subtleties and tricks of deception. We cannot but think that one of the causes of the falling off in the high standard of excellence in our profession in Maine, may be traced to the abrogation of nearly all the forms of pleading; — when they were in force, one could not be a good lawyer who was not tolerably well versed in them. Sir William Jones says, "Our science of special pleading is an excellent logic; it is admirably calculated for the purpose of analyzing a cause, of extracting, like the root of an equation, the true points in dispute." Again, "It is reducible to the strictest rules of pure dialect; and if it were scientifically taught in our public seminaries of learning, would fix the attention, give a habit of reasoning closely, quicken the apprehension, and invigorate the understanding; but," he adds, "it may unquestionably be perverted to very bad purposes." It was observing the "bad purposes," that made Lord Mansfield an avowed enemy of *special pleaders*, if not of the science.

Mr. Hopkins was for several years a leading member of the bar, and had more business than any other member in the early part of this century. As an advocate, he was zealous, ardent, and impassioned. His faults were, too much excitability and too much expansion. He entered with his whole soul into the cause of his client, and spared nothing which thorough investigation and untiring industry could accomplish for his success. A short time previous to the appointment of his legal instructor, Mr. Davis, as Solicitor General, he formed a partnership with him, which continued until Mr. Davis left the State, in 1804.

During the existence of the Federal party, Mr. Hopkins entered zealously into the controversies of the day in support of its principles. His addresses at public meetings were ardent and impulsive; at times, eloquent, and on occasions of high excitement, often overwrought and violent. In the latter portion of his life, he took no active part in politics, but quietly and steadily pursued his literary and legal labors with the love and interest which had guided his early studies.

For industry and patient labor he was a pattern to young men who are seeking preferment in life. When not engaged in the active duties of his profession, he devoted himself to study and general improvement. He wasted no time in mere amusement. He was fond of antiquarian researches, and it gave him particular pleasure to trace pedigrees, and to examine ancient titles. With a warm imagination and fondness for labor, he prepared, in his leisure hours, a work of fiction, in two volumes, founded upon the early settlement of Portland, which was highly interesting as a historical novel. It was never published. His taste in this department of research was also displayed in an address which he delivered before the members of the Cumberland bar in 1833, which was published in a pamphlet of seventy-nine pages. The work exhibits careful investigation, and preserves valuable memorials relative to law and lawyers in Maine. A single extract will show the tendency of his own studies. In speaking of some libraries in the last century, he says they contained "Good store of black-letter learning, a few volumes of which, modern notions notwithstanding, are worth a multitude of recent publications."

During the latter period of his life, he was engaged in the preparation of a work on Insurance, which was nearly ready for the press; but the full and accurate volumes of Mr. Phillips of Boston, on the same subject, had so entirely occupied the ground that he did not deem it advisable further to pursue his work. Mr. Hopkins also left copious notes and memoranda on the law of real estate; and his manuscripts show an immense amount of labor in the examination of titles, and in explaining and illustrating the records.

He was three times married. His first wife was Mary, a daughter of John Bagley of Portland, to whom he was married December 18, 1801. She died within three months of their union. In December, 1804, he married Dorcas, a daughter of Capt. Daniel Tucker of Portland, by whom he left three daughters who are still living, and are his only surviving children. Mr. Hopkins had a younger brother, Thomas, who read law with him, and a few months with Judge Wilde at Hallowell, and was admitted to the bar of Cumberland in 1805. We quote the following tender memorial of him from the Address to the Bar above referred to: "He commenced practice in Bridgton, where he remained about a year, and then removed to Portland in ill health, which continued and increased until his death, Dec. 8, 1807. Cut off in the morning of his days, he had but little opportunity of showing his professional qualifications or acquisitions. What he was, and what he promised to be, it should be the office of some other to declare. He was my brother."

GEORGE WASHINGTON WALLINGFORD. 1798—1824.

George W. Wallingford was born at Somersworth, in New Hampshire, February 19, 1778. His father, Samuel Wallingford, was killed in a naval engagement between the Drake and Ranger in April, 1778. This engagement was one of the daring actions of the renowned naval commander, Paul Jones. It took place in April, 1778, off Belfast, Ireland. Jones had been cruising on that coast, and by his many bold enterprises had struck terror into the minds of the people in that neighborhood. To stop his marauding, the sloop-of-war Drake, of twenty guns, was prepared for sea, on board of which a large number of volunteers entered for a holiday expedition, making her crew one hundred and sixty men, so determined were they to get rid of this pest. On the morning of April 24th, Jones's ship, the Ranger, of eighteen guns, was off the harbor, and the Drake immediately proceeded to get under way, and came slowly out to sea. The Ranger ran down toward her, and, hauling up her courses, lay to, to await her arrival. On her coming up, Jones sheered across her bow, and poured into her the first broadside. The engagement was maintained with great energy and obstinacy at close quarters for more than an hour, when, the captain of the Drake receiving a musket ball in his head, the crew called for quarter, and the action ceased. The captain and lieutenant of the Drake died of their wounds, and forty-two of her crew were killed. The loss on board the Ranger was the brave and noble Lieutenant Wallingford, and one seaman killed and six wounded. The prize was taken to Brest, with two hundred prisoners, being double the number of his own crew, and Jones was greeted with lively demonstrations of joy by the American commissioners, in which the French court heartily joined.

One incident honorable to the humanity of Lieut. Wallingford, we cannot forbear to mention:—Jones, just previous to the above-named battle, had entered Whitehaven harbor in the night, with the intention of destroying the town and a large fleet of vessels lying there. He assigned to Wallingford the duty of firing a portion of the fleet, while he scaled the forts and spiked the guns. Having entirely accomplished this object, he was surprised not to see the shipping on fire. Meeting Wallingford on the pier, he inquired as to the failure of his part of the plan. He stated that his light had gone out, and besides, he did not see that anything could be gained by burning poor people's property.

Left in infancy an orphan, the son was compelled to endure hardships and to struggle through many trials. He was educated at Harvard College, from which he took his first degree in 1795, having for his classmate Bishop Dehon of South Carolina, Benjamin Gorham of Boston, and Caleb Bradley and Joshua Wingate of Maine. The last survivor of this class of forty was Caleb Bradley, a clergyman, who died in Westbrook, June 3, 1861, at the ripe age of eighty-nine.

On leaving college, Mr. Wallingford entered the office of Dudley Hubbard in South Berwick, and became an attentive and diligent student. He was admitted to the bar in 1798, and established himself in the profession at Kennebunk in 1800. Joseph Thomas was the only practitioner in the village, then a part of the town of Wells, since incorporated as a separate town by the Indian name of Kennebunk. Mr. Wallingford had an advantage over Mr. Thomas, in that he was a good advocate and a forcible and pleasing speaker, while Mr. Thomas rarely argued his own cases to the jury. But Wallingford, two years after, was encountered by a competitor, his equal in all the qualities of a lawyer, advocate, and a man, the late Joseph Dane, although not gifted with the courage and impulsiveness of the former. These qualities, with a firm will and a determined resolution, very useful, if not necessary to the advancement of a lawyer, oftentimes placed Wallingford in the van of his competitor. He was ardent, bold, and independent, both as a lawyer and politician; and as an active member of the Federal party, he took a prominent position in the contests which fiercely raged in the early part of the century. In 1813, he was elected one of the representatives of Wells to the General Court, and was successively re-elected during the continuance of our connection with Massachusetts. Here he took an active part in the discussions of the great questions which agitated the country, advocating with boldness and ability the leading measures of the Federal party. In 1816, he was chosen a member of the Brunswick Convention, and united with those who protested against the action of the majority, in declaring that the conditions of separation had not been complied with. They did not consider that the requisite majority had been obtained. And this view was sustained by the Legislature. He was also a member of the Convention held in Portland, in October, 1819, which adopted the Constitution under which we now live. He bore his part ably in the debates, and from his experience in the rules of deliberative assemblies, he was a useful and honored member of the Convention. He did not, however, sign the Constitution, from objections to some portions of it, which he and thirty-one other members, who also declined subscribing it, were unable to have amended in conformity with their views. Among these were all the delegates from Wells, four in number, and the five delegates from Portland, which included Judges Whitman and Emery, Messrs. Asa Clapp and Isaac Ilsley. The principal objection was to the apportionment of representatives, which the minority considered unequal and unjust, as it deprived the inhabitants of large towns of their just proportion of members in the legislative body. The discussion on this subject was long and learned, in which the most able delegates in the Convention took part, as Judges Bridge, Thacher, and Green, Mr. Holmes, Mr. Whitman, Allen of Norridgewock, Ames, Wallingford, Parris, &c.

As may be inferred, Mr. Wallingford was not an advocate for the separation; he preferred a connection with Massachusetts, which, with Maine, constituted a large and powerful State, until our resources, population, and wealth should be so much increased as to give us some consideration in the confederacy. Another argument with him undoubtedly was of a political nature: he preferred the conservative character and the high moral standard of the Old Bay State, to swinging off into the control of the Democratic party, which would have charge of affairs in the new State.

His membership in the Convention was his last public office with the exception of his representation of his town in the legislature of Maine in 1823. The next year, January 19, 1824, he died, much honored and lamented, at the age of forty-eight, in the midst of his vigor and usefulness.

He was a good lawyer, a popular advocate and debater, and a man of stern principles and rigid integrity. He was earnest and forcible in contending for truth, or maintaining his principles, or advocating the rights and interests of his clients. He enjoyed the confidence of his fellow-citizens, and was esteemed as a conscientious public man.

In September, 1806, he married Miss Abigail Chadbourne of Berwick, a sister of Ichabod R. Chadbourne, the respected lawyer of Eastport, by whom he had one daughter, who married and died without issue. His wife died in 1808. He married for his second wife, Mary, a daughter of Dr. Jacob Fisher of Kennebunk, by whom he had one son and four daughters, who survived him.

JUDAH DANA. 1798—1845.

Judah Dana was the first lawyer that ventured into that part of Maine now embraced in the county of Oxford. He established himself at Fryeburg, in September, 1798. The town had then about seven hundred inhabitants: it had but one thousand and four by the census of 1810: the whole county of Oxford in 1800 had but nine thousand nine hundred. The town was granted in 1762 to General Joseph Frye, from whom it takes its name, and was occupied the same year by Osgoods, Bradleys, and others, principally from Concord, New Hampshire.

Mr. Dana was the son of John Winchester Dana and Hannah Pope Putnam, a daughter of General Israel Putnam, the celebrated Major General of the Revolution, and was born at Pomfret in Vermont, April 25, 1772. Judge Dana's father was one of the first settlers of that town. He graduated at Dartmouth College in 1795, having among his classmates Heman Allen of Vermont and Judge Nicholas Emery of this State. The present generation may be pleased to know the style of dress which graduates wore at that day. Judge Dana thus described his own,—"a black coat, vest, and small clothes with large silver knee-buckles, black silk stockings and shoes, with silver shoe-buckles; black silk gloves, and the head surmounted with a black three-sided cocked hat. The hair was queued down the back almost to the hips with a black ribbon—hair dressed and powdered white as snow." Thus, in a strange masquerade, with the exception of the hat, the young graduates appeared on the stage at Commencement: the small clothes continued sometime into the present century for dress garments.

On leaving college, Mr. Dana took charge of Moore's Charity school at Hanover, and at the same time entered the office of Benjamin I. Gilbert of that place, a sound lawyer and good classical scholar, who was known by the *sobriquet* of *Baron* Gilbert, from his namesake, the distinguished Chief Baron. In September, 1798, having completed his studies, he was admitted to the bar of Grafton County in New Hampshire, and determining to settle in Maine, he came to the district the same month, and was admitted to the bar in Lincoln County. Thus furnished and equipped, he entered upon the practice in the town which for nearly half a century continued to be his place of residence. The nearest lawyer to him in Maine was at Portland, fifty miles distant, so that he had the range of the forest and the plain, and most energetically and successfully did he pursue his game. His business extended into New Hampshire, which Fryeburg adjoined, and he attended the courts of that State held at Dover, as well as those of his own county held at York, to which his town belonged;—to reach which places he pursued his long and solitary way on horseback. He became a leading advocate, and as he was a careful and intelligent student, he acquired a high reputation at the bar of his own county, and practiced with success in Cumberland, where he encountered the able men of that bar, whose names have in part been recorded.

His first competitor, who settled in a neighboring town, was his classmate, Nicholas Emery, at Parsonsfield. But there soon came into his immediate neighborhood another, to divide the same loaf which was hardly enough for one hungry practitioner to enjoy. Jacob McGaw from New Hampshire, and two years after him in college, opened an office along side of him in 1801, and a vigorous rivalship took place, which certainly did not diminish the business nor the excitement in the efforts of the young and ardent aspirants for legal fame and an honorable support. These lawyers attended the courts in New Hampshire, at York, and in Cumberland, and they had many sharp encounters on lesser matters before local magistrates at home. But Mr. McGaw was not satisfied with this limited field of labor, and left it in two or three years for Bangor, where we shall have the pleasure of another meeting with him. He was succeeded by Samuel A. Bradley, a graduate of Dartmouth of 1799, who for a long series of years was a competitor in law and politics with Mr. Dana.

In 1805, Oxford County was established from territory in the northern parts of York and Cumberland. It was the seventh county in the State in the order of its organization, following Kennebec, which was established in 1799. Paris was appointed the shire town, and two terms a year of the Common Pleas and Sessions were granted to it, but its issues in the Supreme Court were tried in Portland. The two lawyers of Fryeburg found places in the Probate Court, — Mr. Dana as Judge, and Mr. Bradley as Register. Judge Dana also received the appointment of County Attorney, which he held until he was raised to the bench of the Common Pleas. No other persons in any of the offices in the county were lawyers.

Judge Dana continued to practice with increased success, both in the Common Pleas of his own county, and in the Supreme Court at Portland, and he was engaged on one side or the other of every cause, civil or criminal, tried in Oxford from June, 1805, to August, 1811. It is said that he maintained himself with ability in his conflicts with the leaders of the Cumberland bar, Hopkins, Longfellow, Whitman, and others, until 1811, when he was appointed Associate Justice of the Court of Common Pleas for the first eastern circuit, under the reorganization of that court by Governor Gerry's administration. Benjamin Greene of South Berwick was Chief Justice, and William Widgery of Portland, second associate. This office he held until 1822, when the government of Maine established a new court for the whole State, consisting of three judges, of which Chief Justice Whitman was placed at the head.

Judge Dana was a well-read lawyer, of a judicious, well-balanced, and discriminating mind. His perceptions were quick and ready, and he discharged the duties of his official stations with integrity, urbanity, and sound legal intelligence. He was fond of his office, had a high sense of the obligations it imposed, and labored earnestly and devotedly in a faithful discharge of its duties. From these he returned to the bar with unabated zeal, and entered into its conflicts with the energy of his early life tempered by the calmness of judgment which the exercise of the judicial office is wont to impart.

In 1819, he was a member of the State Convention which framed the Constitution of Maine, and was one of the Committee to prepare that instrument, which was composed of some of the most prominent men in the State. He took an active part in the debates.

He was appointed to several political offices. In 1833, he was one of the Executive council in the administration of Governor Smith; in 1836 and 1837, he was one of the Bank Commissioners. In 1836, he was appointed by Governor Dunlap, United States Senator for the remainder of Judge Shepley's term, who resigned that office on being appointed a judge of the Supreme Court; his colleague was John Ruggles. While a Senator, he engaged in the debates of that body, one of the most exciting of which was that on the resolution of Mr. Benton to expunge from the record the censure on Gen. Jackson.

I am indebted to an intimate friend of Judge Dana for the following estimate of his character and powers: "He was a ready speaker, urbane and conciliating, but of unquestioned firmness. In all public positions, he was true and faithful, and fully equal to the demand upon him. In private life, no gentleman could be more genial. Time and chance were never wanting with him to say and do kind things to every one within his circle. In a large sphere of professional life, Judge Dana could have acquired a more brilliant reputation, but he loved the country and its retirement, and there chose to act his part, keeping fresh, however, in the world's history, living and past." He labored effectually to promote the educational interests of his adopted town, and contributed to other improvements to make it a desirable place of residence. He was one of the Trustees of Bowdoin College from 1820 to 1843.

Such was the genial character and reputation of Judge Dana that his office became the resort of many young men who were pursuing the study of law. Among these were Daniel Webster, for a short period; General Samuel Fessenden; Peter C. Virgin of Rumford; Gen. Eleazer Wheelock Ripley; Joseph Howard; Philip Eastman of Saco; Henry B. Osgood, and several others.

Mr. Webster graduated at Dartmouth College in 1801, and afterwards had charge of the academy at Fryeburg; during this time he had his name in Judge Dana's office. A letter from him to his teacher, which we are permitted to use, will give us a little insight into his pursuits while there. "Boston, December 29th, 1804,—Dear Sir,—Circumstances exist which render it desirable to me to be able to show that during the eight months in which I instructed in the Fryeburg Academy, *I considered myself destined for the profession of the law, and had access to the library of a practitioner.* If you can, *salvo honore*, say this of me, it would gratify me that you should. A 'student at law' I certainly was not, unless 'Allen Ramsey's Poems' and 'Female Quixotism' will pass for law books. Besides, I should not expect a man of your habits to certify *me* to have been a *student* at *anything* during the time which I loitered away in your country, perusing rather my male and female friends than my books. To be serious, however, you would really oblige me by writing me a line, and stating in it, if you can, that while I was in the academy six hours in the day, you understood me to have made choice of the law as a profession, and that I had access to your library. I will immediately excuse you if there is anything in this request incompatible with propriety."

Judge Dana replied, saying: "The precise time of your residence in Fryeburg, as preceptor of the Academy, I cannot now ascertain, but I think you came in November or December, 1801, and returned the September following, so as to make up the term of your eight months. On your arrival, you informed me you intended, as you had commenced, to pursue the study of the law, and wished for the privilege of using my books, and during said term you had access to my library."

Judge Dana was twice married; his first wife, and the mother of all his children, was Elizabeth, the youngest daughter of Professor Sylvanus Ripley of Dartmouth College, and grand-daughter of the first President Wheelock of the same college. Generals Eleazer W. and James W. Ripley were her brothers. His second wife was the widow of General John McMillan of Fryeburg. His only son who survived infancy, is the Hon. John W. Dana, former Governor of Maine, and late Minister to Bolivia. Of his several daughters, one married Judge Howard of Portland, another is the widow of the late Henry B. Osgood, and now the wife of Judge Goodenow of Alfred.

He died in December, 1845, at the age of seventy-three, with a consciousness of having endeavored to discharge the duties of life, and with a firm religious trust; leaving a handsome estate, the fruit of his labor, his care, and judicious management.

NICHOLAS EMERY. 1798—1861.

Nicholas Emery, the classmate of Judge Dana, opened his office in Parsonsfield at the same time his friend established himself in Fryeburg,—the autumn of 1798. Parsonsfield lies in the northwest corner of the county of York, and on the boundary of New Hampshire, west, and Oxford, north. This is a large and unbroken township of land, and contained, when Mr. Emery commenced practice there, about twelve hundred inhabitants; it was a flourishing and growing town, aud that part of the county being destitute of any member of the profession, afforded much encouragement to a young practitioner. Mr. Dana was the only lawyer in that part of the State north of him, and the only ones on the south in the county were at Biddeford, Berwick, Kennebunk, and Saco,—the whole number not exceeding six or eight: Mr. Dana, who was his next neighbor, was not nearer than twenty miles, the others thirty miles at least. This range might be considered sufficiently large to give ample employment to one lawyer.

Mr. Emery was born in Exeter, New Hampshire, September 4, 1776. His first American ancestor was Anthony Emery of Romsey, England, a carpenter, who came over, with his brother John, in the James of London, in the spring of 1635, arriving in Boston in June. John settled in Newbury, Anthony in Kittery. The descent is through Daniel Emery of Kittery, whose will on York records bears date November 8, 1722. Daniel had four sons, three of whom he named from the Patriarch of the Deluge and his two sons,—Noah, Shem, Japhet: he wisely substituted the name of a beloved apostle for that of the despised Ham. Noah, the eldest, married Joanna, a daughter of Nicholas Perryman, a lawyer of Exeter, and of his wife, Joanna Dudley, a descendant of Governor Thomas Dudley of Massachusetts.

These were the grand-parents of the subject of our notice; his father, Noah, their second son, married Jane Hale, by whom he had six children, all of whom are dead but John and Jane, now residing in Exeter. Their father, Noah, was many years clerk of the judicial courts for the County of Rockingham. Their father's sister, Margaret, a woman of remarkable powers of mind and an ever-ready flow of wit, is still living at Exeter, in her ninety-first year, having been born in October, 1772. Nicholas was the third child. He entered the far-famed academy at Exeter, at the age of twelve years, in 1788, the same year that the renowned and beloved Benjamin Abbott commenced his course of instruction in that seminary; which continued with eminent success through a period of fifty years. His long term of service closed with a jubilee which brought together a large number of his surviving pupils, to bear honorable testimony of their affection for their venerated instructor. After a diligent pursuit of his preliminary studies, Mr. Emery entered Dartmouth, from which he took his degree with the honors of the college, among able competitors, in 1795, at the age of nineteen: he appeared on Commencement day in the same style of dress which we have described in the sketch of his classmate, Judge Dana.

On leaving college, Mr. Emery, having decided upon the law as the occupation of his life, determined to seek the best advantages which his State afforded for instruction. He therefore wisely placed himself under the tuition of Edward St. Loe Livermore of Portsmouth, son of Chief Justice Samuel Livermore, an accomplished lawyer. Mr. Livermore was afterwards a judge of the Supreme Court of New Hampshire, and united to extensive knowledge of his profession, large general information, and a most happy faculty of interesting his students in their studies, and leading them to elevated principles in the administration and practice of law.

Mr. Emery always acknowledged his obligations to Judge Livermore for his kind guidance through the mazes by which the grand edifice of jurisprudence is reached, and the genial and urbane spirit which he manifested toward him. After two years' study in Judge Livermore's office, he became for a year in 1797, an assistant instructor in Exeter Academy.

On completing his studies, he was admitted to the bar in the autumn of 1798, and immediately proceeded to Parsonsfield and entered upon the practice. The name of Emery was traditional at the bar of York. Noah Emery, one of his family, was the earliest resident lawyer in the State, having commenced practice about 1725, and continued near forty years almost the only lawyer in the State, enjoying a large practice. In 1750, Caleb Emery, another member of the same family, came into the bar, and continued through the Revolution alone in the county, after Judge David Sewall was raised to the bench. A John Emery was also a practitioner at that bar, commencing prior to the Revolution. This new comer, therefore, of the same name, had a sort of prescriptive right to a respectable practice on the old field which had for so many years been trodden and cultivated by his race.

His accomplishments as a lawyer, and his easy, pleasant manners, soon brought him into notice. Numerous and profitable engagements extended his practice from his own county into the adjoining county of Strafford in New Hampshire. After seven or eight years' successful practice in this section of the country, which required much labor and long travel, and being about to form a matrimonial connection with a most admirable woman, used to all the refinements of life, he determined to seek a more eligible position. In the spring of 1807, he, therefore, moved to Portland; and in the autumn of the same year, he married Ann T., the eldest daughter of the worthy and honored Governor Gilman of New Hampshire, a lady admirably qualified to give dignity, grace, and happiness to the domestic circle.

Mr. Emery now entered upon a course of uninterrupted success. The business of the courts in Cumberland County was never greater than in the year he came to Portland; the number of entries on the docket of the Common Pleas was two thousand four hundred and twenty-two: it was the year of numerous failures, and the laws for the collection ef debts were harsh, giving creditors the power to seize upon the property without exemption, as well as the person of the debtor. In repeated cases, the household furniture of respectable but unfortunate merchants, who had done large business and handled heavy masses of property, was sold under the hammer by relentless creditors, not sparing, in some instances, the beds on which the care-worn and depressed family sought repose. Attachments were numerous under this system, and some of the principal lawyers made more than one hundred entries a term.

A favorable opening into this ample field was made for Mr. Emery by the death of two of the most prominent lawyers;— Salmon Chase died in August, 1806; he had the largest practice of any attorney in the State: William Symmes died in January, 1807; and the accomplished and successful Parker, having been appointed to the bench of the Supreme Court, had moved to Boston. There were left twenty-nine lawyers in the county, of whom thirteen were in Portland: among them were the able and eloquent Mellen, recently moved from Biddeford; the sagacious Whitman; the keen and logical Orr; Longfellow, Hopkins, and the young but promising Greenleaf, all skillful and ingenious in the profession. Into competition with such men, did Mr. Emery enter, to wage forensic battle: ably and manfully did he sustain himself for more than a quarter of a century, engaged in the best cases, and acquiring reputation and property.

In 1834, Chief Justice Mellen having retired from the bench of the Supreme Court, Judge Weston was promoted to his place, and Mr. Emery, with the general assent, was appointed to fill the vacancy; the court then consisting of Chief Justice Weston, Judge Parris, and himself. He faithfully and promptly discharged the duties of this official station during the constitutional term of seven years. A cotemporary and friend, the Hon. Mr. McGaw of Bangor, who still lives at an advanced age, thus speaks of him as a judge, "With honorable fidelity and capability he discharged its high functions through the constitutional term of seven years." "Since closing the duties of his eminent judicial station, Judge Emery has not participated in the honorable strife that gentlemen feel who are contending for pre-eminence as advocates at the bar." The opinions of the court, as drawn and delivered by Judge Emery during the time he occupied a seat upon the bench, are recorded in the eight volumes of the Maine Reports from the twelfth to the nineteenth, inclusive. They show careful and diligent research, and just conclusions. An able opinion drawn by him on the question of excluding a witness for want of belief in a Supreme Being, was published in the Law Reporter of November, 1841, Vol. 4, p. 268. In this case it was decided that, by the statute of Maine, a belief in the Supreme Being is a pre-requisite to the admission of a witness to testify; but, he says, the court will require a clear, open, and deliberate avowal of disbelief before rejecting a witness. The judge reviewed numerous decisions in this country and England on the subject.

Judge Emery was devoted to his profession, and was thoroughly read in the law, in which he kept himself fresh amidst the ever-varying changes which the progress of society rendered necessary in the rules of jurisprudence and the modes of administration. He had seen special pleading, in which he took pleasure, gradually giving way before the cogent demands of the people for more plainness and simplicity in the forms of proceeding. He accommodated himself to these changes, and though cautious of innovation, he did not reject a measure because it was new. But caution was the tendency of his mind, and he was slow and reserved both in forming and giving an opinion ; he desired to look at a question on all its sides, and it may be said of him, as of the great Chancellor, Eldon, that, after the widest examination and the most careful reflection, he still doubted. A cotemporary of his early life, in speaking of Judge Emery at that period, said, " He was eloquent and ingenious as an advocate, and made an impression on the jury and the bench, but after a severe sickness which he had, his powers seemed to be less acute and vigorous."

Judge Emery seldom took part in political affairs, but was occasionally drawn into them from his more quiet and congenial pursuits. In 1816, he was a member of the Brunswick Convention on the question of separation ; and in 1819, he was again chosen a delegate from Portland to the convention which formed the present Constitution of Maine. He engaged in the debates on important questions. On the new government's going into effect, he was one of the three representatives chosen from Portland, his colleagues for this and the following year being Asa Clapp and Simon Greenleaf. These were the most important years in the annals of the State, for the government had to be organized, and the laws adapted to the new relations in which the people were placed. The whole body of the statute law in force in the State was arranged and digested by a board of jurisprudence, consisting of Judges Mellen, Preble, and Weston, who made their report at the session of the Legislature in 1821, which was revised, amended, and adopted by that Legislature. His services, in conjunction with those of Judge Potter of Portland in the Senate, and Simon Greenleaf in the House, were of great value in the preparation of this important compilation. He was an active and useful member in these initiatory sessions. In 1832, he was appointed one of the commissioners of Maine with Judge Preble and Reuel Williams, to negotiate with the government of the United States, for a cession of the disputed territory, under the treaty of 1783; and signed an agreement for an arrangement of the controversy on the basis of receiving compensation in land for the territory yielded up. His public life closed with the termination of his judicial office.

In his domestic life, Mr. Emery was no less fortunate than in the outward relations in which he appeared and acted before his fellow-men. The amiable, wise, and judicious woman with whom he lived near forty years, was of the genuine type of womanhood. Of a pure blood, coming down through ancestors among the most distinguished in her native State, she proved and maintained its title to distinction: she inherited the virtues and fine qualities of the stock from which she descended, and left it when she died, as living she had borne it, unsullied. Her death, which took place in 1848, at the age of sixty-eight, was an irremediable loss to her surviving companion, who felt the shock through his own remaining years. The latter portion of Judge Emery's life was passed in an almost unconscious state; and his shattered frame yielded at last to the gradual decay of time, on the 24th of August, 1861, in the eighty-fifth year of his age. Of his six children, one son and two daughters only survive.

Margaret, the sister of Judge Emery's father, who is mentioned in the former part of this article as living, has died before this sheet comes from the press, October, 1862, in the ninety-first year of her age.

Judge Emery, when he died, was the oldest but one of the Cumberland Bar; the oldest, Chief Justice Whitman, still lives, having entered upon his eighty-seventh year, in his native town, East Bridgewater, Massachusetts. Both, at the bar and on the bench, were honored, and in private life respected and trusted. They were connecting links between the present and the future, having passed through the whole period of our existence as a nation, thus far, and witnessed the wonderful changes which have taken place in the ever increasing volume of our imperial greatness.

THOMAS BOWMAN. 1797—1800.

About the time that Judges Dana and Emery commenced practice in York County, three young candidates for the honors and profits of the profession commenced their course in Kennebec County, — Thomas Bowman, Nathan Bridge, and Samuel P. Glidden. Bowman was the youngest son of Judge Jonathan Bowman of Dresden, who, for many years, was Clerk of the Court of Common Pleas for Lincoln, and afterward judge of the court, and Judge of Probate at the same time, while his son, Jonathan, Jr., was clerk of one court and register of the other. And it so happened that Thomas, the subject of this notice, a graduate of Harvard in the class of 1794, also became the first Register of Probate in the County of Kennebec, which was organized in 1799. He was born in Dresden, May 20, 1774, studied his profession with James Bridge at Augusta, and was admitted to practice in 1797. His practice was inconsiderable, and having afterward the office of Register of Probate, which furnished him a pleasant occupation; and having married a daughter of Samuel Howard, one of the oldest and most respected families of Augusta, by whom, and with the considerable patrimony he inherited from his father, he was made independent, he became careless of the emoluments of the profession. Without such stimulant, we cannot expect much effort through the dark and tedious mazes of the law to the higher rewards it has to offer to its votaries; and only to the patient, persistent, toilsome laborer and devotee, will she vouchsafe her noble muniments and honors. Mr. Bowman was placed above the necessity for exertion, and although of fine parts, and of remarkably attractive personal appearance and address, he willingly let go the prizes which he might have gracefully worn. Wilde and Allen, Bond and Rice and Boutelle, won the fame and the rewards with which a faithful, worthy, and devoted service to the law seldom fails to crown the victor in this honorable pursuit.

He lived and died in the old Fort Weston at Augusta, which had a traditional name, as being a frontier post many years: it had for a while the only plastered room in the town, and was the office of William Lithgow, Jr., the distinguished predecessor of Bowman in the practice. He died June 3, 1837. He had five children by his wife, whom he married November 3, 1799. His daughter Mary married Llewellyn W. Lithgow of Augusta, May 25, 1825; and Sarah married first, November 12, 1833, Dr. Sherman, a physician of Dresden, and after his death in 1847, Edward T. Baker of Dorchester, Massachusetts. Mr. Lithgow was a grandson of the celebrated John Gardiner of Pownalboro', barrister at law, by his daughter Ann. His father was James Lithgow, son of Judge William Lithgow. He has no children. Mrs. Baker has children.

A genealogical account of the Bowmans is given in my sketch of Jonathan Bowman, the father of Thomas, which will appear in subsequent pages.

NATHAN BRIDGE. 1798—1825.

Nathan Bridge was a younger son of Sheriff Edmund Bridge, and born in Dresden, September 25, 1775. After pursuing the usual rudimentary studies, not having received a liberal education, he entered the office of his brother James, in Augusta. Having been admitted to the bar in 1798, he established himself in that part of Pittston which lies upon the western side of Kennebec River, and is now Gardiner, the division of the town having taken place in February, 1803. He was the first lawyer in the town, and the only one between Hallowell and Bath. The whole town on both sides of the river contained a population of about one thousand two hundred in nearly equal proportions. By the census of 1810, Pittston had one thousand and eighteen inhabitants, and Gardiner one thousand and twenty-nine. Being the only lawyer for this extensive territory, he had a large business for several years, principally in matters concerning real estate, acting as the agent of absent proprietors of large tracts of land. "Mr. Bridge was highly instrumental in bringing to a successful conclusion many contests and controversies in which the value of his personal and local knowledge was very apparent, and was conspicuously displayed."

He kept his office in the second story of an old building erected by Dr. Gardiner of Boston before the Revolution, which is thus humorously described by an old resident. It was "the exact counterpart of the old Pownalboro' court house in Dresden, still standing on the bank of Kennebec River: the rest of the upper stories was used for dwellings, and the lower portion for pigs and wood, the boards and clapboards of this portion having been taken off and used for fire-wood. You would not expect a learned lawyer in full robes from such a receptacle."

Mr. Bridge never had much fancy for his profession, and therefore did not take sufficient pride in it to seek its higher rewards. He was not very able as a lawyer, not being grounded in a sound preliminary education, and he was no advocate. In 1808, he invited Frederic Allen, who was then settled at Warren, to become his partner, and on his accepting the situation and becoming familiar with the business, Mr. Bridge retired. In 1810, he engaged in land speculations, and subsequently, about 1815, moved to Wilmington, North Carolina, where his brother Edmund was successfully engaged in mercantile business. He returned in a few years, on the death of his brother, with improved means, purchased a small farm, on which he erected a neat cottage, about a mile from the river, where he resided in a quiet, unostentatious manner, until the close of his life, which took place in 1827, September 15, at the age of fifty-two. Mr. Bridge was a man, as Mr. Allen says, "of much kindness and active benevolence. He was strictly honest in all his transactions, and was emphatically the poor man's friend. His conduct and deportment were ever marked with a high sense of honor in all his business, as well as social relations." He never was married.

WILLIAM WIDGERY. 1788—1798.

On the list of lawyers which I have annexed to these sketches, I have put down the name of William Widgery, who was no lawyer, and yet had a considerable practice in New Gloucester, where he lived many years. His name is also contained in a manuscript list of lawyers prepared by William D. Williamson. This eccentric man came to this country, in his boyhood, from England, before the Revolution, poor, friendless, and uneducated. We find him serving on board a privateer as lieutenant, in the Revolutionary War. During the war, he settled in New Gloucester, where he married; and by the natural force of his mind, and the energy of his character, supplied the deficiencies of his early life, and rose to places of distinction and wealth. He was chosen the representative of New Gloucester to the General Court, in 1787, and held the office by repeated elections eight or nine years. In 1788, he was elected a delegate to the convention of Massachusetts which adopted the Constitution of the United States, and strenuously opposed the adoption, frequently speaking on the subjects under discussion. In 1794, he was a senator in the Legislature of Massachusetts from Cumberland, and many years a Justice of the Peace. It was in the exercise of the latter office, that he acquired some knowledge of the forms of legal business, and undertook to practice law in the courts, before any regular lawyer was settled in New Gloucester. His good common sense guided him in his practice. In technical law and legal principles and decisions, he was without any knowledge or skill. In 1791, being a member of the Legislature, he procured a term of the Court of Common Pleas to be held in New Gloucester, in January of each year, which continued until 1805. He quitted practice near the close of the last century, and moved to Portland; where his energies found more ample scope in commercial business, which he carried on largely and with success.

In 1810, he was chosen a representative to Congress from the Cumberland District, and supported earnestly the measures of Mr. Madison's administration. He voted for the war against the strong wishes and interests of his constituents, which rendered him very unpopular; and his return home from that session was greeted with loud manifestations of disapprobation. His place was supplied in the next Congress by George Bradbury.

In 1812, he was appointed an associate justice of the new Court of Common Pleas by Governor Gerry, and held the office until 1822, when the court was abolished. He died the same year.

He was twice married; his first wife was Miss Randall, by whom he had all his children. His daughter Elizabeth, born in New Gloucester in 1779, married Elias Thomas of Portland, and died in 1861, leaving a large family. His eldest son, William, was drowned in the Hudson River, in 1805. His second wife was the Widow Dafforne of Boston. At the time of her marriage, she had a daughter, Eliza, who became the wife of Nathan Kinsman, a successful lawyer in Portland, and the mother of John Dafforne Kinsman, who succeeded his father in the same profession in the same place. These persons are all dead.

Mr. Widgery is a striking example of what may be done by perseverance, untiring energy, and self-confidence. Without any intellectual cultivation, or any knowledge, except that acquired by experience, he placed himself along side of practical statesmen and learned jurists; and had his say, whatever it may have been, in the halls of legislation, and in courts of justice. His manners were rough, his language unrefined and ungrammatical, and his expressions confused. Yet he made his way through all these difficulties and embarrassments, never daunted, never abashed; and always hopeful, cheerful and jubilant. And, having enjoyed the distinctions of society, he died at a good old age, leaving a large estate, the fruit of industry and good management.

CHAPTER XV.

JOHN HOLMES—EZEKIEL WHITMAN—LEONARD MORSE—JOSIAH W. MITCHELL—JOHN P. LITTLE—BOHAN P. FIELD—ANDREW GREENWOOD—DANIEL P. UPTON—TEMPLE HOVEY—HENRY V. CHAMBERLAIN—EBENEZER BRADISH—SAMUEL DAGGETT—NUMBER OF LAWYERS: THEIR INCREASE, AND COURSE OF PROCEEDINGS IN COURT—LAWYERS IN PRACTICE IN 1800.

JOHN HOLMES. 1799—1843.

In 1799, two lawyers came into the State who were destined for many years to exercise a large influence in the civil as well as legal interests of this community. These were Ezekiel Whitman and John Holmes. They both originated in the Old Colony, Mr. Holmes in Kingston, and Mr. Whitman in East Bridgewater; and they both were educated at Brown University, from which one graduated in 1795, the other in 1796. I propose to speak of these two prominent men somewhat at length, and for Mr. Holmes I shall borrow largely from a biographical notice which I contributed, soon after his death, in 1843, to the Law Reporter, Vol. 6, p. 145.

Mr. Holmes was the second son of Malchiah Holmes, and was born at Kingston, Massachusetts, in March, 1773.

His early life was passed as a manufacturer in the extensive iron works of his father at that place. He was seen toiling at the furnace by a collegian, the temporary schoolmaster of the village, who, being attracted by his intelligence, advised his father to educate him. The hint was improved, and in December, 1792, at the age of nearly twenty, he took his first lessons in Cheever's Latin Accidence, at the town school. His friend, on leaving the school in the spring, commended young Holmes, who had made very rapid progress in his studies, to the instruction of Rev. Zephaniah Willis, the venerable minister of Kingston. He was admitted at Brown University one year in advance, in 1793, where he pursued his studies with great assiduity, and was a good scholar, although he labored under serious disadvantage, for want of early training. He enjoyed the friendship of his college companions by his good humor, his frank and amiable manners. The same fearlessness, the same easy and independent manner, characterized him there, as in the subsequent periods of his life. Among his classmates were Tristram Burgess of Rhode Island, Chief Justice Aldrich of Vermont, Dr. Benjamin Shurtleff of Boston, and Dr. Benjamin O. Simmons of South Carolina. He was graduated with a respectable appointment in 1796, and immediately entered upon his professional studies with Benjamin Whitman, who then resided at Hanover, and was in full and distinguished practice in the Old Colony. He was a diligent student, and fully bent on success in his profession.

On being admitted to the bar, in 1799, he resolved to seek his fortune in the eastern country, as affording to the enterprising and intelligent adventurer an eminent promise of success, and an ample field of professional labor. He established himself in September, 1799, at Alfred, in the county of York, then a district of the town of Sanford, and containing but about eight hundred and fifty inhabitants. It was not incorporated until 1808 ; still, it afforded a very favorable opportunity for a talented young man to rise in the profession. He was for several years the only lawyer in the neighborhood. The titles to land in that part of the country were in an imperfect and unsettled state ; the settlers had made their *pitches* upon vacant spots, in what was called the *Fluellen* or *Phillips* Grant, and made their improvements without a shadow of title: the proprietors had just begun to make an investigation of their rights. Mr. Holmes was employed by them for this purpose, and pursued the inquiry and the prosecution of the claims with great industry and success. Many actions were necessarily brought, and much and exasperated litigation was the consequence, which called forth great legal talent from Maine and Massachusetts, and settled some very important questions in the law of real estate. The statement of one of these cases, in which Mr. Dane of Beverly appeared as counsel, may be found in 7 Dane's Abridgement, 697. The discussion of the points in this case produced some little excitement between Chief Justice Parsons and the counsel, particularly with Mr. Dane, toward whom the judge expressed himself with some impatience, in regard to the plea of *not guilty* to a writ of right. These cases brought Mr. Holmes into extensive practice, and a familiar acquaintance with the law of real estate ; and his fees were not inconsiderable. The counsel upon the other side complained to him that he received all the emoluments, while they had to bear heavy burdens. At the time Mr. Holmes commenced practice, the Supreme Court was composed of Chief Justice Dana, and Justices Paine, Bradbury, Nathan Cushing, and Dawes, and was held at York once a year. The Common Pleas consisted of Nathaniel Wells, Edward Cutts, Jonas Clark, and Simon Frye, none of whom were educated as lawyers. There were three terms a year of this court, held at York, Waterboro', and Biddeford.

The courts in York, beside their own lawyers, were attended by the late Chief Justice Parker, Mr. Symmes, and Solicitor Davis of Portland, some New Hampshire lawyers, and occasionally by a professional gentleman from Massachusetts, and were made the occasion of a great deal of mirth and hilarity. The judges and the lawyers, on account of the badness of the roads, generally performed their circuits on horseback, and often met with poor fare and rough usage; but when they could not get a good dinner, they would contrive to have a good laugh, to which Judge Paine, Mr. Davis, and the late Judge George Thacher contributed no little of the Attic seasoning. The mail was also transported on horseback. It is related that a respectable lawyer, on one occasion, as he was passing through Saco woods, met the mail-carrier, and expecting a letter from Boston by the mail, which only came once or twice a week, he expressed to the post-rider his desire to obtain the letter. He took off his mail-bag without hesitation, poured the contents upon the ground, and they both went to work searching for the desired object. The letter having been found, the carrier quietly deposited the remaining budget in his bag, and pursued his way. This collection of lawyers, jurors, suitors, and witnesses filled up the small villages in which the courts were held, and the public houses could not afford comfortable accommodation for the persons that thronged them. It was quite a privilege, enjoyed by few, to obtain a separate bed, far more a separate chamber. These meetings were the occasion of much dissipation, in which many members of the bar were no ascetics. The gravity and dignity of the bar, in that day of the robe and the wig, were very apt to be left in the court room—they were seldom seen in the bar room. Mr. Holmes contributed his share to the amusement of his associates.

The number of lawyers in Maine, at the time of Mr.

Holmes's accession to the bar, was forty-five, of whom ten resided in the county of York, which then included Oxford, and was the most populous county in the district.[1] Those in York were the late Chief Justice Mellen and George Thacher in Biddeford; Cyrus King in Saco; Dudley Hubbard, Ebenezer Sullivan, and Edward P. Hayman in Berwick; Joseph Thomas and George W. Wallingford in Kennebunk; Judah Dana in Fryeburg; and Nicholas Emery in Parsonsfield. Beside these, the bar of Maine then contained the names of Chief Justice Parker, Justice Wilde, and Solicitor General Davis, afterwards of Massachusetts; Chief Justice Whitman, then of New Gloucester; William Symmes; Salmon Chase of Portland; and Silas Lee of Wiscasset, who was afterwards a member of Congress, and fourteen years United States Attorney for Maine. These all were distinguished in their profession, and most of them in public life.

Mr. Holmes was a good lawyer, but not of the first order. He handled the weapons of wit with more skill and effect than those of a severe logic, although he was not deficient in that prime quality of a sound jurist. The force of his argument was sometimes weakened, or at least appeared to be less close and stringent, by the propensity he had, and which he seemed not able to control, of mingling in his texture the threads of wit and anecdote. He was quick of perception, and seized readily upon a weak point of his adversary, which, by a great facility of language and infinite good humor, he turned to the best account. Whenever an opportunity occurred of exhibiting his opponent in a ridiculous position, no person could better avail himself of the occasion. An opportunity of this kind was furnished him in the discussion which took place in the Senate of the United States, on some subject connected with nullification.

---

[1] The population of York County was then thirty-four thousand; of Maine, one hundred and fifty-one thousand.

Mr. Tyler, we believe, alluding to the satirical remark of John Randolph, some years previous, which designated certain active politicians as partners, under the name of "James Madison, Felix Grundy, John Holmes, and the Devil," inquired, with a view to reproach Mr. Holmes, what had become of that celebrated firm. Mr. Holmes immediately sprung upon his feet, and said, "Mr. Speaker, I will tell the gentleman what has become of that firm: the first member is dead, the second has gone into retirement, and the last has gone to the Nullifiers, and is now electioneering among the gentleman's constituents! and thus the partnership is legally dissolved." The laugh produced on this occasion was wholly at the expense of Mr. Tyler.

In his discussions at the bar, Mr. Holmes often carried the exercise of this talent too far for good taste or ultimate benefit to his client. To raise a laugh at the expense of an opponent is not always to gain a cause: he was yet very successful with the jury, and a popular advocate, and became and continued for several years the leader of the York bar. Wit and humor were the characteristics of his mind, and he delighted in their display. An instance or two, at random, will exhibit this trait more perfectly. He was once assisting a client in the survey of a parcel of land, about which he was quarreling with his neighbor. Neither of the parties was of unimpeachable character. As they were passing through a portion of the disputed territory, they came to a swamp covered with bushes and almost impassable. One of the litigants said to Mr. Holmes, "This, Squire, is the Devil's hop-yard." "Ah!" said Mr. Holmes, "then I think the Devil must be dead, for I see his sons are quarreling for the *inheritance*." "Then you expect to prevail," said the opposing counsel, "as your client is the oldest heir." "It is not certain," said he, "my client, to be sure, is the *oldest*, but yours is the most *deserving*." Mr. Holmes was equally happy in the relation of anecdotes. The Rev. Mr. P., some years since, delivered a lecture at Alfred on the subject of *slavery*, and took for his text the words, "Remember them that are in bonds as bound with them." After he had finished his discourse, which was an able one, Mr. Holmes observed that, whatever might be justly said against the institution of slavery, he did not think the text ever had or was intended to have any application to the subject; it related to a very different affair. The application of it to domestic slavery reminded him of a clergyman who preached from this text, "And David took from the brook *three* smooth stones." "Now, my hearers," said the preacher, "by these words I intend to prove, explain, and illustrate the doctrine of the *Trinity*." "It was *five* smooth stones," said the deacon, in a low tone, very respectfully. "We will see," said the preacher, opening the book with some excitement, and read deliberately, "And David took from the brook *five* smooth stones." "Well, my hearers," said he, "I made a small mistake in the *fact*, but it makes not the slightest difference in the *argument*."

During a portion of the time of Mr. Holmes's practice, Joseph Bartlett also practiced at that bar. He was a graduate of Harvard, of the class of 1782, and settled first in Woburn, Massachusetts: he came to Saco in 1802. In some respects he resembled Mr. Holmes: he was a better scholar, and of a more polished wit: his manners were insinuating, and he possessed a peculiar sway over the minds of young men. In other respects he was far different from Mr. Holmes; he was treacherous to his friends, abandoned in his morals, and miserable in his end. Yet the early part of his career was brilliant and promising.

Mr. Bartlett, while he resided at Saco, had a libel suit against the publisher of the *Argus*, a democratic paper published at Portland, and another upon the jail bond, given by the defendant in this case, growing out of political questions. The latter case, which was a very severe one for the defendants, was argued by Solicitor Davis and Samuel Dexter, for the plaintiff, and by the famous Barnabas Bidwell and the late Judge Story of Massachusetts, for the defense; a report of it is contained in the Massachusetts Reports, volume 3, page 86. The former was conducted by Mr. Mellen, Mr. Emery, and Mr. Holmes for the plaintiff, and Cyrus King and Judge Wilde for the defendant. There was much irritation and sparring between the counsel: the case was closed by Judge Wilde for the defendant, in a clear, concise, and highly finished argument, which produced a deep sensation. Mr. Mellen was also very able in his closing argument for the plaintiff.

One of the principal competitors of Mr. Holmes at the bar and in politics, was Cyrus King, of Saco, a fine lawyer and an accomplished scholar; a man of ardent temperament, inflexible principle, and elevated moral character. Mr. Holmes frequently took advantage of his temper to gain advantages over him at the bar. By the coolness of his own temper, he often succeeded in this attempt.

Mr. Holmes was not content with the quiet pursuit of his professional duties, although he had an extensive and profitable business. "The gladsome light of jurisprudence" w as not brightand warm enough for him:—he loved law, but he loved politics more: he was ambitious, and like too many of the profession, he abandoned the embraces of the most noble of sciences for the strife of politics. How many thousands who have embarked their proud hopes and anxious expectations upon this wild and stormy sea, after a course of imposing but transient grandeur, have been swept away into entire forgetfulness, while the names of the upright judge and the learned jurist, the Hales, the Mansfields, the Parsons, and Marshalls, continue fresh and fragrant, as the benefactors of their race.

Mr. Holmes was of a sanguine temperament, and ambitious of distinction. He began life as a federalist of the old school, and was not backward in making his principles known and felt. He was elected by that party in 1802 and 1803 to the Legislature of Massachusetts, from Sanford and Alfred. But the federal policy, although it had the ascendency in Massachusetts, was not to the taste of the people of his town or county, nor, indeed, of the majority in Maine. He could not, therefore, succeed any more as the candidate of the party; still, he labored on in the cause with great ardor, hoping against hope, through the exciting periods of the embargoes and non-intercourse, when, finding there was no stemming the tide of democratic principles, he yielded to the storm like many of his cotemporaries, and trimmed his sails to the prevailing wind of popular favor.

In this connection, we cannot forbear presenting our readers with a specimen of Mr. Holmes's poetical talent. In 1810, a democratic caucus was held at Kennebunk for the selection of candidates. It was said by their opponents, that, disregarding the modern rule of total abstinence, they determined to try the efficacy of treating at the election. Mr. Holmes, with a good deal of tact, seized upon this topic, and published the effusion in six stanzas, from which we copy the first and last:

KENNEBUNK CAUCUS.

SONG.

"The York County *Demos* of late had a meeting:
The object was great, but the party was small.
The marshal had issued his circulars greeting,
To tag, rag, and bob tail to meet at his call.
He called for attention
While he made objection

To Gore's re-election,
  And wished they'd be *mum;*
But while he was stating
The cause of the meeting,
The caucus was prating,
  And calling for—*rum.*[1]

So, bribing the printer, and treating the voters,
  Was the plan they adopted the election to carry,
And ride, by the help of those tipsy supporters,
  Into office, by votes they had purchased for *Gerry.*
When all shouted applause,
To the Jacobin cause,
And declared, by the laws,
  They would never be dumb;
And most solemnly swore,
Than to re-elect *Gore,*
They had rather give more
  Than a hogshead of *rum.*"

The four other stanzas make pointed reference to the leading Democratic politicians of York County, such as Marshal Thornton, Judge Green, William Moody, Stephen Thacher, &c.

In the latter part of 1811, he became the advocate of the national administration, and the war measures of Mr. Madison. And immediately on the next election, he was returned a representative to the General Court of Massachusetts from Alfred. So high stood his reputation with his new friends, that he was their candidate for Speaker of the House, in opposition to the old incumbent, Timothy Bigelow. A large majority of the House were the political friends of Mr. Bigelow, and he was re-elected; but Mr. Holmes became an untiring assailant of the measures of the majority, and a vigorous partisan and active leader of the party which he had espoused. He was elected to the Senate of Massachu-

---

[1] "The historical election anecdote of the purchase of *rum* to carry on the elections in *York* County is well known."

setts in 1813, and continued a member of that body during the trials and excitements of the war, boldly sustaining the policy of the national government, and contending with unabated ardor against all the anti-war measures of Massachusetts. He was appointed Lieutenant Colonel in Col. Lane's Regiment, United States Army, in 1813, but declined the appointment.

Ths situation of Mr. Holmes in the Legislature was one which would have exceedingly embarrassed a man of ordinary firmness or less buoyancy of mind. The suddenness of his change of sentiment, and the zeal with which he advocated the cause to which he had devoted himself, became the subject of severe rebuke on the part of his former associates. The keen severity of Daniel A. White, the polished irony of Harrison Gray Otis, the caustic humor of Josiah Quincy and Judge Putnam, were not spared in the frequent and sharp encounters which the political heats of the day engendered. And it would be doing great iujustice to Mr. Holmes not to say, that he sustained himself with great ability in these trying and unequal contests. For wit he returned wit, and full measure; for argument, argument, although his dialectics were not of the most compact form; and on all occasions he preserved his coolness. He was a ready debater, never taken by surprise, and when argument was deficient or unavailing, he pressed into his service the auxiliaries of wit and satire.

In 1815, he was appointed by Mr. Madison, commissioner under the fourth article of the treaty of Ghent, to make division between the United States and Great Britain, of the islands in Passamaquoddy Bay. The next year he was elected a representative to Congress from York district to succeed Mr. King, and re-elected in 1818 without opposition, having received eleven hundred and six out of eleven hundred and eighty-two votes. This latter was a period when parties were in a transition state, and little excitement agitated the public mind. While he was discharging the duties of commissioner and member of Congress, he was actively engaged in effecting the separation of Maine from Massachusetts. He not only labored in this work, but he led in it, and as a leader he had to bear the blame of whatever measures of his party were injudicious or unjustifiable.

In the proceedings of the Brunswick convention, in 1816, which reported a constitution, on the assumption that the requisite majority of five-ninths had been obtained, he sustained a liberal share of abuse. He was not, however, the author of the political arithmetic which converted five-ninths of the aggregate majorities of the corporations into a majority of five-ninths of the legal voters of the district. He indeed signed the report of that committee as the chairman, and thus the paternity of that calculation was cast upon him. It is unnecessary to say that the plan did not succeed, the Legislature of Massachusetts not being inclinedto sanction so palpable a perversion of the plain import of language. The next attempt, however, at separation, succeeded; and a convention met at Portland, in October, 1819, composed of the most prominent and able men in Maine, to form a constitution of government. Mr. Holmes was appointed chairman of the committee which drafted the instrument, and took a conspicuous part in all the discussions which led to the adoption of the constitution under which the people of Maine now live.

In 1820, he was elected the first senator to Congress from the new State, and continued to hold that honorable station, by renewed election, until 1827. In 1828, he was again elected to the Senate, for the unexpired term of Judge Parris, who was appointed to the bench of the Supreme Court, in June, 1828. In 1833, his Congressional life ceased, and he returned, with all the freshness of youth, to the practice of the law, after an uninterrupted and most successful political career of over twenty-two years, in which there was not a year when he was not occupying some public station. In 1836 and 1837, he was elected a representative from Alfred to the Legislature of Maine, and, in 1841, he was appointed, by President Harrison, attorney of the United States, for the Maine district, in which office he died, July 7, 1843.

Few persons have had their ambition more fully gratified than Mr. Holmes. The road of public life was freely opened before him, and he appeared to have attained whatever in that direction he most desired. That he acquired a very exalted or enviable reputation cannot be awarded him: he may rather be considered a skillful partisan than an able statesman: he directed his energies to skirmishing and hanging upon the flanks of his political opponents, rather than striking out any great and permanently useful measures. His popularity at one time in Maine was very great, and he managed matters in his own way. In reviewing the life of such a man, we may perhaps derive a useful reflection upon the danger, not to say folly, of leaving the broad highway of an honorable and profitable profession, for the fitful and the exciting pursuits and the unsubstantial rewards of the mere politician. That Mr. Holmes had as much of popular favor and its fruits as falls to the lot of men, none will deny; that they furnished him the satisfaction and the rewards which he would have acquired in the quiet progress of his profession, we do not believe.

Whatever estimate may be formed of Mr. Holmes's public life, there is no diversity of opinion in regard to his private and domestic qualities. He was a kind husband, a tender and judicious parent, and a good neighbor. As a townsman, he was exceedingly vigilant in promoting the interests of his fellow citizens in the matters of education, internal improvements, and whatever related to their municipal interests. From the time he settled in Alfred, he never ceased his exertions until he procured all the courts of York County to be held in that place, which was finally accomplished in 1833. He also succeeded in having the route of a railroad from Portland to Dover laid out through his adopted town, but failed in raising the means to complete it.

Mr. Holmes was twice married: his first wife was Sally Brooks of Scituate, to whom he was united in September, 1800. By her he had all his children, two sons and two daughters. His eldest daughter married the Hon. Daniel Goodenow, Judge of the Supreme Court of Maine: she died a few years since. His second wife was the widow of James Swan, son of Col. James Swan of Boston, and the accomplished daughter of General Knox, to whom he was married in July, 1837. He moved the next year to her seat in Thomaston, the late residence of her father, where he continued the principal portion of the time, until his appointment as district attorney, when he divided his residence between Portland and Thomaston. He devoted that period of his life to the preparation of a digest of public and private law, which he published in 1840, under the name of the "Statesman," in one octavo volume. In this work he passes rapidly through the circuit of jurisprudence, contenting himself by presenting a succinct statement of general principles in constitutional and municipal law.

It is satisfactory, in closing this account of a man who has occupied, for many years, so large a space in public opinion, to be able to say that the last scenes of his life were calm and delightful—life's fitful fever was over: the pageantry had passed before him in all its gaudy drapery: his heart was weary of it, and sought that rest which only can be found in a close communion with its divine author. His intellect was clear to the last; his faith was unclouded; he

Ezekiel Whitman

At the age of 80 years

knew in whom he trusted, and exhausted nature surrendered up the spirit, without a murmur or a struggle, to the hand that gave it.

The United States District Court being in session, the morning after Mr. Holmes's death, Judge Emery, the only survivor of the York bar, when Mr. Holmes entered it, except Judge Dana of Fryeburg, communicated to the court, in a highly appropriate manner, the intelligence of the decease of the United States attorney. Judge Ware briefly replied, expressing his high sense of Mr. Holmes's merits, and his sympathy with the bar on the occasion, and observed that he was ready to unite with them, in paying the last tribute of respect to his memory. The court was immediately adjourned, and the bar then adopted appropriate resolutions, and attended his remains, the next day, to their final resting place. Appropriate services were performed in the High street church, which he attended, and he was buried under Masonic honors.

EZEKIEL WHITMAN. 1799—1822.

Ezekiel Whitman was born in East Bridgewater, Massachusetts, March 9, 1776. He was of the sixth generation of the descendants of John Whitman, who came to this country about the year 1635 from England, and settled in Weymouth, Massachusetts, where he died at an advanced age. His descent was through Thomas, the eldest son of John, who was born in England, and came over with his mother at the age of about twelve years, several years after his father's migration. In 1662, Thomas moved to Bridgewater, where he died in 1712, aged about eighty-three. Nicholas was the third son of Thomas; Josiah was the eighth son of Nicholas; and Josiah's third son, Josiah, was the father of Ezekiel, the subject of our memoir. The descendants of Thomas Whitman contain examples of remarkable longevity. His daughter Susannah, who married Benjamin Willis of Bridgewater, died at the age of ninety-eight; his grand-daughter Sarah was ninety-four; four grandsons averaged eighty-six years; one great-grand-daughter lived to be ninety-five; and one great-grandson, John of East Bridgewater, died in 1842, at the great age of one hundred and seven years; the ages of twelve great-grandchildren of Thomas amounted to one thousand and sixty-four years, giving an average of eighty-eight and two-thirds years; and four great-great-grandchildren are now living, of whom Chief Justice Whitman is one, and his sister, another, whose average age is eighty-four and one-half years. Judge Whitman's father, Josiah, died in 1777, a year after his birth, at the age of twenty-four years. His mother was Sarah, a daughter of Caleb Sturtevant of Halifax, Massachusetts, by Elizabeth Smith, a daughter of Ezekiel Smith of Hingham, from whom he derived his Christian name. She was a lineal descendant of Elder Robert Cushman of Plymouth. Judge Whitman is of the seventh generation from Elder Cushman, and in the same degree from Samuel Sturtevant of Plymouth in 1643, the ancestor of the families of that name. His mother was left poor, with two infant children, a son and daughter. And she did not survive to superintend the education of her children, nor to enjoy the prosperity and honor which her son achieved.

His life, thus begun in sorrow, was continued many years through a hard struggle with poverty. At the age of seven, the Rev. Levi Whitman of Wellfleet took charge of him, and gave him the rudiments of an education, and treated him with a kindness which he never forgot, and which he repaid to the venerable elder when in old age their circumstances were reversed. The children, also, of his uncle, he received into his family, and made provision for them. At the age of fourteen years he became uneasy at his state of dependence, and determined to go to sea; but his uncle resolutely opposed that mode of life, and persuaded him to pursue the preparatory studies for a liberal education. For this purpose he was placed with the Rev. Kilborn Whitman of Pembroke, who afterwards became a lawyer of considerable practice in Plymouth County.

He was, however, a wayward student, apt to learn and quick of discernment, but not very diligent in the routine methods of that day. His life had been so desultory that he had not formed habits of patient industry. But it was no great affair at that time to pass through the preliminary preparation for college. A little knowledge of Virgil and Cicero, in Latin, and of Luke and the Acts, of the Greek Testament, seem to have been sufficient in the classical department; so, after fifteen months' study, our young student, in 1791, offered himself at the door of Brown University for admission, and was freely received.

This college had been in operation twenty-six years. The first President, Dr. Manning, ceased from the presidency and life in 1791, and the next year was succeeded by the learned Dr. Maxcy, who had been professor of Divinity. He presided over the institution until 1802, when he entered upon the presidency of Union College in New York. The standard of education was at that time low in all our colleges, as was also the scale of expense, in comparison of both at the present day. The tuition at Brown University was six pounds lawful a year; the charge for board, sweeping room, and making the bed was six shillings eight pence a week; a load of wood, six shillings eight pence, and candles nine pence a pound. The cost of books for the whole college course, need, as a manuscript letter of a deceased scholar informs me, not exceed three pounds. The same letter observes, "The studying weeks are thirty-nine in a year, but if a scholar will study at home, he need not be here more than two-thirds of that. I think that twenty pounds per annum might largely defray all the necessary expenses, and that the scholar might keep school every winter to earn some part of that. Scholars are allowed to be gone a year or more at a time, only they don't rise while they are gone, if they can't pass examination with their class when they return." The letter referred to was written by Martin Parris, uncle of the late Governor Parris of Maine. Martin Parris was afterwards settled in the ministry at Marshfield. He graduated at Brown University in 1790; was born in Pembroke, and died in Marshfield, 1839, aged seventy-two.

The class into which Mr. Whitman entered, numbered twenty-six members, and was the largest which graduated at the college until 1802. During the vacation of his first year, and the winter following, he taught school in Marshfield. It was on one of these occasions that he practiced a joke upon the minister which had nearly cost him his situation. The Rev. Mr. Leonard was troubled with a painfully hesitating manner of delivery: at a particular time he was unusually beset with this infirmity over some word, on which our schoolmaster became impatient, and spoke in an audible whisper, "Spell it." A solemn pause threw young Whitman, then but sixteen years old, into confusion at his rashness, which was only relieved by a severe rebuke from the minister.

His funds being entirely exhausted, he was forced to leave college in his senior year, and he had to resort to school-keeping to recruit his means for completing his course: returning just previous to commencement, he was, after examination, admitted to his degree. A letter written to me some years ago by Mr. Whitman's classmate and a particular friend, the late Peleg Chandler, of New Gloucester, shows the hardships which young men in narrow circumstances were obliged to endure in order to obtain an education. Mr. Chandler had been pursuing his studies with the Rev. Mr. Briggs of Halifax: when the time approached for his examination, he says he turned his face toward Providence: "I traveled on with rather low spirits until I got into a village in the south part of Bridgewater, called Titicut. It was a monstrous hot day, the last of August, 1792. While musing along on my old Rosinante, I saw a person some fifty rods ahead. As he approached, I saw he was a young man with a large bundle tied up in a bandanna handkerchief hung over his back on a cane; he had on no coat, nor jacket or stock. He wore an old pair of nankeen breeches, and I think he had his stockings and shoes in one hand, suspended by his garters. When he got within two or three rods, he sat down under the shade of an oak. As I approached him, he saluted me by saying, 'I guess you are going to college, aint you? You had better get off and take comfort with me under this shade.' This man is now Chief Justice of Maine (1843), and this was the first time I ever saw or heard of him. We laid on the ground under this tree three or four hours. I told him who I was, and all about my difficulties, and my fears that I should not be able to enter college. He gave me words of courage, gave me the key to his room, for he had been there the freshman year, and we agreed to chum together." "Whitman was at that time sixteen, and I was almost nineteen. I found him an agreeable chum, and the class respected and loved him. He was in many things eccentric, but never vicious: he had a mind of his own, and always pursued that mind. He was slow of speech and motion; never went to morning prayers if he felt sleepy; got the monitor to excuse him three or four times, and me, when the roll was called, to speak for him. The monitor would put him down tardy sometimes, and then he would say that he started in season; this created a smile with the President, who knew how moderate his momentum was. He stood high with President Maxcy, as he invariably told the truth, let the consequence be what it would. I don't believe there was one in our class in whom the government had more confidence than in him. He hated the studies of Latin and Greek, and did not excel in them, but in all the other branches he stood high on the first half of the class."

This trait of truthfulness, exact and without prevarication or reservation, he carried through life, and left the impress of it on all his children. I may be permitted to add, from the same trusty and worthy correspondent, who died in 1847, some further traits in the character of this remarkable man. "Whilst a boy, he was one of the most agreeable companions I ever met with; as a man, he was generous and honorable and kind. He was obstinate in his own opinions, but his opinions were always, or nearly so, right. If roused by insult or abuse, the storm would break out, and time alone could calm the elements of his mind."

On taking his degree, Mr. Whitman's funds were at their lowest ebb. He was absolutely penniless, and various plans for immediate relief passed through his imagination: one of these was to go upon the stage. Powell, who was a familiar star sixty or seventy years ago, was playing then at Providence; and the vagary came into his mind to join his company. How many young men of genius and poverty in the old country have tried this unfortunate expedient! His friend Chandler, never truer, urged every argument to dissuade him from this course, and his own better judgment coming to the rescue, he abandoned the project, and also the one, almost as bad, of going to sea. He at last, after many struggles, came to the resolution of studying law, and immediately entered the office of Benjamin Whitman of Hanover, where he remained a short time, and then went to that of Nahum Mitchell of East Bridgewater. Nothing could have been more propitious. Mr. Mitchell was a good lawyer, a general scholar, and a man of most admirable qualities. He was elected a member of the Eighth Congress, was afterwards a judge of the Court of Common Pleas in Plymouth County, and held other places of distinction. Mr. Mitchell, finding in his student a young man of solid judgment, quick perceptions, and rare ability, confided to him many cases before magistrates and referees, in which he always acquitted himself in a manner to give his instructor not only satisfaction, but a sure token of future success.

He had acquired so good a character, while engaged in his legal preparation, that he was employed on an important mission into the far distant regions of the South-west. A gentleman of Bridgewater had purchased a quantity of Virginia land warrants, which that State sold with unbounded liberality at very low prices, the locations to be made in what is now the State of Kentucky. In consequence of these indiscriminate sales, the greatest possible confusion occurred in making locations and securing the titles. In some instances, the same land was covered by several surveys loosely and indefinitely made, so that no purchaser knew what was his own, unless he took and kept open and actual possession of it. Kentucky was separated from Virginia in 1790, and admitted to the Union in 1792. The purchaser of whom I am now speaking had procured a large quantity of land to be surveyed and located under his warrants, but died before the conflicts in regard to his rights were adjusted. Mr. Whitman was sent out, by his heirs, in 1796, to gather up the wrecks of the property, and close the settlement of the estate. He traversed the whole distance on horseback; spent the year in Kentucky, in accomplishing the object of his journey, and returned in the same manner through Cumberland Gap, Virginia, Maryland, &c. On his return he passed through Washington, and was there at the opening of the special session of Congress on the subject of the French violations of our neutrality. He was much impressed with the dignified and imposing appearance of the Senate, which contained Langdon, Ellsworth, Hillhouse, Aaron Burr, and Jefferson. He said that President Adams personally addressed the convention of the two houses in a very forcible, eloquent, and graceful manner, on the subject of our rela tions with France. He was dressed elegantly, in the style of high officials of the early day. It was while he was on this journey, that he passed through a village in which a court was holding its session. Desirous of seeing the forms of proceeding in that country, he tied his horse at the door, and stepped into the court room. He had not been long there before, a vacancy occurring in the jury, he was summoned as a talesman to supply the place. He prayed to be excused, as he was a traveler on a long journey, and could not conveniently be delayed. But the court would not excuse him, and he was obliged to take his seat. It was not long, however, before the jury were dismissed for a short time, when he, considering his detention unreasonable, availed himself of the opportunity, mounted his horse, and pursued his journey, leaving the court and the parties to manage the cause without his aid.

Mr. Whitman was admitted to the bar in Plymouth County in the spring of 1799, and determined to seek his fortune in Maine, to which territory his attention had been recently directed as a promising field of labor. If Josiah Quincy's sarcasm was true in regard to the Old Colony, Mr. Whitman was right in leaving it. Judge Mitchell observed to Mr. Quincy that "people lived to a great age in the Old Colony." Mr. Quincy said "he wondered that people there should want to live long, there was so little to live on, or live for." This was something like Daniel Webster's answer about New

Hampshire, "that it was a good State to go from." The population of Maine was then one hundred and fifty-one thousand, having in the preceding ten years increased over forty-seven per cent., of which twenty-five thousand was by immigration. Cumberland County then embraced a large part of the present county of Oxford, contained about thirty-seven thousand inhabitants, and had ten lawyers; viz., John Frothingham, Daniel Davis, Wm. Symmes, Salmon Chase, Isaac Parker, afterwards Chief Justice of Massachusetts, James D. Hopkins, George E. Vaughan, all of Portland; Peter O. Alden of Brunswick; and Samuel Thatcher of New Gloucester. The whole number of lawyers in the District of Maine at that time was thirty-seven or thirty-eight, among whom were George Thacher and Samuel S. Wilde, afterwards Judges of the Supreme Court of Massachusetts; Prentiss Mellen, late Chief Justice of Maine; Silas Lee and Jeremiah Bailey of Lincoln; James Bridge of Augusta; and William Wetmore and Job Nelson of Castine. In Massachusetts, the bar contained the names of men who had not only adorned the profession, but given glory to the country: James Sullivan, Harrison Gray Otis, John Lowell, John Q. Adams, Josiah Quincy, Fisher Ames, Theophilus Parsons, William Prescott, Nathan Dane, Charles Jackson, Samuel Dexter, Levi Lincoln, Caleb Strong, and Theodore Sedgwick. Why should we name more?

In April, 1799, Mr. Whitman pursued his solitary way on horseback, from the Old Colony into the wilds of Maine, the only comfortable mode of traveling at that time in this part of the country, on account of the condition of the roads. On his way to Turner, his place of destination, he stopped a few days to visit his classmate and chum, Chandler, where he obtained several engagements for the next court in Portland. He encountered a snow storm on the 7th of May, as he journeyed to Turner, and found there the ground covered with snow and good sleighing, which did not give him a favorable impression of the climate after residing in the comparatively genial one of Plymouth County. Few attornies, on entering practice, were better qualified for its duties than Mr. Whitman: he had been well instructed and disciplined in the profession, and taught to exercise and rely on his own powers. His whole apparatus of books to guide him in the intricacies of the law were that most happy and comprehensive work, Blackstone's Commentaries, a universal authority, and in every lawyer's hands; the Nisi Prius Digest of Mr. Espinasse, which had recently been published, embracing the substance of Justice Buller's work with additional cases; the Statutes of Massachusetts; and the four books of forms published by our worthy townsman, Samuel Freeman, styled "The Clerk's Assistant, "Probate Auxiliary," "Town Officer," and "Justice's Assistant." These books were indispensable to a young lawyer, and had a general circulation among the profession. Mr. Freeman had exercised, practically, nearly all the offices for which he had prepared his useful forms. He was a most remarkable man. He was constantly at work in the numerous offices he held, and in the preparation of books, from the time he came upon the stage, previous to the Revolution, to near the close of a very long life. He held the office of Clerk of the Court in Cumberland County forty-six years, and at the same time was Register of Probate twenty-eight years, and Judge of Probate sixteen years coincident with the clerkship. In 1776, he was also appointed Postmaster, which office he held twenty-nine years, and was all the time an active magistrate; for twenty-five years was one of the selectmen, and most of the time chairman; was several years President of the Maine Bank, the first in the State; a number of years President of the Board of Overseers of Bowdoin College, and its Treasurer, and a leading man in the principal benevolent institutions of the town, and forty-five years deacon of the church. It is fitting and proper that we should state that he discharged *all* these offices faithfully, promptly, and well.

Such was the humble apparatus with which our eminent lawyers began their career: no books of American reports had then been published in this country, unless we except Mr. Justice Washington's first volume of his Virginia Reports, 1798, and no elementary works except republications of a few English books. The principles of practice were unsettled, and the application of the common law had to be adapted to our new and varied and peculiar institutions. The first elementary book published by an American author was Judge Sullivan's History of Land Titles, in 1801. Coleman and Caines's Reports, New York, appeared in 1804; Day's in Connecticut the same year; and the first volume of the Massachusetts Reports not until 1805.

One consequence of this dearth of authorities was brevity in arguments and pleadings: they seldom exceeded half an hour either to the jury or the court, and were occupied in a close and direct application of the testimony and the law to the case without amplification and tedious repetition. Chief Justice Parsons was particularly rigid in repressing any discursive displays of rhetoric: he wished to confine the advocate to points bearing on the case. He did not need the enlightenment of an argument, and often prepared his opinions in advance of the argument. One of these occasions occurred in a case of Mr. Whitman's: after the opposing counsel had finished his argument, Judge Parsons called on Mr. Whitman to reply. As he arose, he whispered to his associate, " It is of no use to argue the case, for the old fellow has got his opinion already drawn up, in his pocket." And so it afterwards appeared. Judge Parsons was himself an example of the rule he wished to enforce. His son, in his memoirs of him, says, " His arguments were always very brief. I have heard it said that he *never* exceeded an hour. Usually he was much less than an hour; and I have heard, from good authority, that he was less than half an hour oftener than he was more." Of his manner, his son thus speaks: "There was no studied beginning nor ending, nothing of the manner, or the tricks, or the graces of the orator. His business was to persuade those twelve men of the truth of certain propositions; and he did his work in the most direct, the plainest, and the simplest way."

In September, 1799, Mr. Whitman moved to New Gloucester. Samuel Thacher had practiced about two years in that place: his removal to Warren, in September, 1799, left a vacancy for Mr. Whitman. When at Turner, he was the only lawyer in what now constitutes the county of Oxford, except Judah Dana at Fryeburg. On the 31st of October of that year, he married Hannah, a daughter of Cushing Mitchell of East Bridgewater, and sister of his legal instructor, Nahum Mitchell. She was born Feb. 2, 1781, and died March 28, 1852, depriving him of the society of an affectionate companion of more than fifty-two years of close and fond alliance. By her he had three children, a son and two daughters.

Mr. Whitman's business and reputation as a lawyer, and his popularity as a man, continued to increase, so as to encourage him to enter upon a larger field of operation. In January, 1807, he established himself in Portland, the largest town and the principal place of commercial business in the District. Here he entered upon a very extensive practice, enjoying the confidence of the community, and sharing the best business with Mellen, who, a few months before, moved to Portland from Biddeford, Longfellow, Orr, and Hopkins. Several bright luminaries of the Cumberland Bar had been withdrawn; Parker, appointed to the bench of the Supreme Court, and moved in 1806 to Boston; Chase, who had the largest practice of any lawyer at the Cumberland Bar, died August 10, 1806, at the age of forty-five; and Symmes, but a little later, January 7, 1807, at the same age. The removal of these distinguished men left large spaces to be filled; and those who came to supply them were fully equal to the demand. Mr. Symmes was not only a lawyer in the first class, but an ingenious advocate and a brilliant scholar. It was told us by one of his students, who says *he knew*, that "great confidence was felt in his opinions on all questions, and especially on legal questions. *I know* that the judges of the Supreme Court used to consult him on making up some of their opinions." His wit, too, and quickness of repartee, added to his agreeable qualities.

Theophilus Parsons received his appointment of Chief Justice, as successor to Chief Justice Dana, in the spring of 1806, and held his first term at York, in this State, in July, but did not, in that year, come further east. At the May term, 1807, he presided at Cumberland for the first time, having Sewall and Thacher his associates. He gave opinions in every case reported, but one, which were elaborate and exhaustive of the subject. The business of Portland in 1806 and 1807 was very large: many ships of heavy burden were owned here, and the town was rapidly increasing in substantial tokens of wealth and prosperity. Lawyers partook of the genial gale. The entries of civil actions for these two, and the two following years, were larger than they had ever been, or were ever after: in 1806, they were one thousand six hundred and seventy-eight; in 1807, two thousand four hundred and twenty-two; in 1808, two thousand two hundred and ninety-three; in 1809, one thousand eight hundred and fifty-five. In the latter part of 1807, numerous failures took place, in consequence of the restrictive policy of the government in the embargo and non-intercourse measures, and suits for the security of property by attachment were greatly multiplied. Mr. Whitman was accustomed to make over one hundred entries a term. At that time, there was no exemption of property from attachment, and it was often the case that the last bed was taken from under a man's family; and many of our merchants, who had lived in luxury, were, by a reversal of fortune, without their fault, deprived, by the execrable law of debtor and creditor, of the humblest articles of necessity.

Mr. Whitman's name appears in the first volume of Massachusetts Reports, 1805, although he had been at the bar but six years, and never ceased to be represented in those valuable records of jurisprudence, and those of Maine, on questions of high importance, until his final retirement from the bench in 1848. The quality of Mr. Whitman's mind was clear, solid, and practical; his judgment was cool and impartial, and his perceptions of the true and the false were quick and keen. He stripped every cause with which he was concerned of its shams and disguises, and held it up in the light of naked, simple truth.

In his arguments he presented the material points of the case with great clearness and force, without any rhetorical display, or any amplitude of language. It might be said of him, as Prof. Parsons said of his father's elocution, "His strength lay in his reasoning. But there was an actual, and, I rather think, a studied absence of all appearance of eloquence, and even of technical logic." "It was, as I believe, his opinion that eloquence is a great hindrance to a lawyer, and of no great value anywhere." In this latter judgment, however, we do not concur.

Mr. Whitman always had great weight with the jury from his calm, quiet, and candid manner. He never attempted to dazzle their minds or darken their understandings. He made no show: he treated the case simply, and talked with the jury as though he was a friend, endeavoring to satisfy them as to the real merits of the pending controversy, and thus disarmed prejudice, if any existed, and conciliated their favorable consideration of his positions. His tall and manly figure, his honest and intelligent countenance, gave great force and power to his addresses to the jury. His early associates at the bar were also men of fine personal appearance. Mellen and Chase, as well as himself and General Fessenden, were over six feet in height, Judge Thacher and Orr were quite or nearly that: Symmes, Davis, Judge Parker, and Longfellow were more compactly built, but were all men of easy, graceful manners, of readiness of speech and well-endowed minds. It would be very difficult to point to a bar of its size anywhere, which contained at that time more eminent lawyers or polished gentlemen.

Mr. Whitman was successfully employed in advocating claims of our merchants under the treaty with Spain of 1819, and attended upon the commissioners at Washington for that purpose. He also was engaged for clients under the convention with France of July, 1831, by which France appropriated twenty-five millions of francs to pay American claims. I have a printed argument of his in the case of Cobb and Clapp of Portland, presented to the Commissioners, occupying twenty-one octavo pages. The claim was for the seizure of the cargo of the ship North America at Antwerp, by the French. The argument was able and successful.

In 1832, he had printed for his own use and private distribution, an octavo pamphlet of forty-four pages, containing a genealogical account of the numerous descendants of John Whitman, their first American ancestor, prepared by him. This was a valuable contribution to that department of knowledge.

Mr. Whitman's large and important business drew around him numerous students, desirous of imbibing his spirit and instruction. Among these were Simon Greenleaf, long a popular advocate at the Cumberland bar, and professor in the law school at Cambridge; Josiah W. Mitchell of Freeport; Albion K. Parris, afterwards Representative and Senator in Congress, Governor of the State, and Judge of the Supreme Court of Maine; Levi Whitman of Norway; Levi Stowell of Paris; John Mussey, John P. Boyd, and Nathaniel Deering of Portland.

The appreciation in which Mr. Whitman was held in his county is shown in the effort of his friends to bring him into political life. In 1806, Gen. Peleg Wadsworth, who had represented the Cumberland District in Congress fourteen years, declined a re-election, and Mr. Whitman, then residing in New Gloucester, was selected as the candidate of the Federal party, against Major Daniel Ilsley, a staunch Democrat of the Jefferson school, and father of Isaac Ilsley, the collector of the port. Mr. Ilsley was elected by a small majority: the vote of Portland being for Mr. Whitman three hundred and seventeen, for Mr. Ilsley two hundred and twenty-six.

At the next election for member of Congress in 1808, political excitement ran high: the embargo, laid December, 1807, had been destructive of the commercial interests of this section of the country, and the administration had become unpopular. The same persons were candidates for Congress, and Mr. Whitman was elected by about three hundred majority: the vote in Portland, where both candidates then lived, stood, — for Whitman, five hundred and thirty-six, Ilsley, two hundred and twenty.

There were three sessions of Congress during this term; the first commenced May 22, 1809, and held thirty-six days. It was the first year of Mr. Madison's administration; and this extra session was called to make some modifications in the restrictive laws upon commerce, in consequence of Mr.

Erskine's unfortunate and unrecognized arrangement for a relaxation on the part of Great Britain, of her orders in council. The next session commenced on the 27th day of November, 1809, and continued to May 1, 1810. The third session commenced December 3, 1810, and continued to March 4, 1811. The subjects which occupied the attention of Congress principally during these sessions, were the rupture of negotiations with Great Britain, on the refusal of that power to carry into effect the arrangement entered into with her ambassader, Mr. Erskine; the quarrel with his successor, Mr. Jackson; the renewal of the non-intercourse system; and subjects connected with our commercial relations with the two great belligerent nations. The question of re-establishing the National Bank, removal of the seat of government to Philadelphia, and the admission of Louisiana to the Union, which was opposed by Josiah Quincy in an able and eloquent speech, and by other Federalists, — were also topics of excited discussion. Mr. Whitman acted with the Federal party, but does not appear to have taken an active part in debate. He, Josiah Quincy, and William Bailies of West Bridgewater are believed to be the only surviving members of that Congress. Mr. Quincy is over ninety, the other two in their eighty-seventh year, in 1862.

At the election for the Twelfth Congress, which took place in November, 1810, the contest was severe, between Mr. Whitman and William Widgery. The result was a precise equality, each party having one thousand six hundred and thirty-nine votes. Scattering, one hundred and fifty-one. In Portland, the residence of both candidates, the vote was,— Whitman, three hundred and forty-seven, Widgery, two hundred and forty-nine. On the next trial, in April, Mr. Widgery was elected by a small majority.

Mr. Whitman returned well pleased to his profession, for he had no taste for these protracted absences from a home to which he was devotedly attached: he preferred the quiet pursuits of private life to the agitations and acrimony of politics. During the seven years, 1811 to 1817, he devoted himself to the practice of law, having a very large business; the amount of which, and the estimation in which he was held by his fellow citizens, may be inferred from the fact that in this period he argued at the law terms in Cumberland County more than half of all the causes which were presented to the court.

In 1815 and 1816, he was a member of the Executive Council of Massachusetts; and in 1816, a member of the Convention held at Brunswick on the subject of the separation of Maine from Massachusetts,—which was to take place on the event that a majority of five-ninths of the votes of the people pronounced in favor of separation. This proportion was not obtained, the vote being eleven thousand nine hundred and twenty-seven in favor, and ten thousand five hundred and thirty-nine against separation; still, the Convention met, and by a peculiar construction put upon the language of the act, taking the majorities of the corporations instead of the individual votes, the Convention, by a small majority, decided that the requisite condition was complied with, and thereupon raised committees to draft a Constitution, and to apply for admission as a State. It is unnecessary to say that this erroneous and violent construction was wholly discountenanced and repudiated by Mr. Whitman; and a minority of the Convention signed a protest against the proceeding, and had it entered upon the records, declaring "the exercise of further powers to be usurpation." The Legislature of Massachusetts sustained the views of the minority, and resolved, "that the powers of the Brunswick Convention have ceased." William King was President of the Convention, having ninety-seven votes to eighty-five given to Mr. Whitman.

In 1816, Mr. Whitman was again elected Representative to Congress, and re-elected for the two following terms of 1819 and 1821, the Fifteenth to the Seventeenth Congresses.

His experience in political life, the soundness of his judgment, and the integrity of his character, gave him influence in the councils of the nation. The years in which he held his seat in Congress were among the most critical and important in our history. When he entered Congress for the second time, 1817, the nation was but twenty-seven years old. It had passed through severe trials: a sharp and expensive war with a powerful nation, preceded by harsh commercial restrictions, had just been honorably concluded: a new course of policy, growing out of the altered state of the country, had to be instituted. It will be sufficient, on this occasion, to indicate some of the prominent measures proposed. These were,— Internal Improvements, a Bankrupt Law, Revolutionary Pensions, Renewal of the Charter of the United States Bank, and a Tariff having reference to the important question of giving protection to our manufacturing industry, which had begun to extend over the middle and northeastern States, and was employing a large amount of capital. The Florida question, involving the occupation of that territory under the Spanish rule, and the attack of Gen. Jackson upon the Fortress of Pensacola in pursuit of the Seminole Indians; and the execution of the two Englishmen, Arbuthnot and Ambrister,—led to long and acrimonious discussions, in which Mr. Whitman took a conspicuous part. But the most exciting and important questions, which occupied much time in 1819 and 1820, grew out of the attempts to restrict slavery. The first important battle on this great issue was then fought. It commenced by the introduction of the proposition to amend the bill for the admission of Missouri, by inserting a clause prohibiting slavery in the State. Maine, in 1819, having applied for admission as a State, a bill for the purpose passed the House in the usual course. On reaching the Senate, it was amended by a clause admitting Missouri without restriction, which, after a most able and ardent debate, passed the Senate, February 15, 1820, — yeas, twenty-three; nays, twenty-one. Mr. Mellen of Portland, and Mr. Otis of Boston, the Senators from Massachusetts, strenuously opposed the unnatural connection. In the House, the vote on striking out the restriction from the Missouri bill was equally close, ninety to eighty-seven. Mr. Holmes and Mark L. Hill alone, from Maine, voted in the affirmative; Mr. Whitman and the other three representatives from Maine voted against removing the restriction, and Mr. Whitman spoke earnestly against it. Only twelve members from the Free States voted to strike out the restriction. The Southern vote was unanimous. Rufus King of New York, as Mr. Quincy observes in his Life of Adams, "delivered two of the most well-considered and powerful speeches that this Missouri question elicited." Mr. Adams in his Diary says, "I heard Mr. King on what is called the Missouri question. His manner was dignified, grave, earnest, but not rapid or vehement. He laid down the position of the natural liberty of man, and its incompatibility with slavery in any shape: he also questioned the constitutional right of the President and Senate to make the Louisiana treaty. The great slave-holders in the House gnawed their lips and clenched their fists as they heard him." Again, he says, "They call his speeches seditious and inflammatory." The result was produced by the adroitness of Mr. Clay, and some other prominent men, in proposing and enforcing the compromise line of thirty-six degrees and thirty minutes, which carried members from the Free States sufficient to adopt the measure. Mr. Adams on this result remarks, "In this instance the Slave States have clung together in one unbroken phalanx, and have been victorious by means of accomplices and deserters from the ranks of Freedom. Time only can show whether the contest may ever, with equal advantage, be renewed."

Mr. Whitman's opinion then was, that the North ought to have stood firm and united against sanctioning the introduction of slavery in Missouri; and has expressed his belief, that, had such been the case, the question which has been productive of so many evils, and such unmitigated calamity to the country, would have been successfully terminated. Mr. Whitman also took an active part in the discussions on the tariff bill: he advocated the reduction of the enormous duty of ten cents a gallon on molasses, but without effect; and moved successfully an amendment to reduce the duty on printed books from thirty-five to twenty per cent., *ad valorem*. He offered other amendments, and entered into the debate with earnestness and ability by the side of his friend, Nathaniel Silsbee, the able commercial member from Salem, Massachusetts. In 1818, he delivered an able speech of about an hour in length in favor of a bankrupt law, which failed by a vote, eighty-two to seventy. Although Mr. Whitman frequently spoke on important subjects, he was so careless of fame that he never took the trouble of preparing reports of his speeches for the press. On the exciting question growing out of the invasion of Florida by Gen. Jackson, I was informed by his colleague, the late Joseph Dane of Kennebunk, that Mr. Whitman made one of the speeches which that agitating measure drew forth, that he literally stormed the character of Jackson, and denounced the act as arbitrary, and a violation of neutral and national law. His friends urged him to prepare his remarks for the press, but he declined doing it.

On the 4th of February, 1822, the new State of Maine passed an act establishing a court of Common Pleas for the State, to consist of a chief justice and two associate justices. Gov. Parris constituted the court by the appointment of Mr. Whitman chief justice, and Samuel E. Smith, afterwards Governor of the State, and David Perham of Penobscot County, associate justices. Mr. Whitman, in consequence of this appointment, resigned his seat in Congress, and retired from political life. He continued to discharge the duties of principal judge in the Common Pleas with great fidelity and ability, with unimpeached integrity, and to the public approbation, until December, 1841, when he was appointed chief justice of the Supreme Court, as successor to Chief Justice Weston.

At the head of the highest judicial tribunal of the State, Chief Justice Whitman devoted himself with untiring diligence, and undiminished powers of mind, to the arduous duties of the office for a period of nearly seven years. He resigned the office in October, 1848, at the age of nearly seventy-three, while yet in vigor and unimpaired intellectual strength, the result of a uniform system of temperate habits, self-restraint, and moderation of life. He had held the office of judge twenty-six and a half years, and his retirement from the bench was regarded as a public misfortune.

No man ever presided in a court of justice with a sounder judgment, with more calm self-possession and dignity of deportment. Every party which appeared in his court was allowed full opportunity to exhibit his case; but he always felt it his duty to let the jury understand clearly and distinctly what were his views on the evidence submitted, which he fully presented to them. He endeavored, in the conducting of cases before him, to confine the counsel to the true points in issue; and when these were unsupported by testimony, he would so rule as to abridge the labor of parties, save the time of the court, and promote the cause of justice. Sophistry, and fraud, and cunning shifts, found no encouragement and no shelter under his administration;

for his own mind was free from all guile, or equivocation, or pretension. Although naturally of a very ardent, and perhaps excitable temperament, he had early acquired a complete control over himself; and his deportment upon the bench was calm, patient, and imperturbable, except when attempts were made to practice collusion, deception, or fraud, when his latent feeling would manifest itself in a manner not to be misunderstood.

The judicial opinions of Chief Justice Whitman are contained in nine volumes of the Maine Reports, from the twenty-first to the twenty-ninth, inclusive, reported by Mr. John Shepley. They are characterized by great simplicity and plainness of language, and directness of application to the real points in issue. They are remarkably free from fine-spun verbosity, or attempts at ornamentation. There is no mistaking the law which it is the design of the court to establish. In a note to decisions in the Supreme Court of Maine, published in the Law Reporter, 1848, volume eleven, page seventy-two, it is said, "It was with melancholy interest that the Bar remembered that this was the last law term which the learned and venerable Chief Justice would hold in the county. Having presided in this court and the Court of Common Pleas for twenty-six years, with a dignity and impartiality rarely equaled, he will this year, by the expiration of his Constitutional term, retire from the bench. The lessons of sound juridical knowledge, clear, practical wisdom, and impartial justice, which have so long flowed from his lips, giving force to truth and confidence to virtue, will never again be heard." As the expression of cotemporaneous opinion may be considered the fairest exponent of the estimation in which Judge Whitman was held by the community in which the best part of his life was spent, we again offer the testimonial of the Law Reporter of January, 1849, in an article on "Judicial Changes in Maine." The writer says, "Judge Whitman is nearly the last of the old-school lawyers among us; and he retains more of the plainness and simplicity which we associate with the earlier time than any we are acquainted with. Born in the year in which our independence was declared, he is a connecting link between the present and the Revolutionary age, and presents an admirable specimen of the union of the two. No judge in our day has presided in the courts with more calm dignity, more independence, firmness, and integrity, than Judge Whitman. He commanded on the bench universal respect; no restlessness or impetuosity disturbed the uniform current of his deportment. As deep waters flow calmly and strongly, without ripple or commotion, so the vigorous and self-poised mind conducts its operations without noise or turbulence."

These testimonials indicate the public favor which waited on his judicial life. We believe they were well deserved and uniform during the whole period. And yet he was no less popular as a man. Without any of the arts which are practiced by those who seek attention and applause in the community, he was attended by both. An eccentric lawyer in Windham in his county, well remembered at our bar, once said to him, "How is it, Whitman, that you contrive to make yourself so popular, when you go along, taking no notice of anybody; while I get no popularity, although I bow to everybody?" This was a peculiarity of Judge Whitman, that in passing through the streets he would scarcely recognize his acquaintances, and had none of that address which wins so many sunshine friends. His was the popularity which Lord Mansfield, in his great speech, said he desired, and which he admirably described as "that which follows, not that which is run after — that popularity which, sooner or later, never fails to do justice to the pursuit of noble ends by noble means."

Without pretension or courtly arts of any kind, he was

always gentle, affectionate, and simple in his manners and conversation, never thrusting himself into notice on any occasion, but always sustaining himself when pressed, and coming up to any required emergency. He was willing to wait for that approbation which surely rewards the efforts of an honorable and useful life.

He read much, but was never fond of writing. The only work he ever prepared for the press was a genealogical account of the "Descendants of John Whitman," his ancestor, and the first immigrant of the name to this country, 1635. This was printed in a pamphlet of forty-four pages, with biographical sketches, for private distribution.

On retiring from the bench, Judge Whitman engaged in those quiet and peaceful pursuits which became his age and his unambitious habits. Study, and gentle labor in his garden, sufficient to keep up the tone and vigor of his constitution, gave repose and serenity to his mind. In March, 1852, occurred one of the severest afflictions which had ever befallen him, the sudden death of his wife, who was struck with paralysis, and died in a few hours. He had lived with her in kind and affectionate companionship near fifty-three years. She had brought up her three children, all of whom were born within five and a half years of her marriage, and who survived her. She had passed with him through privations and trials to scenes of independence and comfort, and had made for him a home of unalloyed domestic happiness. Her death made that home desolate, and, not long after, yearning for the land of his birth and early life, he removed in October, 1852, to East Bridgewater, his native place, to repose and find relief in the associations of his early years. There he still lives, tranquil and serene, remarkably exempt from the sharp trials of old age, waiting for the summons which comes inevitably to all, to appear at the tribunal of the final judge.

"Rectius occupat
Nomen beati, qui Deorum
Muneribus sapienter uti."

LEONARD MORSE. 1799—1815. JOSIAH W. MITCHELL.

The same year, 1799, which gave to our State Chief Justice Whitman at New Gloucester, John Holmes at Alfred,— the first lawyer in that place,— witnessed also the coming of Andrew Greenwood to Bath, John Park Little to Gorham, Bohan P. Field to North Yarmouth, and Leonard Morse to Freeport, being the first persons who established themselves in the profession at those places. Three of them graduated at Brown University; viz., Little in 1794, Whitman in 1795, and Holmes in 1796; Field, at Dartmouth, in 1795.

Leonard Morse was a graduate of Harvard in 1796, with Dr. Woods of the Andover Institution, John Pickering, and Dr. Jackson of Boston. He was born and educated at Cambridge, and established himself in Freeport in 1799. He remained there until 1815, pursuing the ordinary duties of the profession, without arriving at any distinction as a lawyer or an advocate. His habits had previously become so bad that business left him. He died in 1823, leaving a family. His widow married a second husband, Simonton, and is living. She was a Porter of Freeport.

He was succeeded in the profession there by Josiah W. Mitchell, who was the son of Jacob Mitchell, and born in East Bridgewater, Massachusetts, in 1785. He was not liberally educated, but pursued his legal studies with Judge Ezekiel Whitman, first in New Gloucester and then in Portland, and was admitted to the bar of Cumberland County in 1807. He had an extensive business in Freeport and the neighboring towns, and was a sound lawyer and good advocate. He died in December, 1852, suddenly, leaving a wife and a large family of children. He was twice married, first to Sally, a daughter of Oakes Angier, an able lawyer in West Bridgewater, by whom he had one son and two daughters. His second wife was the widow of Elisha P. Cutler, the eloquent lawyer of North Yarmouth, of whom we speak in another place. By her he had three sons and two daughters. Six of his children and his widow still survive. His mother was also the mother of Chief Justice Ezekiel Whitman. He represented the town of Freeport in the General Court of Massachusetts four years; viz., 1812, 1816, 1817, and 1818. He was a Federalist, and sustained with ability the policy of that party. He also represented his town, subsequently, in the Legislature of Maine.

JOHN PARK LITTLE. 1799—1809.

Mr. Little was the son of John Little of Littleton, Massachusetts, where he was born. His mother's maiden name was Park, from whom he derived a portion of his own. His father cultivated a large farm, on which his son was brought up, until he left the occupation for one more congenial to his taste. He graduated at Brown University in 1794: after which he pursued his legal studies in the office of Timothy Bigelow at Groton, who was the legal instructor of several prominent lawyers in Maine, such as Samuel Thatcher and Thomas Rice. Probably Mr. Little had charge, as some other of Mr. Bigelow's students had, of the Groton Academy. Mr. Little was admitted to practice in Massachusetts in 1799, and immediately came to Gorham. He was the first, and for several years the only lawyer in the town. So great was the opposition to the settlement of a lawyer in Gorham, that the people met after church, on Sunday, in the meeting-house, and voted almost unanimously against Mr. Little's settling there. But he went, notwithstanding, and proved one of the best citizens who ever settled in Gorham; a man of great worth, very popular, and a pillar in the church. The same opposition existed to his successor, Col. Whittemore, who also, ultimately, became popular. He was a native of Gorham.

We learn from Mr. Hopkins, who was his contemporary, that "he was industrious, and attentive to the duties of his profession. He had an extensive practice, and enjoyed the full confidence of his clients and his friends. He was not so much distinguished as a lawyer or an advocate, as for his private worth. He was a man of strict integrity, and his moral and social virtues rendered his death a source of grief to an extensive circle of acquaintances and friends, and a loss to the community."

Mr. Little married Mary Jackson Prescott, daughter of Judge Prescott of Groton, by whom he had one son, born in March, 1808, who survived his father but one year. Mr. Little died March 26, 1809, leaving a character without reproach. His widow married, for a second husband, the honorable and excellent Lathrop Lewis, and still survives, in 1862, in the eighty-eighth year of her age. She had three children by Mr. Lewis, who are all dead. She is erect and vigorous, walking regularly to church, and enjoys excellent health.

BOHAN PRENTISS FIELD. 1799—1843.

Bohan P. Field was born in Gill, Massachusetts, April 23, 1774, and was educated at Dartmouth College, from which he took his degree, in 1795, with the reputation of good scholarship, and a taste for classical studies, which he retained through life. He pursued his legal studies under the care of the Hon. Samuel Dana of Amherst, New Hampshire, afterwards a distinguished judge of that State. On being admitted to the bar in New Hampshire, he came to North Yarmouth, in this State, in 1799, and was the first lawyer who took up his residence in that place. The next year, 1800, he moved to Belfast, and became the pioneer of the profession in that thriving town. Belfast is in the Waldo Patent, and was then part of the county of Hancock. It was incorporated in 1773, and contained, in 1800, but six hundred and seventy-four inhabitants: it now contains, by the census of 1860, five thousand five hundred and twenty inhabitants. Mr. Field lived through the period of its growth from its humble beginning, forty-three years, and beheld it a flourishing commercial city, having contributed, by his enterprise, good judgment, and active exertions, to promote all the interests of his adopted town.

On the organization of the county of Waldo, in 1827, Mr. Field was appointed chief justice of the Court of Sessions for the county by Gov. Lincoln, although they were on opposite sides in politics; and continued, for a term of ten years, to discharge the duties of that office with industry, and to the satisfaction of the people of the county.

He was a well-read lawyer, and his opinions were regarded as of good authority, and entitled to much weight. He rarely, however, appeared as an advocate, but when he found it necessary or expedient to address the jury, he did it with force and clearness, without any display of rhetoric, arguing for the cause and not for outside effect. He was valued, in the community where he lived, most for his general intelligence, his integrity of character, and the soundness of his judgment. The following tribute to his memory is from the pen of Mr. Williamson of Belfast: in speaking of him as a magistrate and referee, in which capacity he was often employed, he says, "No man entered on the investigation of the rights of parties freer from passion or prejudice, and no one exercised a sounder judgment. Hence, his decisions were uniformly correct and satisfactory. Such was his known integrity of character and singleness of purpose, that he received a thousand unsought tokens of public favor and confidence. Few men ever died more highly respected and esteemed by all who knew him."

Mr. Field died March 13, 1843, aged sixty-nine.

ANDREW GREENWOOD. 1799—1816.

An ancestor of Mr. Greenwood, in the direct line, lived at Norwich, England, in the time of Charles I., and tradition assigns to him the honorable posts of lieutenant and chaplain in Cromwell's army. Nathaniel, the son of this Myles Greenwood, was born in England in 1631, and, before Cromwell had an army, or thought of power, came to this country young, married Mary Allen, daughter of Samuel Allen of Braintree, and died in 1684. We have an account of three sons left by him, viz, Samuel, Isaac, and Nathaniel. Samuel was the father of Isaac Greenwood, Hollis Professor of Mathematics in Harvard College from 1727 to 1738, grandfather of John Greenwood, who lived in Portland before the Revolution, and great-grandfather of the Rev. Francis William P. Greenwood, late minister of the Stone Chapel in Boston. From Nathaniel, another of the three sons of the first American Nathaniel, came Andrew Greenwood, the subject of this notice. The second Nathaniel was twice married, first to Elizabeth Venteman, by whom he had seven children. The youngest was Miles, the father of Andrew, who became a wealthy East India merchant in Salem; he owned much shipping and some privateers in the Revolution, one of which he commanded. He afterwards met with disasters by the loss of vessels and cargoes; and, being reduced in his circumstances, he became a clerk in the Old Massachusetts Bank in Boston, and died in that service. By his first wife, Miss Hale of Medford, he had several children. The eldest, Miles, born in Salem, 1769, died in Cincinnati, in 1831, and was the father of the present Miles of that city, the largest iron manufacturer of Ohio. The second son, Andrew, the fifth in the line of descent from Myles, the Cromwellian chaplain, became the lawyer in Maine.

Mr. Greenwood was born in Salem, in 1776, and was educated at the Dummer Academy in Byfield, under charge of the celebrated Master Moody, by whom he was fitted for college, expecting to be offered at Harvard, where six of his family had been educated, from 1685 to 1739. But the reverse in his father's fortune turned the tide against him, and he was obliged to give up the further pursuit of his classical studies. While at the academy he had made good use of his opportunities, and letters are in existence, from Master Moody, speaking in flattering terms of his proficiency, and of his being fully qualified to enter college.

Disappointed in his hopes of a public education, he did not relinquish his plan of life; but, returning to Salem, he at once commenced the study of law, and pursued it through the regular term, when, being admitted to the bar, he proceeded to Charleston, South Carolina, where he made many friends; but, his health failing, he undertook a voyage to the West Indies, to restore his energies, whence he returned to Salem. Soon after, he came to Maine and established himself at Bath, the first lawyer who occupied that field. Bath was incorporated in 1781, and in 1800 contained a population of one thousand two hundred and twenty-five, which has been continually increasing to the present day. It more than doubled in the ten years following 1800.

Among this enterprising people, having no lawyer nearer, on one side, than Wiscasset, and Topsham on the other, Mr. Greenwood went, well furnished with natural gifts and acquired knowledge, to adorn the profession, and gain distinction for himself.

Soon after he was seated here, a competitor entered on the same field, John Winslow, son of Dr. Winslow of Marshfield, educated at Brown University, from which he graduated in 1795. He established himself at Bath in 1800, having previously practiced in Northborough, Massachusetts. Mr. Greenwood, either thinking that the place did not offer sufficient business for two lawyers, or desiring a larger scope, went to Portland the same year to try his fortunes there. Here he remained about two years, when he returned to Bath in the latter part of 1802 or early in 1803. Winslow in turn took his departure for Louisiana, just then become a territory of the United States, where he entered into wild and ruinous speculations, which crushed the fortunes of his father and other friends, who had become involved with him. He died, a victim to the climate, at an early age.

Mr. Greenwood earnestly engaged in his profession, which his age, experience, and ability enabled him to do with success. He was not only a good lawyer, but an eloquent advocate: by his ready wit, his easy manners, and graceful utterance, he swayed an audience at his will to laughter or to tears. In an argument to a court or a jury, his strong memory gave him great facility of illustration, and the application of authorities to the points in issue. It is said that he knew Blackstone's Commentaries almost by heart, and was constantly referred to by members of the bar for facts and dates.

In addition to the power which these qualities gave him, he extended his influence by his rare conversational talents, by which his society was courted, and by which he made himself a most agreeable companion. But it may well be doubted whether these social qualities contributed to advance him in his profession, or to give him an elevated position at the bar. A lawyer can become eminently distinguished only by an abnegation of those agreeable attributes which grace the saloon or which make a man the coveted guest at the dinner table. There are undoubtedly exceptions to this rule, and we can readily recall the names of Chief Justice Parsons, Solicitor General Davis, Daniel Webster, and Judge Story as equally great and happy in the forum and at the social board.

Mr. Greenwood's success at the bar was made manifest by two beautiful houses which he built in Bath, one occupied by Colonel Robinson, the other by himself during his life, and now, I believe, by the Hon. Freeman Clarke. His taste in architecture was not confined to his own buildings, but displayed itself in the structures of other persons who sought his advice, and in some public buildings. His influence was felt in the erection of a church for Dr. William Jenks, his pastor, now the venerable antiquarian in Boston.

In 1809, Mr. Greenwood received from Bowdoin College the honorary degree of A. M., which was a proper tribute to his literary and classical attainments. In 1800, he had delivered a eulogy on the death of Washington at Bath, and had shown himself on other occasions to be possessed of a highly cultivated mind. Frederick Allen, an early contemporary at the Lincoln Bar, says, "Mr. Greenwood lived in Bath when I first knew him: he had a very good practice, and was considered one of the most prominent and successful lawyers of that place."

In 1813 and 1814, he represented the town of Bath in the General Court. At the first term, an animated debate took place on the answer to the Governor's speech. It was then the practice in Massachusetts and some other States, as well as in Congress, and as it now is in England, for each branch of the Legislature to prepare an address responsive to the suggestions of the chief magistrate's speech. This was in approval or reprobation, as the views of the speech suited the majority. On the present occasion, the Democratic minority in each house entertained a bitter hostility toward Governor Strong, in consequence of his opposition to the war and Mr. Madison's administration. Mr. Otis reported the answer in the house, which, of course, approved of Governor Strong's policy, and a very animated debate took place, in which the leading men on both sides engaged, among whom were the late Chief Justice Shaw, General Fessenden, then of New Gloucester, and Mr. Otis. Mr. Greenwood being a warm Federalist and a hearty supporter of Governor Strong, advocated the sentiments of the address with great zeal and eloquence: the newspapers of the day remark that his speech "was replete with spirit and independence." It was while he was a member that the subject of the famed "Hartford Convention" was introduced, and the measure adopted and carried through, under a tremendous fire from the opposition ranks. Mr. Greenwood, of course, bore his part in the encounter with spirit and success, aided by other Federal members from Maine, as General Fessenden of New Gloucester, Jeremiah Bailey of Wiscasset, Samuel Thatcher of Warren, Isaac Adams and George Bradbury of Portland. In 1814, Stephen Longfellow was on the Portland delegation, instead of George Bradbury, who was sent to Congress. Probably there was never a brighter display of forensic ability in the General Court than during the three years of the war with England. Bigelow was Speaker of the House, John Phillips, President of the Senate; among the members were Otis, Daniel A. White, Samuel Dana, Erastus Foote, in the Senate; the late Judges Jackson and Shaw, James Savage, the Pickmans, and John Pickering of Salem,

John Holmes, General Fessenden, Josiah W. Mitchell, Thatcher, Calvin Selden, Wallingford, and other prominent men, in the House.

In 1809, Mr. Greenwood married Ann Harrod of Newburyport, who, with two daughters, survived him. One of the daughters, Sarah Miles, married the Hon. George Lunt of Massachusetts, and died in 1858 ; the other married first, Hayward Pierce of Bangor, and second, the gallant General Buford of Illinois, who distinguished himself at Island No. 10, and has performed other services in the war. She and her mother are now living in Illinois.

Mr. Greenwood died in Bath, in the house built by him and afterwards owned and occupied by the Hon. Freeman Clarke, November 15, 1816. The following extract from a letter written by his daughter, Mrs. Buford, will be interesting in this connection : "In a visit at Bath a few years ago, I was surprised to find my father's memory still fresh and green in the hearts of his friends. I was carried to the church he did so much to erect, — Dr. Jenks's. The two fine houses he built,—one occupied then by Colonel Robinson, and the other where he lived and died, occupied by Mr. Freeman Clarke,—both show a fine taste and a true love of proportion in architecture. Judge Wilde of Boston has often spoken to me of his eloquence, and his power over any audience he addressed, — also of his conversational powers and ready wit."

DANIEL PUTNAM UPTON. 1800—1805.

Among the young men of talents and promise who came into Maine, near the close of the last century, was Daniel Putnam Upton, who established himself, the first lawyer, in Eastport, the frontier town of the State and the United

States, in 1800. Mr. Upton was descended from John Upton, who was a blacksmith in Salem Village, now Danvers, as early as 1658: from which place he moved to Reading, Massachusetts, where he died in 1699. He had three sons, William, Caleb, and Samuel, from the latter of whom, the subject of this notice descended, being in the fifth degree from the first American ancestor. Amos, the son of Samuel, who was born in 1716 and died October 6, 1780, a man of great energy and stern Puritan principles, was his grandfather; and Benjamin, the fourth of the seven children of Amos, was his father. Down to 1810, there was no family in New England by the name of *Upton*, but the descendants of *John*, through his three sons above named. The mother of Daniel P. was Rebecca, a daughter of Deacon Daniel Putnam, a refined and cultivated woman, who died in 1785, at the age of thirty-four, too early to leave the full impress of her character upon her young family of five children, of whom Daniel was the second, and then but eleven years old. Mr. George B. Upton of Boston, the son of Daniel, made the following striking statement to me: he said, "I remember to have seen my grandfather's mother: she lived to be ninety-nine years old. She told me that she had seen and talked with people who were here prior to 1650." This seems to be bringing the foundations of our country very near to us. Mr. Upton also gives me another anecdote of historical interest connected with the family, taken from the Massachusetts records: "December 21, 1717, William and Samuel Upton liberate Thomas, who had faithfully served their father, John Upton of Reading; and give security to the treasury that they will meet all charges which may come against said black man."

Daniel P. Upton was born in Reading, August 12, 1774; he took his first degree at Harvard College in the class of 1797. This was a marked class, containing the memorable names of Horace Binney, William Jenks, Chief Justice William M. Richardson, Prof. Asahel Stearns, Dr. John C. Warren, and Daniel Appleton White. Of this class of fifty-four persons, who left the halls of the university sixty-five years ago, five survive, in 1862; among whom are Binney and Dr. Jenks. On leaving college, Mr. Upton pursued the study of law, and part of the time with Phineas Bruce of Machias, who was then the only lawyer in Washington County. Machias had a population of less than one thousand, and the whole county less than four thousand. What inducements turned Mr. Upton's attention to that remote and ungenial region, we are not informed. Machias was the shire-town of the county, and the Common Pleas held one term a year there; the Supreme Court going no farther east than Wiscasset. But there was some good society in the place: in addition to Mr. Bruce's family, were those of Sheriff John Cooper, of George Stillman, and Judges Jones and Avery.

Mr. Upton was admitted to the bar of the Common Pleas in Machias at the August term, 1800. The certificate of Mr. Bruce, as to the qualifications of his student, according to the custom of that day, bears date July 23, 1800. On being admitted to the bar, he selected Eastport, the most eastern part of the State, in which to commence the practice of his profession. That town had a population of only five hundred and sixty, and then included what is now Lubec. It had communication with outside civilized society, almost wholly by water, as a dense and continuous forest cut it off from other parts of the State. The town is the smallest in territory in the State, is situated upon an island, and contains but one thousand nine hundred and ten acres. The road from there to Machias, the shire-town in the county, was not laid out until 1806; and Jonathan D. Weston, the successor of Mr. Upton in the practice there, in his interesting account of Eastport, says, that he was the first person who went the whole distance between those towns by land, which was in August, 1806. He also says that the first two-story house was built there in 1802: this was two years after Mr. Upton moved to it, and there were but two in the town until 1805.

The encouragement for a professional man, and the stimlant to the literary tastes and pursuits of a scholar, accustomed to the refinements of the society existing in the neighborhood of Boston, Cambridge, and Salem, must have been, on this frontier post, of the most humble character. Only one court a year was held in the county, and that at a considerable distance; so that he had rare opportunities to meet his professional brethren: it is not therefore surprising that his spirits and health failed, under the adverse circumstances in which his fortunes were cast. He was admitted to the Supreme Court, held at Castine, on the fourth Tuesday of June, 1803, a term of this court having been granted to Hancock County in 1801. He was commissioned as a justice of the peace, May 10, 1804. But he did not long remain at his post after this last appointment. The next year he returned to Reading, his native place, where he died December 31, 1805. Mr. Williamson, the historian of Maine, in a manuscript notice of him, says, "He had talents to render him distinguished, had he the industry requisite to put them in vigorous operation; but he had no competitor in his profession near him to awaken and excite his emulation. Yet he was a very accurate lawyer." His early death deprived the profession of a member, who, under more favorable auspices, would have been its ornament and a valuable acquisition to the State. Mr. Upton was a man of good personal appearance, of easy address and manly character. His widow never ceased to speak of him with the tenderest affection, and to the end of her long life, with tears. This excellent woman was Hannah Bruce, sister of Phineas Bruce, and daughter of George Bruce of Mendon, where she was born December 27, 1768. She survived her husband more than fifty years. She is said to have been a woman of rare intellectual endowments, gifted with uncommon conversational powers, and of a cheerful, happy temperament. Her mind was well cultivated, and her retentive memory, stored by careful reading and by an experience extending far back to the scenes of the Revolution, rendered her a most agreeable companion.

By her, Mr. Upton had two children, who survived him. One, bearing his own name, Daniel Putnam, was a successful ship-master, having by his merit risen early to the command of a ship, and in this capacity was twenty years in the service of Enoch Train of Boston, commanding his packet-ships, of one of which, the Washington Irving, he was captain when he died, at the age of forty-six, May 2, 1849. He was not married. The following expressive words are from an obituary which appeared in a newspaper, immediately after his death: "As an experienced and judicious ship-master, a faithful and correct business man, and, above all, as a whole-souled sailor, Capt. Upton had few equals."

His other son is George B. Upton of Boston, one of the enterprising and honored merchants of that city, who lives to do credit to the memory and perpetuate the virtues of most worthy parents. He has children, one of whom bears the name of his grandfather, Daniel Putnam, another his own, and thus combines, as George Bruce Upton, the blood of his first American ancestors, Upton and Bruce. The son is a graduate of Harvard in the class of 1849.

Mr. Upton, the subject of our notice, was buried in Reading, but, by the considerate regard of his surviving son, his remains now rest in the beautiful shades of Mount Auburn, by the side of his long-parted wife, and their deceased son.

Mr. Upton was succeeded at Eastport by Jonathan Delesdernier Weston, a graduate of Harvard in the famous class of 1802, who, after an honorable course of practice, died in that place in 1834.

TEMPLE HOVEY. 1800—1803.

Temple Hovey was the son of Dr. Ivory Hovey of South Berwick, and a descendant of the Rev. Ivory Hovey, a learned and faithful minister of Plymouth and Rochester, in the Old Colony, who died in 1803, at the age of eighty-nine. Mr. Hovey was not publicly educated; but, passing through the usual routine studies under the care of Dudley Hubbard, he was admitted to the bar in 1800. He did not live long enough to make any figure at the bar, or to indicate what his future might have been. He died in about two years after his admission to practice.

HENRY VASSAL CHAMBERLAIN. 1800—1808.

Henry Vassal Chamberlain was the first lawyer who settled in that part of the county of Kennebec which is now embraced in the county of Franklin. He was born in Worcester, Massachusetts, about 1778, and established himself in Farmington in 1800. I have not been able to find his name on any of the catalogues of the New England colleges, and cannot state how or where he was educated. I am informed by one who knew him in early life, that he was well educated. He was tall, erect, with an agreeable countenance, pleasant manners, and an exceedingly interesting personal appearance. With such rare advantages, in a new country, where they could be made peculiarly valuable, he was largely patronized, and found friends and business rapidly flowing towards him. He soon married, and built the most elegant house in the village. He was popular, engaged actively in the affairs of the town, and, having a fine taste, he introduced many improvements, whose benefits have been felt to the present day.

Farmington was incorporated in 1794, and the county in 1838. The population of the town in 1800, when Mr. Chamberlain went to it, was nine hundred and forty-two; in 1860, it was three thousand one hundred and six. Mr. Chamberlain remained in Farmington but eight years, all of which were prosperous, and afforded encouragement to future usefulness and honor; but this advantage he lost by one false step, produced by dissipated habits into which he had fallen, which involved a heavy pecuniary loss, and seriously damaged his reputation. He therefore left the country in 1808, and sought in far off Mobile, to retrieve the fortunes he had sacrificed here. It is but justice to say that in his new home, he acquired a high reputation and a large estate: he became collector of the port, and surrogate of the county, and held other honorable offices, which he discharged with fidelity. In social life he was hospitable and kind, and became an honorable, useful, and acceptable citizen of the place to which he moved, and in which he spent the greater portion of his life. In 1841, he made a visit to Farmington with his wife, where he renewed his acquaintance with his former friends: he died about 1855, leaving a family. His wife, whom he married while in Farmington, was Miss Tarbel of Groton, Massachusetts. His son, Henry Vassal, is a lawyer, has been mayor of Mobile, and judge of the Orphan's Court of that city.

EBENEZER BRADISH. 1796—1799.

Ebenezer Bradish, son of Ebenezer Bradish, a lawyer in Cambridge, Massachusetts, graduated at Harvard College, in 1792. He came to Hallowell and commenced practice in 1795 or 1796. The only information I have of him, I derive from the late Thomas Rice of Winslow, who, in a letter to me in 1851, thus speaks of him, and some other of his contemporaries: "Amos Stoddard located himself as a lawyer in Hallowell, a short time before I came to this place, and in two or three years he was followed by Nathaniel Perley and Ebenezer Bradish. Stoddard and Bradish did not possess much reputation as lawyers. Bradish was the son of Ebenezer Bradish, a lawyer in Cambridge, was graduated at Harvard, 1792. He staid in Hallowell three or four years, and then, I believe, removed to the far west." I do not find Mr. Bradish's name in the Registers of that period; and, although his name is starred in the college catalogue, the time of his death is not given. His father graduated at Harvard, 1769, and died 1818.

SAMUEL DAGGETT. 1783—1798.

On the annexed list of lawyers prior to 1801, is the name of Samuel Daggett. The only information I have concerning him is derived from a manuscript catalogue of lawyers by Mr. Williamson, the historian of Maine, whose entry is, "Samuel Daggett, 1783, Pittston, now Gardiner, removed hither from Boston. Exitus, 1798." I also find his name in the Massachusetts Register of 1793, as an attorney of the Common Pleas of that year in Pittston. But I do not find his name in the catalogue of any New England college, nor in the history of Gardiner by Mr. Hanson, nor in the tax lists of that town from 1785 to 1803. I therefore infer that there was no such lawyer in Pittston, or that he was a mere bird of passage.

LAWYERS TO 1800: THEIR INCREASE.

I have, in the preceding pages, brought to notice every lawyer who resided in Maine previous to the present century, and I think all of any distinction who attended our courts from other States. The whole number of resident and regularly educated attornies was seventy-nine, and of those actually in practice at the close of the last century, fifty-three. The names of the latter class will appear at the close of this chapter. At the same period, 1800, the Suffolk Bar contained thirty-three members, thus classed: five barristers, twenty attornies in the Supreme Court, and eight in the Common Pleas. At the time of the Revolution, 1775, there were but eight lawyers in Maine. Their increase during the next quarter of a century was not rapid; but after that time their multiplication far outstripped the proportion of other classes. In early times, the increase of attornies in England was so great that the legislature interposed at different times to check it. In the reign of Henry VI., the number was actually limited to six in Norfolk, six in Suffolk, and two in Norwich. The limitation did not last long. Lord Coke says, "When the statutes gave way to appear by attorney, it is not credible how, with attornies and their multiplication, suits in law, for the most part unnecessary and for trifling causes, increased and multiplied." In England, in 1800, the number of barristers was seven hundred and seventy-three; in 1851, it was three thousand two hundred and seventy-four. During the same time the attornies increased from five thousand one hundred and nine, to about ten thousand. The population during that period nearly doubled, while the barristers increased four-fold.

In Maine, a similar increase took place. In 1800, when the population was one hundred and fifty-one thousand seven hundred and nineteen, the number of lawyers was fifty-three.

In 1820, the date of separation, the population had nearly doubled, being two hundred and ninety-eight thousand three hundred and thirty-five, but the number of lawyers had increased to two hundred and seven, more than quadruple in the twenty years. In 1840, they had more than doubled the number in 1820, being four hundred and thirty-seven, — of whom Aroostook had four; Cumberland, sixty-six; Franklin twenty; Hancock, twelve; Kennebec, fifty-nine; Lincoln, forty-nine; Oxford, twenty-six; Penobscot, seventy-four; Piscataquis, ten; Somerset, twenty-five; Waldo, twenty-nine; Washington, twenty-nine; York, thirty-four. Bangor, with a population of eight thousand, six hundred and thirty-four, had forty-eight; while Portland, with a population of fifteen thousand, two hundred and eighteen, had thirty-seven. In 1860, the number enrolled in the profession was five hundred and twenty-nine, and the population of the State was six hundred and twenty-eight thousand, eight hundred and one.

As the lawyers increased to a multitude, the customs of the bar and the mode of conducting business changed. The respect that was due and paid to the court diminished, and there was less decorum among the members of the bar. In the early day, bar meetings were regularly held; and the opening of the courts was always attended by a procession of the judges and lawyers, preceded by the sheriff and his deputies, the former in his official costume, with staff, sword, cocked hat, blue coat, and buff vest.

In the proceedings of the court, the lawyers were more concise in their arguments, both to the court and jury. Mr. Parsons, in his interesting memoir of his father, the distinguished chief justice, says, he was seldom over half an hour in his addresses to the jury, and these were directed without ornament, to make plain and clear to their minds the precise points of the case. And Chief Justice Mellen, in an article written for Colman's Miscellany in 1839, observed, "Thirty or forty years ago a cause was argued in half an hour, or an hour at the most, which now demands half a day; and in accomplishing the task there is as much circum-round-about declamation, phraseology, and traveling backwards and forwards, as there was in Corporal Trim's story to Uncle Toby, about the King of Bohemia and his seven castles."

This brevity in argument, and the mode of conducting causes, still prevails in England. Mr. Hillard of Boston gives us an illustration of this in an article to the Law Reporter in 1849. He attended several of the courts in England, and thus speaks of an important trial: "The case was argued ably and thoroughly. It was conducted with much more temperance, moderation, and smoothness, than would have been the case in a question of similar magnitude here. The trial lasted about seven hours, and I am persuaded it would have taken three days in our country. The addresses to the jury would have been three or four times as long; there would have been more repetition, more vehemence, more declamation. On that occasion, there was not a single word spoken. But the difference was still more marked in the examination of witnesses. Very few questions were asked — none that were not strictly pertinent — and the cross-examination was very brief, and not in the least degree teasing. Without wishing to draw any invidious comparisons, I will also observe that I was most favorably impressed with the tone of decorum and good breeding which presided over the whole trial. The presiding judge was dignified and generally silent. On the part of the counsel, there were no snappish interruptions, no unseemly vociferation, no angry snarls, no vulgar crimination and recrimination. The gentleman was never, for a moment, sunk in the advocate."

These remarks are respectfully commended to the consideration of the profession in Maine. They represent something of the practice in this country a half century ago, to which a return would be most honorable and refreshing. We also commend the subject to the consideration of the bench as well as the bar, that their deportment and their influence may be employed in this work of salutary reform. Let them rigidly preserve the decorum which is due to the cause and the place. Let me use the language of Lord Bacon: — "The parts of a judge in hearing are four: to direct evidence; to moderate length, repetition, or impertinency of speech; to recapitulate, select, and collate the material points of that which hath been said; and to give the rule or sentence." Again, this wise judge gives further advice, which should be heeded: "Let not the counsel at the bar chop with the judge, nor wind himself into the handling of the cause anew, after the judge hath declared his sentence; but, on the other hand, let not the judge meet the case half way, nor give occasion to the party to say his counsel or proofs were not heard."

In connection with an account of the practice and proceedings in court at the close of the last century, I present a statement from Mr. Rice, an active member of the bar at that period, as an interesting historical record. He says: "I will now speak of the Court of Common Pleas, as connected with the Court of Quarter Sessions. The Court of Common Pleas consisted, I think, of five judges, for the trial of all civil suits. They received, as a compensation for their services, a part of the entry fee paid the clerk. The entry fee for each action, in those days, was one dollar and ninety cents. The clerk and court, after the term closed, met at their chambers; the list of entries was brought forward by the clerk; and the sum total then divided between the clerk, court, and sheriff. In addition to this sum, the judges received pay as justices of the sessions. The Court of Sessions consisted of all the Justices of the Peace in the county, together with the justices of the Common Pleas. Justices were not so plenty then as now. As many of these justices as chose assembled two or three days during the term, and attended to criminal trials, and those matters and things in which the county was more immediately interested, such as taxes, roads, and jails; and they passed upon all accounts against the county; the Common Pleas being considered a quorum to do business, if no others appeared. They received a small per diem pay of about four shillings for their services. In those times, the juries were paid by the cause: no cause, no pay. When a case was opened, the plaintiff advanced eight dollars as jury fee, to be paid to jury, sheriff, and crier. Sometimes the jurors would attend a whole term, and not try more than two or three causes; and sometimes, after the writ was read, the case would be taken from the jury, and demurred or defaulted. In such cases, the jury fee was not paid. There was a practice, in early times, of appealing from defaults. The Supreme Court sat but once a year in Lincoln, and all persons, sued on demands not disputed, who chose, would be defaulted in the Common Pleas, and then appeal to the Supreme Court, merely to give them time of payment. The cost attending those appeals was equal to that of an original action in the Supreme Court. The record in the Common Pleas would stand thus: The defendant, though solemnly called, did not appear, but made default; the court then rendered judgment. The defendant afterwards came into court, and appealed from that judgment; a complaint was entered at the next Supreme Court, for affirmation or judgment, the appellant not having entered his appeal. One day's attendance and travel was allowed in those cases, besides the entry and clerk's fee for copies. At some terms, twenty of these entries would be made by one person, and would be productive of nearly as much fees as original actions. The justices of the Common Pleas were none of them lawyers: they were plain, sound-sense men, aiming to do their duty faithfully. I believe, without speaking disrespectfully of any other court, that the business of the counties, by the courts thus organized, was as faithfully performed, and with as much satisfaction to the community, as it has since been, and at much less expense."

In the old wooden court-house in Portland, there were wings extended on each side of the judge's seat, for the accommodation of the sessions justices, who frequently appeared in considerable number during the terms of the Common Pleas.

LAWYERS IN PRACTICE IN 1800.

The following table contains the names of all the lawyers who were in practice in Maine in the year 1800, arranged alphabetically by counties:

CUMBERLAND.

Alden Peter Oliver,
Angier Charles,
Chase Salmon,
Davis Daniel,
Frothingham John,
Hopkins James Dean,
Little John Park,
Morse Leonard,
Parker Isaac,
Symmes William,
Vaughan George Elliot,
Whitman Ezekiel.

HANCOCK.

Field Bohan Prentiss,
Gilman Allen,
Leonard Oliver,
Nelson Job,
Sparhawk Thomas Stearns,
Story Isaac,
Wetmore William.

KENNEBEC.

Bridge James,
Bridge Nathan,
Bowman Thomas,
Chamberlain Henry Vassal,
Glidden Samuel P.,
Kidder Reuben,
Perley Nathaniel,
Rice Thomas,
Whitwell Benjamin,
Wilde Samuel Sumner.

LINCOLN.

Bailey Jeremiah,
Greenwood Andrew,
Hasey Benjamin,
Langdon Timothy,
Lee Silas,
Merrill John,
Stebbins Josiah,
Smith Manasseh,
Thatcher Samuel,
Winslow John.

WASHINGTON.

Bruce Phineas,
Upton Daniel Putnam.

YORK.

Dana Judah,
Emery Nicholas,
Hayman Edward Payne,
Holmes John,
Hovey Temple,
Hubbard Dudley,
King Cyrus,
Mellen Prentiss,
Sullivan Ebenezer,
Thacher George,
Thomas Joseph,
Wallingford Geo. Washington.

CHAPTER XVI.

JACOB McGAW—BENJAMIN ORR—STEPHEN LONGFELLOW—WILLIAM LAMBERT—BENJAMIN GREENE—WILLIAM ABBOTT—WILLIAM CROSBY—BARRETT POTTER—ERASTUS FOOTE.

JACOB McGAW. 1801—1836.

The first ten years of the present century witnessed the accession of many enterprising and talented young men to the bar of Maine, who were destined to occupy eminent positions in their peculiar department, as well as in public stations. Among these were Stephen Longfellow, Benjamin Orr, Benjamin Greene, Samuel Hubbard, Jacob McGaw, Joseph Dane, William P. Preble, Timothy Boutelle, A. K. Parris, Benjamin Ames, William Crosby, William Abbott, Reuel Williams, S. A. Bradley, Simon Greenleaf, Samuel Fessenden, Nathan Weston, Frederic Allen, Ether Shepley, Charles Davies, and others, whose names will find a place in our subsequent pages. To many of these distinguished men, the society, the social institutions, and the public prosperity of Maine are largely debtors. Their liberal and genial culture, their elevated tone of character, their sound practical wisdom, have made an indelible impression upon the character, the laws, and institutions of our State. The names of such men should not be suffered to die. Let us attempt to do something to keep the record of their services and merits fresh amidst the perishable memorials of time.

In 1801, no less than eight young men entered into the practice in Maine,—Jacob McGaw at Fryeburg, John Abbot at Castine, William Lambert and Benjamin Green at South Berwick, Benjamin Orr at Topsham, Stephen Longfellow at Portland, Barrett Potter at North Yarmouth, and William Jones at Norridgewock.

Jacob McGaw was the first adventurer of the new century. He came to Fryeburg in January, 1801, where Mr. Dana had been in practice nearly three years, and to that time the only lawyer in what is now the county of Oxford. Mr. McGaw was of that noble old stock which has infused so much energy into the Saxon blood of America. His father, Jacob McGaw, born in the north of Ireland, in 1737, came to this country at the age of twenty-three, arriving in Boston in 1760. His companion in this emigration was his cousin, Robert Means, afterwards the Col. Robert Means of Amherst, New Hampshire, who had the honor to be the father of the three remarkable women, wives of Jeremiah Mason, the distinguished lawyer of New Hampshire and of Boston, the Rev. Jesse Appleton, President of Bowdoin College, one of whose daughters is the wife of the late President of the United States, Franklin Pierce; the third daughter of Col. Means married the late Amos Lawrence, the merchant of Boston, who was no less distinguished in his sphere, than the others in theirs.

These two cousins, McGaw and Means, embarked their little fortunes together, and carried on their business as partners, in Merrimac, New Hampshire, until 1770, having all things in common. Mr. Means then sold out his interest in the firm to his relative and partner, McGaw, and moved to Amherst, where he married and commenced a successful trade.

At this time, it happened that John Orr, another descendant of the Scotch-Irish immigration, whose father, following the exodus of a portion of his race from the old and renowned Londonderry, of the north of Ireland, to the new Londonderry of America, lived at Bedford, a few miles from the residence of Mr. McGaw, with his sister Margaret. These families, originating in the same locality of the old country, and having a common faith, the Presbyterian, which knit the souls of these emigrants firmly together, and endeared them to one another in this land of their adoption by kindred associations, became intimate. And as our friend, Mr. McGaw, happily said, "This acquaintance resulted in the important and very happy relation of husband and wife between my father, Jacob McGaw, and Margaret Orr."

The fruit of this happy union was four sons and three daughters. Two of the sons were educated at Dartmouth College, and became lawyers; two were merchants; the three daughters were married to gentlemen of much respectability. The children received the best education it was in the power of their parents to bestow. Jacob, the subject of this notice, was born in 1778, at Merrimac, and having passed through the usual preparatory studies, entered Dartmouth College, from which he took his degree in 1797, at the age of nineteen. In December of the same year, he entered the office of the Hon. Thomas W. Thompson of that part of Salisbury, New Hampshire, which is now Franklin, and, after passing the regular *curriculum*, he was admitted an attorney of the Common Pleas in January, 1801. Being now legally qualified to enter on the practice of law, he lost no time in putting himself in a position to make his talents and his privileges available. He had vigorous health, he had an ardent mind, a good education, and high hopes.

Armed with these, he only needed opportunity. He proceeded at once to Fryeburg, and opened his office there in January, 1801; thus beginning the year and the century in this wide but cheerless field of professional labor. We will permit Mr. McGaw to look back from his eminence of four-score, and narrate some of the experiences of this period of his life:

"The Hon. Judah Dana had preceded me about three years, and was the only practicing lawyer in all that part of the county of York that was situated north of Ossipee River, and south of the Canada line, and had no competitor within the territory that now constitutes the county of Oxford. A considerable portion of northeastern New Hampshire was without any lawyer resident in it. Although the limits of country within which the principal part of our practice originated was extensive, yet the population was sparse. The terms of the courts were all holden at great distance from Fryeburg, which caused practice in them to be laborious. York was eighty miles distant from my office, and Waterboro' forty, Dover in New Hampshire seventy, Rochester and Gilmanton about sixty each. At all these places I necessarily attended at every term of the court, and occasionally at Haverhill and Plymouth, New Hampshire. As a matter of course, the litigation originating within a considerable distance around Fryeburg was managed by Judge Dana and myself on opposite sides.

"This state of things called into exercise such debating powers as each of us possessed, and tended to cause a more thorough study of principles and authorities than would have been likely to have happened had we been within reach of older and abler lawyers." Their wits were undoubtedly sharpened by this self-reliance. One anecdote I have heard of their practice which was amusing. On one occasion, they had a very sharp conflict in a trial before a magistrate in a neighboring town, in which the counsel became much excited. Not getting through the case in season to return home, they were obliged to stop at the tavern, in which the trial was held, for the night. When bed-time arrived, the simple country girl who lighted them to their chamber, expressed great surprise that they should be put into one room. She thought it could not be safe for persons who had quarreled so bitterly in the day-time to be shut up together at night. Judge Dana, however, quieted her fears, and told her that lawyers were like two sides of a pair of shears; they did not cut one another, but only what was between.

I borrow further from Mr. McGaw's manuscript letter to me: "In 1805, the county of Oxford was organized, and the first term of a judicial court was holden at Paris, the shire-town, in June of that year. Much of the extensive region both north and west of my residence was composed of the White Mountains and their branches, which rendered it incapable of compact settlement or valuable productiveness. This fact, with some other considerations, led me to the conclusion that Fryeburg would not be the most favorable place for a permanent residence. My professional business had been equal to any just claim that I could make to public patronage, yet it seemed to me that some other location might furnish a better promise for the future. With this feeling, I visited the Penobscot River and Bay, and, having determined to adventure into that new country, I closed my business in Fryeburg, and moved to Bangor in the last days of October, 1805."

The numerous acquaintances he had formed by his long residence in various places in New Hampshire, and his later practice in that State and Maine, and the reputation he had acquired for business talents, and as an advocate, very soon introduced him to a good and an increasing business. He says, "Within a period of two years, my docket was respectable when compared with the business of the most successful practitioners in the then very large county of Hancock, which extended to the Canada line from the sea. All the terms of the courts were held at Castine; and the Supreme court, sitting at Castine, had appellate jurisdiction of all appeals from the Common Pleas of Washington County, and so continued as long as Maine was united to Massachusetts. At the first term of the Common Pleas, holden at Castine, which I attended, I was invited by a professional brother to argue a cause for him impromptu, in a matter of small amount, but in which there were some doubtful points. I accepted his proposal gratuitously, and gained a verdict. And as it was a case where the court had final jurisdiction, I supposed that the verdict ended the suit. But the opposite counsel, vexed and disappointed, filed a bill of exceptions to the ruling of the court, under the statute of Elizabeth, and brought a writ of error to the Supreme Court. This was then an extraordinary process, and it was the first case of the kind I ever heard of." He argued the exceptions in the Supreme Court in a manner to elicit commendation from the court, although the cause was decided against his client. This effort of the new lawyer in the growing county gave him a reputation which increased his business, and opened the way for more profitable engagements. He thus speaks of his progress:

"In 1810 or 1811, I was appointed to attend the courtsat Machias, in Washington County, to manage some litigated causes pending there. Although the distance from Bangor, as the road was then traveled, was more than one hundred miles, yet I found compensation for the labor of the tedious journeys and attending the courts during twenty succeeding years. The late John Wilson of Belfast and myself were opposing counsel in most of the causes which were tried during that period in that county.

"My competitors in practice, after moving to Bangor, were principally the Hon. William Crosby, until he was appointed Chief Justice of the Common Pleas, Hon. John Wilson, Allen Gilman, Esq., and the Hon. William D. Williamson. After Maine became a separate State, professional business increased very much. Some of my former rivals either died or were employed in new directions, and younger men, as Gov. Edward Kent, John P. Rogers, and Judges John Appleton and Jonas Cutting, took the places which had been occupied by the gentlemen before mentioned. Through many years, and until my health suffered by too much confinement and too little exercise, my uninterrupted employment as an advocate was not less than that of any other gentleman of the bar in the county where I resided." In 1816, on the organization of the county of Penobscot, he was appointed county attorney, an office which he held and most faithfully discharged, until the establishment of the new government in Maine, when he was succeeded by Allen Gilman.

In 1834, Mr. McGaw was obliged, by the failure of his health, for the causes above indicated by him, to relax from his severe labors; and in 1836, he relinquished his engage ments as an advocate, and for the most part his other profes sional employments, and retired to the quiet enjoyment of private and domestic life. This great change in the habits and pursuits of an active and busy career of over a third of a century did not disturb that cheerfulness and serenity of mind which had ever characterized the early and riper years of this most estimable and uniformly honored man. And now, at the age of fourscore and four years, he enjoys the peaceful rewards of a well-spent life, and calmly and patiently waits the inevitable summons to the higher bar.

Mr. McGaw is a man of fine personal appearance, of ardent and impulsive temperament, and agreeable conversational powers. As an advocate, he was, during his active practice, the leader at the bars in which he was employed, and the securing his services was considered almost as equivalent to success. He had great influence with the jury by his easy, pleasant manner, and the happy tact of introducing anecdotes, and applying familiar incidents and facts to illustrate his argument. He retired from the bar with the honors of the profession upon him, and with the respect and affection of his professional brethren, his clients, and the community.

Soon after his removal to Bangor, Mr. McGaw married Miss Poor, a daughter of Ebenezer Poor, of Andover, in Maine, and a sister of the father of John A. Poor. The latter gentleman became a partner of Mr. McGaw, and succeeded to his business. Mr. McGaw has one daughter living, the wife of John B. Foster, a merchant in Bangor.

BENJAMIN ORR. 1801—1828.

A most fitting accompaniment and companion piece to the sketch of Mr. McGaw, will be that of his kinsman, Benjamin Orr. Of the same honored descent, originating in the land and under the principles of the great reformer, John Knox, their ancestors brought to this country the inflexible religious ideas and stern self-poised characters which distinguished the disciples of that rigid teacher. Their families, by inter-marriage, became more nearly allied, the aunt of Mr. Orr becoming the mother of Mr. McGaw. The parents of both transmitted to their children the firm resolution, the intellectual power, and the unbending integrity which they received from their own. This Scotch-Irish stock, mingling the current of its blood with that of Saxon origin, has diffused itself over the whole country, with a vigorous growth, imparting a vital, elevating tone to the population of the land.

The following extract from a *jeu d'esprit* was written for the centennial celebration in Bedford, in 1850, by George Kent. Mr. Kent is a son of New Hampshire, a member of our profession, and late of Bangor, now absent on a foreign appointment. He thus speaks of the race.

"A hundred years! what hopes and fears
Are crowded in its pages!
What scenes to thrill of good or ill,
In glancing down the ages!
Than Scottish stock, not Plymouth Rock
Can boast of nobler scions;
Whose mixture good, of Irish blood,
Speaks true Scotch-Irish "lions."

Not *lions* they, which, in our day,
Might pass for "just the *dandy*;"
But stern old stuff, in aspect rough,
Yet always shrewd and handy.
From Ulster's coast, a valiant host,
They crossed the deep blue waters,
And refuge found on Yankee ground,
Sires, mothers, sons, and daughters.
Hither our *Macs* had made their tracks,
Our *Orrs*, and *Goffs*, and *Pattens*;
Their housewives, too, of good 'true blue,'
Undecked with silks or satins."

The father of the subject of this notice was John Orr, born in 1749. He was an officer in the army of the Revolution, and served as a lieutenant under General Stark at the battle of Bennington, where he was severely wounded, and rendered a cripple for life. He died at Bedford, New Hampshire, in 1823, aged seventy-four, leaving the reputation of a sound and vigorous mind, and of an exemplary Christian character. He was the son of John Orr, who came from the north of Ireland, in 1726, to Londonderry, in New Hampshire, with a brother Daniel and sister Janet. He died in 1754, and his wife a week after, leaving his son John a lad of five years old. At the age of nineteen, John, the son, came to Maine with some other young men, and engaged in the occupation of a carpenter, where he remained two years, and then returned to Bedford. In two years after, he married Jane, the daughter of Benjamin Smith, and earnestly engaged in conducting a saw and grist mill, and in improving his farm.

His oldest son, Benjamin, was born in Bedford, December 1, 1772. When he arrived at years of discretion, he expressed a desire to receive a liberal education; but his father, having eight sons to provide for, was not able to comply with his wishes, and apprenticed him to a housewright. He labored in this capacity for two or three years, when he purchased a release from his indentures, and worked on his own account, keeping steadily in view the prominent idea of his life, — to qualify himself for a learned profession. With this intent, his head and hands were constantly busy, working at his trade, pursuing a course of study, and keeping school. Some buildings in Portland, Fryeburg, and other places, were pointed out by him, in after life, as the work, in part, of his hands, and they did him credit. He excelled no less in mechanical art in early life than he afterwards did in the higher art of the law; and such was his genius, that, if he had not preferred the more elevated walks of a profession, he would have been no less eminent as a mechanic. By keeping steadily in view his great plan of life, his mind was constantly educating itself amidst his daily mechanical toil, by close attention and constant discipline, superior far to the mere formula and routine study of schools. When in Portland and other towns in which courts were sitting, he embraced the opportunity to spend what time he could spare in listening to their proceedings, hearing the arguments of counsel and the rulings of the court, and thus increasing his stores for improving the operations of his own mind.

In these early pursuits and struggles, he exhibited the qualities which ripened to the rich fruits of mature years, and gained him the affection and attachment of the companions of his labors. In his studies he received much aid from Paul Langdon, a graduate of Harvard, and some time preceptor of Fryeburg Academy, who gave direction to his preparatory efforts. With such assistance, and his own unbending perseverance, he was enabled, in 1796, to enter the *junior class* of Dartmouth College. During the last year of his college life, he was attacked with a severe disease, one of the consequences of his unremitted application; which had the effect of inducing his father to procure means to assist his son, on returning health, to complete his college course, without further extraordinary exertions. While in college, so earnest was Mr. Orr to get forward in life, that he entered his name in a lawyer's office, as appears by the following certificate, which we insert to show the form of that day: "State of N. H., Grafton ss. I hereby certify that the bearer, Mr. Benjamin Orr, lodged his name as a clerk in my office on the 27th day of April, 1797. That at the next term of the Court of Common Pleas in September following, he was regularly received into my office as a candidate for the bar, and continued therein one year, to September, 1798, during which period he attended with diligence and constancy to the study of law, and made every proficiency therein which could be expected in that term. Attest, William Woodward, attorney at law, and secretary to the bar of said county." The following certificate continues the history of his apprenticeship: "N. H., Cheshire, ss. This certifies that Mr. Benjamin Orr, at September term of the Court of Common Pleas in 1798, was, by the consent of the bar of this county, admitted a student in the office of Samuel Dinsmore, Esq., of Keene. Attest, Samuel West, clerk of the bar of Cheshire County."

On taking his degree in 1798, he entered the office of Samuel Dinsmore, late governor of New Hampshire, and continued there something over a year; when, thinking that Maine would be the best field for his future labors, he proceeded to Hallowell, and placed himself under the tuition of the late Judge Wilde. In the autumn of 1801, he was admitted to the bar in Lincoln County, and immediately opened an office in Topsham, where Mr. Hasey was then the solitary practitioner. In 1803, he was admitted to practice in the Supreme Court, and from the position he at once took at the bar, his practice became very extensive in his own, and the adjoining county of Cumberland. Some interesting letters from Judge Wilde to him at this period, show a sincere attachment between these distinguished men. April 9, 1801, Judge Wilde writes, "I am happy to learn, by your favor of the 28th ult., that you are not dissatisfied with the place you have chosen for your professional exertions. The man who is accustomed to dwell with gloomy despondency upon the present scenes and views of life, will derive but little satisfaction from the future. However elevated his situation, however splendid his talents, he will find it difficult to eradicate that canker of the mind which the restless spirit of early life had formed, and which had been nourished by the habits of succeeding years. The high objects of honorable enterprise are not obtained by brooding over the present evils of life with a morose and gloomy mind, but by activity, industry, and energy, which will not be exerted when surrounded by the horrors of disappointment and discontent." In the same letter he confided his business to him. "As my attendance in this county will be indispensable, I must be indebted to the candor of my brethren in the disposal of my actions in Lincoln. I shall beg the favor of you to take a list of my actions, and to which, if you have no objections, you will have the goodness to attend." "If I shall have it in my power to be of any service to you, either professionally or otherwise, I shall be happy in the occasion, as it will evince the sentiments of esteem with which I am, my dear sir, your obedient friend and servant." In November, 1801, "The only objection that I can see to your coming to our December term is business, which is not to be neglected. I am rejoiced that you receive so large a share of it, as I have your interest and prosperity very much at heart." In December, 1802, he writes, "I hardly know what to say to you on the subject of separation. I have always been friendly to the measure, but I very much doubt if the present time be the most favorable for bringing it into view." He then states some objections to the measure, among which was the seditious spirit which was prevailing among the squatters in Kennebec and Lincoln Counties. He adds, "Upon the whole I see difficulties in the way, which, I think, cannot be removed; and I think, with great deference to the better judgment of many of my friends, that it would be better to wait for a more favorable opportunity." He closes the same letter with the following remarks: "Mrs. Dutton, the mother of our friend, lately died on her passage from this place to Penobscot, under circumstances peculiarly distressing to her friends. Poor Dutton writes in great distress on the occasion. I most sincerely sympathize with him. Mrs. Samuel Howard is likewise almost the same as dead—there is hardly a forlorn hope left. Thus death plays the tyrant about us. We must all soon feel that his power is not to be resisted by force, or softened by entreaties. While we remain, however, let us 'act well our parts,' in doing which I shall always remain, I trust, most sincerely your friend."

Mr. Orr's first appearance in the reports is in the second volume of Greenleaf, in a case argued by him on a bill of exceptions to the ruling of Judge Thacher at *nisi prius* against him, in which he gained his case; Lee and Mellen on the other side; Parsons, chief justice, delivering a learned opinion. From that time onward, to his death in 1828, he had continual employment in the best causes argued in the State; attending the circuit of the Supreme Court in the several counties. Here he came in competition with lawyers and advocates of the highest powers in Maine: Mellen, Wilde, Whitman, Longfellow, Lee, Boutelle, Emery, McGaw, Wilson, Crosby, Greenleaf, and Fessenden. On one occasion, he encountered the able and distinguished Jeremiah Mason of New Hampshire, in a bill in equity before the Circuit Court of the United States. The case was of great importance, as may be supposed by the engagement of such an advocate as Mason. "His success was complete and triumphant," and he was highly complimented by Mr. Mason for the manner and ability with which he conducted the cause. In chancery practice, which came in principally with the introduction of the Circuit Court into this State, in 1820, favored by Judge Story, Mr. Orr became quite eminent. This practice was not familiar to our lawyers, who joined, on that account, probably, in the general prejudice against equity jurisdiction. They had, no doubt, the opinion which Selden expressed many years ago, when he said, "For law we have a measure, and know what to trust to; *equity* is according to the conscience of him that is chancellor, and as that is larger or narrower, so is equity. 'Tis all one as if they should make the standard for the measure a chancellor's foot. What an uncertain measure would this be! One chancellor has a long foot, another a short foot, a third an indifferent foot. It is the same thing with the chancellor's conscience."

In this department, Mr. Orr is said to have been without a rival in the State, and was consequently much employed in causes arising under it. He pursued his large and successful practice without interruption by extraneous employments, except for two years from 1817, when he represented the Lincoln District in Congress. His heart was in his profession. He sought it for the love he bore it, and he rendered to it a most devoted affection, and the honor of a most upright and chivalrous service. Although a firm and conscientious member of the Federal party, he had no taste for political life: he did not like the paths that led to it — they were winding and crooked and narrow. He, however, yielded his private inclinations, and was elected to the Fifteenth Congress, being the first of Mr. Monroe's administration, and took his seat December 1, 1817. During the first session, he did not much engage in debate: some running observations, taken from his familiar correspondence, will convey the impressions which these new scenes made upon him. December 15, 1817, he writes, "Debates begin to grow lively, and some good things are said. For my own part, my propensity is very strong to be silent." December 17, he says, "The oratory of the western mountains and wilderness is as vociferous as themselves, full of foam and rhetorical flourishes. But amidst these, there is occasional relief from the well-timed and judicious observations of men of thought and weight of character." "Mr. Speaker Clay, I feel well satisfied, has no cordiality for the administration. He does not appear to wish to hide his feelings." December 30, "I do not as yet feel any inclination to enter the list of debaters, and am very much amused to see so many around me set up for orators." It was at this session that a change was made in the compensation of members, from six dollars to eight dollars a day, and excited a good deal of controversy and debate. Mr. Orr touches the point of the subject in a few words. He says, January 8, 1818, "On the business of compensation, there has been some little stir among us, and it is truly amusing to see men *wriggling* between ambition and avarice. Many who would do every thing but cheat in such manner as to become legally criminal, are extremely anxious to have their votes for cheapness recorded, so that the people who chose them may see and approve. The Speaker, Clay, appointed a committee of seven to prepare a law on the subject, and put Holmes at the head of it. When they retired to consult upon the business, they were all very ready to give their opinions except Holmes: he said he was not under any obligation to give an opinion, and did not. The rest of the committee agreed to report a bill for nine dollars, which was afterwards, in the house, reduced to eight." Mr. Holmes, on the passage of the bill, uniformly voted against increasing the compensation. The claim of Massachusetts for a remuneration of her war expenses was another question which engrossed the attention particularly of members from Massachusetts and Maine. In regard to this, Mr. Orr writes, January 25, 1818, "The question of the Massachusetts claim worries my mind a good deal. Every one who knows me will expect me to advocate that claim in Congress, in some measure suitable to its merits. I feel entirely incompetent to the task; yet, I suppose, with my colleagues, I must attempt it. There is more than eight hundred thousand dollars depending, and pretty strong prejudices existing against the allowance of it." The question did not, however, come up. But he says, under January 29, "The Speaker has seen fit to appoint three of us from Massachusetts,—Mason, Whitman, and myself, on the committee to investigate the claims of Massachusetts. There are four others joined with us from other States. It is my design to give every attention to the subject."

Two other questions of importance occupied the attention of Congress at this session: one was a uniform system of bankruptcy, which Mr. Orr sustained, and on which his friend Whitman made an able speech; the other was the first movement toward committing the government to "Internal Improvements within the States of the United States." On this measure, Congress and the people were much divided. The Federal party generally opposed the employment of government money in work of this character, as a contravention of the powers with which it is clothed, and of the letter and spirit of the Constitution. Mr. Orr, on the 13th of March, made an able speech in opposition to the resolution, which declared that it was the duty and in the power of Congress to authorize the making of post, military, and other roads and canals within the several States. The resolution was, however, adopted, by a vote of ninety to seventy-five; Mr. Holmes voting in favor, and the Federal members from Maine, Orr, Whitman, and Wilson, against it. The next day, March 14, Mr. Orr obtained leave of absence, on account of sickness in his family, and returned home.

Before leaving this portion of Mr. Orr's life, we will cite another passage from his Congressional correspondence, which will express, better than I can, the natural diffidence which pervaded his character. Under January 3, 1818, he writes, "There is one thing relating to my station here that I would be glad were otherwise: that is, the people who sent me will expect me to make speeches, and will perhaps think it part of my duty, on topics, particularly, which regard their interest. My reluctance to engage is really very great, and to overcome it will require an effort. There is pride in this, I acknowledge, for our greatest talkers are evidently the most vain and shallow part of our body, and I do not like to belong to their number. I understand it is the trade, or a part of it, of Gales, the editor of the National Intelligencer, to prune, correct, and revise, as well as publish speeches; and he often trims a very shabby thing in such a manner as to save it from a great portion of the ridicule which is due to the original."

The members from Maine in the Fifteenth Congress were John Holmes, Mr. Orr, Ezekiel Whitman, John Wilson, Thomas Rice, A. K. Parris: the latter being appointed judge of the United States District Court in January, 1818, resigned his seat, and was succeeded by Enoch Lincoln.

At the next session, many subjects of an interesting and exciting nature occupied Congress. Among these were the Seminole War; General Jackson's conduct in seizing the forts in Florida, and executing Arbuthnot and Ambrister; amending the charter of the bank of the United States; the application of the territories of Alabama, Arkansas, and Missouri to form constitutions preliminary to their admission as States, which involved a warm and lengthened discussion on the restriction of slavery, and in which the Missouri compromise line was first proposed, having been intro duced by Mr. Taylor of New York. On the Massachusetts claim, which was received and again postponed, Mr. Orr made a speech, and also on a bill relating to the coasting trade, in which he spoke twice, as did Mr. Whitman, from Portland. Their remarks were characterized by sound sense, conciseness, and entire pertinency to the subjects under discussion. Mr. Orr was a useful member, by his clear perceptions, his promptness and fidelity to the duties of his station, and the ability with which he treated every subject to which he gave his attention. At the next election, there was no choice on the first trial, and he withdrew from the contest, as not worth to him the struggle to obtain the office. Col. Head of Waldoboro' became the Federal candidate, but was defeated by the election of Mark L. Hill of Phippsburg.

This was the last public office which Mr. Orr held. The practice of law suited him far better, and was better adapted to his powers, his education, and his inclinations. He sought it in his highest forms: it gave full scope to his clear and comprehensive mind, and his severe dialectic talent. And he pursued it with elevated aspirations and lofty endeavors, which would have no fellowship with meanness in any shape. The following lines from *Maynard's XII Wonders of the World*, 1611, well describes Mr. Orr's principles and practice:—

" The law my calling is,
  My robe, my tongue, my pen,
Wealth and opinion gaine,
  And make me judge of men.
The knowne dishonest cause
  I never did defend;
Nor spunne out sutes at length,
  But wisht and sought an end;
Nor counsaile did bewray;
  Nor of both parties take,
Nor ever took I fee
  For which I never spake."

He adhered with scrupulous exactness to the letter and spirit of his oath, "to do no falsehood, nor consent to the doing of any in court," "nor wittingly or willingly promote or sue any false, groundless, or unlawful suit, nor give aid or consent to the same."

As an advocate, Mr. Orr was concise, logical, and forcible. He seized upon the salient points of a case, and pressed them with a power that was invincible. He did not waste his strength in efforts to sustain the weak points of his cause, but poured a concentrated light upon its strong features. The manner in which he viewed this style of managing a cause may be inferred from his reply to an anxious client, who, sitting by him as he was closing a splendid argument, in which, with conciseness and force peculiar to himself, he had presented his case to the jury, suggested to him some point which he had not touched upon : "I have argued your cause, sir, and cannot stop to pick up the chips." As a lawyer, his mind was clear, discriminating, and exact. He readily scattered the mists of sophistry and fraud from the body of truth, and presented it in its simple proportions. As he grew in experience and reputation, his business rapidly increased, and his services were called for in all parts of the State. In September, 1819, he writes to his wife from Castine, "I have as much business as I had any reason to expect, and shall be able to render a good account of myself when the fall terms are over." In June, 1823, he writes from Bangor, "I have just got through the argument of a tedious cause, and have left the court house while Brother Wilson manages his side of the case. I have had as much business since I have been here as I could well turn my hand to, and am glad to have a few moments' leisure, while Wilson is endeavoring in a long speech to undo what I have done, for I believe I have convinced the jury that I had the right of the case; but it is not certain they will continue of that mind when another long speech is made to them. If they do not, poor Upton of Dixmont will have to pay the doctor, whom he is contending with, for speaking the truth of him." In May, 1825, he again writes from Bangor, "With regard to my prospects in business in this town the present court, I have no reason to complain. I have got old Father Bussy for a client here. I like such; but he is so sociable and vain that I have to double my patience." "I expect to be very busy this week, and that is what I wish to be. This place grows in every way; hence the business of the court increases, and will probably continue to increase so long as I shall be able to follow my profession."

But in the midst of this high career of business and fame, he died, in 1828, in the fifty-sixth year of his age.

The death of such a man, in the vigor of life and the full maturity of his powers, was a serious loss to the bar and to the profession. The manner in which it was noticed was honorable to his memory. Immediately after his death, Chief Justice Mellen, in a charge to the Grand Jury, September, 1828, spoke of him as one "who had long stood, confessedly, at the head of the profession of our State; who had distinguished himself by the depth and solidity of his understanding, by his legal acumen and research, by the power of his intellect, the commanding energy of his reasoning, the uncompromising firmness of his principles, and the dignified and lofty sense of honor, truth, and justice which he uniformly displayed in his professional career, and in the walks of private life." The writer of an obituary notice in the newspaper, who was competent to judge and describe his character, observed, "At the bar, he was always a pleasant and honorable practitioner, indulgent and obliging towards his younger brethren, and not at all disposed to take advantage of any mistake of theirs arising from want of experience. In his addresses to the jury, he would sometimes, it was thought, animadvert with too much severity on a witness who he believed had suppressed the truth, or intentionally prevaricated in his testimony. On such occasions, he would pour out his keen and biting satire in short, pithy sentences of concentrated sarcasm on the supposed delinquent. But his powers appeared to the most advantage in discussing points of law to the court. Here, laying aside all display of wit and sarcasm, all superfluous illustration and circumlocution, all skirmishing at the outposts, he seized at once on the question at issue. His argument was dense and brief; proceeding in regular progression from commencement to conclusion, so that it was dangerous for one who would comprehend its full force, to withdraw attention from it for a moment."

Mr. Orr, residing in the vicinity of the principal college of our State, did not decline to render it his services and counsel at all times. He was first appointed one of its overseers, and in 1814 was chosen a trustee, which office he held at the time of his death; and during this time, for one or two years, he held the office of treasurer.

In 1805, Mr. Orr married Elizabeth, a daughter of Capt. Richard Toppan, who had moved from Newburyport to Topsham. She was a descendant from John Robinson, the Leyden pilgrim, and venerated pastor of the Plymouth church before its migration; by her he had eleven children. "She was a lady of fine manners, and well-fitted to preside in a family where hospitality and generous friendship were extended to their utmost limit." The death of this excellent lady in 1828, to whom he was most tenderly attached, struck a severe blow upon Mr. Orr, from which he never recovered. His letters to her when he was absent in Congress, or upon the circuit, were filled with expressions of anxious solicitude for her health, of deep interest in her comfort, pleasure, and welfare. And when she was taken from him, he ceased to find consolation or support. She had been to him the right arm of his domestic life, and the sympathizing friend of his struggles, his successes, and his fame.

Two sons and five daughters survived their parents: the sons, John and Henry, were educated at Bowdoin College. One graduated in 1834, the other, Henry, in 1846. John is settled in the ministry at Alfred, and Henry is in the practice of law. The five daughters married as follows: Elizabeth to John A. Poor of Portland, and died without issue, June 2, 1844, aged thirty-two; Margaret to Alfred I. Stone of Brunswick; Jane to William H. Noble, a civil engineer; Catherine to Mr. Gregg of Andover, who is dead; and Laura to John W. Davis, a lawyer now living in Wellfleet, Massachusetts. The daughters are all living but Elizabeth.

STEPHEN LONGFELLOW. 1801—1849.

Mr. Longfellow was a successful rival and an honorable competitor of Mr. Orr for more than a quarter of a century, at the bar of Cumberland County; and was, like him, a wise counsellor, an able advocate, and an honest man. He was born in Gorham, Maine, March 23, 1776. His father, who was born in Falmouth, and his grandfather, removed to Gorham from Falmouth, on its destruction by the British fleet in October, 1775, and remained there during their lives. His early days were spent in that town, on the farm of his father, and in studies necessary to prepare him for his future occupation. Sometimes, in his addresses to the jury, he adroitly drew illustrations from his farmer's apprenticeship, to point his argument or secure their favorable attention. I once had great fear of losing a case by one of these apt allusions, in speaking of his carrying butter to market in Portland.

He was descended in the fourth degree from William Longfellow, the first of the name who came to this country and settled in the Byefield Parish, in the old town of Newbury, and who married there, in 1678, Anne Sewall. She was the daughter of Henry Sewall and Jane Dummer, and born September 3, 1662. After the death of her first husband, Longfellow, she married Henry Short; and as Savage says in his Genealogical Dictionary, "had both Longfellows and Shorts." His father, grandfather, and great-grandfather were all named Stephen; derived from Stephen Dummer, the father of Jane, the first William Longfellow's wife. His

S. Longfellow

grandfather, the first immigrant to Maine, graduated at Harvard College in 1742, and came to Portland, then Falmouth, as the Grammar School Master, in 1745. He filled many offices of honor and trust, and exercised an important influence in the affairs of the town and county. He was fifteen years Grammar School Master; twenty-three years Parish Clerk; twenty-two years Town Clerk; and fifteen years Register of Probate and Clerk of the Judicial Courts; several of which offices he held at the same time. His son Stephen held the office of Judge of the Court of Common Pleas, and died much respected, in 1824, at the age of seventy-four. The grandfather died in 1790.

The subject of our notice entered Harvard College in 1794, at the age of eighteen, and at once took an honorable position with the government and his college companions, by the frankness of his manners, and his uniformly correct deportment. His scholarship is attested by his election to the *Phi Beta Kappa* society. I have the privilege of offering the satisfactory testimony of his associates concerning this period of his life. His classmate, Humphrey Devereux, now living at Salem, in a letter, says of him, "On entering college, Longfellow was in advance in years of many of us, and his mind and judgment, of course, more matured. He had a well-balanced mind, no part so prominent as to overshadow the rest. It was not rapid in its movements, nor brilliant in its course, but its conclusions were sound and correct. He was inclined to think, compare, and weigh closely: he did not soar into the regions of fancy and abstraction, but kept on the *terra firma* of practical common sense. In his habits, he was studious and exemplary, free from every contaminating influence. In a class which had its full share of talent and scholarship, he held a very reputable rank among its high divisions, and shared its honors in the assignment of the college government, and in the estimation of his classmates. In his temperament, he was bright and cheerful, and engaged freely in the social pleasures of friendly meetings and literary associations. His manners then, as in later life, were courteous, polished, and simple; springing from a native politeness, or a generous, manly feeling. He was born a gentleman, and was a general favorite of his class."

The venerable Daniel Appleton White, of Salem, two years his senior in college, lately deceased, writes, "Mr. Longfellow was a general favorite with his classmates. The Rev. Dr. Channing used to speak in high terms of his excellent classmate: he said to me in one of his eulogiums, that he possessed great energy of character." He again says, "I never knew a man more free from everything offensive to good taste or good feeling; even to his dress and personal appearance, all about him was attractive. In his deportment and manners, he was uniformly courteous and amiable. He was evidently a well-bred gentleman when he left the paternal mansion for the university. He seemed to breathe an atmosphere of purity, as his natural element, while his bright intelligence, buoyant spirits, and social warmth diffused a sunshine of joy that made his presence always gladsome."

These high tributes to the youthful character of Mr. Longfellow were fully sustained in his riper years. He graduated in the class of Dr. Channing, Judge Story, Professor Sidney Willard, Dr. Tuckerman, and other distinguished scholars, of whom but three in a class of forty-eight, now remain.

On leaving college, he immediately entered on the study of law with Salmon Chase of Portland, who was then engaged in the most extensive practice of any lawyer at the Cumberland Bar; and was admitted to practice in 1801. He established himself at Portland, where the field was already occupied by seven lawyers in a population of thirty-eight hundred. These prior occupants of this field were John Frothingham, who commenced practice there in 1778, and was for a while the only lawyer in the county; Daniel Davis, a polished gentleman and popular advocate; William Symmes, a good scholar and lawyer, but of very formal manners; Isaac Parker, afterwards Chief Justice of Massachusetts — all these were from the old Bay State; Salmon Chase and George E. Vaughan, from New Hampshire; and James D. Hopkins, a native of England, but whose parents immigrated to Portland soon after the peace of 1783. There were but two other members belonging to the Cumberland Bar at that time, who were Ezekiel Whitman, then practicing at New Gloucester; and Peter O. Alden, at Brunswick. Of these, not one survives but the venerable Judge Whitman, who was born in the same month and year with Mr. Longfellow, and is now enjoying, in his native town, East Bridgewater, Massachusetts, a serene old age, the ripe fruit of temperance, self-control, and a virtuous life. The county then contained a population of about thirty-two thousand.

Notwithstanding this array of able counsellors, Mr. Longfellow, fearless of the competition, earnestly engaged in the struggle which such a rivalship exacted. The forensic efforts and encounters were conducted with more regard to courtesy and the dignity of the bar at that period than at the present time. The members of the bar, and the judges on the bench, carried into their official deportment, the dignified and somewhat formal manners of the old school. Levity or vulgarity could not exist in the presence of that personification of dignity, the learned Chief Justice Dana; nor would rudeness or degrading personalities be tolerated by his more learned but less polished successor, Chief Justice Parsons, and his associates, the pure-minded Sewall and the stern and reserved Sedgwick.

Parker, Davis, Chase, and Whitman could not do otherwise than welcome to their association a brother, kindred to them in all elevated qualities. Mr. Longfellow soon secured a successful and honorable practice, and took a commanding position at the bar, by the urbanity of his conduct, his legal ability, and the integrity of his principles. One of his contemporaries at the bar recently said to me, "Longfellow had a fine legal mind, he was industrious, attentive, courteous, and got into business at once. His first address to the jury was plausible and ingenious, and almost as good as any one he afterwards made." On the death of Chase and Symmes, and the removal of Judge Parker to Boston, all which occurred in 1806 and early in 1807, he became one of the leaders in the practice, which, as he advanced, continually increased, until its accumulated weight bore too heavily upon his over-taxed powers; and he was admonished by a fearful attack of epilepsy, to withdraw for a while from the excitements of business and its overwhelming cares. He gradually, although most reluctantly, quitted a field which had been to him a source of happiness and fame, and on which he had conferred dignity and honor.

No man more surely gained the confidence of all who approached him, or held it firmer; and those who knew him best, loved him most. In the management of his causes, he went with zeal and directness of purpose to every point which could sustain it: there was no traveling out of the record with him, nor a wandering away from the line of his argument after figures of speech or fine rhetoric, but he was plain, straight-forward, and effective in his appeals to the jury, and by his frank and candid manner won them to his cause. And I may truly offer him as an illustration of Fuller's "good advocate," whom he thus describes, "He makes not a Trojan siege of a suit, but seeks to bring it to a set battle in a speedy trial. In pleading, he shoots fairly at the head of the cause, and having fastened, no frowns nor favors shall make him let go his hold." But with all this, although firm and unyielding when he believed himself to be right, he never forgot the duties of a gentleman and a Christian, nor lost his suavity of manners in the ardor and bravery of action.

A man of such estimable qualities was not permitted to give his whole time to his profession: the people demanded the exercise of his eminent ability and practical talent for their service; and in 1814, a year of great excitement and danger to the republic from war with England,—a large fleet hanging upon our coast, and a well-disciplined army menacing our northern frontier,—he was sent to the Legislature of Massachusetts, and while there he was chosen a member of the celebrated Hartford Convention, in company with Judge Wilde from this State, George Cabot, Harrison Gray Otis, and other distinguished Federalists from Massachusetts and the other New England States. In 1816, he was chosen an elector of President, and with Prentiss Mellen, and the other electors of Massachusetts, threw his vote for the eminent statesman, Rufus King, a native of Maine. Mr. Monroe, the candidate of the Democratic party, was elected for this, his first term, by a majority of one hundred and nine votes; for his second term, from 1817 to 1821, he received every electoral vote but one, which was thrown for John Quincy Adams, by Gov. Plumer of New Hampshire.

This was the era of good feeling; or, as John Randolph called it, the "era of indifference." Political harmony prevailed, such as had not existed since the days of Washington: the old Federal party, which had embraced many of the wisest and best men of the country, whose names are now canonized, then ceased to exist; all parties united to render a sincere and hearty support to the federal constitution, opposition to which, in the early days of the government, had created the anti-federal party.

In 1822, Mr. Longfellow was chosen to the Eighteenth Congress, the closing two years of Mr. Monroe's second administration, where he was associated with Lincoln of Maine, Webster of Massachusetts, Buchanan of Pennsylvania, Clay of Kentucky, Barbour and Randolph of Virginia, McLane of Delaware, Forsyth of Georgia, Houston of Tennessee, Livingston of Louisiana. Henry Clay was Speaker of the House, and John Chandler and John Holmes were Senators from Maine. Having served out his term faithfully and well, and by his voice and vote resisted the general and profuse expenditure of public money for indiscriminate internal improvements, he took leave of political life, which had no charm for him. The remainder of his years, so far as his health permitted, he gave to his profession. How well he served it, the first sixteen volumes of the Massachusetts Reports, and the first twelve of the Maine Reports, extending through a period of more than thirty years, bear ample testimony: they exhibit his ability as a learned jurist, and his skill as an ingenious dialectician. In 1828, he received from Bowdoin College the honorable and merited distinction of Doctor of Laws. He was one of the trustees of that institution from 1817 to 1836. In 1826, he represented Portland in the Legislature, with Isaac Adams and Gen. Fessenden. In 1834, he was President of the Maine Historical Society, having previously held the office of Recording Secretary. He died August 3, 1849, in the seventy-fourth year of his age.

In his domestic life, Mr. Longfellow was as exemplary as he was able in public and professional relations. In January, 1804, he married Zilpah, daughter of General Peleg Wadsworth of Portland, with whom he lived in uninterrupted happiness for more than forty-five years. She was a woman of fine manners, and of great moral worth. By her he had eight children, — four sons and four daughters. The sons are destined to transmit the name with new luster to posterity, in lines divergent from the parental profession, — poetry, divinity, and science. The elder surviving son, Henry Wadsworth Longfellow, by his sweet and eloquent verse, has not only made his name vocal throughout his own land, but has found genial echoes on the other shores of the ocean, and his numbers will be repeated in distant lands and times, like the songs of the bards that have floated down to us through the centuries, which have preserved naught else.

In all the relations of private and public life, Mr. Longfellow was a model man; kind and affectionate in his family, prompt and efficient in business, courteous uniformly, ready with money or service, whenever properly required, and filling large places in benevolent and religious institutions. His death was deeply mourned, and the people grieved most of all that they should see his face no more.

A life so adorned could not have been withdrawn from its sphere of usefulness without making a palpable void; and I only express the universal sentiment that was felt at his departure, that an able, upright, and Christian gentleman had gone: one to whom may be applied language used in regard to an eminent English lawyer, "that he cast honor upon his honorable profession, and sought dignity, not from the ermine or the mace, but from a straight path and a spotless life."

The Bar, at a very full meeting, took an honorable and appropriate notice of the death of their deceased brother. Professor Greenleaf, the particular friend and admirer of Mr. Longfellow, and who for many years practiced with him at the Cumberland Bar, in reply to a letter from another friend, inviting him to attend the meeting, said, "Dear Brother Daveis: Many thanks for your kind letter and kind remembrance. It warms and cheers me. I am strongly tempted to go down to the Supreme Court in November, especially as the meeting you anticipate will draw out the *quæ extant* of the Cumberland Bar, as it was in our youth. We shall see Whitman and Potter, possibly Southgate; but where are Orr, and Mellen, and Hopkins, and the rest of that day, and now at last, Longfellow? It will be a scene of lights and shadows."

Professor Willard, in his "Memoirs of Youth and Manhood," in speaking of his classmate, Longfellow, thus remarks: "He was a young man of remarkable maturity of judgment, and of quiet, affable, and gentlemanly manners and demeanor, from his first entrance within the college walls to his exit. His kindness and courtesy were so unostentatious and sincere that they seemed to be innate. So early was his ability as a counsellor and advocate of his younger fellow-students, perceived by them and confided in, that in cases of doubt or difficulty in matters of conduct, his advice was often sought and followed.

During his long career of professional service in Portland, he was distinguished and respected no less for the excellence of his social character, and for his judgment in matters of municipal and civil concerns, than for his talents and integrity in the business affairs of his chosen vocation, as a counselor at law. It may truly be said of the conduct of his life, "His own example sanctioned all his laws." Before the meeting of his class at the expiration of the half century from the year they graduated, his constitution had become greatly impaired, and his consequent absence was deeply regretted."

WILLIAM LAMBERT. 1801—1824.

The same year were admitted to the bar in York County, William Lambert and Benjamin Greene, who both studied with Dudley Hubbard, and settled in South Berwick by the side of their teacher. Mr. Lambert was born in Rowley, Massachusetts, July 22, 1778. Having been fitted for college at the celebrated Dummer Academy, he entered Dartmouth College, from which he took his degree in 1798, a classmate of Mr. Orr, of whom we have spoken in preceding pages. Mr. Lambert, deciding on the practice of law as his profession, was attracted to the office of Mr. Hubbard in Berwick, whose reputation as an advocate was widely spread. Having passed through the regular course of study, he was duly admitted to the bar, and opened an office in South Berwick. Mr. Lambert confined himself principally to office business, and rarely appeared as an advocate. His business was of a profitable character, and was promptly attended to by him and to the satisfaction of his clients. He was a man of quiet habits, of good personal appearance, and a worthy citizen of the town. He died December 11, 1824, aged forty-six.

He was twice married, first to Rhoda Hastings of St. Johnsbury, Vermont; second, to Abigail, daughter of Ebenezer Ricker of Somersworth, New Hampshire. He left two children, a son and a daughter: the son is the Rev. Thomas Ricker Lambert, Rector of the Episcopal church in Charlestown, Massachusetts; the daughter is the wife of the Hon. John P. Hale, Senator in Congress from New Hampshire.

Mr. Lambert's son, the Rev. Thomas Ricker Lambert, prepared himself for the profession of law, and was, for a time, in the office of Judge Emery in Portland. But a change coming over his views of life, he devoted himself to Christ and the church. He received from Brown University the honorary degree of A. M. in 1845.

BENJAMIN GREENE. 1801—1837.

Benjamin Greene was the second son and fourth child of Benjamin Greene and Martha Brown of Waltham, Massachusetts, and was born in that place May 5, 1764. He graduated at Harvard College in the class of 1784, which contained the honored names of Professor Abbott of Bowdoin College, Silas Lee, Chief Justice Mellen, Benjamin Pickman of Salem, and President Webber of Harvard College. He studied divinity, and was settled in Medway, Massachusetts, in the ministry, June, 1788. He was dismissed from the pastoral office in 1793, and went to Marblehead, where he remained a few years engaged in teaching. In 1797, he was invited to take charge of the Berwick Academy: accepting this proposal, he moved to that place, and entered upon the course of instruction in that seminary. While pursuing the duties of Preceptor, he had his name entered in the office of Dudley Hubbard as a student at law. In 1801, he closed his vocation as an instructor of youth, was admitted to the bar, and entered at once, full fledged for law and politics, on a hearty pursuit of both.

Mr. Greene commenced practice with great advantages; he had a mature, well-cultivated mind; he had large knowledge of the world, and varied experience; he had a good voice, easy manners, was a fluent speaker, and had abundant confidence in himself. He therefore moved forward with considerable rapidity; he took an active part in the various interests of the town, parochial and educational, in which his experience gave wisdom to his counsels. In 1809, he was elected a representative to the General Court, and was re-elected in 1810, 1811, 1813, 1815, 1816, 1817, and 1819: he was a member of the convention of 1819 which formed the Constitution of Maine, took an active part in the debates of that learned body, and was one of the committee to make application to Congress for the admission of the State into the Union.

While a member of the Legislature in 1811, in the administration of Governor Gerry, the old Court of Common Pleas, which had existed from the days of the charter, was abolished, and a new system was established called the "Circuit Courts of Common Pleas," by which the Commonwealth and Maine were divided into circuits, in each of which a chief justice and two associates were appointed. Maine was divided into three circuits, "the first Eastern Circuit," embraced the counties of York, Cumberland, and Oxford; over this branch Mr. Greene was appointed chief justice, and Judah Dana and William Widgery, associates. Judge Greene entered with vigor and vivacity upon this new sphere of action, and discharged its duties with great promptness and fidelity. He magnified his office, and upheld the dignity of the bench with scrupulous exactness; was somewhat formal and precise in his manner, not to say, pompous, and although not a very learned judge, he conducted the business of the court with urbanity, impartiality, and integrity. He held the office until the establishment of the new Court of Common Pleas, which took place under the act of Maine, passed February 4, 1822. He had been, for several years before this appointment, a special justice of the old court of Common Pleas for sessions business, and held the office of county attorney.

In 1824, Judge Greene was again called to represent his town in the Legislature, and was chosen Speaker of the House. In September of the same year, he was appointed by President Adams, Marshal of Maine, as successor to Thomas G. Thornton of Saco, who had held the office from 1803. This was his last public service, which, ending in 1830, he moved to Athens, in Maine, where his son, Dr. Benjamin F. Greene, then resided, and passed the remainder of his life in a peaceful retirement, to its close, October 15, 1837, in the seventy-fourth year of his age. His wife had died in 1830.

Judge Greene was short in stature, and of a full figure; his features were large, and his complexion dark. He was an easy and rather graceful speaker, used good language and had a powerful voice; his manner was inflated, and his gesticulation somewhat overdone. But he was, in general, popular as a speaker, and did not avoid occasions for display. He was not a profound lawyer, but presided very well in a court which was not called upon to pronounce final decisions.

Judge Greene married Lydia Clark, daughter of the Rev. Jonas Clark of Lexington, Massachusetts, the worthy minister of that town for half a century, through the trying conflicts of the Revolution, who died in 1805. His daughter Lydia was born there in 1768. By her Judge Greene left five sons; he had no daughters. His oldest son, Benjamin Franklin, a physician, who resided at Athens, now at Parkman; and Frederick, a lawyer at Saco, — only survive. His son Charles, born at Marblehead, Feb. 21, 1796, graduated at Dartmouth College in 1811, a classmate of Judge Shepley, Judge Parker of the Cambridge Law School, and other prominent men, was a successful lawyer, first in South Berwick and then at Athens, Maine; was a senator in the Legislature in 1835; councillor in 1836, and several years judge of Probate for Somerset County. He married Sarah Sawtelle of Norridgewock, by whom he had several children. He died August 24, 1852. Another son, Henry Bowen Clark, was a distinguised physician in Boston, where he died in 1848. His other son, Bowen Clark, was a lawyer in Saco.

WILLIAM ABBOT. 1801—1849.

For the following interesting sketch, I am indebted mainly to the hand of a relative and friend of the subject. It was my good fortune to know Mr. Abbot with considerable intimacy, and I take much pleasure in adding my testimony to this just and beautiful tribute to his memory.

William Abbot was born at Wilton, Hillsboro' County, New Hampshire, November 15, 1773. His father, William Abbot, was a native of Andover, Massachusetts, where he married Phebe, daughter of Timothy Ballard, also of Andover, who was the mother of the subject of this notice. Mr. Abbot, the father, moved, early in life, from Andover, the place of his nativity, to Wilton, where he settled as a farmer, and where he died, in 1793, in the full vigor of his powers, at the age of forty-six years, having the unqualified respect of his fellow-citizens. He was a member of the State Convention of New Hampshire, which, in 1788, adopted the constitution of the United States. He was a descendant in the fifth degree from the American ancestor of the family, George Abbot, who, in 1644, emigrated from Yorkshire in England, and was one of the first settlers of Andover. The farm originally taken up by him remains in the Abbot family to the present time.

Young Abbot passed his early years upon the paternal farm in Wilton; and there he probably acquired the love for horticulture which he carried with him through life. He began preparation for college in his native town, in 1790, in the town school, under the care of Jonathan Fisher, then an undergraduate of Harvard College, and subsequently settled in the ministry at Bluehill, Maine. After due preparation, he entered Harvard College, where he ever maintained a high character for industry and moral worth. He was graduated at the Commencement in 1797, delivering a poem on the occasion on his favorite subject, "Music." Among his classmates who subsequently arose to eminence, were the late Dr. John C. Warren, and the Hon. Horace Binney of Philadelphia, who was Mr. Abbot's room-mate. With both of these gentlemen, he maintained relations of intimate friendship to the close of his life.

Mr. Abbot had a fine natural taste for music, and in his

early years he taught vocal music in Connecticut and Massachusetts. On leaving college, he commenced the study of law with William Gordon of Amherst, New Hampshire, an eminent lawyer, and a graduate of Harvard, in 1779. Having completed a full course of professional study, in 1800, he was admitted to the bar. He removed from his native State to the then District of Maine, in 1801, and commenced the practice of law at Castine, in Hancock County, where he remained for nearly thirty years, assiduously engaged in the practice of his profession. In May, 1802, Mr. Abbot married Rebecca, daughter of Dr. Israel and Rebecca (Stevens) Atherton; he was a distinguished physician, residing in Lancaster, Massachusetts.

In a brief biographical sketch, by Hon. Jacob McGaw, a distinguished member of the Penobscot Bar, in reference to Mr. Abbot's professional life at Castine, he says, "His entire devotion to all the proprieties of life, and his constant attendance at his place of business, did not pass unobserved by the merchants and other energetic men, among whom he had come to live. All of his surroundings indicated that he was worthy of the confidence of a virtuous people. His subsequent life supplied complete confirmation of the correctness of its foreshadowings."

Mr. Abbot enjoyed the confidence of the people among whom he had taken up his residence, not only in their business relations, but also as a public agent. He held the office of Register of Probate eighteen years from 1803, until the separation. In 1816, he was appointed one of the electors of President and Vice President, on the ticket with Christopher Gore, Prentiss Mellen, Israel Thorndike, William Phillips, and others: the vote of the college was given entire to Rufus King, who received but thirty-four out of the two hundred and seventeen votes cast. In 1816, he was chosen a member of the Brunswick Convention. His town, Castine, was strongly opposed to separation, having given seven votes in favor to sixty-five against the measure: he, of course, represented the sentiment of his people, and denounced the action of that body. In 1819, he was a member of the convention which met at Portland and framed the constitution under which we live, and was on the committee to select the baptismal name of the new State.

He was a representative in the first Legislature of the State, and in those of 1823, 1826, and 1827, in all of which he was an industrious, useful, and intelligent member, watching carefully, as it was our fortune to know, with deep interest all that related to the honor and welfare of the new republic.

"In 1829, Mr. Abbot removed to Bangor, where he soon established for himself the substantial and dignified reputation he had previously earned, and worthily worn in the county of his former labors." Here the popular confidence in him was soon manifested by his election to places of public trust. He was, for a considerable time, a member of the Board of Selectmen of the town before its adoption of a city government; and chairman of the board when that change was made. He was chairman of the committee chosen to draw up a charter for the prospective city, and the charter adopted was almost wholly his work. He had been a member of the superintending school committee of the town of Bangor, and after the adoption of the city charter, he was chairman of the board some twelve years. In connection with his official labors in this department, the sketch before quoted from, continues, "Under his fostering care, a system and grade of schools, teachers, and tasteful structures, which it is believed has no superiors in the State, was developed and completed. A beautiful plat, containing about three acres, was purchased by the city, stocked with handsome shade trees, and ornamented with pleasant gravel walks.

Then, by a vote of the city council, it received the honored and merited appellation of 'Abbot Square.' The plat is set apart for the exclusive use of schools, with suitable play grounds for the children. Confidence in this estimable man was further manifested by his being elected to the office of mayor of the city in the year 1848. Again, in the succeeding year, he was elected with great unanimity to the same office. But he soon finished the work that had been assigned him on earth. In August of this year he died, and was deeply mourned."

The intellect of Mr. Abbot was clear, strong, and discriminating, rather than brilliant, imaginative, and original. It was well-balanced and logical; its pre-eminent characteristic was practical common sense, constituting the possessor of it a man of sound, reliable judgment. As an advocate and a public speaker, he was not an eloquent man, in the popular sense of that word. His eloquence consisted in his earnestness, his sincerity, his deep conviction. But he possessed great influence with juries, whose reason and sense of moral right he addressed, rather than their feelings or their prejudices. He never allowed the advocate's desire of success to obscure or prevail over the moral convictions of the man; and therefore, when he expressed an opinion, unqualifiedly, to the jury, they knew it to be the sincere conviction of the man, not the partial view of the advocate. He was regarded by his legal brethren and compeers as a sound lawyer, thoroughly read in his profession, learned, astute, and able, and was greatly respected by them.

In his opinions and in his character, Mr. Abbot, both by nature and by habit, was conservative. Yet a rational, not a blind conservatism — one which not only receives, but demands progress; a conservatism which will not accept all change as progress, nor all destruction as improvement; but a conservatism which, while putting forth its aspirations and its efforts for the higher and the better, still labors to "prove all things," and to "hold fast that which is good."

In politics, Mr. Abbot was a disciple of Washington, Hamilton, Jay, and Ames, — a worthy and consistent member of the old Federal party, the principles and measures of which had been inaugurated, developed, sustained, and adorned by the efforts and toils of those illustrious patriots. Of this party he continued to be a member so long as it existed as a distinct organization. In the latter years of his life, he was a member of the Whig party.

In his religious views, from examination and conviction, he was a firm and decided Unitarian Christian of the school of Noah Worcester, Channing, and the Wares. In the formation of his opinions, he was independent. Eminent names had but little influence over him. Upon all subjects which he regarded as important, he formed his opinions slowly and with much caution. And when, after thorough and patient examination, he had come to adopt an opinion through conviction of its truth, he held it persistently. Yet he was not a bigot, but he was always ready to receive and honestly weigh new evidence, to accept new light upon every subject. Firmly as he held his own views, he was always tolerant, liberal, and courteous to those from whom he differed.

The universal respect awarded to Mr. Abbot, and the confidence and trust reposed in him by those who differed most widely from him upon political, theological, and other subjects, bear unquestioned testimony to his sound judgment, and not less to his disinterestedness, his integrity, his sincerity, and his conscientiousness. Throughout his whole life, from childhood to old age, he maintained a pure and well-balanced character. He was singularly unselfish, liberal, and public-spirited. With a native delicacy of feeling, and reserve amounting almost to diffidence, he was liable to be regarded as unsympathetic and cold. Yet those who were acquainted with him in his family relations, and in the intimacies of private friendship, knew how quick and broad were his sympathies, and how strong and enduring were his attachments.

In person, Mr. Abbot was fully six feet in height, of rather spare form, but of remarkable muscular power. The natural expression of his countenance when in repose was dignified and grave; but when moved by the gentle emotions, its expression became amiable and beneficent, with a peculiarly winning sweetness. "He is a good man," was the earnest exclamation of a child who had received one of his pleasant smiles; and when excited by quiet humor, of which he had a keen appreciation, it lighted up with mirthful animation.

Upon the Sunday after his interment, a just and discriminative discourse upon his character was preached by Dr. F. H. Hedge, then in charge of the Unitarian Society in Bangor. An extract from that discourse will conclude this notice.

"As a public functionary, Mr. Abbot was distinguished by entire devotion to the trust assigned him, by a wise regard to the public good, and a conscientious discharge of the duties he assumed. It is not, however, as a public officer, whatever the ability, his knowledge or his zeal, that we love best to remember him, but as a private citizen — as a man. His character was remarkable for its harmony; a character in which no passion or sentiment was unduly prominent, but all combined in just proportion, each in its order, each within bounds, each subservient to all the rest, and all subjected to the moral sense which reigned supreme in his heart and life. Characters so constituted are not apt to become famous, unless placed by accident in a commanding position; but place them where you will, they act with beneficent effect on the sphere in which they move; they are the strength and marrow of the state. It is the prominence of some one quality that makes the great man; it is the balance of all the qualities proper to humanity that makes the useful man.

Mr. Abbot was not ambitious; he sought no distinction, he sought no office. In these days of selfish competition, when the spoils of party and the lust of place are tempting so many from the paths of useful industry, and making politics a scramble for prizes and a name for intrigue, he was content to labor from year to year, with no other emolument than the slow returns and ordinary gains of his profession; and while in politics he took a decided stand, he did it from conviction, and not from calculation; and asked nothing from government, but to leave him undisturbed in the peaceful pursuit of his calling. He coveted no man's goods, he asked no man's vote, he sacrificed nothing to popularity, nothing to the fear or favor of men. Whatever of popularity he enjoyed, was unbought and unsought. Too proud to beg, too honest to intrigue, too meek to claim, he lived by labor, and continued to labor at threescore years and ten, as he had labored at two-score, and "honest poverty" preferred to "gainful perjury." A conscientious man, quick to perceive, and strict to interpret, the claims of duty; a man whose chief aim and constant study it was to do right and to render unto all their dues. If I should say that he was an honest man, I should do imperfect justice to my conception of his character in this regard. Let me rather say, a man in whom honesty was incarnate; whom no conceivable bribe could have tempted to swerve from the strict integrity of his life; with whose character aught of meanness or obliquity refused even in imagination to combine. Honor and probity composed the aroma of his name.

Mr. Abbot was a religious man, a Christian by confession and by practice; uniting the performance of Christian ordinances, and exhibiting the best fruits of the Christian spirit in his character and life. While, for his own part, he embraced, with his whole soul, that form of doctrine which is commonly called Unitarian, he was tolerant of all opinions, honestly formed and sincerely held, and sought the proofs of the Christian character, not in the creed but in the life. It is no small praise to say of any man, what in strictest truth may be said of him, that he was blameless, and led from the first commencement of his active existence until its close, a blameless life. To be possessed of some one distinguished virtue is less infrequent than to be without reproach. He was one to whom no scandal or breath of suspicion could ever attach,—whose pure fame no obloquy ever dared to assail,—whom to know was to respect, whom to name was to praise."

WILLIAM CROSBY. 1802—1830.

We cannot better follow our notice of Mr. Abbot than by introducing here a brief biography of one of his contemporaries of the same admirable qualities which we have shown that he possessed. Judge Crosby was his contemporary in college and at the bar. They were of strong kindred sympathies in religion and politics, and were guided in all their conduct by the same sterling principles in morals.

Judge Crosby's earliest American ancestor was Simon of Cambridge, who came over in the Susan and Ellen in 1635, at the age of twenty-six, with Ann, his wife, and son Thomas, but eight weeks old. His son Simon, born in 1637, moved to Billerica, Massachusetts, and was the head of that branch of the family. Thomas, the eldest son of the first Simon, born in England, was the head of the Cape Cod family; and Joseph, born in 1639, was head of the Braintree stock, the ancestor, as Gov. Crosby informs me, of the *Major Crosby*, an acting justice of Billerica, in whose court the elder President Adams first fleshed his maiden sword; and also of the several Professors Crosby, of considerable literary fame.

The Governor adds, "I have heard my father remark that if any of his descendants ever attained to any eminence, it would be through their own merits, not those of their ancestors; for that the highest position in church or state ever occupied by any of his ancestors, was that of first selectman, deacon, or captain of a military company; adding that he found comfort in the fact that no one of them, to his knowledge, had ever been hung!" This is a pleasant piece of badinage, but not exactly true, for we find that even the first Billerica Simon was several times chosen a representative to the General Court, first in 1692, at a time when the office was really a mark of distinction; other honors have waited on the family.

Judge Crosby was born in Billerica, June 3, 1770. His father was a farmer in moderate circumstances, and his son William was destined to the same occupation; but at the age of seven years, one of those events occurred, which, as in numerous other cases, so much so as to seem *Providential*, changed the course of his future life. Playing about a cider mill while in operation, his right hand was caught in the machinery, and his arm was drawn in nearly to the shoulder, and so crushed as to cripple it for life. This disqualified him for manual labor, and he could not even use it in writing — he always wrotewith his left hand.

This event, seemingly sad and disheartening, was full of precious hopes and results: the necessary resort was an education, for which he soon began to prepare. But he had to struggle with poverty and adverse circumstances. At the age of seventeen, he began to teach school and prepare for college, the latter portion being accomplished at the Phillips Academy, Andover, then under the care of Master Pemberton. He entered Harvard College, 1790, and took his degree in regular course, in 1794. Among his classmates were Rev. Timothy Alden, William Bigelow, better known among his college companions as "Sawney" Bigelow, and the late Professor McKean of Harvard. Not one of the class is living: Rev. Isaac Braman was the last survivor. The class was made somewhat famous by Bigelow's "classology," or class song, which was sung and remembered many years after, through the college halls: it preserves, like Goldsmith's "Retaliation," some striking characteristic of each scholar. The rythmical measure was in imitation of the "Heathen Mythology," a popular song of that day, "Songs of Shepherds in rustical roundelays." A few stanzas of this Bacchanalian extravaganza will show its spirit and character:

"Witty *George Appleton*,[1] high blooded *Atherton*,[2]
Rigadoon *Atkinson*[3] joined the high *Go*.

Here little high *Sawney*,[4] call'd Bigelow, appeared in view,
Amid the full chorus distending his lungs.

Now jovial *Channing*[5] kindled merriment fanning,
Was never for ganging while liquor would flow;
And *Crosby*, the blood, would be damn'd if he would,
Sneak off if he could, and not join the high *Go*.

---

1 Appleton died in 1808.

2 Charles H. Atherton, a distinguished lawyer of New Hampshire, and Representative in Congress, died 1853.

3 John Atkinson died 1838.

4 William Bigelow died January 12, 1844, in Boston, aged seventy. Allen, in his Biographical Dictionary, says of him, "He was a wit, writer of poetry, editor of several periodicals, and author of a history of his native town, Natick, and of Sherburne. He unhappily disregarded the laws of Temperance."

5 Francis Dana Channing, brother of Rev. Dr. Channing, died in 1810. He was a lawyer in Boston.

While *Braman*[1] split razor, buffoon of pleasure,
Made fun without measure, to assist the high *Go*.

From Pike's learned page, came *McKean*[2] in a rage,
The full vessels to guage, boys, and bless the high *Go*."

Mr. Crosby, on leaving college, took charge, for a year, o the Aurian Academy at Amherst, New Hampshire, on a salary of seventy-five pounds lawful money a year: after which he pursued the study of law two years in the office of William Gordon, a very prominent lawyer in Amherst. His third year was spent under the care of Samuel Dana at Groton, when he was admitted to the bar in Middlesex County in 1798, and immediately opened an office in his native town. He remained here three years, but being desirous of changing his location, he made a tour of exploration into Maine, which then seemed to be a land of promise to young lawyers, a promise often broken to their hopes; not, however, to the hopes of the truly persevering and meritorious, as our record fully shows. He at first proposed to settle in Bangor, which then was a wild and uncultivated field; but finally determined on Belfast, to which place he moved January 2, 1802. Mr. Crosby was the second lawyer who settled in Belfast: Bohan P. Field had preceded him a short time. It was then a small place, containing but about eight hundred inhabitants, but was favorably situated on a beautiful harbor and bay, which gave encouragement of a rapidly increasing business. The town belonged to Hancock County, the shire of which was Castine, on the opposite side of Penobscot Bay. This connection continued during nearly the whole of Mr. Crosby's

1 Rev. Isaac Braman, pastor of the church in Georgetown sixty-one years, died in 1858, aged eighty-eight, honored and respected.

2 Prof. McKean of Cambridge, died in 1818, eminent for learning and piety.

practice, the bar containing many able lawyers. It was at this bar that Chief Justice Parker, Isaac Story, William Abbot, and John Wilson commenced their professional lives; and here, as young practitioners, early came Allen Gilman, Jacob McGaw, and William Crosby. Abbot, Wilson, Gilman, and McGaw were the competitors through a series of years in the practice of Hancock, which embraced also what is now Penobscot County, and also in Washington County on the east, and Lincoln on the west. On this large circuit, these and other lawyers traveled and labored, and there often encountered the adroit and experienced advocates of the older parts of the State,— Mellen, Wilde, Orr, Lee, &c., who were accustomed to travel the circuit. In this honorable competition, Mr. Crosby ably sustained himself, not only as a sound and honest lawyer, but as an ingenious and popular advocate. For several years, in the early part of his practice, he was county attorney, which made him familiar with the criminal side of the court. A gentleman of the profession,[1] a townsman, and competent to speak on this point, said in a well-prepared notice of his death, "As a sound, practical lawyer, he filled the largest space in the community, and will the longest be remembered as the safe counsellor, the able advisor, and the eloquent advocate. His clear, logical mind readily comprehended the most complicated questions. He at once analyzed and seized upon the strong points of the case, enforcing his views and positions upon the minds of the jury with that clearness of illustration and that force of reasoning which were always effective and often irresistible." Another lawyer, and a competent witness in the case, thus speaks of his merits: he says, "There was one trait in the character of Mr. Crosby as a lawyer, which contributed much to secure

[1] Hiram O. Alden.

the high reputation which he had acquired. No considera-tion would induce him to undertake the prosecution or defense of an action, unless morally convinced that the ground of his client was maintainable." Again, the same writer says, " As an advocate, he possessed a clear, musical voice, and a happy power of illustration. He was lucid and logical in his reasoning, fluent in his enunciation, never at a loss for the most appropriate language to express his ideas. He knew how to seize and dwell upon the strong points in his cause. He could be playful or witty, or embellish with the flowers of rhetoric as occasion might require: his elo-quence was of the most attractive character." Mr. McGaw, whose competency to pronounce nobody will deny, says, " Mr. Crosby was generally deemed to be the ablest advo-cate and best lawyer then living in the large county of Hancock."

In 1811, on the reconstruction of the Court of Common Pleas, Mr. Crosby was selected as the chief justice in the third Eastern Circuit, embracing the counties of Hancock, Washington, and Penobscot. Nothing could have been more complimentary, for he was a firm and well-known oppo-nent of the administration of Gov. Gerry, by whom the appointment was made. He was the only lawyer on the bench of this circuit; his associates were democratic politi-cians,—Martin Kinsley of Hampden, and James Campbell of Harrington in Washington County. Kinsley was that year in the council, and Campbell was often a senator. This office Judge Crosby held until 1822, when a new court was constituted by the State under its separate organization, consisting of but three judges for the whole territory; of which Ezekiel Whitman was appointed chief justice, and Samuel E. Smith of Wiscasset, and David Perham of Brewer, associates. The administration being in the hands of the democratic party, it was deemed to be a State necessity, or rather a party necessity, that a majority of that court, as of the Supreme Court, should be on that side in politics. The Federalists having the chief justiceship in each court, the associates were consequently taken from the supporters of the administration. Judge Crosby's qualities for the distinguished office he had held for eleven years were of a high order. Calm, patient, learned, and discriminating, he carried to the investigation of causes a clear judgment and a most upright mind. The writer whom we have before quoted, Mr. Williamson, thus speaks of him as a judge: "On his elevation to the bench, he more than equaled public expectation as a judge. Quick in his perceptions, learned in the law, nice and discriminating in his judgment, and placing a cause in the clearest light before a jury, he was not exceeded by any judge in the State." Surely, the State ought not to have parted with the services of such a man and such a judge. But the law of party is inexorable; rotation has its victims while it exalts its worshippers.

Judge Crosby returned to the bar in 1822, and continued the practice of his profession with eminent success until 1830, when he carried into effect a resolution which he had long before adopted, to retire from all active business at the age of sixty years. Having reached that grand climacteric, he gave up his office and all professional engagements to his accomplished son, William G. Crosby, afterwards Governor of the State, and retired to his books, his philosophy, and his farm. With admirable complacency and self-denial, did this philosophic man, in full health and the maturity of his powers, give up the honors and emoluments of his profession and the blandishments of a popular life, for the quiet pursuits of friendship and study, which were congenial to his tastes. He was a good scholar, and pursued his investigations into almost every department of science. His examinations into some of the branches of natural philosophy are said to have been acute and valuable. "As a naturalist, few men have devoted more patient study to the mechanism of nature." In a letter from his son to me, before referred to, he says, on his retirement, "The remainder of his days was passed in the society of his books — he was a constant reader; in the preparation of manuscript on various topics; and in agricultural and horticultural pursuits, of which he was passionately fond." In this manner glided on the last twenty-two years of his life. He died of paralysis, March 31, 1852. "Until two years before his death," says his son, "he had enjoyed almost uninterrupted, vigorous health. His was truly a 'green old age;' and no man ever enjoyed life more than he did." His death was serene and tranquil as his life had been.

> "The stream is calmest when it nears the tide,
> The flowers are sweetest at the even-tide,
> The birds most musical at close of day,
> And saints divinest when they pass away."

Soon after Mr. Crosby became established at Belfast, on October 12, 1802, he took a wife from his native town, who continued, during his long life, to be his partner and companion, and the light and blessing of his domestic circle, and who survived him to mourn a great bereavement.

Judge Crosby had no taste for the excitements of politics. "He was a Federalist, a title which, to the very last," says his son, "he claimed to be proud. In his religious faith, he was a Unitarian. In neither politics nor religion was he a bigot, but in both liberal to an extent which some men count a fault." His party, both in religion and politics, was generally in a minority; but as he did not form his opinions for the profit of them or the honor, but from a sincere conviction, it mattered not to him what the world thought or believed: nothing did or could move him from his conscientious convictions. He was once elected to the Senate of Massachusetts, in 1815. In 1812, he was chosen an elector of President and Vice President, on the board with General Heath, Harrison Gray Otis, Nathan Dane, Lothrop Lewis, Israel Thorndike, and others. Massachusetts cast her twenty votes for DeWitt Clinton, in opposition to James Madison. I know of no other political office held by him.

I will close this notice with a few extracts from Mr. Alden's remarks, as he was his neighbor and knew him well: "As a companion, he was cordial and communicative; as a neighbor, kind, social, and accommodating; and as a citizen, just and humane. As a benefactor, Judge Crosby occupied a high position, taking the lead in most of the charitable, educational, and religious enterprises of the day. The erection, in 1818, of the spacious church of the First Congregational Society, Unitarian, in Belfast, and the installation therein of the Rev. William Frothingham, were objects in which he felt a lively interest and took an active part. There, in the sanctuary of his own erection, and with the pastor of his own choice, he was a regular and constant worshipper for a period of more than thirty years."

BARRETT POTTER. 1801—1822.

The Potter family were early immigrants to this country. John and William, each with a wife and two children, were of the company of the eminent and Rev. John Davenport, one of the founders of the New Haven Colony. They arrived in Boston in 1637; and the next year, 1638, the company proceeded to the place which is now New Haven, where they laid the foundation of that thriving community.

William Potter was the ancestor of the subject of this notice. His grandson, Daniel, was born in North Haven, in 1685; his son Daniel, born June 9, 1718, married Martha Joes, March 11, 1741, and soon after moved to Plymouth in Connecticut: he had five sons and three daughters: all the sons, viz., Jared, Elam, Isaiah, Lyman, and Daniel, were educated and graduated at Yale College, between the years 1760 and 1780. Isaiah, the father of Barrett Potter, took his degree in 1767, in company with the honored John Trumbull, and Governor Treadwell of Connecticut, and the famous theologian, Dr. Nathaniel Emmons of Franklin, Massachusetts. He was settled in the ministry at Lebanon, New Hampshire, and soon after married Elizabeth, a daughter of Colonel John Barrett, a native of Boston; but who moved first to Middletown in Connecticut, thence to Springfield, Vermont.

Their son, Barrett, was born March 8, 1777, at Lebanon. After passing through the usual preliminary studies, he was admitted to Dartmouth College, from which he received his degree in 1796: Bishop Chase of Illinois was one of his classmates. Deciding upon the profession of law as the future business of his life, he entered the office of Benjamin Gilbert, a leading lawyer in Hanover, New Hampshire, where he remained about a year, when he went to his uncle John Barrett's, in Northfield, Massachusetts, where he completed his studies, and was admitted to practice in the autumn of 1801. He immediately came to North Yarmouth, in this State, where he opened his office in November of that year. Here he remained until March, 1805, when he moved to Gorham, built him an office (still used as an office), and earnestly pursued his professional duties.

In 1806, the appointment of Judge Parker of Portland to the bench opened the way for some enterprising lawyer in that town. The late Chief Justice Mellen determined to improve the opportunity, and with that view invited Mr. Potter to take his office at Biddeford, — his business being then the most profitable, probably, in the county of York,—

worth two thousand dollars a year. But Mr. Potter having, about the same time, an offer from Mr. Chase of Portland, who was overwhelmed with business, and exhausted with its care, to form a connection with him; he preferred this situation, moved to Portland in June, 1806, and entered into partnership with that distinguished gentleman. But, unhappily for Mr. Potter, Mr. Chase survived this new arrangement but about two months, having died suddenly in August. But Mr. Potter, by his devotion to business, his skill and intelligence, retained much of the business, especially the collecting part, which was very considerable, arising from clients and correspondents in Boston and other places, who had reposed the utmost confidence in Mr. Chase. Mr. Potter, also, had the settlement of the estate of Mr. Chase, and the guardianship of his children: trusts which he executed with great exactness and integrity, both as regarded their education and their estates.

At the time Mr. Potter moved to Portland, the only lawyers in the town were Mr. Chase, William Symmes, both of whom died within a few months; Isaac Parker, appointed judge, and soon after moved to Boston; James D. Hopkins, Stephen Longfellow, Horatio Southgate; and Woodbury Storer, Jr., recently admitted. Law business was large and increasing, the trade and commerce of the town was extensive, never more so for many succeeding years than at that time. The tonnage of the port was thirty-nine thousand, and the amount received for duties at the custom house in 1806, was three hundred and forty-six thousand four hundred and forty-four dollars. A large trade was carried on with the West Indies in shipping lumber and provisions, and importing sugar, molasses, and rum. Mr. Potter's office business was lucrative, and occupied most of his time; he was not much employed as an advocate, but whenever his own cases needed that service, he did not shrink from performing it, and he presented them in a sensible, intelligent manner, without display or pretension. He had the entire confidence of his clients, and discharged his duty toward them with faithfulness for their best interest and to their satisfaction, so that he could justly say, on retiring from practice, that he had conscientiously endeavored to do his duty to his clients, to the courts, and to the community in which he lived.

In 1819, Mr. Potter was chosen a member of the Executive Council of Massachusetts, and in 1820, to the Senate of Maine from Cumberland County. That being the first Legislature which assembled in the new State, much important and responsible duty devolved upon it. The judges of the Supreme Court had been appointed commissioners to prepare a digest of the statute laws in force in the State: their report was made to the January session, and Mr. Potter, with Timothy Boutelle and Daniel Rose, were appointed a committee on behalf of the Senate to revise the report, and submit such alterations and suggestions in regard to the laws as the altered circumstances of our State seemed to require. This laborious task was promptly and ably attended to; and the laws published in 1821, under the superintendence of the judges of the Supreme Court, were the result of the action of the two committees. Judge Potter is now the only survivor of the Senate of that year, and Chief Justice Weston only remains, though much younger than Judge Potter, of the board of jurisprudence. The Legislature chosen in 1820, by a provision in the Constitution, held over to January, 1822: in that year he was withdrawn from political life by his appointment as Judge of Probate, successor to Judge Parris, who had been chosen Governor of the State in place of Governor King. This office Judge Potter held a quarter of a century, and retired from it in 1847, at the age of seventy, with intellect unclouded, his natural force scarcely abated, and with a just consciousness that he had administered his office with strict integrity, with unimpeached impartiality, and for the rights of the numerous classes of persons among whom the Judge of Probate stands a wise arbiter and a judicious friend, having a large discretionary power in relation to the widow and orphan, requiring that a tender compassion should be regulated and controlled by a sound judgment. Judge Potter brought to this office the admirable qualities which enabled him to discharge its duties with justice and equity.

In July, 1809, Judge Potter married Ann Titcomb, a daughter of the Hon. Woodbury Storer of Portland, by his first wife, who was a daughter of Benjamin Titcomb, and grand-daughter of Moses Pearson, honored citizens of Portland through a period of seventy years. By her he had three daughters,—Eliza, now living with her father unmarried; Mary, the first wife of Professor Henry W. Longfellow; the third, Ann, the wife of Peter Thacher of Rockland, a respected member of the bar of Knox County. Mrs. Potter was a lovely woman, but of frail and delicate organization: she died at the age of forty years in 1821.

ERASTUS FOOTE. 1801—1856.

Erastus Foote was one of the few lawyers who came to this State from Connecticut: he was born in Waterbury, in that State, October, 1777. That town was a place of some importance for its manufacturing and agricultural resources: it was the birth place of the celebrated Samuel Hopkins, D. D., the founder of the sect which took his name sixty years ago, the *Hopkinsians*. Mr. Foote was not educated at college, but after receiving ample advantages of preliminary study, he entered the office of Judge Samuel Hinkley at Northampton, at the age of nineteen, and having diligently pursued his studies under the instruction of this distin guished lawyer four years, he was admitted to the bar in Hampshire County, in 1800, and commenced practice in Northampton.

After a short experience at that place, he removed to Camden in Maine in 1801, where he was the successor of John Hathaway, who died in 1799, and was the second lawyer in the town. Its population did not then exceed one thousand, but his business was drawn from a much larger space of country, and from other persons than those who lived in that narrow circle. Mr. Foote was an enterprising and aspiring man, of considerable ability, and a power of displaying what he had to the best advantage. He was a handsome man, of florid countenance, a cheerful expression, tall, of a fine figure, and with a self-reliance amply sufficient to set off these qualities. His manner was somewhat pompous, and his arguments verbose, but he had no difficulty in saying what he wanted to say, and making himself understood. He was kind and genial in his disposition, and of a sanguine temperament: he made himself agreeable to the younger members of the bar. He was quite successful in his practice. In 1811, he succeeded Benjamin Ames as county attorney,—an office which enlarged his practice and increased his experience. He held this office to the time of separation, and was prepared by it for the duties of the higher criminal office to which he succeeded. In 1812, he was elected a senator to the Legislature of Massachusetts from Lincoln County on the Federal ticket; but the war breaking out with England while he held this office, he gave his adhesion to the National administration, and sustained the war measures of Mr. Madison. He was appointed the same year to the command of the fifth regiment of the second brigade, eleventh division of the militia of Massachusetts, and was called into service in 1814, when the British threatened the whole coast, and effected a landing at Castine and some other places. His exploits as a military man did not add to his reputation, and were made the theme of much raillery by the party which he had abandoned, whenever his name was brought forward for political office. He was an unsuccessful candidate of the Democratic party for Congress at that time.

After the war was ended, Mr. Foote, in 1815, moved to Wiscasset, the shire town of the county where he had married his wife. The question of separation from Massachusetts was now agitated, and Mr. Foote took sides with its advocates. He was elected to the House of Representatives of Massachusetts in 1819, and supported vigorously the measures proposed to accomplish that favorite object. He was elected to the first Senate which convened in Maine, in 1820, and before the close of his term, received the appointment of attorney general of the State. Gov. King, who made the appointment, carefully canvassed the qualifications of various candidates, and remarked that he knew no man better qualified for the office than Col. Foote. He had large experience as a criminal lawyer, as well as in other branches of practice, and other departments of business. He entered, therefore, upon its duties with great advantages, and is entitled to the commendation of having faithfully, ably, and promptly filled all the expectations of his friends in its discharge. The late William D. Williamson, the historian of Maine, in speaking on this subject, said, "Col. Foote held the office about fourteen years, a very correct, able and faithful prosecuting officer. It is said that he never lost but a single indictment for defect in form." Mr. Orr, a very competent judge in such matters, is reported to have said, "It is almost impossible to wrest a criminal out of the hands of Brother Foote." While in office, he made valuable suggestions to the government, which led to improvements in the criminal law. Mr. Foote was succeeded, in 1832, by Jonathan P. Rogers of Bangor, and returned to the bar, where he continued with almost youthful ardor to pursue the duties of his profession. He died July 4, 1856, at the age of seventy-nine, and was the oldest practicing lawyer at that time in the State.

Mr. Foote was a public-spirited citizen ; ready at all times to promote good objects ; he was kind and benevolent; prompt with his counsel and his purse for the relief of the distressed, and exemplary in all the relations of life. As early as 1820, he was elected a trustee of Bowdoin College, the duties of which he discharged for twenty-four years: in 1821, the college conferred upon him the honorary degree of Master of Arts. He was a friend of education, and was himself a cultivated man.

Mr. Foote married two daughters of Moses Carlton, an honored citizen of Wiscasset, who survived his son-in-law, and died the same year, aged ninety-one. By his second wife, he had one son, bearing his name and adopting his profession, a graduate of Harvard in the class of 1843, and several daughters.

CHAPTER XVII.

EBENEZER THATCHER — JOSEPH DANE — HORATIO SOUTHGATE — WILLIAM JONES — SAMUEL A. BRADLEY — JOHN WILSON — GEORGE HERBERT — JUDAH McLELLAN — NATHAN CUTLER — JOSEPH BARTLETT.

EBENEZER THATCHER. 1802—1841.

Ebenezer Thatcher, a younger brother of Samuel Thatcher, of whom we have, in previous pages, given an account which embraced the origin and descent of the family, was born in Cambridge, Massachusetts, October 9, 1778. He was educated at Harvard College, under the shadow of whose venerable halls he was born, and graduated in the class of 1798, which contained such illustrious names as Channing, Longfellow, Story, Tuckerman, Willard, and maintained such rank as to entitle him to membership of the Phi-Beta-Kappa Society. Professor Willard, in his interesting "Memoirs of Youth and Manhood," in describing the members of his class, says, "He was a young man of more than common talents and literary ambition, but somewhat self-distrustful. He acquitted himself well, however, in the performance of the tasks prescribed by the professors and tutors, and maintained a respectable relative rank in his class." He was something of an athlete in college: at that day it was the custom for the sophomore class, on the first or second week after the entrance of the freshman class, to give them a challenge to a wrestling match, and thus introduce them to the fellowship of this peculiar community. On the entrance of the class which graduated in 1800, containing the names afterwards renowned, of Allston, Buckminster, Boutelle, Lowell, Chief Justice Shaw; the sophomores, embracing Professor Cleaveland, Willard Hall, General Sumner, John Wilson of Belfast, &c., extended the customary challenge, which was, of course, accepted. The form was for all the classes to be present on "the play ground;" the seniors and juniors forming a circle, in the center of which, the combatants met for the Olympic game. The victory was generally in favor of the older class, but on this occasion, 1796, the freshmen routed the sophomores utterly: Weed, an agile, muscular young man of the freshman class, brought up on a farm in the county of Essex, stood triumphant, having thrown out every competitor. When such an event happened, it was usual for the junior class to enter the list and contest the victory. On this occasion the juniors put forth, as their champion, Ebenezer Thatcher, and the contest now rose to a high pitch of excitement. After a severe struggle, Weed, exhausted by his previous unparalleled efforts, was finally thrown by Thatcher, and to the juniors was awarded the victory. But so animated had been the contest, and so manfully did the freshmen sustain themselves, that the seniors invited them to a handsome supper as a token of approval for their manly bearing. At this jovial feast, one of the "*Noctes ambrosianæ*," there were sixteen toasts drank, among which were the following, "The students of Harvard University, — May their social disposition strew flowers of pleasure in the paths of science. The Freshman Class,—May its late victories animate it to encounter the sons of science. The Members of Harvard,—Never may the scorpion sting of envy and hatred rankle in their breasts." Weed was afterwards, for fifty years, a beloved physician in Portland.

After pursuing his regular course of legal studies, Mr. Thatcher commenced practice in Boston in 1801. But the next year, probably attracted by the success of his brother Samuel, at Warren, he came to Maine, and opened an office in Newcastle, and was the first lawyer who attempted practice in that place. At that time, it contained about one thousand inhabitants. In three or four years after this, he married Lucy Fluker, a daughter of General Knox of Thomaston, and soon after moved to that town. His classmate, and a friend of his early days, Professor Willard, says, in his "Memories," "The last time and place at which I saw him was in the year 1807 in Thomaston, at the house of Mrs. Knox, the widow of General Henry Knox, to whose daughter Thatcher had been recently married. As I was looking from her magnificent dwelling-house at the wide domain around it, and expressing my pleasure at the view, Mrs. Knox uttered a few words of just eulogy upon her deceased husband, who had died within a year preceding,—on his enlarged soul, his generous heart, his gentleness of demeanor, and his expansive benevolence."

Mr. Thatcher represented Thomaston in the General Court in 1814, being then one of the associate justices of the Circuit Court of Common Pleas for the second Eastern Circuit, to which he was appointed in 1812: the court consisted of Nathan Weston, Jr., chief justice, Benjamin Ames and himself, associates. Soon after his marriage, he resided a few years in Warren, and was there chosen a captain of artillery, from which he rose, through different grades, to the rank of brigadier general.

Mr. Thatcher, although of a cultivated mind and well-read as a lawyer, was not successful as an advocate. His natural diffidence, or "self-distrust," as his classmate Willard describes it, was a clog which embarrassed him, as it has many a brilliant scholar and lawyer before and since his day. Few men come to the bar, however well endowed in legal principles, who have the happy faculty of commanding their thoughts and the full sway of their powers, when the eyes of the court, the jury, the bar, and numerous spectators are all leveled at the only person "who has the floor." We have alluded to this embarrassment in the cases of Salmon Chase and Chief Justice Parker, both eminent as lawyers.

Mr. Thatcher held the office of judge during the period that Maine continued united with Massachusetts. By the reorganization of the courts under the new government, the circuit system was abolished, and a court for the State established, consisting of a chief justice and two associates, and new judges were appointed. Judge Thatcher returned to the practice, in which he continued, at Thomaston, Mercer, and Bingham, until his death, June 9, 1841, at the age of sixty-three. His widow died October 12, 1854, aged seventy-seven. They had a large family. The various places to which Judge Thatcher moved, viz., Newcastle, Thomaston, Warren, back to Thomaston again, Mercer, and Bingham, indicate a degree of instability which was unfavorable to progress or accumulation. "A rolling stone gathers no moss" is a proverb applicable to him: for some reason or other the fair prospects of his early life were not answered by the results of his later years. He died in a remote place, and poor.

JOSEPH DANE. 1802—1858.

Joseph Dane, who for fifty years was a distinguished member of the York County bar, and a prominent citizen of Maine, was descended from John Dane, who came from Essex County, England, to Roxbury, Massachusetts, in 1636, bringing two daughters and a son, John, born at Colchester in England, in 1613. John, the son, settled in Ipswich, Massachusetts, and was the direct ancestor of the eminent lawyer and statesman, Nathan Dane of Beverly, and of his nephew Joseph, the subject of the present notice. His parents were John and Jemima (Fellows) Dane of Beverly, where he was born October 25, 1778. His parents were natives of Ipswich, and died, the father in 1829, in his eightieth year; the mother in 1827, aged seventy-six.

Mr. Dane was fitted for college at the academy in Andover, and graduated at Harvard College in 1799, with the second honors of his class. His class contained such men as Parker Cleaveland, Willard Hall, Samuel D. Parker of Boston, William H. Sumner, John Wilson of Belfast, and Dr. Rufus Wyman. Mr. Dane was one of the best scholars in his class. In the commencement exercises he had an oration on "Speculation." Cleaveland had an English dissertation on "Modern Philosophy, or Universal Patriotism." On leaving college, he entered the office of his uncle, the distinguished Nathan Dane of Beverly, as a student at law, and was admitted to practice in Essex County, in June, 1802. The large practice and great learning of his uncle, and the association with the eminent men then coming upon the stage, Prescott, Jackson, Putnam, Story, all at the Essex Bar, could not but have animated the aspiring student with high and honorable motives of action, and an ardent desire to become distinguished in his profession.

Immediately after his admission, he opened an office at

Kennebunk, then a part of Wells, and soon became prominent as a sound lawyer, an able advocate, and an upright man. There were then in practice in that county, Prentiss Mellen, Cyrus King, Dudley Hubbard, Benjamin Greene, Joseph Thomas, John Holmes, and George W. Wallingford, all men of note at the bar and in public service, and who preceded him in the crowded funereal procession to the tomb. He continued in practice until 1837, having maintained for more than a third of a century, a character of spotless integrity, and of great honor and ability in his profession; and during the latter portion of the time, was a leader at the bar of York County.

Although his modesty and reserve caused him to shrink from public employments, he was induced, by the earnest application of his fellow citizens, occasionally to take office. In 1816, he was a member of the abortive convention at Brunswick, on the subject of the separation of Maine from Massachusetts; and in 1819, of the convention which formed the constitution of the State, and was one of the very able committee appointed to draft that instrument. In 1818, he was chosen one of the two members of the Executive Council of Massachusetts, then allowed to Maine, but he declined accepting the office. In 1820, he was chosen a member of the Sixteenth Congress, for the unexpired term of Mr. Holmes, who had been raised to the Senate; he was re-elected to the Seventeenth Congress, and having served out his term, he declined being again a candidate. He served his town as a Representative in the Legislature of the State, in the years 1824, 1825, 1832, 1833, 1839, and 1840, and the county in the Senate, in 1829. At the close of the session of 1840, he retired from public life altogether, having declined the appointment of commissioner to revise the public statutes, and the office of executive councillor, both of which were honorably tendered to him. He preferred the enjoyments of private life, and the repose of his own excellent family, to the bustle and excitement of political life. He was thoroughly and essentially conservative in all his views, and he had a great abhorrence of a demagogue and an intriguing politician, in whatever guise they might appear. He was a valued member of the old Federal party while it existed, but in the latter part of his life he took but little interest in politics. In every public office, and in every act of private life, his conduct was characterized by a firm, undeviating sense of right, and a conscientious determination neither to do nor to submit to what was unjust or wrong. No man or statesman's record is clearer than that of Mr. Dane, among all our public men or fellow citizens, through the more than half a century that he dwelt in our community.

In October, 1808, he married Mary, a daughter of the Hon. Jonas Clark of Kennebunk. Mr. Clark was a son of the Rev. Jonas Clark of Lexington, Massachusetts; and his wife was Sarah, a daughter of Dr. Edward Watts, a prominent physician of Portland before the Revolution, and a son of Judge Samuel Watts of Boston. Mrs. Dane is a lady of great excellence of character, and still survives. They had two sons and one daughter. His eldest son, Joseph, succeeded to his business, and in 1856, served as one of the Bank Commissioners. His second son, Nathan, is a farmer in Alfred. He represented his county in the Senate of the State in the years 1857 and 1858, and is now Treasurer of the State. From a stock so sound and healthful, we should be justified in expecting no other than excellent fruit.

He bore his last sickness, which was attended with considerable suffering, with cheerfulness and patience; and surrendered his parting breath with Christian resignation and trust. He died at Kennebunk, where the preceding fifty-six years of his life had been passed, May 1, 1858, aged seventy-nine. The death of such a man, although full of years, was felt as a public loss; and the community in which he lived, mourned with unfeigned sorrow the departure of a wise counsellor, a true friend, and an honest man. His death preceded that of his classmate, Prof. Cleaveland, just five months and a half; and but five from a class of forty-four now remain alive. Ebenezer Clapp and the Rev. William Frothingham, beside those before mentioned, John Wilson and Prof. Cleaveland, adopted our State, at an early period of their lives, as their place of residence; and all died among us, after enriching our community with the fruits of their wise and varied experience. The law, theology, and science are their debtors for large contributions made by them, in the early period of our commonwealth, to the departments they ably represented. In our zeal for the new, and the present, and the pressing, let us not forget those wise pioneers and vigorous men who strengthened the foundations of our young society, and defended its battlements through the struggles of our earlier and weaker day.

HORATIO SOUTHGATE. 1802—

Horatio Southgate was admitted to the Cumberland Bar at the October term of the Common Pleas, in 1802, held at New Gloucester. By the influence of William Widgery, who resided in New Gloucester, and was a leading justice of the peace, an active politician, and one of the irregular practitioners at the bar, a term of the Common Pleas was established at New Gloucester in 1791. It continued there until 1805, when it was removed to Portland; and the three terms were ever after, annually, held at the latter place, until that court was abolished. Davis, Symmes, Chase,

Hopkins, Greenwood, and Longfellow from Portland; Whitman of New Gloucester; Little of Gorham; Potter of North Yarmouth; and Morse of Freeport, attended the courts there, and were the only lawyers in the county at that time.

Mr. Southgate was the son of Dr. Robert Southgate of Scarboro', a practicing physician in that town, and one of the judges of the Common Pleas. He came from Leicester, Massachusetts, in 1771, with all his worldly gear in a pair of saddle-bags, on the horse which bore their possessor through the forests of Maine to that place. This worthy man, the father of several beautiful and accomplished daughters, died in 1833, at the age of ninety-two years. His wife, the mother of Horatio and his other children, was Mary, the daughter of Richard King of Scarboro', and sister of the renowned statesman, Rufus King.

Her son, of whom we are speaking, was born in Scarboro', in August, 1781. At the age of thirteen years, in 1794, he was placed at Exeter Academy, where he had for his associates, Henry Wadsworth, who gallantly perished before Tripoli, in 1803; Leverett Saltonstall of Salem, Massachusetts; the accomplished Joseph S. Buckminster, afterwards the pastor of Brattle Street Church, in Boston; Augustine and Bushrod Washington from Virginia; and Daniel Webster.

After the preparatory course at this celebrated institution, he entered the office of Salmon Chase in Portland, where he pursued the regular term of study prescribed by the rules, and was duly admitted to the honors and duties of the profession. He opened an office in Portland, but spent a portion of his time in Scarboro' assisting his father, who, in addition to the routine of his busy profession as a physician and his duties as judge, owned a very extensive farm; to this, and to all the neighboring lands and marsh where it was situated, he was giving additional value by the construction of a turnpike road over the very extensive marsh, forming the most direct and convenient route for the travel from Portland to Boston. This excellent road, long used for common travel, is now the bed of the railroad on the same route.

Mr. Southgate had his office in the building erected by the Portland Bank, now owned and occupied by the Canal Bank. His office, for many years, was on one side of the entrance to the banking-room, and Judge Whitman's on the other; and here he continued to practice until 1815, when, at the instance of Judge Whitman, a member of the Council, he received from Governor Strong the appointment of Register of Probate for the county of Cumberland. In this office he was retained twenty-one years, during the closing period of Judge Freeman's administration as judge, the whole of Judge Parris's, and a large part of that of Judge Potter. This fact alone is a sufficient testimonial to his accuracy and fidelity, to which I can properly add, that no man ever discharged the duties of the station with more promptness, integrity, and honesty than did this incumbent. The records during that period are a model for neatness and correctness.

In 1830, Mr. Southgate prepared "The Probate Manual, containing Forms adapted to the Practice of Probate Courts in the State of Maine," also the laws relating to the subject. This compilation was much needed, was well prepared, and is still in constant use.

Mr. Southgate, after the death of his father and mother, took possession of the homestead farm in Scarboro', where he continues to reside, enjoying a serene and vigorous old age.

By his three wives, he has had a large family of children, sixteen sons and daughters, but of whom only five are living. Among the sons, five were educated at Bowdoin College, and all became clergymen; viz., Robert, of the class of 1826, is minister at Ipswich, Massachusetts; Horatio, late Bishop of Constantinople, is settled in New York; Frederick and John B. are dead; and William S., of the Episcopal Church, is settled at Litchfield in Connecticut. His second wife was a daughter of Noah Webster, the renowned lexicographer; his first, a daughter of Major Hugh McLellan of Portland; his third, Miss Neal of Portland.

He made to me, recently, the following statement: "There is one fact respecting the Cumberland Bar, of which, I believe, it would be difficult to find a parallel instance in any other bar. It is this: in 1861, there were four of its members living, the youngest of whom was past eighty years of age." These were Judges Whitman, Emery, Potter, and himself. Emery is since dead. I can add to this singular fact the names of Samuel Thatcher, now living at Brewer, Maine, at the age of eighty-six; and Chief Justice Weston, now eighty, living at Augusta,—both of whom began practice in New Gloucester, and were members of the Cumberland Bar: also Judge Ware, now eighty, whom entered the Cumberland Bar in 1817; and General Fessenden, aged seventy-eight, whose membership runs from 1809. So that there now survive seven persons who were members of the Cumberland Bar, the youngest of whom is seventy-eight; three, eighty-six; one, eighty-one; and two, eighty years old.

WILLIAM JONES. 1801—1813.

William Jones was the first lawyer who settled in Norridgewock, if we except the itinerant and shattered remains of the once brilliant man, Timothy Langdon, who made that town his occasional residence for about two years, from 1795 to 1797. Langdon had practiced at Pownalboro', as we have before mentioned, prior to the Revolution, during which he acted as judge of the Admiralty Court for Massachusetts; and who, afterwards, by his dissipated habits, became a wanderer and an outcast, and died a pauper. Jones established himself in Norridgewock in 1802. He was the son of a worthy farmer in Concord, Massachusetts, and was born there in 1768. He was educated at Harvard College, from which he took his first degree in 1793, in a class containing the distinguished names of Judge Charles Jackson of Massachusetts, Francis C. Lowell, the Rev. Dr. Coffin of Buxton in this State, the Rev. Dr. John Pierce of Brookline, and Samuel Thatcher of Brewer. The latter is the only surviving graduate of the class. Mr. Jones was a man of fine natural abilities, and of very handsome personal appearance. His father spared no pains to give these qualities their highest advantages: he was placed under the tuition of one of the best lawyers in the county of Middlesex. Being trained well for the bar to which he was admitted in due course, he opened an office in his native town. But he had scarcely entered the practice before the war with France startled the whole country with its clarion notes, and the excitable and ardent young men, and many elders rose respondent to the shout. We have seen that a number of our profession in Maine laid down their law books, and put on the harness of war. Major Stoddard of Hallowell was a prominent one, and he died in the service after this impromptu war was over. The war of 1812 had the same inspiring effect, and we find Gen. Ripley and Col. Larned of our State eagerly entering the army; and so it is in the present unhappy conflict all over the North. Members of the profession are quitting the peaceful pursuits of the forum for the great arbitrament of battle. Col. Shepley and numerous others of Maine, we trust will adorn their names with the trophies of the field, as they have with those of the bar.

Jones was fired up with military zeal. He had devoted much time to the study and practice of belligerent tactics, and having a fine military bearing and considerable knowledge of the art, he received a commission as major, and proceeded with his regiment to Oxford, the head-quarters of the army. But this brief war was terminated as it begun, on the sea, by a series of brilliant actions, such as have illustrated the naval history of our country from its origin to the present day. On the disbanding of the forces, Mr. Jones returned to the bar, less fitted for the practice of his profession than when he broke away from it. He never could exorcise his military visions, and after he moved to Norridgewock, he paid more attention to the parade than to the bar; was chosen first a colonel, then a brigadier general; rode a horse elegantly, and made a very showy officer. He practiced in Concord until near the close of 1801, when he went to Warren in this State, and the next year to Norridgewock. Norridgewock was incorporated June 18, 1788, and had, in 1802, about six hundred and fifty inhabitants. It is a beautiful town, the county seat, lying on both sides of the Kennebec River, and contained, by the census of 1860, one thousand nine hundred inhabitants. Here he had a large farm, which he carried on in connection with his law business, of which, for a time, he had a full share. His manners were easy and popular; he won the affection of the people; and if he had devoted himself to either his farming or his profession, he might have retained his patrimony, which was respectable, and made large additions to it. But, fond of social life, fond of sports, proud of his gay horse and his own fine person, he mingled in assemblages of the people, and thus run out his business, and run down his farm, until he found himself dependent upon the good will of his friends for the support of himself and family. When Calvin Selden opened his office by the

Samuel A. Bradley

side of him in 1809, Mr. Jones had to seek other resources to sustain himself.

In 1809, the county of Somerset was organized, and the friends of Mr. Jones succeeded in procuring for him the offices of clerk of the courts and judge of Probate. He held the clerkship to the time of his death, except for a period of about ten months during the administration of Gov. Gerry in 1811, who made a pretty general sweep of all the opponents of his administration. He resigned the office of judge of Probate a short time previous to his death, which took place January 13, 1813, at the age of forty-five.

Mr. Jones was a man of wit, ready talents, and popular manners: his mind was capable of a high degree of improvement. On all public occasions, and as presiding officer at meetings of the people, he officiated with dignity and ease. And had he given to his profession the same time and effort which he permitted to run wild in other channels, he would have been a distinguished ornament to the bar. There can be no doubt that his youthful diversion to the army had an unfortunate influence upon the future success and results of his life.

SAMUEL AYER BRADLEY. 1803—1844.

Mr. Bradley was a descendant from the branch of the Bradley family which established itself in Concord, New Hampshire, as early as 1729, among the first settlers, when the plantation yet bore the Indian name of Penacook. His first American ancestor probably was Daniel, who, according to Savage, came in the Elizabeth from London, in 1635, at the age of twenty; settled in Haverhill, Massachusetts, where he was killed by the Indians, August 13, 1689. Daniel, probably his son, with his wife Hannah, and daughters Mary and Hannah, were also killed by the Indians, March 15,

1697. Joseph, of Haverhill, who is known to have been the ancestor of Samuel, the subject of our sketch, was surprised in his garrison house, at Haverhill, February 8, 1704, and his wife was a second time taken captive, and carried away by this relentless enemy: showing a series of sufferings and disasters seldom accumulated in one family.

Abraham, the son of Joseph, was the first of the name who settled in Penacook. He was one of the pioneers who moved up from the lower towns on the Merrimac to the rich meadows and intervals higher up this beautiful river. Among them were the Abbots from Andover; Ayers, Bayleys, Bradleys, Clements, Eastmans, Emersons, Hazens, &c., from Haverhill; Osgoods, Parkers, and Stevens from Andover; Hall and Stickney from Bradford; Peabody from Salisbury, &c.,—than whom no better colonists occupied the virgin soil of New England. Abraham Bradley died in 1754, having had ten children by his wife, Abigail Philbrick. His seventh son, Samuel, was the grandfather of the subject of our notice. He, too, was inhumanly massacred by the Indians in 1746, leaving by his wife, Mary Folsom of the Exeter family, a son, John, born February 13, 1742, and a daughter, Mehitabel, born 1745. John married Hannah Ayer, by whom he had nine children; viz., Robert, born June 17, 1772, who, by his wife, Abigail Bailey, was the father of our prominent citizens,—the late distinguished lawyer, Samuel Bradley of Saco, Dr. Israel Bailey Bradley, and the late Alexander Ramsey Bradley of Fryeburg; the other children of John were Samuel Ayer, Mary, John, Moses Hazen, George, Anna, Richard, and Ann Ayer who married John S. Barrow of Fryeburg. Richard, the only surviving son of this large family, was born February 28, 1790, and is now living in Concord in the enjoyment of a handsome estate, and the honor of a well-spent life.

Samuel Ayer Bradley was born in Concord, November 22,

1774. His father, John Bradley, was justly esteemed for his many virtues and the usefulness of his life. Mr. Bouton, in his valuable History of Concord, says he was "one of the most upright, useful, and honored citizens of the town." He died in 1815. He was the owner of large tracts of land at and near Fryeburg, to improve which three of his sons, Robert, John, and Samuel, emigrated to that town, where they became useful and respected citizens. Samuel went there about 1794, and in company with Asa Eastman, father of our respected brother of the bar, Philip Eastman of Saco, went to Cold River Valley, about fifteen miles north of Fryeburg Village, erected a log cabin, and spent one summer in the forest, felling trees and clearing lands preparatory to making farms and a permanent settlement. But the discomforts and privations of this mode of life, and the annoyance of the mosquito and black fly, were too severe a discipline for a young man of good taste and ardent aspirations. Returning to Fryeburg in the autumn, he placed himself under the instruction of Paul Langdon, a graduate of Harvard in the class of 1770, and the first preceptor of the academy at Fryeburg, by whom he was prepared for college, and entered Dartmouth in 1795. Perhaps it is not too much to say that the bar and the forum are indebted mainly to the mosquitoes and black flies for the services of Mr. Bradley, as they drove him from the pioneer life of the forest. In fitting for college, he was a schoolmate of the late Benjamin Orr, who had been occupied in his trade of joiner in Fryeburg. They both boarded at the house of Col. Page, about a mile from the academy, on the other side of the river. As it was something of a task to ford or ferry over the river in a canoe, boarders took their dinner with them. One day, their good landlady made for their lunch a large custard in a dish. Orr and Edmund Page, son of the Colonel, thinking to play a trick upon Bradley, slily put *tea-*

spoons in their pockets. This, good Mrs. Page observing, privately supplied Bradley with a *table*-spoon. So, when they sat down in the pine grove to eat their dinner, Orr and Page exultingly produced their spoons, and began eagerly to invade the custard: judge of their surprise when Sam brought out his table-spoon to get his share of the savory dish. They felt that the joke was a failure.

Mr. Bradley took his first degree in 1799. Among his classmates were Charles Coffin and Nathan Kinsman, subsequently lawyers in this State; and Roswell Shurtleff, long the distinguished professor of divinity and moral philosophy in the college. He soon after commenced the study of law in the office of Samuel Greene of Concord, afterwards a judge of the Supreme Court of New Hampshire, and finished his studies in Boston, partly in the office of John Heard, and was admitted to the bar of Suffolk.

Mr. Bradley, whose acquaintance with Daniel Webster commenced in college, was two years his senior. Their friendship continued through life. Mr. Bradley was quite sick in Concord in 1800, when Mr. Webster came down from Salisbury, watched with and attended upon him. The families of their parents were on intimate terms. Capt. Eastman, an aged relative, remarked that when the news of the battle of Bunker Hill reached Salisbury, Ebenezer Webster, the father of Daniel, was aroused, and the next day started fully equipped for the scene of action. On his way, he called at the house of John Bradley, father of Samuel, and said to him, "Who goes from Concord?" "I go," replied Mr. Bradley; "get off your horse, and spend the night, and we will start early in the morning." So prompt were the patriots of that day. Mr. Webster and Mr. Bradley kept up a correspondence for many years, and Mr. Bradley's friends have numerous letters of the distinguished statesman to him, beginning in 1801. At that time, Mr. Webster had charge of the Fryeburg Academy, was a student in Judge Dana's office, and was helping himself along by writing in the Registry of Deeds. It was when Mr. Bradley was in Boston, in 1801, that Mr. Webster wished him to procure some office in that town in which he could pursue his law studies. Bradley applied to Christopher Gore, then the most prominent lawyer in Boston; but Mr. Gore declined receiving him, although Mr. Bradley persevered in his application. At last, he carried to him one of Mr. Webster's literary productions, I think a Fourth of July oration, and requested Mr. Gore to read it, and then see if he would not change his decision. Mr. Gore took it with some impatience, saying he was very pertinacious, and dipped into it here and there, finally commenced at the beginning, and read it through; then said, "Bring your young friend along, and I will see him." Mr. Gore received him into his office, and frequently afterwards, when meeting Mr. Bradley in the street, would speak to him pleasantly for bringing that young man to his office.

We transfer to our pages a specimen of the correspondence of these friends, Mr. Webster to Mr. Bradley, genuine and racy. "Boscawen, August 19, 1806. Dear Sir,— Circumstances do not permit me to see you this week at Gilmanton. I am late from Boston, and at present am greatly pressed in my time by some little affairs. I have made up my mind to escort you to Commencement, if you desire to take that mode of conveyance. I have a comfortable chaise and an ordinary horse, that can draw us from this to Hanover in a day. If you have a nag to put before him *to open the cause*, mine, I think, would bring up the rear of the argument pretty well. However, we shall do tolerably well with one horse.

I shall expect to see you this way on Friday or Saturday, when we will make a definite arrangement. I should choose to be early at Hanover, and leave immediately after Commencement. Thursday and Friday are languid days. Dr. Perkins is expected this way to-morrow. His wife is at Hanover, and so is Mrs. Ticknor. I hear of many people who think of visiting Commencement,—probably because they know you and I will be there, and the collection, I fancy, will be numerous. Yours verily, D. WEBSTER.

P. S. Rebecca—Miss Rebecca McGaw, has just ridden by my window, going to Commencement. How the girls expect *us!*"

An anecdote of these two young lawyers and friends may not be out of place. They had been attending court at Sanborn, New Hampshire. After the adjournment, Mr. Bradley took Mr. Webster in his sleigh on their return home. He had a fine, large horse, justly called "Old Mars." As they were rising a hill toward night, they overtook a feeble old man who was struggling up the hill with a load of wood drawn by a poor, broken-down horse. The man, in turning his horse from the path to let the travelers pass, found his team sunk in the deep snow on the side, from which neither man nor horse seemed able to get clear. Webster and Bradley saw the sad plight and sadder countenance of the poor woodman, and without a moment's delay, they took their powerful horse off their sleigh, and, putting him into the woodman's team, soon extricated it, and moved it safely up the hill, to the infinite joy of the poor man, and their own happy consciousness of a good deed promptly done. They had a hard struggle to get the load out of the deep snow. Mr. Webster used a rail behind the load, and Bradley led the horse. The latter, in relating the story in after years, said, "Webster lifted like a giant."

Mr. Bradley established himself in Fryeburg, in the practice of law, in the latter part of 1803, or early in 1804, finding there Judah Dana and Jacob McGaw, making a large supply of legal talent for the small population. But, then, nearly all the lawyers in the county were concentrated at that point, there being but three others within its limits. Mr. McGaw moved to Bangor in October, 1805, and left Judge Dana and Mr. Bradley for some time alone: of them, one, Dana, was appointed judge, and the other register, of Probate, on the organization of the county of Oxford, in March, 1805. There was much rivalship between these gentlemen, not only at the bar, but in political life; for Mr. Bradley was a very ardent Federalist, and Judge Dana became, from a Federalist, a zealous Democrat; and the town, in its political character, was nearly divided. Mr. Bradley had numerous family connections in and about Fryeburg, which, with his legal ability both as a lawyer and advocate, secured for him a large business. He attended the courts of the three counties,—Oxford, York, and Cumberland, and maintained a respectable rank in competition with the leading lawyers in those bars. In 1810, he resigned the office of register of Probate. Mr. Bradley carried the ardor of his character into the practice of his profession: he identified himself with his client to such a degree as to believe him the abused party, and entered into his case as if vindicating his own: he often contributed from his own purse to pay the expenses of his client's suit. He was an exceedingly honorable practitioner, and it is believed that he never engaged in a cause which he considered unjust; although, from his kindly sympathies or impulsive temperament, he was liable to be deceived. Pursuing the profession on such principles, it was not a money-making business with him, nor was it a very favorite pursuit: there was much in the details of practice which he did not like. He took more interest in politics — it had a larger sweep; and during the exciting periods of the embargo, the war of 1812, and the discussions on separation, he threw himself with all his warmth of feeling into the conflicts of party. He was five years a member of the General Court from Fryeburg, from 1813 to 1818, and took a very prominent part in the debates of the house. He was a violent opponent of the war with Great Britain, and of the separation of Maine; and wrote and talked and pleaded on these subjects with all the energy of a man who was in earnest. His speeches were long, minute, and loaded with illustration and facts. Their fault was too much prolixity; but he was so fully imbued with the spirit of his subject that he was not willing to let it alone: he presented it in all ways, and repeated his thoughts in new language. His town voted against the separation in 1816, sixty-five yeas to seventy-six nays, and he was returned a delegate to the Brunswick Convention as an opponent of the measure. It is needless to say that he repudiated the mathematics of the majority of the Convention, which endeavored at that time to accomplish the separation by an ingenious construction of the condition requiring a majority of five to four of the votes cast to be in favor of the object. A renewed effort for the separation immediately followed the former defeat; and no measures were left untried by its friends to give it success. Their writers and actors were unwearied. Mr. Ware, now the learned judge, was invited from Boston to aid the cause by his vigorous pen: his articles in the Eastern Argus did essential service to it. The vote was taken in July, 1819, and resulted in a large majority for the affirmative — seventeen thousand and ninety-one in favor, and seven thousand one hundred and thirty-two against it. The vote of Fryeburg was seventy-eight yeas to seventy nays. This decisive vote settled the question, and there remained nothing further than to adjust the affairs and laws of Maine to its new condition. The opponents of separation had, therefore, to submit to the fate of unsuccessful combatants in a hard contested battle. Mr.

Bradley retired from the field, and his political life was ended.

About the year 1825, he moved to Portland, and engaged in speculations in timber lands, and other employments outside of his profession. He was very successful in his operations, making large purchases of land; and having some familiarity with the business, and the value of such property, and giving his personal attention to it, it became a source of profit and wealth to him. In 1825, he took much interest in the centennial celebration of Lovell's Battle, as it was called, which occured at Pickwacket, now Fryeburg, in May, 1725, by which the noted tribe of Indians seated at that place suffered severe loss in the death of their leader, Paugus. Capt. Lovell was also killed, and but eight of his company, which consisted of thirty-two men, returned to report the distressing tidings of the disaster. The effect of the battle, which lasted all day, was so discouraging to the Indians as to induce them to abandon the favorite resort of the tribe. The event was thought worthy of commemoration, and the people of Fryeburg united in a celebration worthy of the occasion. Ebenezer Fessenden, the oldest son of the Rev. William Fessenden, was the presiding officer. On the appointed day, a large concourse of people assembled at Fryeburg, coming not only from neighboring towns, but from Portland and other distant places. A numerous procession was formed in the village, and moved to the pond, which was the scene of the principal fight; and there Col. Bradley, resting upon his crutches, for he was suffering from a fractured leg, in an enthusiastic and eloquent manner, addressed the assembled crowd, describing the battle, and pointing out the places at which various incidents of the bloody engagement took place. The procession then returned to the village meeting house, where an elaborate and beautiful oration was pronounced by Charles S. Daveis of Portland, to a very large auditory. The ceremonies of the day closed by a public dinner, in which the important event, the historic scenes, and the progress of society through the hundred intervening years, were freshly remembered and recounted. Col. Bradley was a leading figure in this joyous festival, and largely contributed to its inception and consummation.

Mr. Bradley, in his prime, was a tall, well-made, and well-proportioned man, of handsome person, and easy, pleasant address. His personal appearance was not unlike that of the venerable Josiah Quincy. In the latter part of his life, he suffered a good deal from lameness, caused by the fracture of his leg in being thrown from a carriage in 1824 or '25. He alludes to this in his will: after speaking of the soundness of his mind and memory,—"for which," he says, "and all the unmerited favors, mercies, and blessings conferred upon me, I desire to be grateful to my Heavenly Father"—he adds, "but feeling sensibly the debilitating effects of the severe bodily injuries I have suffered, at different periods of my life; and of the protracted and wasting sicknesses of which I have been the subject within the last thirty-eight years;" he thinks proper to make his will. This was in 1838: in July, 1841, feeling the need of more kind and affectionate attention than he could receive at a boarding-house,—for he, unhappily, never enjoyed the patient, watchful, and assiduous care of wife and children,—he returned to Fryeburg; and died at the house of his brother Robert, September 24, 1844, at the age of sixty-nine years and ten months.

Mr. Bradley was a large-hearted man: wherever occasion offered, which demanded his aid and met his approval, he was ready with his money and his personal services for the emergency; and to his particular friends in distress, or to those who presented peculiar claims to his benevolence, it seemed as though he could never do enough. In the case of the late Mr. Cushman, who had been thirty years preceptor of the academy in Portland, and had broken down his constitution by devotion to his calling, he took unwearied pains to obtain an office for him, when Gen. Harrison came into power. Among other means employed, he wrote to his friend, Mr. Webster, a most earnest appeal, saying that he did not ask office for himself, — he wished for nothing, — that he should not, probably, live to see another Presidential election; and besought him by their long friendship, and as the last request he would make of him, to bestow the sought-for office on Mr. Cushman. The office was obtained; and the hearts of these two worthy men, Bradley and Cushman, and those of their friends, were greatly cheered. In performing these acts of kindness, Mr. Bradley was very peculiar: if he drew a check on the bank for a person he was assisting, he would often cover the back of the check with a writing expressive of his motives for drawing it, and the object of the charity; or, his views in general. This profuseness of language, both in speaking and writing, was a failing in Mr. Bradley, which rendered him sometimes prolix and prosy; but this was all forgotten in the acts of sympathy and benevolence which he amply displayed in his life-time; and which are perpetuated in his will, wherein he remembered numerous living friends, and the children of those who were dead. Among these were,—Gen. Fessenden, Judge Mellen, Mr. Orr, Mr. Hopkins, Mr. Longfellow, and Mr. Daveis, his companions at the bar; and many others who had his sympathy and regard. His benefactions went to the whole extent of his property, and were only limited by the amount of his estate: his good wishes far transcended that.

JOHN WILSON. 1803—1848.

John Wilson was another of the strong-minded men and able lawyers of the Hancock Bar, contemporary with McGaw, Gilman, Abbot, Field, Crosby, and Herbert. They were all immigrants: all received a liberal education: four were from New Hampshire, and three from Massachusetts. They were competitors at the bar, and in the struggle for life; and all, men and lawyers of honor, ability, and success.

Mr. Wilson was of Scotch-Irish descent: his first American ancestor, James Wilson, came from the north of Ireland, about 1722, to Londonderry in New Hampshire. The family afterwards established itself under the shadow of the Grand Monadnock, in the new settlement of Peterborough; which was occupied about 1750, principally by settlers of the Scotch-Irish race, — the Morrisons, the Cunninghams, the Wilsons. Here Mr. Wilson was born in 1777: here, too, was the birth-place of Jeremiah Smith, governor and chief justice of New Hampshire, — eminent for his learning and wit; and the Steeles, a governor, a general, and a judge. The Wilsons took prominent rank among the distinguished men whom this town has produced, for strong intellectual powers, fine physical organization, and persevering industry. After passing through his preliminary studies, Mr. Wilson entered Harvard College, from which he took his degree in 1799, in the class with Professor Cleaveland of Bowdoin College; Rev. William Frothingham, the esteemed minister of Belfast; Joseph Dane of Kennebunk; Gen. Sumner and Dr. Wyman of Massachusetts.

On leaving college, Mr. Wilson entered the office of his elder brother, James Wilson, at Peterborough, who was a graduate of Harvard in 1789; a member of Congress, 1809 — 1811; a distinguished lawyer of New Hampshire; and who died at Keene in 1839. With the high qualities of Mr. Wilson, and the advantages he enjoyed in his brother's office, he made substantial progress in the knowledge of the law, which he had the intellectual ability to appreciate and comprehend. At the end of three years' study, he was admitted to the bar; and in 1803, came to Belfast to commence the practical business of his life. Here he found two other young lawyers of talents, industry, and enterprise, who were earnestly pursuing the occupation destined to give them an honorable support. He fearlessly entered into this competition: he perceived that the field was broad, and its prospective growth encouraging. The beautiful harbor, set like a gem on the margin of the bay, invited commerce: the ample country, with its old forests around, hardly touched by the woodman's axe, gave assurance that enterprise and industry would awaken their echoes through the surrounding woods and along the ever-resounding waters of the sea. Mr. Wilson was sanguine and courageous: his heart gave token to the intellect, and he bravely put on the harness which, for a quarter of a century, he kept untarnished, and only laid aside on the requirements of physical inability. Hancock County extended on both sides of the Penobscot River to the Canada line, on the west side from Camden, and on the east side from the sea: it embraced Belfast, Bangor, Castine, Bucksport, and other flourishing towns. In that early day, there was a very small sprinkling of lawyers in Washington County, so that persons who had acquired some note at the bar in adjoining counties, were accustomed to attend the courts in that county, a long and weary way, as the road then was through unbroken forests and across the open bay. The lawyers from Bangor and Belfast regularly attended the courts of the county which were held at Castine, and extended their circuit on to Machias, in Washington County.

It was not till 1800 that a term of the Supreme Court

was held as far east as Hancock, then one term a year was held at Castine for the counties of Hancock and Washington. And Washington County had no term of the Supreme Court held within it until after the separation. Living in the same town with Mr. Crosby, and sharing with him the principal business of the place and adjacent country, they were usually employed on opposite sides of important questions. Mr. Wilson sustained himself successfully and honorably in these forensic contests, which were always conducted, as we might suppose from the elevated principles which guided their conduct, without resort to the tricks which inferior minds are apt to employ to accomplish their purposes. Their struggles were often severe, but always manly: intellectual forces were the weapons, and the contest was for the right, for truth, and justice. This rivalry continued until Mr. Crosby was placed upon the bench in 1811. Soon after, in 1812, Mr. Wilson was elected to the Thirteenth Congress, which held three sessions in 1813 and 1814, during his term, occupying three hundred and seventy-one days, it being the busy time of the war with England. At the next term, he was defeated, but returned to the Fifteenth Congress, 1817—1819. These interruptions withdrew him much from practice, but he returned from this political episode with new vigor, which continued undiminished until 1823.

In the early part of the winter of 1823 and 1824, he was exposed, without an overcoat, to a severe squall, with damp snow that filled his ears, and so completely enveloped his neck and face as to produce in him such severe cold and fever as to confine him to his house, amid great suffering, through several succeeding months. But a small portion of his accustomed labors were performed by him in the next succeeding summer, though he argued some causes pending in the Supreme Judicial Court in his own and two other counties, with respectable ability.

In September, 1824, while engaged in court at Machias, soon after the opening to the jury of an action in which he was senior counsel for the plaintiff, he, unexpectedly to everybody, exhibited evidence of total aberration, or obliviousness of the subject in which he was engaged. The cause was stopped, and he retired with a friend to his lodgings, and in a few minutes, recovered his consciousness, but not his usual physical or intellectual force. Within three or four days, he was able to return to his family and home at Belfast, though in feeble health. But the truth that his whole system was shattered, and that fragments only of the strong man remained, became from year to year, painfully obvious to his numerous friends.

The blow was then struck to the efficiency and successful effort of this brilliant, powerful man. He lingered through gradually decaying years, until his life happily closed on the 9th of August, 1848, at the age of seventy-one years. His early friends deeply mourned over the ruins of the once able lawyer, the ingenious advocate, and the inflexible, upright man.

One of his contemporaries thus speaks of him: "Mr. Wilson was a strong man; but for his eminence at the bar, he was more indebted to keen observation and a retentive memory than to a knowledge of books. For a great many years, until his health failed, he took the lead of the bar, having a large practice, extending into the counties of Lincoln, Hancock, Washington, and Penobscot. He displayed wonderful tact and ingenuity in the management of jury trials. Although Mr. Wilson was accused, by some, of being rather slow in his enunciation and long in his addresses to the jury, yet no man was listened to with more gratification, especially by his clients. A friend once asked Mr. Wilson if he did not think his arguments were too long. His answer was, 'Did you ever hear my clients complain of the length of my arguments ?' Mr. Wilson possessed another very important trait in the character of a counsellor ; viz., coolness and self-possession. No man ever saw him moved by anger in the trial of a cause."

Another gentleman, Mr. McGaw, to whose recollections I have been greatly indebted in the preparation of my sketches, who knew Mr. Wilson from the beginning to the end, remarked, " Mr. Wilson's ability and worth as an advocate was, in the early period in his practice, known and appreciated in the adjoining county of Washington, where, for more than twenty years, he argued one side of nearly every action that was tried by a jury. His memory was so uncommonly retentive that nothing presented in evidence that could have the slightest bearing on the cause in hand, was forgotten or omitted in argument. Indeed, extreme minuteness was sometimes attributed to him as a fault ; but his application of all the facts in a case on trial made him a difficult adversary to be encountered."

In regard to Mr. Wilson's social qualities, which give the rounding off to the finished man, his townsman, Mr. Williamson, shall touch the canvass : " He took an early interest in agriculture and its products ; and having a most retentive memory, he would recollect, for years, everything about the quality of horses and oxen in his neighborhood. This brought him into acquaintance with farmers far and near, who were surprised as well as gratified to perceive his minute observation and judgment in such matters. At all times, in his most palmy days as a lawyer, even while in Congress, he was perfectly free from pride or ostentation. It mattered not who approached him, the high or low, rich or poor, young or old, he was alike accessible to all. He had a word for each and all, whether it related to the affairs of the nation, a patent right, or the quality of a yoke of oxen ; and in all this familiar intercourse with all classes of people, it is remarkable that he never lost one jot of that dignity of character which belonged to his standing as a public man. Under all circumstances, at home or abroad, he uniformly maintained, in whatever company he chanced to fall, even to the last moment, that native politeness and gentlemanly bearing in his deportment which were peculiar to him."

GEORGE HERBERT. 1803—1820.

George Herbert, the only son of George and Honor (Dickinson) Herbert, was born in Deerfield, Massachusetts, August 18, 1778. His father, also, was an only son of the Rev. John Herbert, who came to this country about the middle of the last century, as a chaplain and surgeon in the English army. He is said to have spent the latter years of his life as a missionary in Maine, and died in that service about 1780. The father and mother of Mr. Herbert died in his infancy, and he was left an orphan at an age when the care and solicitude of parents are especially needed to guide the infant footsteps; but this duty devolved upon his maternal grandparents, which, from the results of after life, would seem to have been faithfully applied. He spent the early years of his life in his native village, where he was marked for gentleness of manners, united with high mental endowments, studious habits, and great skill in athletic exercises. It being desirous to give him a collegiate education, he was sent to the academy at Petersham, where he was duly qualified for and admitted to the freshmen class in Dartmouth College, in 1796. We have the testimony of two friends and contemporaries as to his college standing: William Abbot says, "He was distinguished at college for the regularity of his conduct, and his progress and taste in classical literature." Mr. McGaw, his senior, during his freshman year, says, "He became a pet in his class, and acquired the friendship of many members of other classes. Respectability of character for scholarship, and gentle, manly deportment, was awarded him throughout his collegiate course." Among his classmates were Prof. Dean, Prof. Dr. Cyrus Perkins, and Eleazer W. Ripley, afterwards a lawyer in Maine, and a general in the War of 1812.

On leaving college, he entered the office of Theodore Sedgwick, who, in 1802, was appointed judge of the Supreme Court of Massachusetts, under whose valuable instruction and extensive practice he acquired a knowledge of his profession, and a faculty for business, which enabled him to enter with advantage and success on the practical duties of life. He was admitted to the bar in 1803, and established himself at Ellsworth in the autumn of that year.

Ellsworth was then a new town. It was not incorporated until 1800, and then it contained but two hundred and twenty-seven inhabitants. But it embraced a large territory, and had great advantages for business by its water power, its neighborhood both to the sea and the forest, and the enterprise of the men who laid the foundation of the present flourishing settlement. Mr. Herbert was its first lawyer, and the only one until 1809, when John G. Deane, afterwards distinguished for his services on the northeastern boundary question, settled there. Mr. Deane was a graduate of Brown University, in the class of 1806; and was descended from John Deane, one of the original purchasers and settlers of Taunton, Massachusetts, to which he removed in 1639. Mr. Deane became eminent as a statesman and lawyer. He moved to Portland in 1835, and died in November, 1839, at the age of fifty-four; leaving a widow and several children, some of whom are following their father's profession.

When Mr. Herbert took up his residence in Ellsworth,

there were but four lawyers in what now constitutes the county of Hancock ; viz., Job Nelson and William Abbot at Castine, Thomas S. Sparhawk at Buckstown, and Nathaniel Coffin at Surry ; and in the county of Washington but two, Phineas Bruce at Machias, and Daniel P. Upton at the land's end—Eastport ; none of whom were within twenty miles of him. But if the lawyers were few and far between, so were the people, their resources, and their business connections : the whole county contained, in 1800, but about one thousand three hundred inhabitants ; and the lawyers, like the other settlers, all new and fresh upon a virgin soil, had need to wait until they could build up a society and institutions, and generate quarrels on which the lawyers could live. But Mr. Herbert was no stirrer of strife : he was literally a peace-maker—a healer of strife ; and the concurrent evidence of those who knew him well all through his professional life, places the stamp of truth to the statement furnished by Mr. McGaw : "The gentleness of Mr. Herbert's manners, and the purity of his morals, soon won for him the confidence and friendship of those persons with whom he had business relations, and the respect of the whole community. Professional avocations soon occupied so much of his time as he chose to devote to them, and were as profitable as could reasonably be expected in so new a region of country. Mr. McGaw continues, "Among the early clients of Mr. Herbert was Col. John Black, the very efficient agent of the proprietors of the 'million acres.' The services rendered by his counsel were highly satisfactory to Col. Black, and were introductory to his employment for other persons in the courts of Hancock and Washington Counties, in which the million acres were situated, during the life of Mr. Herbert."

This seems to afford me a fit opportunity to say a word of the excellent man whose name I have just mentioned. Col.

Black was a native of England, and born in London, July 3, 1781. At an early age he was employed in the banking house of Hope & Co., one of whose members was interested in the Bingham Purchase, or *million acres*, as the tracts were called, lying in Maine. The late General David Cobb of Gouldsboro', in Maine, and John Richards of Boston, were, in 1798, appointed agents for the sale and settlement of these large tracts. John Black was, fortunately for himself and the proprietors, although only seventeen years of age, sent out with Mr. Richards, then in London, as their clerk. He went first to Gouldsboro', but finally settled in Ellsworth, in 1809. On the death of Gen. Cobb, in 1830, he became his successor, and when Mr. Richards died, the sole agent; in which responsible and arduous trust he acquitted himself with the highest integrity and skill, and to the entire satisfaction of his employers. Col. Black's first wife was a daughter of Gen. Cobb, and his second wife a granddaughter. He died October 25, 1856. After the death of Mr. Herbert, Mr. Deane was Col. Black's confidential counsel and attorney.

In the political years 1813, 1814, and 1815, Mr. Herbert represented his town in the General Court of Massachusetts. He was a decided Federalist in his politics, and acted uniformly with that party. That he truly represented the sentiment of Ellsworth may be judged from the unequivocal state of parties in that town: its vote for Gov. Strong, at the first election of Mr. Herbert as representative, was sixty-three to six for Varnum, the opposition candidate. In 1816, he was appointed county attorney of Hancock, as successor to William D. Williamson of Bangor, whose office became vacant by the incorporation of Penobscot County in that year. Mr. Herbert's practice, already large, became extended by this appointment, which he held at the time of his death. This took place at Ellsworth, by consumption of the lungs, January 2, 1820, at the early age of forty-one.

We cannot give a better summary of Mr. Herbert's life and labors than by adopting the proceedings of the bar of Hancock at the next term of the court after his decease. The bar, at the March term, 1820, adopted the following resolutions unanimously:

"*Resolved*, That they deplore the loss they have sustained in the death of their lamented brother, George Herbert, who, by his kindness, ability, and integrity, had obtained in a high degree their esteem and confidence; and as a mark of their regard for his memory, they will wear the usual badge of mourning on the left arm during the term of the court.

"*Resolved*, That Mr. Nelson, Mr. Wilson, and Mr. Abbot be a committee to address a letter to Mrs. Herbert, expressive of the feelings of the bar upon this melancholy occasion; and that a copy of the foregoing resolution with an extract from the charge of the Hon. Judge Crosby to the Grand Jury be therein inclosed."

The remarks of Judge Crosby so fully describe the character of Mr. Herbert, that they cannot properly be withheld from this notice. He says, "It is my melancholy duty to announce to you a vacancy in the office of county attorney, by the decease of George Herbert, Esq., late attorney of this county. The worth and character of this man do not permit me to pass over them in silence, and yet the time and occasion will not enable me to do them justice. He received his classical education at Dartmouth, and pursued the study of the law under the late Judge Sedgwick. I have heard that great man speak of Mr. Herbert in terms of high eulogy and affection. His professional life was spent in Ellsworth. For several years, he represented the town in the State Legislature, and has sustained the offices of magistrate and county attorney with integrity and ability. In whatever period of life, and in whatever station we view him, we find him the same,—unassuming, industrious, persevering, enlightened, and just. If he had any fault, it was excess of zeal in any cause he deemed to be just, and that required his services. In such a cause, he spared neither his time nor his talents, his health nor his happiness. He was susceptible of the purest and most permanent friendship, and few men had more friends than usually surrounded him. Although not bred a physician, his superior knowledge in this department of science, and his humanity, made him the physician of his neighborhood. I have myself witnessed his gratuitous labors of love and sympathy among his neighbors and townsmen. When sickness and death were before him, he forgot his own concerns, his professional pursuits, and even his own family, and devoted himself to the bedside of the sick and the dying. He was the father of the fatherless, and every youth whom fortune threw under his roof was his child and the object of his tenderest care and solicitude. In the relation of a parent, he exhibited an example scarcely imitable, and which no language can describe. He studied the character of infancy and youth with assiduity, and gave a practical example in his family, at how early a period the principles of science, obedience, and virtue may be implanted in the youthful mind.

As a counsellor and advocate, his character is too well known in this county to require a particular delineation. He seldom, if ever, misled his clients by his advice, and in the management of his causes, was faithful and persevering almost to a fault. Although minute in argument, he never discussed without point or object, and never quitted his subject without taking every possible view of which it was susceptible. These are but a few outlines of the character of Mr. Herbert. The loss to his family is irreparable. His fellow townsmen will not find another more devoted to their interest and welfare; and his county must feel the loss of so valuable a character."

To this honorable tribute to the memory of Mr. Herbert, from so wise and truthful a man as Judge Crosby, little need be added. His particular friend, Wm. Abbot of Castine,—to have such a friend is proof of merit,—in a brief obituary, said, "At the bar, he was distinguished for his correct knowledge of the law, for ardor and perseverance in the causes in which he was engaged, for fair and honorable practice, and for perfect integrity. As a man, he was firm and undeviating in the pursuit of what he thought right, without regard to private interest; and he held in contempt that popularity which was not the consequence of correct views and motives." Of his private life, Mr. Abbot thus speaks: "In this point of view, the character of the deceased was peculiarly interesting, and embraced a rare assemblage of the milder virtues. Integrity, benevolence, and reverence for the Supreme Being, formed the great outline of his character. Memory will recur with delight to past scenes, and fill these outlines, and complete a picture which must forever remain dear to his afflicted family and friends."

Mr. Herbert was excessively fond of music, in which he thoroughly harmonized with Mr. Abbot, whose soul was attuned to the divine art. Mr. Abbot's son Charles writes me that he well remembered Mr. Herbert when he resided in Ellsworth. "Before the division of the counties," he says, "the late Allen Gilman of Bangor, and Mr. Herbert, attended the courts here. They passed court week at my father's. All three were very fond of music; and glees, songs, and other music were usually the order of the evening."

From another source,—a lady,—who was an acquaintance, we have another view into Mr. Herbert's character. She says, "He was quite eccentric, though kind-hearted, very sociable and companionable, yet sometimes taciturn. He was fond of music and society, and his literary attainments and tastes were of a superior order." She adds, "One of his eccentricities related to his attending court. These were held part of the time at Castine, some thirty-four miles from Ellsworth. Instead of starting in the early part of the day, or after dinner, with others whose business called them to court, he would wait until after tea, start off alone on horseback, and ride through by night. Often the family of Mr. Abbot, where he usually stopped, would be aroused in the night for his admission: sometimes, unwilling to disturb them, he would sleep in the barn until the family were astir."

Mr. Herbert was of medium size, had dark hair and eyes, and his manner, we are told, was somewhat quick and abrupt.

On the fourth of December, 1807, Mr. Herbert married Miss Charlotte Tuttle, a daughter of William Tuttle, Esq., of Littleton, Massachusetts, by whom he had four children, who all survive. His eldest son, George, is a lawyer in Chicago, Illinois, having commenced practice in Ellsworth: his second son, Rev. Charles Dickinson Herbert, was educated at Bowdoin College, from which he graduated in 1841, and is now residing in Newburyport: his eldest daughter, Mary, married the Rev. Mr. Peabody, a foreign missionary, but now resident in Newburyport, as are also her mother and sister Charlotte. They all retain a most lively and affectionate remembrance of the virtues and high qualities of the distinguished and honored man who has been the subject of our present notice.

JUDAH McLELLAN. 1803—1860.

The immigrant lawyers to Maine came principally from Massachusetts and New Hampshire. But occasionally a stranger from Connecticut lighted among us, to seek his fortune in this remote region. Among these, was the late Attorney General Foote of Wiscasset, Oliver Bray of Portland, and Judah McLellan of Bloomfield. Mr. McLellan was born in Thompson, the northeast corner town of Connecticut, in 1779; and is said to be of the same lineage, and a near relative of George B. McClellan, recent commander of the Army of the Potomac. He was graduated at Brown University in 1799, in the class with the late President Chaplin of Waterville College, Senator Dixon, and Judge Pitman, both of Rhode Island. He had faithfully improved his opportunities at college, and on leaving it, was well qualified to enter successfully upon the study of law. He immediately came to Maine, and became a student in the office of Judge Bridge at Augusta. While pursuing his studies, he amused himself by writing for the newspapers. His articles were principally of a political character; and, being a warm Federalist, he often bore severely upon the merits of the candidates on the other side, for office. In 1802, he wrote some personal strictures against Dr. Martin Kinsley, who had been named as a candidate for Congress in the Eastern District, at which the doctor took offense, and came to Augusta to seek satisfaction. When he ascertained who the author of the offensive article was, — only a student at law,—he disclaimed, as he said, to have anything to do "with the insignificant young puppy." At this, McLellan came out with a card over his own signature, posting Kinsley as a poltroon and a coward, who came all the way from Penobscot to the Kennebec to fight a duel, and when he got there, did not dare to do it.

After being admitted to the bar in 1802, Mr. McLellan proceeded to Canaan, on the Kennebec River. This was a large town, in territory, lying around Skowhegan Falls, incorporated in 1788, and embracing what is now included in the three towns of Canaan, Bloomfield, and Skowhegan. Bloomfield was separated in 1814, and Skowhegan in 1823. It was in the latter named town that Mr. McLellan fixed his residence as the first lawyer, and where he has continued to live through the sixty intervening years.

Mr. McLellan devoted himself to his business, and soon acquired an extensive and lucrative practice. He connected with his professional duties the management of a farm, which grew in size and value by his skillful and intelligent care, so that he justly had the reputation of being at the same time a sound lawyer, a safe counsellor and advocate, and a thriving, practical farmer. He was a man of great decision of character: he watched carefully the genuine improvements in agriculture, which he not only reduced to practice, but extended by lectures in the lyceum and before agricultural societies, and in earnest and enlightened efforts to introduce valuable breeds of cattle and sheep, improved tools and modes of cultivation. For a period of fifty years, he occupied in his town and county a prominent position as a lawyer, an intelligent farmer, and an enlightened and patriotic citizen. And after half a century of steady devotion to the duties of life, he retired from the toils and cares of business, at the age of about seventy-five, to the enjoyment of the ease of which a competency, the fruit of his own exertions, afforded him the means.

During this period, he was ten years or more one of the directors of the Skowhegan Bank, and several years, from 1820, county attorney for Somerset. In 1811, on the formation of the new court, he was offered a seat on the bench of the Circuit Court of Common Pleas for the Second Eastern District; but he declined accepting the position, preferring the quiet pursuits of his home to the responsibilities of office, and influenced, too, in a measure, by a sense of delicacy in regard to his political opinions. In 1815, he represented his town in the General Court of Massachusetts: with these exceptions, he abstained from political and public life, for which he was well qualified by the integrity and firmness of his character, and his general intelligence. In fact, after the breaking up of the old Federal party, to which he was sincerely attached, he found no place where he could fix his unsettled opinions, and he became quite disgusted with the whole game of politics: it is said that for the ten years after retiring from business, he cast but one vote for governor,—that was for Dr. Ezekiel Holmes, the anti-slavery candidate.

Soon after he found himself established in his business at Canaan, to complete the arrangements for his future life, he formed a matrimonial connection with Elizabeth White, the daughter of Samuel White, a worthy farmer of the place. She was well educated, accomplished, and handsome, and became the happy mother of an excellent and useful family. One son, Samuel, graduated at Waterville College, and is settled as a lawyer in Dexter: several other sons are merchants, some doing business in New York; one daughter married Abraham Sanborn, Esq., a lawyer in Bangor, and is dead. Mr. McLellan is still living, past eighty-three, but is entirely prostrated in health and intellect, the wreck of the once active and vigorous laborer in numerous fields of industry.

NATHAN CUTLER. 1803—1861.

A contemporary of Henry V. Chamberlain at Farmington, — whom we have before described, — was Nathan Cutler, who seated himself beside his competitor in 1803. Mr. Cutler was descended from James Cutler, one of the early settlers of Watertown, Massachusetts, whom we find there as early as 1635, but who moved to Lexington about 1648. His father, Joseph Cutler, was born in Lexington, in 1733:

in 1755, he married Rebecca Hoar; who dying, in 1758, he married, in 1759, Mary Read, who was the mother of the subject of this sketch.

Mr. Cutler was born in Lexington, May 29, 1775. His father was a farmer, in very moderate circumstances: the country, at the time of his birth, was just entering the seven years' war of the Revolution, in which the first blood was shed in his native town, less than a month before he came into this breathing world. His father could do little for the education of his children, and was unwilling that they should be at the expense of acquiring more than was necessary to make good farmers. He offered Nathan a small farm, but his mind was bent on a profession; and he succeeded in spending some time at Leicester Academy, where he fitted for college, and then passed to Dartmouth. Here he employed his time diligently; and took his degree in 1798, in the same class with Benjamin Orr, afterwards the distinguished counsellor in Maine. Mr. Cutler had to make his own way, receiving but little aid from his father— alternately working and keeping school; and by the exercise of a rigid economy, with good courage and cheerful hope, he was carried forward.

After leaving college, he took charge of the academy in Middlebury, Vermont, — which has since grown into a college, — and at the same time, pursued the study of law in the office of Judge Chipman of that place. He completed his studies in Worcester, Massachusetts, and was admitted to the bar in Worcester County, in 1801. He opened an office, first in Lexington; but being attracted by accounts of the rising prospects of Maine, he came to see if it afforded any opening for him. He visited New Gloucester, then a flourishing village, where Judge Whitman was then practicing, who advised him to go to Farmington. He adopted the suggestion, established himself there in 1803, and it ever after was his place of residence. In speaking of this occurrence, his son-in-law lately observed to me, that, "his esteem and respect for Judge Whitman were life-long and unqualified."

Mr. Cutler immediately entered upon a good business, for which he exhibited the necessary and reliable qualities. He entered into the improvements of the village which became his abode, and exercised his taste and means in making it the beautiful and desirable resort of a cultivated society. In 1807, he was instrumental in procuring a charter for an academy in that town; and was one of the trustees and secretary of the Board. He continued a trustee during his life, and was the president at the time of his death.

In 1811, he was appointed a trustee of the ministerial and school fund, and the treasurer: the three following years, he was the treasurer of the town. He represented the town in the General Court of Massachusetts, in 1809, 1810, 1811, and 1819: in the latter year, he was a delegate to the convention which formed the constitution of the State, and was one of the committee on "the style and title" of the new State. In 1812, the appointment of judge of the Circuit Court of Common Pleas, for the Second Eastern Circuit, was tendered to him, which he declined. He was a member of the senate of Maine, in 1828 and 1829, from Kennebec County: in the latter year he was president of that body, by virtue of which office, he became acting governor of the State for the unexpired term of Governor Lincoln, who died October 8, 1829. In 1832, he was one of the electors at large for President and Vice-President, when Maine threw her ten electoral votes for Andrew Jackson for President, and Martin Van Buren for Vice-President. The last public office held by Mr. Cutler, was as the representative of his town in 1844.

These various stations of responsibility and trust, show

the confidence which his fellow-citizens entertained of his capacity and integrity. An obituary notice written by his pastor, says, "Few have done more than he, in the last half century, to mold the character and advance the interests of the community in which he lived."

In September, 1804, he married Hannah Moore of Weston, Massachusetts: she became the mother of his nine children, — seven sons and two daughters, — and died in 1835. Three sons and the two daughters survived him. His eldest son, Reuben, occupies the paternal mansion in Farmington, and is a respectable merchant of that place: another son, John L., a graduate of Bowdoin in the class of 1837, is a lawyer in Augusta: the other is a clergyman. Robert Goodenow, a respected lawyer of Farmington, married one of the daughters.

Mr. Cutler died June 8, 1861, under the burden of eighty-six years, which he carried with meekness and with honor. He was a diligent student, a well-read and good lawyer, but not at all distinguished as an advocate. He generally presented his cases to the jury so as to secure their attention; but he was diffident, and dry in his manner. In special pleading, he was a proficient, having few superiors at the bar. He was faithful to his clients, honest and honorable in his dealings, a conscientious and religious man. He was successful in his profession, because he devoted himself to it; and he had the confidence of those who employed him, and of the whole community. He retired from its active duties in 1835; but his counsel was sought to his last days, by those who respected his judgment and experience.

JOSEPH BARTLETT. 1803—1810.

Joseph Bartlett was one of the eccentric men and wits of the bar. He was a native of Plymouth, in Plymouth County,

Massachusetts, and was born June 10, 1762. He graduated at Harvard College in 1782, in honorable standing: his scholarship entitled him to membership in the highest literary society of the college, — the Phi-Beta-Kappa. He pursued the study of law at Salem for a while; but soon after the ratification of the treaty of peace with England, he went to that country, where he led, for some time, a wild, irregular life, to which he was introduced by a set of companions, gay like himself, to whom his wit and reckless manners made him acceptable. He was one evening attending, at the theater, the representation of a play written by Gen. Burgoyne, in ridicule of the Americans, when he rose in the pit and exclaimed "Hurrah! Great Britain beaten by a nation of barbers, tailors, and tinkers!" The effect was electric: the bold sally pleased the house prodigiously, and gained him applause and new acquaintances among the wags of the metropolis. He passed his time in London in gambling and dissipation, in which he spent all his money and got in debt, for which he was sent to prison. Here he turned his wits to some account. He wrote a play to procure his release, and went himself upon the stage as one of the actors in it. After this incident, he procured, upon credit, a cargo of merchandise, and set sail for America, with a view to engage in commercial business. But the vessel which took him and his cargo was wrecked on Cape Cod. He had freely avowed infidel opinions on the voyage, and, when he was in the peril of shipwreck, and was laughed at for his cowardice, he parried it off by saying that he was not afraid to die, but could not bear to be found dead in such a dreary place as Cape Cod.

Being cast upon the world again, without means of support, he joined the forces raised by Massachusetts to put down Shays's rebellion, and was appointed a captain of volunteers. After the war was over, he returned to the law, and commenced practice at Woburn, Massachusetts, from which place he moved to Cambridge in 1796 or '97. Here he entered zealously into the affairs of the town and college, and in 1799 he delivered a poem before the Phi-Beta-Kappa Society, on physiognomy, which contained many personal allusions, and was satirical and witty. While he was residing in Cambridge, he was employed to argue a case which arose on a quarrel between a mother and her son, at Plymouth. It was tried before referees, and Bartlett made a serio-comic argument which cut both ways. He commented on the sadness of such a quarrel between a parent and child, and said it was a shame such a thing should occur "here in the old town of Plymouth, under the shadow of the hill on which were the graves of the forefathers, and on which I have, myself, often picked huckleberries."

In 1803, he came to Saco. Cyrus King was then the only lawyer there, and Prentiss Mellen the only one on the other side of the river, at Biddeford, who were able and popular competitors. But Mr. Bartlett, by his long experience, his readiness as an advocate, and his facetious and agreeable manners, became very popular, and for awhile had a great run of business. He took the popular side in politics, was an ardent Democrat and demagogue, as he had before been a Federalist. By his eloquence and his arts, he succeeded in getting elected to the Senate in Massachusetts in 1805; and afterwards, by his ambition to become a leader of the party, involved himself in a quarrel with other persons who had been accustomed to manage the party tactics of the county, as Dr. Thornton and Richard Cutts. He undertook to set up Daniel Cleaves, as a candidate for Congress in opposition to Richard Cutts, who was first elected from that district in 1800, and held the office by six successive elections, through the administration of Mr. Jefferson and part of that of Mr. Madison.

Of course this power, supported by great wealth and influence at home and abroad, was too firmly established to be moved by a new man, and a fresh aspirant for place, who had none of the auxiliaries which surrounded his more fortunate opponents. The party, however, was distracted by his efforts and intrigues, and consequently he became the object of very severe animadversion. The Portland Argus, the leading democratic organ of the State, opened its galling fire upon him, and his influence and business were pretty thoroughly cut up. The abuse in this paper was so personal, that Bartlett commenced an action of libel against the proprietor, and recovered judgment against him for one thousand five hundred dollars damages, four hundred eighty-seven dollars and ninety-five cents costs; which, refusing to pay, he was committed to jail, having only the narrow limits of the yard, under a bond of nearly four thousand dollars. From this place of almost close confinement, so rigid were the laws then relating to debtors, the debtor sent forth his weekly missiles, until, unfortunately, on one unlucky winter night, he went from the jailor's house to the pump outside of the picket fence which surrounded the jail, to get some water, the pump inside the fence being frozen. The creditor, who had kept, by his employes, a constant watch over his prisoner, improved the occasion, and brought an action for the penalty of the bond, against the debtor and his sureties, who were very responsible men in Portland. The whole affair was brought into the arena of politics, and mingled in the stirring excitements of the day. This action, therefore, added to the fire: it was contested at every step, and when a verdict was rendered in favor of the plaintiff, on the bond, a new trial was moved, and the questions of law, raised in the case, were argued in Boston with great ability by Samuel Dexter and Solicitor General Davis for the plaintiff, and Attorney General Bidwell and Joseph Story, then leading

Democrats, for the defendants. The principal point in the case made by the defendants was that the pump to which the debtor went, was not out of the limits of the jail yard. A distinction was made by the plaintiff in regard to the time of going to the pump; the condition of the bond being that the debtor should have the liberty of the yard in the *day-time*. Chief Justice Parsons delivered a long and learned opinion in favor of the plaintiff, at the July term of the court, 1807, in Cumberland, adjudging the bond to have been broken, and giving judgment for the whole penalty. So severe was then the law of creditor and debtor, that, even under a heavy bond, the debtor could not leave the narrow limits of the yard connected with the jail, without a forfeiture.

But the proceeding, although it put money in his pocket, had the effect to destroy the business of Mr. Bartlett in Saco; and he moved immediately after to Berwick, and in 1809 or '10, he left the State and became a wanderer: we find him sometimes in Portsmouth and then in Boston, but without clients and without business, subsisting by expedients and by desultory literary efforts. It was in these latter days, when he had lost all his clients, that he brought a low and trifling action for a negro named Cæsar, and being asked by some one how he came to take up such a suit as that, he replied that he had not seen a client for a month,—he couldn't help it; it was "*aut Cæsar aut nullus.*"

After drifting about in various places, he finally went to Boston, his last station, and there continued his literary efforts. July 4, 1823, he delivered an oration in the hall of the Exchange Coffee-house, and on the same occasion recited an ode, styled the "New Vicar of Bray," which attracted considerable attention: for the following extracts from which, we are indebted to Mr. Loring's "Hundred Boston Orators:"

"We now see much upon the earth,
  Especially in Boston,
Which gives to man a vigorous birth,
  And keeps our souls in motion.
Boston a city now is made,
  Our officers elected;
'Tis best for every class and trade,
  Our mayor will be respected.
Our Quincy now, by all admired,
  The city's pride and glory;
May he the difference never know,
  'Twixt Federalist and Tory."

The same year, 1823, Mr. Bartlett published an edition of his poems, dedicated to John Quincy Adams, to which he added "Aphorisms on Men, Principles, and Things," the result of his various experience.

While he resided in Saco, he edited a paper called "The Freeman's Friend," in 1805, and July 4th of that year, he delivered an oration at Biddeford. He wrote with ease, and his communications for the papers and his desultory efforts were numerous. As an advocate, when he gave his attention to business, he was fluent, and at times eloquent, but very unequal and often whimsical: he could not be relied upon; and his skill as a lawyer was quite insignificant,—he had not industry nor steadiness of purpose sufficient to accomplish any important object, or to obtain any valuable reputation. In his last days, he had become a burden to his friends and acquaintances, and closed his irregular and useless life at Boston, October 27, 1827, at the age of sixty-five He wrote the following epitaph upon himself:

"'Tis done! the fatal stroke is given,
And Bartlett's fled to hell or heaven;
His friends approve it, and his foes applaud,
Yet he will have the verdict of his God."

When attending the funeral of John Hale, a worthy citizen of Portsmouth, he improvised the following epitaph:

> "God takes the good,
> Too good by far to stay,
> And leaves the bad,
> Too bad to take away."

Mr. Bartlett was profuse and prodigal in his expenses, when he had money, and never halted in his reckless career, as long as he could obtain means by borrowing or other expedients, to indulge his extravagant habits; and he never paid debts when he could avoid it. The large amount he received on his verdict against the proprietor of the Argus, was soon squandered in improvidence and dissipation, and some, at least, of those who assisted in the prosecution, failed of getting their fees. Yet, with all his faults, and he had an unusual share, he was an agreeable and pleasant companion: his wit and vivacity, and his general information, made his presence welcome at the social meetings of the bar, until he had become too degraded to regard the decencies of respectable company.

Mr. Bartlett married, in early life, Ann Witherell of Kingston, Massachusetts, a beautiful girl, daughter of the tavern keeper in that place, but left no children. He died unlamented, as he had lived unhonored.

Reuel Williams

AT THE AGE OF 77.

FROM A BUST BY PAUL AKERS.

CHAPTER XVIII.

REUEL WILLIAMS—THOMAS BOND—TIMOTHY BOUTELLE—WOODBURY STORER—ELISHA P. CUTLER—FREDERIC ALLEN—WILLIAM B. SEWALL—SAMUEL HUBBARD—BENJAMIN AMES—NATHAN WESTON—WM. D. WILLIAMSON.

REUEL WILLIAMS. 1803—1862.

The lawyer who is now to engage our attention, was so totally different from the one with whom our last chapter closed, that they scarcely seem to belong to the same epoch of time, or the same profession. The life of one was a wild and reckless vagary; that of the other was filled with devoted industry and eminently practical results — the lights and shadows of life.

Mr. Williams was one of the most successful men who have risen in Maine. He was a native of the State, born in Augusta in June, 1783, and from the most humble origin. By the inherent force of his character, he overcame all disadvantages, and rose to the highest stations in the forum and the State. Who his first American ancestor was, and when he first came to this country, we have not been able to ascertain. He probably descended from Richard of Taunton, whose son Benjamin married there in 1690. The Williams name is very numerous and extensive. It is supposed to be of Welsh origin. Roger, the earliest champion of the rights of conscience, and founder of Rhode Island, was from Wales. To the year 1825, Farmer, the distinguished antiquary, says, " One hundred and forty-seven of the name of Williams had graduated at the colleges in New England, New Jersey, and Union in New York." By the last catalogue of Harvard, eighty-six of the name were borne upon it, being larger than that of any other.

Seth Williams, father of Reuel, was born in Easton, Plymouth County, Massachusetts, to which place the family moved from Taunton. His father united the trades of tanner and shoemaker. When the expedition was fitted out from New England, 1779, to retake Castine, which the British had seized and fortified, commonly called the Bagaduce expedition, he, with a brother, enlisted in the army, and proceeded to that place. The disastrous and disgraceful defeat of our forces in August of that year, sent our dispirited men homeward, with loss of all their supplies as well as their reputation. They landed on the west shore of Penobscot Bay, and pursued their way through the wilderness and tangled forests which then covered the country. The march was long and tedious, and the sufferings of the men intense: many died from hunger and fatigue. Seth Williams, with his brother, reached Fort Western in August or September of 1779; and, finding persons there who came from the neighborhood of his own home, and pleased with the situation, he concluded to remain and try his fortunes there.

He established himself on the eastern side of the river, commenced his two trades, tanning in summer, shoemaking in winter, and found his prospects sufficiently encouraging to induce him, by a marriage alliance, to lay the foundation of a family, which was destined to confer honor and benefit on the town and the State he had adopted. In the winter of 1780, he married Miss Zilpha Ingraham of Augusta, by whom he had eleven children, six sons and five daughters. Hartwell, the eldest, was born November 15, 1781. The father died in 1817, at the age of sixty-one. Reuel, the second son, was born June 2, 1783. At that time, the town formed part of Hallowell, and was called Fort Western, the Indian name was *Cushnoc*, and had a very small population. In 1790, when the first United States census was taken, the whole territory embracing Hallowell and Augusta contained but one thousand one hundred and ninety-four inhabitants, the majority of whom were within the limits of that part which was Hallowell, but now divided into several other towns. Augusta was incorporated in 1797, and in 1800 its population was one thousand two hundred and eleven.

Seth Williams was able to give his children only such education as the common schools afforded, and as they became old enough, they assisted their father in his occupation. The year 1797 was a great occasion for Augusta; it was then incorporated, and the bridge across the Kennebec River was completed — the first which was erected over that river. It was finished in the autumn, and as but a short time remained before the river would be frozen over, which afforded a natural bridge for the people, they looked for some person to gather the toll without much expense: a smart boy, fourteen years old, offered and was employed, and here Reuel Williams begun his *public life*. He attended to this duty diligently and faithfully, and it was a hard service, for the weather was cold, often stormy, and no toll-house had as yet been provided. But he contrived by threshing his hands, and stirring about, to keep warm. A distinguished man, whose office stood near by the bridge, had watched the faithful boy, and when it was cold and stormy, he gave him shelter in his office. No man loved to see faithfulness and diligence more than Judge James Bridge, and he was attracted to young Williams by these qualities, and more so, when he saw his quickness and general intelligence. He took these opportunities to talk with him about his studies, recommended reading for him, and advised him to go to the academy in Hallowell to improve his mind. These lessons fell like good seed, and being pressed upon his father, he concluded to send him to the academy. This was a happy day for this hopeful youth, and the year spent at that institution and profitably improved, bore ample fruits in after life.

The good work which Judge Bridge had thus begun, he continued, by receiving young Williams into his office, as a student, at the age of fifteen years. A better school of instruction for practical life could not be found in Maine. Judge Bridge was both a scholar and a lawyer. The principles of the science, he had from his law teacher, the wise and profound Parsons, who was as good a disciplinarian as he was scholar. Mr. Bridge was doing a very extensive business, the only lawyer in Augusta, dealing largely in questions and facts relating to landed property and the laws applicable to real estate. Mr. Williams had therefore the great privilege of enforcing upon his mind the principles of this large and profitable department of legal practice, by its minute details. At the end of the five years devoted to these preliminary studies, he came to the bar in 1802, fully equipped for the manly service of life; and so useful had he made himself to Judge Bridge that he retained him as a partner in his business. What young man had ever a fairer start in life than this? How he improved it, the experience of sixty years of uninterrupted success, has given ample demonstration. In less than six years, the little shivering toll-gatherer has become a lawyer in full practice, having the confidence of the best men about him! and the most fortunate adventitious circumstances to aid the force of his own character.

The business of the office was pursued with great energy and success for a quarter of a century, Mr. Williams, after eight or ten years, having the chief burden of it; for Judge Bridge was a little nervous, could not bear the court-house, disliked the office, and as the affairs of it were conducted with promptness and ability, he was quite satisfied to enjoy the profits, which he did for thirty years, without engaging much in the labor. A contemporary lawyer has informed me that more business was done in that office than any other in Maine, especially in what related to real property, and that Mr. Williams, for a considerable period, filled more writs than any other lawyer in the State. He was indefatigable; up early and down late; he gave himself no rest; he was not only the legal adviser, but the practical agent of large absent real estate owners; he was the attorney of the Plymouth Proprietors, whose large tract of land lay on each side of the Kennebec River for fifty miles, occasioning numerous conflicts with settlers, squatters, adverse claimants, and requiring constant labor in making contracts, sales, and in various legal proceedings. Those who live in these quiet times, when all these proprietary rights and conflicts are settled, can form no idea of the passion, the litigation, and bitter feeling which prevailed in that part of the State forty or fifty years ago.

Mr. Williams, as a lawyer, was sound and quick of apprehension: his mind perceived clearly the relations and obscurities of a case, and he patiently evolved it from its intricacies. As an advocate, he was calm and logical: his arguments to the court and to the jury were clear and concise: he argued directly for his cause, and came directly to his points without display or circumlocution; and he never lost a case for want of taking the proper strategic ground. A more successful professional life we have not to record among our brethren of the bar in Maine; successful in all the results of practice,—reputation, property, political station, and public employment and confidence, sufficient to gratify the desire of the most ambitious.

A gentleman who knew Mr. Williams from the commencement of his practice to the close of it, thus speaks of him: "The judgment with which he managed land agencies committed to him, and the promptness with which he settled his accounts and paid over the moneys he received, tended to give him the agency of the Plymouth Company, and of most of the absentee proprietors owning lands in the Kennebec Purchase. His familiarity with the law of real estate caused him to be employed in every real action that was tried in this, Kennebec, and the two adjoining counties."

Mr. Williams devoted himself exclusively to his profession for twenty years, firmly resisting all attempts to draw him from duties which were engrossing his whole attention. Indeed, so involved was he in the multifarious cares of business, that he could not escape from them without serious inconvenience, and even actual danger to himself and his client. In 1822, he first entered public life as the representative of Augusta in the Legislature; and for the next twenty years, he seems to have been equally engrossed by public business, as he had for the twenty previous years in his private affairs. He was re-elected to the House the three following years, at the end of which he was elected senator from Kennebec County, and re-elected the two following years, making a continued service of seven years in the Legislature, from 1822 to 1828 inclusive. In 1826, he was chairman of the committee on State Lands, and as such submitted a clear and succinct report on the North-Eastern Boundary question, then beginning to assume an alarming importance both to the State and national administrations. In 1828, an able joint committee of the two houses was appointed on this special subject, of which he was a member. John G. Deane, the chairman on the part of the House, drew a report, filling fifty-six octavo pages, in which he reviewed, in a masterly manner, the whole controversy; coming to the conclusion, from historical facts, the configuration of the country, and the concessions of British authorities, that the right of the State to the whole territory in dispute was indubitable, and could not fairly be impugned. The document embraced a long and able report of Charles S. Daveis, agent of the State to confer with the provincial authorities, and correspondence with official and other persons. It was a document exhaustive of the subject.

The political majority of his county being reversed in 1829, he was not re-elected to the Senate that year, but was returned to the House, and again in 1832. In 1824, he had taken the place of Judge Bridge as one of the joint committee of Massachusetts and Maine, to make division of the public lands and other public property belonging to the two States. The committee, of which Levi Lincoln of Massachusetts was chairman, made their first report in 1822; and they made special reports in subsequent years, until the division was completed. The first report in which Mr. Williams took part was made in December, 1825. This was an office of no little labor and responsibility, and for which Mr. Williams had peculiar qualifications.

In 1831, he was appointed commissioner of Public Buildings to complete the State House, which had been commenced by William King, the first commissioner. As early as 1822, a committee was appointed to visit different towns in the State for the purpose of selecting a place the most suitable for a permanent seat of government: the committee consisted of Daniel Rose and Benjamin Greene. They reported in favor of Augusta in 1823. Nothing further was done on the subject until 1827, when the Governor and council held a session in Augusta, and selected the site on which the State House now stands, as the location of the future Capitol. In 1828, William King was appointed "Commissioner of Public Buildings," and authorized to procure plans and estimates for the structure. Twelve and a half townships of land were appropriated to defray the expense. Charles Bulfinch of Boston furnished a plan precisely like the Massachusetts State House, of which he was the architect, but of reduced size, to be completed at an estimated cost not exceeding eighty thousand dollars. The models and plans were adopted, and the work commenced in 1829. Mr. Williams, who had been an indefatigable advocate for establishing the Capitol at Augusta, succeeded to the unfinished work, and pushed it rapidly to a completion; so that the session of the Legislature for the first time occupied it in January, 1832. So wild were the original estimates, that, instead of eighty thousand dollars, the cost of the building, including furnishing and fencing, reached the sum of one hundred and thirty-nine thousand dollars, while the proceeds of land, nearly three hundred thousand acres, brought into the treasury but sixty thousand, two hundred and sixty-six dollars and eighty cents, not half the cost of the work. This was not an uncommon experience: it seems to be the infirmity of architects to frame estimates which become decoys to the unfortunate persons who undertake to construct public or private edifices. If any one has has ever been built within the amount estimated, it would be a pleasure to know it. This was no fault of Mr. Williams, who pursued his part of the task with skill and prudence, such as he would employ in his own transactions. Another unfortunate circumstance in this concern was the hurrying the sale of the land. If it had been kept five or six years longer, the sales would have doubled the whole expenditure upon the public buildings. Individuals reaped the large profits at the expense of the State.

In 1853, Mr. Williams, William P. Fessenden, and Elijah L. Hamlin were appointed by the Legislature, commissioners to negotiate with Massachusetts for the purchase of all lands owned by her in this State. In pursuance of this commission, a contract was entered into, and approved by both governments, by which the old commonwealth released to Maine all her interest in lands belonging to her, lying within this State, for the sum of three hundred and sixty-two thousand five hundred dollars. This act met with general approbation, as it gave us entire control in the regulation and management of the public domain, and settled questions of partnership which often gave trouble in their adjustment. As a pecuniary arrangement, the purchase may at least be considered a doubtful one.

In 1836, Mr. Williams was chosen one of the electors at large for President and Vice President, and united with the college in casting the ten electoral votes of the State for Martin Van Buren, President, and Richard M. Johnson, Vice President, of the United States. The next year he was elected to the Senate of the United States, and took his seat in the Twenty-fifth Congress at the extra session held in September, 1837. Judge Shepley had resigned this seat in 1836, on being appointed judge of the Supreme Court, and Judge Dana had been appointed to fill the vacancy for the unexpired term. John Ruggles was the colleague of Mr. Williams during the first portion of his term, and George Evans from 1840. There was a great political change throughout the country in 1840, which brought the Whig party into power in the National and State governments, occasioned by unpopular measures of the administration in regard to the Sub-treasury, the National Bank, the Florida

War, the Slavery Question, the pecuniary distresses of the country, &c.

Mr. Williams acted with the Democratic party through his whole period of service. He had been a Federalist while that party had an existence as a distinct organization, and as a Whig, supported the election and administration of John Q. Adams. The history of this change of sentiment belongs to the annals of the time. In 1829, Peleg Sprague, who had been a Representative in Congress from the Kennebec District, was elected to the Senate of the United States. Mr. Williams had been previously urged by his Whig friends in the Legislature, to become the candidate for Governor of the State, as successor to Enoch Lincoln; but he absolutely declined, from disinclination for office, and it was supposed that he did not wish to continue in public life. But on the occurrence of the vacancy in the Congressional District, he was informally nominated in the newspaper at Augusta for the vacant place: George Evans was also nominated in the same informal manner. They both, as it was supposed, belonged to the same party; and no convention of the people was called to name or confirm a candidate. The election was appointed on very short notice, to be held at the annual town meeting in March. At that time, the traveling was very bad, the vote light, and no choice was effected, Mr. Williams having a small plurality: the Democratic candidate had votes enough to defeat the election. A new trial was ordered to take place in July. The canvass now became very animated. The Augusta papers, the only ones printed in the district, strenuously advocated the election of Mr. Williams; but the friends of Mr. Evans called a convention, which the supporters of Mr. Williams declined attending, and Mr. Evans received its unanimous nomination. Both sides now entered into one of the most exciting electioneering campaigns which had taken place in that district. There was no other candidate in nomination. The vote was very large: Augusta gave nearly its whole ballot, over seven hundred to eleven, for Mr. Williams; while Gardiner, the place of Mr. Evans's residence, gave almost its entire vote to him, five hundred and ninety-three to three. Hallowell also voted strongly for Mr. Evans, and the towns above Augusta supported Mr. Williams, and he also received the votes of the Democratic party. The result was the election of Mr. Evans by about two hundred majority. After that defeat, Mr. Williams joined the advocates of Gen. Jackson, and became the uniform supporter of his administration, and labored earnestly and successfully in the ranks of the Democratic party, of which he became one of the leaders in Maine.

Taking his seat in the Senate in 1837, the first year of Mr. Van Buren's administration, he gave his constant support to all its measures. In the great revolution of parties, which took place in 1840, Maine joined the ranks of the opposition to the administration of Mr. Van Buren. Edward Kent was elected Governor, and the Legislature of 1841, having a strong Whig majority, passed a series of resolutions on the Currency, a National Bank, the Independent Treasury, and national affairs generally, severely condemning the course of the administration. In one of these, they referred to the published declaration of Mr. Williams, "that it is the duty of the elected to carry into effect the will of his constituents, if he is instructed what that will is, or else resign his trust;" and added, "We, therefore, hereby instruct him that the foregoing resolutions express the will of his constituents." These resolutions were passed near the close of the session in April, 1841, and the February following, 1842, Mr. Williams sent in his resignation. Gov. Fairfield was elected to fill the vacancy. The Senate never, perhaps, contained abler men than occupied the seats at that time, and graver questions had not before engaged their attention. There were Webster, Clay, Calhoun, Crittenden, Berrien, Silas Wright, Buchanan, Southard, Rives of Virginia, Preston of South Carolina, Benton. Among the important measures which were discussed in that period, beside those before alluded to, were the annexation of Texas; a general bankrupt law; abolishing slavery in the District of Columbia; the Cilley duel; the gag law, as it was familiarly called, by which all petitions relating to the abolition of slavery were to be laid on the table without debate, which passed the House one hundred and thirty-five to sixty; repeal of the sub-treasury, which passed the Senate twenty-nine to eighteen, Williams against the repeal, Evans for it; the Canada troubles, growing out of the burning of the Caroline and the arrest of McLeod; and the North-Eastern Boundary question, which was adjusted by Mr. Webster and Lord Ashburton in 1842, and was the consummation of Mr. Webster's diplomacy as secretary of state, and for which, alone, he had retained office, when his colleagues of the cabinet resigned under President Tyler. Mr. Williams occasionally took part in debate, and when he spoke, it was to the matter in issue, and not to the country; and his speeches were characterized by the same terseness, brevity, and force as were his arguments at the bar. He voted in the Senate against the ratification of the Ashburton treaty. It was a critical point: there was a tremendous excitement in the country, on apprehension of a war with England on the boundary question. A portion of the delegation from Maine, supposing their constituents were opposed to the treaty, were resolved to resist it. The commissioners from the State, then in Washington, viz., Messrs. Preble, Kent, Kavanagh, and John Otis, had, in a midnight session previous to the day when the question of ratification was to be submitted, agreed to refuse the assent of Maine to its terms, and a paper containing their refusal was actually drawn up by Gov. Kent. Mr. Webster, having received a hint of this action, procured a conference of the delegation, in both houses, from the State, with the commissioners, which, after a long and anxious discussion, resulted in a revision by the commissioners of their paper, and a reluctant assent to the ratification of the treaty. Mr. Williams did not attend the conference, and when the question of ratification came up in executive session, he voted against it. Mr. Evans rendered very active and effectual service in favor of the treaty, as did the other Whig members from Maine. The delegation then consisted of Messrs. Williams and Evans in the Senate, and Messrs. Elisha H. Allen, David Bronson, Nathan Clifford, William P. Fessenden, N. S. Littlefield, Joshua A. Lowell, Alfred Marshall, and Benjamin Randall, in the House. The grand difficulty with our members was a mistaken notion that the popular sentiment at home was so hostile to the treaty that it would bring its supporters under severe condemnation.

Mr. Williams's retirement from political life only changed the course of his duty and labor. His own large affairs required much attention, and he was soon called upon to lend his aid in various ways toward the construction of the railroad extending from Portland to Augusta, with a branch to Bath. The original charter was granted in 1836, but nothing having been done under it, it was renewed in 1840, at a time when public attention was directed to these great improvements in the means of transportation. The plan was to form a connection direct with Boston, by connecting at Portland with the road from that place to Portsmouth. The embarrassments of the country, and the large amounts required to move such expensive projects, delayed operations until 1847, when the work commenced in earnest, Mr. Williams putting his shoulder to the wheel and his hands in his pockets to help forward the enterprise. He was made president of the corporation as successor to George Evans; and, by his influence, he obtained subscriptions to the stock in large sums at Boston, and along the line of the road: the Portland, Saco, and Portsmouth corporation subscribed one hundred thousand dollars to secure the connection with their road; and gentlemen in Boston subscribed largely to the stock. Mr. Williams devoted himself with great energy to the accomplishment of this object, which was expected to give increased wealth and importance to the cities of Augusta and Bath, and promote the prosperity of the country through which it passed. It was opened from Bath to North Yarmouth, where it met the Atlantic and St. Lawrence Road, July 4, 1849, and to Augusta in 1851, the whole length of road being seventy-three miles. Mr. Williams continued to be its chief manager for about twelve years, and although he spent a vast deal of labor and capital upon it, it has never been a remunerating investment, owing to competing means of transportation, and the heavy cost of construction.

Mr. Williams was a faithful and devoted son to the town which bore and nurtured him. He labored in season and out of season to promote her prosperity, and to adorn and enrich her. The public improvements which have been made to cluster there, are largely due to his efforts and influence. Nor did he withhold his ample means to endow and establish institutions and companies to advance the moral and material interests of the place. When the mill-dam was laboring for the needed help, he was the person to be called upon; when the railroad wanted funds, Mr. Williams had to advance or procure them. In 1834, a resolve passed the Legislature appropriating twenty thousand dollars for the erection of an asylum for the insane, provided a like sum was contributed from individual sources within a year. Two gentlemen promptly responded to this urgent appeal: these were Benjamin Brown of Vassalboro', and Reuel Williams of Augusta, who each subscribed ten thousand dollars to secure the condition. This noble institution stands now on the banks of the Kennebec, at or near the spot where Mr. Williams was born, a perpetual monument to his liberal benefaction. It was not money alone, however, that Mr. Williams contributed to this admirable object: he gave it his constant supervision, and was one of the first trustees. He made himself perfectly familiar with its details, and was anxious and watchful that the institution should become a blessing to the unfortunate class so long neglected and ill-treated; nor did he relax his efforts, until he found that the hospital had outlived the prejudices excited against it, and had wholly gained the confidence of the public. He then, in 1859, resigned the office of trustee. But we cannot dwell upon his numerous acts of beneficence. "They are registered where every day you may turn the leaf to read them." "His fellow-citizens," says the gentleman before quoted, "entertained the highest opinion of his business capacity, and when the Augusta dam, in which his friends and connections were deeply engaged, was twice carried away, he was told that he must engage in it, as he was the only person who could carry it successfully through. He accepted the presidency of the corporation. The dam was completed, and though it has been unfortunate for the stockholders, it has added largely to the population and business of the place."

The last public act in which Mr. Williams engaged was in 1861, when he proceeded to Washington with Vice President Hamlin and John A. Poor, under a commission from Gov. Washburn, to invoke the prompt action of the national government in fortifying the sea coast of Maine. They enlisted the attention and interest of the government in the subject, and a system of measures was initiated which will result, probably, in giving efficient protection to prominent points of our coast. But, during his absence, he took a severe cold which prostrated him, and caused a sickness which at one time threatened sudden dissolution. He, however, rallied from it, but with health and a constitution naturally firm and rugged, considerably impaired. He had a relapse which still further prostrated him, and his strong constitution at length wholly gave way, and he ceased to live July 25, 1862, at the age of seventy-nine. He died calmly, and in a firm religious trust.

Although Mr. Williams did not enjoy the advantages of a liberal education, he ever felt the importance of encouraging the cause of education in the State, and contributed to promote it. He was thirty-eight years one of the trustees of Bowdoin College, from which in 1820 he received the honorary degree of A. M., and that of LL. D. in 1855. In 1815, Harvard College also gave him the degree of A. M. On resigning the office of trustee of Bowdoin, which he had faithfully filled for so long a period, he presented to the institution the sum of three thousand dollars.

The same good fortune, or good Providence; perhaps we should say, which waited upon Mr. Williams in his varied and numerous active pursuits, accompanied him in private and domestic life. He early obtained for a companion and friend, and the head of his household, a daughter of Judge Daniel Cony, an eminent citizen of Augusta. Judge Cony was born in Sharon, Massachusetts: he held civil and military offices in his native town and State, during and before the Revolution: in 1778, having been married but two years, he moved to the infant settlement of Augusta. Here he enjoyed the favor of his fellow-citizens, was elected for twelve successive years to the House or Senate or Executive Council of Massachusetts, was ten years an active member of the committee for the sale of eastern lands, twelve years a judge of the Court of Common Pleas, and seventeen years judge of Probate. He died January 21, 1842, in the ninetieth year of his age. Judge Cony had four daughters: one, Sally, married to Mr. Williams; another, Abigail, to Rev. John H. Ingraham; the others, Susan and Paulina, to Samuel Cony and Chief Justice Weston.

Mr. Williams had a large family of children, eight daughters and one son; and we know of no truer test of a parent's domestic qualities than the respect and affection entertained for him by his children. Mr. Williams will not suffer when measured by this standard. His only son, Joseph H. Williams, is a lawyer in Augusta: in 1857, he was President of the Senate, and acting Governor the greater part of the year, on the resignation of Gov. Hamlin to take his seat in the Senate of the United States. He was nominated for the office of judge of the Supreme Court in 1862, but declined the situation. Five daughters of Mr. Williams married as follows; viz., Sarah, to James Bridge; Paulina, to Charles Jones; Zilpha, to John L. Cutler; Jane, to the Rev. Mr. Judd; and Helen A., to Dr. John T. Gilman: his youngest daughter, Anne, remains single. Mrs. Jones and Mrs. Cutler died before their father. Mrs. Williams has ever presided over this happy domestic circle with dignity and good sense, dispensing hospitality and liberal gifts with unfailing hand. Long may its open palm continue, and her life and health be spared.

THOMAS BOND. 1804—1827.

The contemporaries and competitors of Mr. Williams during the early period of his practice at the Kennebec Bar, who attained distinction, were Thomas Rice of Winslow, Timothy Boutelle of Waterville, Judge Wilde, Thomas Bond and Nathaniel Perley of Hallowell, Judge Bridge of

Augusta, Nathan Cutler of Farmington, and Frederic Allen of Gardiner. At a later period, 1815, Peleg Sprague, and in 1818, George Evans, came in and took a high position, as the others were gradually retiring from this scene of their labors. Of this talented group, none remain alive, in 1862, but Allen, Sprague, and Evans.

Thomas Bond, who had a brilliant career at the bar, was descended from William Bond, the first American ancestor, who was born in Suffolk County, England, in 1625, came a young man to Watertown, Massachusetts, and was the founder of most of the families by the name of Bond, in New England. The grandfather of Thomas was Amos of Watertown, a weaver, who died in 1762. His father, Thomas, was born in 1761, moved to Groton in 1773, married Esther Merriam of Concord in 1777, and moved with his family to Augusta in 1796, where he died March 15, 1815. Thomas was his oldest son, and was born in Groton, April 2, 1778. Soon after moving to Augusta, he entered Harvard College, from which he took his first degree in 1801, having among his classmates, Timothy Fuller, R. H. Gardiner, Dr. Gorham of Boston and Archdeacon Stuart of Canada; among whom he held a high rank. On leaving college, he entered the office of the late Judge Wilde at Hallowell, as a student. Having diligently improved his time and the very favorable opportunity he enjoyed in the office of so genial and distinguished a practitioner as Mr. Wilde, he was thought worthy, on being admitted to practice, to be received by his respected teacher into partnership. No better proof can be furnished of the high qualities of Mr. Bond than this substantial token of his merit. Mr. Bond now entered upon a career of successful practice and full employment. His partner was drawn away into all the eastern counties by his popularity as a lawyer and advocate, and was necessarily much absent from his office. The responsibility, therefore, of conducting the office business, devolved upon the junior partner, who proved himself to be fully competent to the duty. The partnership continued until Mr. Wilde was raised to the bench of the Supreme Court of Massachusetts, in 1815, when Mr. Bond took charge of the whole business. His labors became now severe and responsible: it was a hard task to sustain the structure which had rested on the athletic shoulders of Wilde; but Mr. Bond acquitted himself with ability both in the details of the office, and the wider field of the forum. For more than twenty years, he maintained a high and honorable position at the bar and in society, faithfully fulfilling all trusts, and acquiring the reputation of a sound lawyer, ingenious advocate, and an upright man. He had great weight with the court and jury, by his candor, honesty, and ability.

He was a firm and unwavering Federalist in his politics; and when the war with England brought up the conservatives in Maine and throughout New England, he was chosen to represent Hallowell in the General Court, in the years 1813 and 1814. He acted decidedly with his party, but was entirely free from the tricks of a partisan or demagogue. In the latter year, his friend and partner, Mr. Wilde, was chosen by the Legislature, a member of the Hartford Convention, and served in that body. In 1822 and 1823, Mr. Bond was a member of the Senate of Maine, from Kennebec County, and in the latter year was appointed one of the committee, with Daniel Rose and Benjamin Ames, to select a suitable site for a State's prison. In 1826, he was appointed on the part of the Senate a commissioner to revise the penal code. In 1824, he was chosen one of the trustees of Bowdoin College, and continued in the office to the time of his death.

In 1805, December 1, Mr. Bond married Lucretia F. Page, a daughter of Dr. Benjamin Page, a distinguished physician of Hallowell, by whom he had three children, viz., Francis

Eugene, Lucretia Page, and Caroline Mary. The son was born February 7, 1808, graduated at Bowdoin College in 1828, became a lawyer, and practiced awhile in Darien, Georgia, but came to Bangor in this State, where he died, September 5, 1840. Lucretia married Dr. Franklin Page: they resided some time in Cuba, but returned to Bangor, where she died in 1846. Caroline married Thomas H. Sandford, a merchant in New York. She died in Brooklyn, New York, January 11, 1853, aged thirty-seven, leaving two daughters, the only representatives of Mr. Bond now living. His widow is living, in 1862, at Brooklyn. In domestic life, he exhibited the same generous qualities which he displayed in his public and professional deportment. He died suddenly, of an acute disease, in 1827, in the forty-ninth year of his age, greatly lamented by his fellow-citizens.

Mr. Allen, in his sketches of the deceased members of the Kennebec Bar, in the sixth volume of the Maine Historical Collections, furnishes the following comprehensive summary of this gentleman's character: "Mr. Bond was remarkable for his integrity, for the urbanity of his manners and deportment. He was familiar with the principles of the common law, and with the rules of practice. He was a very safe counsellor and adviser, and was a highly reputable advocate. His practice was extensive, and no one was more beloved and esteemed by his fellow-citizens. His habits and modes of life were unexceptionable."

TIMOTHY BOUTELLE. 1804—1855.

Timothy Boutelle occupied for fifty years a prominent position among the lawyers and intellectual men of the State. He was descended from James Boutell, who came from England and settled in Salem, as early as 1635, and died in 1651. The name is variously spelled in our annals,—Boutell, Bout-

J. H. Bufford's lith. Boston.

TIMOTHY BOUTELLE.

At the age of 75.

well, and Boutelle. George S. Boutwell, late Governor of Massachusetts, and now commissioner of revenue, is of this family. The father of Mr. Boutelle, Col. Timothy, was a respectable farmer in Leominster, Massachusetts, where our late honored fellow citizen was born, November 10, 1777: his mother's name was Rachel Lincoln. His father served in the army during one or two campaigns of the Revolution, and in 1785, commanded a regiment called out to suppress the Shays insurrection.

Mr. Boutelle when young had delicate health, and therefore seemed incapable of rugged labor; but showing considerable mental power, his father was induced to give him a liberal education. After receiving the preliminary preparation, he entered Harvard College in 1796, from which he took his degree in honorable standing in 1800. His class contained many men whose names have not been permitted to perish. Among them were Washington Allston; Loammi Baldwin; President Bates of Middlebury College; Joseph S. Buckminster, the accomplished and learned minister of Brattle Street Church, Boston; Rev. Dr. Lowell of Boston; Chief Justice Shaw; Dr. Lincoln of Brunswick, and Dr. Weed of Portland. Of the forty-seven members of the class, two only survive, — Dr. Lincoln and Col. Samuel Swett of Boston. In college, he was the chum of Chief Justice Shaw. His scholarship may be inferred from his having been a member of the Phi-Beta-Kappa Society, the highest literary institution of the college.

Immediately on leaving college, Mr. Boutelle became the assistant preceptor of Leicester Academy, then under charge of Ebenezer Adams, late professor of mathematics at Dartmouth College. He remained there one year, and then entered the office of Abijah Bigelow in his native town. Mr. Bigelow was a graduate of Dartmouth, 1795, and a man of some note. He represented his district in Congress from

1810 to 1815, and was many years clerk of the courts in Worcester County. Mr. Boutelle completed his studies in the office of Edward Gray in Boston. On being admitted to the bar in 1804, he came to Waterville, which was ever after his place of residence. The only lawyers then in the neighborhood were Reuben Kidder of Waterville, and Thomas Rice of Winslow, the town opposite. If the lawyers were few, the population and business were small; Waterville was incorporated in 1802, and contained a population of only eight or nine hundred, and the whole county, including Somerset and Franklin, which were not then established, only about twenty-five thousand. His business, small at first, went on gradually increasing, as the country increased, and his merits became known, until by his legal acquirements, his earnest and eloquent advocacy of his cases, his genial manners and firm principle, he rose into the front rank of the profession. Chief Justice Shaw, in noticing the death of his classmate, makes the following remarks: "When Mr. Boutelle entered the profession of law in Maine, he placed himself within the circle of distinguished counsellors and advocates, most of whom, like himself, had gone from Massachusetts: among these were Parker, Wilde, Mellen, Davis, the Thachers, the Whitmans, and many others, since known as the bright ornaments of the legal profession. He soon established a good practice in the counties of Kennebec and Somerset, to which his attention was principally limited. In a bar eminent for talents and learning, he had the reputation of being a well-trained and well-read lawyer, with a quick apprehension and a power of legal discrimination, which enabled him to discern and apply the sometimes nice distinctions of the common law, to involved and intricate combinations of fact, with peculiar force and effect."

After the county of Somerset was established in 1809, he regularly attended the courts in that county, and occasionally went into other counties. His business became very large, hardly surpassed by any lawyer at the Kennebec Bar. As an advocate, he was eminently successful; industrious and faithful in the preparation of his cases: honorable in his practice, with a mind acute and comprehensive, and well-stored with legal principles and standard authorities, he could not fail to command a full share of the best business, and the commendation of the whole community. A writer of an article previous to his death, thus speaks of his manner and effect in court: "In addressing the court or jury, he did not aim at mere rhetorical display. His manner was earnest, energetic, forcible: his arguments were clear, logical, conclusive; and his object manifestly was to serve his client with the utmost fidelity, rather than to exhibit himself and gain applause. He uniformly had the respect and confidence of the court as a sound and able lawyer, and was influential with the jury because he presented his views with clearness and force, and appeared before them with the moral power of an honest man." Mr. Boutelle never, in the most active period of his life, neglected the cultivation of his various intellectual powers. He was a great reader both of history and general literature, and few men were better informed, in regard to the progress of society and the current events of the world, than he was. He was free to impart his knowledge: easy and social in his manners, of happy conversational talent, he freely communicated from his ample stores of information to all who were desirous of enjoying them.

In his early practice, Mr. Boutelle refrained entirely from public life. The only office he consented to fill, before the separation, was that of elector of President and Vice President in 1816. Christopher Gore was at the head of the college, and his associates from Maine were Prentiss Mellen, John Low, Stephen Longfellow, William Abbott, and Josiah

Stebbins. The vote of Massachusetts, then including Maine, was cast for Rufus King, who received but thirty-four votes out of two hundred and seventeen cast: the remainder were for James Monroe. Soon after this, the discussions for the separation of Maine from Massachusetts became more animated. Mr. Boutelle gave his influence in favor of the measure; and when it was finally accomplished in 1820, he was elected the first senator from Kennebec for that and the following year. These were the most important years in the legislation of Maine, for the new government was to be inaugurated, and a code of laws was to be formed, adapted to the peculiar circumstances of the State.

During the twenty years following the separation, Mr. Boutelle was repeatedly called into public life: he served, in this period, six years in the Senate, and six years in the House, and was a judicious and able member of important committees, especially of the Judiciary Committee, of which he was often chairman, on which the most responsible labors of legislation rested. His experience, his legal and general knowledge, rendered his services peculiarly valuable to the State. He entered into the debates on important questions, which he discussed with earnestness, directness, and force.

In 1829, he made a report on the North-Eastern Boundary, clear and able, thus stating the position of Maine: "The people of Maine have a constitutional right to claim, and do claim, of the government of the United States, that they will not suffer the integrity of our State to be violated — that they will assist us in preserving our ancient land-marks, and in vindicating our undoubted right to all the territory assigned to us by the treaty of 1783." In 1838, as chairman of the judiciary committee, he made a very able report on the subject of divorces by the Legislature, which checked an evil that had become prevalent and was increasing, of making the Legislature a court for the dissolution of the bonds of matrimony. He concludes as follows: "The Legislature is not, then, a branch of the judiciary, as known to our constitution, nor is it a court in the last resort, having the right, in divorce cases, to prescribe and apply to each particular case, such principles as suit its pleasure — acting, in fact, above and beyond the law. Sufficient has been said, as your committee believe, to establish the position, that the Legislature cannot, in any case, nor under any circumstances, rightfully undertake to dissolve the marriage contract." Notwithstanding the soundness of this doctrine in law, and its reasonableness in practice, cases are annually pressed upon the Legislature for special action on this subject.

In 1821, he procured a charter for Waterville College, or rather a change of its name from that of "The Maine Literary and Theological Institution," by which it was first incorporated, to its present title. Mr. Boutelle was one of the trustees appointed the same year, and continued an active and useful member of the board during his life. He was ever watchful for its interests and its honor, and promoted in every practicable manner its advantages and usefulness. In 1839, he received from it the deserved distinction of Doctor of Laws. He lived to see the college take a prominent position among the literary institutions of the country, and administered by men of industry, worth, and learning.

From the year in which he established himself in Waterville, Mr. Boutelle devoted himself with energy and intelligence to promote the prosperity, elevation, and happiness of that beautiful village. In the department of education, were the college and the schools; in its pecuniary concerns, he took the like interest; and, in 1814, assisted in procuring a charter for the Waterville Bank, with a capital of one hundred thousand dollars, the first established on the Kennebec River above Augusta; the bank in that town having been incorporated at the same session. He was a director from its organization, and for more than twenty years its president, managing its affairs with great skill and prudence.

In 1847, he was an efficient agent in procuring a charter for the Androscoggin and Kennebec Railroad, connecting with the Atlantic and St. Lawrence Railroad at Danville, and extending fifty-five miles to Waterville. He was made the first president, and by indefatigable exertions, he was able, with the assistance of a competent board of directors, to carry the enterprise through, so that in three years the road was opened for travel, at a cost of over two millions of dollars, and at a time when the pressure for money on the market was unusually stringent. By this great avenue of traffic and transportation, Waterville was put in connection with Portland and the great cities west and south of it; and its trade and general welfare largely promoted. He felt now as if he might, at the age of seventy-three, ask relief from the wearing toil and responsibility of this laborious office; and he declined, after three years' service, a further election. Since that time, the road has been extended to Bangor, and is now under successful operation: by a consolidation accomplished in 1862, with the Penobscot and Kennebec road, it forms one line one hundred and ten miles long, under the new name of Maine Central Railroad Co. This route, by its various connections, furnishes ample facilities for transportation by rail to the great lakes in Canada, to and beyond the Mississippi at the west, and to the Gulf of Mexico at the south.

Such are some of the claims of Mr. Boutelle to the affectionate remembrance of his fellow-citizens. His elevated moral character, his sterling religious principles, his noble public and private example, entitle him to the warmest commendation of the whole community which he adorned and advanced by his high social virtues.

Mr. Boutelle's domestic life was no less commendable than were his public and professional services. In 1811, he married Helen, a daughter of Judge Rogers, of Exeter, New Hampshire, by whom he had a large family of children. His excellent wife, to whom he was tenderly attached, and who was a most devoted friend, with two children, survived him. His son is a physician in Waterville; and his daughter is the wife of Edwin Noyes, a lawyer in Waterville, and the able superintendent of the Androscoggin and Kennebec Railroad.

Mr. Boutelle closed his long and busy life, November 12, 1855, at the ripe age of seventy-seven years and two days. We cannot more aptly conclude our notice of this estimable man than by adopting the language of his classmate and life-long friend, Chief Justice Shaw: "Active, energetic, and public-spirited, he was ever ready to engage in any enterprise which, in his judgment, would tend to promote the best interests of the public; and in all situations of influence and trust, and in all the offices and employments of political and public life, he enjoyed, in a high degree, the confidence of those associated with him."

WOODBURY STORER. 1805—1860.

If the services of one's ancestors against the enemies of the country were a title, in former times, and in kingly nations, to the distinctions of nobility, surely in our days, and under our institutions, the descendants of those who saved the colonies from the destructive inroads of French and savage invasion, and afterwards established the independence of the nation, are entitled to the civic honor of respectful commemoration. It cannot fail to have impressed those of our readers who have reflected on the subject, that the ancestors of a large proportion of the persons whose lives have been sketched in this volume, bore prominent parts in the Indian wars of our early annals, or in the later Revolutionary struggle. Such men are the true nobility of a country.

Among these, were the ancestors of Mr. Storer, both on the maternal and paternal side. His great-grandfather was Joseph Storer, who was an active officer in the second Indian war, and his house in Wells was a garrison, which gave protection to all within its reach; and his great grandmother, Hannah Hill, wife of Joseph Storer, belonged to a family that was constantly engaged for the defense and progress of the early communities. His grandfather, John Storer, was a prominent man in the affairs of York County many years: he married Mary, a sister of Woodbury and Gov. John Langdon of Portsmouth, New Hampshire, by whom he had six sons; viz, John of Wells; Samuel of Portsmouth; Bellamy, who died in the Revolution; Capt. Seth of Saco; and Ebenezer and Woodbury of Portland. The name of Woodbury, as a Christian name, came into the family in this way. Elizabeth, daughter of the Rev. Samuel Dudley of Exeter, a descendant of Gov. Joseph Dudley, married, in 1674, Kinsley Hall of that town: their eldest son, Josiah, married a Woodbury of Beverly, by whom he had two children,—Elizabeth, wife of Tobias Lear, the grandfather of the Tobias Lear who was aid to Washington, and consul general to Tripoli; and Mary, wife of John Langdon. She became the mother of Woodbury, Gov. John, and Mary Langdon, who was the mother of Woodbury Storer, the father of the subject of the present notice. Our Woodbury Storer, therefore, combined the blood of the Dudleys, the Hills, the Woodburys, and the Langdons, with that of the Storers.

He was born in Portland, July 12, 1783. His father came to Portland from Wells before the Revolution, a young man, and entered the store of John Archer as a clerk. He was serving in that capacity when the town was burned by the British fleet under command of Capt. Henry Mowat. Mr. Archer's stock of goods was hastily moved to the neighboring town, and Storer, the young clerk, stood sentry over it with his musket till it could be safely secured. After the war was over, Mr. Storer, the father, engaged very largely in commercial business in company with his brother Ebenezer, who had been an efficient officer in the army, and was true to the martial traditions of the family. This alliance of blood and business was still farther extended by their marriage of sisters, daughters of Deacon Benjamin Titcomb of Portland, and grand-daughters of Moses Pearson, who served with honor in the Louisburg expedition, and was the first sheriff of Cumberland, and subsequently one of the judges of the Common Pleas. Anna, the second daughter of Deacon Titcomb, was married to Mr. Storer's father in 1780, and died in 1788, leaving one son, Woodbury, and two daughters. The daughters were married, one to William Goddard of Portland, afterwards a prominent merchant in Boston; the other to Judge Barrett Potter, who is still living, and a widower. By a second marriage with Margaret, daughter of James Boyd, the elder Woodbury Storer had a large family of sons and daughters, who have taken honorable positions in the communities where they have established themselves: the Rev. John Parker Boyd Storer, late minister in Syracuse, New York, now deceased; Judge Bellamy in Cincinnati; Robert, a merchant, and David Humphreys, a physician, both in Boston, highly respected and valued citizens.

Woodbury Storer, the subject of our sketch, received his preliminary education at Phillips Exeter Academy, then the highest seminary of its kind in the United States, and under the charge of that admirable instructor and disciplinarian, Benjamin Abbot, LL. D., whose fifty years' service was rounded off by a splendid jubilee, which called around this venerable seat of juvenile study, a large proportion of the older and younger pupils. Daniel Webster presided. Edward Everett, Benjamin Merrill, Sparks, Palfrey, and other distinguished *savans* graced the occasion. This school was then, in the dearth of educational advantages in Maine, the favorite resort of her sons seeking a higher education. Young Storer entered it in 1798: we find upon its catalogue from Maine about that time, Lyman from York; King and Pierson from Biddeford; two Titcombs, Fosdick, Cobb, Hunnewell, and Henry Wadsworth, the martyr of Tripoli, from Portland; Chandler from Fryeburg; Page from Hallowell; Cook from Wiscasset; and numerous others from different parts of the State, showing a degree of popularity in the institution then unsurpassed.

Mr. Storer continued about two years at Exeter, and then entered the office of William Symmes in Portland. Mr. Symmes had graduated in 1780 at Harvard, had resided sometime in Virginia as a private tutor, and had been a member of the convention of Massachusetts which had adopted the constitution of the United States. He had been in practice in Portland ten years, and was confessedly at the head of the bar in Maine, as a lawyer, an advocate, and a general scholar. The fellow-students of Mr. Storer were Thomas E. Hale, who died in Castine, and William Freeman, son of Judge Samuel Freeman of Portland, a graduate of Harvard with high honors, in 1804. Mr. Storer faithfully and diligently pursued his studies under the favorable circumstances offered by the large practice of Mr. Symmes, and the fellowship of as fine a society of talented young men as ever assembled in Portland. They were attracted there as students by the reputation of Symmes, the late Chief Justice Parker, Daniel Davis, and Salmon Chase. Here were then gathered as students, James Savage and the late Gen. Eustis of Boston; William B. Sewall of York; William Freeman; Edward Payson, then preceptor of the academy; Horatio Southgate; James C. Jewett; Samuel D. Freeman; and John Wadsworth.

Mr. Storer continued with Mr. Symmes five years, the period required of those students who had not received a collegiate education, and was admitted to the bar in 1805. He commenced practice in Portland, where he had the benefit of a large circle of business connections, who could give to a person commencing life, the encouragement which ambitious young men need to stimulate their exertions, and develop their powers.

Mr. Storer had a steady, regular business: he was not an advocate, and rarely addressed the court or jury, but he was a careful, judicious, and honorable practitioner. For more than fifty years, he pursued a uniform, consistent, and upright course of life, by which he secured the confidence of his clients, and the respect of the community. He was much employed in the administration of estates as executor, guardian, and trustee, in which capacities he had large experience and the entire reliance of those who obtained his services. At the time of his death, which occurred June 24, 1860, at the age of seventy-seven, lacking eighteen days, he was the oldest member of the Cumberland bar, with the exception of Jonathan Morgan, then eighty-two years old, and still surviving. Gen. Fessenden, the next oldest member of that bar, and one year younger than Mr. Storer, still survives.

Mr. Storer did not attempt great and brilliant achievements, but he performed good and honest ones. Clients felt safe in his hands: his life and practice cast no shade upon a uniform career of gentleness, moderation, and useful endeavor. The widow appealed to him in her perplexity; the orphan confided in him; and they were never betrayed.

He walked uprightly, and worked righteousness, and spoke the truth in his heart. He was, from his youth, a religious man, sincere and conscientious, and many years one of the deacons of Dr. Dwight's church, the Third Parish, in Portland.

Being a native of the town, and always a resident in it, he took a deep interest in its affairs: he was particularly engaged in promoting the great railroad enterprises, which have extended their advantages to different parts of the State, and especially in the Atlantic and St. Lawrence Rail-Road, which he watched with anxiety from its inception to its completion, aiding it by his counsel and his purse; and, when it went into operation, he was made one of the trustees of the sinking fund, which place he held at the time of his death.

Mr. Storer, in 1811, married Miss Mary Barrett of Greenfield, Massachusetts, niece of Judge Barrett Potter of Portland, and grand-daughter of Col. John Barrett of Boston, afterwards of Springfield, Vermont. He left no children, and his widow survives.

ELISHA POMEROY CUTLER. 1805—1813.

The same year which introduced Mr. Storer to the bar of Cumberland, witnessed the introduction of Mr. Cutler, a young lawyer of fine talents and brilliant expectations. Mr. Cutler was son of Dr. Robert Cutler, a distinguished physician of Amherst, New Hampshire, where he was born in 1780. He received his public education at Williams College, which he entered, a sophomore, at the age of fifteen years, and graduated in 1798. He pursued his legal studies in the office of Judge Samuel Dana of Groton. On being admitted to practice, he opened an office at Hardwick, in the county of Worcester, where he remained about three years, and then moved to North Yarmouth, in this State, where he opened his office in 1805.

His adoption of North Yarmouth as his place of residence was one of those accidents, or providential occurrences, which often shape the destinies of men, "rough hew them as they will." He accidentally met in Boston Dr. Ammi R. Mitchell, the loved and genial physician of North Yarmouth, who represented that town in the Legislature in 1805. Mr. Cutler was there in search of a place more eligible than Hardwick for the pursuit of his profession. Dr. Mitchell was so much pleased with him that he recommended North Yarmouth to him, and urged him to make that his future abode; and, as an inducement, he offered him a home in his own house. The offer was gratefully accepted, and Mr. Cutler ever found the good doctor a firm and constant friend to him and his family.

This was a very flourishing town: its inhabitants were a well-cultivated and thrifty people, of a good Puritan stock. It afforded as much encouragement to a good lawyer as any inland town. Judge Potter, who had been practicing there four years, had, in this year, moved to Gorham, leaving the field entirely open. Mr. Cutler entered under favorable circumstances: he was a well-read lawyer, an agreeable speaker, and a man of fine person and manners. He became very popular, not only in the town but in the adjoining country, and at the shire-town. He had not been three years in the place before he was elected to represent the town in the Legislature, and was re-elected the two following years, 1809 and 1810. During this brief period, he distinguished himself as an excellent debater, and would have made a figure in political life, as well as at the bar, as a lawyer and advocate, had he not been cut down in the midst of usefulness and the prime of life, by a pulmonary complaint, which terminated his days in August, 1813, at the age of thirty-three years.

Mr. Hopkins, his contemporary at the bar, and his friend, in an address to the Cumberland Bar twenty years afterwards, thus speaks of this worthy gentleman: "Mr. Cutler was a good lawyer, and had just begun to distinguish himself as an able advocate. Few gentlemen have entered into the practice with a fairer prospect of usefulness and of eminence. And he was equally respected in private life: he was popular in his place of residence. Mr. Cutler was, in his principles and deportment, firm, manly, and independent. His integrity, outward circumstances had never shaken; and I believe it may be said, they would have no power to shake it. He never sought popularity: it sought him; and he died in full possession of the confidence, and of the high esteem of all who knew him."

In 1811, he married Elizabeth, daughter of Capt. Judah Delano of Portland, who came from Plymouth, Massachusetts. By her he had one son, who bears his father's name, and is a merchant in Boston. His widow still lives, having married, for her second husband, Josiah W. Mitchell of Freeport, a lawyer, and a friend of Mr. Cutler, by whom she has had a large family of children.

FREDERIC ALLEN. 1805—

Among the early and eminent lawyers of Kennebec County, was Frederic Allen of Gardiner, who happily still lives, 1862, to reflect back upon the half century of his honorable and prosperous practice, the genial light of his recollections and careful observation. He was born in Chilmark, on Martha's Vineyard, where his ancestor, James Allen, settled, in 1668, having become the proprietor of the Manor of Tisbury, containing two thousand acres purchased by him of the sachem of the island. The wife of James was Elizabeth Perkins, by whom he had numerous children, two of whom, daugh-

AT THE AGE OF 50

ters, were born in 1665 and 1667, at Sandwich, Massachusetts, where he first settled. The accurate and indefatigable Savage supposes this James may have been the son of George, who is found in Lynn, Massachusetts, in 1636, and the next year in Sandwich. He moved to Tisbury in 1668, where he had eight children, and died, in 1714, aged seventy-seven. His son John, born in 1680, married, in 1716, Margaret Homes, daughter of the Rev. William Homes of Martha's Vineyard, a Presbyterian minister of the Scotch-Irish stock, who was settled in Chilmark in 1715, and whose descendants are numerous. By her, he had five sons and three daughters. The second son, Jonathan, was educated at Harvard College, from which he took his degree in 1757, and became a lawyer, to the practice of which, his father had given some attention, and a portion of whose law books, as well as those of his son, are now, as heir-looms, in the hands of the subject of our sketch. He married Deborah Gardiner of Newport, a descendant of Joseph Gardiner, one of the first settlers of Narraganset in Rhode Island, by whom he had five sons and two daughters, and died in 1783. Frederic, the youngest of the sons, was born in 1780. He is thus in the fourth degree from the first James of Martha's Vineyard, through John and his wife, Martha Homes; and Jonathan and his wife, Deborah Gardiner, by which marriage and his own he has a twofold connection with the family of Dr. Sylvester Gardiner, who was, for many years, a large proprietor of lands in Maine, and a liberal benefactor to her religious and educational institutions,—a practice which his grandson, Robert Hallowell Gardiner of Gardiner, has not forgotten to exercise.

Mr. Allen's father died when he was but three years old, by which he was deprived of the guidance and the education which the father was competent to give, having himself received the advantages of Harvard, and a regular legal training. The Allens seemed to have taken to Harvard College in a remarkable degree: I find the number borne on its catalogue of 1860, to be forty-three, of whom nineteen were in the last century, having but seven names larger; viz., Williams, eighty-six; Smith, eighty-four; Adams, eighty-two; Parker, sixty-six; Brown, fifty-six; Rogers and Russell, forty-five each. The name is also among the highest on the Bowdoin catalogue, containing nineteen, Smith only exceeding it. Mr. Allen, by the circumstances of his family, was deprived of these advantages, and was obliged to avail himself, in the intervals of labor, of such instruction as he could obtain at Chilmark, aided by his brother, Homes Allen, and his brother-in-law, Dr. Allen Mayhew. At an early age, he came to Maine, where his sister, the wife of Dr. Tupper, lived, at the head of Swan Island, and was a clerk in a store. On his return, about the age of eighteen, he entered the office of his brother Homes, who was a practicing lawyer in Barnstable, and a gentleman of great ability and promise, but who died at the early age of thirty-four. After spending two years with his brother, he went to the office of Benjamin Whitman, who then resided in Hanover, Massachusetts,—a very eccentric gentleman, whose peculiar appearance, with a squint in one eye, and his nankin breeches, used to attract my attention when a student in Boston. He had considerable practice in the country, and hoped to extend it by moving to Boston. Mr. Allen accompanied him to that city, and has often remarked that the six months which he spent there were more profitable to him than any other portion of his studies, as he had an opportunity of attending the courts, and seeing and hearing the great lights of jurisprudence which then adorned the Suffolk Bar: these were Sullivan, Parsons, Lowell, Dexter, Gore, Fisher Ames, Otis, &c.

On being admitted to the bar, Mr. Allen, like other enterprising young men, looked to the new and growing district of Maine as furnishing a prospect of the most speedy advance in the profession; and, coming into it, he stopped first at New Gloucester, to seek the advice and aid of Judge Whitman. He accompanied him to Windham and other neighboring towns, but not being particularly satisfied with these places, he proceeded to Waldoborough, and there pitched his tent, in 1805. Waldoborough had been a half shiretown, from 1786 to 1800, when the courts were moved to Wiscasset. It had no lawyer at the time Mr. Allen went there, and we have no evidence of there having been any after the death of Roland Cushing, in 1789. The population, about two thousand, was largely of German descent, and the town was flourishing: it now has a large commercial marine, and a population of four thousand five hundred and sixty-nine. But Mr. Allen was scarcely initiated in business when he had an encouraging offer from Nathan Bridge of Gardiner to form a partnership with him. This he concluded to accept, and moved to Gardiner in 1808: his connection with the Gardiners, established there and owning large estates, probably afforded an additional inducement. This was ever after the place of his residence.

Mr. Bridge was no advocate, and not much of a lawyer; but he had large transactions for absent landed proprietors, for whom he was a faithful agent. Mr. Allen heartily engaged in the business, attending the courts and managing his causes with skill and legal accuracy, while the out-door work was done by Bridge. The latter, however, withdrew gradually from the duties of the profession, which were not agreeable to him, and in three or four years after the commencement of the partnership, left it entirely. Mr. Allen secured, by his good management, the business of the firm, and continually gained new: he was a diligent student, a careful and accurate lawyer; and, although not what would be called eloquent, he presented his cases clearly and urged them strongly upon the attention of the jury. His arguments to the court were sound and forcible, and had great weight from the perspicuity of his statement, and the force of his logic. He did not deal in rhetoric, nor was he in the habit of employing the graces of style; but he went directly to the points in issue, and threw upon them the strong light of authority and illustration. His practice extended from his own county into Lincoln, Somerset, Franklin, and all the eastern counties, where, after Judge Wilde left the bar, he had for competitors, Bond, Reuel Williams, Boutelle, Orr, Sprague, Belcher, and George Evans. As the elders of these died, or retired from the practice, he rose to the head of the profession in those counties, where he devoted himself through near fifty years to the stern and wearing labors of a responsible and arduous profession. He did not even indulge himself in the recreation of politics, which has fascinated so many lawyers, and led them into labyrinths that have bewildered them from the quiet and peaceful pursuits of professional life.

After the separation of Maine from Massachusetts, his business rapidly increased, and carried him into all the counties of the State east of Cumberland. It seemed surprising, that with so few adventitious charms of oratory, he should have acquired such an extensive business; and we can attribute it only to the faithfulness and zeal with which he devoted himself to his clients' interest, his sound knowledge of law, and his integrity and strictly honorable practice. The manner of his arguments and addresses was dry and somewhat desultory; but, as one of his contemporaries has observed, he would get the whole case out, and make the jury comprehend it, although in a way peculiar to himself. Sometimes he would rise into a flight of eloquence, but this was exceptional, and sometimes a joke or anecdote would come from him exceedingly apt and effective, and the more so because not common. He was persevering and tenacious, understood his case, and worked till he made others understand it. We must award to him, looking to his long course of successful practice, and the high reputation he obtained, the praise of the "Good Advocate," who "finds God's blessing on his provisions and posterity." Mr. Allen, in 1820, received from Bowdoin College the honorary degree of A. M., and in 1847, the more distinguished and deserved honor of LL. D. He is and has been for some years one of the overseers of the college.

Another branch of the Allens of Martha's Vineyard came into Maine at the close of the last century,—William Allen, who settled with his family in a log cabin in the town of Industry. His son William, now of Norridgewock, and well known throughout that region of country as William Allen, Jr., an ample promoter of good works, was born on the Tisbury manor in 1780, the same year which gave birth to his kinsman of whom we have been speaking. Before we close our sketches, we shall have more to say of this early clerk of the courts of Somerset, and valuable citizen. Another relative of Frederic, a sister, much older than himself, came to the Kennebec before the Revolution with her husband, Dr. Tupper of the old Vineyard. They settled on a farm at the head of Swan Island on the Kennebec River. He was quite an eccentric character: being in the midst of a timber country, he conceived the idea of constructing a raft of timber sufficiently compact and strong to be transported across the ocean. Having obtained the aid of some persons of wealth in Boston, he commenced his raft in front of his house on the river. He piled the timber, stick upon stick, into a solid mass, shaped as nearly as possible in the form of a vessel. She was rigged as a ship, and taken to Boston, before proceeding on her voyage. She excited great attention in that place. Mr. Gardiner informs me that he visited her with other boys who joined the crowd of curious spectators. Dr. Tupper proposed to go to Liverpool in her himself; but his partners dissuaded him; and, being highly insured, she left the harbor for her adventurous voyage, amidst the apprehensions and conflicting opinions of the people. She never reached her destination: she was abandoned by her crew off the coast of Labrador, and as she was afterwards discovered, in good order, and with a plentiful supply of provisions, it was suspected that her desertion was fraudulent, and without sufficient cause. Mr. Gardiner, who furnished me with this anecdote, observed, that two other similar attempts were made some years afterwards, and both vessels went safely across the ocean, but were foundered on the coast of England, with the same suspicion of fraud as attached to the other case.

Dr. Tupper was very peculiar in his religious views, as well as in some of his temporal concerns. He was a high-toned Federalist, and joined to the full in all the measures of that party. He one day visited the office of Mr. Glazier, the publisher of the Hallowell Gazette, a warm Federal paper, and said to him, "Mr. Glazier, I advise you not to publish your paper any more." "Why so?" said Mr. G.; "I am doing very well — have a good list of subscribers, and my paper is well received." "Yes," said Dr. Tupper, "but you know that in heaven people follow the same business in which they have been employed here, and a Federal newspaper will never be tolerated in that place."

Mr. Allen himself had some eccentricities of character: he was often absent-minded: sometimes in his office, in the midst of deep study, he would suddenly jump up, thrust his hands into his pockets, move rapidly about the room, and break out on topics wholly irrelevant to those which had, apparently, been engaging his attention. He has been known to arise from his bed at night, and go to his office, examine a law book, and return to his bed again. But this may have been a ruling passion, rather than an eccentricity, — the effect of deep study and abstraction.

Mr. Allen was a good citizen, a good neighbor; just and honorable in all his dealings; genial and social in his intercourse with society, and an honor to the profession which his whole life has richly illustrated. His peculiarities, his absent-mindedness, may be attributed to an abstraction occasioned by a too exclusive confinement to professional duties: he read and thought and meditated on law, until he became absorbed in it to the exclusion of other objects, which, if indulged in, would have given a more perfect finish to the fullness of his character.

In 1859, Mr. Allen prepared for the Maine Historical Society, sketches of the early lawyers in Lincoln and Kennebec Counties, containing reminiscences of his contemporaries. A portion of this was read at a meeting of the society, and the paper forms an interesting article of the sixth volume of its collections. In the editor's introduction to the paper, it is observed: "Mr. Allen was elected a member of the society in the year of its incorporation, 1822. It is a graceful act of his ripened years, to revive the memories of the able predecessors and contemporaries who have dignified with him the same field of arduous and useful labor. Among his competitors at the bar, were the late judges, Bridge, Wilde, Bailey, and Crosby; Samuel Thatcher, Bond, Reuel Williams, Lee, Boutelle, John Wilson, Orr, Peleg Sprague, and George Evans: of whom, besides himself, Thatcher, Sprague, and Evans only survive." We may add the names of McGaw and William Abbot of the Penobscot Bar: the former still lives at Bangor, of the same age with Mr. Allen.

In 1812, Mr. Allen married Hannah Bowen, a daughter

of Oliver Whipple of Portsmouth, New Hampshire, and a grand-daughter of Dr. Sylvester Gardiner. Mr. Whipple was a native of Rhode Island: he graduated at Harvard College in 1766, and settled at Portsmouth in the practice of law. His professional engagements often led him into Maine; and during and after the Revolution, his employment as the agent and attorney of Dr. Gardiner, and of his executors, required his frequent presence in the courts of Lincoln and York Counties. Just previous to the Revolution, Mr. Whipple married Abigail, the sixth child of Dr. Gardiner; and as the family was distinguished in Boston for wealth and social position, the occasion was made one of considerable notoriety. We have happened to see a list of the wedding calls for the three or four days after the marriage; and as some of the names are of historical interest, I will introduce a few of them: these were, Admiral Graves and his lady; the Hallowells; the Lechmeres; Capt. Montressor, his wife and daughter; Mr. and Mrs. Vassal; Secretary Fluker, the father of Mrs. General Knox; General Gage and his aids; Mr. Pepperell, Mr. Whipple's classmate, afterwards Sir William, and his wife; Miss Auchmuty, and Colonel Waldron. These are sufficient to indicate the standing of the family in the society of the then most aristocratic city in the colonies.

All the persons we have named above were loyalists, in which party were Dr. Gardiner and most of his family and acquaintances. There was, however, one striking exception, and that was the doctor's son John, afterwards the eminent barrister in Maine, a memoir of whom appears in preceding pages. We may be pardoned, if, to show this fact, we introduce here an extract of a letter written by him to his father from St. Kitts, January 18, 1783, just previous to his return to Boston,—his father being then a refugee in England. He says, "I am a staunch, thorough,

Revolution Whig, you know, and abhor all king-craft and priest-craft. Such have been my principles since I could judge for myself; and such, I trust, will be the principles I shall carry with me to the grave. I have, however, borne a place here under his most christian majesty, which I have discharged the duties of with the utmost fidelity and integrity, and without the least view to gain; and in such a manner as I would have served his Britannick Majesty, had I been entrusted. And it is with gratitude I mention it, I have received every protection and every mark of friendship from his Excellency, Count Dillon, and the French officers here, insomuch so that time shall not obliterate my regards to them."

St. Kitts was alternately in the possession of the French and English, until it was ceded to the English in the peace of 1783.

Mr. Whipple died suddenly at Washington, of apoplexy, in 1813. His wife was the sister of Hannah, the wife of Benjamin Hallowell, who was the mother of Robert Hallowell Gardiner, our respected fellow citizen, now enjoying, in the town of Gardiner, a ripe, hale, and serene old age.

Mr. Updike, the historian of Narraganset, in a recent letter to Miss Allen, daughter of Frederic Allen, thus speaks of Mr. Whipple: "I knew your grandfather, Col. Oliver Whipple, well. He was a fine looking and accomplished gentleman, with a highly expressive countenance: he was six feet in height or very near it, erect and straight: he was corpulent, and in manner dignified and courteous: his society was always agreeable and interesting. He was grand master of the Masons in New Hampshire."

By the marriage of Mr. Allen with Miss Whipple, he had three sons and three daughters. Two of the sons, Charles Edward and Augustus Oliver, graduated at Bowdoin College in 1835 and 1848, and are lawyers in Boston. His oldest son, Frederic, having received his medical education at Harvard, died in 1840, at the entrance of his profession. His daughter Eleanor married Dr. Martin Gay of Boston, and died in 1858. The other two daughters reside in Gardiner. Mr. Allen's wife was a lady of talents, cultivation, and taste. She died a few years since, leaving her companion of many years, to pursue his solitary way alone; and yet not alone, for his path is still lighted by his own genial disposition and the kind attentions of children and friends.

WILLIAM BARTLETT SEWALL. 1806—

No name was more familiar and honored at the bar, and in the courts of Massachusetts and Maine, for more than a century, than was that of *Sewall*. From 1692 to 1819, — a period of one hundred and twenty-six years, — one of the family had a seat upon the bench of the highest courts for one hundred years, about twenty-five of which, as a chief justice: these were, Samuel, Stephen, David, and Samuel, all descendants from Henry, the first American ancestor, who came to Newbury, in Massachusetts, from Coventry, England, in 1634. Beside these, were Jonathan, attorney general, before the Revolution, and Daniel and Henry, in this State, clerks, time out of mind. They seem to have had a prescriptive right to the bench and bar, and places in court. Nor were they much less prominent in the church, whose pulpits they have filled with eminence, all along the course of our history. Few names in our annals have had higher rank and distinction than theirs.

William B. Sewall, the subject of this notice, was the only son of Daniel Sewall, the time-honored clerk of the courts in York County, who descended from the first Henry through his second son, John: he was born in York, as he humorously said, "about 2 o'clock, A. M., according to the

Yours truly
W. B. Sewall

At the age of 80.

best of my recollection and belief, December 18, 1782." His mother was Dorcas Bartlett, daughter of John H. Bartlett of Kittery. Of his father I will not say more at present, because I intend to devote a distinct article to him, in connection with the ancient clerks.

At the time Mr. Sewall was obtaining the rudiments of knowledge, a grammar school was kept, the principal part of the year, in the central district of the village of York, although not always by a college graduate. To this school, Mr. Sewall was sent. When he began to fit for college, he commenced the "Latin Accidence," under the guidance of Nymphas Hatch, a graduate of Harvard in the class of 1797: Mr. Hatch afterwards became a clergyman, and died in 1850. Hatch left before young Sewall had made much progress, and he completed his studies under direction of Mr. Briggs, the minister of the parish, who offered his pupil for admission to Harvard College in 1799. In regard to this village school, Mr. Sewall remarked, "It has been privileged with some of the most distinguished teachers of their day or any other: Prof. Cleaveland was one; and his successor, Mr. N. Lord, afterwards Register of Probate of Essex County, may be named as another: they were remembered with gratitude by all who enjoyed the privilege of their instructions."

Mr. Sewall pursued his studies in college with diligence and success: his classmates were young men of ambition and ability: their names will not soon die: among them were,— Benjamin Ames, well known in Maine forty years ago; Dr. Asa Eaton of Salem Street Church, Boston, whose venerable appearance in the latter part of his life attracted universal attention — he died in 1858; Prof. John Farrar of Harvard College; Rev. Nathan Parker of Portsmouth; Rev. Dr. Payson of Portland; James Savage of Boston, whose works will live after him; and the good and venerable

Samuel Willard, D. D., of Deerfield. Savage had the first part at Commencement, an English oration: the subject was, "The Patronage of Genius." Ames and Payson had a conference with Lewis Strong; Daniel Waldo Lincoln, a poem; Farrar, an English dissertation.

In competition with such men, the dullest wit might be quickened, and the quickest sharpened. Ames, Eaton, Farrar, Parker, Savage, Sewall, and Willard were among the seventeen who were deemed worthy of membership in the Phi-Beta-Kappa Society, and of course must have had a good college rank.

On leaving college, Mr. Sewall, determining on the law as his profession, and naturally enough, for his father, being register of probate and clerk of the courts, and who also practiced law himself, was steeped in legal forms and proceedings, wisely selected the office of the eminent jurist, Isaac Parker, at Portland, in which to pursue his studies. He says, "When I went to Portland in December, 1803, the students in Judge Parker's office were,—Samuel D. Freeman, John Wadsworth, and James Savage: Freeman was, for the most part, with his father in office business; and Wadsworth was absent considerably from ill health, part of the time at Washington, his father being representative from Cumberland. In 1804, Abraham Eustis was added to our number; and not long afterwards, Lemuel Bryant, a nephew of Major Weeks, began his term of five years. We were all dispersed by the appointment of Judge Parker to the Supreme Court, in February, 1806. Eustis went to Boston, and was in the office of Mr. Gore, but was appointed a captain in the United States Artillery, before, I believe, he had completed the term of office-study,—certainly, he never entered on the practice. Bryant afterwards went into trading business. Wadsworth was admitted to the bar, and had an office in Portland, in 1808 or 1809: he afterwards moved to Hiram, where he died in 1860. When I first went to Portland, Mr. Parker's office was in the upper story of a wooden building on Fish Street, belonging to Mr. Widgery, in a place where Neal kept an insurance office below. Soon afterwards, he removed to the then new brick building, so long occupied as a custom house, insurance office, &c.,— now Cumberland Bank, Lowell & Senter's, &c." He adds, "Horatio Southgate, James C. Jewett, and Woodbury Storer, Jr., were, I think, admitted before I went to Portland. Bray came from Connecticut, and was a short time in Symmes's office, before being allowed to practice in this State: he was in practice when I first came, in Kellogg's building."

Mr. Sewall was, for a short time, in the office of Prentiss Mellen, who moved to Portland from Biddeford, in February, 1806, about the time Judge Parker retired from the bar; but completed his studies with Edward St. Loe Livermore, at Newburyport; and was admitted to the bar of the Common Pleas in Essex County: he came back to Portland, opened an office there, and was admitted to the Supreme Court in Cumberland County. As Mr. Mellen spent much of his time in attending the courts in other counties, where his reputation as an advocate gave him numerous engagements, he invited Mr. Sewall into his office as a partner. Here he devoted himself to the business of the office, while Mr. Mellen was occupied in the courts.

Mr. Sewall was a good lawyer, had a clear and discriminating mind, and had great accuracy and familiarity with the forms of practice, and the art of conveyancing. But his extreme diffidence and modesty deterred him from making any exhibitions in court, or taking any position as an advocate. Perhaps the circumstance of his connection with Mr. Mellen, in the early years of his practice, restrained him from aiming at, or acquiring any experience as an advocate. Mr. Mellen argued all his own causes, as well as many of those commenced by other lawyers, with rare zeal and ability, so that a junior partner could have no opportunity to acquire facility in the art. Experience shows us that the longer one has been at the bar without speaking to a jury, the more difficult it is to open his mouth,—he becomes startled at the sound of his own voice, while the eyes of an audience are pointed steadily at him. Ease and facility in public speaking are the offspring of practice and habit. Mr. Sewall, too, had great delicacy and sensitiveness of taste: nothing commonplace or inferior could ever satisfy the demand of his own criticism; and this, I think, in his case, as well as in that of many other young lawyers, has proved an embarrassment, and sometimes an insuperable one to excellence as an orator. I would not say of Mr. Sewall, as Robert Hall once said of a very timid man, "He is so nervously modest, that he seems to be always asking pardon of everybody for being in the world." This diffidence, I think, is natural to the family: his father and uncles Jotham and Henry had it; so had the excellent judge, David Sewall, and the wise and modest chief justice, Samuel Sewall, who died while holding court at Wiscasset, in 1814. It does not arise from lack of knowledge so much as an overfullness, which, as in Addison's case, finds difficulty of expression.

Mr. Sewall was a scholar and a ripe one, of cultivated taste and fine thought. He preferred the quiet pursuits of the scholar to the wrangles of the bar, and devoted much time to poetry and prose composition, which illuminated the columns of newspapers and periodicals. In connection with the wits about town, Savage, Payson, Lear, Davies, Deering, Carter, Wright, and others, Portland was kept in good humor; and the "Pilgrim," "Prowler," "Night Hawk," and "Torpedo" flashed with merriment, which would have done honor to the "Salmagundi," or to the modern "Punch."

When he came to Portland, in 1803, he found his classmates, Savage, and Payson, afterwards the distinguished preacher, but at that time preceptor of the new academy, pursuing their studies there; and to amuse themselves, they were writing a series of articles in the "Old Portland Gazette," then edited by Isaac Adams, over the signature of "*Pilgrim.*" They immediately pressed Sewall into the service, and he became a joint contributor to those agreeable literary productions, which instructed and amused the town; and were continued until Savage was called away by an invitation from his kinsman, Mr. Tudor, to go to the West Indies, and assist in introducing the ice business into the islands. The "*Prowler*" followed, and these more formal essays were interspersed with many a squib and New Year's Hudibrastic verses, which lightened up the prosaic columns of the Gazette.

Mr. Sewall had a great fondness for mathematical studies, which he pursued to a large extent in college, and was rewarded for his attainments in that branch, by an assignment of "Exercises in Mathematics and Astronomy," at Commencement, with two others of his classmates, Nathan Parker and Daniel Swan. This taste was probably imbibed in early life from his father, who had quite a genius for mathematical calculations, which manifested itself in the preparation of almanacs and the like labors. Both father and son worked much in that line, in which they took pleasure and made great proficiency. The son, when young, assisted his father in almanac-making; and when in the practice of his profession, beguiled the leisure time in preparing a Register for Maine, which he published several years after the separation from Massachusetts. In connection with Judge Bourne of Kennebunk, he prepared the

Register of Maine for 1820. This being the first published in the new State, was very full, and contained a vast deal of useful information, in a compact form. It contained a chronological account of the various settlements in Maine from the earliest time, with notice of early grants, &c.; the act of separation, the new constitution, and list of delegates to the convention; tariff of duties, army and navy register, besides the usual matter embraced in such works. He continued the publication of the Register several years; for the labor, care, and investigation in which, the sales poorly compensated. These humble, but very valuable statistical works, are not appreciated in their day so much as they ought to be. Nor is the labor and skill necessary in their preparation sufficiently estimated. A full series of these works is invaluable to one who is collecting materials for history, or who desires to see the form and pressure of the times long gone by.

In all works of this kind, and others, involving statistical habits or knowledge, Mr. Sewall had few equals among us in his day: what he did, he did thoroughly and well; and he was constantly busy about something useful or amusing. He was one or two years secretary of the Senate, soon after the separation, which gave him facilities in his favorite pursuit; and he was afterwards often employed by members and committees to draft and prepare bills and other papers to be laid before the Legislature, in which his clear and concise method rendered him a model worthy of all imitation: it would have promoted the accuracy and precision of the statutes if this practice had been continued.

He was always cheerful, social, and often gay: his humor was racy, and the play of his mind was lambent and genial. In 1819, on the death of his first wife, which took place that year, he moved to Kennebunk, and re-occupied, with his aged father and sisters, the old homestead. He assisted his father in the duties of his offices as clerk and register of probate, during the remainder of the time he continued to hold them. Afterwards, in 1823, he returned to Portland, and took charge of the editorial department of the Advertiser, which he continued to conduct several years, and to which was added during his management the issue of the semi-weekly edition. In 1837, he went back to Kennebunk, formed a second matrimonial connection with a lady of that town, practiced law moderately as opportunity offered, and still enjoys, at the mansion of his late honored father, with his wife and a sister, the calmness and serenity which wait on a genial temper, and follow, toward its setting, a life of gentleness, purity, and uniform benignity. He has no children.

SAMUEL HUBBARD. 1806—1810.

Among the lawyers who commenced practice in Maine, and afterwards became distinguished in Massachusetts, was Samuel Hubbard, late of Boston. Mr. Hubbard was born in Boston, in 1785, and graduated at Yale College, in 1802, at the early age of seventeen. He studied his profession in New Haven, in the office of Judge Chauncey, for two years, and completed his studies with Charles Jackson, the eminent lawyer and judge in Boston. On being admitted to the bar, in Suffolk County, he embraced the favorable opportunity offered by the removal of Judge Mellen to Portland from Biddeford, and took his office and his business at that place, in the autumn of 1806. Judge Mellen had resided in Biddeford fourteen years, and had acquired an extensive practice, — said to have been worth two thousand dollars a year, which was very remunerative for those days. But this was accomplished in part by his reputation as an advocate; and which a young lawyer, but twenty-one years old, and just entering practice, could not expect to retain. Mr. Hubbard was, however, the only lawyer in the town, although in the flourishing village of Saco, on the other side of the river, there were three attornies, viz., Cyrus King, the eccentric Joseph Bartlett, and Jeremiah Bradbury. He continued there, the only lawyer, doing a successful business, until September, 1810, when he returned to Boston.

He formed in that place a connection with his former teacher, Judge Jackson, which was probably the inducement which drew him from Maine. This continued until the appointment of Mr. Jackson to the bench, in 1813. From that time, he had a full and extensive practice, taking an honorable position among the eminent lawyers who, for the third of a century in which he occupied his place at the bar, came in competition with him: these were,—Prescott, Otis, Shaw, Sullivan, and Webster, among the seniors; Gallison, Loring, Dexter, Fletcher, and Fuller, among the juniors. After a long course of a first-class practice, in which his mind had become thoroughly disciplined by study and forensic conflicts, he was elevated to the bench of the Supreme Court, in 1842, to fill the vacancy occasioned by the death of Judge Putnam.

This station he occupied to the acceptance of the bar and the community until his death, which took place in Boston, December 24, 1847, at the age of sixty-two. His qualities as a lawyer and a judge are thus described in a notice which Chief Justice Shaw took of his death, when it was announced from the bar: he said, "As a counsellor and advocate, he was extensively employed and trusted; and he devoted himself to his professional duties with a fidelity and assiduity which showed how worthy he was of the trust reposed in him. He was remarkable among his contemporaries for his power of patient and thorough investigation, which enabled him to unravel the most complicated cases. * * * His mind was thoroughly imbued with a knowledge of mercantile law, not merely the municipal law which governs one State or one country, but that qualified international law, which, for general convenience and almost by general consent, governs the commercial world. * * * The judicial qualities of Judge Hubbard, during the few years that he has held this office, have been too conspicuous and too highly appreciated to require any remarks at this time. Coming to the bench in the full maturity of his powers, after a long course of study and practice; thoroughly acquainted with the rules and principles of law, in all its departments, and familiar with all the forms of proceeding, he needed no preparation, but was ready to enter at once upon the duty of a judge. The same qualities of mind, the same acute and persevering investigation, which we have already noticed, were brought to bear here with eminent success."

On the same occasion, Charles G. Loring, an eminent practitioner of the Boston Bar, in addressing his associates, observed, "that he had the pleasure of completing his studies under the guidance of Judge Hubbard, and entered the forensic arena under his auspices, as his associate in the profession; and how grateful and refreshing will ever be that recollection of the kind manners, the honest love of truth, and gentleness of spirit with which he exercised his high powers."

Judge Hubbard occasionally engaged in political life, being pressed into service by his fellow citizens as their representative in the General Court. On one of these occasions, in 1838, he drew a report relating to the disastrous failure of the Commonwealth Bank, with the testimony of witnesses examined by the legislative committee: this was a sound and able exposition of the affairs of that institution, and of banking operations.

He was also for many years one of the Board of Commissioners for Foreign Missions, and rendered this extensive and important cause most efficient and valuable service. In whatever capacity Judge Hubbard employed his powers, he was prompt, able, and effective. He was active, intelligent, and conscientious. His private life, as well as his public career, was adorned with the fruits of sound religious principle: his profession and practice were blended in harmonious action in all the varied relations of life.

He was twice married, and has left a family of children: his first wife was a daughter of Gardner Greene of Boston.

His merits were publicly recognized by his own college, Yale, and also by Harvard, in bestowing upon him the honorary degree of Doctor of Laws; in which they were amply sustained by public sentiment.

BENJAMIN AMES. 1806—1835.

For the following interesting sketch of Mr. Ames, I am indebted to John H. Sheppard of Boston, who, practicing at the same bar, had abundant opportunity of becoming acquainted with his subject.

Benjamin Ames, formerly of Bath, was born in Andover, Massachusetts, October 30, 1778. He was the son of Benjamin Ames, a respectable inn-holder of that place; and the rank to which he rose in after life, so far from disparagement on account of his humble origin, should rather reflect honor on his character. His case is not without precedent: for Macaulay tells us[1] that the famous Prior "passed his boyhood in drawing corks at a tavern."

Mr. Ames was educated at Harvard University, which he entered late, at twenty-two years of age, and graduated in

[1] History of England, vol. v.

1803. One of his classmates described him to the writer as a student of correct habits, not of a genial temperament, always plodding over his book, fond of logic and metaphysics, but without any taste for the classics of Greece and Rome. At commencement, he had one of the higher parts, and belonged to a class of which the venerable and distinguished genealogist, James Savage, Esq., of Boston, took the lead in an English oration.

He studied law in the office of Samuel Dana of Groton, Massachusetts,—a man of note in that day, particularly as a zealous partisan. He was president of the senate two sessions, and afterwards was appointed one of the judges of the Court of Common Pleas. This gentleman was a member of the legislature, when the election of Caleb Strong, for governor, was so hotly contested; and he was very strenuous and urgent to reject a number of votes, because the t, in some of the written suffrages for Strong, was not crossed. In the result, however, he must have felt the force of my Lord Coke's adage, "*Qui hæret in litera, hæret in cortice.*" Probably it was under such an astute special pleader, that his pupil Benjamin was initiated into mysteries of politics, and drank deep of the waters of Meribah.

Having been admitted to practice as an attorney in 1806, he opened an office in Bath, with high recommendations for talents and acquirements. At that time, party spirit was raging like a pestilence, and the whole community was divided into federalists and democrats. Then there was no middle clique of hard-shells, know-nothings, and abolitionists; no grades of political distinction, nor prismatic colors in either party: white and black were the only hues to designate either side. So violent and fierce was the contention between these two national belligerents, that in many towns and villages there was neither friendly intercourse nor even courtesy between them. Houses, in many instances, were literally divided against themselves; families were estranged from each other; and instead of love to our neighbor, a burning hatred reigned in the bosom of the partisan. To stand neutral was out of the question;—it drew down the vengeance of both parties; and, in a word, there was a state of civil war without battle-field and without bloodshed.

It was during these political excitements that an amusing incident occurred. General Joshua Wingate, a man of generous and hospitable character, was collector of the port of Bath. His wife, daughter of Gen. Dearborn, late Secretary of War, and one of the most beautiful women Maine ever produced, was desirous of giving a genial welcome to their numerous acquaintance in their new house: cards were issued; the drawing-rooms were filled; and ladies and gentlemen of both parties there met face to faee. But the elegant and fascinating Mrs. Wingate was almost overwhelmed with anxiety and despair. She saw there was no conversation—no smile—no kind looks at each other. What could she do? How could she make her guests happy? A bright thought suddenly sprung from her warm heart. "Wingate," as she always called her husband, "send for Terpsichore, let us have music and dancing." It was done. The instruments struck up; hands and feet were soon in lively and graceful motion; and though few and short were the words which were spoken, yet federalists and democrats long remembered that happy evening.

The picture I have drawn of those times is no exaggeration. Such a state of things had been coming on for some years; and it culminated at its gloomiest height, when the embargo, like a paralytic shock from the invisible world, dismantled every ship in the harbors of the United States, arrested the trade of the country, and overshadowed the land with fear and perplexity. It made tens of thousands poor: it made no one rich, except the satellite of power, or some feeder at the public crib. But this is neither the place nor the hour to discuss the wisdom or policy of a measure which seemed so suicidal. For the actors in that drama are all gone; and that great and wonderful man, who filled the world with terror, and under whose impulse the embargo was said to have originated, has long since passed away and finished his destiny. Napoleon Bonaparte — of whom the eloquent Fisher Ames said in 1806, "Fourteen centuries have gone back over our head, and Attila, the scourge of God, has come again," — now only lives in the history of the past.

The town of Bath — now a flourishing city — was not exempt from the common fate. She had her full share of dissension, and Mr. Ames seemed to have migrated from the school of law in Groton, to the school of politics in Bath, where master spirits stood ready, and were too successful in training him in their legerdemain and tactics, — to his sorrow at a future day.

The two great parties at this emporium of the Kennebec, were marshaled under distinguished leaders: Gen. King was at the head of the democrats; Samuel Davis, the greatest merchant then in this section of the country, was the leader of the federalists. These two dignitaries, with their families and friends, kept up a perpetual feud. On every occasion the hostility broke out — in church or state — at the polls or on the exchange.

It is said that in the blaze of this domestic war, it so happened that Mr. Davis, with some of his pious friends, seeing that a large and stately house of worship was needed in Bath, erected a church on the north side of the county road to Brunswick. It stood on the top of a craggy hill, looking down upon the city. At the sight of this conspicuous edifice, looming up on the bank of the beautiful river, Kennebec, like a light-house in the narrow path to Heaven, Gen.

King experienced the throbbings of great seriousness; his heart was touched to the quick; and he said within himself; "Shall mine adversary build a temple to the Lord, and thereby get into Paradise before I do?" Thought and action with the General were synonymous; he summed up the profits of his voyages, contributed largely, and with a troop of his religious friends, built a church on the same hill, on the other side of the road, within a pistol shot of the first one. It was similar in size and architecture: one faced the east, the other the West; one was called the North, the other the South church.

For a long time, the two Congregational societies, who separately assembled in these twin churches, were bitter opponents, though both Orthodox. At last, that eminent and much beloved divine and learned scholar, the Rev. William Jenks, D. D., now of Boston, was induced to take charge of the North church; and having also preached occasionally at the South, he was instrumental in reconciling the two societies. This was in 1812–1817. Since then, the South church has been burnt to the ground by an anti-Catholic mob, and the North church left in a dilapidated state;—a melancholy monument of other days, while several new and elegant houses of worship adorn this eastern city, so famous for fine ships.

When a young lawyer first begins practice, he needs some powerful friend to introduce him to the world; and fortunate is he if he meet with a patron who will whisper kind things in his behalf, in the ears of the people. Such was Gen. King to Benjamin Ames; and under a prestige so auspicious, he rose rapidly into notice. Let us turn aside a moment from the beaten path, to contemplate this patron who gave him the right hand of fellowship so cheerfully.

William King, the sultan of Bath, was a very remarkable man. He belonged to the first order of strong, energetic intellect. He was the seventh child of Richard King of Scarborough, who had been a great exporter of lumber, and died wealthy. William was born in that place February 9th, 1768, and his early advantages were poor and limited. While his half-brother, Rufus King, was laying the foundation of a great and splendid eminence in the academic groves of Cambridge, and his brother, Cyrus King, was preparing himself for distinction at the bar, William was tending a saw-mill in Saco, and there, perhaps, learnt the mystery of log-rolling, so essential to success in political life. The want of education was a misfortune and not a fault; and many a learned sophister who made sport of his blunders in grammar, rhetoric, or orthography, was infinitely beneath him in original thought and deep power of reasoning. He had studied the heart of mankind, and his knowledge of human nature seemed intuitive. His ambition was lofty, and his perseverance was untiring and inexhaustible. He felt that he must rely upon himself in making his way in the world, and he did. In business, as a merchant, he acquired a fortune, and built a spacious house near the water's edge, where, as one of the greatest ship-owners in the United States, he could often hear the mariner's joyous song from his window, in the morning, or look out at his vessels moored at the wharf. In politics, he was the head of the democracy in Maine; and although, touching the management of an electioneering campaign, there are many things to be considered, such as a newspaper, club-room, caucus, town, county, or State convention, out-runners for candidates, and distributors of circulars and speeches, yet there must be some master-spirit behind the curtain, like a fly-wheel to regulate all this machinery; and William King was pre-eminently the man for that. Had he only been blessed with a finished education, he would have been one of the first men in the United States; for he had the skill of Talleyrand, but much more virtue.

His influence in bringing about the separation of Maine from Massachusetts, and in the formation of her excellent constitution, was powerful; for he wielded the democracy of Maine, and managed the helm with great prudence. Such was his popularity, that, with an immense majority, he was elected the first governor; and, laying aside all party feelings, he administered that office with much ability, wisdom, and fairness. His selections were excellent. Before the term was out, he resigned the chair of state, for an appointment at Washington, as commissioner under the Spanish treaty. He was afterwards collector of Bath,—1831–1834.

In his person, he was tall and of a striking figure; and with a finely-formed head, strongly-marked features, high forehead, and black, impending brows, he had a natural and majestic air of command, which impressed every beholder with respect; and more especially when the general was arrayed in his military cloak of blue and red. He had his faults; but he had warm friends and many admirers. He was unfortunate in his old age, not only in the loss of property and in domestic trials and afflictions, but in the decay of his own mind, once so active and vigorous. His sun went down in great darkness.

I remember, a long time ago, when stopping one night in Portland, at Paine's hotel, that, having been called up at four o'clock on a cold winter's morning, to take the stage to Boston, I heard a window open in the next room, and a loud voice hailing a passenger in the yard who was in the eastern stage just arrived:—"Ah! Major Wood, is that you, what is the news from Boston? How go the votes?" It was Gen. King's voice. Such was this extraordinary man — an early riser, wide awake, and long before the dawn, watching the course of political events. In a brief sentence, his character may be summed up: if riding out on horseback for pleasure, he met a beggar asking alms, he would relieve him in a moment; but let him be in hot haste after some distant object, and the grand old general would ride over that very mendicant, nor cast a lingering look behind. He died June 17th, 1852, aged eighty-four.

Few young men have ever commenced the practice of the law under patronage so powerful, and influences so encouraging to an aspiring advocate, as Benjamin Ames. He made but one step from poverty to the emoluments of his profession. In a few years, he stood in the front rank of the lawyers of Maine. His docket was the largest, and he entered a longer list of suits than any one of the forty lawyers of Lincoln County, and his defenses were numerous. He seemed to glory in this ostentatious display. Perhaps his brother Nathan Ames, for a long time a deputy sheriff, was in some degree instrumental to such large practice. Be that as it may, he brought many suits where neither plaintiff nor defendant was worth the clerk's fees,— a species of suit pauper vs. pauper. This is not profitable litigation, and though he worked harder, yet he laid up less money than many at the bar whose talents were inferior to his.

With all these errors of judgment, however, Mr. Ames was looked up to as an astute lawyer and able advocate. He was an easy and ready speaker, and a close reasoner, for he had a logical brain. When necessary, he could spin a thread fine as ever spider wove, to catch the unwary. He studied a case for trial with unwearied industry, and prepared his testimony with such skill, that every strand of evidence was wound and warped into a cord, which, like the lasso, seldom failed to entangle his adversary. But, with all his ingenuity and the cunning forms of logic, though often successful, he was not a great advocate nor orator. He had no genius; no one could recollect a brilliant flash of wit that came from him; and as to imagination,— that power of summing up the past before the mind's eye,— his soul was a stranger to it; his fancy was as "dry as a remaining biscuit after a voyage." And yet, on many accounts, he had no superior at the Lincoln bar — save one, whose profound legal knowledge, original talents, and peculiar power over the jury, placed him far beyond and above him. Benjamin Ames, though a tall man as a debater in court or caucus, seemed small indeed, when he walked in the shadow of Benjamin Orr's magic eloquence.

With an overflowing practice and economical family, Judge Ames ought to have acquired a handsome competency, and been free from pecuniary embarrassments long before he had passed the meridian of life. But he had no idea of the day-book and ledger, in his business and expenditures. He seemed ignorant of the value of money. Early and late he was found at his office, and was a working-man in the hardest sense of the word. Perhaps his intense devotion to politics absorbed all thoughts of prudence, and made him forget that popularity is transient and fleeting as a dream, and when a gray-headed politician has once grown poor in public service, he is forgotten by his friends, and regarded by his foes as a pauper. The time came when he felt this truth; but repentance came too late.

For many years he was one of the leaders of his party. His zeal in their cause secured him, under Governor Sullivan in 1807, the office of county attorney for Lincoln; and again, in 1811, that of judge in the Circuit Court of Common Pleas, under Governor Gerry. This station he resigned in 1814, for the sake of a mercantile cruise in a brig to Bermuda; others say to the Provinces down east, disguised in a large wig, for it was war time. Being an able special pleader, he escaped the enemy who were hovering over our coast, and after some months' absence, returned home to his old office. And here he continued in practice for several years. In 1820, having been elected to the first legislature of Maine, he was chosen speaker of the House. He was re-elected the three following years, and acquitted himself with honor. In 1824, having been chosen a senator from Lincoln, he was made president of the senate, an office which he filled but one year, not being again returned to that body. In 1827, he was again chosen a representative from Bath, and it was his last appearance in public life. For some cause or other, among all the appointments to lucrative offices in the new State, not one fell to him. With his talents, legal attainments, and skill as a logician, he might, by more attention to his profession and less subservience to party, have attained to a seat on the bench of the Supreme Court, or any office in the gift of the people. But he was restless, uneasy, impulsive, and strangely deficient in stability of character. He was far from being a happy man: he had no taste for the literature of Greece or Italy or old England; and he was therefore laying up no delightful memories for the solitude of old age.

Judge Ames was twice married: his first wife was Mary Boynton, who died of a decline November, 1810, leaving no children: he afterwards married her sister Sally, by whom he had three children, two daughters, and a son, George, who was educated at West Point, then went to the far west, and after a short probation of study, was admitted to practice law; but by his conduct and dissipation he lost the confidence of his friends, and no one knows his whereabouts.

The ladies he successively married were sisters of Abel Boynton, Esq., who opened an office in Lisbon, Maine, 1809, and removed to Bath in 1811, where he became a partner with his brother-in-law. Mr. Boynton was the son of Col. Abel Boynton of Westford, Massachusetts, and was born May 4th, 1783.[1] He was highly esteemed by all who knew

[1] Genealogical Register of the Abbot Family, 1847.

him as a gentlemanly, honorable man. He married Sarah Leland, daughter of Joseph Leland of Saco. His prospects were flattering: with a charming wife, whose aunt was Mrs. Gen. King, with prosperous business, and many friends, who were attached to him, he seemed to have years of felicity marked out for him in the calendar of life. But it was otherwise ordered in the inscrutable movements of Providence. He was attacked by consumption — that destroyer of so many of the finest flowers in the garden of friendship. He failed rapidly, and, by the advice of his physician, embarked in the autumn of 1816 in a vessel bound for the West Indies, for the benefit of a milder climate. On the eve of his departure, the Rev. Dr. Jenks, who took a deep interest in the welfare of a young man so promising, presented him with Wilberforce's Practical View of Christianity. *The seed fell on good ground.* He returned home only to die; but he told Dr. Jenks that this book was the first which ever called up his attention to religion. He was admitted into the church and his pastor administered the sacrament to him on his dying bed: he died January, 23d, 1817, aged thirty-three. The Columbian Centinel of February 1st, 1817, makes this obituary notice of him: "To his friends his loss is irreparable, and society has seldom lost a brighter ornament." He left no issue.

Some writer has said that the old Roman adage, "Nil de mortuis nisi *bonum*," should have been, Nil de mortuis nisi *verum*. Be it so. And yet the truth about the dead, though told with much reserve and great caution, may sometimes wound the feelings of the innocent, and do no good. When, however, the course of life in one we lament, has led to difficulty and unhappiness, it may be made a warning to others. Every step in the daily journey to another world must convince any one that integrity, sincerity, prudence, and temperance are blessed with rich rewards. Judge Ames had many fine qualities; but in making political honors the grand object of his life, he entered upon the path of intrigue, where corruption and insincerity usually prevail. He quarreled with his old and best friend, Gen. King, about the collectorship, and they were at swords' points. They mutually accused each other of supplying the enemy in the war of 1812. Their recriminations were violent. They raked open the ashes of the old wig and the brig and the flour and potatoes, which had been carried down east, and for many years had been outlawed and forgotten. It is not fifty years since, and both parties have gone to that unseen world where the truth only is known.

He perceived with sorrow that his office business was passing into younger hands. He became involved in debt. Something must be done to keep the wolf from the door, and he cast his eye anxiously toward the *Far West.* Having obtained credit, and made provision for his family for one year, he went to Cincinnati, and there opened an office. This was 1827–9. What clients he found, or success he met with, is unknown to the writer. The fame of his eloquence, even if it ever charmed a county court, could not have reached the magnificent banks of the Ohio; and there was no King there to smile upon his professional labors. The first news we heard of him was from Rhode Island, where, having reached Providence, on a journey to Bath, he was somewhat delayed; and from over-anxiety to get along, he became excited, the blood rushed to his head, and he was struck down with a paralysis of the brain. From this visitation he never fully recovered. His mind in a great degree had wandered from him.

This took place in 1831–2. His brother-in-law, Captain Benjamin A. Boynton, U. S. A., at that time had command of the military station at Houlton, a village, then just incorporated as a shire town of Aroostook County, on a branch of the St. John River. Here, broken down in body and a mere wreck in mind, he with his family were taken care of by that generous and noble relative, while he lingered three years, until September 28th, 1835, when he ended his unhappy life at the age of fifty-seven. Judge Ames was a member of the church of Christ; and may we not hope, in charity, that after years of restless ambition, and much disappointment and suffering, he has found a home in that city which needs not the light of the sun nor of the moon to lighten it.

NATHAN WESTON. 1806—

Chief Justice Weston may be treated rather as a judge than as a practicing lawyer, for he had not been long enough at the bar to establish a business, or a high reputation, before he was raised to the bench. And his career as a judge, of thirty years' continuance, was commensurate with his legal life.

Judge Weston was descended from John Weston, who came from Buckinghamshire, England, to Salem in 1644, at the age of thirteen years: he subsequently moved to Reading, Massachusetts, where he died in 1723, over ninety years of age. His son, Stephen, died in Reading in 1753, at the age of eighty-eight. He had a son, Stephen, who died in Wilmington, a town adjoining Reading, in 1776, in his eighty-first year. These were all substantial men and honored citizens of the towns in which they lived. The last named Stephen was the father of Nathan, and the grandfather of the subject of our present notice; who thus appears to have been in the fifth degree from the first American ancestor.

Nathan Weston, father of the chief justice, was the fifth son of Stephen, and born in Wilmington in 1740. In 1781, he married Elizabeth, a daughter of Samuel Bancroft of Reading, and sister of the Rev. Aaron Bancroft, for more than fifty years the honored and beloved minister of Worcester, and father of George Bancroft, the historian. She was his third wife, and the mother of the chief justice. Mr. Weston served in the French War a short period; after which he came to Maine, engaged in the lumber business about Merrymeeting bay, and finally established himself in trade at Augusta toward the close of the Revolutionary War, 1781. He represented the town two years in the General court of Massachusetts, and was subsequently, in 1806 and 1807, a member of the Executive council: he died in 1832 at the age of ninety-two.

His son, Nathan, was born in Augusta July 27th, 1782. He pursued his studies at the Hallowell academy, an institution then recently opened and placed under the care of Samuel Moody, who became a distinguished instructor for many years in that academy. In due time he entered Dartmouth College, then administered by President Wheelock, and diligently and honorably pursued his studies, acquiring a high standing in a class of forty-four, which numbered among its members Drs. Hall, Mussey, and Shattuck, Calvin Selden and Henry Hubbard. He was chosen into the Phi-Beta-Kappa society of the Alpha of Dartmouth. On leaving college, he entered the office of Benjamin Whitwell in Augusta, in which he remained a few months, when he sought a wider field of excitement and observation, and entered the office of George Blake of Boston. Mr. Blake was District Attorney of the United States, to which office he was appointed in 1801, and which he held through all changes of administration until 1828. He was a learned lawyer, an able advocate, and a leading politician of the democratic school. He died in 1841. Mr. Weston had here an ample opportunity for instruction and improvement; among which, the privilege of hearing the eminent lawyers at the Boston Bar may be ranked. The most prominent of these were Parsons, Sullivan, Dexter, Gore, and Otis. On completing his studies, he was admitted to the Suffolk Bar in July, 1806, and soon after opened an office at Augusta. Mr. Blake invited him to remain in Boston, and have charge of his office, but he preferred to take his chance in the rising fortunes of his native State.

The following spring, Mr. Weston was induced to remove to New Gloucester, where an opening was made by the removal of Judge Whitman to Portland. Mr. Whitman's business there had been very large, he was the only lawyer, and the vacant place promised many advantages. He had a successful business, and was chosen a representative from the town in 1808, but the next year, 1809, having formed a matrimonial connection with Miss Cony, a daughter of Judge Daniel Cony of Augusta, he returned in 1810 to that town, which has since been the place of his residence.

In 1811, Elbridge Gerry, the democratic candidate for governor, having succeeded in his election over Gov. Gore, and being sustained by majorities in both branches of the legislature, his administration made radical changes in men and measures of the old commonwealth. As they could not reach the judges by removal, and as Mr. Jefferson said of office-holders generally, "Few die and none resign," the majority undertook to abolish the old Court of Common Pleas, which had stood unchanged from the time of the charter of 1691, and thus getting rid of an army of veteran officers, their places were supplied in the new "Circuit Courts," for the greater part, by the friends and supporters of the administration. And the clerks, who had always been appointed by the respective courts previous to that time, and were considered as official guardians of the records and papers of the courts, under the order and direction of the judges, were, by an act passed at the same session, made subject to executive appointment. The existing clerks were displaced, and in future were to receive their appointment from the Governor and Council. These great changes made quite a commotion through the State; the removal of so many officers of all departments rallied an opposition to the administration of Mr. Gerry, which it could not withstand, and it was overthrown the next year by the election of Gov. Strong and his political friends to power. Another of the obnoxious measures of Mr. Gerry's administration was making a new division of districts for the election of members of Congress. For the purpose of securing a democratic representative from the county of Essex, a singular and unnatural arrangement was made of the towns in that county. Major Russell, the editor of the Boston Centinel, to show the absurdity of this arrangement, made a map of the county, designating by a particular color the towns composing the new district. This he hung in his office, where Gilbert Stuart, the great painter, happening to see it one day, said to Russell, that it formed a picture resembling some animal. He took his pencil, and with a few touches put on what represented claws. "There," said he, "that will do for a salamander." Russell looked at the hideous figure, and exclaimed "Salamander! call it Gerrymander." It was so named, and became a by-word. An engraving was made of it, and it was used with considerable effect in the next political canvass.

Under the law altering the Court of Common Pleas, which was entitled "An act establishing Circuit Courts of Common Pleas within this Commonwealth," three circuits were formed in Maine: the first including the counties of York, Cumberland, and Oxford, and called the "First Eastern Circuit;" the second embraced Lincoln, Kennebec, and Somerset, and was called the "Second Eastern Circuit;"

the third circuit included the two eastern counties, Hancock and Washington. In the second circuit, Mr. Weston was appointed chief justice, Benjamin Ames of Bath and Judah McLellan of Bloomfield, associates. McLellan declined the office, and his place was supplied by Ebenezer Thatcher.

Judge Weston had been at the bar less than five years, and was but twenty-nine years old, when he received this appointment. He had not had a great amount of practice, nor had he distinguished himself at the bar; but he was a warm friend of the administration, and had friends at court. Notwithstanding the political character of the change, and the censure it received from the opposition, the new court was certainly an improvement on the old one. A court consisting of three judges and all lawyers, was substituted, in this second circuit alone, for three courts and ten judges, each county having its own court, of whom not one was a lawyer. The system of paying the judges by fees levied on the business, was continued during the existence of the court, and was not superseded until after the separation. This led to the undignified practice, at the close of every court, for the judges and clerks to make an adjustment of the fees, and apportion their compensation. They counted over the entries and the cases opened to the jury, the number of appeals, &c.; for each item there was a specific charge. The fee bill at that time allowed to the judges the following items, viz., for the entry of each action eighty cents, and where issue was joined, one dollar in addition; appeal twenty cents; surrender of bail twenty cents; proving deed twenty cents; petition and order for partition seventy-five cents; accepting partition forty cents; accepting report of referees when contested, sixty cents; when not contested, thirty cents: these were in addition to the fees allowed the clerk, as, for instance, fifty cents for the entry, taxing cost, and filing papers. Soon after the organization of the court in the second circuit, then consisting of Chief Justice Weston, Ames, and Ebenezer Thatcher, who had succeeded Judah McLellan, the court made an order that no action should be continued unless "issue be joined:" this sudden order took the bar by surprise, as it subjected them, as will be perceived by the above extract from the fee bill, to heavy additional taxation; that is, one dollar for every case, and gave the same additional compensation to the judges. The indignation of the members of the bar was equal to their surprise, and a successful effort was made to the Legislature to overrule the order: an act prohibiting such taxation was passed in June, 1813.

Judge Weston presided in this court with dignity and ease, faithfully and promptly discharging the duties of the office, to the acceptance of the bar and the people, until 1820, when, on the organization of the new State, Judge Weston was appointed one of the associate justices of the Supreme Court. He was commended to this honorable position, by the side of the able jurists Mellen and Preble, by his experience and the satisfaction he had given in the discharge of his official functions in the Common Pleas. This office he held till near the close of 1834, fourteen years, when Chief Justice Mellen, having arrived at the age of seventy years, then the constitutional limit of the office, Judge Weston was elevated to the chief justiceship in October of that year, as the successor of this eminent jurist. His associates at this time were Judges Parris and Emery. Chief Justice Weston continued to preside in this court for the term of seven years, at the end of which, a constitutional amendment having been adopted, limiting the judicial tenure to seven years, he retired, in October, 1841, from the bench. The administration of the State being then in the hands of the whigs, they took this occasion to place at the head of its highest judicial tribunal, Chief

Justice Whitman, who had presided in the Common Pleas a period of nearly twenty years. Chief Justice Weston was nominated as his own successor by Governor Kent, but was not confirmed by the council.

Chief Justice Weston presided in this court with dignity and impartiality: he was not a profound lawyer, but he had industry and long experience, and discharged the duties of the responsible office to general satisfaction. He was patient in the trials of causes, and his opinions were clear and to the point. These opinions, as an associate and chief, are recorded in the first twenty volumes of the Maine reports, embracing Greenleaf, Fairfield, and a part of Shepley's series. They are lucid expositions of the law applicable to the cases heard and determined.

At *nisi prius*, Judge Weston presided with calmness and ability: his long experience enabled him to rule promptly upon such points of law as were raised at trials. He was patient and unruffled in the hearing of causes, and his charges to the jury were clear, full, and methodical. To the members of the bar, he was frank and courteous.

Chief Justice Weston was so early placed upon the bench, that he was removed from the field of political action, and is rarely found in its offices. He was always and firmly, a member of the democratic party; and the only political offices we know of his having filled were those of representative of New Gloucester in 1808, and a delegate to the Brunswick Convention in 1816: in the latter body, he was one of the committee on the Constitution, and supported the measures of the majority of the convention.

Judge Weston was appointed one of the trustees of Bowdoin College in 1820, under the law of Maine, which gave the governor and council power to appoint twelve of the trustees of that institution; which office he continues to hold. In 1843, the college conferred upon him the honor-

Wm. D. Williamson.

ary title of LL. D., in which they had been anticipated by both Dartmouth and Waterville. He also held the office of trustee of Waterville College thirty-two years. He married a daughter of Judge Daniel Cony of Augusta, a woman of fine manners and admirable qualities: by her he had a large family of children: he is left a widower, and now spends the evening of his long day in the management of his private affairs, and the genial courtesies and amenities of life. He has been a great reader of works in all departments of knowledge, and having a tenacious memory, he has accumulated large stores of valuable information. By an easy conversational talent, he makes himself a very agreeable companion both to old and young, to whom he freely imparts, from his ample resources, useful and pleasant information, with interesting reminiscences running through a large part of a century. Those who have enjoyed the privilege of his society, remember it with gratification.

Judge Weston has had seven children, four sons and three daughters: his sons, Nathan, Daniel Cony, and George Melville, were graduates of Bowdoin College, and were educated for the bar; but Daniel C. is now in the ministry at Stonington, Connecticut; Charles, the youngest, has served both in the navy and army.

WILLIAM DURKEE WILLIAMSON. 1807—1846.

One of the prominent men in the fraternity we have been describing, was William D. Williamson, the lawyer, the politician, and the historian, who established himself at Bangor, then in the county of Hancock, in 1807. Mr. Williamson was born in Canterbury, Connecticut, July 31, 1779. He was educated at Brown University, from which he took his degree in 1804, at the age of twenty-five, and at once commenced the study of the profession which he had adopted, in the office of Samuel F. Dickinson, at Amherst, Massachusetts. On being admitted to the bar, he immediately entered on the practice, at Bangor. Mr. Williamson commenced the active pursuits of life under unusual advantages: he was older, and had had more experience than young men generally when entering on their profession: he had great activity of mind, an ardent, sanguine temperament, and a persevering industry: qualities like these rarely fail of success, and we find in this case no exception to the rule: his prosperity was uninterrupted. At the time he went to Bangor, there were three lawyers in the town, — Allen Gilman; Samuel E. Dutton, who soon after moved to Boston; and Jacob McGaw; and sixteen in the county, embracing Hancock, Penobscot, and territory now included in several other counties. Mr. Williamson did not lack confidence or perseverance: his competitors for the prizes of the law were very able, — many of them eloquent men: he pushed his way among them, acquired a large business, which he managed with skill: he attended the courts regularly at Castine, and in the neighboring counties, and established a good reputation at the bar, and in the community. His advance was greatly aided by his appointment, in 1811, as county attorney for Hancock, an office which the administration of Governor Gerry, by an act passed that year, restored to the patronage of the executive. It had passed through several mutations within a few years. It was originally bestowed by the courts; but in the political struggles for power, in the early part of this century, it was made the foot-ball of parties: in 1807, under Governor Sullivan, the Democratic party gave the appointment to the executive: under Governor Gore, in 1809, it was restored to the courts: in 1811, under Governor Gerry, it was again given to the executive, as were also the clerkships of the courts. Mr. Williamson was the most active democratic lawyer in the county, while a majority, including the most prominent and influential members of the profession, were of the federal party. This office he held, and faithfully discharged its duties, until it became vacant by the establishment of the county of Penobscot, in 1816, when Jacob McGaw was appointed for Penobscot, and George Herbert of Ellsworth for Hancock. The same year, however, he was elected to the Senate of Massachusetts, and held the office by successive elections until the separation of Maine from Massachusetts. When this event took place, he was chosen the first and sole senator from Penobscot to the Legislature of Maine, and elected president of that body, as successor to Gen. John Chandler, who was chosen the first senator of the new State in Congress. By another change, during his term of office, he became the acting governor of the State, in place of Governor King, who was appointed commissioner under the Spanish treaty, and resigned the office of governor. But in this busy time of political mutation, he did not even hold the office of governor through the whole term, for having been elected to Congress from his district, he resigned the former office to take his seat in the House, in December, 1821. This position he held but one term, when, by a new division of the State into districts, the election fell to another portion of the territory: David Kidder, a lawyer in Somerset County, was his successor.

But Mr. Williamson did not long remain without the honors and emoluments of office: in 1824, he was appointed judge of Probate for the county of Penobscot, which office he held until 1840; when the amendment of the constitution having taken effect, which limited the tenure of all judicial offices to seven years, he retired from a station which he had filled with promptness, fidelity, and ability for sixteen years. If any one could be gratified by success in politics, surely Mr. Williamson should be that man: he entered into office almost at the commencement of his professional career, and continued in possession of one or another, during the whole meridian of his life. It may have satisfied the ambition of the time, but we doubt whether it produced the happiness, — we know that it did not the fame, — which attended the steady and quiet pursuit of all his leisure hours.

His History of Maine was the great labor of his life: to this the best powers of his mind were given; and on this he labored with an earnestness and ardor which gave joy to his heart and light to his understanding. Wherever he went, upon whatever subject he was engaged, his eye and his pen were intent upon his great work. He was indefatigable in his labors, and explored all sources of knowledge which would be likely to inform or illuminate his page. He collected a vast mass of materials, and rescued from oblivion treasures, which, had it not been for his exertions and industry, would have passed out of human observation and memory. The work was published in two large octavo volumes, the first edition in 1832; and a second issue, with corrections, was made in 1839, with a portrait of the author. The title is, "The History of the State of Maine, from its First Discovery in 1602, to the Separation, A. D. 1820, inclusive:" pp. 660, 714. The work is not skillfully or conveniently arranged, and the style is defective: it is an ample collection of valuable facts, but does not rise into the rank of an elegant or a philosophical history. We could not now spare it; and the student of the history of Maine could not do without it. This State and all the States are greatly his debtor for this fruit of his unwearied and abundant labor. How low do the rewards of his political life sink, when compared to this enduring monument to his memory and fame! His political acts have perished in the using: the history will be his perpetual record.

Mr. Williamson was an original member of the Maine Historical Society; and many of his valuable manuscripts, prepared while collecting materials for his history, are now preserved in the archives of the society, — the gift of his nephew, Joseph Williamson of Belfast. His mind had a tendency to detail, and he gathered up and arranged statistics with great facility and fondness, the results of which appeared in various forms.

Mr. Williamson finished his useful and varied life on the 27th of May, 1846, at the age of sixty-six. The Penobscot Bar passed appropriate resolutions on the occasion, and attended his funeral.

CHAPTER XIX.

SIMON GREENLEAF — CALVIN SELDEN — SAMUEL FESSENDEN — WILLIAM ALLEN HAYES — EDMUND FLAGG — ALBION KEITH PARRIS — HIRAM BELCHER.

SIMON GREENLEAF. 1806—1834.

Among the distinguished lawyers and advocates who have adorned the Cumberland Bar during its century of existence, from the organization of the county in 1760, we may rank Professor Greenleaf, who for twenty-seven years was one of its able champions. He descended from Edmund Greenleaf, who was born in the parish of Brixham, Devonshire, England, about the year 1600, and came to Newbury, Massachusetts, in 1635, with his family. One of his descendants, the Rev. Jonathan Greenleaf of Brooklyn, New York, in his well prepared genealogical account of the family, to which I am largely indebted for many facts, remarks: "It is believed that the ancestors of the Greenleaf family were Huguenots, who left France on account of their religious principles, sometime in the course of the sixteenth century, and settled in England. The name was probably translated from the French name '*Feuillevert*,' which means in English a green leaf." His wife was Sarah Dole. The table of descent in a direct line to Simon is as follows:

1. Edmund,	. . .		died in Boston, 1671.
2. Stephen,	born in England,	1630,	drowned 1690.
3. John,	"	June 21, 1682,	died June 21, 1734.
4. Daniel,	"	Dec. 24, 1690,	drown'd Jan., 1729.
5. Jonathan,	"	July, 1723,	died May, 1807.
6. Moses,	"	May 19, 1755,	" Dec. 18, 1812.
7. Simon,	"	Dec. 5, 1783,	" Oct. 6, 1853.

The grandfather of Simon, the Hon. Jonathan Greenleaf, was the sixth child and second son of Daniel, who was drowned when his son Jonathan was a little over five years of age, leaving his family quite destitute. At the age of seven, Jonathan was apprenticed to a ship carpenter, which was the principal occupation of his life, and by which he accumulated a large estate. And as he was a very upright, honest man, it is very probable that the high character of the ships built at Newburyport, and on the Merrimac River, may be owing to the integrity of the men who were engaged in this employment. Jonathan Greenleaf rose into political life and influence: he was a member of the Provincial Congress, and after that, of the House of Representatives, the Senate, and Council of Massachusetts. He was of dignified manners and popular address, and from the gentle, silvery tones of his voice, he was distinguished from others of the name by the title "silver-tongued Greenleaf." His second son, Moses, father of Simon, was also bred a ship-carpenter, but on the breaking out of the Revolution, he entered the army as a lieutenant: the next year he was promoted to a captaincy, and served nearly through the war. In 1781, he formed a connection in ship-building with his father; and from that time to 1790, the firm built twenty-two ships and brigs. In the latter year, he moved on to a farm in New Gloucester, where he died December 18, 1812. He was a well-proportioned man, with a military air, walking erect with a firm step. His wife, whom he married in 1776, was Lydia, a daughter of the Rev. Jonathan Parsons of Newburyport, a woman of remarkably benevolent and self-denying spirit. They had five children, viz., Moses; Clarina, married to Eleazar A. Jenks, a printer in Portland; Ebenezer; Simon; and Jonathan, who was born in 1785, and is the only survivor. He studied divinity with the Rev. Francis Brown of North Yarmouth, and was ordained at Wells, Maine, in 1815; and in 1843 was installed pastor of the Wallabout Presbyterian Church in Brooklyn, New York. While residing in Wells, he published in 1821, "Sketches of the Ecclesiastical History of Maine from the Earliest Settlement to the Present Time," a work admirably executed and of standard authority. Their eldest brother, Moses, was also gifted with high intellectual qualities: in 1816, he published "A Statistical View of Maine." This, in 1829, he enlarged into an octavo volume of four hundred and sixty-eight pages, entitled, "A Survey of the State of Maine, in reference to its Geographical Features, Statistics, and Political Economy: Illustrated by Maps." Accompanying this was a large map of the State, and an atlas exhibiting various features of the State, titles to land, &c. These works were of high authority and very valuable.

Simon Greenleaf, the subject of our notice, was born in Newburyport, December 5, 1783. He did not accompany his father's family to New Gloucester in 1790, but was retained by his grandfather for the advantage of the better schools in his native town. He was educated at the "Latin School" in Newburyport, then under charge of Michael Walsh, who was well known in his day, and for many years in the early part of the present century, as the author of the "Mercantile Arithmetic," which was not only a popular text book, but a counting-house companion. Mr. Greenleaf rapidly improved his advantages, acquired a very thorough knowledge of the Latin and English languages, and great facility in the use of them. On leaving the academy, he went to New Gloucester, and entered the office of Ezekiel Whitman as a student, and boarded in his family. I am happy to be able to give the testimony of so discriminating an observer as Judge Whitman to the early character of Mr. Greenleaf: he said, "When he came to me in New Gloucester, he was an excellent English and Latin scholar, and became a very faithful and devoted student." He added, "When business called me from home, I intrusted my office business to him, placing entire confidence in him, and was never disappointed or deceived." In his family he was kind, patient, and considerate, and won the affection of all the members of it. He was admitted to the bar of Cumberland in 1806, and commenced practice in Standish, but the next year he moved to Gray. Being the first and the only lawyer in the place, he soon acquired a very considerable practice, which he retained and enlarged by his fidelity and skill. As his family increased, he desired to extend the range of his business and increase its emoluments, and in 1818 he removed to Portland. At that time, the two leading members of the bar had been drawn aside from their profession into public life: Judge Mellen was in the United States Senate, and Judge Whitman in the House of Representatives; and Mr. Orr, who had a large practice in Cumberland, was also in Congress. This encouraged the accession of other prominent men to Portland: of these were Mr. Greenleaf and the late Judge Preble, who came the same year. Mr. Greenleaf was not disappointed: his business and his fame increased, and the larger and more cultivated society, and its superior advantages in other respects, stimulated his susceptible powers to higher efforts. He now took rank among the foremost men at the bar, and by his winning manners, and his persuasive style of speaking and address, accompanied by the skill and ingenuity of his arguments, established his reputation and his practice on a firm basis.

In the act of the new State, establishing the Supreme Judicial Court, passed June 24, 1820, the governor and council were required "to appoint some suitable person learned in the law, to be a reporter of the decisions of the Supreme Judicial Court," whose duty it was made to obtain true and authentic reports of cases decided by the court, and publish them, whenever they would compose a suitable volume. His compensation was fixed at six hundred dollars a year salary, and the profits arising from the publication. Mr. Greenleaf was immediately appointed reporter under this act, and entered on his duties at York, August term, 1820. He continued faithfully, promptly, and very ably to discharge the duties of this arduous and responsible office for twelve years, closing with the July term at Waldo in 1832. The cases determined during this period are contained in nine volumes, the last embracing a table of cases, and a digest of the whole. The judges were,—Mellen, chief justice, and Weston, judge, through the whole period; Judge Preble to 1828; and Judge Parris the remainder of the time. The reports are distinguished for the clear and concise manner in which the points of law are stated, and the arguments of counsel given: they took high rank in this class of legal productions, and were received as standards of authority throughout the Union. They were deservedly considered among the most valuable of American reports, and so highly were they esteemed that a new edition was demanded by the profession, — a very rare thing in this class of works, — which was published with annotations by Mr. Abbot of Cambridge, a short time previous to Mr. Greenleaf's death.

In 1821, while engaged in his office of reporter and his extended practice, increased by his attending the circuits through the several counties, he employed himself in the preparation and publication of "A Collection of Cases, Overruled, Doubted, or Limited in their application, Taken from American and English Reports." Professor Parsons of the Cambridge Law School, in a notice of Professor Greenleaf's death, gives the following interesting account of the origin of this useful little work. He says, "His first law book sprang, as we have his own authority for saying, from this circumstance. Very early in his professional career, he had given an opinion, and argued a case which grew out of his opinion, upon the authority of an English decision, which seemed to be applicable and decisive. But the court informed him that this case had been overruled, and had no authority whatever. He determined at once to ascertain, as far as he could, which of the apparently authoritative cases in the reports had lost their force, and to give the information to the profession. The idea was original, the execution good, and the book very useful." But Prof. Parsons observes, if he could have had access to a more complete library of Reports, he might have made it more full and useful.

By his unceasing application, his genius, and his increasing experience, Mr. Greenleaf advanced himself into the foremost rank of the profession: the eminent lawyers who had been moving onward with him, were gradually withdrawing from the bar,—Judges Mellen, Whitman, and Preble to the bench, Mr. Longfellow by ill health, and Mr. Orr in 1828 by death; thus making a larger opening for the learning and talents of the younger members who were pressing forward for distinction: among these were Mr.

Greenleaf, Gen. Fessenden, Mr. Davies, and others still younger. So conspicuous had Mr. Greenleaf become about the time that he closed his duties as reporter, that the attention of Judge Story, then at the head of the law school at Cambridge, was turned to him, as the most suitable person to supply the vacancy in that department of the university, rendered vacant by the death of the lamented Prof. Ashmun. We are indebted to Prof. Parsons's address before quoted, to a little private history on this subject, which it may not be uninteresting to our readers to review. Mr. Parsons says, "He succeeded Prof. Ashmun in 1833, as Royall Professor. It was, as I have always understood, at Judge Story's suggestion that Mr. Greenleaf was solicited to leave Portland, and take upon himself these new duties. I have been told, but not by Mr Greenleaf, that Judge Story, holding his court in Portland, had there an interesting case in admiralty. At that time, this branch of the law was known only in our largest commercial cities, and not to many of the profession there. And Judge Story was surprised when he found that Mr Greenleaf brought to this case, a thorough acquaintance with this very peculiar system of law, which he himself deemed of great importance, and which, foreseeing its constantly increasing value, he wished to make prominent in the instruction of the school. And he immediately determined to bring Mr. Greenleaf to Cambridge, if he could."

The case above referred to as attracting the notice of Judge Story, was similar, perhaps, to one of which the following anecdote is related. Mr. Greenleaf's father was not only a ship-carpenter, but an accurate draughtsman, and he took much pains in teaching his boys the art of constructing a vessel. Simon, in this, was his most apt scholar: the benefit of which was shown in his legal practice. On one occasion, he was engaged in an insurance cause: the vessel insured had been injured by pounding upon the bottom or side while lying at a wharf. The defense was, that the injury was occasioned by carelessness in the insured in not securing her to the wharf, alleging the damage to have been in her side and not her bottom. One of the witnesses for the plaintiff was a master-builder, who had repaired the ship, and who, having testified that the injury was on the bottom, was thus cross-examined by Mr. Greenleaf. "You are a ship-carpenter, and master of your trade?" "Yes." "In building a vessel, after laying your keel, you place a row of crooked timbers cross-wise, securing them to the keel with iron bolts?" "Yes." "These you call *floor timbers?*" "Yes." "Between these floor timbers the end of another crooked timber is inserted, as you would insert the fingers of one hand between those of another, and these you call *foot hook* (futtuck) timber?" "Yes." "And so you proceed, filling in rows of crooked timbers, until you reach the top, calling the third the *rising timber*, then the *naval timber*, and then the *top timber?*" "Yes." "Now," said Mr. Greenleaf, "state to the jury, on your oath, what kind of a timber you furnished for the repairing of that vessel. Was it a floor timber, a foot hook, a rising or a naval timber?" "It was a naval timber," said the witness. The case was clear, the jury saw it at a glance. The injury was on the *side* of the vessel, and not on the *bottom:* it was from carelessness and not accident, and the defense was sustained. For this anecdote I am indebted to his brother Jonathan, and it well illustrates his ingenuity and the advantage of his early attention to the details of the mechanic arts, in which he was quite proficient.

He entered upon the important duties of his professorship, a new and untried course of life, in 1833, when there were but about fifty students in the school, and closed his labors in it by resignation in 1848, when the number was about one hundred and fifty.[1] The duties of his professorship, and those which he voluntarily assumed and performed, were too much for his health, and he retired from his office with a shattered constitution. For thirteen years, from 1833 to 1846, he and Judge Story labored together to build up this valuable school. To use the language of Prof. Parsons, "They worked harmoniously and successfully, and perhaps the more harmoniously, because they were so entirely different. With much in common, for both were able, learned, and of the most devoted industry, there were other traits that belonged to one or the other of them exclusively. Greenleaf was singularly calm, finding strength in his very stillness, always cautious, and therefore always exact; Story was as vivid and impulsive as man could be. His words flowed like a flood; but it was because his emotions and his thoughts demanded a flood as their exponent, and Story's manner was most peculiar: everybody listened when he spoke, for he carried one away with the irresistible attraction of his own swift motion. And Greenleaf,— somewhat slow and measured in his enunciation,—by the charm of his silver voice, the singular felicity of his expressions, and the smooth flow of his untroubled stream of thought, caught and held the attention of every listener as few men can." In connection with this office, Mr. Parsons again says, "If Mr. Greenleaf could himself have directed the course of one who was to construct a memorial of him, assuredly he would have given special prominence to that which was not only the scene of his long-continued usefulness, but the object with which he

---

1 "The exact number of students who have been in the Law School during Mr. Greenleaf's connection with it is one thousand three hundred and five. During the same period, upwards of ten thousand volumes have been added to the library, at the cost of over twenty-six thousand dollars."—Law Rep. 11,190.

was most earnestly, most devoutly, and most successfully identified." In 1846, after the death of Judge Story, he was appointed as his successor in the Dane Professorship, in which he continued until his resignation in 1848.

The current of testimony was strong and uniform to the very able and satisfactory manner in which he discharged the duties of his professorship. The numerous pupils, who, during his labors, partook of the benefit of his instruction and his counsel, scattered all over our country, cherish a sweet recollection of the eloquent and persuasive lessons which it was their privilege to receive from him. The Faculty of the college were most unwilling to lose his services, but yielded to a paramount necessity. And they bestowed upon him the honorary title of *Emeritus* Professor, which he bore as long as he lived. They also bestowed upon him the degree of LL. D. in 1834, in which they were followed by Amherst in 1845, and Alabama in 1852.

The whole life of Prof. Greenleaf was filled with useful and honorable labor,—" *Actis ævum implet, non segnibus annis.*" — But the fifteen, nay, the twenty years in which he resided in Cambridge were the most busy portion of his life. In addition to his lectures and the duties incident to his professorship, he was incessantly at work upon his books. During this period, he published a second edition of his Reports with notes; in 1842, his first volume "On the Law of Evidence;" in 1846, the second volume; and in 1853, the third volume. In 1849, appeared the first volume of his edition of "Cruise's Digest of the Law of Real Property;" and in 1850, the second and third volumes — all these volumes were in royal octavo. In 1841, he prepared, at the request of the Cumberland Bar, a memoir of Chief Justice Mellen, which was published as an Appendix to the seventeenth volume of the Maine Reports. In 1845, he delivered a eulogy on Judge Story, which was published. This was a beautiful tribute to the memory of a great man, an honorable literary effort. In a notice of it in the Law Reporter for December, 1845, is this remark: "It is entirely free from the defects of extravagant and indiscriminate praise, to which eulogies are peculiarly exposed. It is calm and conscientious. It is also a production of much literary merit. It has that simplicity and transparency of style which we always notice in Prof. Greenleaf's publications." His discourse on his inauguration in 1833, was published in that year. Several communications from him appeared in the Law Reporter, viz., in 1839, I., 345, "Remarks on the Exclusion of Atheists as Witnesses;" in the April number, 1847, "The Rule of Damages in Actions ex Delicto." In 1845, he published "Testamentary Counsels and Hints to Christians on the Right Distribution of their Property by Will: By a Retired Solicitor." In 1846, he published "An Examination of the Testimony of the Four Evangelists by the Rules of Evidence administered in Courts of Justice; with an account of the Trial of Jesus." This was republished in London in 1846. Besides these, he printed "A Catalogue of a Select Law Library;" "A Course of Legal Studies;" "A Letter to a Lawyer: By a member of the Profession," which was published as a tract by the American Tract Society.

The continued pressure upon mind and body in the preparation and publication of these valuable works could not but make serious inroads upon a system of the strongest model, much more upon one not gifted with the highest physical properties. No wonder that the silver cord was loosened by the great tension upon it, or that the golden bowl which fed the lamp of life was broken. He gave no margin of his life to recreation, except from one field of mental activity to another: the consequence was that he fell exhausted by life's toil: he was cut down suddenly, with his harness all on, in the midst of his labors. He died on the 6th of October, 1853, at the age of seventy, " in the full maturity of his powers, and the meridian of his fame."

Mr. Greenleaf had neither leisure nor taste to engage in politics. His political opinions were always firm and decided as a federalist of the old school, and he never hesitated to express them. But he was no partisan, and the farthest remove from a demagogue. In 1816, he was proposed as a candidate for the Senate of Massachusetts from Cumberland County, with Lathrop Lewis, but the opposition candidates were elected by a small majority. In 1820 and 1821, he, with Asa Clapp and Nicholas Emery, represented Portland in the Legislature of Maine. As these were sessions when the new government was put in operation, the duty was responsible, and to a lawyer who was expected to pass upon the code of laws to be adopted on careful revision, arduous. Mr. Greenleaf was faithful to his trust, and beneficial to the country. With this experience, he retired at once and forever from political office.

Mr. Greenleaf, in August, 1806, married Hannah Kingman, a daughter of Capt. Ezra Kingman of East Bridgewater, Massachusetts, by whom he had fifteen children,— eleven of whom died in infancy. The survivors are two sons and two daughters: the daughters married Episcopal clergymen,— Charlotte Kingman, the Rev. Samuel Fuller; and Caroline Augusta, the Rev. Andrew Croswell: of the sons, Patrick Henry graduated at Bowdoin College in 1825, was educated for the bar, and practiced sometime in Portland,— he afterwards became, and is now, an Episcopal minister: James graduated at Dartmouth College in 1834, was a merchant in New Orleans at the breaking out of the great Rebellion, and now resides in Cambridge, Massachusetts: he married a daughter of his father's cherished friend, Stephen Longfellow.

As a writer and author, Professor Greenleaf stands deservedly high, and may be ranked, among American authors, in the class with the learned jurists, Kent and Story. The estimation in which his works are held, and their merits, may be inferred from the following remarks of Professor Parsons: "His reports are among the most valuable of American Reports: his edition of Cruise has entirely superseded, for American use, the English edition. It is, however, in his work on the Law of Evidence, that we find the best proof of his industry, his learning, and his sagacity. He certainly intended it, at first, mainly as a manual for students. But the profession took it up; and, as repeated editions were demanded, it grew upon his hands; and has grown equally in public favor, until it has overcome all competition, and become *the* book which every student and every practicing lawyer must have. How completely it has monopolized the public favor, may be inferred from the fact, that of the several volumes, there have been printed in this country, — if we include the second edition of the third volume now going through the press, — but very little less than thirty thousand copies."

It may be interesting to those who never saw Mr. Greenleaf, to have a portrait of him, drawn by a familiar hand.[1] His brother Jonathan, in his "Genealogy," says: "Mr. Greenleaf was a grave, sedate-looking man, and very quiet in his movements. He was about five feet ten inches in height, rather stout built, full face, with a small, sharp eye, nearly black. His original hair was very dark brown." I may add from my own personal observation, that his complexion was sallow, his posture a little stooping, with his head projecting forward: his countenance was expressive of

---

1 Since writing this memoir, we have been able to obtain an excellent portrait of Prof. Greenleaf to adorn our volume, to which we take pleasure to refer our readers.

Simon Greenleaf

benignity and intelligence. His brother thus continues his personal description: "Religion was not with him a dry system of doctrines, but a living and active principle of love to God and love to man. For the last thirty years of his life, he was one of the most spiritually-minded men, evidently intent on walking humbly with God, and doing good to the bodies and souls of his fellow-men. Thus he moved quietly on as years increased upon him, with the evidence of his piety becoming brighter and brighter, especially to those who saw him in private life."

Some other traits of character we notice in a brief biographical sketch published in the Cambridge Chronicle immediately after his death. "As an instructor, he was greatly beloved, and his lectures were clear, distinct, and practical. As a counsellor, he was clear, safe, and practical. His advice was always characterised by a weight of common sense as well as legal skill. As a man, he possessed a weight of character which insured for him the esteem of all who enjoyed his society, or came within the circle of his influence. Affable, polite, courteous, frank, and liberal-minded, he secured the confidence of his fellow citizens and neighbors. Combined with varied and legal attainments, he possessed great simplicity of character, which seemed to set off as in bold relief, those characteristics for which he was so truly distinguished."

The bar of Suffolk and Cumberland, on receiving tidings of the death of Prof. Greenleaf, immediately held meetings, and adopted appropriate and feeling resolutions. At the assemblage of the Suffolk Bar, the venerable Justice Wilde presided, and made some suitable remarks on the professional life, eminence, and character of Mr. Greenleaf. Charles G. Loring submitted the resolutions with a few introductory observations. One of the resolutions was as follows: "That as Americans, we owe him a debt of gratitude, for by his science and erudition, he has illustrated the judicial literature of his country at home and abroad, and added another American name with those of Story, Kent, and Wheaton, to the great legal authors of Christendom. That by his laborious, genial, and successful services as teacher of the law, in the school at Cambridge, he has deserved the gratitude of his country." Judge Hoar, in response to the resolutions presented in court, said, "Among those eminent lawyers, who have never held judicial station, the name and opinions of Mr. Greenleaf stand highest as authority, in all matters of law. I consider his death a great public loss."

Judge Emery presided at a meeting of the Cumberland Bar, held October 11th, and Charles S. Daveis presented the resolutions, which paid a high tribute to the intellectual and moral worth of Mr. Greenleaf, and an affectionate recollection of the kind and social relations that had existed between them. One of the resolutions thus speaks: "Resolved, That under a sense of the solemn impression produced by his lamented loss, and the length of time to which his works may last, we could not better express our affectionate regard for his worth, and render more justice to his memory than by the inscription suitable to be placed on his monument, that it was the aim of his instructions and writings, in accordance with the purpose of his life, to improve the tone, and raise the standard of professional morality, no less than the scale of legal excellence; and that he sought to sustain the solemn sanctions of the divine law, by exhibiting confirmed grounds of evidence in attestation of Christian truth."

Mr. Daveis spoke feelingly to the resolutions, and in high commendation of Mr. Greenleaf, as did also Judges Emery and Parris, Gen. Fessenden, and others.

CALVIN SELDEN. 1808—1859.

Calvin Selden of Norridgewock died November 29th, 1859, at the age of eighty. Mr. Selden was a descendant, in the sixth degree, from Thomas Selden, one of the company of the Rev. Thomas Hooker, who came over to Cambridge, Massachusetts, in October, 1633; from which place he migrated to Hartford, Connecticut, in 1636, and was made freeman in 1640. The parents of Mr. Selden were Joseph and Susannah (Smith) Selden of Haddam, Connecticut, where he was born February 28th, 1779.

Mr. Selden spent the early part of his life on his father's farm; but having a desire for an education, he changed the course of his pursuits. His father wishing him to become a minister, he prepared for college, and entered Dartmouth, from which he took his degree in 1803, at the age of twenty-four. A certificate from President Wheelock, at this time, is so honorable to this graduate, that I will not withhold an extract from it. "He is a young gentleman of talents and unblemished moral and religious character, of respectable acquirements in the different branches of collegiate literature, and of accomplishments in music."

He immediately after took charge of the Gilmanton Academy in New Hampshire, which he kept for two years, at the same time pursuing his studies in divinity. He was duly licensed as a preacher, and officiated in several parishes, but his performances not coming up to his own ideal of excellence, he suddenly abandoned that profession, and devoted himself to law. On being admitted to the bar, he came to Norridgewock in the autumn of 1808, at a most favorable juncture. Efforts were then making for the establishment of a new county from the territory constituting the northern part of Kennebec, which resulted in the incorporation of Somerset County, March 1st, 1809, with

Norridgewock for its shire-town. At that place, a large trade was carried on by Messrs. Ware and Sawtelle, who with ample means were extending their business in every direction. Mr. Selden entered at once upon a successful course of practice, to which he brought a high character for integrity, considerable experience, and good business qualities. He soon acquired the confidence of the whole community, and took a prominent position at the bar and among the people. In 1810, '11, and '12, he was chosen to represent the town in the Legislature, and again in 1829; and acquired reputation in this department, so that in 1812 his name was proposed for one of the justices of the Court of Common Pleas, to fill the vacancy occasioned by the declension of Judah McLellan. He failed to obtain the appointment, not for want of the necessary qualifications, but the greater influence which was brought to bear in favor of another candidate, Ebenezer Thatcher. He was, however, soon after appointed chief justice of the court of sessions, and one of the commissioners for building a court-house for the new county. He was also much employed in the financial and prudential affairs of the town, as agent, clerk, and selectman. In all these public employments, Mr. Selden sustained the character of an able, honest, and faithful servant, looking always carefully and judiciously after the public interests, and giving entire satisfaction in the numerous and various concerns intrusted to his management.

Mr. Selden was a many-sided man, and seems to have had wonderful facilities of adaptation to the different positions which he was called to fill, or to which he gave his energies. After successfully practicing law a few years, he formed a partnership with Mr. Fairfield, to whom the law business was gradually intrusted, while he engaged in trade as a partner in the prosperous house of Messrs. Ware &

Fletcher, which was doing the most extensive business of any firm in that part of the country. Here he rapidly accumulated property, sufficient, it would seem, to satisfy his humble ambition; for in about eight years he quitted mercantile and for most part his legal employments, and devoted himself heartily and practically to the cultivation of the soil. In this primitive and most independent pursuit, he was no less successful than in the various other employments to which he had given his attention. He changed so readily from one staple pursuit to another that it would seem to indicate instability or fickleness of character; but the success which attended each change justified his course, and helped him on in the career of usefulness and prosperity, and thus confirmed the soundness of his judgment. On the formation of the Agricultural Society of Somerset, in 1821, he was chosen its first president, and was the most efficient member in introducing improvements in the various departments of agricultural labor.

In 1812, Mr. Selden formed a matrimonial connection with Harriet, a daughter of Mr. Sawtelle, the former partner of Mr. Ware, by whom he had five children, two daughters and three sons. One daughter, Sarah S., married James McCobb, Esq., of Portland; the other, Mary W. S., the Rev. Mr. Burgess of Portland, and is dead. Edward C., the oldest son, died in California in 1862. Henry I. is commission merchant in New York, and James R., in San Francisco.

This aged and respected man — the preceptor, minister, lawyer, merchant, magistrate, and farmer — *facile princeps*, died at the age of eighty years and nine months.

The bar of Somerset, still holding on to him as a member of their fraternity, and valuing the traditions of his connection with them, at a meeting held for the purpose, on the ensuing term of the court, adopted very complimentary resolutions in relation to their deceased brother, which were ordered to be placed on the records of the court. Mr. Hutchinson, one of the elders of the bar, and since dead, in announcing the death, spoke of him as the oldest member of the bar, and said that, although he had left the active duties of the profession for several years, "he was never wholly absent from the courts, up to the time of his death, but was with us at every term."

Among his classmates were Henry Hubbard, late M. C. from New Hampshire; the distinguished physicians Drs. Mussey and Shattuck, and Chief Justice Weston of our State. I cannot more fittingly close this brief sketch, than by adopting the language of Chief Justice Weston, written a few days after the death of Mr. Selden. He says:

"We graduated at Dartmouth College in 1803: Mr. Selden was a few years older than myself. * * In our junior year, we were both members of the Phi-Beta-Kappa Society. He was highly respected by the faculty and by his fellow students, for his application to study, and for the faithful discharge of his various duties. He maintained there, as in after life, the character of a man eminent for prudence and discretion. While at college, he was a professor of religion, and I think never lost sight of the high and solemn duties the profession imposed. He steadily manifested, in his deportment and social intercourse, a strict attention to the proprieties of life, and a kind and friendly regard to others. He was modest in his deportment, but not wanting in self-respect, which no one in his presence would ever presume to invade. He was manly, but genial.

He was not a man of display, seeking distinction as a scholar, and was, therefore, not stimulated to the severe labor and exertion with which it is generally purchased. The same moderation in his aspirations attended him in after life. The path of ambition had few attractions for

Samuel Fessenden

1830 at the age of 46.

him, either as a literary, professional, or political man. Few men have had a more prosperous career through a long life. Health, friends, ease, comparative affluence, and the respect of the community, were his. These were elements of happiness, the value of which he appreciated; and with these he was satisfied.

It is nearly two years since I saw him. He was then about eighty; erect, vigorous, and very little changed in person from the period of our first acquaintance. I have never known a man so little marked by the hand of time for sixty years."

SAMUEL FESSENDEN. 1809—

The venerable Samuel Fessenden, now, with one exception, the oldest resident member of the Cumberland Bar, was the early contemporary of Mr. Greenleaf, and a competitor, of equal ardor and ability, for the practice, in the interior of Cumberland County.

Mr. Fessenden — or, as we shall call him, General Fessenden, for he is universally known by that title — was the son of the Rev. William Fessenden, of Fryeburg, Maine, where the General was born, July 16, 1784. His father was descended from Nicholas Fessenden, who was born in England, in 1651, and came to Cambridge in New England, previous to 1674.

John Fessenden, the first of the name who came to this country, was one of the first settlers in Cambridge, Massachusetts, and was admitted a freeman in 1641. He was by trade a saddler, and died without issue. Nicholas, his nephew, was his heir, and probably came over to settle and enjoy the estate: he had fourteen children by his wife, Margaret Cheney. His son Benjamin, educated at Harvard College, went to Sandwich, and is the ancestor of the Fessendens in that quarter. The branch in Maine descended from William, born in 1693, who married Martha Wyeth in 1716, and had eleven children. His oldest son, William, born December, 1718, and graduated at Harvard College, 1737, was a schoolmaster, and licensed to preach, but did not follow the vocation. He married Mary Palmer, March 31, 1740, by whom he had six children: one of whom was William, the father of Samuel, who was born November 3, 1747, old style, and graduated at Harvard College in 1768. He was settled the first minister of the first parish in Fryeburg, October 11, 1775; in which office he continued about thirty years, to the time of his death, May 6, 1805. He was a man of sterling qualities, earnest and devout, and died deeply lamented. He was twice married: first to Sarah Reed of Dunbarton, New Hampshire, in 1771, who with one child early died. In August, 1774, he married Sarah Clement of Boscawen, New Hampshire, — the wise and genial woman who long survived him, and was the mother of nine children: several of whom have left the imprint of their honorable and useful lives upon the pages of the times through which they passed. Ebenezer, a farmer in Fryeburg, though dead, lives in a family of lawyers, merchants, and physicians, who descended from him and survive him; Thomas was a respected lawyer in New York; Joseph Palmer, the well-known clergyman of South Bridgton, died in 1861, at the age of sixty-eight; Sarah was the wife of Dr. Oliver Griswold; and Mary Palmer, the wife of our late esteemed brother of the bar, William Barrows, and mother of our no less esteemed brother and judge of probate for Cumberland County. His distinguished son, Samuel, the subject of this notice, was born in Fryeburg, July 16, 1784; and was brought up at Fryeburg, receiving instruction in the fundamental principles of virtue and religion from his excellent parents, as well as the rudiments of the education, afterwards pursued at Fryeburg Academy, an institution established in 1792, by the influence of his father and other gentlemen of that town. He afterwards taught school in his native town, before going to college; and while in college, he pursued the same occupation at Paris and Boscawen, to help out the means of finishing his college course. Entering Dartmouth College, he devoted his time diligently to the acquisition of knowledge, and took his degree, with a high reputation as a scholar, in 1806. Among his classmates were his future brother-in-law, William Barrows; Judge Richard Fletcher of Massachusetts; the late Governor Harvey of New Hampshire; and the late Governor Parris of Maine.

On leaving college, Mr. Fessenden entered the office of the late Judge Dana at Fryeburg, where he faithfully pursued his studies, and was admitted to the bar in 1809; when he opened an office in New Gloucester, where Judge Weston and Daniel Howard were then in practice. This was in the central part of the county, and was then the center of a considerable trade. Mr. Fessenden entered upon the practice with earnestness, and having a strong mind, well furnished by literary and legal study, and in the vigor of life, and with the advantages of a well developed and handsome person, he soon took the lead in the practice of his town and neighborhood. A fortunate concurrence of events or some trifling incident often gives a sudden turn to a man's life, and hastens on his advancement or decline. Such an incident happened to General Fessenden soon after commencing practice in New Gloucester. He was called to attend a trial before a magistrate in a neighboring town, in the course of which, one of the witnesses opposed to him, somewhat excited by liquor, was contradictory in his statements, and prevaricated, to favor the party by whom he was summoned. Mr. Fessenden, perceiving this, cross-examined him so closely as to make him appear ridiculous, and to destroy the force of his testimony: this so provoked the witness that he determined to be revenged on the attorney; and when Mr. Fessenden went out of court, he found the bully waiting for him, and with his shirt sleeves rolled up, he made a sudden assault upon his adversary. The General coolly dealt him a left-handed blow, not a slight one, and at the same time dextrously applied his foot, so that the culprit was laid quivering on the ground. The General went to him, and quietly said, "If you are satisfied, I will go home, as I am somewhat in a hurry." The crowd raised a deafening shout, and told the General he had vanquished the greatest bully in the town, and he should have their business. His popularity was thus secured, and the next term of the court he made thirty entries.

His most powerful competitor was the late Prof. Greenleaf, who lived in the adjoining town of Gray, and who had already acquired popularity and reputation for his ingenuity and eloquence. The encounters of these two young men, struggling for mastery in the profession, and for an honorable livelihood, were often sharp and interesting, as they took place before country magistrates, as well as on the broader field of the Common Pleas and Supreme Courts. One anecdote of their country practice often amused the bar. Mr. Greenleaf usually brought his justice actions before 'Squire Perley of Gray, and Mr. Fessenden was occasionally called there in the defense. In one of those trials, which had occupied the forenoon, and was contested with considerable feeling, the justice had thrown out intimations favorable to the plaintiff, which, Fessenden perceiving, endeavored to avert by the most courteous treatment: they adjourned for dinner, after which the magistrate was to render judgment. On meeting again in the afternoon, to the surprise of all but General Fessenden, and most of all to Mr. Greenleaf, the case was given in favor of Mr. Fessenden's client. On their way home, the two counsel were commenting on the decision, in which Greenleaf expressed astonishment at the sudden change of opinion in the magistrate, and asked Fessenden if he could imagine the cause. The only reply Fessenden made, was to show Greenleaf a package of blank writs signed by Perley, which satisfied him that the prospect of getting a new customer had produced a striking development in the mind of the justice.

The oft-repeated skirmishes of these sharpshooters on the outposts prepared them for the sterner conflicts on the larger arena of the courts. They were thus trained and disciplined: both ardent and ambitious, — Greenleaf keen, ingenious, insinuating, and fluent; Fessenden solid, moderate in manner, pertinacious, and persevering, — and both having great weight with the jury, but by different approaches. Their forensic encounters, from their rivalship and ability, were listened to by the bar and the court with much interest: in these were displayed copious resources of legal knowledge and cultivated powers of elocution. Greenleaf's manner was more plausible, Fessenden's more ingenuous: each having peculiar effect in his own way. Fessenden did not arrive at his points and conclusions so directly as Greenleaf: he had more circumlocution and repetition, but he reached his point, and every point, before he quitted his subject, and nothing was omitted that could give light to the jury. Greenleaf's manner was extremely pleasant, his elocution easy and graceful, and his arguments more concise. In learning and ability, it was difficult to choose between them. For more than twenty years, this rivalry existed between them in a larger degree than with any other members of the Cumberland Bar, because their competition in the country was brought to Portland, to which place they both moved, bringing their clients, and retaining those local feelings and prejudices, which they had not escaped in their early practice. Gen. Fessenden moved to Portland in 1822; Mr. Greenleaf had preceded him four years; their fame went before them, their business followed them; and they advanced in both with a firm and steady step to the highest ranks in the profession, gaining and securing the confidence of their brethren of the bar and on the bench, and the respect of their fellow citizens. They were both men of high honor and integrity, professors of religion, Christian men, and Christian gentlemen. Such men were an honor to the bar, and a blessing to the community in which they lived.

When Gen. Fessenden moved to Portland, he formed a connection in business with Thomas Amory Deblois, who was born in Boston, the son of Stephen Deblois, and grandson, by the mother, of the wealthy and respected merchant, Thomas C. Amory. He graduated at Harvard College in 1813, and prepared for the bar in the office of Samuel A. Bradley at Fryeburg. He was admitted to the bar in 1816, and after practicing a short time in Windham, he moved to Portland. This professional partnership continued to 1854, a period of thirty-two years, and was one of the most successful ever established in the State. The junior partner had numerous friends in Boston, his native place, with which our State was largely connected in commercial transactions, which brought large accessions to the office; while the senior's popularity in the country secured many clients from that quarter; and the attention, promptness, and ability which they gave to their business, secured all the clients and correspondents whom they had once received. Gen. Fessenden was particularly familiar with the law of real estate, which formed much of the controversy, and the gravest part of it, that occupied our courts. He was largely employed in this branch of business, and managed it with skill, learning, and success. Both parties were able advocates, and held conspicuous rank, during this period, at the bar.

He dissolved his connection with Mr. Deblois in 1854, in order to take his son Daniel into partnership, and the new firm continued until his son was elected clerk of the courts in 1861, when, advanced in years, and with the honors and burdens of more than fifty years' professional life, and the respect of the community upon him, he retired from the courts and all active duty, to the repose of private and domestic life, which his enfeebled health imperatively demanded. He happily now survives at the age of seventy-eight, the oldest member, but one, of the Cumberland Bar, and for many years its honored president. And as he leaves with pain these scenes of his labors and his triumphs, he speaks emphatically of the high regard he carries with him, for the profession in which he was so long and honorably engaged.

He found at the bar of Cumberland, when he entered it, Mellen, Whitman, Longfellow, Hopkins, Emery, Henry A. S. Dearborn, Potter, — all of Portland; Orr of Brunswick; Cutler of North Yarmouth; Greenleaf of Gray; besides other lesser lights: Freeman was clerk and Waite sheriff, time-honored attendants. Of all these whose names I have mentioned, Whitman and Potter are the only survivors, one in his eighty-sixth and the other in his eighty-seventh year, still enjoying the mellow fruits of temperance, moderation, and virtuous lives.

General Fessenden's literary attainments were very respectable: in early life he had cultivated his classical taste, and stored his mind by a course of general reading with copious knowledge, which he subsequently improved as the duties of his profession would admit. His standing in college was among the best scholars, and this rank he sustained in after life, and received a public acknowledgment, in his election in 1828 as a member of the Maine Historical Society, and in 1846, by the degree of LL. D. conferred upon him by Bowdoin College. In 1828, he was spoken of as president of Dartmouth College, on the death of President Tyler; but his aversion to change his mode of life, suspended further effort in that direction.

General Fessenden early took a deep interest in the political affairs of the country, as his father had before him, who had represented his town in the General Court. They were strong and undeviating federalists of the Washington and Hamilton school; and the whole family being ardent, earnest persons, threw themselves zealously into the conflicts which occurred between the opposing parties in the early part of the century. The year after he settled in New Gloucester, he was invited by the federalists there to deliver the 4th of July oration: Francis Eaton, another lawyer of the town, was the orator of the democratic party. The town was strongly federal, and that party erected a flag staff in front of the house in which their oration was to be delivered, on which they hoisted the national flag. Col. Foxcroft, the democratic leader, sent word that the flag must come down; which, when Mr. Fessenden heard, he stationed two men at the foot of the staff, first asking them if they would see that the flag was not lowered during the delivery of the oration. They replied that it should not come down, unless they passed over their dead bodies. It is needless to say that the banner floated unmolested. It was on this occasion that Parson Mosely, the minister of the parish, and a high federalist, read the hymn beginning thus:

> "Break out their teeth, Almighty God,
> Those teeth of lions dyed in blood."

General Fessenden was a representative from New Gloucester to the General Court in 1814, 1815, and 1816, and a senator from the county in 1818 and 1819, in which year the State swung away from her ancient moorings by the side of the old commonwealth into independent life. In these years, he steadily advocated the principles of the federal party, and often with great eloquence and power. It was in 1814, in the discussion of the proposition to send delegates to the *Hartford Convention*, that he made his famous speech against the national administration, in which he uttered the memorable declaration, that he was "ready to take the constitution in one hand and a sword in the other, and demand at Washington the constitutional rights of the people." He held a high position in the Legislature, and was considered during this period of public life, being but thirty years old when he entered it, one of the most promising of the young men in the District of Maine.

It was while he was senator, in the political year of 1818, that a sharp controversy occurred on the floor of the Senate between him and General King, a senator from Lincoln county, which was subsequently continued before the people in the public papers, and had an influence on political events. It arose on the question of making a grant to the "Maine Literary and Theological Institution," now Waterville College. The trustees had petitioned the legislature for aid: at the same session, the subject was referred to a committee of which Gen. King was chairman, who made a report accompanied by a bill granting four townships of land, and $3,000 a year for several years to the institution. The bill was postponed to the next session, an opposition being manifested to it. During the summer, the Baptist denomination was roused by Gen. King to an effort in favor of the passage of the bill, and printed petitions were prepared by General King, and sent through the State for signature. These were presented at the January session, and were so objectionable by their offensive language, that it had an unfavorable effect upon the application and the object of the grant. They demanded the passage of the bill, and made disparaging reflections upon other literary institutions. When the subject came before the Senate, General Fessenden and others objected to the passage of the bill, on the ground that it granted too much; and General Fessenden, in a speech on the occasion, in order to obviate the effect of the offensive language of the petitions, observed that they did not emanate from the board of trustees, nor have their assent. This was immediately denied in a very excited manner by General King, who pronounced the statement false. General Fessenden replied that the information had been given him by a member of the other house, who was also one of the trustees of the institution, and he had no doubt of its correctness. King re-affirmed, with great vehemence, that the statement was untrue, and that the petitions were submitted to the trustees, and approved by them, with one exception. After much angry discussion, the bill was defeated; and the battle was renewed on the broader arena of the public press. The Eastern Argus threw itself warmly into the controversy, and sustained the position of General King with keenness of sarcasm, for which the editor of that paper, Mr. Ware, had acknowledged talent. And it was used as one of the arguments in favor of separation, that as Massachusetts and the federal party withheld a just favor and patronage from the literary institutions of Maine, the District should place itself in a situation to bestow a proper endowment upon her own institutions. The argument had great weight, especially in the Baptist denomination, to which the Waterville institution belonged.

Gen. Alford Richardson, the representative from North Yarmouth, was the member who furnished the information to General Fessenden on which he made his statement: he and General King were both members of the board of

Trustees of the Waterville Seminary, and were thus brought in direct issue on the question of veracity. General Richardson, in 1822, published a pamphlet in which he thoroughly examined the whole subject, produced copies of the records of the trustees and various correspondence and facts, in order to vindicate himself from the charge of falsehood. He was a man of great purity of character and incapable of falsehood; and now that the principal belligerents are dead, King and Richardson, and the party issues which gave interest and importance to the controversy, entirely effete, we may justly say, that General Richardson stands relieved from the imputation, hastily and harshly cast upon him. As for General Fessenden, his vindication was made on the spot, and was triumphant and successful. The college, by this injudicious management, was the principal sufferer.

General Fessenden's powers, physical and mental, seemed peculiarly to qualify him for a prominent position in a deliberative assembly: his commanding figure, his full round voice, his emphatic and graceful elocution, could not but make a deep impression upon such an audience. He distinguished himself so much in the Legislature, that, in 1818, while holding the office of senator, he was elected by both branches, major general of the 12th division of the militia of Massachusetts. This office he held fourteen years, and took great pleasure in it. At that time, the militia was held in respect, and scarcely a year passed but he had reviews of different portions of his division, which embraced the whole county. He collected around him as his staff, gentlemen of high standing in the community, and his parades were brilliant and attractive. His figure and appearance were in a high degree military and commanding. In a manuscript note of Mr. Williamson, the historian of Maine, who was his opponent in politics, we find these comments: "He is a man of very good intellectual powers, a thorough lawyer, an able advocate, and a safe and faithful counsellor. He is in person above the usual size, has an expressive countenance, and his manners are elevated, and his bearing military. Though he is a high-toned federalist, he was popular, for his principles were pure — a man of accredited piety. He was emulous to excel, and his example worthy to be imitated."

The separation, and his removal to Portland, soon after, threw him for awhile out of public employment, especially as his strong party biases were obnoxious to the ruling power in the new State. But in 1825 and 1826, he represented Portland in the Legislature, and did good service in that capacity: his colleagues the first year were Joseph Adams and Joshua Richardson; the second year, Stephen Longfellow and Isaac Adams. After this, he became more engrossed in business which occupied all his time. He early became a member of the Masonic Order, and rose through its various grades to its chief position in the State; for a number of years he was Grand Master of the Grand Lodge of Maine.

General Fessenden followed the federal party in its various changes; to national republican, under John Quincy Adams, and to whig, when Clay led off the party. But, at length, when the anti-slavery power was acquiring force, and taking a firm stand for the emancipation of the African race on this continent, General Fessenden, with his accustomed ardor, and from sincere conviction, entered the ranks of that party, and did yeoman's service in its cause. For a long time, it was very unpopular in Portland: the municipal authorities refused the public halls for their meetings, and when they did assemble, they encountered an exasperated mob. The General became quite obnoxious for his earnest advocacy of the cause, but nothing intimidated or discouraged, he struggled on through evil report and good report, holding up the banner of freedom for all men, not whites alone, but blacks as well. It was a matter of principle with him, and he was regardless of what men might say, if it conflicted with his sense of right. He received colored persons into his house, he took them with him to church, he visited them in their families, and encouraged them in every way to give them self-respect and a place in society. In 1844, he introduced a colored man, Macon B. Allen, into the court-house, while the District Court was in session, and moved the court that he be admitted to practice as an attorney and counsellor at law, under the law then existing in Maine, which rendered any citizen eligible to admission, who produced a certificate of good moral character. Allen was rejected on the ground that he was not a citizen. He afterwards applied to be admitted on examination; he was thereupon called before the examiners, a committee of the bar, and having sustained a satisfactory examination, he was recommended and admitted. He, however, never entered upon the practice in Maine, but went to Boston, and made repeated applications for admission to the Suffolk Bar, but was uniformly rejected.

General Fessenden has always been extremely popular with those people, not only from his great benevolence of character, but from the strong, undeviating interest he has taken in the race. One of them, to show his affection, at a festival which they held, gave the following toast: "General Fessenden — though he has a white face, he has a black heart." He has advocated the anti-slavery cause consistently and uniformly, from a deep conviction, but is far from entering into the ultra radical views of those who would sacrifice the Union and all other of our political blessings to this one issue. He is governed by enlightened views of freedom, not freedom from law and just restraints, but a large liberty in which man may exercise his freedom of thought and speech, under the salutary restraints of just laws, which guarantee the rights and give their protection to others, as well as himself. His maxim is, "*Et sentire quæ velit, et quæ sentiat discere*,"—he is willing to grant to others what he claims for himself.

In 1841, and several other years, General Fessenden was the candidate of the anti-slavery party for governor of the State; and he has always enjoyed their confidence, and stood high in their esteem as a firm friend and wise counsellor. He has lived to see the sect which was despised and rejected, come to be high in public consideration, and courted for its popular influence; and its orators, who once encountered hisses and reproaches, now greeted with huzzas and applause, not the faintest of which are bestowed upon those really gifted men who advance up from the ranks of the colored race itself.

As might be inferred from the uniform benignity and kindness which have ever warmed the heart and guided the steps of this excellent man, the purest source of his enjoyment, and the kindliest influences of his life, were to be found in the domestic circle. No man ever made a better husband or a better father than he; and in response to this sentiment, his cherished wife, and his eight living children, seven sons and one daughter, all respectably settled in life, will rise up with one accord, and do him homage. His children numbered eleven, nine sons and two daughters; two sons and one daughter are dead. Eight of the sons were educated at New England colleges,— five at Bowdoin and three at Dartmouth. Four of his sons were educated for the bar, three for medicine, and one for the pulpit. Three are now in Congress,—Samuel C., a representative from the third congressional district in Maine; and William Pitt, the distinguished senator from our State; and his son Thomas

A. D., recently elected from the Oxford District, for the unexpired term of Judge Walton. William Pitt, the oldest son of the General, has had a splendid career: born in 1806, he early manifested remarkably quick perceptions and strong mental power. He entered college before he was thirteen years old, and graduated in 1823, before he was seventeen. He studied his profession with Charles S. Daveis in Portland, whose kind and able counsel, and the peculiar line of his practice, cultivated and developed that activity of mind and those brilliant powers that carried him, with undeviating step, to the head of the bar in Maine, and to the leadership in the Senate of the United States; and would have given him the highest seat on the bench of the Supreme Court of the State, if he would have been willing to sacrifice the noble aspirations of political life for the quiet and solid rewards of judicial office. His first appearance in public life was as a representative from Portland in 1832, at the age of twenty-five; and being repeatedly elected to the House, where he distinguished himself by the keenness of his intellect and his graceful and powerful elocution, he was selected by the whigs of Cumberland District, in the exciting campaign of 1840, to represent that district in Congress. In this first portion of the first whig administration, he at once took a prominent stand on the floor of Congress, and acquired a reputation that did honor to himself and the district which he ably represented. His professional engagements, which were numerous and important, and the claims of a young family, induced him to decline a re-election. After this, he was returned four times to the Legislature from Portland, and in 1853, was elected United States senator for a full term of six years, as successor to James W. Bradbury. During this term, he served on the finance committee, of which Mr. Hunter of Virginia was chairman; much of the labor, therefore, of this important committee devolved on Mr. Fessenden, and he signally distinguished himself during the whole of his term, embracing the administration of Franklin Pierce, and the first half of James Buchanan's, by wisdom in council and eloquence in debate. He resisted with undeviating firmness and skill, the deep and insidious machinations of the slaveholding party to fasten their supremacy on the country, and with equal ability, illustrated the financial policy of the government, and the other varied and multifarious interests of the country. His merits and services were justly and handsomely acknowledged by a re-election for a second term of six years, in 1859. His large experience in political life, and especially on this broad field of national politics, engrafted on intellectual powers and resources of the highest quality, all united to a dialectic skill rarely equalled, have justly given him that prominence in the national councils, which the public award and his colleagues concede. In the exciting and deeply interesting discussions and measures which have grown out of the great rebellion, he has proved himself no less an unflinching enemy to treason, than friend to a sound and wise conservatism, which seeks the re-establishment of the Union upon the basis of the old and venerable and venerated constitution. As chairman of the committee of finance in the Senate, his labors, his rare powers and resources, in this period, when the highest financial ability of the country is put in requisition to meet the unparalleled demands upon the treasury, have proved equal to the emergency, and he has shown himself to be a chancellor of the exchequer admirably adapted to the urgent demands of the great republic.

In addition to his own labors in council, three of his four sons, all educated at college, promptly entered the army. Two remain in the service ; but his youngest, Samuel, nobly perished on the field in the great battle near Centreville, in August, 1862, while serving as an aid to General Tower.

The mother of his children was Ellen, the youngest daughter of James Deering, Esq., of Portland: her lamented death in 1857 deprived him of a loved companion and a dearly cherished friend. In 1858, Senator Fessenden received from Bowdoin College the degree of LL. D.

These are some of the claims which General Fessenden has to public gratitude, and had he given no more than his children to his native land, he would deserve the thanks of the present and future time. He has devoted to their education and support, the resources of a large income, which has been invested beyond the reach of casuality or depreciation, and become a large benefaction to his country.

And should some envious, or superficial, or curious person ask, "Where are his jewels? where is the pecuniary result of fifty years' professional labor?" he would have more reason than the mother of the Gracchi, to point to his sons and say, "They are here." It is a source of unalloyed satisfaction to the venerable Fessenden, to have lived to this day, and to be a witness to the honors, the respect, and prosperity which have attended upon all of his surviving children, without a single exception. Standing upon the verge of life, he may well exclaim with the ancient seer, "Lord, now lettest thou thy servant depart in peace, for mine eyes have seen thy salvation."

WILLIAM ALLEN HAYES. 1809—1850.

Mr. Hayes, who long filled places of honor and trust in the county of York, was the youngest of the three sons of David Hayes of North Yarmouth. He was born in that town October 20, 1783. The family was of Scotch descent: his first American ancestor, John, was in Dover, New Hampshire, as early as 1680, and married there in 1686. The grandson of the first John having the same name, who was grandfather of the subject of our notice, was the first of the name who settled in North Yarmouth, and was among the early immigrants who went there on the revival of the town in the early part of the last century.

His mother died when he was nine years old, and his father when he was but twelve. Deprived of these guides and guardians of their early years, the three brothers were thrown upon their own resources, and manfully did they sustain themselves. The eldest son was but fifteen, yet they kept the household together, without assistant or domestic. William worked with the others on the farm in summer, and attended the district school in the winter; and so well did he improve his opportunities, limited as they were, that at the age of fifteen, he was invited to become the teacher of the school. This encouragement and reward stimulated him to seek a liberal education: this determination was no sooner formed, than, with the energy which ever characterised him, he commenced and prosecuted the studies preliminary to a college examination, with the Rev. Tristram Gilman, the worthy pastor of the church in North Yarmouth. Mr. Gilman was a graduate of Harvard in the class of 1757, with Edward Brooks, his predecessor in the ministry, Judge Theophilus Bradbury, and other distinguished men. He was ordained in 1769, and died in the ministry in 1809. Under the guiding and friendly influence of this excellent man, young Hayes was well prepared for college, and was admitted to Dartmouth in 1801. He passed through his collegiate course with honor, and graduated in 1805, with the highest distinction of the class, although it contained such names as Francis Brown, afterwards president of the college; the Rev. Samuel Osgood of Springfield, lately deceased; and the learned and Rev. Henry Coleman of Salem. With these gentleman he was ever on terms of intimate friendship; and we have heard that this friendship, especially in the case of Dr. Brown, was transmitted to their children, two of whom, twenty-six years later, entered the same college as classmates, and graduated in 1831: these were the Rev. Samuel G. Brown, professor of oratory at Dartmouth College, and John L. Hayes, Esq., distinguished for his scientific attainments.

On leaving college, Mr. Hayes took charge for a year, of Moor's classical school at Hanover, an institution established by the elder Pres. Wheelock, in connection with the college. After that time, he devoted himself to the study of the law with his wonted ability and earnestness. He spent his first year with Ezekiel Whitman at New Gloucester, then a short time with Dudley Hubbard at South Berwick, and finished his course with Artemas Ward of Charlestown, a celebrated lawyer of the Middlesex Bar, afterwards chief justice of the Boston Court of Common Pleas, who was a sound lawyer, with a very large practice. He was admitted to the Middlesex Bar in 1809, and immediately opened an office at South Berwick, which place for the remainder of his life became the field of his usefulness, his labor, and fame.

Mr. Hayes, as might have been anticipated from his habits of industry and method, from his acquirements as a scholar and a lawyer, from his acknowledged ability and perseverance, immediately took a prominent position in his profession and society. At the time he commenced practice, the only lawyers in Berwick, which then embraced a very large territory now divided into several towns, were Dudley Hubbard, whose business, by inattention, was fast receding; Benjamin Green, who was more fond of politics than law; and William Lambert, a very easy, quiet man, who made little effort for business. A good opening, therefore, existed in this thriving community for an enterprising lawyer, and Mr. Hayes was the man for the place and the time. He soon acquired a large business, which he managed successfully, accumulated property, won the confidence of the public, and earnestly engaged in promoting the various interests of the community in which he had cast his lot. He succeeded not only to the business of Dudley Hubbard, who died in 1816, but to his elegant mansion and farm, and made it one of the most beautiful and highly cultivated spots in the county. He was a thoroughly experimental farmer, and his experiments being in the line of intelligence and progress, were successful. Whatever he did, in the different walks of life, he did well: the head always came to the aid of the hand, and working together, they produced the results which always must follow intelligent labor. God helps those who help themselves.

The forty years of his busy life at South Berwick is well described in the following brief summary, which we take from an obituary notice of Mr. Hayes, published soon after his death. "During this period, he received repeated testimonials of respect and confidence from his brethren of the bar and fellow citizens. For more than twenty-five years he was President of the South Berwick Bank, about the same period President of the bar of York County: he was many years President of the Board of Trustees of the Berwick Academy, and for twenty years Judge of Probate for York County. (1828–1847.) In all these multiplied relations, he maintained the character of a faithful, upright, wise, and good man." He did not engage much in general politics: he was a representative to the legislature in 1822, and we do not know that beside this he held any political office. His business and private affairs, and his numerous engagements, as indicated above, engrossed his time and thoughts.

When his cares and labors had greatly increased, he found a partner, and an able coadjutor, in a young man of fine talents and business capacity, whom he took into his office, — Charles N. Cogswell.

Charles Northend Cogswell, the son of Northend and Elizabeth Cogswell, was born in Berwick, April 24, 1797. He was educated at Bowdoin College, from which he graduated in 1814, at the early age of seventeen. He became a student in the office of Mr. Hayes, and on being admitted to the bar in 1817, he entered into partnership with his teacher. And a most successful partnership it proved: both members of the firm were possessed of high intellectual and moral gifts, were endowed with a large capacity for affairs, and for many years more business was done in their office than in any other in the county. Mr. Cogswell, like Judge Hayes, enjoyed the confidence of the community, and was often selected to represent the town, as well as the county, in the Legislature. After an active and honorable course of life and practice, he died very suddenly on the eleventh of October, 1843, in the forty-seventh year of his age. Judge Goodenow, in reply to the application to place upon the records of the court the resolves of sympathy adopted by the bar, observed, "In a professional career of twenty-five years, few, very few, have accomplished it so well. His talents for business were indeed extraordinary, and he was most diligent in the employment of them. His memory was retentive, and he was exceedingly accurate in all his transactions in his office and in the courts. His whole demeanor was amiable and exemplary."

Mr. Cogswell was twice married; first, to Elizabeth, daughter of Elisha Hill of Portsmouth; second, to Margaret E. Russell, daughter of Edward Russell of Portland: by the latter he left one son, now a member of Harvard College. Judge Hayes survived his junior partner eight years, still finding active employment as president of the bank, in the management of his farm, and in ministering to his large family of twelve children, in the midst of whom he moved with affectionate interest, training them to usefulness and honor. In these various and beneficent duties, and while fully competent to their discharge, he calmly, and without a struggle, sunk to his final repose, April 15, 1851, in peace and charity with all men, at the age of sixty-seven years.

EDMUND FLAGG. 1810—1816.

FROM THE PEN OF JOHN H. SHEPPARD, ESQ.

Edmund Flagg of Wiscasset was born in Chester, New Hampshire, in 1786. He was the son of Josiah Flagg of that place, who was in the Revolutionary War, an adjutant, one year under Washington. On the return of peace, he went back to Chester, lived on a farm, and did much business as a justice of the peace. He died of consumption April 25, 1799, aged fifty-one; his wife, Edmund's mother, died May 1, 1799, aged forty-nine. His uncle, Dr. John Flagg of Lynn, was a Cambridge graduate, a colonel in the Revolution, and an eminent physician, who died in 1793. His grandfather was the Rev. Ebenezer Flagg, who was born in Woburn, 1704, graduated at Harvard College in 1725, was settled over the First Congregational Church at Chester, 1736, and, after a faithful ministry of sixty years, died, as the Columbian Centinel of November 26, 1796, has remarked, on the fourteenth of November, aged ninety-three; leaving an example, "worthy to be imitated, of public, domestic, and social virtues." This venerable man lived in those days of conservative piety, when the pastor and his people were united by love, and he could look forward to a sepulcher among his kindred and friends.

Edmund graduated at Dartmouth College in 1806, and was distinguished as a scholar. He was a classmate of the Hon. Richard Fletcher, LL. D., of Boston, an eminent counsellor, and recently one of the judges of the Supreme

Judicial Court of Massachusetts, of Gov. Parris and Samuel Fessenden of this State. He studied law with Francis D. Channing, a lawyer of high rank in the Boston Bar, who died in 1810. After his admission to practice in 1810, he settled in Wiscasset, and within a year he had the good fortune to form a partnership with Silas Lee, District Attorney of the United States and Judge of Probate. He was immediately engaged in the lucrative business of collecting the debts of that able and successful practitioner, to whom the arrears of fees amounting to thousands of dollars were due. He was appointed Register of Probate for the county of Lincoln on the third of August, 1812, — an office not incompatible, and even favorable to a young man's prospects in the profession. He wrote a fair and ready hand, did his own recording, was a working man, industrious, persevering, and economical; and in the harvest before him he beheld the harbinger of future independence.

He now saw his way clear to connubial happiness, and in 1813, married Harriet, daughter of Colonel Payson of Wiscasset, a pretty woman, and one of the belles of a seaport renowned for the beauty of her girls, her social circles, and well-conducted assemblies, in the days of her prosperity. He purchased a small cottage, and fitted it up prettily and neatly: it stood a little out of town on the Bath road, in the midst of rural scenery, where the distant water — which is the eye of a landscape — added to the picturesque effect of his white mansion among the trees. Here, with a flood tide of business, and growing reputation at the bar, he appeared to be a happy man, destined to years of felicity. But Providence otherwise ordered. His parents died of a decline, and the son inherited this disease. He had a fair and florid complexion, indicating, too often, a hectic temperament.

On the fourth of July, 1815, he was suddenly attacked

with a feverish cough, rapidly fell sick, and was confined to his room. He was advised to seek a warmer and more salubrious climate, and in October following, left his family, and sailed in a packet for the West Indies. It was a voyage of hope in pursuit of health. I saw him shortly before his departure: his large blue eyes had the well-known brilliancy of consumption; his cheeks were deeply flushed, and his voice, naturally so clear and cheerful, could only whisper through his hoarseness a parting word. It was a sad sight to see him there, as he reclined his slender form on the sofa, and looked round on his once happy home, his fond partner, his little playful daughter, Harriet, with a trembling hope that seemed bordering on despair; and I came away from the house remembering that the leaves of autumn were dropping, and the fir tree of the north would soon wear its mourning verdure on the snowy hills; but where would he be then? Alas!

> "Linquenda tellus, et domus, et placens
> Uxor."

He reached a foreign port in safety; but in the Columbian Centinel of February 7, 1816, was this melancholy notice among the obituaries: "On the island of St. Croix, on the fourteenth of December last, Edmund Flagg, Esq., late of Wiscasset, counsellor at law, aged thirty. In the hope of a restoration of health in a climate more mild, he left his family and friends last autumn. He was a member of the church of Christ, a good citizen, and a kind and affectionate husband."

The loss of this amiable and talented young man was much lamented. He was a member of the church of the late Rev. Hezekiah Packard, D. D., of Wiscasset. As a lawyer, he was well read, and familiar with our reports. He conducted a suit skillfully, was gifted with fluency of ideas and words, and grew fast in reputation. He left a

J.H. Bufford's Lith. Boston.

Albion K. Parris

At the age of 80.

widow and two children, — Harriet, who died in 1860, and Edmund, born in 1815, soon after his father left home. It would have been a source of the purest joy could he have lived to see his name ennobled by this virtuous and excellent son, who is now a writer of no mean rank among the literati of our country.

Young Edmund graduated at Bowdoin Collage in 1835, and I have understood, went south and studied law with the witty and renowned George D. Prentiss, in Louisville, Kentucky, where he was admitted to practice. With Mr. Prentiss he was connected in editing the Louisville "Literary News Letter:" he also edited other papers, and wrote several books,—"The Far West" in two volumes, "Carrero," and a number of novels. He went to Berlin as secretary of the Hon. Edward A. Hannegan, Minister to Prussia, in 1848, and on his return in 1850, was appointed United States Consul at Venice. In that place of such time-honored memories, his pen was not idle; he gleaned from the Italian literature — that sweet and exquisite language — a rich mass of historic facts, and gave, as the fruit of his studies on the shores of the Adriatic, "The City of the Sea" in two volumes; which is highly spoken of as a reliable history of "glorious old Venice."

If the manes of our departed friends have ever been permitted to look down from the unknown world upon those dear kindred they have left below, what must be the joy and gladness of the father to see such a son, cheering the declining days of his widowed mother, and adorning society by the light of his genius, and the labors of his pen?

ALBION KEITH PARRIS. 1809—1857.

The life of Judge Parris was one of uniform success: his aspirations in every department seemed to have been promptly answered. He was born at Hebron, Maine, the only child of Samuel Parris and Sarah Pratt of Middleborough, Massachusetts. He descended from Thomas Parris of London, who had four sons living in that city in 1660, viz., John, Thomas, Samuel, and Martin. John was a minister of the Reformed church at Ugborough, near Plymouth, England. Samuel was the unfortunate minister of Salem village in New England, in whose family the witchcraft tragedy commenced. Thomas, son of John, the minister, sailed from Topsham in Devonshire, for New England, June 28, 1683. He went first to Long Island, New York, where he married, and afterward moved to Boston, and there losing his wife, he moved to Pembroke, Massachusetts, and married a Miss Rogers, by whom he had four sons and three daughters. He died in 1752. His son Thomas, born May 8, 1701, married Hannah Gannett of Scituate, by whom he had four sons, and died September 7, 1786. Benjamin, one of these sons, born August 27, 1731, married Millicent Keith of Easton, Massachusetts, July 4, 1753, and had five sons and three daughters. He lived in Pembroke, Massachusetts, and was much employed as an instructor of youth: he died November 18, 1815. Samuel, the eldest son of Benjamin, was born August 31, 1755: he entered the army in 1775, and performed much service as an officer both on land and at sea. On the close of the war, he married Sarah Pratt, and had one child only, Albion Keith, the subject of the present notice, who was born in Hebron, Maine, January 19, 1788, and was, as it thus appears, in the seventh degree of descent from Thomas of London, through John, Thomas, Thomas, Benjamin, and Samuel, his father. Samuel had a brother Martin, a graduate of Brown University in 1790, who settled in the ministry at Marshfield, and died in 1739. After the Revolutionary War, Samuel, the father of Albion, moved to Hebron, then an incorporated plantation, and was one of the first settlers of the town. He held the office of Judge of the Court of Common Pleas for Oxford County, several years; was repeatedly chosen a representative from Hebron; and in 1812, he was chosen by the Federal party one of the Electors of President, and united with the other Electors of that State in casting the vote of Massachusetts for DeWitt Clinton. He died in Washington at the residence of his son, September 10, 1847, aged ninety-two.

Governor Parris worked on his father's farm until he was fourteen years old, when he began to prepare for college, and entered in advanced standing at Dartmouth in 1803. He graduated in 1806, in the class with William Barrows and General Fessenden of our State, John Harvey of New Hampshire, and Judge Fletcher of Massachusetts. He soon after commenced the study of law with Chief Justice Whitman, who was then in practice at New Gloucester, and who next winter removed to Portland. He pursued his studies with great diligence, and was admitted to the Cumberland Bar in September, 1809. He immediately established himself in the practice of law at Paris in the county of Oxford: from that period, his course was one of uninterrupted success.

In 1811, he was appointed county attorney for Oxford. In 1813, he was elected to the General Court in Massachusetts from Paris. In 1814, he was chosen a senator for the counties of Oxford and Somerset; and in November, 1814, he was elected to the Fourteenth Congress of the United States, for the years 1815 and '16, and again to the Fifteenth Congress; and while holding this office of representative to Congress, he was appointed Judge of the District Court of the United States for Maine, in 1818, at the age of thirty, as successor to the venerable Judge Sewall, who had held the office from the organization of the government.

On receiving this appointment, he moved to Portland, from which place, the next year, 1819, he was chosen a member of the convention to form a constitution for the new State, then seeking admission into the Union. This body was composed of the most able and prominent men in the State, over which William King was called to preside. Judge Parris took an active part in its proceedings and debates, and was a member of the committee which drafted the constitution, Mr Holmes being chairman. Among the members of this important committee, were Messrs. Dane of Wells, Whitman of Portland, General Wingate and Chandler, Judge Bridge and Judge Dana. Mr. Parris was also appointed treasurer by the convention.

On the adoption of the constitution, and the admission of the State into the Union, of which it became the twenty-second member, Mr. Parris, then holding the office of District judge, was appointed Judge of Probate for Cumberland County, under the new dynasty, succeeding the venerable Samuel Freeman, who had held the office sixteen years as successor to Judge Gorham. While in the enjoyment of these honorable and responsible trusts, public opinion designated him for the highest office in the State as successor to Governor King, who having been appointed in 1821, one of the commissioners on Spanish Claims, resigned the office. This nomination was not unanimously accepted by the democratic party, some of whom preferred General Joshua Wingate, and a triangular contest resulted of considerable harshness and asperity. Governor Parris was elected, and entered upon the discharge of the duties, before he had quite attained the age of thirty-three years, and was continued in the office by successive elections, five years. In his annual message in 1826, he peremptorily declined another nomination. Governor Parris administered the government with ability and faithfulness: it was a period of repose — there were no exciting questions to irritate the public mind. The most important subjects calling for attention were those relating to the common property owned with Massachusetts, and the disputed northeastern boundary. The latter subject was, toward the close of his administration, becoming of serious import, and had begun to create alarm as to the final result. In his annual message in 1826, Gov. Parris called the attention of the Legislature to the subject, as one unexpected, and for the discussion of which, the government needed the evidence contained in documents, reports of commissioners, and maps, and recommended that copies of such needed papers should be procured. Immediate action was taken by the Legislature, and Reuel Williams, chairman of the committee in the Senate, made a clear and able report on the subject, concluding with resolves authorizing and requesting the Governor to procure "all such maps, documents, publications, papers, and surveys, relating to the northeastern boundary of the United States, as he may deem necessary and useful for the State to be possessed of."

The interests of education, religious culture, and temperance were often and earnestly urged by Gov. Parris upon the attention of the Legislature, and received respectful consideration. In 1825, Lafayette visited the State, where his reception was most cordial, and where he found some of his old companions in arms to welcome their illustrious ally and friend. He was warmly greeted and entertained by the Governor. His visit to the State extended as far as Augusta. He was the guest of the State by invitation of the executive, under a resolve of the Legislature expressed in cordial and complimentary terms. The report on the subject was signed by the most respectable gentlemen of the Legislature, — James Campbell, James W. Ripley, Robert P. Dunlap, General Fessenden, Timothy

37

Boutelle, Daniel Goodenow, Parker McCobb, and others. His journey was a triumphal progress, and he was received everywhere with the warmest expressions of gratitude and respect.

Governor Parris was not permitted to enjoy repose from official life. The last year of his administration had not expired when he was elected to the United States Senate in place of John Holmes, whose term of service ended on the 3d of March, 1827.

But he had scarcely become familiar with his new position, when in June, 1828, he was appointed Associate Justice of the Supreme Court of our State, in the room of Judge Preble, who resigned the office on his appointment as Minister to the Hague. Judge Parris having been for several years withdrawn from practice, and never having had much experience in the routine of his profession, on account of his early and steady employment in the public service, found himself somewhat rusty in regard to the decided cases and the progress of legal science. But with his accustomed industry and facility, he applied himself to the study of the reports and the learned elementary treatises, until he thoroughly qualified himself for the arduous and important duties of the bench; and it is but justice to say, that he received unqualified testimony from the bar and the community, of the ability, promptness, and impartiality which graced his judicial life.

He was not, however, destined to grow old upon the bench, for he had hardly ripened his judicial powers and opened the way to judicial fame, before he was transferred, I cannot say to a higher sphere — but to one of more emolument and ease. In 1836, by the favor of Mr. Van Buren, he found an honorable position and a salary of three thousand dollars a year, as Second Comptroller of the Treasury of the United States. This office he held thirteen years until 1849, and discharged its duties with the utmost fidelity and promptness, through the administrations of Mr. Van Buren, Gen. Harrison, John Tyler, and President Polk. On retiring from this station, he returned to Portland, of which city he was chosen mayor in 1852, declining a second nomination. This was the last public office he held, and for the remainder of his life he reposed quietly upon his many and well-won laurels.

This career of public duty, continued through a period of thirty-six years, never for an hour interrupted, is extraordinary, not to say unparalleled in recent times — offices, too, of the highest importance and responsibility. A member of Congress at the age of twenty-eight, Judge of the United States Court at thirty, Governor at thirty-three, prove him to have early acquired an unusual popularity. Without brilliant talents, or a large accumulation of knowledge, he proved himself equal to every office he was called to fill, and to every emergency which required his action. The secret of his success lay in his industry and close application to the duties of every office confided to him, his promptness and fidelity, his sagacity, his general suavity of manners, and an easy adaptation of himself to every situation: in short, it may with truth be said of him, that he faithfully and acceptably filled all the offices, however varied their duties, to which he was successively called.

For several years previous to his death, he had been troubled with difficulty of breathing and sharp pains in the region of his heart, when making any considerable exertion: this increased the last year, and terminated in his sudden death on the morning of February 11, 1857. The City Council of Portland and the Bar of Cumberland promptly expressed their sense of their own and the public loss, and their sympathy on the occasion; and a general and honorable sentiment went up from the press of Maine, and from our citizens throughout the State, in honor of this faithful public man.

In 1810, Governor Parris married Sarah, eldest daughter of the Rev. Levi Whitman, of Wellfleet, Massachusetts, who, with three daughters and two sons, survives him. Governor Parris always led a regular and exemplary life: punctual at church as he was at his office, he gave the entire influence of his example to the observance of the Sabbath and all moral duties. On his return to Portland from Washington, he became a consistent member of the High Street Congregational Church, took his place as a teacher in its Sunday school, and was observant of all the practical duties of religion. He died at the age of sixty-nine, in the full assurance of a higher and better life.

HIRAM BELCHER. 1812—1857.

Among the most worthy and honored members of the Kennebec, and of the Franklin Bar, after the division of the county in 1828, was Hiram Belcher of Farmington. He was the son of Supply Belcher, who was of Stoughton, Massachusetts: he served in the war of the Revolution, and claimed to be of the Governor Belcher branch of that family. Soon after the close of the war, he came to Augusta in this State, where his son Hiram was born in the winter of 1790. In the next winter, while the son was yet in his mother's arms, the enterprising father sought a still more remote region, and pitched his tent in the wilderness of Sandy River, now Farmington, forty miles from Augusta. This settlement was commenced by Stephen Titcomb of Topsham, who built the first log house there in 1780, and lived to see a rich and productive country rise up under the hand of intelligent labor and persevering industry, until it has become a garden in Maine.

Here Hiram Belcher's early and latter days were spent; the former in honest labor on the farm, which expanded his body and gave him a vigorous and muscular frame; the latter in a higher range of exertion. His father rose to posts of honor in his town, was a magistrate, and represented the town in 1798, 1801, and 1809, was the first town clerk and selectman, and died respected, at the age of eighty-four, in 1836. When young Belcher was old enough to appreciate the value of an education, he was sent to the excellent academy at Hallowell, where he attained the first rank in his class, among competitors over whom victory was a distinction. Among them were William Clark, William C. Wilde, and Dudley Norris. After receiving a good academical education, he entered the office of Wilde and Bond of Hallowell, and devoted himself earnestly and steadily to the pursuit of a profession which was to become the source of his future emolument and honor. He was admitted to the bar in 1812, well prepared to enter on the work of his life.

He immediately established himself in Farmington, where he continued to reside until his death, which took place May 6, 1857, at the age of sixty-seven. That country was very prosperous: its fertile valleys and intervales had invited an energetic class of immigrants, who, by their operations in the forests and the fields, and in trade, had rapidly transformed the whole region from a state of nature to a fruitful, thriving, and well-settled country. Its business gave encouragement to numerous traders, and the lawyers partook of the general prosperity. At that time, there were but two lawyers besides himself in all that part of Kennebec County which now constitutes the county of Franklin: these were Nathan Cutler and Elnathan Pope. There had been in the town for about six years, a lawyer named Zachariah Soule, a man of fine promise and brilliant wit: he was from Halifax in Plymouth County, a graduate of Brown University in the class of 1799: he tried his fortune first at Paris, then at Farmington, where he settled in 1806; but his habits became very dissolute, and he returned to Massachusetts, in 1812, a wreck, and subsequently died in a poor-house. Of Mr. Cutler we have before spoken: Mr. Pope was from Freetown, Massachusetts. He opened an office in Farmington in 1809, where he continued in the practice until 1828, when he moved to New Sharon. About 1840, he became a preacher and farmer, and died in 1861, aged eighty years. He was honorable and respected in his profession, of sound judgment and good common sense.

Into this field Mr. Belcher entered with the ardor of youth, and with the confidence of well-cultivated powers. He was a zealous federalist, while Mr. Cutler espoused the democratic side, and this had some influence on the division of business, as parties at that time ran high: both the town and county were democratic by a small majority. Mr. Belcher soon took a prominent position at the bar; his ability and integrity carried him steadily forward; there was no cessation to his onward progress; he was a good lawyer, a successful advocate, and above and beyond all, an honest man. He was faithful and true to his clients, and well-grounded in the solid learning of his profession: he never stooped to any doubtful, or dishonest, or disreputable course, to win a cause or to gain or gratify a client. A friend who knew him well through his whole life, thus speaks of him: "He was no time-server nor demagogue, watching the weather-cock; but in his public and private life, he formed his opinions with an honest mind, and carried out his convictions with a courageous independence and unwavering fidelity. He made no pretensions; but secured without artifice or profession, the respect and friendship of all, by his solid qualities and unquestioned integrity." He had a quick apprehension of the vain, assuming, and absurd in men, which he had a happy faculty of showing up by his keen and quiet wit, of which many instances occur to the memory of his friends. The venerable William Allen of Norridgewock, from whom we derive these facts, adds, "Happy in his domestic life, he lived among his neighbors and friends beloved for his Christian character and his social virtues, doing his duty as a citizen in all the relations of life."

To this, we may add the testimony of Frederic Allen of Gardiner, whose practice with him at the bar enabled him to speak of his legal standing. In his brief notice in the sixth volume of the Maine Historical Collections, he says, "He possessed talents far above mediocrity. He was frequently employed as an advocate, and was not an unsuccessful one. He had an excellent and well cultivated mind, and much benevolence of disposition. He was remarkable for his amusing and quiet sallies of wit and dry humor, occasionally interspersed in his forensic discussions, as well as his private intercourse. He was a man of large stature, in height over six feet, rather thin and spare of flesh, and not very compactly formed."

Mr. Belcher held the office of town clerk of Farmington from 1814 to 1819, and represented the town in the Legislatures of 1822, 1829, 1832: in 1838 and 1839, he was a member of the Senate of Maine. In 1846, he was chosen a representative in the Thirtieth Congress, and served the two years, 1847 to 1849, during the last half of President Polk's administration. Mr. Belcher supported the measures of the whigs, and of the seven representatives and two senators from Maine, he was the solitary whig member of the whole delegation in both houses of Congress. During this term, the Mexican war was closed by a treaty which largely increased the territory of the United States, and opened new issues for party strife. It is hardly necessary to say that Mr. Belcher was opposed to the Mexican War and an increase of territory, and all schemes whose tendency was to enlarge the area of slavery, of which he was an earnest opponent. Mr. Belcher would probably have been re-elected had not his health failed, which induced him to withdraw from active duty. He had received his son Hannibal, who was admitted to the bar in 1839, into partnership with him, who now took the principal charge of the business of the firm.

Mr. Belcher, after a life of great purity, usefulness, and honor, died on the sixth of May, 1857, at the age of sixty-seven. He married a niece of Judge Daniel Cony of Augusta, by whom he had five children: Hannibal, an only son, and four daughters; viz., Charlotte, who died young; Abigail, married to John L. Cutler, son of Nathan Cutler of Farmington, who died in 1845; Susan, wife of Joseph Fairbanks; and Mehitabel, wife of Mr. Abbott, the accomplished principal of the excellent school at Farmington. The memory of Mr. Belcher is held in fresh regard and consideration by his numerous friends in the town and county in which his useful life was passed.

CHAPTER XX.

CHARLES S. DAVEIS — CHARLES SHAW — LUTHER FITCH — WILLIAM P. PREBLE — SAMUEL E. SMITH — ETHER SHEPLEY — PELEG SPRAGUE — ASHUR WARE.

CHARLES STEWART DAVEIS. 1810—

Among the best read and most highly cultivated lawyers in Maine, we may justly rank the gentleman whose name we have placed at the head of this article. For many years, he was a leader in the admiralty and equity practice of the United States courts, and with the earliest who labored to introduce the equity system, as it now exists, into the courts of our State.

Mr. Daveis was born in Portland, May 10, 1788. His father, Captain Ebenezer Davis, was an officer in the army of the Revolution, and became a member of the Society of Cincinnati: he was a native of Haverhill, Massachusetts, and came to Portland on the close of the war, where he died in 1799, leaving but this one son. He was a large and well-proportioned man, with a military air, and the easy manners which the officers of the army either possessed or acquired in the profession. His mother was Mehitabel Griffin, a daughter of Deacon Ebenezer Griffin of Bradford, Massachusetts, whose grandmother was the second child of Richard Hazen, a descendant of Edward Hazen, the first American ancestor of the name, who came from England and settled at Rowley, Massachusetts, as early as 1650. Hazen's son Richard married Mary Peabody of Boxford, whose daughter Priscilla was the great-grandmother of the subject of our notice, by her marriage with Benjamin Kimball of Bradford; and thus he bears the blood of Hazen, Peabody, Kimball, Griffin, and Daveis, flowing through honored channels from the foundations of the country,— *ab urbe condita.*

Mr. Daveis received the rudiments of his education at the common schools in Portland; but in 1802 he was sent to the Phillips Academy at Andover, of which Mark Newman was then, and many years after, the accomplished preceptor, and John Abbot the assistant: Mr. Abbot being afterwards, during the residence of Mr. Daveis, translated to a professorship at Bowdoin, was succeeded by Samuel Greele, Harvard College, 1802, who has lately died. Mr. Daveis was destined for the twin academy at Exeter; but there being no vacancy in that celebrated institution, he proceeded to Andover.

In 1803, he became a member of Bowdoin College, in the second class which had entered that institution. His class consisted of but two others besides himself, who were Robert Means from Westbrook, and Seth Storer, then of Saco and now of Scarborough. The first, or prior class, which entered in 1802, graduated seven, only one of whom, Mr. O'Brien of Brunswick, now survives. The college was then under the instruction of the learned and excellent Dr. McKeen, who had been called from his pastorate in Beverly to take charge of the infant institution; and John Abbot as Professor of Languages and Librarian. But while Mr. Daveis was passing through his *curriculum*, and as new classes entered, numbering six in 1804, five in 1805, and twelve in

1806, the corps of instruction was enlarged by the accession of very able men, who afterwards occupied prominent places in the community: in 1804 came Samuel Willard, subsequently the venerated pastor of the church in Deerfield; Parker Cleaveland, *clarum et venerabile nomen*, as Professor of Mathematics, subsequently of Chemistry; and Nathan Parker, the respected and beloved pastor of the first church in Portsmouth, New Hampshire. These instructors, as well as Professor Abbot, were all graduates of Harvard. President McKeen received his education at Dartmouth, the college of his native State. But this excellent guide, teacher, and friend did not live to preside at the graduation of this second class: his sudden death, a short time previous to the commencement of 1807, cast a gloom over the halls of the college and the community, where his name was greatly venerated and beloved.

Mr. Daveis faithfully improved his time and opportunities at Brunswick, and always, in after life, fondly cherished the kind and constant attentions of the President, Professor Cleaveland, and Tutor Willard, in directing his studies and moulding his character. In the exercises of Commencement, each of the three scholars had two parts,—Storer the Latin salutatory, and a forensic with Means; Means also had an English oration; Daveis delivered a *poem* on "Tradition," and the valedictory oration.

He left college well furnished with the apparatus for enlarged and useful application, and immediately entered the office of Nicholas Emery, who had recently removed to Portland from Parsonsfield, with a high reputation as a lawyer and advocate. Here he pursued his legal, with the same assiduity that he had his literary studies. Yet he didn ot deny himself to the muses, nor cease to yield to the blandishments which literature lends to the graver lessons of the law. In his recreations from Coke and Blackstone, he wrote poetry and poetical prose; and what talented young man ever passed through the formative processes of life without wooing the muses, and getting up poetry that has made him blush in after years to find in print or the albums of friends? Mr. Daveis was a frequent contributor to the "old Portland Gazette," both in the grave and serio-comic style; while the staple of his time was devoted to his preparation for the bar. It was during this period of preparation for the stern realities of life that he laid the foundation of a literary fame which never forsook him. This was in an oration delivered before a literary society of Bowdoin College. The subject was Greek Literature. Dr. Jenks, now the venerable antiquary of Boston, but who was then a minister in Bath, and connected with the college, was so much pleased with the performance that he procured its publication in the "Monthly Anthology," then the leading literary periodical in the country. It appeared in the June, July, and August numbers of that review. It was brilliant and classical, rather overloaded with classical allusions and illustrations. The editor of the Anthology thus introduces the article: "The following communication upon Greek Literature we have received from the District of Maine, a part of the country which, in our local pride, we have supposed to be nearer Bœotia than our own; but after perusing this charming rhapsody, we were forced to suspect, that in obedience to the call of the motto, *Iomen eis Athenas*, the young author of this piece would have less ground to traverse than some of us who fancy that we live within sight of Athens." A few brief extracts from the address must suffice. It thus commences:

"In the evening the Grecian exiles used to sing, 'Let *us* return to Athens.' Let *us* return to Athens this evening, for *we* are exiled from Greece by two great seas, and two thousand years."

"It is possible that in Greece we shall find a great many

memorials of Greece. We shall be able to discover strong traits of her ancient genius, and some remains of her former greatness."

"What if we first search the modern Greeks for some token of their descent? It will take but a moment, and they are living monuments. It will then be in our power to reply to them, who taunt us, as the Corinthians taunted Themistocles, with the ruins of Athens, that though Athens is destroyed, there are Athenians alive."

"It is hard to discover the son of a Greek in the slave of a Turk. And there is a long time to redeem since the taking of Athens! Yet we are willing, like Cæsar, to spare the living Greeks for the sake of the dead."

Mr. Daveis took his Master's degree in 1810, on which occasion he delivered an oration on "the Genius of our Political Liberties," of which the Portland paper thus spoke: "The oration by Daveis happily and novelly blended the exuberant fancy of the poet with the deep research of the statesman and lawyer."

Thus trained and furnished, with a reputation going before, Mr. Daveis was admitted to the bar in 1810. He commenced practice in his native town, which has ever been the scene of his labors, his triumphs, and his trials. He devoted himself to study and the duties of his profession. Not contented, as too many young lawyers are, with the preliminary studies and admission to the bar, he made continual additions to his stores of legal knowledge and general literature.

Mr. Daveis was among the first to engage in equity practice in the State. The system was unpopular both on the bench and at the bar. The old lawyers were prejudiced against it, principally, perhaps, because they were unacquainted with its forms and principles: they had been brought up in the common law practice, with which they were familiar, had found it to work well with them, and they desired no change: they were afraid of the large discretionary power which was supposed to belong to equity jurisdiction. There was no equity practice in the courts of Massachusetts, prior to the separation, except in cases of mortgage; and bills of equity under them were rare. The statute of 1817 gave jurisdiction to the Supreme Court in cases of trusts arising under deeds, wills, and the settlement of estates. This power was adopted by the statute of Maine in 1821, to which was added, "and all cases of contract in writing, where a party claims the specific performance of the same, and in which there may not be a plain, adequate, and complete remedy at law."

As late as 1821, 17th Massachusetts Reports, the court say that they had no jurisdiction in bills of discovery, previous to the statute of 1817, and by that statute they had jurisdiction of trusts created by deed or will. They also say in the same case, that the Supreme Court has no jurisdiction in equity, except such as has been given by statute. The same court also decided as late as 1839, 22d Pickering, that no equity jurisdiction to reform or rectify contracts had been conferred upon the court. The practice in equity worked very slowly: I think no bills in equity were commenced in Massachusetts before the separation except on mortgage: in 1823, equity jurisdiction was given to the Supreme Court of that State in cases of copartnership and tenants in common, and in 1827, it was extended to nuisances, &c. Maine followed Massachusetts in these improvements. How slow the progress was, may be seen by reference to Greenleaf's nine volumes of reports, where, in the space of twelve years, we find but five or six cases arising under the equity powers of the court, aside from mortgages and the relief in chancery against penalties and forfeitures, a power which has always existed in the court. In the Circuit Court of the United States, that jurisdiction had long been exercised, and was encouraged by Judge Story, who was partial to the system.

Into this practice and that of the admiralty court, Mr. Daveis introduced himself, and became an adept, which extended his business and his reputation so much, as that his services were eagerly sought by those who were unfortunate enough to desire the aid of the law and the courts in their emergencies. He was a very close student of law and equity, and probably no person in the State was more familiar with the science in equity and admiralty and the forms of practice in those courts, than he was, until that department of jurisprudence had attained sufficient importance to attract other lawyers to its study. He brought to the discussion of his causes all the learning of the books, and his arguments were amply freighted with authority and precedent. He presented his causes to the jury and the court with great minuteness of detail, leaving nothing to conjecture or imagination, and great fullness of illustration. If there was fault in his arguments, it was in their overfullness and minuteness, overloaded, indeed, with illustration and citation. He was not, therefore, an eloquent advocate in the popular sense, for his object was to convince, rather than persuade. In lighter efforts and occasional speeches outside of the forum, he displayed amplitude of resources, and variety and beauty of illustration from classical literature; and these were also abundantly displayed in conversation, for which he had great readiness and facility. His playful wit was often summoned to the amusement of the bar in their hours of recreation. It was on one of these occasions that he penned the following *jeu d'esprit*. Mr. Longfellow, when opposed by a remark or statement from the court, adverse to the position he was arguing, would attempt to parry its force, by admitting the principle as stated by the court, and saying, "But, your Honors, there is this distinction between the case you state and the one before us." This often occasioned a laugh at the bar, and once when a dull argument was going on by a prosy member, the idlers busied themselves writing epitaphs on one another. Mr. Daveis, prompt on such occasions, thus hit Mr. Longfellow's peculiarity:

"Here repose
The mortal remains of Stephen Longfellow;
born ——, died ——.
But there is this distinction,
That such a man never dies."

For many years, Mr. Daveis was a most skillful and successful practitioner in the admiralty and equity courts, where he came in competition with the best lawyers and advocates at the Cumberland Bar, as Whitman, Longfellow, Orr, Greenleaf, Fessenden, and others, as well as several strong men from bars of other counties and States. Nor was his practice confined to these departments of the law: he was no less learned in the principles of the common law. His practice in this branch was very respectable, as frequent recurrence of his name in our early reports sufficiently prove. For the ability which he manifested, we need only to refer to the reports, and especially to the exhaustive argument submitted by him in the case of Fosdick v. Gooding and al, in the first volume of Greenleaf's Reports, on the subject of Dower, in which he was opposed by Mr. Whitman, afterwards chief justice. Probably no argument in the volumes of Greenleaf shows more labored research into the fundamental principles and authorities than this.

Mr. Daveis has lived to see the equity system become part of our code, cultivated as a science by our lawyers, and become a favorite system for exposing frauds, correcting mistakes and reaching the conscience, where remedies at common law would fail. He had the aid, the friendship, and sympathy of Judge Story, who had a high opinion of his sagacity and learning.

Mr. Daveis was not so much absorbed by his professional pursuits as not to indulge in the genial recreations of literature. He kept up fully with the rapid progress which literature was making among us, and his associations with cultivated persons in different parts of the country gave tone and freshness to his mind. He was a copious writer: our newspapers and periodicals attest the vigor of his pen, and the sprightliness of his style. He was a frequent contributor to the public journals, and was often called upon for occasional addresses. Among these, was an address before the Portland Benevolent Society in 1813, of which he has for many years been one of the managers: in 1825, he delivered a long, able, and interesting historical discourse at Fryeburg, to commemorate the centennial anniversary of Lovewell's battle with the Indians, which was published. In 1826, he was selected to pronounce the funeral oration on Adams and Jefferson, whose death taking place on the same day, July 4th, 1826, produced a profound sensation throughout the country: this also was published. In 1839, he delivered a Latin address at Brunswick on the inauguration of Dr. Woods as President of Bowdoin College. Some years after, he prepared a long and very able historical discourse at the dedication of the new chapel at the college, in which he embodied many interesting facts and incidents relating to the origin, progress, and history of the institution. This was read by the Rev. Mr. Abbot, the health of Mr. Daveis not permitting him to deliver it himself, as part of the services of dedication. This occurred in September, 1854. About the same time, he prepared a biography of Governor Gilman of New Hampshire, in the form of an address, delivered at Exeter, which is a part of the transactions of the Historical Society of that State, which the subject of the memoir long adorned by his life and counsels. In 1845, Mr. Daveis's good friend, Judge Story, ended his life and usefulness on earth, at the age of sixty-six, deeply and universally lamented. Of this learned judge, a writer in the Law Reporter of October, 1845, says, "A greater than Sir Samuel Romilly has fallen in the midst of us. The death of Mr. Justice Story will create a void in the judiciary, in the professor's chair, and in the social literary circle, which no living man can fill." The bars of several counties and States honored the memory of this distinguished judge by grateful tributes. In Cumberland County, the resolutions were drawn up by Mr. Daveis, and presented at a meeting of the bar of the Circuit Court of the United States, at which Mr. Longfellow presided. They were full of sympathy, grateful acknowledgment, and classical purity. We will present in one of them a single specimen. "We rejoice that it was eminently his fortune to carry out so near to its natural close, a career rarely equalled in the judicial life of a single individual, rewarded by so many results, and crowned with such celebrity. The sun knoweth his going down. And although painful and unexpected, we may not feel it to be otherwise than a final harmonious felicity, in keeping with his signal lot, that he should have breathed his last before he retired from the bench. *Felix non vitæ tantum claritate, sed etiam opportunitate mortis.*" To the resolutions, Judge Ware made an elegant and feeling reply.

In 1855, Mr. Daveis was appointed by the mayor and aldermen of Portland on a large committee, to investigate the causes of a serious riot which occurred in Portland in June of that year, and which resulted in the death of John Robbins, one of the rioters. It grew out of the enforcement of the liquor law by Mayor Dow. The committee was engaged several days in this delicate duty, and their report was published in a pamphlet of fifty pages. Mr. Daveis, in a very elaborate article published in the Law Reporter, vol. 18, p. 361, reviewed in a clear and able manner, not only the pamphlet, but the whole subject, in all its bearings of morals, philosophy, and law. In 1859, Mr. Daveis prepared the article on the Society of Cincinnati, which occupies several columns of the American Encyclopedia, and presents in a clear and concise form, and in the best manner of Mr. Daveis, a history of this renowned institution, of which he is a member, as successor of his father, and president of the Massachusetts branch. These are some of the literary labors for which the public are indebted to the industry of this learned gentleman. Nor does this comprise the whole of their obligation to him, for in his many-sided character and pursuits, he did not shun politics,— a favorite field of American lawyers and scholars.

He early engaged with ardor in the discussions relating to our northeastern boundary in the conflict with the British government, and pursued the investigation with the skill and research of a lawyer, and presented the results in clear and able arguments. In 1827, Mr. Daveis was appointed by Governor Lincoln, under a resolve of the Legislature, agent of the State to inquire into facts relating to aggressions upon the rights of the State and individual citizens, by inhabitants of the Province of New Brunswick. In pursuance of this commission, he proceeded to New Brunswick in 1827, and having attended to the arduous duties assigned him, embodied the result of his inquiries in a report to the Executive which occupies twenty-five octavo pages in the documents of the Legislature. In consequence of his familiarity with the subject, and the useful information he had acquired in examining this perplexing question, he was sent, in 1829, with dispatches from the United States to

Judge Preble, who then represented the government at the Hague, the king of Holland having been appointed arbiter in the dispute between the two countries on that subject. This gave Mr. Daveis a favorable opportunity to enlarge the sphere of his observation by foreign travel. In 1838, the services of Mr. Daveis were again invoked, and he was appointed a special agent "to co-operate with our delegation in forwarding the views of the Legislature and the people, and in urging our claims and our determination upon the attention of the government." Of the manner in which this mission was conducted, Governor Kent's message will tell. It thus speaks: "Mr. Daveis immediately repaired to Washington, and performed the duties required with great zeal, discretion, and ability, and to my entire satisfaction, with equal honor to himself, and benefit to the cause." In 1841, Mr. Daveis was a senator from Cumberland in the State Legislature, and was appointed chairman of a joint select committee upon the northeastern boundary. In this capacity, he submitted a report on the thirtieth of March, which occupies fifty-five octavo pages in the printed copy of the resolves of that year. It is a clear, calm, thorough, historical and legal argument in support of the justice of the claim of Maine to the whole of the territory under the just and fair construction of the treaty of 1783, and embraces a justification of the conduct of the State in vindicating her lawful rights against the hostile acts of the people of New Brunswick.

The merits of Mr. Daveis in the various capacities in which we have presented him, have not passed unnoticed by an observant and appreciating community. In 1828, he was chosen a member of the Maine Historical Society, and more recently, an honorary member of the Massachusetts Historical Society. In 1814, he was chosen a member of the Phi-Beta-Kappa Society of Harvard College, the privileges of the society not having then been extended to Bowdoin. In 1836, he was appointed one of the trustees of Bowdoin College, having been several years prior, one of the overseers, and has served the institution which nourished him, with most devoted assiduity and affection: the honor she conferred upon him in 1844, of the degree of Doctor of Laws, was no less due to him for his literary and scientific position in the domain of learning, than his ardent love for his literary mother. He has stood by her in season and out of season, joying in her prosperity and sorrowing in her trials, for more than half a century. He has felt with her, and labored for her, during the whole period of her existence — now sixty years.

We have to look at Mr. Daveis in one phase more before we take leave of him, and that is in his interior life — his life of life. He had got well under way in business; the war of 1812, which had prostrated Portland, was fully over, and the star of peace was shining through the broken clouds, when he united himself to the excellent and lovely woman who became his dear and cherished companion for nearly forty-five years that she remained by his side. He was married in June, 1815, to Elizabeth, a daughter of Governor Gilman of New Hampshire, whose three other daughters were married to Nicholas Emery, the Rev. Dr. Nichols of Portland, and Dr. John G. Cogswell, late of the Astor Library — all highly distinguished in their several walks in life. Their wives, coming from a fine ancestral stock, the aristocracy of New Hampshire, — and the genuine republicanism, too, — were distinguished for their refinement, their purity and elevation of character, and the highest type of womanly virtues. They are all dead; Mrs. Cogswell being the first, and Mrs. Daveis the last to leave the earth — her lamented death having taken place April 3d, 1860. Four children survived her, two sons and two daughters, all in prosperous circumstances in life, the sons educated, one to medicine, the other to the law. Mr. Daveis, thus left alone, with a system enfeebled by an attack of paralysis, pursues his solitary way, looking upward and onward, with the hope and trust which are a perpetual benediction to the human soul. This attack occurred in 1851, and impaired the use of his limbs on the right side, and affected his speech. He did not sufficiently recover to engage again in the duties of his profession; but he was not disabled from enjoying society: the genial play of his mind continued to interest and gratify his friends. His habit of writing, too, was a source of enjoyment: he not only kept up a copious correspondence, but, as will be perceived by our previous statements, some of his best and most matured articles were written after his bodily prostration. Our best wishes attend this accomplished gentleman through the remainder of his declining years, which, we trust, in the midst of his genial family of children and grandchildren, will cheerfully and calmly pass on, until the leaves fall gently, at last, from the ripened stock.

CHARLES SHAW. 1810—1828.

John H. Sheppard of Boston, who long practiced in Lincoln County, having been a student of Judge Wilde and Thomas Bond of the Kennebec Bar, and who has furnished me many interesting materials for the legal antiquities of the Lincoln Bar, has contributed the essential portions of the following tribute to the accomplished Shaw. He says:

One gentleman, once a member of the Lincoln Bar, who left us and went South, you do not mention. If he comes within the circle of deceased Maine lawyers of some note, perhaps an account of him may not be superfluous. I refer to Charles Shaw, once more known as a ripe scholar and fine writer than as a lawyer.

Charles Shaw was born in Bath, February 20, 1782, the son of Major Joshua Shaw, a respectable merchant of that town, who was born in Braintree or Weymouth, Massachusetts, in 1755, and came to Bath with his father, Elisha Shaw, a young man. After being thrice married, and having by his three wives a large family of children, he died at Phippsburg, in 1809. One of his sons was Dr. Moses Shaw, a physician, an active politician, and Collector of Wiscasset under the administration of President Harrison: he died in Wiscasset, in 1847.

Charles, the oldest son, was educated at Harvard College, and took his first degree in 1805, having the distinction of the salutatory oration, which is the second assignment in order of scholarship in that college. He afterwards studied law with Nathaniel Coffin at Bath, and then opened an office in Jefferson, about 1810 or '11, an obscure village at the head of Damariscotta Pond, where there were some mills — then thought to be the *Ultima Thule* of civilization. Mr. Shaw was an elegant *belle-lettre* scholar, a man of refined taste, and a practical master of music; but though married, he found his lot dreary enough in this hamlet of woods, waters, and grog-shops,— among lumberers and mill-men,— where the piano of his beautiful wife astonished, but never could tame the rough natures around him. Yet the location was a hot-bed of suits,— with Nat. Bryant, a noted magnate of Nobleboro', for his client,— and would have been eligible if he could only have got his pay.

A few years he struggled and suffered in this situation, and then removed to Montgomery, in Alabama, where he was appointed a judge of one of their courts, and died in 1828. I knew him well: he was one of the best Latin scholars I ever saw, and was among the very few who could scan the odes of Horace, and reduce their prosody to sweet and melodious cadences of the voice. He wrote in college, an elegant elegiac piece or ode on the death of President Willard, for which he received the *triple mark* of Professor Pearson: it was published and much admired. He wrote a book called, "An Historical Description of Boston," which was published in 1817; and, in its day, was much valued both for its style and matter. He was a man of great reading and pleasing manners; too modest to make his merit known at the bar, and too refined to enter the arena of mental gymnastics in a court of law; but his talents and education were of a high order. He was a member of the Antiquarian Society of Worcester.

LUTHER FITCH. 1810—

The Fitches, Ffytche, as the name was spelled, in at least one branch of the family in England, came to this country from the county of Essex, England. There were several branches in that county, whose coats of arms were similar, with slight variations. They all bore on the shield a leopard or a leopard's head, and the crest was a leopard's head, *or*, or *cabossed* (full-faced) *or*.

Two brothers, Thomas and James, established themselves in Connecticut in 1638, and were the ancestors of a numerous race in that State. Others of the name came to Massachusetts as early as 1635: among these, was Zechary or Zechariah, of Reading, who was made freeman September 7, 1638. He had a large family, seven sons and one daughter, whose names are mentioned: among these was Zechary, who was born March 6, 1647. From this stock, descended the subject of our memoir, whose father and grandfather both bore the name of Zechariah. His father was born in Bedford, formerly a part of Billerica, in 1732, and moved in early life into Groton. He, with his brother William, were members of the celebrated corps of Rangers, under

J.H.Bufford's Lith. Boston.

Luther Fitch

At the age of 75.

Major Rogers in the French War, and made successful raids on the frontier, in which William lost his life. Zechariah rose in his military service to the rank of captain. In 1767, he married for his third wife Sybil Lakin, a descendant of Sergeant Lakin, one of the original proprietors of Groton. By his three wives, he had a large family of sons and daughters, several of whom migrated to Maine in the early part of this century, or near the close of the last, and became enterprising and useful citizens. By his fourth wife, whom he married at the age of seventy-five, he had no children. He died in 1820, in the eighty-eighth year of his age. His son Luther, the subject of the present notice, was born in Groton, Massachusetts, January 28, 1783, and was the youngest son of his third wife. Having received his preliminary education in the good schools of his native town, and especially at the Groton Academy, of which Mr. Richardson, afterwards chief justice of New Hampshire, was the preceptor, he entered Dartmouth College, from which he took his degree in 1807. His class contained men who afterwards became distinguished in life, — Joseph Bell, LL. D.; Timothy Farrar, treasurer and librarian of the college; Col. Thayer, formerly chief of the Military Academy at West Point; and the learned George Ticknor of Boston. Dartmouth has furnished many eminent lawyers to the profession in Maine: we need only mention Wilde, Salmon Chase, Dana, Emery, McGaw, Fessenden, Parris, Orr, Bradley, Herbert, and Shepley. Mr. Fitch commenced the study of his profession with Dudley Chase, brother of the honored Salmon Chase of Portland, and the late Bishop Chase of Illinois. Mr. Chase lived in Orange County, Vermont, was ten years senator in Congress, and chief justice of the Supreme Court of his State. Mr. Fitch continued with him eight months, and then completed his term of study in the office of Dana and Richardson in Groton, and was admitted to the bar of Middlesex in 1810.

Having friends and relatives in the county of Cumberland, he came immediately to Westbrook, then a part of Falmouth, but incorporated in 1814, and opened an office in the village of Saccarappa. This was then a very flourishing place, lying on the Presumpscot River, about half way between its mouth in Casco Bay, and its large and unfailing reservoir in Sebago Pond. From the first settlement of the country, the village and the falls of the river over which it spreads, have been improved for manufacturing purposes; first, in all the processes of converting the abundant and beautiful growth which covered the surrounding country, into various descriptions of lumber, and afterwards, in manufacturing the more valuable fabrics of cotton, and wool, and paper. It was an admirable station for a lawyer, for in such a population, especially devoted to the irregular operations of lumbering and milling, the habits of the people, particularly in that period, were apt to be wild and disorderly, and led to litigation, and the final arbitrament of the courts. Saccarappa was no exception to the rule. Mr. Fitch was, at the time he commenced practice, the only lawyer there. He succeeded Peter Thacher, a son of the Rev. Josiah Thacher of Gorham, who studied his profession with William Symmes, was admitted to practice in 1804, and opened an office in Saccarappa. He remained there about five years, when he returned to Gorham, leaving the field entirely open to the new comer.

Mr. Fitch was well trained, thoroughly furnished, of ripe age and matured powers, and well calculated to enter upon the rugged duties which the practice, in such a community, required. He was intelligent; he was persevering and resolute; and he steadily pursued his practice, commanding the business of the village and its vicinity, and drawing towards him from the interior parts of the country, business relating to lumbering operations; for the practice of which, he had, by study and experience, acquired much skill. He had well studied the peculiarities of this branch of business, and had the tact effectively to apply his knowledge. There are good real estate lawyers, and there are good commercial lawyers: we have given striking examples in the foregoing sketches, of eminent and successful practitioners in these important branches; as Bridge, Wilde, and Williams in real estate, and Whitman, Greenleaf, Longfellow, and Hubbard as commercial lawyers. The law regulating the cutting, hauling, driving, and sawing of timber is quite different from either of the others, and trains another class of minds; and it is especially pursued by lawyers living by the side of our water-falls, where this kind of business centers. Among lawyers thus situated and disciplined, were Mellen from the Saco, Orr from the Androscoggin, and Boutelle from the Kennebec. In this line of practice, Mr. Fitch, living in the midst of a very busy and thrifty lumbering population on the Presumpscot, was very successful, and accumulated property, which was considerably increased by a fortunate marriage and prudent management. He was not an eloquent advocate, but he was a shrewd, discriminating lawyer, comprehending the strong points of his own causes and the weak ones of his opponent, and he pressed both with vigor and perseverance during the fifteen years that he was in the practice.

In 1820, on the organization of the new State, he was appointed attorney for the county, by Governor King; and in 1825, the Municipal Court for Portland, the first of the kind introduced into our State, having been established, he was appointed the first judge. By a special provision in the law, constituting this tribunal, "The judge shall not, in any case, act as counsellor or attorney in any court:" he was thus, by the acceptance of this office, withdrawn from the practice. He soon after transferred his residence from

Westbrook to Portland, which was ever after to be the scene of his labors.

As a judge, Mr. Fitch was faithful, strictly scrupulous and conscientious; his decisions were well considered, sound, and approved; he listened attentively and calmly to evidence, patiently investigated the facts, and deliberately arrived at conclusions, generally correct and satisfactory. His court had, besides its civil matters cognizable by justices of the peace, jurisdiction also in the worst and most vexatious cases on the criminal side,—all simple larcenies under twenty dollars, all offenses against the by-laws of the city, complaints for keeping houses of ill-fame, riots, drunkenness, &c.,—which brought before him the lowest characters in the community, with whose disorders and irregularities he had often very sharp contention. The manner in which he discharged the disagreeable duties of this responsible office, cannot be better proved than by the fact that he held it by successive appointments, through all changes of administration, for a period of twenty-nine years, to 1854, at which time he had arrived at the age of seventy-one years. Mr Williamson, the historian, in a manuscript note to a list of lawyers prepared by him, says, "Luther Fitch was a good lawyer, and a worthy, well-esteemed man; was city judge of Portland, and filled the office to his own credit and the public satisfaction." The remark we know to be true, for we had occasion to appear in his court often during the whole term of his official life, and can add, that he was an honest and impartial judge, and that his uniform endeavor was, in every cause, to render a just and impartial judgment.

Judge Fitch married Almira Titcomb, June 23, 1816. She was a daughter of Andrew Phillips Titcomb, the oldest son of Deacon Benjamin Titcomb, an old and most respected citizen of Portland, who died October 15, 1798. Her

Wm P. Preble

mother was Mary Dole, a daughter of Daniel Dole, also a citizen of Portland, whose wife, as also Benjamin Titcomb's, was a daughter of Moses Pearson, the first sheriff of Cumberland County. They all, Pearson, Titcomb, and Dole, immigrated to that part of Falmouth which is now Portland, many years before the Revolution, from Newbury, Massachusetts. Judge Fitch and his wife, and their eight children, five daughters and three sons, are all living. The eldest daughter married Dr. Josiah Blake of Harrison; another, Samuel F. Perley of Naples; a third, Henry E. Perley; and the youngest, Henry Willis, both of Portland: one daughter is unmarried. Of the three sons, one is a physician in California, another a surgeon in the army.

WILLIAM PITT PREBLE. 1811—1857.

The first of the Preble family in Maine, and the ancestor of all of the name in the State, was Abraham Preble, who came to Scituate in Massachusetts, prior to 1637, from England, and was one of the first settlers of that town. He was in this State as early as 1642, in which year he purchased of Edward Godfrey, the agent of Gorges, a tract of land in Agamenticus, now York, and continued to reside in that town until his death, which took place in 1663. He sustained during his residence in Maine, some of the most considerable and responsible offices in the Province: in 1645, he was one of the councilors of Sir Ferdinando Gorges, and continued to hold the office as long as the government of that proprietor was maintained. He was a member of the General Court of the Province; one of the commissioners to hold county courts; treasurer sometime; and the chief military officer of the Province. His descendants have been distinguished in our history since that time: his son Benjamin filled many important offices; and his great-grandson, Brigadier-General Preble of Portland, was not only conspicuous for half a century in our annals as a military officer and magistrate, but was the father of the renowned Commodore Edward Preble, and also of Ebenezer and Henry, distinguished merchants, and Enoch, an able shipmaster.

Judge Preble, the subject of our present notice, was in the same degree of descent from the common ancestor as Commodore Preble, — the fifth or great-great-grandson, — his grandfather, Samuel, being the son of the second Abraham. His father, Esaias, was a whig of the Revolution, a captain in the service, and a member of the convention of Massachusetts to ratify the Constitution: he voted against it. Judge Preble was born in that part of the town of York which is called Scotland Parish, from its being settled principally by Scotch people, November 27, 1783. He was fitted for college by the Rev. Rosewell Messinger of York, for many years the blind preacher; and graduated at Harvard in 1806, in a very distinguished class, — containing such names as Dr. Bigelow of Boston; Dr. Burroughs of Portsmouth; Dr. Cogswell of the Astor Library; Alexander H. Everett; Prof. Oliver; and Ebenezer Everett of our own State. Among these scholars, Mr. Preble took high rank, especially in the mathematics, — which led, in 1809, to his appointment as tutor in that branch at Harvard, — successor to the late Dr. Ichabod Nichols. This situation he retained for two years, associating in the duty of instruction and the intercourse of literary fellowship with Professor Farrar, Professor McKeen, Professor Willard, and the accomplished scholars, Tutors Frisbie and Ware.

Mr. Preble having pursued the study of law, partly in the office of Benjamin Hasey in Topsham, and partly in that of Mr. Orr in Brunswick, commenced practice, first in York, whence, in a short time, he moved to Alfred, and was there appointed, in 1811, County Attorney for York. In 1813, he moved to Saco: in 1814, he received from President Madison the appointment of United States Attorney for the district, as successor to Silas Lee, who died in that year. In 1818, he moved to Portland, which ever after continued to be his place of residence. He entered the profession with a clear, discriminating mind, and high logical powers, and consequently made rapid progress to its higher eminences. He had a faculty of presenting his cases both to the jury and the court, in a concise and perspicuous style, which left no doubt on their minds as to his meaning: in this respect, he caught the manner of his teacher, Mr. Orr, whom he resembled in his mode of argument. He aimed to convince the judgment, rather than by persuasive eloquence to seduce the passions. In a few years, he rose to the front rank of the profession in Maine, and became a competitor with the distinguished men who then honored the bars of the several counties,—Dane, Mellen, Whitman, Holmes, Longfellow, Wilde, Allen, Greenleaf, Fessenden, Crosby, McGaw, and many others. And so prominent had he become, that on the separation of the State, in 1820, from Massachusetts, he was selected, although only nine years at the bar, as one of the three judges of the highest judicial tribunal of the new State.

Judge Preble continued on the bench but eight years. The decisions of the court of which he was a member, are contained in the first five volumes of Greenleaf's Reports. The majority of the opinions were drawn up by Chief Justice Mellen: those which appear in the name of Judge Preble exhibit the soundness of argument and perspicuity of statement which characterize all Judge Preble's written communications. He was undoubtedly a learned, clear-minded judge: his defects on the bench were those of the temper: he was hasty and irritable, which rendered him impatient occasionally, and disturbed the calmness and equanimity of mind which are high qualities in the judicial office. The Supreme Court of Maine was never more able than during the eight years in which Judge Preble was a member of it, with Chief Justice Mellen at its head. Its decisions were learned, and commanded the respect of judicial tribunals in all parts of the country.

Judge Preble retired from this honorable position in 1828 to enter upon a diplomatic service. The state of the country was alarming from the agitation of the northeastern boundary question: the governments had agreed to submit the controversy to the arbitration of the King of Holland, and Judge Preble was associated with Mr. Gallatin, who was the American Minister at London, to prepare the case for a hearing; and the same year, he was appointed by Gen. Jackson Minister Plenipotentiary to the Hague, to represent the interest of the country in that important case. It is well known that the King of Holland made his award in January, 1831, and instead of deciding the controversy upon its merits and the proof, recommended a compromise line, to follow the course of the river St. John to its tributary, the St. Francis, thence to the source of the southwest branch of that river, thence on a line due west to the agreed boundary line. The question submitted, was to determine the *highlands* of the treaty, which the Dutch king seems not to have been able to find, except in the bed of a river. Judge Preble made a very severe protest against this award, in January, 1831, and returned the same year to his own country to resist its acceptance by our government. The protest, after quoting from the treaty the description of the boundary line to be adjusted, observes, "The manner of carrying this exceedingly definite and lucid description of boundary into effect, by running the line as described, and marking the line on the surface of the earth, was the subject, the sole, exclusive subject, submitted by the convention of September 1827, in pursuance of the treaty of Ghent, to an arbitrator." Again it says, "In the present case, especially, as any revision or substitution of boundary whatever, had been steadily, and in a spirit of unalterable determination, resisted at Ghent and at Washington, they had not anticipated the possibility of there being any occasion for delegating such powers." Judge Preble was sustained in his opposition to the decision of the arbiter, by the government and people of Maine: John G. Deane, on behalf of a committee of the Legislature, drew an able argument against the reasoning and principles of the award, concluding with a recommendation that the United States "will not consider themselves bound on any principle to adopt it."

Judge Preble returned to Maine in 1831, and was appointed an agent of the State to proceed to Washington, for the purpose of enforcing her rights. There was a disposition on the part of the government to accept the award: they were embarrassed by the controversy, and wished to have it closed. The subject was long agitated in executive session of the Senate; and it was proposed, that, to relieve the government and save the honor of our State, Maine should cede the territory lying north and east of the line of demarcation by the King of Holland, to the United States for an indemnity, and thus enable the United States Government to settle the matter on the basis of the award. Commissioners were appointed by Maine in 1832 to negotiate with the United States on the subject: these consisted of Judge Preble, Reuel Williams, and Nicholas Emery. Under this appointment, an agreement was entered into between the commissioners and the agents of the United States in July, 1832, by which Maine was to cede to the United States the jurisdiction and territory of the land in controversy, and to receive a grant of a million acres of land in Michigan. In the meantime, renewed negotiations were opened with Great Britain for the establishment of the line upon the basis of the treaty of 1783. These were protracted; irritation increased to exasperation on both sides of the line, until it broke out in what was called the Aroostook War in 1839: the difficulty was not finally settled until the English government, in 1841, sent over Lord Ashburton with full powers to adjust by compromise or otherwise the vexed question: this resulted in the Webster-Ashburton treaty of August, 1842, and the establishment of a conventional line; for which the British government paid an equivalent money consideration. Judge Preble's agency in this difficult and perplexing question did not terminate until the controversy was thus closed: his last act in it was as one of four commissioners chosen by the Legislature in 1842, to adjust the terms of settlement with this State. This was his last political act.

In 1844, Judge Preble engaged with youthful ardor in a great work, which he considered one of the most important of his life: this was the grand project which was to connect by railway the waters of the St. Lawrence and the Great Lakes with the sea at Portland. Those who enjoy or observe the advantages which that magnificent work is now conferring upon the two countries which it connects, can have no conception of the toil, the care, the exhausting efforts which were required to give it motion and continue its progress. After the completion of the railroad to Portsmouth from Portland in 1842, public attention was called to similar improvements which should afford facilities for transportation from the interior to the seaboard at Portland. Incipient measures were taken to explore routes to the northward and westward, and communications appeared in the papers, showing the advantages and feasibility of a railroad extending in that direction to the St. Lawrence. In September, 1844, a very large and enthusiastic public meeting was held in Portland on the subject, which resulted in the appointment of Judge Preble and Josiah S. Little as a committee to proceed to Montreal to procure, if possible, the concurrence and aid of the government and people of Canada to open between the two countries an international highway. They made their report on the eighteenth of October, to a very large public meeting in Portland, giving a favorable account of their reception, and of the encouragement tendered to the project. This was followed up by a reconnoisance of a route by James Hall, an engineer, and a charter for a company, styled the Atlantic and St. Lawrence Company, which was incorporated February 10, 1845, with a capital of three millions of dollars. While this bill was being carried through the Legislature, John A. Poor proceeded to Montreal, to stir up the public mind there, and was followed by Judge Preble on the twelfth of February, with the charter, in the depth of winter, by express teams, through untried paths of wilderness and forests. These extraordinary efforts were deemed necessary, because of incessant exertions and misrepresentations of persons interested in rival routes, having their termini in Massachusetts. These movements of the committee were conducted with great skill, and were crowned with entire success. A charter was granted by the Canadian Government to a company, for a connecting road dated March 18, 1845, with a copy of which Judge Preble and Mr. Poor returned to Portland.

In June, subscription books were opened for the stock, and on the first of September, it was announced that the sum requisite for organization was subscribed. On the twenty-fifth of September, the shareholders, representing six hundred and twelve thousand five hundred dollars, assembled at the City Hall in Portland, and organized the company. Judge Preble was unanimously chosen president.

On the thirtieth of November, 1845, Judge Preble sailed for England to advocate the interests of the company. There he had to encounter the same malign influences which he had met in Canada. Emissaries were in London to create a prejudice against the route to Portland, and to divert it to Boston; incredible efforts were made for this purpose; and it was with great difficulty that Judge Preble could get a hearing. The minds of leading men there had been prejudiced by misrepresentations, which it required the presentation of solid facts and able argument to refute and remove. In this mission, he was greatly assisted by Mr. Galt, the able representative of the Canadian road, and their exertions were partially successful. He returned in February, 1846, and the next movement in this grand enterprise was to settle the terms of union with the Canada company. This was accomplished to mutual satisfaction in April, by which a uniform gauge of five feet six inches was agreed upon, together with the points of termination of the two roads, the place of junction, and other conditions necessary for a harmonious and united action of the two companies. The convention was signed by George Moffatt, Augustin N. Morin, and Samuel Brookes, on behalf of the Canada Company; and by William P. Preble, John Mussey, and John B. Brown for the American Company; and constituted the basis of their mutual action.

Proposals were now issued for contracts, which were closed on the first of July, 1846, and on the fourth of July, ground was broken at Fish Point in Portland harbor, amidst an immense assemblage of persons, who filled the air with shouts of gratulation as Judge Preble threw out the first spadeful of earth to inaugurate the work which was thenceforward to go on to a happy and successful consummation. He accompanied his act by words well suited to its importance. In the evening, there was a beautiful display of fireworks, in honor of the occasion.

Among the papers which Judge Preble wrote in connection with his services for the railroad, were, "An Address to the Citizens of Montreal," in 1845; "An Address to Mr. Gladstone, the English Colonial Secretary," 1846, and "A Memorial to the Governor General of Canada," in 1847; all able state papers.

Judge Preble, in his report to the shareholders, July 22, 1848, remarks, "It is now just two years since the first shovelful of earth was moved in the ceremony of breaking ground. You will remember that the first twelve miles of our road, including the depot grounds, extending into the deep waters of Portland harbor, present more obstacles to be overcome, and require a greater outlay by nearly a hundred per cent., than any other like number of consecutive miles of the road between Portland and the Canada line. These obstacles, however, have been overcome, and your road is now in successful operation to the town of North Yarmouth." He states that the road was in good advancement to Minot, thirty-six miles from Portland, and would be opened in the fall. He then gives the following sketch of the features of the road: "As we pass on northerly from Portland, we gradually ascend a gently inclined plane, about one hundred miles in length, attaining at its northern termination an elevation of eleven hundred and fifteen feet above the tide waters of Portland harbor: thence by an almost imperceptible descent, we fall into the valley of the Connecticut, losing in a distance of some twenty odd miles about two hundred feet only of elevation, where we reach the bank of the main stream. Strictly speaking, with this single exception, we pass in our whole course, no dividing ridge separating waters flowing in different directions."

With this report, Judge Preble's connection with the railroad ceased: the great exertions he had made, and the exposure he had endured, in the inception and progress of this grand enterprise, had broken down his health, and he found that he needed repose from all active employment; he therefore retired to private life, still retaining a deep interest in the prosperity of an improvement which he had effectually labored to accomplish. He made frequent and urgent appeals through the newspapers to arouse the public mind to the importance of the undertaking, and to induce the people to come forward to aid the work; and he lived to see it fully achieved, and bearing the fruits of a large and successful operation, extending from the Atlantic Ocean at Portland eleven hundred miles, passing on the northern shores of the St. Lawrence, of Lake Ontario, of Lake Erie, to the far off Lake of the Hurons.

The road was opened to South Paris, January 1, 1850, and to Island Pond, its point of connection, early in 1852; and the whole line to the St. Lawrence was completed early in 1853. Mr. Little, the president of the road, in a report in March, 1855, observed, "The act incorporating the Atlantic and St. Lawrence Railroad Company was approved by the governor, February 10, 1845. At that time, not a dollar of capital had been raised, or pledged, for the prosecution of the enterprise; nor had a spade been put into the ground on account of it. Now, we have more than four hundred miles of railroad in actual and successful operation, connecting the waters of the Atlantic Ocean at Portland, with the waters of the St. Lawrence at Montreal, and also at Quebec. Add to this, that in this whole distance of continuous rail, there is no gradient in either direction, exceeding sixty feet to the mile, even for the shortest space."

Judge Preble was one of the most prominent and influential politicians of the State. He began life as a zealous federalist; but with many other active and intelligent young men, Holmes, Parris, Ware, and others, previous to the separation from Massachusetts, he veered into the democratic ranks, and became as ardent on that side of the question as he had before been opposed to it. He advocated the cause of his new friends with the zeal and ability which characterized all his other efforts, and sustained the cause of the national administration by an efficient service, which made him a successful candidate for the office of attorney of the United States for the district of Maine, to which he was appointed in 1814, when but three years in practice. His political efforts were especially directed to effect a separation of Maine from Massachusetts; and no person labored more ardently and effectually to accomplish that object than he did. The attention of leading men had been devoted to this subject from time to time, ever since the peace of 1783; and conventions had been held to promote the object. The people were nearly equally divided on the subject, and in the last movements it had become a party question. The old commonwealth was strongly federal, while Maine was democratic; consequently the federal party bore sway: it was the policy, therefore, of the democratic party, to establish a separate government, that they might have the benefit of official patronage. There were many men, however, independent of party, who believed the affairs and interests of the district would be better managed by a local government than by the more remote one in Massachusetts; and these cast their influence into the scale of the friends of separation. During the session of the Legislature in 1816, numerous petitions were presented to that body, praying for the separation, which were referred to a committee, who reported in February, recommending that the question be submitted to the people. The act on the subject was not passed until the June session: in this, the terms on which the separation was to take place were specifically set forth. Among the conditions was that determining the majority required: the inhabitants of the towns in the district were to assemble on the first Monday in September then next, to give their votes on the question, whether it is expedient to form the district into an independent State, which votes were to be returned to a convention, to assemble on the last Monday of the same September, delegates to which were to be chosen at the same time that the vote was taken. The act proceeds to say, "If it shall appear that a majority of five to four, at least, of the votes so returned, are in favor of separation, the convention is to proceed in forming a constitution, and not otherwise." During the intervening time, the discussion was very animated. Judge Preble wrote strongly and earnestly in favor of the measure; the papers in Massachusetts, as well as those in Maine, entered zealously into the conflict; for it cannot be disguised that the old Commonwealth was very reluctant to lose so valuable an appendage to her sovereignty, her territory, and her political rank in the Union. The vote of Saco was two hundred and fifteen for separation, and sixteen against it, and Mr. Preble was elected one of the delegates. But the vote of the county was not so decisive; there were one thousand seven hundred and twelve in the negative. Wells and Lyman, strong federal towns, gave large majorities against separation, viz., Wells three hundred and seventy-four to forty-seven, Lyman one hundred and seventy-nine to six. The federal towns were generally opposed to the measure, but Lincoln and Hancock Counties were the only ones which gave a majority of votes in opposition: Hancock stood four hundred and seven for, and one thousand two hundred and fifty-seven against, separation; and Lincoln, one thousand seven hundred and fifty-two in favor, and two thousand three hundred and fifty-seven against it. The whole vote was nearly divided, and was eleven thousand nine hundred and twenty-seven in the affirmative, and ten thousand five hundred and thirty-nine in the negative: evidently, the measure was not carried, and the convention met under this disheartening cloud. But the mind of Judge Preble was fruitful in expedients, and with more casuistry than force of logic, he endeavored to show that the five-ninths majority had been obtained. John Holmes was chairman of the committee to examine the votes, and submitted the report, which is understood to have been drawn by Judge Preble, and came to the result that the requisite majority had been obtained. We quote the following passage, as a specimen of the ingenuity of the report. "By recurring to the second and third sections of the act concerning the separation of the District of Maine from Massachusetts proper, and forming the same into an independent State, we find that the convention is authorized to form a constitution, provided a majority of five to four, at least, of the votes returned, are in favor of the measure. The meaning of the word *majority is doubtful.* This word is sometimes understood to mean the excess of one number over another, and sometimes the excess of half the whole number. Exclude the words 'a majority of' in the second and third sections of the act, and no doubt remains but five yeas to four nays, or *five-ninths* of the votes returned, would be required. But your committee do not feel authorized to say that these words have no meaning." "In the report of the committee prefixed to the act, it appears to have been the intention, that the expediency of separation should have been decided by an assembly of men, charged with the most solemn duties, meaning, no doubt, a *convention of* *delegates chosen by towns.* Here the delegates would have been in proportion to the number of majorities in each corporation, and not in the aggregate majority of all the votes returned." It then draws the following conclusion: "As the delegates must be apportioned according to the respective majorities of their towns, so on the question of separation, the majority of *yeas* in the towns and plantations in *favor* must be to the majority of *nays* in those opposed, as *five* to *four* of the votes returned. * * * In this way only can your committee give a meaning to the word *majority* as contained in the second and third sections of the act."

After having rejected the votes of Lyman, which, as we have seen, were one hundred and seventy-three majority against separation, because the meeting called to have the house polled before voting, the committee thus state their sum:

Whole number of votes,		22,316.
The yeas are,	11,969.	
The nays are,	10,347.	

The whole aggregate majority of yeas in the towns and plantations is six thousand and thirty-one. The whole aggregate majority of nays in the towns and plantations opposed is four thousand four hundred and nine. Then, as *five* is to *four*, so is six thousand and thirty-one to four thousand eight hundred and twenty-five, the nays required, but the majority of nays is four thousand four hundred and nine only. Hence it appears that upon this construction of the act, there is a majority of five to four, at least, of the votes returned, in favor of said District's becoming an independent State."

So earnest was the majority of the convention to accomplish the work which they had assembled to do, that they adopted the report of the committee, and proceeded to perform the other duties consequent upon the act. But the minority, consisting of seventy-one members, among whom were some of the most honored names in the District, were not convinced by this ingenious ciphering, and although some of them were favorable to separation, they entered into a solemn protest against the report, its reasoning, and its principles, and against further proceeding on the subject. Judge Stebbins of Alna presented the protest, which is supposed to have been drawn by him. After stating the facts which show, by a reasonable construction, that the requisite majority had not been obtained, it says: "Nothing, therefore, remains to be done by the convention. The only duty in this event, assigned to them by the Legislature and their constituents, here terminates. The exercise of further powers by this convention we are constrained to consider as *usurpation*. To proceed to form a constitution, is, in our view, at once a violation of express law, and an invasion of the rights of our constituents."

The Legislature of Massachusetts took the same view of the law and the powers of the convention which the protestors did, and declined proceeding further in the matter. So this attempt, like former ones, failed from a sufficient unanimity of the people in accomplishing the object.

Judge Preble and Messrs. Holmes of Alfred and Davis of Augusta were appointed a committee to publish an address in answer to the protest. Judge Preble was also one of the committee to make application to the Legislature of Massachusetts to carry into effect the act of separation.

This latter committee presented a memorial to the Legislature which held a session in November, 1816; and it was referred to an able committee, on which were Messrs. Otis, Pickman, and Pickering. Numerous remonstrances were also presented against separation from different parts of Maine, as were, also, petitions for it. The committee made a long report adverse to the application, accompanied by two resolutions: one was, that the contingency upon which consent was given to the separation had not happened, and that the powers of the Brunswick Convention have ceased; second, that it was not expedient for the present General Court to adopt any further measures in regard to the separation. The report and resolves were adopted. After this, the subject of payment to the members of the convention for their travel and attendance was introduced and referred: the committee reported that it was not expedient to take any action on the subject; and thus, for that time, the movement for a separation was suspended, only to be revived with new ardor the following year, with a successful result.

In the convention of 1819, which prepared the constitution, Mr. Preble was a delegate from Portland, where he then resided, and took part in the debates, especially on the subject of apportionment of senators and representatives, in which his mathematical talent was again invoked. He was chairman of the committee on the name of the State. Of the seven delegates from Portland, he and Judge Parris only signed the constitution: the other five declined signing it, because they believed the apportionment of representatives to have been unequal and unjust to Portland and other large towns.

In 1820, Judge Preble was chosen one of the trustees of Bowdoin College, the duties of which he promptly discharged for twenty-two years, until his resignation in 1842. In 1829, the college bestowed upon him the honorary degree of LL. D.

Judge Preble was twice married: his first wife, to whom he was united in September, 1810, while he was a tutor at Cambridge, was Nancy Gale Tucker, the second daughter of Joseph Tucker of York, who was at one time the collector of that port. Her only sister, Mary Ann, married, the same year, Louis A. DeCreney, a French gentleman, connected with a considerable family in France.[1] By this marriage, Judge Preble had two daughters and one son: the son bears the same name with himself, and now resides in Portland, and is Clerk of the District Court of the United States. The eldest daughter married Stephen Longfellow, Jr., a lawyer in Portland: the youngest married Lieut. Allen of the United States Army. Mr. Preble's second wife was Sarah A. Forsaith, a daughter of the late Thomas Forsaith of Portland, by whom he had one son, who with his mother survives.

The constitution of Judge Preble, considerably shattered by hard use, at last gave way, and he closed his busy, unquiet life October 11, 1857, at the age of seventy-three. The following summary of his character was furnished by John A. Poor, in an obituary notice, which appeared in a Portland paper soon after Mr. Preble's death, — "All his published writings display the most marked exhibition of labor and care of preparation. He never allowed anything from his pen to appear without subjecting it to the most elaborate preparation. But little, however, remains that will serve as an enduring record of his labors. His reported opinions as a judge do not give any adequate idea of his power as a lawyer. He had a reputation for intellectual power far beyond any measure of success that he obtained; and those who knew him best, were aware of his peculiarities of temperament and of temper that were drawbacks to popular favor. He appeared to best advantage in the oral argument of legal questions. He stated his propositions with a clearness and force rarely

[1] Mr. DeCreney died in 1818, his widow in 1836; having had three sons and one daughter: the daughter married Henry C. Lovell of Portland, and is dead: one son is living in Portland, another in France.

equalled. When all his faculties were raised into activity by the excitement of a great occasion, his mind worked with the greatest ease, and he was capable on such occasions of bringing out an argument, that by its strength of reasoning, force of illustration, and effective eloquence, gave him the mastery over others."

SAMUEL EMERSON SMITH. 1812—1860.

Samuel Emerson Smith died at Wiscasset, March 3, 1860, aged within nine days of seventy-two. He was the seventh child and third son of Manasseh Smith, a native of Leominster, Massachusetts, and Hannah Emerson, a daughter of Daniel Emerson of Hollis, New Hampshire, at which place he was born, March 12, 1788. His father was born in 1749, a graduate of Harvard College in the class of 1773, and was for a while a chaplain in the army: he afterwards pursued the practice of law in Leominster and Hollis, and subsequently at Wiscasset in Maine, to which place he moved in 1788. Before this time, he had been clerk of the Supreme Court in Massachusetts. He died in 1823. A more full account of him is given in preceding pages of this work.

We may infer that Manasseh Smith, the father, was entirely satisfied with the college in which he was himself educated, and the profession which gave him his living, by the fact that his four sons were graduates of Harvard, and became lawyers. Manasseh, the eldest, Harvard College, 1800, established himself at Warren, where he died a prominent citizen in 1822; Joseph E., Harvard College, 1804, long a respected lawyer in Boston, and died there in 1837; Edwin, the only survivor, Harvard College, 1811, is still living in Warren.

Samuel, with whom we have now to do, pursued his

preparatory studies at Groton Academy, and received his degree at Harvard in 1808, in the class with Rev. Ralph Sanger, recently deceased, Benjamin Rand, the distinguished lawyer of Boston, and other prominent men. He studied his profession, partly with Samuel Dana of Groton, and partly with his brothers, Manasseh and Joseph; and was admitted to the Suffolk Bar, February 25, 1812. The same year, he established himself in practice at Wiscasset.

Mr. Smith early took a prominent position at the bar, as a sound and discriminating lawyer. His mind was clear and acute: he had disciplined it well in mathematics and metaphysics, studies which he cherished and pursued through life, and devotion to which was the act of his last hour: he left his study at eleven o'clock at night, after having been several hours engaged in solving a problem in algebra, and an hour later he had ceased to breathe.

He also engaged earnestly in politics: his father and all the members of his family were zealous adherents to the old democratic party, and he was early brought into public life. In 1819, the last year of our connection with Massachusetts, he was elected a representative from Wiscasset to the General Court, and the next year to the Legislature of Maine. On the separation of the State from the old commonwealth, he was removed from the sphere of political action by his appointment, in 1821, as chief justice of the Circuit Court of Common Pleas for the second circuit, as successor of Judge Weston, who had been raised by the new government to a seat on the bench of the Supreme Court. He had then been but nine years at the bar, and there were in his circuit much older practitioners; as Stebbins, Ames, Allen, Wheeler, Bridge, Fuller, Williams, Bond, Cutler, Belcher, &c. In the reorganization of this court in 1822, by which the circuit system was abolished, he was appointed an associate judge of the new court, with

Ezekiel Whitman as chief justice. He continued to discharge the duties of this office with great fidelity, intelligence, and to public acceptance, until 1830; when, having been elected governor of Maine, he resigned it. The decisions of Judge Smith were impartial and wise; and I have heard it said by competent authority that his judgments were rarely overruled by the ultimate tribunal.

He held the office of governor, by annual elections, three years, — 1831, 1832, and 1833. During his administration, the public mind was greatly excited on the subject of the northeastern boundary. The question in controversy, after ineffectual negotiation, had been submitted to the King of the Netherlands. Our fellow citizen, Judge Preble, had been sent by the general government to the Hague to manage the cause. That umpire, in January, 1831, rendered his award; and, instead of determining the question submitted to him, viz., what was the true boundary line by a fair construction of the treaty of 1783, determined that the line ought to extend north from the source of the St. Croix River to the middle of the channel of the St. John River, thence up that river to the St. Francis, and through the middle of that river to the source of its southwest branch. This singular departure from the terms of the submission, and the plain language of the treaty, which placed the line upon a ridge of highlands and not in the bed of a river, gave just indignation to the people of this State, and led to an entire repudiation of the award.

A long correspondence and discussion took place on the subject between the executive of this State and the authorities in Washington, in which were distinguished Governor Smith, and our fellow citizens, — Judge Preble, John G. Deane, Charles S. Daveis, Governor Evans, and Governor Kent. The United States Government was desirous of having the award accepted, and was willing to conciliate

Maine by an equivalent in money or land for their loss of territory. Much historical research and ability were displayed on the part of the persons in Maine who warmly engaged in the discussion. The messages and communications of Governor Smith were sound and judicious, and met with public approbation. The agitating and unpleasant controversy was not finally arranged until 1842, when Maine, through her commissioners, assented to a conventional line, established by the Ashburton treaty, yielding a large portion of territory, for which she received an inconsiderable remuneration: the treaty provided that the general government should satisfy Maine and Massachusetts for the expenses incurred by them in protecting the disputed territory, and making a survey thereof, and to pay them the further sum of three hundred thousand dollars in equal portions, "on account of their assent to the line of boundary."

Another measure of importance occurred in the administration of Governor Smith; that was the removal of the seat of government from Portland to Augusta. The Legislature commenced its first session at Augusta, in January, 1832: on which occasion, the chief magistrate, in his annual message, congratulated the people "upon the possession of a capitol, which is an ornament to the State, and in beauty of materials and style of execution, inferior to no building for a similar purpose among our sister States." The building and furniture cost something over one hundred and twenty-five thousand dollars; but to raise this sum ten townships of land had been appropriated, seven of which were sold for forty-five thousand two hundred and thirty dollars, sixty cents, or an average price of twenty-nine and a half cents per acre. The other three sold at a less price: the whole fell far short of meeting the expenditure, or even the estimate of its cost by the architect, Charles Bulfinch of Boston, which was eighty thousand dollars. Mr. Bulfinch was the architect who planned and constructed the Boston State House, having for his model St. Peter's Church at Rome, which he had visited. Our State House was a copy of that of Massachusetts, on a smaller scale.

In the third and last year of Governor Smith's administration, the country was greatly disturbed by the nullification movements of South Carolina, and agitations concerning the charter of the United States bank, and a modification of the tariff. In regard to the nullification, the governor took firm ground in support of the national executive. In his annual message of 1833, he says, "In this alarming crisis of our national affairs, we cannot but rejoice that the executive department of the national government, sustained, as it is, by a vast majority of the American people, has announced its determination to support and carry into effect the constitution and laws of the United States."

At the expiration of his third term of office, Governor Smith returned to private life; but in 1835, his services were again required by the State, and he was restored to the bench of the Common Pleas. He continued to discharge the duties of the office until 1837, when he finally withdrew from the bench. In October of the same year, he was appointed with Chief Justice Mellen and Ebenezer Everett, Esq., one of the commissioners to revise and codify the public laws: the first edition of the Revised Statutes was the result of the labors of this commission.

In 1832, while Governor Smith was residing in Augusta as chief magistrate, he married Louisa Sophia, a daughter of Henry Weld Fuller of that city. By her, he had five sons, who, with their mother, are now living.

Governor Smith was one of the forty-nine corporate

J.H.Bufford's Lith. Boston.
Ether Shepley

members of the Maine Historical Society, of whom, after a period of forty years from its organization, ten survive. Their names are worthy to be placed on record, viz., William Allen, late President of Bowdoin College, now living at North Hampton, Massachusetts; Rev. Jonathan Cogswell, professor in a college of New York; Robert H. Gardiner of Gardiner; Dr. Isaac Lincoln of Brunswick; Jacob McGaw of Bangor; Judge Sprague of Boston, the youngest of the number; Chief Justice Shepley and Judge Ware of Portland; the Rev. Benjamin Tappan and Chief Justice Weston of Augusta.

The remainder of Governor Smith's life was passed in literary ease and retirement, and in the enjoyment of an independent estate. And it closed calmly, and without sickness or pain, when threescore and twelve years had been nearly completed. He was a genial, pleasant companion, and freely commnicated with the young, as well as old, from the ample stores of his richly furnished mind.

ETHER SHEPLEY. 1814—

Chief Justice Shepley was the second son of John Shepley of Groton, Massachusetts, and Mary, widow of Captain Therlow of the Revolutionary army, a daughter of Deacon Gibson of Stowe; was born in Groton, November 2, 1789. The family was early settled in Groton; we find it there as early as 1700, in which year a son of John and Lydia Sheple, as the name was written all through that century, was born. From that ancestor, Judge Shepley was of the sixth degree. As early as 1637, a John Shepley, as Farmer informs us, was in Salem, and was probably the ancestor of the John who established himself in Groton. He had a son John born in 1637, and moved to Chelmsford. The family always maintained a prominent position in that ancient and respectable town, which contained such names as Ames, Bancroft, Farwell, Fiske, Lawrence, Prescott, Parker, Sawtelle. In the History of Groton, Captain John Sheple, the ancestor above named, appears to have been a representative to the General Court six years, between 1716 and 1728: in 1718, we find his name as one of the selectmen of the town. His son, Jonathan, was town clerk in 1730, and from 1734 to 1744. Joseph, another member of the family, in 1773, was on a committee with Oliver Prescott, Amos Lawrence, and others, to consider the grievances under which the colony was laboring by an infringement of their rights and liberties, and to instruct their representative. He was also a member of the convention of 1788, for adopting the constitution of the United States, and, with his colleague, opposed it. In Worcester County, there was a very strong opposition to the constitution: of its fifty delegates, forty-three voted against it. Judge Shepley's father was an only son of John and Abigail (Green) Sheple; he was an orderly sergeant and clerk of a company in the Revolution; he held several town offices in Groton, was a farmer, fond of reading, and a man of general information. He had three sons: John, the eldest, born October 16, 1787; Ether, November 2, 1789; and Stephen, in 1791. John is remembered as reporter of the decisions of the Supreme Court of Maine for many years, contained in volumes thirteen to thirty-one, from 1836 to 1849. He entered Harvard College in the class which graduated in 1806, but left college, with a portion of his class, in his senior year. He afterwards practiced law in Rutland and Fitchburg in Worcester County, and, in 1825, came to Maine. He had been a senator in the Legislature of Massachusetts, and a member of the convention for amending the constitution of that State. He formed a partnership with his brother on his coming to Maine, and they conducted a very extensive business in the profession. He died in 1858, leaving, by his wife Abigail, a daughter of Nathaniel Fellows Cunningham of Lunenburg, Massachusetts, two daughters and one son, a graduate of Bowdoin College, and now in the practice of law in Minnesota.

This branch of the family restored the original orthography of the name: they found on examination of English registers and documents, that the name was early, and almost invariably, spelled with a final *y*, as it was pronounced. As early as 1316, a record appears, in which "John de Shepley" signed a certificate as "Lord of the township of Shepley in the county of York." Being satisfied that such was the correct mode of writing the name, it was then adopted, and has ever since been retained. The christian name, *Ether*, was adopted from Joshua xix. 7, the designation of one of the villages of the Canaanites in the south of Judah, allotted to Simeon. The word in Hebrew means a stone.

Mr. Shepley received his elementary education at Groton Academy, under the instruction of Caleb Butler. Thence he proceeded to Dartmouth College, from which he took his degree in 1811. Among his classmates were Professor Nathaniel H. Carter, Bezaleel Cushman, and Nathaniel Wright, who were all instructors in Portland after leaving college; Mr. Cushman, for thirty years, having had charge of the academy. Dr. William Cogswell; Daniel Poor, the celebrated missionary; Professor Parker of the Law School at Harvard; Amos Kendall, Postmaster-General under President Jackson; and other distinguished men, — were members of that class.

On leaving college, Mr. Shepley entered the office of Dudley Hubbard in South Berwick, where he remained two years, under very favorable circumstances. The large collection business of Mr. Hubbard was suffering for want of attention: Mr. Shepley took serious hold of it, and by his activity and intelligence, revived it, and left it in a favorable condition. He was urged by Mr. Hubbard to continue his services, but he preferred a change, and successively read in the offices of Zabdiel B. Adams in Worcester County, and Solomon Strong in Hampshire. On being admitted to the bar, he came immediately to Saco, where he commenced practice in July, 1814. With the experience he had gathered, and the habits of business he had acquired, he was more than usually advanced over young practitioners in the knowledge of his profession, and in the use of its machinery; and early entered upon a successful and lucrative practice, which his industry, close application, and practical ability made secure, and gave to him a prominent place in the community in the midst of which he resided.

In 1819, the subject of the separation from Massachusetts was earnestly discussed in this State, and Mr. Shepley zealously entered into it: he was elected to represent Saco that year in the General Court, and the same year was chosen a member of the convention which formed the constitution of Maine. In February, 1821, he was appointed United States attorney for the District of Maine, as successor to William P. Preble, who was placed on the bench of the Supreme Court of the State. This office he held until his election as one of the senators in Congress from Maine, in 1833. The duties of that office, in connection with his very extensive practice, he discharged with great promptness and fidelity, of which no better evidence can be adduced, than the length of time he was permitted to retain it, — through the four closing years of Mr. Monroe's administration, the whole of Mr. Adams's, and four years into General Jackson's, and left it at last, only for a more exalted station. In 1833, he was elected to the Senate of the United States, as successor to John Holmes. In this body, he sustained the administration of General Jackson by his votes and his voice. On the great and exciting question of removing the deposits from the United States Bank, he made two earnest and able speeches in January, 1834, vindicating the course and policy of the President. In one of these, he paid a glowing eulogium to his classmate Amos Kendall, who was then the agent of the government in relation to those deposits. But the office of senator, however favorable and agreeable, the good opinion entertained by the government of Maine of his legal ability, did not permit him long to retain; for in September, 1836, a vacancy having occurred on the bench of the Supreme Court, by the resignation of Judge Parris, who had been appointed by President Van Buren, second comptroller of the treasury, he was immediately appointed to that place. It was apparent from the studies and habits of Judge Shepley, that the quiet pursuits of professional duties, and especially in their highest forms as an expositor of the law, were more suited to his tastes than the turmoil of politics. As a judge, both at nisi prius, and in the law department, his ability, his industry, and integrity fully justified the partiality and good judgment of the administration of Governor Dunlap, by which the appointment was made. In 1848, he was appointed chief justice, as successor to Chief Justice Whitman, with the general concurrence of the bar and public sentiment. His long experience as a jurist and a judge, and the fidelity and legal acumen which he had displayed in his long judicial service, placed him prominently before the public, as a fit successor of the eminent judge who had preceded him. He continued in this high office until the autumn of 1855, when his constitutional term of seven years having expired, he retired from the bench, his ermine unsullied, and closed his long judicial life. No judge ever more faithfully or more promptly discharged the duties of the bench than Judge Shepley; and the ability which characterized his judicial career is amply illustrated in the twenty-seven volumes of the Maine Reports from the fourteenth to the fortieth inclusive. His opinions are drawn with clearness, directness, and force; and no one can mistake the point which he endeavors to establish. That Judge Shepley was devoted to his professional and judicial life, and clung with strong attachment to his domestic joys, we can have no better proof than the firmness with which he resisted the allurements held out to him to accept positions under the general government: while on the bench, he was urged to accept official stations by authorities at Washington, which he uniformly declined, preferring the comforts of his home, and the steady and calm pursuits of the duties of a judge, which he could not but feel were useful to his fellow citizens, to offices of more notoriety and higher compensation, which would interfere with his domestic arrangements.

The last public office Judge Shepley was called to perform, was that of sole commissioner to revise the public laws, to which he was appointed by Resolve of April 1, 1856. And notwithstanding the injudicious instruction to complete, and cause his report to be printed, on or before the fifteenth day of November following, he accomplished the almost herculean task, and prepared a very full index of the whole body of the public statutes, which constitutes what is now cited as the "Revised Statutes of Maine," published in 1857. If more time had been allowed, we should, of course, had a more complete and perfect work, with the benefit of the wise and learned suggestions of an experienced and sensible judge, upon the discrepancies inconsistencies, and imperfections in the great body of our law. Defects and contradictions undoubtedly exist, which can only be remedied by the most careful investigation and comparison, by a sound and experienced jurist. But in this, as in many other cases,—an American fault,—our people seem to regard more the having things done quickly, than well done. They had better follow the Shakespearian rule, "If it were done when 'tis done, then 'twere well it were done quickly;"—we add, but not otherwise.

Judge Shepley has uniformly, through his long life, been the firm friend and supporter of good order, and a just administration of law: he has given substantial aid to the cause of religion, good morals, and general education, and has himself practiced upon the rules he has prescribed for others. He has been thirty-three years a trustee of Bowdoin College, having been chosen in 1829; and he has been a careful observer of its affairs, and a faithful counsellor in its emergencies. He has fulfilled all the numerous trusts, private and public, intrusted to him, uprightly, diligently, and well, for the good of the people and the individuals in whose service he has been employed. And after a well filled public life of thirty-six years, and at the age of seventy-three years, he may very properly lay aside the armor, which has been worn worthily and with honor, through the conflicts of political contention, the sharp strifes of the forum, and the calmer struggles with the subtleties and nice discriminations of legal investigation, where the arms are reason and judgment, against the keen logic of the masters of rhetoric. He has received from Dartmouth College the honorary degree of LL. D.

In 1816, Judge Shepley married Anna Foster, with whom he has lived in the most affectionate relations to the present time. By her, he has had five sons; three of whom, only, survive: John R., educated at Bowdoin College in the class of 1837, and now a prominent lawyer in St. Louis, Missouri; George Foster, a graduate of Dartmouth in 1837, well known as a distinguished lawyer in Maine, who entered the army as colonel of the twelfth regiment of Maine volunteers, and is now acting brigadier general and military governor of Louisiana. The third son is Leonard D., a merchant in Portland, Maine. They all have families. The Chief Justice, too far advanced to take a part in active hostilities in support of the government of his country, sustains the cause by his words, and co-operation in its efforts to put down the rebellion. And to enable his son to fight freely, and unencumbered by his numerous engagements at home, he has taken his place anew in the courts, and burnished up the forensic armor for fresh contests on the field of his former struggles. "E'en in his ashes live his wonted fires."

PELEG SPRAGUE. 1815—1835.

Among the lawyers who rapidly acquired eminence in politics, as well as in law, in the county of Kennebec, was Peleg Sprague, now the distinguished judge of the District Court of the United States for the District of Massachusetts. Judge Sprague was the son of Seth and Deborah Sprague of Duxbury, Massachusetts, where he was born, April 28, 1793. His first American ancestor was William Sprague, who is supposed to have come over in the fleet with Rev. Mr. Higginson to Salem, in 1629. His elder brothers, Ralph and Richard, of Charlestown, certainly arrived with that company. William settled in Hingham, and for a time lived in Marshfield. The descent was through Samuel, son of William, born in 1640, and his son Samuel, born in 1674.

Mr. Sprague was educated at Harvard College, from which he took his degree in 1812. His class contained men who have since become distinguished in civil life: among them were, — Franklin Dexter; James H. Duncan;

AT THE AGE OF 51.

Dr. Homans; Charles G. Loring; the late Bishop Wainwright of New York; George Downes and Dr. Nourse of Maine. Judge Sprague maintained a high rank in college, was a member of its brightest literary society, and graduated with prominent honor. His performance at Commencement was a dissertation "on the Superiority of Modern Europe." Loring had the salutatory oration; and Henry Ware, Jr., a poem on the pursuit of fame. On leaving the halls of the university, he, with some others of his classmates, proceeded to the law school of Judges Reeve and Gould, in Litchfield, Connecticut, which then offered advantages, under those distinguished lawyers, superior to any other in the country; for, at that time, none of the colleges had introduced into their courses of study, a department for legal instruction. After leaving Litchfield, he spent the remainder of his term, partly with Judge Hubbard in Boston, and partly with Levi Lincoln in Worcester: he was admitted to the bar in Plymouth County, in August, 1815.

He immediately opened an office in Augusta, where he remained about two years, when he removed to Hallowell. The bar of Kennebec contained at that time able lawyers and advocates: among them were Judges Bridge and Fuller, Reuel Williams, Frederic Allen, Thomas Bond, and Timothy Boutelle. It required industry, perseverance, and a high ambition, as well as intellectual powers, to compete successfully with such men, who had acquired the confidence of the communities in which they lived, by ability and honorable practice. But Mr. Sprague, nothing discouraged by such an array of talent, but rather stimulated by it, steadily and patiently waited for the success which was sure to follow a persistent and earnest endeavor to attain the higher ranks and honors of the profession. His agreeable and eloquent manner as an advocate, and his acknowledged ability as a lawyer, soon introduced him to a profitable business; and within five years from the commencement of his practice, we find him taking his position in the reports as the manager of causes at the law term of the Supreme Court. He appears in the first volume of Greenleaf in 1820; and each subsequent volume of the Maine Reports contains his arguments, while he remained in the State, showing a steady progress in the magnitude and importance of his business. The death, in 1827, of Mr. Bond, of the same town, who was enjoying the entire confidence of the people, in his profession, gave an accession to the engagements of Mr. Sprague, and a more prominent position.

Mr. Sprague's style of speaking, both at the bar and in public assemblies, was so entirely different from what the people in the county had been accustomed to hear, that it attracted them by its novelty, and interested them by its beauty. The addresses at the bar in that county had been particularly plain and simple; the great lawyers there — Wilde, Bridge, Bond, Williams, and Allen — made no pretensions to oratory; they did what they undertook to do, presented their cases to the jury and the court in a brief, comprehensive, unvarnished manner, bringing out every material point in the case, and laboring solely for that purpose. But a young man came among them, highly educated and cultivated, ambitious of distinction, and capable of making a figure, and introduced a style of elocution, showy and rather declamatory, accompanied by gesticulation which attracted by its gracefulness as well as peculiarity, and rendered the advocate extremely popular.

And his popularity was not confined to the bar, but extended through the community, and made him a desirable candidate for public office. He had come into Maine a democrat, sustaining the principles and traditions of his family;—he joined the dominant party in the State in favor of separation: his adopted town threw a strong vote in favor of the measure, three hundred and forty-four to ninety-six; and he was elected a representative from Hallowell to the first Legislature, in 1820, of the new State, and re-elected the subsequent year. His political course was now onward. In the severe presidential contest of 1824, he gave his concurrence, but not very hearty exertion, in favor of the election of John Quincy Adams: parties, it is well remembered, were strangely divided in this quadrangular contest between the four great candidates, who had their partisans in their respective portions of the country. Maine cast her whole electoral ballot for Adams. Mr. Sprague was elected to Congress the same year from the Kennebec District, and then, through the whole of the administration of Mr. Adams, gave to it his hearty and valued support. He was again elected to the Twentieth Congress. During both of these terms, he engaged in debates on important questions, and always attracted attention by his able and eloquent advocacy of the measures which he espoused.

So acceptable were his services in Congress during these four years, and so popular had he become in the State, that on the resignation of General Chandler, to accept the collectorship of Portland in 1829, Mr. Sprague was chosen his successor, and was succeeded in the House by George Evans, who had commenced, in his own State, a brilliant political as well as legal career, which was continued through eighteen successive years in Congress, twelve as a representative and six as a senator, to 1847, a period of political life in Congress unparalleled in our State.

In the Senate, Mr. Sprague took a very prominent position as an opponent of the administration of General Jackson. On the protective system and on the measures of hostility to the national bank, he stood by Mr. Clay, and made able speeches on the subjects. He defended General Jackson's policy on the nullification scheme of South Carolina, and with Mr. Webster, sustained the administration in its prompt and vigorous action against that rebellious movement. In January, 1834, he made an eloquent speech on Mr. Clay's resolutions adverse to the removal of the deposits from the bank of the United States. In speaking of what he denounced as the arbitrary acts of President Jackson, he said, "A king of England or France, who should, at this day, disregard the acts of the Legislature or the decrees of the Judiciary, would not only shake their thrones to their foundations, but might soon behold in their stead, the bloody scaffolds of Louis and of Charles! Shall a *republican* president have prerogatives over both?" Again, he says, "Such are the delusions which have placed the iron scepter in the hands of the Cæsars and Bonapartes of past ages, and overwhelmed or jeopardized all the free governments of the earth."

His reputation stood high as an able and eloquent statesman; but the friends of President Jackson had acquired ascendancy in Maine, although, on his first election, he had received but one out of the nine electoral votes of the State. A quarrel soon arose between the majority party in the Legislature and our senators in Congress, — Messrs. Holmes and Sprague, — on the subjects of national dispute which were agitating the country. This was gentle at first, but increased in the four years of its continuance to a storm. The first movement on the part of the Legislature was a resolution, approved February 23, 1832, instructing the senators, and requesting the representatives, to vote against the renewal of the charter of the United States Bank. This monition was unheeded, the members following their own predilections on the subject. Early in the next session of the Legislature, January, 1833, a series of resolutions was passed, denouncing the United States Bank and a protective tariff, and declaring "that the people of Maine disapprove of the conduct of both their senators in the Congress of the United States, relative to the renewal of the charter of the bank of the United States, and relative to the tariff; and in consequence of the utter disregard by said senators of the instructions of the last Legislature," * * * "each of said senators has forfeited the confidence of his constituents." They further declared the right of the Legislature to instruct their senators, and "to exact of them a strict observance of such instructions." They close with a resolve that the governor transmit "a copy of the resolutions to the president of the Senate, and to both of the delinquent senators from Maine."

This blast, too, was ineffectual to move the senators from their places, or to change their votes, founded on their own convictions. Mr. Sprague wrote a long and explicit letter to the Legislature, explaining his views and motives of action, and the reasons on which his votes were based. The letter was laid before the body to which it was addressed, but never published. Mr. Holmes also wrote a letter which he caused to be published in the National Intelligencer, and which the speaker of the House in Maine undertook to read; but it reflected so severely on the members, that the *further reading was dispensed with*, and both documents went to the tomb of the Capulets.

The next year, 1834, the Legislature renewed the attack among the first business of the session; repeating their hostile expression against the national bank, and again instructing the senators, and requesting the representatives, to oppose the restoration of the deposits, and the renewal of the charter. Still in vain, as regarded Mr. Sprague and the whig members of the House, who sat quietly in their seats, while the storm was fiercely raging without, and casting their votes according to the convictions of their own minds.

Mr. Holmes, whose term expired in 1833, was succeeded by Judge Shepley, a firm supporter of General Jackson's measures. Mr. Evans was the only whig member of the House from Maine, at that time.

In February, 1835, the Legislature again adopted a series of resolutions on the same subject, approving of those before adopted, and giving similar instructions. Mr. Sprague, having, in the meantime, been defeated as the whig candidate for governor, and having determined to move to Boston, then resigned his office as senator, and established himself in the profession in Massachusetts, previous to the expiration of his term. While he held the office of senator, he faithfully discharged his duty, maintaining a high rank in that distinguished body, and gave entire satisfaction to his political friends. The mooted questions of obedience to instructions, according to the varying phases of political ascendancy, in the ever-shifting and transitory state of parties, remains unsettled, and I must leave it to the casuist to decide. Subsequently, in the case of Mr. Williams, the card was changed, and instructions as fierce were hurled against him, by the party which had sustained Judge Sprague. It is a political game of shuttlecock, which is adopted to get rid of an opponent from an influential sphere, for the purpose of supplying the place with a friend of the ruling party.

Mr. Sprague continued in the practice at Boston until 1841, when in July of that year, the venerable and honored Judge Davis, having retired from the bench of the District Court of the United States, which he had occupied over forty years, Mr. Sprague was at once appointed to the office. We have before noticed the remarkable similarity in the history of the District Courts in Massachusetts and Maine. They were both created by the same law of Congress, passed in September, 1789, and their first judges were appointed at the same time, viz., John Lowell for Massachusetts, and David Sewall for Maine. Since that period, but three judges have filled the seat of either court. Judge Lowell was succeeded by Judge Davis, in 1801; and he, after an illustrious service of forty years, resigned the office, which has since been filled by the present incumbent. In Maine, Judge Sewall held the office twenty-nine years, until 1818, and was succeeded by Judge Parris, who relinquished it in 1822, to take the governor's chair: since which time the place has been honorably filled for over forty years by the present occupant, Judge Ware — in each court, three judges filling the space of seventy-three years! It is but justice to say, that the judges who are now occupying those important positions, will not suffer in comparison with their distinguished predecessors. Judge Sprague has exhibited through his judicial course of more than twenty-one years, great clearness of judgment, sound discrimination, and legal acumen and accuracy, combined with unquestioned purity and integrity of principle, and urbanity of manners. In a commercial community like Massachusetts, the principles of admiralty law are in constant requisition, and of large magnitude, creating a demand for legal talent, and deep and varied research in the solution of intricate and perplexing questions. The business of that court is very large, taxing almost to excess the physical and mental powers of the judge. Judge Sprague has conducted it most ably through difficulties which would have discouraged many a man of less firmness, perseverance, and intelligence. When it is considered what wise and learned opinions this eminent judge has delivered, notwithstanding his eyes have for years been overshadowed in darkness, our admiration of the judge can only be exceeded by our regard for the man; and constrains us to utter the wish that his judicial life may not fall short of that of his learned predecessor.

No volume of reports has issued from the District Court of Massachusetts; although we cherish a hope that for the sake of the profession and the mercantile community, the judge himself, or some other able hand, will collect the opinions of the court as prepared by that able judge, scattered, as they are, like the leaves of the sybil, and give them a permanent place by the side of the learned decisions of the Circuit Court, with which he is connected. Many of his opinions have appeared in the Law Reporter and other periodicals, and may be studied by lawyers and students as models of reasoning and of judicial style. In 1847, Harvard College justly and properly bestowed upon Judge Sprague its highest honor, that of LL. D.

In August, 1818, Judge Sprague married Sarah Deming of Utica, New York, but a native of Berlin, Connecticut, by whom he had three sons and one daughter. Charles F., the eldest son, died in 1840, aged twenty-one. Seth Edward is clerk of the United States District Court in Massachusetts, a graduate of Harvard, 1841, and of the Law School, 1843. The youngest son is Francis Peleg, a graduate of Harvard Medical School, in the class of 1857. His daughter Sarah is the wife of George P. Upham, a merchant in Boston.

ASHUR WARE. 1817—

In the class at Harvard, of 1804, graduated Ashur Ware, the time-honored Judge of the District Court of the United States for Maine. His class was a brilliant one: it contained sixty-one names, among which were those of Colonel Aspinwall, who lost an arm in the war of 1812, and was long consul at London; Rev. Samuel Carey, loved and early lost; Rev. Dr. Chapin, late President of Waterville College; General Eustis; William Freeman, son of the late Judge Freeman of Portland; the late Benjamin Merrill of Salem; Andrews Norton, the Christian scholar; and Rev. Samuel C. Thacher of Boston. In this talented company, Mr. Ware gained high honors as a scholar, a place on the rolls of the Phi-Beta-Kappa Society, and a forensic at Commencement with Joseph E. Smith. Such was the foundation on which his future labors and fame were to rest. The subject of his forensic seems to point to a study which he afterwards pursued to high results: it was, "Whether the law of nature be equally applicable to individuals and nations." Thacher, a beautiful and polished scholar, had the first part, an English oration; Norton, an English oration on "Duelling;" and Freeman, a poem on "Credulity."

Judge Ware's first American ancestor was Robert Ware, who came to Dedham, Massachusetts, about 1640. He was a Puritan of the "Round-head" party; and for his zeal in that cause, tradition leads us to believe that his safety rendered it necessary or convenient for him to leave the mother country. He came from the eastern part of England, near Boston. I think the family is from Ireland: the family in Devonshire and Essex Counties has the same coat of arms as that of Ireland. Robert Ware of Dublin, at the close of the last century, was great-grandson of Sir James Ware, Knight, the eminent Irish historian and antiquary. Judge Ware was the sixth degree from Robert of Dedham, through John, second, Joseph, third, John, fourth, Joseph, fifth, Ashur, sixth. His grandfather, John, moved to Sherburne, Massachusetts, where he had ten children, of whom Joseph, the father of the judge, was the eldest, and Henry, for forty years the eminent and learned Professor of Divinity at Harvard, was the youngest. Joseph, the father of Ashur, was a man of note in his native town: he held many municipal offices, was in the army of the Revolution, and lost an arm in the battle of White Plains. He had two brothers in the battle of Bunker Hill, George and Benjamin. He died in 1833, aged eighty-four. He had three sons, Alpheus, Ashur, and Henry; and two daughters, Betsey and Patty, by his wife Grace Coolidge of Sherburne.

Judge Ware was born in Sherburne, February 10, 1782: he was fitted for college, partly by his father, who had passed through the preliminary studies for admission to college, and finished with the Rev. Mr. Brown of Sherburne, and was admitted in 1800.

It may be mentioned, in this connection, and as a fact worthy of preservation, that the college and the country are indebted to the liberality of Joseph and John, the father and uncle of Judge Ware, for the education of their younger brother, Henry; whose learned labors and devout life have adorned the college and blessed the country, not only by the many pupils who have received his particular care and instruction, but by his excellent and learned sons, Prof. Henry, Jr., Dr. John, Rev. William, and Charles; and his many daughters, who have transmitted the blood and the Puritan principles, received from this beloved progenitor, to their posterity. His father, being in narrow circumstances, could not afford the means of accomplishing this work, which was happily undertaken by the affectionate brothers.

Of the class of Mr. Ware, we have briefly spoken. After leaving the venerable halls of the university, he spent one year at Exeter, as assistant in the academy, under charge of the distinguished Dr. Abbot. He then returned to Cambridge, where his uncle Henry had, in the meantime, been appointed professor of theology, to succeed Professor Tappan, who died in 1803, and entered his family as a private tutor. He remained in that situation about a year, when, in 1807, he was appointed tutor in Greek at the college; and in 1811, raised to a professorship in the same language, which he continued to hold until 1815. As a teacher in Greek, he was thoroughly furnished: he had an ardent love of the language, and a critical knowledge of it, which he retains by repeated recourse to his classics. During this period, between four and five hundred pupils received instruction from him; among whom, we may number eminent scholars: the late Governor Smith of Maine, Francis C. Gray, Judge Phillips, Octavius Pickering, Edward Everett, Judge Sprague, Charles G. Loring, Bishop Wainwright, Charles Folsom, William H. Prescott, Presidents Sparks and Walker, Dr. Palfrey, George Bancroft, and Caleb Cushing.

And as one of the Faculty, he was in the midst of a constellation of bright particular stars: the genial Kirkland, the grave Ware, the brilliant McKean, Professors Willard and Farrar, the late Dr. Nichols and Judge Preble of Portland, the copious Frisbie, the polished Everett, and the beloved Samuel Cooper Thacher. At that time, commons were held in a hall on the first floor of old Harvard: its well sanded stone floor grated under the tread of the busy feet, as they rushed to the pine, red-painted tables, which extended from the walls on each side of the hall to the aisle which passed from the door to the end of the room. At the upper end of the room were elevated tables for the tutors and officers, who lived in commons; and the classes were ranged in order of seniority from these tables of honor to the door, and were divided into messes,— sixteen, I think, occupied each table, constituting two messes. To each mess were assigned two pewter mugs for drinking vessels, which contained cider or water, and the provisions were served and eaten on pewter dishes: crockery and glass were luxuries unknown at that primitive time, and during the whole period of my college life. These were introduced when the commons were transferred, in 1814 or '15, to University Hall. The cooking was carried on underneath, in the basement; and if there was not enough on the table, we could *size*, as it was called, that is, send to the kitchen for more bread or butter, and it was made an extra charge. Such was the style of living in college to as late a period as 1815. But this did not mar the hilarious enjoyment, which made the old commons hall ring with fun and laughter: no dinner tables outside of a college hall ever exhibited more pranks or jokes than did those of Harvard; and these were accompanied often by missiles, — potatoes, or crusts of bread, not to say sometimes a whole pudding, which proved too solid for the teeth and stomachs of the guests. These were not always harmless, as was proved in the case of Prescott, of the class of 1814, whom I happened to see hit with a crust of bread, which nearly destroyed the sight of his eye; but which probably contributed to make the great historian, who has gone to an undying fame.

It was at the high table, or *dais*, that the officers sat to control the exuberant excitement raging below; and here, at one time, were seated Ware and Frisbie, Thacher, Preble, Nichols, and Norton; and as the elder ones dropped out for other stations in life, came in a younger set, Sanger, Everett, Phillips. Among these wits was a table talk, equal, perhaps, to that which gave Holland House, and that of Samuel Rogers in London, their peculiar grace and celebrity. The sparkling wit, the sharp discussion, the learned criticism, not only gave eclat to the repasts, but quickened the faculties for the larger encounters of life. Here Nichols and Frisbie initiated, or cultivated, their splendid gifts in conversation; and Ware and Preble, in graver discussions, polished their armor for the political controversies which largely engaged their attention when they left the college walls. It was Frisbie, whose conversation was easy and flowing, like the monologue of Coleridge, who, at the inauguration of Kirkland, gave the classical toast, so apt and appropriate, "*Jam, jam, regnat noster Apollo*," which was received with unbounded applause. It was Frisbie, who, when the beef upon the commons table was too strong even for a school boy's stomach, allayed the storm by his gentle words, closing with the expression, "Such accidents, young gentlemen, sometimes occur in the best regulated families." This brilliant scholar died in the service of the college, as Professor of Moral Philosophy and Civil Polity, in 1822.

Judge Ware, when he returned to Cambridge in 1805 or 1806, under the influences which prevailed in his uncle's family, had concluded to pursue the study of divinity, and prepare himself for the ministry. But, after a brief experiment, finding the study not congenial to his tastes, he entered his name as a student-at-law in the office of Loammi Baldwin at Cambridge; and, on resigning his professorship in 1815, he moved into Boston, and finished his studies in the office of his classmate, Joseph E. Smith, who had attained an honorable standing at the Suffolk Bar. While in Boston, he took quite an active part in politics as an advocate of democratic principles; and, in company with Henry Orne, another prominent democratic politician, he edited the "Boston Yankee." He was selected by his party to deliver the 4th of July oration in 1816, in which he attacked the measures and policy of the federalists with extreme severity and sharpness of satire. The next year, he delivered another 4th of July oration in Portland, characterized by the keenness and sarcasm which a man of ardent feelings and brilliant genius could array against his adversaries in times of high party excitement. Loring, in his "Boston Orators," thus speaks of these performances: "His brilliant talents displayed in the two orations, show him a devoted champion for the war with Great Britain, and a decided opponent to the Hartford Convention. They are valuable records of the party feeling of the day. He said of Samuel Dexter, that he indignantly frowned on all attempts to impair the Constitution, or sever the Union." He was particularly severe upon Fisher Ames, and expressed sentiments, under the influence of party excitement, which he does not cherish, I think, at the present day.

Judge Ware was admitted to practice in Suffolk County, in 1816: the next year he came to Portland, and was admitted to the Cumberland Bar. Here he found, besides the elders, whose names have appeared in the preceding pages, a class of young men, destined to uphold the high character of that bar, and to adorn the profession. Among these, were Ebenezer Everett of Brunswick; Joseph Adams of Gorham; William Barrows, Jr., of North Yarmouth, whose early death was greatly lamented; Thomas A. Deblois; Bellamy Storer, now Judge of the Supreme Court in Cincinnati; and John Anderson, whose successful career, both at the bar and in political life, was signally marked. Mr. Anderson was a graduate of Bowdoin College, in the class of 1813; studied his profession with Stephen Longfellow, and was admitted to the bar in 1816. He entered at once into an encouraging business; was ardent, impulsive, uniting the Celtic and Saxon blood: he entered actively into politics; and embracing from conviction and tradition the democratic principle, he soon came into political life, and was elected in 1824, a representative to Congress, in opposition to Mr. Longfellow, and held the seat by repeated elections until 1833. From this position, he succeeded without pause, to the office of mayor of Portland, which he held two years. He was very active and efficient in securing the construction of the Atlantic and St. Lawrence Railroad, by his counsel, his eloquence, and money, and was several years a director. His useful life terminated at the age of sixty-one years, in 1853. He left three sons: one a prominent engineer and agriculturist; a second, who takes his place at the bar; the third, deceased, was a physician.

Mr. Ware immediately took charge of the "Eastern Argus," which was the principal inducement of his coming to Portland; and, by his vigorous pen, gave it a character, which it had never attained before, nor has kept up, since he left it. The subject of separation was then the most interesting topic which engaged the public mind, and he advocated it with consummate ability. On this great event being accomplished, Mr. Ware was rewarded by the office of secretary of state, which he held, until the election of Judge Parris to the office of governor; who having resigned his seat on the bench of the District Court of the United States for Maine District, Judge Ware became his successor, in 1822.

Judge Ware had been but six years at the bar, and was a lawyer without briefs; his business in the courts had been very limited; he had devoted himself to politics, which had superior attractions for him, over the law; his taste and his ambition had been turned in this direction; he had not the ease and freedom of public speaking requisite to make a good advocate, although he had the learning and ability to make a good lawyer; and happily for him and the public, he fell into the right place. Or we may more properly say, being in the place, he most amply and happily qualified himself for it.

He has now steadily, faithfully, and with great ability, filled this honorable station forty years; and the learned opinions which he has published through this long period, and the two volumes of reports which have preserved in part the decisions of his court, give abundant and satisfactory testimony to his profound research, his amplitude of learning, and the clearness and extent of his judicial powers. The admiralty law in this State, when he entered upon his office, was in a crude and imperfect condition : there were no settled rules established in regard to it, and no published decisions to determine the law applicable to it, among us. He went to work at once to investigate its principles, and to establish a code of procedure based upon maritime law and usages as promulgated by the leading writers and standard authorities, from the earliest days of commercial enterprise. His numerous decisions on all branches of law and practice, in the department of an obscure and difficult science, have given a permanent form to the law, and placed him among the most eminent jurists of this or any age. The first volume containing the decisions of Judge Ware from 1822, was published in 1839, pp. 540 : the second volume was published in 1849, pp. 443. Besides the opinions contained in these volumes, there were others published from time to time, in the Law Reporter and other periodicals.

Amidst these learned labors, Judge Ware has never lost the relish for classical studies and general literature : he is an indefatigabte student; reading and study are his meat and drink ; he gives himself to them and is absorbed in them. No young man is more engrossed by pleasure, than he is by study: at the age of eighty, his devotion to it seems to increase, and with it, the accumulation of his store of knowledge and erudition. His pen is constantly employed, and upon subjects of the deepest interest to the community. The new edition of Bouvier's Dictionary, now in course of publication in Philadelphia, will contain several articles prepared by Judge Ware. Among them is a treatise on " Admiralty Jurisdiction," a subject which no man in the country can treat with more ability ; another on the " Duty of Masters of Vessels ; " another on " Privileged Debts." We have reason to believe that these important questions are discussed in a thorough and exhausting manner. Another paper recently written, not suited perhaps to the spirit or region of that publication, we hope to see go into a wider circulation than it could have between the covers of a law book: it is a discussion of the limitations of the government of the United States under its constitutional powers. In this essay, the power in regard to slavery receives a calm, judicious, and careful consideration. Judge Ware is a clear and forcible writer; his style is of classical purity; his newspaper communications have been numerous, and attractive from their brilliancy and point. In 1831, he prepared the "Introductory Remarks," to the first volume of the Maine Historical Collections, a beautiful specimen of his style and thought; he was one of the publishing committee of the society: in 1827, he delivered the Phi-Beta-Kappa oration at Brunswick, which was published. This was an argument in favor of classical learning. I may be indulged in introducing some specimens of this beautiful production. "If," he says, "there be a principle in the human mind, which leads us to hold in reverence what is ancient, there is another original instinct of our nature, by which it is limited and controlled. It is that self-love, that complacency, with which we contemplate our own accomplishments; which easily inclines us to the belief, that in no period of time could human attainments have been carried to a higher pitch of perfection than in the age in which we live. Without taking much trouble to examine, we are ready to believe that there is an inferiority, where there is only a difference." Again: "The manly sense, and the natural and graceful beauties of the ancient writers, took the place of the quibbling pedantry and fantastic conceits of the schoolmen. The intellect of mankind, which had long been held in chains, was set free, and received an impulse, of which it still feels the force. The Grecian and Roman writers became the established models of taste. They still continue to be so. If, in some things, they have been surpassed, it has been in following the path which their example had pointed out. And when we consider the intimate connection, the social character, if I may be allowed the expression, of the liberal arts, it may be said without much exaggeration, that they have been our instructors in all the arts which are tributary to the comforts or the elegancies of life,— which elevate its dignity or enlarge its enjoyments." Again: "It may be said without a metaphor, that in Greece, poetry was the daughter of music. Her infant accents were formed in song, and her voice was modulated to harmony by the melting notes which were awakened from the harp, by the hands of Orpheus or Musæus."

"Plato stands as far above all rivals in this particular, as his countryman and disciple, Demosthenes. The easy and graceful movement of his dialogue, the splendid amplification and harmonious numbers of his declamation, and the warm and animated glow of moral enthusiasm which he has thrown over his mystical speculations, render his works the most perfect specimens of philosophical eloquence ever yet produced."

We cannot dwell much longer among the beauties of this classical discourse: the whole of it is an illustration of the deep influence which the studies of this learned scholar had, in forming his own taste and style; but I think my readers will not tire, if I add two more brief extracts from the address. "In an age of so much intellectual activity as the present, all sorts of new opinions are received with favor. The most extravagant have their hour of triumph, until they are chased from the stage by some new absurdity, or until the restless love of change is drawn off to some more startling paradox. This insatiable love of novelty is carried into literature as well as other things. But the principles of good taste are unchangeable. They have their foundation laid deeply in nature and in truth; and the tide of time which sweeps into oblivion the sickly illusions of distempered imaginations, passes over these unhurt. The Bavii and Mævii of former ages, who, like those of later times, enjoyed for their hour the sunshine of fashionable celebrity, have been long ago gathered to their long home; but the beauties of Homer and Virgil are as new as they were at the beginning."

We close our quotations with some passages of the conclusion. "The literature of antiquity, in its prevailing tone and character, is deeply impregnated with the free spirit of the age in which it was produced. Nothing can more powerfutly invigorate those generous feelings which are inspired by the consciousness of freedom, than a familiarity with the historians and orators of Greece and Rome. There is an uncompromising spirit of liberty breathing its divine inspirations over every page." "After the constitutional liberty of the country sunk under the weight of military despotism, its scattered flames still broke out at intervals, in the few great men who arose to throw a gleam of brightness over the surrounding gloom. It showed itself in the pathetic and affecting complaints of Tacitus, and burst forth in the bitter and indignant sarcasms of Juvenal. The venerable father of song declared in prophetic numbers that the first day of servitude robbed man of half his virtue: and Longinus, the last of the ancient race of great men, holds up the lights of fifteen centuries' experience to verify the words of the poet."

These specimens will show that in literary taste and culture, the scholar was scarcely inferior to the jurist.

In 1820, Judge Ware was appointed by the State one of the trustees of Bowdoin College, which office he held twenty-four years. In 1837, that institution very properly conferred upon him the honorary degree of LL. D. In addition to the several offices above alluded to, Judge Ware was President, several years, of the Portland Athenæum; President of the Androscoggin and Kennebec Railroad Company; the first President of Casco Bank, in 1825; and many years a director in the Bank of Cumberland. But his tastes and pursuits were not of a financial character: they delighted most in law and in general literature, with both of which his mind and spirit were deeply imbued.

In 1831, Judge Ware married Sarah Morgridge, who has ever since continued his cherished companion, and borne him three children, a son and two daughters. The son wears the ancestral name, Joseph, is a graduate of Bowdoin College in the class of 1851, and is a lawyer by profession.

APPENDIX.

EARLY CLERKS AND SHERIFFS.

HAVING treated largely of the gentlemen of the bar in the preceding pages, I deemed it not improper that those who attended upon them faithfully in the courts for many years, should still accompany them in this historical procession. I therefore give brief notices of the early clerks and sheriffs.

The clerks were strictly officers of the courts: they were the custodians of their decrees, their judgments, and records. They were uniformly, and by law, appointed by the respective courts. In the statute of 1639, establishing the County Court, the court was authorized to appoint its clerk; and so, when the Superior Court was constituted under the charter of 1691, the same authority was given to that tribunal; and all the courts, by the statutes creating them, were empowered to make rules and orders for the proceedings therein. They all continued to exercise the power of appointing their own clerks until 1811, when that authority was transferred, for a brief period, to the governor and council. In January, 1814, it was restored by statute to the courts. On the organization of the State of Maine, the power was given to the Executive, and continued in him until 1842, when the office was made elective for a term of years, — first, four years, and by the last statute on the subject, 1855, it was limited to three years.

CLERKS OF THE COURTS.

DANIEL SEWALL—SAMUEL FREEMAN—JONATHAN BOWMAN—WILLIAM ALLEN—JOHN H. SHEPPARD—HENRY SEWALL—OFFICERS OF THE COURTS OF THE UNITED STATES FROM THEIR ORGANIZATION.

DANIEL SEWALL.

There are few things so noticeable in the usages of our courts and of the past times, as the long periods for which the officers and the attendants upon the courts held their appointments. When once a man succeeded to an office, he felt secure of its tenure, and could make the arrangements of his business with a comfortable degree of certainty. And not only so, but the multiplication of offices in the same hands was a common fact, and indicated that the number of persons qualified for their discharge was quite limited, or else there were not so many persons ready to serve their country as modern times have turned up. For instance, in the county of York, John Wheelwright was thirty years Judge of Probate and of the Common Pleas; Simon Frost was Register of Probate, Clerk of the Court of Common Pleas, and Register of Deeds twenty years, or thereabout, from the middle of the last century. Daniel Sewall was thirty-seven years Register of Probate, and about thirty years Clerk of the Courts. Ichabod Goodwin was Sheriff twenty-seven years. In Cumberland and Lincoln Counties, the names of Freeman and Bowman as judges, clerks, and registers, and Cushing, Waite, and Bridge as sheriffs, are coeval with the establishment of the counties, and run into the present century. I propose to speak of these time-honored public servants, that the court and the bar upon which they so long attended, should still be accompanied by them in the retirement of these pages.

Mr. Sewall was born in York, Maine, March 28, 1755, and was a descendant in the fifth generation, from Henry Sewall, the first of the name who came to America. That ancestor was the son of Henry, Mayor of Coventry, and arrived at Newbury in 1634, at the age of twenty years. The descent from him is derived through his second son, John, who married Hannah Fessenden of Cambridge; Nicholas, their son, who married Mehitabel, daughter of Samuel Storer; and Henry, son of Nicholas. Henry was the father of General Henry of Augusta; Daniel, the subject of our notice, and the Rev. Jotham, commonly called "Father Sewall;"—all these spent their lives and died in Maine at very advanced ages; viz., Henry, in 1845, aged ninety-two; Daniel, in 1842, aged eighty-seven; and Jotham, in Chesterville, 1850, aged ninety. Their father was a brother of Stephen Sewall, the learned and honored Professor of Hebrew in Harvard College, from 1765 to 1785, and cousin of David, the upright judge of the District Court of Maine. He was by trade a mason, and carried on a farm on which his son Daniel labored, in connection with his trade as a joiner, during his minority. The three brothers above mentioned were in the fifth degree of descent from the first Henry of Newbury.

Daniel had great facility of application, which, united to a vigorous mind aud industrious habits, enabled him to accomplish a large amount of useful and honorable labor. He was a farmer, a joiner, a school teacher, and was awhile in the army of the Revolution, in which his brother Henry honorably served during the war. In all that he did, he was accurate and faithful: he did not slight himself in improving the opportunities which were offered him, meager though they were, to cultivate his mind: he made special advances in mathematical studies, to which he was addicted through life. He became a practical surveyor, and his services were often employed in this branch.

He devoted all his leisure hours to mental culture, and obtained a good knowledge of the most important English branches. Before the close of the war of the Revolution, he employed himself in making calculations for the astronomical department of almanacs. These were contained in the series published by John Melcher in Portsmouth, New Hampshire. Sometimes he assumed the name of Isaac Bickerstaff, Jr., Bickerstaff being the name under which a popular almanac had long been known. He continued this employment many years, and furnished to those invaluable annuals a large amount of useful mathematical information. What is condensed on a page required many hours of careful study to prepare. His son William acquired taste and skill in the same path, which he used at a future period.

Mr. Sewall also engaged in the practice of law so far as to fill writs, and to attend to other duties of the profession outside of the court room. This was common in all the counties while regular lawyers were few and scattered: persons who were familiar with legal proceedings, especially clerks and sheriffs, were employed in such cases: the regularly admitted attornies entered and took charge of the actions in court, until prevented by a stringent prohibitory law.

In March, 1783, Mr. Sewall was appointed by Governor Hancock Register of Probate for York County, and held the office uninterruptedly until 1820, a period of thirty-seven years. While holding that office, he was appointed, in November, 1792, Clerk of the Court of Common Pleas, having been an assistant to the previous clerk, Timothy Frost, eleven years. His first contract with Frost was to work for him, from sun to sun, for a shilling a day; proof of the cheapness of labor and the dearness of money. When, by the law of March, 1797, the clerks of the Common Pleas were constituted, in most of the counties, recording clerks of the Supreme Court, he received that appointment for York County, and held the offices until 1820, with the exception of 1811, when a general sweep was made by Governor Gerry of all the old office-holders, and their places supplied with the supporters of his administration. Jeremiah Bradbury was appointed to the office, and held it one year, when Mr. Sewall was restored by Governor Gore. The separation of Maine from Massachusetts produced a general change in the incumbents of office, and the modes of administration. The tenure became more uncertain, as it was subject to the fluctuations of party, which was ever changing in the State: the doctrine of rotation acquired great popularity with those who were out of office and seeking to be in: the outs constituted the majority, and were incessant in pressing their claims to be in. The system, we cannot look upon but as mischievous to the best interests of the people, as tending constantly to introduce into the service persons without experience, and often with doubtful qualifications; and when they have acquired familiarity with their duties, they must give place to others who are eager for the emoluments.

In 1792, while holding the offices of register and clerk, he was appointed by the Postmaster General, the honored and honest Timothy Pickering, postmaster at York, an office which he held and faithfully filled about fifteen years, thus holding three good offices at the same time. But it must be remembered that the compensation derived from office was much less at that period than the present, and the business much smaller. As an offset, however, to that, the expenses of living were proportionably less, and the habits of the people were more frugal. Luxury and extravagance had not then manifested themselves to any considerable degree in our District.

In 1815, Mr. Sewall moved from York to Kennebunk. In 1820, on the reorganization of the courts by the new State, the old incumbents of office were set aside, and their places filled by a younger generation. George Thacher of Saco, son of the judge, succeeded to the office of register of probate, and Jeremiah Bradbury of York to that of clerk of the courts. Mr. Sewall, now at the age of seventy-five, having occupied responsible official stations thirty-seven years, retired upon a competency to the calm enjoyments of his cheerful and happy family circle, and his books, which had been the refreshment and strength of his youth and manhood, and were the solace of his old age.

Mr. Sewall married Dorcas Bartlett, daughter of John H. Bartlett of Kittery, by whom he had one son, William Bartlett, of whom we have before spoken, and seven daughters, one of whom married Mark Langdon Hill of Phippsburg. He died October 14, 1842, aged eighty-seven years and nearly seven months. His widow died within five months after, aged eighty-four.

In a notice of this most worthy and venerable man, published in the American Almanac of 1844, it is remarked: "The confidence constantly reposed in his ability, of which he received so many marks, was justified by the diligent and faithful performance of every trust. He was a man of remarkable industry and punctuality, of singular fidelity, probity, and perseverance; possessed of great moral courage and firmness, not unmixed, perhaps, with some of those peculiar traits that strike the present generation as belonging to the character and manners of the old Puritan. To that constancy of self-reliance, energy, and determination which constituted such marked points in his character, he joined a firm and unwavering trust in the overruling administration of an all-wise and good Providence, which enabled him to overcome difficulties and obstacles, and carried him successfully through the course of a long, respectable, and useful life."

SAMUEL FREEMAN.

The case of Samuel Freeman was more extraordinary than that of Mr. Sewall, for he held more offices and held them longer. Mr. Freeman was born in that part of Falmouth which is now Portland, June 15, 1743: and if his family was not so illustrious as the Sewalls, though sufficiently so, yet it was more ancient in America, being among the first settlers of Massachusetts, four years prior to the coming of Henry Sewall. His first American ancestor, from whom he was of the fifth degree, came from Devonshire and settled in Watertown in 1630; and he was the great-great-grandfather of Samuel Freeman of Portland. The first Samuel moved from Watertown to Eastham in Plymouth County, and after his death his widow married Governor Thomas Prince of that colony. Enoch, the father of Samuel of Portland, was the eighth son and ninth child of Samuel, the grandson of the first immigrant, and was born in Eastham, May 19, 1706. He was educated at Harvard College, from which he took his degree in 1729, and in a short time after entered the house of Mr. Hall, a merchant in Boston, as clerk, and in 1732, became a partner. His employment called him occasionally to Maine, and his observation led him to choose Portland as the future place of his residence, to which he moved about 1742. His education and enterprise soon gave him a prominent position in this infant community, and offices accumulated upon him with fearful rapidity, as we should consider at the present time. He was appointed in 1748 to the command of the forces on the eastern frontier, and in successive years held the offices of justice of the peace, naval officer, collector of the port, four years representative to the General Court, judge of the Court of Common Pleas on the organization of the county, and register of deeds, which two last offices he held together twenty-nine years, and in 1770, judge of probate; and he also, by way of variety, practiced law, before any regular practitioners settled in the county. To illustrate my remark before made, relative to the multiplication of offices in the same hands, I cannot have a better example than that before me: Enoch Freeman, at one and the same time, held the following offices: judge of the Common Pleas, judge of probate, register of deeds, colonel of the eastern regiment, selectman, and representative to the General Court. What a day was that for office-*holders!*

His son Samuel rivaled him in this respect, as we shall see before we conclude our notice of him. He received the best education the village afforded, and that is saying considerable, when we remember that the first Stephen Longfellow, who came to Portland, and who graduated at Harvard the year before Mr. Freeman was born, kept the grammar school from which he imbibed his early lessons. After leaving school, he himself engaged in school keeping and also in trade, and connected with these the practice of law, which he pursued to a considerable extent, as his father and several other unadmitted gentlemen in different parts of the Province as well as in Massachusetts had been in the habit of doing. This annoyed the regular practitioners, who, having passed through a long and expensive course of preparation for the proper discharge of the duties of their profession, were not pleased to have their compensation abridged, or the honor of their profession degraded by the blunders of uneducated men. And they adopted restrictive rules in different counties on the subject. At a term of the court held in October, 1770, at York, "by the barristers and attornies practicing in that county," the following rule was adopted: "We, the said barristers and attornies, thinking it detrimental to the public that persons, not regularly admitted and sworn as attornies, should be countenanced by us, do agree that we will not enter, argue, or in any manner assist, in the prosecution of causes where the writs shall be drawn by any person not regularly admitted and sworn, except in cases of necessity, which are to be judged of by the majority of the gentlemen of the bar present at term time."

This rule, rigidly enforced and sustained by the court, had the effect to check, if not entirely stop, the outside practice, and seriously impaired the gains of Mr. Freeman and others who had been largely employed in the business in consequence of their fees being much less than those of the regular lawyers. Mr. Freeman expressed his indignation through the public press: he said, "I am the more influenced to address the public in this manner and on this subject, as I was employed at our last Superior Court to assist a widow, whose late husband's estate she employed me to settle, and on that account had an action there, which the lawyers refused to manage because I drew the writ. But what seems more hard and oppressive, their Honors would not allow me to plead the case myself, but even said I insulted them, when I requested permission to do it, in behalf of the widow."

Bar rules were adopted in Essex County in 1768, and are contained in the records of the Suffolk County Bar, in the handwriting of John Adams, second President of the United States, who took great interest in the subject, having been vexed, in his early practice at Braintree, by the evil generation of irregular practitioners. They had been previously adopted in Boston, and contained one similar to that now quoted from York County.

In the preliminary movements of the people previous to the commencement of hostilities with Great Britain, Mr. Freeman took an active part. In 1774, he was appointed one of the committee of correspondence of the town, and a general meeting of these committees was held in Falmouth in September of that year, of which his father was appointed chairman, and himself clerk. The next year, he was elected sole delegate from Falmouth to the Provincial Congress, and was appointed its secretary for that and the two succeeding years, at the same time representing his town in the Assembly for the years 1776 and 1778.

In 1775, while holding a seat in the Congress and secretary of that body, he received the appointment of Register of Probate, and Clerk of the County Court for Cumberland County, in both which courts his father was judge. The office of register he held thirty years, and was then appointed judge of that court, which he continued to hold to the time of separation, being forty-six years steady service in that court. The clerkship of the Common Pleas Court he held to the same period, with the exception of 1811, when his place was filled by Joseph C. Boyd, appointed by Governor Gerry. The fees of the clerkship, as he himself stated, were very small at first: in 1776, they amounted to only fifteen dollars; and for the first twenty years but to an average of one hundred and twenty-three dollars a year. The last fifteen years, the average was one thousand nine hundred and seventy-five dollars a year; and in 1808, a year of extraordinary business, they were four thousand and eighty dollars. The number of entries of actions in different years, during this period, were as follows; viz.,

1776,	9.	1794,	267.	1814,	879.
1780,	20.	1798,	468.	1818,	1224.
1783,	162.	1801,	867.	1820,	1396.
1785,	196.	1803,	1277.	1831,	888.
1788,	52.	1808,	2293.	1840,	1389.

The fees were divided, until the separation, between the judges of the Common Pleas, the clerk, and sheriff.

The same year, 1776, which was a memorable one in his life, as it was in the annals of the country, Mr. Freeman was appointed postmaster of Falmouth, which office he held twenty-nine years, and when he was removed by Mr. Jefferson, he thought it a most unrighteous decree, and loudly protested against it, as did a majority of his townsmen. The mail was sent but once a week from Boston to Portland from June, 1775, to January, 1789, and was very irregular, being brought by a carrier on horseback: from 1789, it was sent three times a week. As late as 1790, a letter was sixteen days coming from Philadelphia, thirteen from New York, and three from Boston. Mr. Freeman's income from the postoffice, for several years, was as follows: in 1776, two pounds, three shillings, six pence, lawful money; in 1779, sixteen shillings, four pence; in 1780, eight shillings, four pence; in 1785, ten pounds, three shillings, which was the highest for the first eleven years; the aggregate for the eleven years was forty pounds, two shillings, five pence. The first year, the letters did not average five a week; in 1783, the number was fifty-seven, and continued regularly to increase: the postage ranged from five and a quarter pence to thirteen pence on a letter.

The confidence of his fellow-citizens in this estimable man was no less than that of the government. In 1781, he was chosen deacon of the church of the First Parish, and continued in the office about forty-five years, to near the close of his life. In 1788, he was elected one of the selectmen of the town, and with the exception of one year, was chosen twenty-five years, in many of which he served as chairman. In 1802, on the establishment of the Maine Bank in Portland, the first, and for several years the only one in the State, he was elected its president, and continued several years faithfully and intelligently to discharge the responsible duties of the office. He was also a number of years one of the overseers of Bowdoin College, and president of the board from 1816 to 1819: he was, also, a trustee and treasurer of the college. In addition to these various and responsible occupations, he was actively employed as a magistrate in the trial of civil and criminal causes, performing the duties which are now devolved upon the Municipal Court. The following curious paper, drawn up by him in 1797, at the age of fifty-four, has come into my hands, and furnishes authentic information as to his offices: "Minutes of the different kinds of business in which I am engaged, September, 1797. *Official*, as Justice of the Peace; Register of Probate; Clerk of the Court of Common Pleas; Clerk of the Court of General Sessions; Postmaster; Selectman; one of the School Committee; Clerk of the Proprietors of Sufferers' Townships; one of the Committee of the Proprietors to settle the towns, ditto to purchase land for settlers; Treasurer of Bowdoin College; Committee to sell townships granted to said college; Clerk of four eastern townships, [Narraguagus lands]; Agent for ditto; Committee for building the jail; Parish Committee and Assessor; Secretary of the Portland Academy; Committee to sell lands in Standish; Administrator and Guardian in several cases."

Who ever held so many and such a variety of offices at one time, before? Yet we are assured, and partly know, from our own observation, that no duty in any of them escaped his attention or was neglected. He was the most industrious of men, and the most exact and faithful. Long experience had given him great versatility and facility; and a firm constitution, regular habits, and persevering labor enabled him to discharge all his responsible and arduous duties with fidelity and correctness. And at this time he employed himself in preparing works for publication, which his office showed him to be needed, and which proved to be exceedingly useful to the profession and others. These were the Town Officer, Clerk's Assistant, a Probate Manual, and Justice's Assistant. At that time, there were no books of forms suited to the wants of our community; and these works, skillfully prepared by Mr. Freeman, and adapted to the various business of the day, had a very extensive circulation, and passed through several editions. His last work, undertaken when he was near eighty years old, was the editing the journal of his venerable pastor, the Rev. Thomas Smith, who was his minister fifty years, whose deacon he was fourteen years, and his devoted friend. The journal passed through a period of sixty-eight years; was written in a small hand, often with abbreviations, the study of which, and the copying and preparation of accompanying statistics, would have been a severe task for a young man, yet was well and ably accomplished, and published in a duodecimo volume in 1821. To show the facility he had acquired in the execution of his varied tasks, I have been told that in his probate duties and clerk duties, he would add up a long column of figures with accuracy almost as rapidly as he could run his eye over it; and he would pass from one kind of business to another without pause and without any relaxation of his mind, as if pursuing the same current of mental operation.

In his private and domestic life, he was distinguished for uniform kindness and conscientiousness. It was based upon religious principle, deeply ingrained by circumspection and habit. In 1773, he united himself with the church of the First Parish, at the age of thirty, and ever remained a constant and consistent member. In 1777, he married Mary Fowle of Watertown, Mass., by whom he had one daughter and two sons,—Samuel Deane and William. The sons were educated at Harvard, Samuel in 1800, and were good scholars. William graduated in 1804, was a member of the Phi-Beta-Kappa Society, and delivered a poem at Commencement. He studied law with Mr. Symmes in Portland, was admitted to practice, but was led off to other pursuits. He is a man of fine character, literary taste, ability, and talents, and is still living at Narraguagus, where he originally was induced to settle by the large ownership of his father in lands there. Samuel became deranged, and died in 1831.

Mrs. Freeman died in 1785, and the next year Mr. Freeman married Betty, daughter of Enoch Ilsley, and widow of Pearson Jones, by whom he had six children, three sons and three daughters. One daughter, Charlotte, the wife of the Rev. John Boynton, only survives. Charles, first a lawyer, afterwards a worthy clergyman, was settled in Limerick, and died there in 1853. George was a very promising law student in Portland, and died in 1815, aged nineteen. They were both graduates of Bowdoin in the class of 1812. Not one representative of this old and most respected family remains in Portland, the seat, for near ninety years, of their usefulness and honor. Mr. Freeman died June 15, 1831, at the close of the eighty-eighth year of his age. He was tall and erect in his person, of a good figure, and a grave but benevolent countenance. His nose was large, considerably broad, and gave a dignified and manly expression to his face. His eyesight continued good to the last, never having had occasion to use spectacles. He continued to wear breeches and shoes and buckles, to the last, and the old-fashioned buckled stock around his neck: he discontinued the wig, cocked hat, and expansive coat and waistcoat when everybody else left them off. We find a memorandum on his father's account book, which shows that before he was ten years old, his head was shaved to receive the wig, the indispensable appendage of that day.

Mr. Freeman was an inveterate snuff-taker: he used to take immoderate quantities before he left the clerk's office, putting the favorite powder in his hand and stuffing it up his nose. One day, Solicitor General Davis called at the clerk's office for some papers, on which Mr. Freeman took out his snuff-box and began his usual draft, when Davis, impatient, cried out, "Come, come, Mr. Freeman, get me the papers and I'll shove up the snuff."

In all his other duties and labors he never forgot the claims of charity: he was a leader in all the benevolent institutions as well as of education, in the town, as long as he was able to attend their meetings or aid their efforts. And he did not go with his hand and heart shut, but open as melting charity. He was not content to give his services only, but his money followed in the same direction. Take him for all in all, Portland never had a better citizen, and it might be said, "We shall never see his like again."

JONATHAN BOWMAN.

No place in Maine, previous to the Revolution, was so distinguished for its able and talented young men as Pownalboro'. It was a large town, extending from the Kennebec to Sheepscot River, and embracing what are now the towns of Dresden, Alna, Wiscasset, and Perkins, that is, Swan's Island. It was incorporated February 13, 1760, and named in honor of Governor Pownal, who was about retiring from the office which he had acceptably filled from 1757 to 1760.[1] Among these young men, who commenced life

[1] Samuel Bridge, a son of Samuel and grandson of the old sheriff Bridge, has recently presented to his native town, Dresden, an admirable portrait of Governor Pownal for its town hall. He has also made the liberal donation of a similar copy to the State, to be placed in the rotunda of the Capitol at Augusta.

in that remote part of civilzation, were Rev. Jacob Bailey, the "Frontier Missionary" of the Church of England; William, Charles, and Roland Cushing; Dr. Thomas Rice; Timothy Langdon; Edmund Bridge, the time-honored sheriff; and Jonathan Bowman. When the county of Lincoln was organized, in November, 1760, William Cushing was made judge of probate, Charles Cushing sheriff, and Jonathan Bowman register of deeds and clerk of the Court of Common Pleas. The town then contained one hundred and fifteen families, and Mr. Bailey, who had been appointed a missionary to the people there, by the "Venerable Society for Propagating the Gospel" in America, was the only ordained minister in the new county. He had been to London to take orders and receive ordination.

Jonathan Bowman derives his descent from Nathaniel Bowman, who came from England in 1630, probably in the fleet with Winthrop. He settled in Watertown first, then moved to "Cambridge Farms," now Lexington, where he died January 26, 1682. By his wife Anne, he had seven children, two sons and five daughters. His eldest son, Francis, married Martha Sherman, by whom he had eight children, and died in 1687: his, Francis's, fifth son, Joseph, born in 1674, died in 1762, at the age of eighty-eight, having had by his wife Phebe, thirteen children. Jonathan, the fourth of this large family, was the father of the subject of our sketch. He was born in Lexington, February 23, 1704; graduated at Harvard College in 1724; was settled in the ministry at Dorchester, Massachusetts, November 5, 1729, and died there March 30, 1775. His wife was Hannah, a daughter of the Rev. John Hancock of Lexington, grandfather of Governor John Hancock, by whom he had seven children. Two of his sons, Jonathan and William, graduated at Harvard College, Jonathan in 1755, and William in 1764: the latter, born in 1744, settled in Roxbury, filling many useful and honorable stations: he married Lucy, a daughter of Governor Increase Sumner, and sister of the late General William H. Sumner, and died in 1818. His son, William, was an officer in Colonel Miller's regiment on the frontier, and distinguished himself in the war of 1812.

Jonathan was born in Dorchester, December 8, 1735: in his class at college were William Browne, the refugee judge of the Supreme Court of Massachusetts; John Wentworth, the refugee Governor of New Hampshire; the patriot judge, David Sewall of Maine; the still more distinguished President, John Adams; Charles Cushing, first sheriff of Lincoln; and the eccentric and unsophisticated missionary, Jacob Bailey. How singular the coincidence, that three classmates, Bailey, Bowman, and Cushing, ingenious and well educated, should have settled at the same place, and near the same time, in the wilderness of Maine. One thing led to another, Bailey first went, William Cushing was already there, and the others followed as office was opened for them under the new county. When hostilities with the mother country commenced, Mr. Bailey adhered to the royal cause, and a bitter feud arose among these old friends, which led to recrimination and persecution. Bailey felt obliged to leave the country, and sought refuge in Nova Scotia in 1779. Charles Cushing was seized at night by a loyalist party, towards the close of the war, under John Jones, a violent tory, and hurried away to the British army at Castine. In July, 1777, Mr. Bailey, in a memorial signed by fifty-four inhabitants of Pownalboro', well affected toward the Church of England, which had been established there under Bailey, says, "Mr. Bowman came here in 1761, invested with several places of profit under government: Colonel Cushing came and voluntarily joined with the church, became a communicant, and was chosen warden." They afterwards became hostile to the church, as Mr. Bailey asserts, charging Bowman and Cushing as the chief actors. He says in the memorial, "Our enemies are determined to ruin us. They have put every churchman in the list for transportation, even the captain of the militia, a most zealous friend for the country." He adds, "The occasion of this petition was briefly as follows: Mr. Bowman seized the land where the church and parsonage were erected, as the property of Major Goodwin; and Cushing, the sheriff, coming suddenly with a number of men to turn me out of possession, I, ignorantly, took a short lease under Mr. Bowman, which so offended Dr. Gardiner, that he declared that he would apply to the society for my removal. Upon which, our people agreed to send this petition to the society." Again he says, "I would further remark, that Colonel Cushing asserts that there are no church people in this place. This is very surprising, when by far the majority of the present inhabitants have been married, baptized, and received the other sacrament in this church." In another letter, dated August 26, 1778, Mr. Bailey says, "Colonel Cushing has declared, in the most positive terms, that I shall never officiate again in this place; and if I attempt to transgress this mandate, that he will take me out of my house with an armed force, and commit me to jail." Mr. Cushing's letter to him of the same date does not sustain this charge so fully as stated: it says, "Sir, I am informed of your arrival, but have not heard what your conclusion is respecting the oath of allegiance to the United States of America. I trust you cannot think of residing here in the exercise of your functions, until you have complied in taking said oath."

The persecution which Mr. Bailey suffered was evidently caused by his hostility to the Revolutionary government: he utterly opposed it, and his influence must have been considerable in keeping up an agitation among the people of the town. He would not take the oath of allegiance, nor abandon his loyalty to the king and the church, nor leave the country. Bowman and Cushing were officials whose duty it was to preserve the peace, to sustain the cause of the new government, and enforce obedience to its laws. Whether they used more harshness in this case than was necessary, we cannot determine until we hear from the other side: it is evident that Mr. Bailey was a pretty obstinate subject to deal with, judging from his own presentation of the case, as we find it in his manuscript letters and papers in the hands of the Rev. William S. Perry, rector of St. Stephen's church in Portland, to whose kindness we are indebted for their use. They remind us of the wretched state of things now existing in this country, where the oath of allegiance finds many a recusant, even in loyal or semi-loyal States.

Mr. Bowman, it appears, went to Pownalboro' in 1760, with commissions in his pocket as register of deeds and clerk of the court: the register, by the act establishing the county, was to be appointed by the governor and council, to hold his office five years, from February, 1761, afterwards to be elected by the people. The clerks of the courts were appointed by the respective courts. On the organization of the county, the officers were as follows: *Judges of the Common Pleas*, Samuel Denny, William Lithgow, Aaron Hinkley, and John North; *Judge of Probate*, William Cushing; *Register of Probate*, Jonathan Bowman; *Sheriff*, Charles Cushing; *Register of Deeds*, Jonathan Bowman. He held the office of register of deeds until 1781. In 1772, he was appointed judge of probate, as successor to William Cushing, who was promoted to the Superior Court. In this office, he was recommissioned by Governor Hancock in 1781, and continued in it until his death, in 1804,—a period of thirty-two years. It appears by the records of the courts, that Mr. Bowman was appointed clerk of the Court of Sessions, March 2, 1761, and held the office until January 12, 1796,—a period of near thirty-five years, when he resigned. On May 26, 1761, he was appointed clerk of the Common Pleas, and continued in the office until 1794: in June, 1791, his son, Jonathan Bowman, Jr., was appointed assistant clerk, and so continued until the resignation of his father, when he was made chief clerk: he continued in the office until September, 1801, when Alden Bradford, who had been the clergyman in Wiscasset, and was afterwards secretary of State of Massachusetts, was appointed. During part of the time, William Bowman, another son of the judge, was assistant of his brother, and afterwards chief clerk of the Court of Sessions. His son Thomas was the first register of probate in Kennebec County, 1799. It appears from the probate records of Lincoln, that Jonathan Bowman was register of probate in November, 1760, and held the office until Judge Cushing, who had been the judge of probate, was elevated to the bench of the Superior Court, in 1772, when Mr. Bowman became his successor. In 1791, his son Jonathan, who had graduated the year before, was appointed register of probate, and held the office until 1803, when Bradford succeeded him. Mr. Williamson, in a note on the organization of Lincoln County, says that William Bryant was the first register: this is not sustained by the records, which contain the name of Bowman as register at that time. Judge Bowman accumulated a large estate by his various offices and speculations. He lived at a beautiful spot on the eastern bank of the Kennebec, about a mile below the court-house. His house remains a conspicuous object to those who sail by on this charming river, whose varied scenery furnishes ever new pleasure to the tourist. He was a man of tall and commanding figure. John H. Sheppard, Esq., the learned librarian of the New England Genealogical Society, to whom I am greatly indebted for my genealogical and many other facts, in this and my notice of Sheriff Bridge, thus speaks of Judge Bowman: "He was a man of tall and striking appearance: his prominent features, silvery locks, full black suit with small clothes, silk stockings, and large glittering shoe buckles, have left their portrait on the memory of one, who, when a small boy, accompanied his father on a visit to the mansion of Judge Bowman."

His speculations were not always successful: he was concerned in the great project of Charles Vaughan, a wealthy merchant of Boston, and a large proprietor of land on the Kennebec; who, in the latter part of the last century, perceiving the resources and advantages of the Kennebec valley, set about to improve them, and to give them an ample development. Like Bingham and numerous other persons, whose familiarity with the high prices of real estate in the old countries conceived the idea that the prices on this side of the Atlantic must greatly increase under the rapid immigration and settlement of the country, he invested largely in the wild lands of Maine, and in building up towns and villages. They were greatly in advance of their age, and found, to their cost, that they could not force population, nor commerce, nor manufactures, out of the natural channels which they would gradually work for themselves, in the steady progress which American society was surely and gradually making.

Mr. Vaughan and his associates, finding no commercial town on the Kennebec, determined to make one: they fixed upon Hallowell as the great city at the head of navigation, and selected Jones's Eddy as the seaport. They spared no expense to give vitality and success to their grand ideas: they built at Hallowell a distillery, a spacious brewery for malt liquor, an expensive flour mill with the most approved machinery, wharves, stores, and houses for the accommodation of these branches of industry. At Jones's Eddy, wharves, houses, and stores were constructed, suited to a large commercial business. But the business did not and would not come; and no advance has been made at the Eddy for more than sixty years, and Hallowell is probably less prosperous than it was when the energetic and public-spirited Mr. Vaughan was striving to build it up as a great metropolis. Jones's Eddy is about nine miles above Hunnewell's Point at the mouth of the river, and about four miles below Bath: it is a snug and quiet nook, well suited by deep water and protecting arms for a safe harbor, but is unsupported by a fertile and productive country. Judge Bowman partook of the disappointment and losses of this premature enterprise.

Judge Bowman was twice married; first, April 26, 1770, to Mary Emerson, daughter of Ebenezer Lowell of Boston; his second wife was Ann Goodwin of Dresden, to whom he was married January 1, 1798. She died in Dresden, January 26, 1856, at the age of ninety-one: he died September 4, 1804, in the sixty-ninth year of his age. By his first wife, he had four children, viz., Jonathan, William, Thomas, and Mary, who was born November 22, 1784, married to Dr. Jonathan B. Parker of Wiscasset, January 18, 1800, and died soon after. His oldest son, Jonathan, was born April 17, 1771, graduated at Harvard College, 1790, of which class the venerable Quincy is the only survivor' and the oldest graduate. He qualified himself for the bar, and opened an office in Wiscasset in 1793, having the year before been appointed clerk of the Court of Common Pleas and Sessions in connection with his father, and register of probate, his father being the judge. He held the office of clerk of the Supreme Court and of the Common Pleas until 1801, when Alden Bradford superseded him, but he continued register of probate two years longer, when Bradford succeeded to that also. In 1803, his brother William was appointed clerk of the sessions.

Jonathan, Jr., married, in September, 1798, Lydia Wood, daughter of General Abiel Wood of Wiscasset, who died, leaving a daughter, an only child. In 1806, he married Sally D. Clough, and died August 21, 1808. His daughter, Louisa Lydia, had a fine taste for music. She married in 1818 Benjamin Sewall, a merchant in Boston, and died in 1828, leaving an only daughter, who married, in 1845, Charles D. Hubbard, a merchant in Boston. She died in 1854, leaving three children.

Mr. Sheppard says of Mr. Bowman, Jr., that "he was a tall and handsome man: he wore his hair powdered, with a queue tied with black ribbon, a fashion of that day. He was a man of high spirit, and fought a duel with Captain James Hodge, and wounded him: the origin of the quarrel is not known at the present day.

William, the second son of Judge Bowman, was born October 2, 1772: he entered Harvard College, but did not graduate. He practiced law at Wiscasset, and in 1803 was appointed clerk of the Court of Sessions, which office he held until 1811: he was also postmaster of Wiscasset. He married Phebe, a daughter of Sheriff Bridge, and died in September, 1826, leaving a daughter born in 1802, who married James Johnson of Dresden, in 1827; and one son, Edmund Bridge Bowman, born August 29, 1804. He graduated at Bowdoin College in 1823, settled first in Bowdoinham as a lawyer, and now resides in Wiscasset, having been recently clerk of the courts for Lincoln County. By his wife Hannah D. Norris, whom he married in 1828, he had nine children.

Thomas Bowman, the third son of Judge Bowman, was born May 20, 1774, a graduate of Harvard, 1794. A particular notice of this gentleman will be found in his appropriate place as a lawyer. He was also the first register of probate in Kennebec County, and completes the remarkable and *unique* case, of a father and all his sons and a grandson having filled the office, for a series of years, of clerk or register of the courts,—the father having held the office of clerk, without intermission from the organization of the county, in 1760, to his death—forty-four years; and always more than one office at the same time. As for instance, register of deeds and clerk of the court, and register of probate; then judge of probate, register of deeds, and clerk; and finally, judge of the Common Pleas and judge of probate, which two offices he filled at the time of his death, having held that of probate from January, 1772, to his death, thirty-two years. So that his family monopolized the offices of clerk of the several courts and register of probate, from 1760 into the present century, and the head of the family passing from the clerkship of the two courts to the bench in each. He was register of deeds from 1760 to 1782.

The following is a transcript of the first entry upon the records of Lincoln County.

"LINCOLN, SC.

Anno Regni Regis Georgii Tertii magnæ Britanniæ Franciæ & Hiberniæ, Primo.

At his Majesty's Court of General Sessions of the Peace, held at Pownalborough within and for the County of Lincoln on the Second Tuesday of May, being the Twelfth day of said Month Annoque Domini 1761.

His Majesty's Justices present are as follows, viz.,

Samuel Denny Aaron Hinkley William Cushing Jonathan Bowman	Esqrs.	Patrick Drummond Joseph Patten James Howard John Stinson	Esqrs.

At a meeting of the Justices of the General Sessions of the Peace for the said County, March the Second 1761 at Georgetown in said County, present Samuel Denny, Esqr., William Lithgow, Esqr., Aaron Hinkley, Esqr., William Cushing, Esqr., James Howard, Esqr., Patrick Drummond, Esqr., and Joseph Patten, Esqr.

Jonathan Bowman, Esqr., unanimously appointed Clerk of said Court of Sessions. A True Copy from the Minutes of said Meeting,—Attest Samuel Denny. Sworn to the said office Before me, Aaron Hinkley, Justice of Peace."

WILLIAM ALLEN.

Mr. Allen, more familiarly known to the old lawyers in Somerset County, and whose name appeared on their writs for several years, as William Allen, Jr., was a native of Chilmark in Martha's Vineyard, where he was born, April 16, 1780, on what was then the manor of Tisbury, by special grant to his ancestor. In 1792, at the age of twelve years, he migrated with his father to the wilderness of Maine, to the place which is now the town of Industry, in the county of Franklin. He speaks of their location as "a log camp two miles beyond any human habitation, and forty miles beyond any incorporated town." To show what hardships the pioneer occupants of the beautiful valley of the Sandy River had to endure, I must use again his graphic description. "We resided in that camp five years, near a large swamp, tormented with musquitoes in summer, and covered with snow in the winter, secluded from society, without any school, and on unproductive land. We then removed four miles east to another log camp, where the land was good, and where by constant labor, we soon could raise corn and grain sufficient for the family, consisting of twelve persons, — father, mother, six sons and four daughters. We lived comfortably till I became of age, when I commenced clearing up a farm for myself in the woods: we had no schools. I succeeded well, raised good crops, and, in 1802, when twenty-two years old, I was able to pay my board six weeks at Hallowell Academy." Such is a specimen of what the early settlers of our backwoods had to endure in opening those fair lands to the light of civilization and profitable culture. It may fairly be considered as the pursuit of the means of living under difficulties.

In our notice of Frederic Allen, the distinguished lawyer of Gardiner, a relative of William, we made some reference to their origin. Their common ancestor in this country was James, who was born in England, in 1636, married to Elizabeth Perkins, and died at Tisbury, July 25, 1714, aged seventy-eight. His second son, James, married Mary Bourn, and died at Chilmark, on the Vineyard, 1724, aged fifty: his eldest son, Sylvanus, married Jane, a daughter of the Rev. William Homes of Chilmark, July 1, 1725, and died 1787, aged eighty-six. The Rev. Mr. Homes was a native of Scotland, born about 1662, and settled in the ministry at Strabane, Ireland: after remaining there twelve years, he came to Martha's Vineyard and settled over the parish there, where he died in 1747. His diary, kept in a beautiful handwriting, has been this year presented to the Maine Historical Society, by the subject of this notice. The oldest son of Sylvanus and Jane (Homes) Allen, was James, born in Chilmark, 1732, married to Mary Athearn, and died in 1815, aged eighty-three: their oldest son was William, who was born 1756, married Love Coffin, and was the father of William, our present subject: he moved to Industry, in 1792, and died in 1842, aged eighty-six. William Allen is, therefore, of the sixth descent from the first James, and the fifth from the Rev. William Homes. John Allen, the great grandfather of Frederick of Gardiner, and Sylvanus Allen, the great grandfather of William of Norridgewock, both married daughters of the Rev. William Homes; and, therefore, they both center in that gentleman, as well as in the first James Allen, as their common ancestors.

At the age of twenty-two, Mr. Allen first had the benefit of a competent instructor to guide him in his studies: this was Samuel Moody, one of a family distinguished for its teachers; and he entered upon the pursuit of knowledge with the earnestness with which a famished man rushes to food. Such was his ardor and such was his mental capacity, that he succeeded in six weeks in obtaining a knowledge of English grammar, plane trigonometry, geometry, and the theory of surveying. And though he did not receive a college diploma, he obtained from his instructor a certificate, which answered all the purpose to introduce him as a teacher to the towns in his county. It certified that "The improvement made in the several studies he pursued was answerable to my highest expectations. I recommend him to be a person of a judicious, penetrating mind, and so far as I am acquainted with him, of a good moral character. His knowledge in reading, writing, English grammar, and arithmetic is such as, I think, qualifies him for instructing in those branches of literature usually taught in a common English school." He says that this diploma was not without its effect, for "On my way home I had applications for teaching two of the best schools in the county, ragged as I was." Schoolmasters were not abroad then as they are now, and the services of a faithful one in that region were diligently sought and highly prized. The immigrants, principally from the old Bay State and New Hampshire, had received the benefit of good common schools, and they desired to impart it to their children. His continued progress I cannot better express than in his own simple style. On his way home from Hallowell, he says, "I took a letter from a land proprietor to a noted surveyor, urging his completion of his surveys of three townships for which purchasers were waiting. I went out of my way to carry the message, with the hope that the surveyor would require my assistance. He did employ me two days at seventy-five cents a day, to complete the plan of one town, and I went home rejoicing, with a dollar in my pocket and ten dollars' worth of instruction in plotting lots fronting on a crooked river, so as to contain equal quantities, &c. I kept school in Farmington, under inspection of Henry V. Chamberlain, who, in visiting the school, spoke encouragingly and in a very gentlemanly manner. I taught in Winthrop the two following winters, and worked on my land in summers. In 1803, the place where my farm was situated was incorporated into a town by the name of Industry. I was chosen first selectman, and served in that office every year that I resided there, until 1813. In the fall of 1805, I was employed by my good friend, Samuel Moody, an instructor in the English department of Hallowell Academy, where I remained two years with increased compensation, when the state of my health and the condition of my farm required my personal attention."

When the county of Somerset was organized in 1809, Mr. Allen was appointed one of the justices of the peace for the county, and living near the border of the county, and but one mile from the line of Farmington, in which near half the county of Somerset did business, he became a popular magistrate for the neighboring towns. He tried the causes of the principal attornies there, and Messrs. Nathan Cutler, Elnathan Pope, Zachariah Soule, Hiram Belcher, and others brought their actions before him, so that in his capacity of judge of small causes, his transactions were quite large: in four years, their entries amounted to two hundred, all of which he recorded at full length. He was also appointed one of the special justices of the Court of Common Pleas, and officiated until that court was abolished in 1811. William Jones, a lawyer of some repute in Norridgewock, had been appointed the first judge of probate and the first clerk of the courts in the new county, but dying in 1813, Mr. Allen was appointed clerk in his place by the Circuit Court, then consisting of Weston Chief Justice, Ames of Bath, and Thatcher of Thomaston: he had previously, in 1812, been appointed temporary clerk during the sickness of Mr. Jones.

The duties of this office he was well qualified to discharge, by his experience as a practical justice and his service on the bench, as well as by his general habits of application and accuracy. He continued in the office twelve years, outliving the old Circuit Court several years, and retiring at last with the consciousness of having faithfully performed his trust, and given satisfaction to those immediately interested in the business of the courts, and all who had occasion to meet him on official business. During this period, he became intimately acquainted with all the lawyers who practiced in that county, embracing those who earliest went there, through a period of more than fifty years,—Wilde and Bond, Boutelle, Rice and Kidder, Chamberlain, Soule, Cutler, Williams, McLellan, Belcher, — besides those from distant counties, who occasionally illuminated that remote bar,— as Mellen, Orr, Greenleaf, &c. The variety of talent and character possessed by these counselors, many of them eminent, made an impression upon his vivid memory which will not be obliterated while reason and memory retain their power in his mind.

After his appointment as clerk, Mr. Allen moved to Norridgewock, the shire town of the county, and the favor which he enjoyed in the town where he had lived for more than twenty years, followed him to his new residence. It was a popularity which followed as well as went before, for it was founded upon integrity of character, intelligence, and prompt business habits. We have mentioned his continued employment at Industry in municipal offices: he had not resided long in Norridgewock before his services in the same line were sought for there. In 1816, he was elected one of the selectmen and assessors, and held the office, by successive re-elections, seventeen years, and five years subsequently, making twenty-two years that he held the office. In 1825 and 1828, he represented the town in the Legislature, and in 1816 and 1819, in the conventions which met at Brunswick and Portland on the subject of the separation of Maine from Massachusetts. In both the conventions, he was one of the committee to draft a constitution. The vote of Norridgewock, in 1816, was sixty-four in favor of separation and sixty-five against it; but on the trial in 1819, a large majority voted in favor of the measure, leaders in both parties struggling to show their zeal, with a hope, probably, to partake of the patronage, as in this last attempt, the accomplishment of the long sought-for end seemed to be a foregone conclusion.

The confidence thus reposed in Mr. Allen by those who knew him best, through a period of more than forty years, sufficiently testifies to his ability, his moral worth, and his capacity for business. And the confidence was well bestowed and never, betrayed, and in the various responsible positions in which he was placed, he was always found equal to the trusts committed to his charge. And he still devotes himself with his accustomed industry, and as far as his health will permit, to the settlement of estates and other probate and legal business, for which his services are much required.

In 1808, Mr. Allen married Hannah Titcomb, a daughter of Stephen Titcomb, the first settler in Sandy River valley. Mr. Titcomb explored the country and took up a lot there as early as 1776, and in 1780 commenced his perilous journey of seventy miles through the forests from Topsham to the log hut he had erected in the woods, with a young wife and two young children, one an infant daughter in her arms. The last habitation on the route was where Readfield Corner now is, a log cabin, twenty-two miles short of their destination. This then infant daughter became the wife of Mr. Allen, and for fifty-one years was the dearly beloved, most worthy, and cherished companion of her devoted husband. She died deeply lamented, March 26, 1859. By her, he had four sons and one daughter. The daughter became the wife of John S. Abbott, a prominent lawyer, and once the attorney general of Maine, now a resident in Boston: she died in 1858. Of the sons, William, Stephen, and Charles were graduates of Bowdoin College: the two latter are able and popular ministers of the Methodist denomination: William and Albert B. died while pursuing the study of law. Mr. Allen has not only given his two sons to the ministry, but has himself been a devoted and exemplary servant, member, and officer of the Methodist Church during his long life; and still lives to give it his support by the influence of his virtues, his labors, and his pecuniary means.

JOHN H. SHEPPARD — REGISTER OF PROBATE. 1817—1834.

Two lawyers of our State were natives of England: of one, Mr. Hopkins, we have spoken in previous pages. The other is the subject of the following notice, who was also register of probate for Lincoln County seven-

John H. Sheppard.

1850.

teen years, under the excellent Judge Bailey. We are permitted to use on this occasion an autobiography, which cannot fail to prove interesting.

I was born March 17, 1789, at Cirencester, Gloucestershire, England,—a town surrounded with a wall by Julius Cæsar, portions of which, two miles in extent, are still visible. There my ancestors lived, and their genealogy, running some ages back, is in my possession. My father, John Sheppard, a merchant, was well educated at an English school, and served his time in a counting-house in London. He married my mother, Sarah Collier of that city, who had been two years under tuition at a convent in France, and excelled in music. They were both young, and emigrated to America about 1793. They went first to Philadelphia, and then to Hallowell on the Kennebec; but I have no recollection of that period. For several years, my father was engaged in trade at the "Hook," so called, — a handsome bend in the river,— where "Sheppard's Wharf," almost at the head of navigation, still preserves his name, while the ancient house where we lived, has vanished from that beautiful spot. He was concerned in a large brewery with Charles Vaughan, Esq., and built a brig named, I believe, the Bermuda, which foundered at sea, uninsured. He was unfortunate, wound up his business, and went as supercargo on a voyage to the East Indies, in which he acquired such a knowledge of navigation and lunar calculations, that he afterwards took the command of a ship belonging to Stephen Higginson & Co., of Boston. In the recent "Commemorative Discourse on the Death of Hon. Edward A. Newton," by the Rev. Dr. Randall, page nineteen, it is remarked that Mr. Newton went to India, January, 1805, "in the capacity of assistant to the captain, who was supercargo." My father was that man; and it is singular that Mr. Newton, a member of our Genealogical Society, on the 7th of February last, upon my being introduced to him at the rooms, should have mentioned the same fact to me. He spoke in the highest terms of my father as an English gentleman of fine figure and appearance, and of my mother, whose voice of music he remembered well, and whom he described as a woman of elegant symmetry and beauty.

My father had many warm friends: among them was that finished classic scholar and man of genius, the late Rev. John S. J. Gardiner, D. D., rector of Trinity Church, under whose care I was at college, and to whom I am indebted for a love of choice reading and literature, which have been a perennial consolation and support in all the changes of fortune. The Hon. Benjamin Vaughan, LL. D., who settled in Hallowell soon after my father, was another friend; and the friendship of such a man, to him and his family, and particularly to myself, is among the halcyon recollections of early life. My father wrote a very handsome hand, and kept a journal when absent, in a style of accuracy, conciseness, and vigor: he was a great reader, and had a fine taste. He died of the yellow fever at Point Petre, Guadaloupe, August 22, 1807, aged about forty, and was buried with Masonic obsequies. I was then a student at law, and when the news reached us, and I thought of a widowed mother and seven children, of whom I was the eldest, being only eighteen, I was seized with a dangerous fever, which laid me on the bed of sickness for a long time, for I was greatly attached to my father.

As to myself, I was seven years under the care of Samuel Moody, preceptor of Hallowell Academy, since deceased, a thorough Dartmouth scholar, and superior instructor. I can see, in the visions of the past, his tall, majestic form, like an admiral on the deck of his frigate, treading the academic floor, arrayed in small clothes, the costume of the time, with his bright blue eye watching over his one hundred pupils at their desks. He was severe at times, but affectionate, and used the ferule as a scepter of righteousness. I loved him and was a favorite, for he let me study the Eclogues of Virgil in school hours under the groves of the Academy. His scholars turned out well in the world. Among them was my friend, General A. S. Dearborn, late Mayor of Roxbury; Nathan Weston, formerly chief justice of the Supreme Judicial Court of Maine; Hon. Reuel Williams; Charles Shaw, author of a history of Boston; Alfred Johnson, late judge of probate at Belfast; Joseph M. Marsh, Esq., cashier of the Exchange Bank, Boston; and many others, since of note in life.

In 1804, I entered Harvard University. My chum was Lloyd Nicholas Rogers of Baltimore, a fine Greek scholar, who died November 30, 1860. My father had been unfortunate, and withdrew my connection in the middle of the junior year; up to which time my collegiate expenses had been generously defrayed by the late George Higginson, Esq., of Boston, who, when I had finished my law studies, gave me a law library worth five hundred dollars. I entered the office of Wilde and Bond, Hallowell, the late distinguished Judge Wilde, who was to me as a father, and whose honored memory I shall ever cherish. Without a degree, the term of study was then four years, during which, in the office, I read all the law library, and at home, went through the Iliad and Odyssey and several Greek authors, acquired some knowledge of French and more of Italian, especially of the Divina Comedia of Dante, and the marvellous style of Boccace. I endeavored to sleep but four hours a day, but my health suffered.

I was admitted at the bar in August, 1810, opened an office in Wiscasset, and for a season almost lost my taste for literary pursuits in a struggle for support. *Nil Desperandum* is the motto on my father's coat of arms, yet I found, for years, the truth of Juvenal's sad remark:

> "Haud facile emergunt, quorum virtutibus obstat
> *Res angustæ domi.*"—Satire III., 164.

In 1817, I was appointed register of probate for Lincoln County (Jeremiah Bailey, judge), by Governor Brooks. I held this office seventeen years, to April 1, 1834, and was also notary public. It enabled me to take care of my mother, three sisters, and young brother, whom I removed from

Portland in 1816. She had taught school since my father's death, and especially music, in Hallowell, and afterwards in Portland under Judge Mellen's patronage. She gave an accomplished education to her daughters; but I saw too plainly her health began to fail after the death of my sister Frances. This fond parent died November 6, 1818, and at the time I had the means to make her more happy. I honor her memory for the noblo spirit with which she bore her sorrows and brought up a large family. She belonged to the Episcopal Church: her religion was noiseless, her spirits cheerful, and so prudent she seldom, if ever, spoke an unkind or disparaging word of any one.

My sister, Harriet Helen, born 1791, died April 10, 1817, aged twenty-six; my brother, George Albert, merchant in Calcutta, married a daughter of one of the directors of the East India Company, born 1793, died 1834; Frances died of a rapid decline, 1814, in Portland, on the eve of a most flattering marriage; Ann Augusta married Dr. P. E. Theobald of Wiscasset, May 23, 1822, and died September 6, 1824; Louisa, born 1806, married Major Samuel Page of Wiscasset, and died October 3, 1833, aged twenty-seven, leaving two children; and Wm. W., born 1807, died of cholera, on the Mississippi, 1834.

I was married to Helen, daughter of the late Abiel Wood, May 13, 1819. We had three children: Hannah Wood, born February 9, 1820, who was married to Dr. Stephen B. Sewall, and recently died, November 19, 1862, aged forty-two, leaving a daughter and son, Helen and Frederic; John H., born March 7, 1822, graduated at Bowdoin College, 1845, and at Cambridge in 1849, M. D.; and Abiel Wood, born March 30, 1827, educated as a merchant. They have long been in California.

I received the honor of A. M. from Bowdoin College in 1820, and was one of the board of overseers for several years, from 1831 to 1852. I was appointed one of the general assignees in Maine, under the last United States bankrupt law, by Hon. Judge Ware. In 1842, on account of my wife's health, I removed to Boston, where this most affectionate partner was taken from me, June 26, 1843. Since that time, I have resided in that city and kept an office, but have never practiced in the courts. In Wiscasset, I had an extensive run of business; at one term of the court, was engaged in almost every jury trial. Before Metcalf's Digest of Massachusetts Reports was published, I had prepared one similar to it, which Judge Mellen examined, and advised me to publish, but after that more elaborate work came out, I was too late. November 13, 1846, I was again married, to Mrs. O. B. Foster, daughter of the late Rev. Ezra Willmarth of Georgetown, Massachusetts. In January, 1861, I was elected librarian of the New England Historico-Genealogical Society, which office I now hold.

NOTE.

We may add to this interesting memoir a few facts, which the author has modestly omitted. The notice of Mr. Sheppard would be incomplete if his efforts and his honors, as a prominent and leading member of the Masonic Order, should have no place in it. Mr. Sheppard in early life, following the example of his father, entered the Order as an apprentice, and has ever since, with the ardor and energy which make part of his character, zealously devoted himself, through good report and evil report, to its service. As early as 1820, he was a member of the Royal Arch Chapter, and was Royal Arch Captain of the New Jerusalem Chapter of Wiscasset. In that year, the Grand Lodge of Maine was incorporated, of which William King, Governor of the State, was made Grand Master, and Simon Greenleaf, Deputy Grand Master. And the Lodge inaugurated its establishment by a grand and gorgeous jubilee in Portland, which had never been exceeded in the State. Mr. Sheppard was present on this occasion, June 24, 1820, and delivered an address. He has delivered several other Masonic orations before the Grand Lodges of Maine, New Hampshire, and Vermont, and on other public occasions, some of which were published, and well received by the Order and the community. The most prominent of these, perhaps, was his "Defense of Masonry," delivered at Wiscasset, June 24, 1831, at a time when the attacks upon the Masonic institution were incessant and severe. This address was published in Boston, and brought down upon its author a shower of crimination and abuse from all the anti-Masonic papers published in the land. The address was received with great favor by the advocates of Masonry: three editions, numbering three thousand copies, were published. Among those who attacked the sentiments of the address, was no less a person than John Quincy Adams: his principal animadversion was against a statement of the address, that John Adams, father of John Quincy, was a friend to Masonry. This his son denied, and made a personal attack in a Boston paper against the author of the address. To this attack, Mr. Sheppard replied in the Boston Gazette, and vindicated his allegation by quoting a letter from the first President Adams to the Grand Lodge of Massachusetts, dated Philadelphia, June 22, 1798. His reply was conclusive, and was republished in other papers as far south as Charleston, South Carolina, and had an extensive circulation.

The Masonic institution survived the staggering, long-continued, and oft-repeated attacks upon it during a period of fifteen years, and is now in a more flourishing condition than it ever has been. This fact was demonstrated by the celebration which took place in Portland, June 24, 1862, in commemoration of the one hundredth anniversary of the establishment of the Masonic institution in the State. This was the most elaborate and gorgeous display ever witnessed in Maine, calling together lodges, and chapters, and encampments from our own and numerous other States. Mr. Sheppard was present as a Knight Templar, and made an address in the evening to a large assemblage.

In 1835, Mr. Sheppard published anonymously an elegy in nine stanzas, on the death of our late distinguished citizen, Dr. Benjamin Vaughan of Hallowell. This was republished in the National Intelligencer and other papers, and had a wide circulation.

Mr. Sheppard still continues to render good service to the cause of letters as well as to Masonry. His labors in the library of the Historico-Genealogical Society, and commuications at its meetings and to its periodical, the "Register," are of permanent value, and will place his name among the benefactors of that useful and respected institution.

HENRY SEWALL. 1789—1818.

The venerable Henry Sewall, who died in Augusta in 1845, at the age of ninety-two, was the oldest brother of Daniel Sewall, the ancient clerk of the courts in York County, and of the Rev. Jotham Sewall, long a valued missionary in Maine, whose labors ceased only with his protracted life of ninety years, in 1850. They were lineal descendants of Henry Sewall, of a highly respected family in England, the first of the name to these shores, which he reached at the age of twenty; established himself at Newbury in 1635; married Jane, a daughter of Stephen Dummer; and was the ancestor of all, or nearly all, of the name in the country. His daughter Ann married William Longfellow, and is the maternal ancestor of all the Longfellows among us. Henry Sewall, the clerk, at the head of our article, was of the fifth degree from the first Henry, who died in 1700, aged about ninety; his second son, John, born in 1654, was the father of Nicholas, and Hannah who married Rev. Samuel Moody of York; Nicholas, born June 1, 1690, married Mehitabel, daughter of Samuel Storer, was a tanner by trade, and died in 1740: he had Henry, born March 26, 1727; Stephen, born 1734, the learned professor of Hebrew in Harvard College; and numerous other children. His son Henry was the father of the aged trio above mentioned, was a mason by trade, and cultivated, besides, a farm in York.

Henry, the subject of this sketch, was born in York, October 24, 1752: he was brought up to his father's occupation, working at intervals upon the farm. He must have received a good education, for he wrote a beautiful hand, and in his letters expressed himself with clearness and force. His relatives, including the Moodys, were among the most respected persons of the town: the Rev. Samuel Moody, the second minister of York, who married his grandfather's sister, was a learned and devoted man, of whom it was said that "his praise was in all the churches of that region:" Mr. Moody's son, Joseph, was the pastor of the second parish in the same town.

When hostilities commenced with Great Britain, the Sewalls of York entered heartily into the cause of the colonies. Henry, at the age of twenty-three, joined the army as a private, and honorably served through the war, having risen through the intermediate grades to the rank of captain, and was at one time an aid to General Heath, but without losing his rank of captain in the line. Under the act of 1828, granting pensions to the officers and soldiers of the Revolution, he was placed on the pension list, and drew the rate as a captain of infantry to the time of his death, four hundred and eighty dollars a year.

On the conclusion of peace he established himself at Augusta, where the remainder of his life was spent in labors useful and honorable, to the church of which he was a most honored member and officer, to the town, the county, and the nation. In 1789, General Sewall was at New York during the session of the first Congress in the summer of 1789. By his letters, from which we make some extracts, he appears to have been an attentive observer of the subjects which were then occupying Congress. On the first of August he writes: "The committee appointed not long since to bring in a report respecting amendments to the Constitution, have performed that service, and the draught of their report is in the enclosed scrap of a newspaper. These proposed amendments do not vary essentially, and scarcely in form differ, from those proposed in June last by Mr. Madison. They are of such a general nature that it is thought they will meet the ready approbation of all parties. By a gentleman of character and information lately from ———, I am informed that there is no ground to expect that that State will come into the present Union. They are confident in the opinion that Congress cannot *compel* them, and that they can have what foreign alliance and assistance they may want for supporting their *independence.*

"The prodigious quantity of copper coin which has been pouring in here from the eastward for more than a year past, has at length produced a revolution. About a week ago, they fell suddenly from twenty to forty-eight and sixty for the New York shilling, and now they are refused altogether. It is judged that there were between fifteen and twenty thousand pounds New York currency, in this city, of copper coin." Another letter to the same correspondent, Mr. Benjamin Shaw of Hallowell, dated August 18, 1789, contains some interesting facts. "For near a week past the attention of the House of Representatives has been engrossed on the subjects of *amendments* to the Constitution. They have taken up the report which was made by the committee of eleven, and have proceeded to pass upon the several articles without any material alteration. Those who were not very anxious for amendments consented that the matter should be brought on now, upon the principle of conciliation to which they seem to be disposed, and to give the subject a fair, open, and candid discussion. Mr. G—— of Massachusetts seems to be disposed to embarrass the House by multiplying not only his motions, but amassing together a crude variety of proposed amendments, which would seem rather to perplex than to facilitate the business. Mr. Tucker of South Carolina also introduced a long list of amendments, principally local, which were rejected by the House. The subject of amendments being now passed upon, it is probable the *judiciary* bill will claim the first attention."

The Mr. G. mentioned by Mr. Sewall, was Elbridge Gerry, who was a member of the Continental Congress from 1776 to 1785, and signed the Declaration of Independence: he was a representative in Congress from 1789 to 1793, Governor of Massachusetts in 1811, and Vice President of the United States, 1813-1817. The name of the State which was not then in the Union is unfortunately obliterated in Mr. Sewall's letter, but as North Carolina and Rhode Island were the two which were not represented in the early days of the session, it must have been one of them,—North Carolina adopted the Constitution in November, 1789, and Rhode Island, May 29, 1790.

The judiciary act was passed September 24, 1789, by which Maine was constituted a separate District, and invested with jurisdiction of all causes cognizable in a Circuit Court, except appeals and writs of error, in addition to the usual powers of District Courts. This jurisdiction it retained until the separation of the State from Massachusetts. Under this act, President Washington nominated, and the Senate confirmed, David Sewall as judge; William Lithgow, Jr., of Augusta, as attorney; and Henry Dearborn of Gardiner, as marshal: their commissions bear date September 26, 1789. The court assembled at Portland on the first Tuesday, being the first day of December, 1789, when the commissions of the judge, attorney, and marshal were read, and the oath prescribed by law was administered to Judge Sewall by four magistrates of Portland; viz., Samuel Freeman, Richard Codman, John Frothingham, and Daniel Davis. Whereupon Judge Sewall appointed his kinsman, Henry Sewall, clerk of the court by the following commission:

"DISTRICT OF MAINE, SS.

To Henry Sewall of Hallowell in the District of Maine, Esquire:

[SEAL.]

Pursuant to a commission from George Washington, President of the United States of America, to me, to be judge of the District Court of Maine, and by virtue of an act of Congress to establish the Judicial Courts of the United States, I do hereby appoint you, the said Henry Sewall, Clerk of the District Court of Maine, to have, hold, exercise, and enjoy the said office, with the profits, perquisites, and emoluments to the same belonging, for and during pleasure. In witness whereof, I have hereunto set my hand and seal, at Portland in the said District, the first day of December, A. D., 1789.

DAVID SEWALL."

The judge then administered the oath to the clerk, and he entered upon the duties of his office.

The records kept by Mr. Sewall have all the neatness and beauty of copper-plate, and are an extraordinary specimen of accuracy. They commence as follows:

"Records of the District Court of the United States, begun and held at

Portland, within and for the District of Maine, on the first Tuesday of December, in the year of our Lord 1789, being the first day of the same month.

The court being opened, the commissions following were read." Then follow the commissions to the officers of the court before mentioned. After which is the following entry: "There being no direction as yet by the laws of the United States, as to the time or manner of serving original writs in the District Court, the court do now order and make a rule thereof, That the same regulations in that respect shall take place and be observed, as by the laws of Massachusetts are prescribed for the service of original writs in the Supreme Judicial Court thereof. And that all barristers and attornies duly admitted and sworn in the Supreme Judicial Court of Massachusetts, *prior* to this time, may practise in this court. And thereupon, on the same first Tuesday of December, being the first day of the same month, the court adjourned without day."

The next term was held at Pownalboro' on the first Tuesday of March, 1790, at which only two entries were made; both by Stephen Smith, collector of Machias, for breach of the revenue laws. The next, being the third term, was held in Portland on the first Tuesday in June, 1790, at which a grand jury and two petit juries were, for the first time, impaneled in this court. Several informations and libels were filed for breach of revenue laws, and a capital trial for *piracy*, the first that had occurred under the new government. The prisoners were Thomas Bird, who is styled late resident of Bristol, in Great Britain, and Hans Hanson, late resident of the kingdom of Norway. They were taken on the coast of Cape Elizabeth, where they had been trading from a small schooner of about thirty tons, commanded by Bird. They were first taken, under suspicious circumstances, before the Supreme Court of Massachusetts, then sitting in Portland; and on examination, it appeared that the vessel they came in belonged to one Hodges of England, which had been trading on the coast of Africa under command of Captain Connor; that in a moment of resentment for abusive treatment, the crew, or a part of them, had risen upon the master and killed him, and then fled to America with the vessel and cargo. The case not falling under the jurisdiction of the court of Massachusetts, the prisoners were remitted to the District Court, where they were tried at the June term, 1790, on a bill of indictment duly presented. To accommodate the large number of persons whom curiosity drew to the trial, the proceedings were held in the meeting house of the First Parish, on Friday, the fifth day of June, when it being fully proved by the testimony of one of the crew and the voluntary confession of Bird, he was found guilty, and Hanson was acquitted. Judge Sewall pronounced the sentence of death on Bird, to be carried into effect on the twenty-fifth day of the same June; and he was accordingly executed on that day, in Portland. Marshal Dearborn presided. Mr. Lithgow, the district attorney, was the prosecuting officer, and the prisoners were defended by John Frothingham and William Symmes, assigned by the court. Mr. Sewall continued to hold the office of clerk until 1818, about twenty-nine years, when he and the judge both retired,— the judge at the age of eighty-three, and the clerk at that of sixty-six. He was a most prompt, faithful, and accurate officer, and his records bear ample testimony to his intelligence, neatness, and accuracy.

Mr. Sewall was succeeded in this office by John Mussey of Portland, who entered upon its duties January 1, 1819. On the establishment of the Circuit Court of the United States in Maine, which took place in 1820, under an act of Congress passed March 30, of that year, Mr. Mussey was appointed clerk of that court also, and held the two offices until 1848,— a period of twenty-nine years and some months. Mr. Mussey was a son of Captain John Mussey of Portland, where he was born, October 15, 1790. He graduated at Bowdoin College in 1809, of the fourth class which left the institution: in his class were President Lord of Dartmouth College, and the late Benjamin Randall of Bath. He studied law with Judge Whitman, and was admitted to the Cumberland Bar in 1812. Mr. Mussey was a most faithful, accurate, and punctual clerk: he did his work promptly and to the satisfaction of the courts, whose officer he was, and retired upon a competency, inherited, and largely increased by his industry and good management, and which he still lives to enjoy.

In 1799, on the organization of the county of Kennebec, Mr. Sewall was chosen register of deeds for the county, and held the office until 1816: for this place he was admirably qualified by the beauty of his handwriting, and his habit of correctness in everything that he undertook.

The military experience and talent of General Sewall were early called into exercise in his new place of residence. On the organization of the militia in Maine, there were two divisions established: one the sixth, embracing York and Cumberland, which was placed under the command of Major General Ichabod Goodwin; the eighth division embraced the counties of Lincoln, Hancock, and Washington, of which William Lithgow, Jr., who had served in the Revolutionary army as major, was commissioned major general, and Mr. Sewall with the rank of colonel, "deputy adjutant general." Henry Dearborn was brigadier general of the first brigade, and Alexander Campbell of the second. After the death of General Lithgow, in 1796, General Dearborn was promoted to the chief command of the division, and Colonel Sewall was made brigadier. And when General Dearborn left the State to enter upon his duties as secretary of war, in 1801, General Sewall succeeded him in the command of the division,— a post which he filled with zeal and intelligence twenty years, until the militia was reorganized under the new State.

On the news being received of the capture of Castine by the British, on the first of September, 1814, and the movement of a portion of the fleet up the Penobscot River, General Sewall called out a portion of his division, and proceeded with dispatch to the Penobscot. Here he found that the enemy had preceded him, and by the disgraceful cowardice and want of combination of the local militia, Hampden and Bangor had been captured, the sloop of war Adams abandoned and burnt, and possession of the river seized by the enemy. By these daring acts, the whole eastern country was aroused, and the militia was collected in large bodies on the river and the whole coast of Maine.

General Sewall was strictly and thoroughly an upright, conscientious, and religious man: when he took office, and he did not accept any that he was not competent to fill, he had no other purpose than to discharge the duties with a single view to their true objects and ends; he was faithful to the letter; he neglected nothing that belonged to the station, whether civil or military, whether in detail or a general principle; and when he retired from them, it was with a clear, unclouded retrospect of unequivocal endeavor to perform his entire duty to every intent. Such a retrospect, from the eminence he had attained in his onward march toward the end of his brilliant campaign of life, was a constant and unfailing source of comfort and joy, to the extreme verge of his ninety-three years' pilgrimage. He died September 4, 1845.

General Sewall was tall, erect, grave, and dignified in person and manners. His step was firm and with a military air; and as he reached old age, his venerable appearance attracted general attention, and presented an embodiment of our ideas of the ancient patriarchs.

He was three times married: his first wife, Tabitha, was his cousin, a daughter of John Sewall of Georgetown; his second, Rachel Crosby; the third, Eliza Lowell of Boston. He had two sons, Charles and William, and several daughters.

This seems to be a suitable place to make record of the officers of the District Court of Maine, from the beginning to the present day; which is accordingly annexed.

OFFICERS OF THE UNITED STATES COURTS IN MAINE.

JUDGES.

David Sewall, . .	appointed Sept.	. 26, 1789;	resigned Jan.,	1818.
Albion K. Parris, . .	" . Feb'y, .	1818;	. " . . .	1822.
Ashur Ware, ...	" . . April, . .	1822;	. . . . .	

CLERKS.

Henry Sewall, . .	appointed	Dec. .	1, 1789;	resigned . .	1818.
John Mussey, ...	" .	Jan'y .	1, 1819;	. " . .	1848.
George F. Emery, Circuit Court,		August .	4, 1848;	. . . . .	
Wm. P. Preble, Jr., Dist. Court,		August .	1, 1848;	. . . . .	

ATTORNEYS.

William Lithgow, Jr.,	appointed	Sept. .	26, 1789;	died, . . .	1796.
Daniel Davis, ...	" .	August	25, 1796;	removed .	1801.
Silas Lee, ...	" .	July .	27, 1801;	died, . . .	1814.
William P. Preble, . .	" .	April .	. 5, 1814;	resigned, .	1820.
Ether Shepley, ...	" .	Sept. .	12, 1820;	. " . .	1833.
John Anderson, . . .	" .	April .	10, 1833;	. " . . .	1837.
Joseph Howard, . . .	" . .	May .	9, 1837;	to	1841.
John Holmes, . . .	" .	February,	1841;	died . . .	1843.
Gorham Parks, . . .	" .	August	25, 1843;	to	1845.
Augustine Haines, . . .	" .	April .	29, 1845;	resigned, .	1848.
George F. Shepley, . .	" .	Nov. .	8, 1848;	to	1849.
Thomas A. Deblois, . .	"		1849;	to	1853.
George F. Shepley, . .	"		1853;	to	1861.
George F. Talbot, . . .	"		1861;	. . . . .	

MARSHALS.

Henry Dearborn, .	appointed	Sept. .	26, 1789;	resigned . .	1794.
John Hobby, ...	" .	Jan. .	28, 1794;	to	1799.
Isaac Parker, ...	" .	March .	6, 1799;	removed . .	1803.
Thomas G. Thornton, .	" .	Dec. .	21, 1803;	died, . . .	1824.
Benjamin Green, . . .	" .	Sept. .	14, 1824;	resigned . .	1830.
Albert Smith, ...	" .	June .	. 1, 1830;	to	1838.
Gorham Parks, ...	" .	April .	25, 1838;	removed . .	1841.
John D. Kinsman, . .	" .	February,	1841;	. " . .	1844.
Virgil D. Parris, . . .	" .	Oct. .	11, 1844;	resigned . .	1849.
Rufus McIntire, . . .	" .	Jan'y .	15, 1849;	removed .	1849.
William Paine, ...	" .	June .	15, 1849;	. " . . .	1853.
George W. Stanley, . .	" .	April .	1, 1853;	to	1857.
William K. Kimball, . .	" .	April .	2, 1857;	to	1861.
Charles Clark, . . .	"		1861;	. . . . .	

SHERIFFS.

JOHN WAITE — ICHABOD GOODWIN — CHARLES CUSHING — EDMUND BRIDGE.

JOHN WAITE. 1776—1809.

The first sheriff of Cumberland County was Moses Pearson of Falmouth, appointed in 1760, on the organization of the county. He held the office until 1768, when William Tyng was appointed, and continued to discharge its duties until 1775, when, joining the royalists, he left the country, and the office became vacant. On the establishment of the Provisional Government in Massachusetts, John Waite of Falmouth, now Portland, the shire-town, was appointed sheriff, and entered upon the duties of the office in 1776. Mr. Waite was the fourth child of John Waite, who was the son of Jonadab Waite, and was born in Newbury, Massachusetts, in July, 1732: his mother was Sarah, a daughter of John Kent of Newbury. His father was born February 6, 1702, married in 1724, and came to Falmouth about the year 1738: his sixth child, Abigail, born February 6, 1739, was the first of his children born in Falmouth,. His prior children, all under age, accompanied him: he was an active and enterprising ship-master, was influential in the affairs of the town, and died, possessed of a good estate, in 1769. He had four sons and six daughters, who, in various relations, have contributed to the honor and prosperity of the town, among whose population his posterity is largely mingled.

John, the fourth child, began life as a mariner, which employment gave occupation to, and formed the energetic character of many of the young men of the town and of the State: the Waites, Prebles, Weekses, Tuckers, Woodburys, Greelys, Jordans, Pattens, and numerous others along our whole sea border, attest the energy and success of this large class of persons. From fore-mast-men they became masters, then prosperous ship-owners and merchants.

In 1759, Captain Waite commanded one of the transports in the expedition under General Wolfe, to Quebec. He sailed from Louisbourg, June 4, 1759, in a company of eight sail of the line, several frigates, and five ships, and about one hundred transports for the St. Lawrence. They arrived at the Isle of Orleans, June 25, and continued in the river, fronting and near Quebec, until after the fall of that city. In a brief diary which he kept, he gives some account of the movement of the troops and the ships. A few extracts may be interesting. "September 7, 1759. This day, General Wolfe marched from Point Levi, in order to join the forces above the town for some secret expedition. This evening passed the town, two ships, two sloops, and one schooner, which caused a very smart fire from both sides, but without any damage on our side. 13th. This morning, about half a mile above Quebec, ensued the greatest battle that ever was fought in America; in which we lost about six hundred killed and wounded, among which was the brave General Wolfe killed, and General Moncton wounded. The enemy left about thirteen hundred on the field, besides a great number taken, among whom was the second in command: General Montcalm was wounded. 14th. We hear that General Montcalm died about seven hours after the battle. 17th. A flag of truce, sent from the town in order to capitulate. 18th. This morning our army took possession of the famous city of Quebec, after a long and tedious siege of near four months,—a day ever memorable to the English nation." His instructions for this voyage are now in his family, dated May 15, 1759, signed by "Charles Saunders," admiral, "on board of his majesty's ship, Neptune, in Louisbourg harbor." He successfully accomplished his voyage, and returned to Falmouth in November of that year. Under November 13, 1759, the Rev. Mr. Smith, in his journal, says, "I was to see John Waite, who is returned from the river St. Lawrence, and who came away with the last of the fleet." After this, he continued to pursue his sea life in foreign and coastwise voyages to near the opening of the grand drama of the Revolution, mingling always in the affairs of the town, in which, from his ardent temperament, he was often found taking a prominent part. In 1763, he and his father's family, becoming disaffected with the venerable Parson Smith, pastor of the only parish in what is now Portland, seceded, with others, from the parish, and formed a new society, which, after a serious conflict, adopted the Episcopal form, the first which had existed in the State since the early days of the colonial government. In this conflict, in regard to the form of worship, Captain Waite and General Preble came to blows. Mr. Smith's journal says, "This evening the signers for the new meeting-house had a meeting, when ——— and ——— quarreled and fought in the street," and pertinently adds, "A foundation for a church was thus laid — the pillars tremble." The venerable annalist was no little troubled at this defection from his society: the Waites were a large and influential family, and drew off much support from the old parish: in his grief, he exclaimed, "I have been discouraged about my enemies: they talk of a new meeting house." He was fearful of the consequences, but his wit did not forsake him — he said, "The parish is like a clock, when the *Waites* are off, it will stop." Mr. Waite became one of the most efficient supporters of the Episcopal Church in Portland, which separated from the first parish, in 1763, and in 1764 voted to adopt the Episcopal form of worship. The Rev. John Wiswall, in 1764, was sent by the society to England for ordination: in their invitation to him, they say, "We desire you would, as soon as may be, apply to his lordship, the Bishop of London, for ordination to qualify you therefor." In December of the same year, Mr. Wiswall wrote to the warden and vestry of the church, addressed to Captain Waite, who was one of the vestry, if not the warden, in which he says, "Your petition to the Venerable Society for propagating the Gospel, was laid before them, and the members were unanimously of the opinion that Falmouth is a very proper place for a church; and they readily agreed to do something toward the support of a missionary there."

Mr. Wiswall kept up the most friendly intercourse with Colonel Waite, until the opening scenes of the Revolution caused a final separation. Mr. Wiswall, in May, 1775, went on board the English man-of-war, Canceau, under Captain Mowat, then lying in Falmouth harbor, from which he wrote an earnest and persuasive letter to his friend Waite, urging him to abandon measures of opposition to the mother country, and apologizing for the course he took himself. He says, "I know the people are acting a very wrong part: I am determined never to join them in a rebellion. Now the sword is drawn, I must obey God rather than man; and agreeable to the dictates of my conscience, though at the hazard of everything that is dear to me. Let me ask you, my dear friend, when you first joined Freeman, Preble, &c., did you suspect that they would ever draw the sword against their king? Why will you rashly engage in these measures which may prove the ruin of yourself, your family, and country? How unhappy shall I be, if the phrenzy of the times should dissolve that friendship between us, which I have thought not death itself would put an end to. Nor shall anything ever make me forget you, cease loving you, praying for you, and exerting my best ability, to promote the spiritual and temporal interest of you and yours."

At the commencement of the troubles with Great Britain, Captain Waite espoused with ardor the cause of the colonies, and took a leading part in the measures of resistance adopted by the town of Falmouth. In 1772, he was one of a large and respectable committee, of which Enoch Freeman was chairman, to prepare instructions to William Tyng, then the representative to the General Court. In 1774, he was chosen a member of a convention, composed of delegates from the towns in the county, "to consider what measures it will be expedient to adopt for the general interest of the county in the present alarming situation of our public affairs." The convention met in September, and summoned Sheriff Tyng before them, who, after being interrogated and signing a declaration satisfactory to the convention, was discharged. They took a general supervision of the affairs and opinions of the people; they were empowered to regulate intercourse and prevent the violation of the non-importation agreement; to check disorders and mob violence; and watch over the liberties and rights of the people. A committee of "inspection" was also chosen, of which Theophilus Parsons, afterwards the distinguished chief justice, was one, and clerk of the body: Captain Waite was one of the committee. I have before me an original record of two meetings of the committee in the handwriting and with the attestation of Mr. Parsons, bearing date in March and April, 1775. The power assumed and exercised by this body was of the most extraordinary kind, and not to be endured except in extraordinary emergencies. They were spies upon all the transactions of the people, and visited with public censure and indignation, and often something worse, those who were found to transgress the rules of this tribunal. They were in constant correspondence with similar committees in Boston and elsewhere. Some of their votes will serve as an illustration: "Voted, that Captain P. [Pote] be ordered to go to the General Court by land, on or before Thursday next, to answer for his conduct with respect to his exporting fish." "Voted, that a committee wait on Mrs. Ross concerning a letter sent her from Boston." "Voted, that —— be a committee to inspect inward and outward bound vessels."

In these transactions, Captain Waite, by his intelligence and activity, acquired a high degree of popularity; and in 1776, honors and office were accumulated upon him. In that year, he represented the town in the Provincial Congress; was chosen town treasurer, and annually re-elected to 1785; was apponited sheriff of the county, and colonel of the first regiment. He was also appointed under the absentee act of 1777, an agent for the estates of absentees in the county of Cumberland. Tristram Jordan was appointed to the same office in York County, and Rowland Cushing for Lincoln County.

It is evident from the secret history of the times, which we get from private correspondence and other sources as it is slowly disclosed, that at the commencement of the war there were two parties among the whigs, one of which was determined to push matters to extremities for the independence of the colonies: another party, more conservative, was fearful of the issue, thought it presumptuous to make the attempt, and hoped for an accommodation of the troubles. These persons were very cautious in the expression of their opinions, but their true feeling is exhibited in their confidential correspondence. One such letter we have before us, addressed to Colonel Waite by Theophilus Parsons, from Byfield, to which place he had retired after the burning of the town. It is dated March 12, 1776, and while it conveys a favorable impression of Colonel Waite, it gives us a little specimen of secret history. We make some extracts from it. "Some designing men among you have overshot their mark, and are now receiving the reward of their doings. I should be resigned to the dispensation, if the innocent did not suffer with the guilty. I can acquit you of being an author of the troubles of the town. I now please myself that the aspect of our public affairs is a little brighter. I believe we shall have commissioners to try to settle the dispute. Most of the people are sick of it, and would gladly terminate it, if left to their own judgment." "I am fully persuaded that many of our present leaders will oppose any accommodation; and some would choose rather to support the war alone, than accept any." He urges him to make interest to go to the next Provincial Congress, as they need conservative men there: he says: "You ought to stand forward—to make interest to go yourself, instead of your present member. I do not mean to flatter you. I suppose others are as capable as you are, but they have not interest sufficient to carry an election; you have." Samuel Freeman was the "present member" referred to. At the next election, four members were returned from Falmouth; viz., Brigadier Preble, Joseph Noyes, Mr. Freeman, and Col. Waite.

Besides discharging the duties of the several offices which were conferred upon him in 1776, he was employed in looking after the defenses of the town, and making provision for the inhabitants who suffered in the conflagration. In a letter of April 24, 1776, addressed to Mr. Freeman at Watertown, where he was in attendance upon the Congress, he says: "The selectmen are preparing tools, agreeable to the militia act, as fast as possible, part of which are already made, and sent to the commanding officer for the men to work with. I need not mention the distress of the poor sufferers in this town which daily increases, and everything in our power ought to be done for their relief."

In 1777, several of the inhabitants of Falmouth, "taking into consideration the glorious victory obtained by the army of the United States," subscribed "to procure a good beef ox to distribute to the families of the non-commissioned officers and soldiers" belonging to the town who were in that battle. [General Gates's victory.] Colonel Waite was chairman of the committee to make the purchase and attend to the duty. They also celebrated the event by a public dinner. In February, 1778, he issued the following advertisement: "Whereas a subscription is opened for the soldiers who enlisted from this town into the continental army, and are now in camp destitute of shoes, stockings, and shirts, I make no doubt but every person who does not (like the Israelites of old) wish to return into bondage again, will contribute either shoes, stockings, shirts, or cash to be sent by Lieut. Lunt, for the immediate relief of said soldiers. Any of the above articles will be received by the subscriber's humble servant, John Waite." We introduce these papers to show the interest and the part he took in the measures to establish the independence of the country. In 1779, his oldest son, Henry, then but seventeen years old, was a volunteer in the Bagaduce expedition.

He was constantly employed in various important services of a public nature through the war, in correspondence with official persons at the seat of government and other places, in raising troops and in furnishing supplies. At the close of the war, he engaged in works for the improvement of his private estate, which was large, and in building up the desolate town.

When he entered upon the office of sheriff, the Court of Common Pleas consisted of Enoch Freeman, who was appointed judge in 1760, and held the office twenty-nine years; Jeremiah Powell of North Yarmouth, appointed in 1763, and held the office nineteen years; Jonas Mason, 1773 to 1777; Solomon Lombard, 1776 to 1781, who took Moses Pearson's place, who retired in 1775, at the age of eighty. Samuel Freeman was the clerk. The business of the courts was very small: the whole number of entries for seven years, from 1776 to 1782 inclusive, was only one hundred and ninety-eight. The last court in Cumberland County, held under royal authority, was July 25, 1775; it was the "Inferior Court of Common Pleas," and the record of the term thus commences, "Cumberland, ss. Anno Regni Regis Georgii tertii Magnæ Britanniæ, Franciæ, et Hiberniæ decimo quinto:" that is, in the fifteenth year of the reign of George III., King of Great Britain, France, and Ireland. The court consisted of Powell, Freeman, Mason, and Pearson; — Stephen Longfellow, clerk. The following memorandum is made: "No jurors returned and empanelled this court. The sheriff nor crier did not attend this court." Tyng, the sheriff, had fled from town, and abandoned his duties. There were no actions entered, and but two continued actions on the docket, in which judgment was rendered.

No Supreme Court was held in Maine that year. All the judges were tories but William Cushing: they were Edmund Trowbridge, who remained in the country unmolested, but went out of office: he died in 1793; Foster Hutchinson, a brother of Governor Hutchinson, who left the country, as did also the fourth judge, William Browne of Salem. There are no records in our public offices of the Supreme Court in Maine, earlier than 1798: prior to that time they were kept in Boston. The term was held in July. In 1798, when our records commence, the term was held by Dana, chief justice, Robert Treat Paine, Theophilus Bradbury, Nathan Cushing, and Thomas Dawes, Jr.

The first term of the Court of Common Pleas, held under the new government, was in October, 1776: the judges were Powell, Freeman, Mason, and Lombard: the latter had been a minister in Gorham. Samuel Freeman was clerk; John Waite, sheriff; Timothy Cutler, crier. The record commences thus: "Cumberland, ss. In the year of our Lord one thousand seven hundred seventy-six. At an Inferior Court of Common Pleas." The first judgment in a criminal cause in this court was rendered at the March term, 1778, and was in the name of the "Government and People." At the October term, 1782, Robert Treat Paine, as attorney general, entered complaints for forfeiture of land, against several former inhabitants of Falmouth, who were refugees in the Revolution. The business of this court was very small at that time, the record of judgments from October term, 1776, to October term, 1782, inclusive, occupying only one hundred and three folio pages.

Colonel Waite held the office of sheriff until 1809, a period of thirty-four years. During that time he led the venerable procession of the judges and the bar, which, at the opening of every term, proceeded with great formality to the court-house, and on the first day of the term to the public dinner, with which the occasion was invariably celebrated. It was at one of these dinners that Chief Justice Parsons gave the toast which Judge Mellen used to tell with a relish. "At a court dinner, composed of the judges and members of the bar, federalists and democrats, Chief Justice Parsons said: 'Gentlemen, before leaving the table I will take one glass of wine, and will give my old toast. I know it is a party one, but I can't help it, we live in party times. Gentlemen, my toast is, *All honest men.*'" We may place along side of this another toast, given by Judge Parsons at a social meeting of the Boston Bar: "The laws of the land, — the *common* law for the *people;* the *civil* law for our *friends;* and the *cannon* law for our *enemies.*"

Col. Waite's official life outlasted that of Cushing, the first chief justice, and those of Foster, Sullivan, Paine, Sargent, Nathan Cushing, Dawes, Bradbury, and Simeon Strong, and the judicial term of David Sewall on that bench. These were the first judges under the commonwealth appointed to 1801. He attended upon the elegant and dignified Chief Justice Dana for twenty years, and his successor, Chief Justice Parsons, who was the sheriff's early companion and friend; upon the dignified Sumner; the severe and blunt Paine; the wise and modest Samuel Sewall, successor to Parsons; Thacher, Sedgwick, and Parker. This procession of eminent men, the sheriff who led them off, the clerk who recorded their doings, and all but two of the members of the bar who followed in this march to the high seat of justice, have gone to a higher tribunal, in which an immutable and eternal Judge pronounces his just and irreversible decrees. The sheriff, as he appeared on these occasions, sixty years ago, stands before me; his venerable figure, which had weathered the storms of seventy years, still erect, of medium height and rather broad, crowned with a three-cornered cocked hat of the Revolutionary model, blue coat with bright buttons, a buff vest, and a sword by his side; his countenance grave, not to say stern, as he seemed to the juvenile mind, which associated harsh duties with his office; heavy, overhanging eyebrows, and his white staff, the badge of his office, in hand, had an imposing effect upon all spectators, old as well as young.

In July, 1809, Colonel Waite, having arrived at the age of seventy-seven, after a correspondence on the subject with Chief Justice Parsons, placed in his hands a letter to be delivered to Governor Gore, resigning his office. In his letter to Judge Parsons, he says: "Infirmity incident to old age is the lot of man; it creeps upon us insensibly. I shall continue to hold the office until a successor shall be appointed." His resignation was accepted, and Colonel Richard Hunnewell was appointed his successor. Colonel Hunnewell had been the first sheriff of Hancock County: his wife was Miss Hall of Boston, a sister of Judge Parker's wife: the two young men commenced life in the new county of Hancock. He held the office there until 1798, when, having been appointed a colonel in the Oxford army under President Adams, he resigned the office, and after the war he followed his brother-in-law, Parker, to Portland, where he died in 1823, at the age of sixty-five.

Colonel Waite survived the resignation of his office several years, and died in Portland in 1820, at the age of eighty-eight. He married, January 15, 1759, Hannah, the second of the three daughters of Phineas Jones, one of the most enterprising and valuable citizens of Falmouth, who died at the early age of thirty-eight in 1743. She was born October 6, 1738: by her he had thirteen children, nine sons and four daughters, the youngest of whom, a daughter, born in 1783, only survives, the widow of Captain Samuel McLellan. Another daughter was the mother of Thomas and Edward Motley, long-honored merchants in Boston, and grandmother of the distinguished historian of the Dutch Republic,—John Lathrop Motley. Of course, the sheriff was his great-grandfather. He survived all his sons, and after a long and varied life, he went to the grave under the burden of many years and many sorrows.

ICHABOD GOODWIN. 1793—1820.

Sheriff Goodwin, like Sheriffs Waite of Cumberland and Bridge of Lincoln, rendered good service to the cause of the country during the war of the Revolution; and they received the reward of their services in the offices which they held: the shortest being near a quarter of a century. It was an honored practice, on the restoration of peace, to confer upon those who had devoted themselves and their property to accomplish the independence of their country, the honors and emoluments of office, as a just acknowledgment of their services.

Ichabod Goodwin, one of these deserving men, was born in what is now South Berwick, May 25, 1743. His father was Captain Ichabod Goodwin, born in the same town in 1700, who was the son of Thomas Goodwin, the first immigrant of the family to the ancient town of Berwick, who came to this country in 1660.

A portion of the land on which this ancestor settled in South Berwick, and which constituted his farm, and on which the sheriff was born, still remains in the family; and traces of the cellar on which the farm house once stood are still visible. It was a beautiful spot, from which could be seen the village of Dover, and a large sweep of surrounding country, through which the Piscataqua River, the boundary of Maine and New Hampshire, pours its fertilizing waters.

In 1754, his father was a member of the General Court of Massachusetts, and on the breaking out of the French war, received a commission as captain in the Provincial army, and raised a company from among his neighbors and friends. In 1758, he was ordered to Lake George, and took with him his son, Ichabod, then but fifteen years old: they were with General Abercrombie in his unsuccessful attack upon Ticonderoga, in which he was defeated, with the loss of two thousand men. Captain Goodwin, the father, was wounded in the battle, and returned home with his son, who received his father's sword as a trophy of the engagement. After his return, he employed himself upon his father's farm, and as a surveyor of land, for which his services were often sought, until the busy scenes preliminary to actual hostilities with the mother country gave a new direction to his patriotic impulses.

In these movements, he was an unflinching whig, and took an active part. In the years 1775, '6, '7, he was a member of the Provincial Congress, and was present when the place of meeting, at Cambridge, was surrounded by British troops, which led to the adjournment to Concord; and then, in April, on account of the attack upon Concord, to Watertown. In November, 1775, he was appointed by the Provincial Council, with Colonel John Baker and several other officers and civilians, to purchase arms for the Provincial troops: in the resolve he is styled captain.

When the prisoners of Burgoyne's army were sent to Cambridge, the regiment of militia belonging to York County was detailed as a guard for the prisoners, and was stationed at Winter and Prospect Hills. Mr. Goodwin was lieutenant colonel of the regiment, which was commanded by Colonel Gerrish. The order book which Colonel Goodwin kept, is preserved, and gives an account of each day's proceedings, until the prisoners were sent to Rutland and otherwise disposed of. The discipline of the camp was strictly maintained, and interesting incidents are recorded, as they occurred during this year of camp service. Among them are several cases of trial by courts martial for desertion and other crimes, in which the sentence of death by shooting was decreed for desertion, and whipping, or fine and imprisonment, for other crimes. The prisoners were allowed many privileges: the officers, especially, were permitted to roam over a large extent of territory, for exercise, under their parole, which was not infrequently abused, and occasional riots occurred, which caused stricter orders to be issued and narrower limits to be prescribed. The following order is taken from this book: "June 11,

1778. A strict and watchful eye is to be kept over the prisoners of war removed this morning from the guard ships to Prospect Hill. They are to be quartered as compact together as possible, and the sentries are to have a particular charge respecting them. No one of them is to be allowed a pass under any pretence of being a servant to any officer, or to come without the chain of sentries on any pretence whatever, without express leave in writing from the general." Lieut. Brown, one of the prisoners, undertook to violate this order, and was driving over the lines in a carriage with two women, one on each side of him, when he was challenged by the sentinel, and informed what his orders were: he recklessly disregarded the challenge, and was driving on, when the sentinel discharged his piece and shot him dead, without injuring the women. A court of inquiry was held in the case, and on the facts being proved, the sentinel was acquitted. The lieutenant was buried under orders from the general, with the marks of respect due to his rank; but the commanding officer, on account of the commotion among the prisoners in consequence of this affair, was required during the funeral ceremonies to have "all the guards under arms at their respective guard houses, and the officers and men off duty, to be at their regimental parades." In 1780, he was appointed by the government of Massachusetts, superintendent of the troops to be enlisted in the county of York for the continental army;— the number for the State then called out was four thousand, two hundred and ninety; for York County, two hundred and two.

After the war, he returned to the peaceful pursuits of private life; but he was soon called again into the public service; first, as major general of the militia of York County, which, under a new arrangement, in 1793, formed the sixth division of the militia of Massachusetts: in 1792, he was chosen the representative of Berwick to the General Court, and the next year was appointed sheriff of the county of York, as successor to Sheriff Moulton. The duties of this office he discharged with honor and fidelity twenty-seven years, with the exception of a few months in Governor Gerry's administration, until the separation of the State in 1820; when, at the age of seventy-seven years, he retired from all official station, having been in public life with only occasional and brief intermissions, for more than fifty years. His first commission as lieutenant, he received under George III., from which he rose under the government of Massachusetts, through various grades, to the highest rank in the militia,— a major general. He was colonel of the second regiment in York County, in 1780. While holding the office of major general, during the war of 1812, his division was called into service, and portions of it stationed, under his superintendance, at Kittery Point, York, and other exposed places. In 1815, after the war, he resigned his commission.

It is alike honorable to General Goodwin and to Governor Sullivan, that in 1807, when Mr. Sullivan was governor, and party excitement was raging bitterly through the Commonwealth, the executive was vehemently urged to remove Sheriff Goodwin, and appoint one of his own party friends. But Sheriff Goodwin was a townsman of Governor Sullivan, of the same age, and they were early schoolmates: he steadily resisted, during the nearly two years of his administration, all efforts to remove the old sheriff: his constant reply was, "I know the sheriff of York County. I cannot remove him." Not so, however, Gov. Gerry, for in 1811, when he came into power, he made haste to remove all the old officers he could reach, sheriffs, clerks, &c., and a general commotion was raised all over the State among the dry bones of the old office-holders. Even the Court of Common Pleas was abolished to bring in new judges, and new participants of public patronage. Among these, in the old counties, were Goodwin, sheriff, and Daniel Sewall, clerk, in York; Hunnewell, sheriff, and Freeman, clerk, in Cumberland; and Bridge, sheriff, and Alden Bradford, clerk, in Lincoln. Colonel Lane, who was appointed sheriff of York in this revolution, sent word to Sheriff Goodwin, that he would meet him in York, and take delivery of the county property under his charge. The old sheriff promptly met him, and after accomplishing the business, invited Colonel Lane to spend the night with him at Berwick, which the new sheriff gracefully accepted, and was hospitably entertained. The next year, Governor Strong returned to power, and the old officers were generally restored to their places; then General Goodwin sent to Colonel Lane, who resided at Hollis, informing him that he had been qualified as sheriff of York, and requested him to meet him at the county seat, and re-deliver the public property: he invited him to come to his house, and they would proceed the following day and attend to the duty. The Colonel, not behind General Goodwin in courtesy, waited upon him at his house, and they proceeded in the kindest manner to perform the necessary duties of the occasion. Pleasant incidents these, in the irritating controversies which cloud party conflicts. In 1800, Sheriff Goodwin was appointed one of the commissioners to adjust the controversy between the Pejepscot proprietors and the settlers upon their land: the other commissioners were Nathaniel Dummer and John Lord. Under their award, about twenty thousand acres were conveyed to the settlers.

Sheriff Goodwin died peacefully, without a struggle and without a pang, of old age, May 25, 1829, on his birth-day, precisely at the age of eighty-six. He had a family of eleven children, five sons and six daughters; five of whom, three daughters and two sons, survived him. His oldest son, Ichabod, died in 1814. Two of his sons, Dominicus and James Scamman, were graduates of Dartmouth College in the class of 1811: Dominicus studied law, and had just opened an office in South Berwick, when he suddenly died from exposure and fatigue in assisting in throwing up defensive works in Portsmouth harbor, in the war of 1812: James studied medicine with Dr. Hazeltine of South Berwick, and at the Dartmouth Medical

School, and now resides in Portland. Governor Ichabod Goodwin of New Hampshire is Sheriff Goodwin's nephew, a son of his brother, Samuel. The sheriff was short in stature and compactly built, erect and muscular: in the latter part of his life, he became very corpulent.

CHARLES CUSHING. 1761—1783.

We have repeatedly spoken in previous pages of Mr. Cushing, in connection with his distinguished brothers, William and Roland, all of whom settled in the county of Lincoln. They belonged to one of the most honored and conspicuous families in New England. They were sons of John Cushing, Jr., of Scituate, who was a judge of the Superior Court of Massachusetts, from 1747 to 1771, and whose father was John Cushing, born in Scituate in 1662, a son of Hon. John Cushing, and was ten years a member of the governor's council, and a judge of the Superior Court of Massachusetts, from 1729 to 1733: they all seem to have been bred in courts. Charles, the subject of our notice, was born in Scituate, August 13, 1734, graduated at Harvard College in 1755, and was educated for the bar. But on the organization of the county of Lincoln in 1760, he was appointed the first sheriff, and came into the county in 1761, about the same time with his brother William, Sheriff Bridge, and Judge Bowman. He was also appointed collector of excise for the county. They all established themselves at Pownalboro', now Dresden, which was made the shire-town, being conveniently situated on the Kennebec River, about thirty miles from its mouth.

Although the country was thinly settled and in a rude state, these gentlemen, and the Rev. Jacob Bailey, an Episcopal missionary, who also settled in Pownalboro' in 1760, under the auspices of the Society for Propagating the Gospel in Foreign Parts, all graduates of Harvard, and three of them classmates, viz., Cushing, Bailey, and Bowman, formed a society, as enlightened as it was genial and courtly. They all had families; Charles Cushing having married, August 25, 1768, Elizabeth, a daughter of Increase and Sarah (Sharp) Sumner, and sister of Governor Increase Sumner of Massachusetts. It would be rare to find at any time, in so small a population, so many refined and highly educated people.

The town was first named Frankfort, from a fort of that name in its limits, and was settled by immigrants from Germany, in the vicinity of the Rhine, who were invited by the proprietors of the Plymouth patent to occupy their vacant land, on favorable terms. They were poor and ignorant, but industrious and honest. Things went smoothly on in this happy community for some time, enlivened by visits occasionally from Governor Pownal; Dr. Gardiner, a large proprietor there, and portions of his family; Mr. Bowdoin;

Mr. Sumner, Mrs. Cushing's brother, and others; by which, and by frequent correspondence with their friends in Boston and vicinity, a knowledge and an interest with the inside world was freshly kept up with those who were on this outer margin. Two letters from Mr. Sumner to Sheriff Cushing, who, to his other appointments, had added the commission of colonel of the regiment, will show the style of this correspondence, and at the same time illustrate some facts. We have not space to introduce them here: they may be seen in the New England Genealogical Register, vol. 8, pages 109 and 110.

By and by, differences arose on religious questions, which extended to the masses. The leading men had all been educated in the Puritan notions of Massachusetts; but Bailey had abandoned these, and become a very earnest Episcopalian. On taking possession of his missionary field, he was the only clergyman for many miles around, and the people must attend upon his ministrations, or lose all benefit from public religious observances. He therefore drew around him the majority of the people, who yielded their denominational preferences to the benefit of religious instruction, although different from what they had been accustomed to. But an opposition gradually arose to the Church of England, which led to very bitter quarrels, extending to controversies in regard to land titles and suits in the courts. These involved the principal men of the town, and distracted that once peaceable society. Mr. Bailey was very strenuous in carrying out his theological and denominational views, and does not appear to have been very conciliatory in his manners in that regard; which brought upon him and his family severe trials. In a letter under date of March, 1773, he refers to them in the following lines:

"Far distant from the pleasing scenes of life,
From all the joys which sacred friendships give:
Amid the sons of malice and of strife,
Where discord rages, I am doomed to live."

He ranked Judge Bowman and Sheriff Cushing among his opponents, and says that at first they voluntarily joined with the Church, but afterwards became hostile to it, and labored to get up a dissenting meeting-house.

But this denominational quarrel was but a trifle, to the violent and exasperated one which grew out of the Revolutionary troubles. Mr. Bailey, Major Goodwin, and many of the prominent members of his parish, adhered firmly to the royal cause; while Bowman, the Cushings, and many others, joined the whigs. The Episcopalians on the Kennebec, as well as in other parts of the country, were loyalists, while the dissenters generally, supported the revolution. Most violent mobs and bloody outbreaks occurred in that once peaceful hamlet: Mr. Bailey and his family were treated with great harshness, which it must be confessed he did nothing to avert. In the progress of events, he stood unyielding: he continued his prayers for the king in 1776, after the Declaration of Independence, though forbidden; he refused to take the oath of allegiance, and refused to pray for the Revolutionary Government, or to adopt any measures of concession; he even named a son, in 1777, for Lord Percy, who fought at Lexington. He was impracticable; and, consequently, was a subject of censure, denunciation, and persecution. It became the duty of Sheriff Cushing, under the law, to silence him, and to use the arm of authority to prevent the influence he was using, through that community, against the *de facto* government of the province. In October, 1778, Bailey was presented to the Grand Jury for preaching treason in a sermon to his people; but, he says, "The jury, however, at the instance of Langdon, the attorney, refused to find a bill." In November, Mr. Bailey undertook to preach again, believing, as he said, that Mr. Cushing had no authority to silence him. He held a meeting the Sunday before Christmas, about which he says, "This indignant magistrate [High Sheriff Cushing] observing a number of people passing by his house in the attendance upon Divine service, sent directly for one of my wardens * * and ordered him to deliver to me the following imperious message: 'Tell the parson that if he presumes to discharge his functions any longer, I will immediately commit him to prison.'" The sheriff, he says, further threatened him, that if he officiated on Christmas day, "he would drag him out of the pulpit." The same scenes of disorder and violence occurred on the Kennebec, as were enacted in other parts of the country, and similar to those which every revolution produces, and which are daily repeated in portions of our country at the present time, under the influence of insane and bitter passion.

Mr. Bailey remained in the country until June, 1779, when, having obtained permission of the Massachusetts government, he moved to Halifax, and forever left this field of his labor and trials,— and thus one source of annoyance to the friends of the Revolution was removed. But still an opposition was kept up,— the snake was scotched, not killed,— John Jones, who had been a surveyor under the royal government, still remained: he was a very active partisan, and controlled a considerable party on the river. In 1781, Jones, with a small force, in the night, proceeded to the mansion of Sheriff Cushing, who had now become a brigadier general, broke it open, and entering the chamber of the sheriff, took him from his bed, compelled him to hurry on his clothes, and hastily and secretly carried him to the British post at Castine, where he was retained for some time as a prisoner. By his vigilance in the discharge of his duties as sheriff and military officer, he had made himself especially obnoxious to the loyalists, which led to this method of revenge.

His functions as sheriff and brigadier general seem to have ceased soon after this time, when he removed to Boston; and he next appears as clerk of the courts in Suffolk County, in 1783. He was succeeded in the office of sheriff by Edmund Bridge, in 1782, and by Colonel McCobb as brigadier general. Mr. Cushing continued clerk of the courts in Suffolk to the time of his death, which took place November 7, 1810, at the age of seventy-six. Mr. Deane, in his History of Scituate, says of him, "He was a gentleman, worthy of his distinguished ancestors." The fact of his occupying responsible public stations from the age of twenty-six to his death, continuously, both under the royal and republican governments,—a period of fifty years,—is sufficient proof of his ability, faithfulness and integrity. His wife died May 31, 1817, aged seventy-four. They had seven children,—one son and six daughters. The two eldest daughters died in infancy, the others were born and married as follows; viz., Elizabeth, born March 9, 1772, married Elisha Doane of Scituate—no issue: Mary, born January 16, 1774, married Eli P. Ashmun, United States senator, first, and Stephen Codman for her second husband—no issue; she died in 1846: Sarah, born November 21, 1777, married Charles Paine, 1797, and had several children; she died in 1848: Lucy, born February 3, 1780, married Henry Sheafe, November 23, 1805, and had several children: Charles, the only son of the sheriff, was born December 22, 1775, married Ann H. Sheafe, daughter of Jacob Sheafe of Portsmouth, March 12, 1805, by whom he had several children: he lived in Portsmouth, where he died August 6, 1849.

EDMUND BRIDGE. 1782—1814.

For the principal part of this memoir, I am indebted to my friend, John H. Sheppard of Boston.

The families of Sheriff Bridge and Judge Bowman of Dresden were descendants of early settlers in Massachusetts, and were of note and influence in their day. Their settlement in Dresden had an important influence upon the town and that portion of Maine.

The towns of Dresden, Alna, and Wiscasset, including Swan Island on the Kennebec, formerly constituted Pownalboro', named after Gov. Thomas Pownal, a noble-hearted man, whose portrait, having been skillfully copied from a very fine mezzotint engraving of Governor Pownal, in the possession of Mr. Drake, author of the "History of Boston," by Henry C. Pratt, was presented to the town of Dresden by Samuel J. Bridge, Esq., late of San Francisco. Pownalboro' was anciently called Frankfort, before Lincoln County, of which it was the shire-town, was incorporated, which was June 19, 1760. In 1794, it lost its name and was divided into Dresden, New Milford, afterwards Alna, and Wiscasset, then called "Wiscasset Point," from that part of it which projected into the bay and was first peopled. Dresden, now chiefly the still and silent abode of the descendants of German farmers, in its early days, when a shire-town, was a place of resort and no small gaiety. Here stood the court-house, where the trials of all cases east of Cumberland County were held. The old building with its three-story front, on a high bank of the Kennebec, embowered by woods, still towers, as a private residence, above the tree tops. Not far from it was Fort Pownal, a block-house like that on the eastern shore of Augusta, built in 1752 by the Plymouth Company, to protect the settlers from the Indians: it has vanished utterly. Here John Gardiner, an eminent barrister at law, father of that celebrated scholar, the late Rev. John S. J. Gardiner, D. D., rector of Trinity Church, Boston, practiced law, arrayed when in court as an English advocate, in wig and gown. He was representative to the General Court three or four years. Here, in this old court-house, Judge Wilde and Judge Bridge gained their maiden laurèls ; and here Edmund Bridge many years presided as sheriff, and Jonathan Bowman served as judge of probate and clerk of the court.

Edmund Bridge was in the fifth generation a descendant from John Bridge of Cambridge, Massachusetts. Let us trace his pedigree.

I. Deacon John Bridge came from the county of Essex in England, 1631, and in 1632 settled in Cambridge, then called "Newe Towne ; " in May 2, of the same year, it was ordered by the General Court henceforth to be called Cambridge. Young, in his Chronicles of Massachusetts, page 519, quotes: "Divers people in Old England of my dear friends, desired me to go to New England, says Rev. Thomas Shepard, there to live together ; and some went before and writ to me of providing a place for a company of us, one of which was John Bridge." He took the oath as freeman March 4, 1634–5. He was chosen a selectman in 1635, and for eleven years after, filling this office the last time in 1652. He was "Deputy" to the General Court in 1637, 1638, 1639, and 1641; and several times was put on important committees to set off towns, make partitions of estates, adjust boundaries, &c., as will appear in the colonial records of Massachusetts.

Cambridge at that time, as now, was the favorite resort of literary and talented men. There dwelt the Danforth family; and also Harlakenden, the wealthiest man in New England, who was a member of the Court of Assistants, 1636–1638. That Mr. Bridge should have been chosen selectman twelve times and a representative four, in such a place, is a strong proof of the high character he sustained, and that the tradition among his heirs, that he took a very active and influential part in promoting education and aiding Harvard College in its first start, is very probable.

In 1638, he bought of John Barnard and Thomas Judd a lot of land in Cambridge, supposed to include the premises on which General Washington had his head-quarters in the Revolutionary army at Cambridge, and where Professor Longfellow now lives. On this spot, he died in 1666. Two sons came out with him from England, Thomas and Matthew, and he had a daughter Sarah, born February 16, 1648, who died soon after. Thomas died in 1656, and the only surviving son

II. MATTHEW BRIDGE, married Anna Danforth, sister of Lieut.-Governor Danforth, 1643 or 1644. He is on the roll of the "Ancient and Honorable Artillery Company" of Boston, 1643. He died April 28, 1700, and his wife December 2, 1704. They had seven children, three daughters and four sons; all the sons died before them except

III. MATTHEW BRIDGE, who was born May 5, 1650, and married Abigail Russell. He removed to "the Cambridge Farms," so called, now Lexington. He had nine children. He died in 1738; his oldest son

IV. MATTHEW, was born March 1, 1694, and married Abigail Bowman, March 22, 1720. He lived on a lot formerly within Lexington, on the boundary line of Waltham, which, at his request, by resolve of the Legislature, was set off to Waltham, making a jog called the "Bridge Farm," in the northwest line of the town. He died March 25, 1761. Of his four children, one was the Rev. Matthew Bridge, born July 18, 1721, graduated at Harvard University in 1741, and settled as a minister of the first parish in Framingham, February 19, 1746. He was a chaplain in the Revolutionary army, and died September 2, 1775, a truly good man.

IV. The youngest son of Matthew III., and last of his nine children, was SAMUEL, who was born May 2, 1705, married Martha Bowman as his second wife, April 22, 1738, and had four children, all sons, of whom Edmund (called Edward by mistake in Bond's Watertown) was his second son.

V. EDMUND BRIDGE, the high sheriff, and the subject of our present notice, was born August 6, 1739. At the age of twenty-one, in 1760, he went into Maine, seeking his fortune, and settled in Dresden. As soon as he got things well prepared, he returned home, and in 1764 married his cousin, Phebe Bowman, then seventeen years old, — described as a "young and tender plant to transfer to the cold soil of a wilderness." Yet this motherly and excellent woman had nine children, lived to a good old age, surviving her husband, and died in 1827, aged eighty-two.

Mr. Bridge settled in that part of Pownalboro' called Dresden, which lies on the "Eastern River,"— a stream of considerable size, rising in Pittston, some twelve miles distant, and from the bridge navigable for coasters to the Kennebec, which it enters after winding for six miles to the foot of Swan Island. The bridge which crosses the stream at the head of tide-water is within half a mile of the fine green interval on which, a few rods from the river, stands the spacious house he built in 1793. This homestead of some generations, which faces the water, with its large barn, where many a stranger's horse has found a welcome bite, has a cheerful and cosy appearance. The farm around it is extensive, the spot romantic; near which arises a series of well-wooded hills from the level plain.

The mansion of Sheriff Bridge was the abode of hospitality. He first settled on the banks of the Kennebec, and was a large landholder in Dresden and Augusta. On his farm by the Eastern River he seemed like Magnus Troil in his castle at Zetland, so finely described by Walter Scott in the "Pirate." The intercourse among neighbors and the customs of visiting were very different from the reserved habits of the present day. There was less cold ceremony, and more warm hospitality; for flocks of visitors would come on a three days' siege, like a flight of birds, to Sheriff Bridge's genial roof. His lady once remarked that one morning she counted twenty-five saddles on the kitchen floor. The poor Indian there found a welcome meal, and was never turned away from that door. There often were seen some of the first men in the land: when Talleyrand visited this country and went to Hallowell, he found on his way a cordial reception at the Sheriff's. The age of dollar distinctions and copper calculations had not then arrived. Gov. Pownal often visited the Kennebec, and always made the Sheriff's house his home.

In those genial and hospitable times after the Revolution, Gen. William Lithgow, one of Washington's aids, was living in Georgetown; Col. William Howard at Augusta; Gen. Henry Dearborn at Gardiner; and Gen. Henry Knox at Thomaston, like lairds of the Highlands in their baronial castles; nor should the generous and convivial families of the Woods and Hodges, the merchant princes of Wiscasset, be omitted, when we wake up the pictorial reminiscences of olden time. But there was a family in Hallowell which should never be forgotten, filling up the outlines of the past with delightful remembrances of elegant retirement, taste, fortune, books, religion, noiseless and without guile, and the courtly manners of the most polished gentleman of the old school. I allude to Benjamin Vaughan, LL. D. He came from England,—had been a member of the British Parliament,—he settled in Hallowell in 1796. He was a ripe and learned scholar, educated at Cambridge, England, and to him, Dr. Priestly dedicated his lectures on History. He had a library of ten thousand volumes, lining the sides of the rooms, and distributed all over his house, except in his front parlors. This house, erected on a conspicuous hill, commanded one of the finest views in Maine, looking up and down on the Kennebec River: his large garden was noted for choice fruit trees and rare plants. He was always doing good to the poor, always studying some learned work like another Prospero in his cell, and always writing letters, for he kept up an immense correspondence at home and abroad. No stranger ever visited Hallowell without letters to him, and none went away without loving him. His death occurred December 8, 1835, in his eighty-fifth year.

Mr. Bridge was appointed Sheriff of Lincoln County, March 2, 1782, by Gov. Hancock, and continued until his resignation in February, 1814, nearly thirty-two years—excepting some six or eight months, when Orchard Cook, of Wiscasset, under Gov. Gerry, held that office. He used to relate an anecdote of the Revolution which showed the bitter and furious feelings of those days when brother rose up against brother, and father against son. Samuel Goodwin had been the King's surveyor: he lived in Pownalboro', near the court-house, and as a matter of course, was a loyalist. His son Sam, aged twenty-five, on the other hand, was a whig, or patriot. Col. Benedict Arnold was on his way in that ill-fated expedition to Quebec, and stopped at this place to obtain a map of the country from the surveyor; but Goodwin strenuously refused to deliver it. Sam interfered; words came to blows; the son got the father down on the floor; the women screamed, and Mr. Bridge, a near neighbor, hearing the noise, rushed into the house, pulled off Sam who was pounding his father, and inquired into the cause of the fracas. The son said, "Col. Arnold wants the map, and the d— old tory," pointing to his father, "won't give it up." But Mr. Bridge soon persuaded the old man, as it was a case of compulsion, to surrender it. Mr. B. took such interest in Arnold's expedition that he advanced him a hundred dollars in silver, taking Continental money in exchange, some of which is still in the family.

After a long life, much respected for his integrity, and beloved by all who knew him, Sheriff Bridge died at Dresden in September, 1825, aged eighty-six. The Columbian Centinel of September 17, 1825, contains this fine obituary notice of his decease: "Another revolutionary patriot is thus added to the long list of those who have passed off the stage of human action and usefulness. * * * He was a firm and zealous patriot; and many instances of his decision are related, while he was Chairman of the Committee of Safety for that town (Dresden); particularly in preventing the British from obtaining a supply of wood and lumber in 1775, when they were besieged in Boston. In 1781, he was appointed Sheriff of Lincoln County; and retained the office until 1815, when he resigned on account of his advanced age. The various and important duties of this office he discharged with fidelity, and to the universal acceptance of the people. No man was more esteemed and beloved by all classes of citizens. As a parent, he was most exemplary. His children were well educated; his house was the seat of hospitality and cheerfulness; and he was an efficient advocate for the Christian ministry and for public schools. He lived for the benefit of his fellowmen, maintained an unspotted reputation, and his death is deeply lamented by a large circle of relatives and friends."

Mr. Bridge was tall in stature, and of an expressive, open, and very benevolent countenance. His wife died in 1827, aged eighty-two. They had nine children, all born in Pownalboro': James, Martha, Edmund, Phebe, Nathan, Samuel, William, Sarah, and Joseph Bowman.

Of his sons, James and Nathan, we have spoken in their place as lawyers, on pages 154 and 270, to which we refer. James, the eldest son of the sheriff, was born September 21, 1765; married Hannah North, July 4, 1797. She was born June 29, 1774, and died April 9, 1822. We take this opportunity to correct some errors in the table of James's children, given on page 158. His son Edmund was born December 6, 1799, and died February 17, 1854. His daughter Margaret was born February 12, 1802. James was born July 17, 1804. Horatio was born April 8, 1806: he entered the navy in 1838 as paymaster, and is author of "The Journal of an African Cruiser." Mary, born May 2, 1808, married Rufus Chandler Vose of Augusta, and died June 13, 1842. Hannah was born September 23, 1810, married Daniel Williams of Augusta, — his second wife. By his first wife, Miss Sawtelle, Mr. Williams had Seth Williams, now assistant adjutant general in the United States army.

We have thought it would be interesting to preserve in this place some further genealogical facts relating to Sheriff Bridge's family.

II. Martha Bridge, born in 1768, was married to Colonel Arthur Lithgow, who was sheriff of Kennebec County from its organization February 20, 1799, to 1809, when General Chandler superseded him. He was sometime an officer in the custom-house, Boston. He died in Roxbury, Massachusetts, August 14, 1835, aged seventy-five years. He was a popular sheriff, and a generous and hospitable man, of large size and gallant appearance. Mrs. Lithgow died in Charlestown, Massachusetts, April 6, 1852; this noble-hearted, cheerful, and excellent woman having reached eighty-four years. Their children were,

1. Arthur Lithgow, born December 25, 1789. He followed the sea for some years as a ship-master, was skillful and expert, and now resides at Hayti with his family.

2. William Lithgow, born July 1, 1792. He used to sail from Boston, an able ship-master, and died November 19, 1826, leaving a family in Boston. His wife was Miss Langdon of New York.

3. Jane Caroline Lithgow, born July 16, 1795. She married Richard Devens, of Charlestown, Massachusetts, now deceased. Mrs. Devens resides in Charlestown.

4. Mary Lithgow, born December 8, 1797, married Charles Devens of Boston, merchant. She died October 3, 1849, leaving two sons, who each graduated at Harvard University; Charles in 1838, and Arthur Lithgow in 1840. Charles, now General Devens, has distinguished himself in the present war with the rebels; and Arthur is a lawyer at Walpole, New Hampshire. The above were born in Winslow, Maine.

5. Frances Lithgow, born in Augusta, December 1, 1800, married John L. Payson, late American consul at Messina.

6. Frederic A. Lithgow, born at Augusta, 1807, died at Havana, February 21, 1821, aged fourteen.

III. Edmund Bridge, born in Pownalboro', March 26, 1773, was an eminent merchant in Wilmington, North Carolina, where he was engaged in extensive business, and died July 17, 1823, after a residence there of fifteen years: he was much esteemed for his public spirit and benevolence. His brother Nathan was with him at the time of his death. He was never married. His funeral was attended by a large procession of all classes, and the colors on the shipping were displayed at half mast.

IV. PHEBE BRIDGE was born March 6, 1771, and died in Dresden, February 27, 1842. She was married to William Bowman.

V. NATHAN BRIDGE was born September 23, 1775; for further particulars of whom I refer to page 270.

VI. SAMUEL BRIDGE was born November 14, 1778, and died at Dresden, December 12, 1821. He was brought up from a lad in the auction store of the late Thomas K. Jones, a noted auctioneer of Boston; whose niece, Margaret Paine, daughter of Nathaniel Paine, he married. He was one of the firm of Robert G. Shaw, Barker, and Bridge; and afterwards, in 1809, of Barker and Bridge. He removed to Dresden with his family, about 1811, where he lived to the time of his death. He was frequently chosen selectman, overseer of the poor, &c., for Dresden. He was respected for his talents, and beloved for his virtues. His widow died in Boston, June 15, 1836. They left three sons and two daughters; viz.,

1. Mary Helen, born in Boston, July 17, 1804, died August 6, 1846, of consumption, after a vain search for health on the shore and among the isles of the Pacific.

2. Samuel J., born June 1, 1809, a merchant early and extensively engaged in business. In 1841, he was appointed one of the appraisers of the United States for Boston, and after more than twelve years' service, in 1853, promoted to be appraiser general for the Pacific coast, which he held until 1862, when the office was abolished. Mr. Bridge is a liberal patron of the arts, having presented to Dresden and to the State of Maine, beautiful copies of an original picture of Governor Thomas Pownal. To him, also, I am indebted for the fine portrait of his uncle, James Bridge, which I have added to this work.

3. Thomas K. Jones Bridge, the third child of Samuel Bridge, was born in Boston, November 16, 1811; was lost at sea in 1842, on a voyage to the Pacific.

4. Nathan W. Bridge, born in Dresden, June 28, 1814, a ship broker in Boston.

5. Jane Paine Bridge, born in Dresden, September 28, 1817, and now living in Boston.

VII. WILLIAM BRIDGE, born May 4, 1781. He commenced business in Augusta, was unfortunate in trade, went to New Orleans, where he died in 1817. He was always an invalid and sufferer from ill health.

VIII. SARAH BRIDGE, born ———, married Hartwell Williams, Esq., of Augusta. She died in 1835, leaving one son and two daughters; the son,

J. Hartwell Williams, formerly United States consul, and now a merchant in Sidney, Nova Scotia; one daughter, Phebe, married Elisha Hathaway of Boston; the other, Isabella, married Rev. Frederic Freeman of Sandwich, Massachusetts, author of the History of Cape Cod.

IX. Joseph Bowman Bridge was born September 19, 1790. He was never married, and for thirteen years has held an office in the United States Public Appraisers' Office, Boston. For several years, he was one of the selectmen of Dresden, and its Representative in the Legislature.

Within three or four years a number of citizens of Dresden selected a picturesque site for a burial ground, and called it "The Pine Grove Cemetery." It is beautifully laid out by Jonathan Mann, the Superintendent of Mount Auburn, and is to be adorned with trees, shrubbery, and flowers, with a fine avenue leading up to it. It lies on a gentle slope toward the south, in view of the river which glides by, and in the midst of a landscape environed by mountains. It does honor to the liberality and taste of Mr. Samuel J. Bridge, under whose eye it was prepared. The last home of our departed friends, should be, if possible, some scenic spot with the sky above and woodlands and water in the surroundings. It is so in this "Flower Garden of the Dead," as Mr. Bridge happily calls it. Here repose the honored patriarch of Dresden, his wife, children, and grand-children, with neighbors they loved and who loved them. Dust to dust, while the spirit has returned to God who gave it.

HENRY WELD FULLER.

1804—1841.

A notice of Judge Fuller having been omitted in its appropriate place, I will not for that reason deny myself the pleasure, in these closing pages, of giving a brief sketch of a gentleman, who, for many years, occupied a prominent position at the Kennebec Bar, and for thirteen years honorably discharged the duties of judge of probate for that county.

About the middle of the last century, in Attleborough, Massachusetts, there was a man of extraordinary virtues, whose piety and eloquence were mentioned with admiration by Dr. Dwight, in his " Travels in New England," and by the celebrated theologian, Dr. Emmons. I refer to the Rev. *Habijah Weld,* who, after a faithful pastorate of fifty-five years, died May 14, 1782. He was born September 2, 1702, and from the untimely loss of his father, when only six months old, his mother gave him the Hebrew name of Habijah, meaning, my father is God. He was great-grandson of Rev. Thomas Weld, a graduate of Cambridge University, England, who came to this country in 1632, and was the first minister settled in Roxbury. Habijah graduated at Harvard College in 1723, was a Boanerges in the pulpit, and his labors were crowned with great blessings from on high, to such a degree, that at one time there were fifty-seven admissions, and the body of the house was so crowded at the eucharist, that part of the communicants were obliged to sit in the gallery.

He married Mary Fox, daughter of Rev. John Fox of Woburn. They had fifteen children; one of whom, Hannah, married Rev. Caleb Fuller, who graduated at Yale College in 1758, was obliged to give up preaching from weakness of the lungs, and died at a good old age in Hanover, New Hampshire. Caleb and Hannah Fuller were the parents of Judge Fuller, the subject of the present notice, who was first named Habijah, but his

N. W. Fuller

name was afterwards changed to Henry by the Legislature. He was born at Hanover, January 1, 1784, and graduated at Dartmouth College in 1801, the classmate and intimate friend of Daniel Webster — a friendship which lasted for life. He studied law with Benjamin Whitwell of Augusta, with whom, on his admission to practice, he became a partner. He was married January 7, 1806, by Rev. Daniel Stone, to Miss Esther Gould, who now survives him: she was a daughter of Capt. Benjamin Gould of Newburyport, and sister of Miss Hannah F. Gould, eminent as a poetess and fine writer, and is her peer in intellectual strength.

He was afterwards a partner, for a time, with Bridge and Williams; was appointed county attorney in 1822, and held the office until 1828, in which year he was appointed judge of probate for Kennebec. This office he held to the period of his death. He was major, and afterwards colonel in the militia, under Major General Henry Sewall, and was in service when the troops were called out to defend the coast, and encamped at Wiscasset in the war with England, in 1814. He was representative from Augusta to the General Court, Massachusetts, in 1817, and in 1828, in the Legislature of Maine. He was also an active and influential member of the Masonic Fraternity.

His practice was extensive and profitable, and he had one of the largest dockets in the county. He was agent of the proprietors of the Hancock, Pitts, and Thwing Rights, and was owner with the late Reuel Williams of the township of Bradford, Maine, which he settled. In trials before the jury, he was brief and cogent, spoke with fervor, and always to the point, and was remarkably successful in his verdicts. He was fond of horticulture and farming, and had a sound taste in architecture. By his influence and example, Augusta, the capital of Maine, was enlarged and ornamented, wide streets made, and their sidewalks bordered with trees. He was a public benefactor in beautifying one of the handsomest localities in the State of Maine. He died suddenly, struck down by the heart disease in Boston, January 29, 1841, much beloved for his integrity, hospitality, warmth of heart, and kindliness of manner: he was a man of great public spirit, and his death was a heavy loss to society.

He had seven children: 1. Frederic Augustus, born October 5, 1806, died January 29, 1849; 2. Louisa Sophia, born March 12, 1808, married, September 12, 1832, Samuel E. Smith of Wiscasset, governor of Maine, who died March 5, 1860, leaving four sons, one of whom, the late Major Edwin M. Smith, was killed at the battle of Fair Oaks, after greatly distinguishing himself at Williamsburgh. 3. Henry Weld Fuller, born January 16, 1810, graduated at Bowdoin College 1828, counsellor at law, married Mary S. Goddard, daughter of the late Nathaniel Goddard, an eminent merchant of

Boston, and is now clerk of the Circuit Court of United States, Massachusetts District. 4. Martha Elizabeth, born June 12, 1812, married Joseph G. Moody, merchant, September 21, 1834. 5. Caroline Weld, born January 3, 1815, married Isaac Farrar, of Bangor, Maine, June 8, 1835. 6. Benjamin Apthorp Gould, born May 23, 1818, married Harrietta Sawtelle, daughter of Daniel Williams of Augusta, April 27, 1843, and is a counsellor at law in Augusta. 7. Lucretia Goddard, born August 9, 1824, married Joseph K. Clark, merchant of Wiscasset, December 27, 1849.

INDEX.